New Perspectives on

Adobe® Dreamweaver® CS3

Comprehensive

Kelly Hart

Mitch Geller

Australia • Brazil • Japan • Korea • Mexico • Singapore • Spain • United Kingdom • United States

COURSE TECHNOLOGY
CENGAGE Learning™

New Perspectives on Adobe Dreamweaver CS3—Comprehensive
Kelly Hart, Mitch Geller

Executive Editor: Marie L. Lee

Senior Product Manager: Kathy Finnegan

Product Manager: Erik Herman

Associate Acquisitions Editor: Brandi Henson

Associate Product Manager: Leigh Robbins

Editorial Assistant: Patrick Frank

Director of Marketing: Cheryl Costantini

Marketing Manager: Ryan DeGrote

Marketing Specialist: Jennifer Hankin

Developmental Editor: Robin M. Romer

Senior Content Project Manager: Cathie DiMassa

Composition: GEX Publishing Services

Text Designer: Steve Deschene

Art Director: Marissa Falco

Cover Designer: Elizabeth Paquin

Cover Art: Bill Brown

Proofreader: Kim Kosmatka

Indexer: Julie Grady

For product information and technology assistance, contact us at
Cengage Learning Customer & Sales Support, 1-800-354-9706
For permission to use material from this text or product, submit all requests online at **cengage.com/permissions**
Further permissions questions can be emailed to
permissionrequest@cengage.com

Some of the product names and company names used in this book have been used for identification purposes only and may be trademarks or registered trademarks of their respective manufacturers and sellers.

Microsoft and the Office logo are either registered trademarks or trademarks of Microsoft Corporation in the United States and/or other countries. Course Technology, Cengage Learning is an independent entity from the Microsoft Corporation, and not affiliated with Microsoft in any manner.

Adobe, the Adobe logos, Authorware, ColdFusion, Director, Dreamweaver, Fireworks, FreeHand, JRun, Flash, and Shockwave are either registered trademarks or trademarks of Adobe Systems Incorporated in the United States and/or other countries. All other names used herein are for identification purposes only and are trademarks of their respective owners.

Disclaimer: Any fictional data related to persons or companies or URLs used throughout this book is intended for instructional purposes only. At the time this book was printed, any such data was fictional and not belonging to any real persons or companies.

ISBN-13: 978-1-4239-2531-6

ISBN-10: 1-4239-2531-9

Course Technology
25 Thomson Place
Boston, Massachusetts 02210
USA

Cengage Learning is a leading provider of customized learning solutions with office locations around the globe, including Singapore, the United Kingdom, Australia, Mexico, Brazil, and Japan. Locate your local office at: **international.cengage.com/region**

Cengage Learning products are represented in Canada by Nelson Education, Ltd.

For your lifelong learning solutions, visit **course.cengage.com**

Purchase any of our products at your local college store or at our preferred online store **www.ichapters.com**

Printed in the United States of America
1 2 3 4 5 6 7 8 9 12 11 10 09 08

Preface

The New Perspectives Series' critical-thinking, problem-solving approach is the ideal way to prepare students to transcend point-and-click skills and take advantage of all that Adobe Dreamweaver CS3 has to offer.

Our goal in developing the New Perspectives Series was to create books that give students the software concepts and practical skills they need to succeed beyond the classroom. With this new edition, we've updated our proven case-based pedagogy with more practical content to make learning skills more meaningful to students.

With the New Perspectives Series, students understand *why* they are learning *what* they are learning, and are fully prepared to apply their skills to real-life situations.

"This text is filled with excellent explanations and activities. My students vary in their abilities, and this text covers exactly what they need in a logical, incremental fashion. It's a great reference book that students will find useful for years."
—Kenneth Wade
Champlain College

About This Book

This book provides thorough, hands-on coverage of the new Adobe Dreamweaver CS3 software, and includes the following:

- A case-based, problem-solving approach to learning Adobe Dreamweaver CS3 in which students plan, create, and publish professional-looking Web pages using graphics, multimedia, tables, CSS, divs and AP divs, timelines, behaviors, forms, Spry elements, and database connectivity.
- Extensive information on how to plan and design a successful Web site—including project management, market research, target audiences, end-user analysis, and information architecture—before students begin creating Web pages.
- A thorough review of the underlying HTML code for each element students add to the Web site.
- Coverage of the newest features of Dreamweaver CS3, including improved CSS functionality, divs and AP divs, prebuilt Spry elements, and Photoshop integration.
- The basics of integrating Photoshop CS3 with Dreamweaver CS3.
- *Guide to Using Adobe Dreamweaver CS3 on the Macintosh* is available in the Student Downloads and Instructor Downloads sections of www.course.com.

System Requirements

This book assumes that students have a default installation of Adobe Dreamweaver CS3, a text editor, and a current Web browser (preferably Internet Explorer 7 or higher). If students are using a nonstandard browser, the browser must support frames and XHTML 1.0 or higher.

The screenshots in this book were produced on a computer running Windows Vista Ultimate with Aero turned off and, for a browser, Internet Explorer 7. If students use a different operating system or browser, their screens might differ from those in the book.

With some Windows servers, the Dreamweaver built-in FTP client might give continuous or intermittent errors. If these errors occur, students should double-check the remote and testing server configuration settings, and review the following documents on the Adobe site: www.adobe.com/go/tn_14834 and www.adobe.com/go/tn_14841.

Tutorial 10 requires students to create or upload a database to a server. This tutorial was written for and tested on both a Linux server and a Windows server. The recommended server configurations for a Linux server are Apache 1.3.26 or higher, PHP 5.x or higher, MySQL 5.x or higher, and any current distribution of Linux. The recommended server configurations for a Windows server are Windows 2003 IIS 5.0 or higher, running .Net 1.1 framework or higher, and the IIS User must have written permission for the database directory.

> "The New Perspectives Series approach, which combines definition and real-world application of content, makes it an easy choice for me when selecting textbooks. I am able to teach concepts that students can immediately apply."
> —Brian Morgan
> Marshall University

The New Perspectives Approach

Context
Each tutorial begins with a problem presented in a "real-world" case that is meaningful to students. The case sets the scene to help students understand what they will do in the tutorial.

Hands-on Approach
Each tutorial is divided into manageable sessions that combine reading and hands-on, step-by-step work. Colorful screenshots help guide students through the steps. **Trouble?** tips anticipate common mistakes or problems to help students stay on track and continue with the tutorial.

InSight

InSight Boxes
New for this edition! InSight boxes offer expert advice and best practices to help students better understand how to work with Adobe Dreamweaver CS3 and build successful Web pages. With the information provided in the InSight boxes, students achieve a deeper understanding of the concepts behind the features and skills presented.

Tip

Margin Tips
New for this edition! Margin Tips provide helpful hints and shortcuts for more efficient use of Adobe Dreamweaver CS3. The Tips appear in the margin at key points throughout each tutorial, giving students extra information when and where they need it.

Reality Check

Reality Checks
New for this edition! Comprehensive, open-ended Reality Check exercises give students the opportunity to practice skills by completing practical, real-world tasks involved in planning and creating a personal Web site.

Review

In New Perspectives, retention is a key component to learning. At the end of each session, a series of Quick Check questions helps students test their understanding of the concepts before moving on. Each tutorial also contains an end-of-tutorial summary and a list of key terms for further reinforcement.

Apply

Assessment
Engaging and challenging Review Assignments and Case Problems have always been a hallmark feature of the New Perspectives Series. Colorful icons and brief descriptions accompany the exercises, making it easy to understand, at a glance, both the goal and level of challenge a particular assignment holds.

Reference Window
Task Reference

Reference
While contextual learning is excellent for retention, there are times when students will want a high-level understanding of how to accomplish a task. Within each tutorial, Reference Windows appear before a set of steps to provide a succinct summary and preview of how to perform a task. In addition, a complete Task Reference at the back of the book provides quick access to information on how to carry out common tasks. Finally, each book includes a combination Glossary/Index to promote easy reference of material.

www.course.com/NewPerspectives

Our Complete System of Instruction

Coverage To Meet Your Needs

Whether you're looking for just a small amount of coverage or enough to fill a semester-long class, we can provide you with a textbook that meets your needs.

- Brief books typically cover the essential skills in just 2 to 4 tutorials.
- Introductory books build and expand on those skills and contain an average of 5 to 8 tutorials.
- Comprehensive books are great for a full-semester class, and contain 9 to 12+ tutorials.

So if the book you're holding does not provide the right amount of coverage for you, there's probably another offering available. Visit our Web site or contact your Course Technology sales representative to find out what else we offer.

CourseCasts – Learning on the Go. Always available…always relevant.

Want to keep up with the latest technology trends relevant to you? Visit our site to find a library of podcasts, CourseCasts, featuring a "CourseCast of the Week," and download them to your mp3 player at http://coursecasts.course.com.

Ken Baldauf, host of CourseCasts, is a faculty member of the Florida State University Computer Science Department where he is responsible for teaching technology classes to thousands of FSU students each year. Ken is an expert in the latest technology trends; he gathers and sorts through the most pertinent news and information for CourseCasts so your students can spend their time enjoying technology, rather than trying to figure it out. Open or close your lecture with a discussion based on the latest CourseCast.

Visit us at http://coursecasts.course.com to learn on the go!

Instructor Resources

We offer more than just a book. We have all the tools you need to enhance your lectures, check students' work, and generate exams in a new, easier-to-use and completely revised package. This book's Instructor's Manual, ExamView testbank, PowerPoint presentations, data files, solution files, figure files, and a sample syllabus are all available on a single CD-ROM or for downloading at www.course.com.

Online Content

Blackboard is the leading distance learning solution provider and class-management platform today. Course Technology has partnered with Blackboard to bring you premium online content. Content for use with *New Perspectives on Adobe Dreamweaver CS3, Comprehensive* is available in a Blackboard Course Cartridge and may include topic reviews, case projects, review questions, test banks, practice tests, custom syllabi, and more. Course Technology also has solutions for several other learning management systems. Please visit http://www.course.com today to see what's available for this title.

Blackboard

Acknowledgments

The authors wish to thank:

Robin Romer, our favorite editor, for keeping us sane while managing the seemingly infinite complexities of this project. Thank you for all your hard work and dedication.

Charlie Lindahl (aka CyberChuck) for introducing us to an *amazing new thing* called the Web on his new Mosaic Version 0.2A browser (1993), and reminding us of why we do this through his never-ending encouragement and enthusiasm.

Richard Strittmatter of Computeam.com for his guidance, friendship and encouragement, and for knowing the answers to our most complex questions.

Mark Chapman for his unique assistance in tracking Adobe developments and changes.

The staff and management of Meshnet.com for graciously providing hosting and support.

The staff of the Sid Richardson Museum and Store (www.sidrichardsonmuseum.org/store) for their support and generosity in allowing us to use images from their collection.

Exquisite Dead Guys and Matthew Skinner of Inner Mission for allowing us to use their music in the book.

The Course Technology team—Erik Herman, Product Manager; Christian Kunciw, Manuscript Quality Assurance, and his team of Quality Assurance testers, John Freitas and Susan Whalen; and Cathie DiMassa, Senior Content Project Manager—for all their support during the creation of this fourth edition.

Mitch would like to thank Edyie and Joe Geller, Pam, Gregg, and the rest of the family for their love and support…you guys rock! He would also like to thank John Knecht, John Orentlicher, and Don Little.

Kelly would like to thank Mary O'Brien for much needed $C_8H_{10}N_4O_2$ infusions and linguistic reality checks along with the rest of the Nu-Design.com team, Tika, Brian, and Matt, for their support.

Brief Contents

Adobe Dreamweaver CS3

Table of Contents

Objectives

Session 1.1
- Explore the structure and history of the Internet and the World Wide Web
- Become familiar with the roles of Web servers and Web clients
- Learn the basic components of a Web page
- Open a Web page in a browser
- Use hyperlinks

Session 1.2
- Review the history of Web design software
- Start Dreamweaver and select a workspace layout
- Create a local site definition
- Explore the Dreamweaver tool set
- Investigate the Dreamweaver Help features
- Exit Dreamweaver

Getting Started with Adobe Dreamweaver CS3

Exploring an Existing Web Site

Case | Cosmatic

Cosmatic is an independent record label in Denton, Texas, just north of Dallas, that was started by Sara Lynn in 2000. Most of the groups affiliated with the label originated as part of the underground Denton music scene, which centers around the University of North Texas. A year ago, Cosmatic created a Web site to promote its bands. Since that time, some of the bands have developed a national following. Sara believes that this success is due, in part, to the exposure from the Cosmatic Web site. She also believes that further development of the Web site will generate more national publicity as well as increase CD sales. Therefore, she wants to redesign and expand the Web site.

Brian Lee, who is responsible for public relations and marketing at Cosmatic, has a background in multimedia development and will head the Web development team. The new Cosmatic Web site will be developed using Adobe Dreamweaver CS3. Brian's team will research the current market trends as well as design and create a new Web site for Cosmatic. You will work with Brian and his team to develop this site.

Starting Data Files

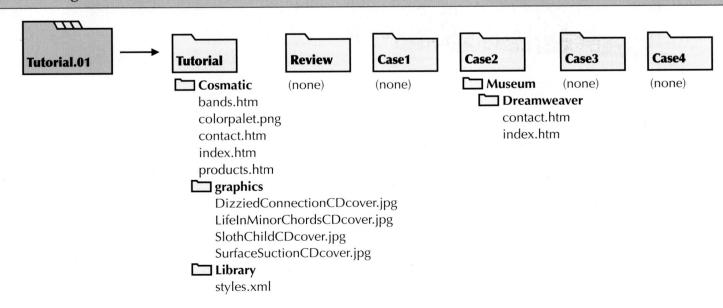

Tutorial.01 → Tutorial

Tutorial
- **Cosmatic**
  - bands.htm
  - colorpalet.png
  - contact.htm
  - index.htm
  - products.htm
  - **graphics**
    - DizziedConnectionCDcover.jpg
    - LifeInMinorChordsCDcover.jpg
    - SlothChildCDcover.jpg
    - SurfaceSuctionCDcover.jpg
  - **Library**
    - styles.xml

Review (none)

Case1 (none)

Case2
- **Museum**
  - **Dreamweaver**
    - contact.htm
    - index.htm

Case3 (none)

Case4 (none)

Session 1.1

Dreamweaver and the Internet

Dreamweaver is a Web site creation and management tool. To better understand what this means, you will need to review some basic terms and concepts associated with Web sites.

The Internet and the World Wide Web

The **Internet** is a huge global network made up of millions of smaller computer networks that are all connected. A **network** is a series of computers that are connected to share information and resources. Within each network, one computer or more is designated as the server. A **server** is the computer that stores and distributes information to the other computers in the network. The Internet provides a way for people to communicate and exchange information via computer, whether they are across the street or across the globe. All of the computers connected to the Internet can communicate and exchange information. Figure 1-1 uses a series of roadways to represent the interconnected networks that make up the Internet.

| Figure 1-1 | Illustration of the Internet |

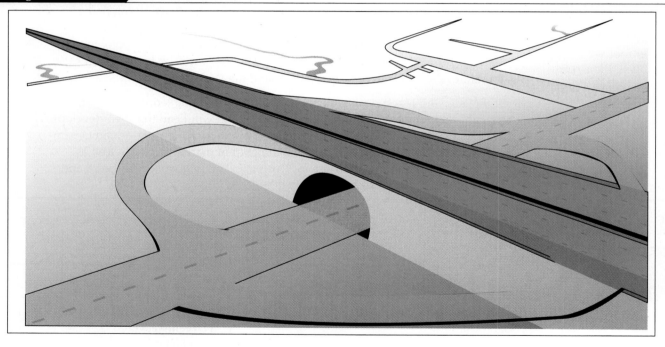

As the Internet has evolved, different protocols have been developed to allow information to be shared in different ways. A **protocol** is a set of technical specifications that define a format for sharing information. Creating an agreed-upon protocol enables a programmer to create software that can interact with all the other software that uses the same protocol. For example, **Simple Mail Transfer Protocol (SMTP)** is an agreed-upon format used by most e-mail software. Without this standard protocol, there would be many incompatible e-mail formats, and you would be able to exchange e-mail only with people who were using the same e-mail software. Another common Internet protocol is **File Transfer Protocol (FTP)**, which is used to copy files from one computer to another over the Internet.

In 1989, Timothy Berners-Lee and his team of scientists at CERN (the European Council for Nuclear Research) invented the World Wide Web as a means for scientists to more easily locate and share data. The **World Wide Web** (**WWW** or **Web**) is a subset of the Internet that has its own protocol, HTTP, and its own document structure, HTML. **HTTP (Hypertext Transfer Protocol)** controls the transfer of Web pages over the Internet. **HTML (Hypertext Markup Language)** provides instructions on how to format Web pages for display. A **Web page** is an electronic document of information on the Web; a group of related and interconnected Web pages is referred to as a **Web site**. Figure 1-2 shows how the Web page vehicles must follow the HTTP rules of the road to travel the Internet roadways. Notice that other vehicles, following other protocols, share the Internet as well.

Illustration of the World Wide Web 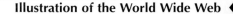 Figure 1-2

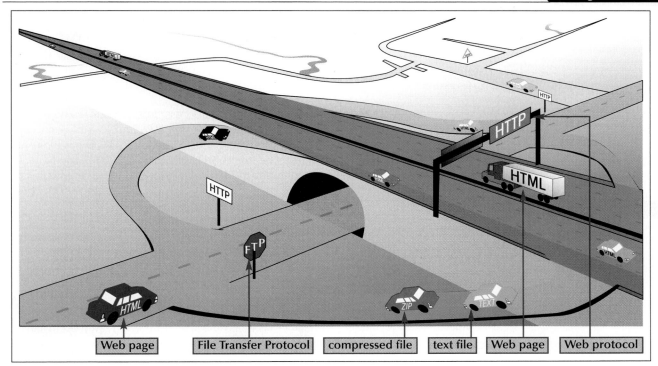

| Web page | File Transfer Protocol | compressed file | text file | Web page | Web protocol |

In addition to standards for transfer and display of information, the Web introduced the technology for hyperlinks to the Internet. A **hyperlink** (or **link**) is a node that provides a user the ability to cross-reference information within a document or a Web page and to move from one document or Web page to another.

Web Servers and Clients

The two general categories of computers involved in accessing Web pages are Web servers and Web clients. When you create a Web page or a Web site, you must post a copy of your work to a Web server to share the page with the world. A **Web server** is a specialized server that stores and distributes information to computers that are connected to the Internet.

A **Web client** (or **client**) is the computer an individual uses to access information, via the Internet, that is stored on Web servers throughout the world. A home computer with Internet access is considered a Web client. You must have access to the Internet to view a Web site. Most people connect to the Internet through an Internet service provider. An

Internet service provider (ISP) is a company that has direct access to the Internet and sells access to other smaller entities. Some large institutions, such as universities, have direct links to the Internet and are, in essence, their own ISPs.

In addition to being connected to the Internet, to view a Web site you must have a Web browser installed on your client computer. A **Web browser** is the software that interprets and displays Web pages. The Web browser enables users to view Web pages from their client computer.

Tip

Two of the most common Web browsers are Microsoft Internet Explorer and Mozilla Firefox.

Common Web Page Elements

Now that you understand what a Web page is and how your computer accesses a Web page on the Internet, you will examine some elements that are common to all Web pages: the Web address, hyperlinks, and content.

Web Address

Every Web page that is posted to the Internet has a Web address. Just as your residence has a unique street address that people use to locate where you live, and as a file on your computer has a unique path used to locate where it is stored, every Web page has a unique address, called a **Uniform Resource Locator (URL)**, that Web browsers use to locate where that page is stored. A URL includes the information identified in Figure 1-3.

Figure 1-3   **Parts of a URL**

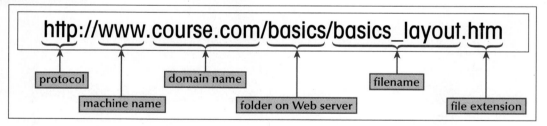

The first portion of the URL indicates the protocol, which is usually HTTP but can be **HTTPS (Hypertext Transfer Protocol Secure)**. HTTPS means that the site is secure because it encrypts data transferred between a user's browser and the server. **Encryption** is the process of coding data so that only the sender and/or receiver can read it, preventing others from being able to understand it. This is important when a user submits confidential or credit card information over the Web.

The protocol is immediately followed by ":// " which originated from UNIX (a server operating system) and essentially means "what follows should be interpreted according to the indicated protocol." When typing a URL into a browser, if you omit the protocol, the browser assumes you mean *http://*.

The next part of the URL is the **machine name**, which is a series of characters that the server administrator assigns to the Web server. Often, the machine name is *www*, but it can be any word, phrase, or acronym. It can even be omitted entirely. For example, the URL *store1.adobe.com* for the Adobe Store - North America uses *store1* as the machine name, and the URL *CNN.com* for CNN omits the machine name entirely. Many servers are configured to route the URL with or without a *www* to the same location. For example, *www.course.com* and *course.com* both go to the same place.

Tip

Because so many sites use *www* as the machine name, include the machine name if you are unsure of a site's exact URL.

The machine name is followed by the domain name. The **domain name** identifies a Web site and is chosen by the site owner. Domain names are often a word or phrase related to an organization or individual. For example, *course* is the domain name for Course Technology, the publisher of this book. What is commonly referred to as the domain name of a Web site is actually the domain name combined with a top-level domain. A **top-level domain** is the highest category in the Internet naming system. The top-level domain might indicate the Web site's type of entity or country of origin. Common top-level domains are commercial (.com), business (.biz), organization (.org), network (.net), U.S. educational (.edu), and U.S. government (.gov). Although .com and .org are generally available to anyone, .edu must be some type of educational entity in the United States and .gov is reserved for the U.S. government. Some top-level domains for countries are .us (United States), .ca (Canada), .uk (United Kingdom), and .jp (Japan). The domain name and top-level domain are combined to create a unique name for a Web site. No two Web sites can have the same domain name and top-level domain. For example, *course.com* is the domain name/top-level domain for Course Technology. No other Web site can use this exact combination of names. However, another site might use *course.org* or *course.uk*, so many companies will purchase all possible domain name/top-level domain combinations and point them all to the same site. Many people commonly refer to the domain name/top-level domain combination as the domain name.

Registering Domain Names | InSight

To ensure that each domain/top-level domain combination is only used once, domain names must be registered for a fee with a domain registrar and are regulated by ICANN (Internet Corporation for Assigned Names and Numbers). Domain names are purchased for one to five years, and the owner has the opportunity to renew the name before anyone else can buy it. After you own a domain name, no one else can use it. At the end of March 2007, at least 128 million domain names had been registered worldwide (*http://www.cnn.com/2007/TECH/biztech/07/23/domain.name.dealing.ap/index.html*). Before you create a Web site, be sure to verify that the name you want is available and then register the name. The more complex the name, the harder it will be for others to remember and enter correctly.

The top-level domain might be followed by nested directories (also called folders) that indicate the location of the file on the Web server. The last name in the series is usually the filename, as indicated by the .html or .htm extension. Each folder and the filename is separated by a slash (/).

The different parts of a URL provide some basic information about the site you are visiting. You can also make an educated guess to determine the correct URL for a site you want to visit.

Opening a Remote Web Page in a Browser | Reference Window

- Click the Internet Explorer icon or your Web browser icon on the Quick Launch toolbar (or click the Start button, and then click the Internet Explorer icon).
- Type the URL of the Web page you want to open in the Address bar at the top of the browser window, and then press the Enter key.

You'll open the main page of the Course Technology Web site by entering a URL because you are accessing the site over the Internet from a remote server. You must be connected to the Internet to view a remote Web page in your browser.

To view the Course Technology Web site in a browser:

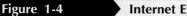 **1.** Click the **Start** button 🪟 on the taskbar, and then click **Internet Explorer**. The Web browser opens and displays the default page. You'll open the Course Technology Web site by entering its URL.

> **Trouble?** If you don't see the Internet Explorer on the Start menu, click All Programs, and then click Internet Explorer. If you still don't see Internet Explorer, press the Esc key until the Start menu closes, and then click the Launch Internet Explorer Browser button on the Quick Launch toolbar or double-click the Internet Explorer icon on your desktop.

> **Trouble?** If you are using Mozilla Firefox or a different Web browser, use the desktop icon or Start menu to open that browser and then modify any Web browser steps in these tutorials as needed.

▶ **2.** Click in the **Address** bar at the top of the browser window to select its contents.

▶ **3.** Type **www.course.com** in the Address bar, and then press the **Enter** key. The main page for the Course Technology Web site opens.

> **Trouble?** If a message appears that Internet Explorer cannot display the Web page, you probably are not connected to the Internet. Connect to the Internet and repeat Step 3. If you do not have Internet access, you will not be able to view the Course Technology site. You can read but not perform Step 4.

▶ **4.** If necessary, click the **Maximize** button 🔲 on the Internet Explorer title bar to maximize the window. See Figure 1-4.

Figure 1-4 ▶ **Internet Explorer Web browser**

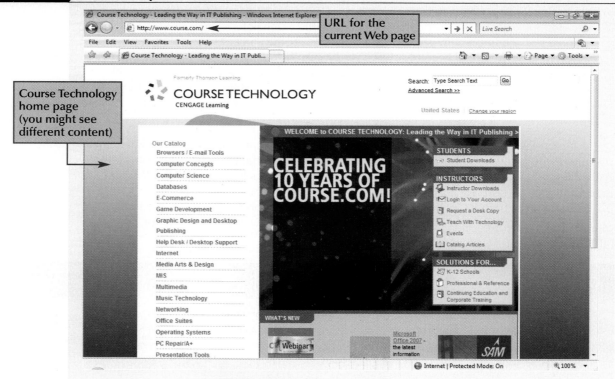

> **Trouble?** If the Web page you see looks different from the one shown in Figure 1-4, the content or layout of the page has changed since this book was printed. Web pages are constantly being modified and updated.

Sometimes you will want to view a Web page that is not posted to the Web. For example, a client might hand you files on a USB flash drive or a coworker may ask you to view a Web page from a local source, such as a computer hard drive or a local network server, before the Web page is posted to the Web. You can view a local copy of a Web page in your browser by typing the file path instead of the URL.

Opening a Local Web Page in a Browser | Reference Window

- Type the file path in the Address bar, and then press the Enter key.
  or
- Click File on the menu bar, and then click Open.
- Click the Browse button, and then navigate to the location where the Web page is stored.
- Click the Web page filename to select it, and then click the Open button.
- Click the OK button.

Brian asks you to view a copy of the existing Cosmatic site. You'll start by opening the Web site's **home page**, which is the main page of a Web site. You do not need to be connected to the Internet to view a local Web page in the browser.

To open the Cosmatic home page in a browser:

▶ **1.** Click **File** on the menu bar of the browser, and then click **Open**. The Open dialog box opens.

▶ **2.** Click the **Browse** button. The Open dialog box opens.

▶ **3.** Navigate to the **Tutorial.01\Tutorial\Cosmatic** folder included with your Data Files, click **index.htm**, and then click the **Open** button.

   Trouble? If you don't have the starting Data Files, you need to get them before you can proceed. Your instructor will either give you the Data Files or ask you to obtain them from a specified location (such as a network drive). In either case, make a backup copy of the Data Files before you start so that you will have the original files available in case you need to start over. If you have any questions about the Data Files, see your instructor or technical support person for assistance.

▶ **4.** Click the **OK** button in the Open dialog box. The home page for the Cosmatic site opens. See Figure 1-5.

Figure 1-5 **Cosmatic home page**

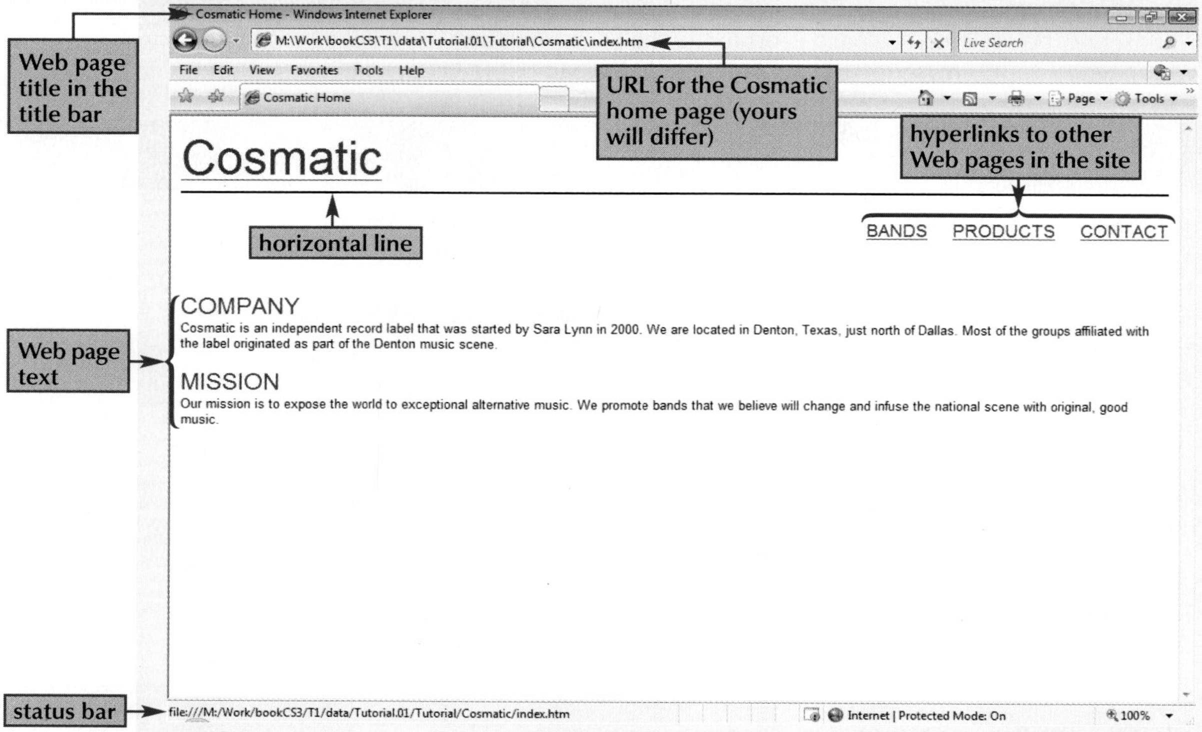

Trouble? If a dialog box opens, indicating that Internet Explorer needs to open a new window to display the Web page, click the OK button and then close all open browser windows when instructed to close the browser.

Trouble? If the Information Bar displays the message, "To help protect your security, Internet Explorer has restricted this file from showing active content that could access your computer. Click here for options." you need to enable the browser to display the page. Whenever this message appears in these tutorials, click the Information Bar, click Allow blocked content, and then click the Yes button in the security dialog box.

Web sites are **nonlinear**, which means that information branches out from the home page in many directions much like railroad tracks branch out from a train station. You can think of the home page as the hub or "train station" of a Web site. Just as people go to a train station to begin a train trip, the home page is where most people start when they want to explore a Web site. The major categories of information contained in the Web site branch out from the home page. Just as different sets of train tracks overlap, the branches of a Web site interconnect through links, and just as one train station is connected to other train stations, your Web site can be linked to other Web sites. So people can take many different routes through your Web site and end up at a variety of destinations.

Hyperlinks

Hyperlinks can be graphics, text, or buttons with hotspots (active areas) that, when clicked, take you to a related section in the same Web page, another Web page in the same site, or on another Web site altogether. This interlinking of information from various places gives the Web its nonlinear nature and even its name.

Links are indicated on a Web page in several ways. When positioned over a link, the pointer will change from ▷ to ⟨ᵐ⟩. Text links are often underlined and appear in a different color to distinguish them from other text. A **graphic** is a visual representation, such as a drawing, painting, or photograph. Images, such as the CD covers on the Products page, are a type of graphic. Usually no visual indicators distinguish graphics that are links from graphics that are not links, although the pointer changes to ⟨ᵐ⟩ when positioned over a graphic link.

The Cosmatic company logo, located at the upper-left corner of the Web page, is also a link. A **logo** is usually a graphic used by a company for the purposes of brand identification. In this case, the company logo is actually formatted text. A company logo is often used as a link to the Web site home page.

Brian wants you to become familiar with the artists that Cosmatic represents and the CDs that it sells. You'll review the Bands and Products pages of the Web site, using links to move between the pages.

To use links to move between pages of the Cosmatic site:

▶ **1.** Point to the **BANDS** hyperlink, but do not click it. The pointer changes to ⟨ᵐ⟩ to indicate that you are pointing to a hyperlink. The URL for the new page appears on the left side of the status bar, which is a banner of details about the window's contents that appears at the bottom of the browser window.

▶ **2.** Click the **BANDS** hyperlink. The Bands page replaces the home page in the browser window. See Figure 1-6.

Bands page　　　　　Figure 1-6

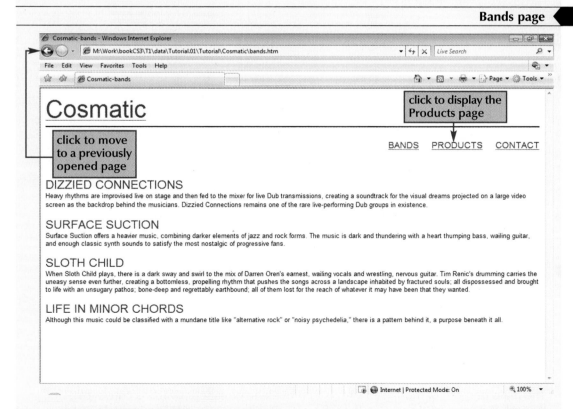

▶ **3.** Click the **PRODUCTS** hyperlink. The Products page replaces the Bands page in the browser window. See Figure 1-7.

Figure 1-7 ▶ **Products page**

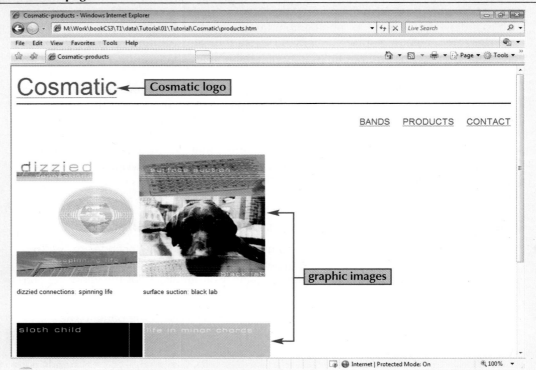

4. Point to the **Cosmatic logo** on the Products page, but do not click it. The pointer changes to 🖑 and the home page URL appears in the status bar.

5. Click the **Cosmatic logo**. The home page reappears in your browser.

After you view two or more Web pages, you can use the Back and Forward buttons on the browser toolbar to move quickly between the pages that you have opened. You'll use the Back button to return to the previous page.

To move between previously viewed pages in the Cosmatic site:

1. Click the **Back** button ⬅ on the browser toolbar. The Products page reappears in the browser window. The Forward button becomes active so you can redisplay the Cosmatic home page.

2. Click the **Forward** button ➡ on the browser toolbar. The Cosmatic home page reappears in the browser window.

Content

The main purpose of most Web sites is to provide information, which is conveyed through the content. **Content** is the information presented in a Web page. A Web page usually contains a combination of text, graphics, and possibly multimedia elements such as video, animation, or interactive content. The blend of these elements is determined by deciding what will most effectively convey the intended message or information. Ignoring the content of a Web site is a common mistake made by inexperienced designers.

Brian asks you to review the Cosmatic site, looking for content and design elements that you think should be added or changed when the Web site is redesigned.

To review the design and content of the Cosmatic site:

▶ 1. Read the content on the home page of the Cosmatic site, considering what information might be appropriate to add and what design changes you would like to see.

▶ 2. Click the **BANDS** hyperlink.

▶ 3. Review the content of the Bands page, considering what information might be appropriate to add and what design changes you would like to see.

▶ 4. Click the **PRODUCTS** hyperlink, and then review the content of the Products page, considering what information might be appropriate to add and what design changes you would like to see.

▶ 5. Click the **CONTACT** hyperlink, review the content on the Contact page, considering what information might be appropriate to add and what design changes you would like to see.

From your review of the Cosmatic site content, you might have a list of changes to suggest to Brian. For example, you might want to add more information to the descriptions in the Bands page. The Products page might also include song titles for each CD. You're done looking at the Cosmatic site, so you will close the site and exit the browser.

To close the Cosmatic site and exit the browser:

▶ 1. Click the **Close** button ☒ on the browser title bar. The Cosmatic site closes and the browser exits.

▶ 2. Repeat Step 1 to close any open browser windows.

Tip

You can also click File on the menu bar, and then click Exit to exit the browser.

In this session, you learned about the Internet, the Web, Web servers, and clients. You explored different components of a Web page. Also, you opened the existing Cosmatic site in a browser, navigated between the Web pages, and reviewed the site's content. In the next session, you will view the existing Cosmatic site from within Dreamweaver.

Session 1.1 Quick Check | Review

1. What is the Internet?
2. What is the World Wide Web?
3. Explain the difference between a Web server and a Web client.
4. What is a Web browser?
5. What is a URL?
6. In the following URL, identify the domain name and the top-level domain: *http://www.course.com/index.html.*
7. Define hyperlinks.
8. Explain the purpose of content in a Web site.

Session 1.2

Evolving Web Design Tools

In the early days of Web design, most Web pages contained only text and were created by typing HTML into documents using a simple text editor such as Notepad or Simple Text. To create a Web page, you had to know how to write HTML from scratch. As the Web evolved, Web authors began to create more complex graphical interfaces. This made creating Web pages from scratch cumbersome. HTML was designed by scientists as a means of sharing information. Using HTML for graphically complex interfaces involves intricate HTML structures that are impractical for most people to type. Furthermore, artists, graphic designers, business people, and nonprogrammers who wanted to create Web pages did not necessarily want to learn all the intricacies of HTML. This led to the development of software packages that allowed people to design Web pages by typing, placing, and manipulating content in an environment that more closely approximated the look of the Web page they wanted to create. The software actually wrote the HTML for them. These software packages were originally referred to as **WYSIWYG (What You See Is What You Get)** programs, because the Web page is displayed in the program window as it will appear to the end user and the code is hidden from sight. Today, the acronym WYSIWYG is not often used because almost all software is designed to show you what you get as you work. The acronym has been critiqued as a bit of a misnomer with Web software because what you get really depends on the specific browser and version used to view the page.

With these Web software packages, people who were not programmers were able to design Web pages, and designers gained even more control over the look of their sites across the various browsers. Dreamweaver grew out of this need for easy-to-use, visual tools that enable Web authors to rapidly develop reliable and well-coded Web pages. Dreamweaver has become one of the most widely used site development and management tools because of its ease of use, accurate HTML output, and powerful tool set. With Dreamweaver, you can successfully create a Web site without knowing any HTML. However, some familiarity with HTML enables you to make the site work better, fix problems that arise, and create elements that are difficult or impossible to create in Dreamweaver.

InSight | **Viewing a Web Page on Different Web Browsers**

When creating Web sites, be aware that aspects of each Web page might display differently in different browsers. For example, text and graphics placement and alignment might differ slightly from browser to browser. These variations occur because browser manufacturers adhere only partially to some of the standards and/or implement them differently. In addition, text might appear more or less sharp and vary in size when viewed on a Macintosh rather than a Windows PC. Images can vary in brightness as well. So test your site on all of the browsers that your intended audience might use. Minor differences are okay. The important things to watch for are layout and functionality errors such as overlapping content, gaps, and cut off or truncated text and graphics.

Starting Dreamweaver and Selecting a Workspace Layout Configuration

To get started, you will need to open Dreamweaver, set the workspace environment, and make sure that it is in the default layout configuration. The Dreamweaver program window consists of several smaller windows, toolbars, and panels. After you start Dreamweaver, you can choose from three preset workspace environments:

- **Designer.** The Designer workspace environment, recommended for most users, is an integrated workspace that uses multiple document interface. **Multiple document interface (MDI)** integrates all of the document windows and panels in one large application window. In this environment, the Document window shows Design view by default, and the panels are docked to the right and below the Document window. You will use the Designer workspace environment in these tutorials.
- **Coder (HomeSite).** The Coder workspace environment uses the same integrated workspace as the Designer workspace layout, but the panels are arranged similarly to Adobe HomeSite and ColdFusion. By default, the Document window shows the Code view. The Coder workspace environment is used primarily by people who are familiar with HomeSite, and it is available only to Windows users.
- **Dual.** If you are working with two monitors, you can display the Document window in your primary monitor and display all the panels on your secondary monitor.

After you select a work environment, you can move windows and adjust the workspace to suit your work style. Dreamweaver opens in the same state it was in when it was last closed, so—depending on the working method of the person who last used the computer—Dreamweaver can open in any of the three environments and in any number of configurations.

You will use the Designer workspace environment in the default layout configuration for these tutorials. If someone else has used your computer and rearranged the position of the panels, you can reset Dreamweaver to the default Designer workspace environment.

The figures in this book show Dreamweaver in the default layout of the Designer workspace environment. As you become more proficient with Dreamweaver, you might find that you prefer a different setup, but you should begin by using the default layout.

To start Dreamweaver and select the Designer workspace environment:

▶ 1. Click the **Start** button 🌀 on the taskbar, click **All Programs**, click **Adobe** or **Adobe Design Premium CS3**, and then click **Adobe Dreamweaver CS3**. Dreamweaver starts with various windows and toolbars displayed.

   Trouble? If you do not see the Adobe or Adobe Design Premium CS3 folder, click Adobe Dreamweaver CS3 on the All Programs menu. If you can't find Adobe Dreamweaver CS3 on the All Programs menu, press the Esc key twice to close the Start menu, and then double-click the Adobe Dreamweaver CS3 program icon on your desktop. If you still can't find Adobe Dreamweaver CS3, ask your instructor or technical support person for help.

   Trouble? If this is the first time Dreamweaver is started on this computer, the Default Editor dialog box opens to show the file types for which Dreamweaver will be the default editor. Click the OK button.

▶ 2. Click **Window** on the menu bar, point to **Workspace Layout**, and then click **Designer**. The workspace environment resets to Designer and all the panels and windows return to their default positions.

▶ 3. Click the **Maximize** button 🔲 on the program window title bar, if necessary. See Figure 1-8.

Figure 1-8 ▶ **Dreamweaver in Designer workspace environment**

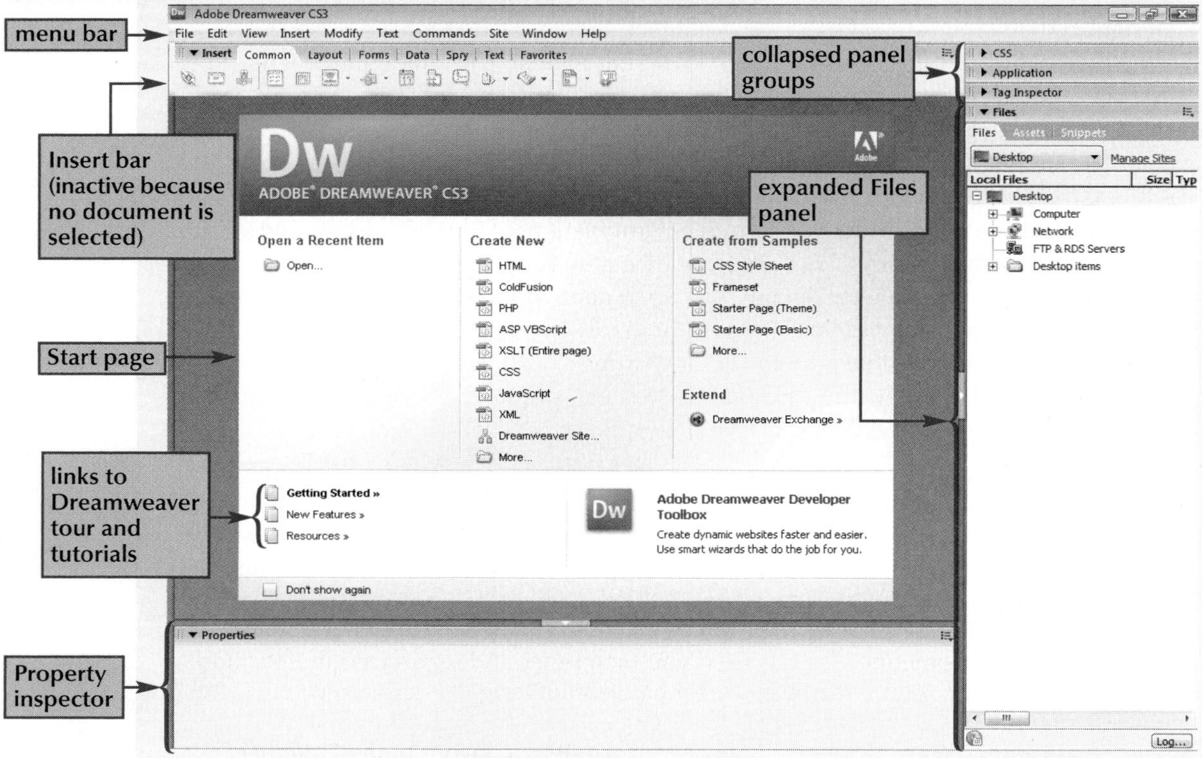

The basic elements of the Designer environment in the default view of the workspace layout are labeled in Figure 1-8. The **menu bar**, located at the top of the work area, is a categorized series of menus that provide access to all of the tools and features available in Dreamweaver. The Text menu, for example, has commands for creating and formatting text.

Each **panel group** on the right side of the screen contains related panels. A **panel** contains related commands, controls, and information about different aspects of working with Dreamweaver. The Start page, which appears when you initially open Dreamweaver, enables you to create a new document, open an existing document on which you have recently worked, and links to the Adobe Help Resource Center where you can learn more about Dreamweaver. You will learn about the other Dreamweaver elements as you use them.

Creating a Site Definition

Working on a Web site is a lot like working on a report. You most often keep the original report locally on your computer and distribute a copy of the report to others to review. In the case of a Web site, you work on the original site on your computer, and then have Dreamweaver post a copy to a publicly viewable space such as a Web server. The original site stored on your computer is the *local version*, and the copy that Dreamweaver posts is the *remote version*. You make all changes and revisions to the local site, and then have Dreamweaver update the remote site. A **site definition** is the information that tells Dreamweaver where to find the local and remote files for the Web site, along with other parameters that affect how the site is set up within Dreamweaver. Dreamweaver stores a local Web site in the same format as it will be posted on the Web. The two main categories in a site definition are the local information and the remote information.

You should create the local information for the site definition (referred to as the local site definition) before you begin working on a Web site. You can wait to create the remote information for the site definition (referred to as the remote site definition) until you are ready to post a copy of the site to a Web server.

Creating a Site Definition | InSight

The site definition is stored in the Windows registry and is *not* kept as part of the site. If you use a different computer for a later work session, you must re-create the site definition on that computer. Be sure to use the most recent version of the site when you create or re-create the site definition.

Configuring a Local Site Definition

A **local site definition** is the information stored on the computer you are using that tells Dreamweaver where the local root folder is located. A **local root folder** is the location where you store all the files used by the local version of the Web site. You can use files stored anywhere on your hard drive or network to create a site; Dreamweaver prompts you to copy these files into the local root folder so that everything you need is in one convenient location. You can place the local root folder on a hard drive or on a removable disk. Working on a site stored on a removable disk can be slower than working on a site stored on a hard drive.

You create a local site definition in the Site Definition dialog box. From the Basic tab, you can access the Site Definition Wizard, which walks you through the process of setting up a site. However, the wizard prompts you to set the remote site definition as well. Another option is to enter the site definition information manually on the Advanced tab. For these tutorials, you will enter the information manually so that you can better understand the process of creating a local site definition.

Creating a Local Site Definition | Reference Window

- Click Site on the menu bar, and then click Manage Sites (or click the Site button on the Files panel toolbar, and then click Manage Sites).
- Click the New button in the Manage Sites dialog box, and then click Site.
- Click the Advanced tab in the Site Definition dialog box.
- Click Local Info in the Category box.
- Type a name in the Site name box.
- Type a path in the Local root folder box (or click the Browse button, navigate to the Web site's folder, and then click the Select button).
- Type a path in the Default images folder box (or click the Browse button, navigate to the Web site's folder, double-click the graphics folder, and then click the Select button).
- Click the Document option button.
- Click the Use case-sensitive link checking check box to check it.
- Click the Enable cache check box to check it.
- Click the OK button.

You'll need to enter several pieces of information and select a few options to set up a local site definition. The following list explains the parts of a local site definition:

- **Site name.** An internal name you give the Web site for your reference. This name appears on the Site menu in the Document window and in the Files panel but is not used outside of Dreamweaver. You'll use Old Cosmatic as the site name for the existing Cosmatic site.
- **Local root folder.** The location where you store all of the files used by the local version of the Web site. You choose where to place the local root folder on your computer, network, or removable disk.

| InSight | **Creating a Logical Folder Structure** |

When creating the local root folder, use a logical folder structure and a descriptive naming system. A logical folder structure helps keep the Web site files organized. For example, it is a good idea to store each project in its own folder and to create a Dreamweaver subfolder within each project folder so that the Dreamweaver files remain separate from any original, uncompressed artwork and working files that you have not yet added to the Web site. You might, for instance, create a Cosmatic project folder that contains a Dreamweaver subfolder. Any text files or graphics that you have not yet added to the Web site would be stored in the Cosmatic folder. The Dreamweaver subfolder would be the local root folder for the new Cosmatic Web site project. Remember that folder names can include any series of letters, numbers, hyphens, and underscores. They should not include spaces, symbols, or special characters, which can cause problems on some servers. Symbols and special characters can also have different meanings on different platforms.

- **Default images folder.** The folder in which you store all of the graphics files used in the site. A good practice is to create a graphics folder within the local root folder as the default images folder.
- **Links relative to.** The option that sets the path of hyperlinks relative to the current Web page (Document relative links) or relative to the root directory of the site (Site root relative links). Dreamweaver inserts relative paths when you create hyperlinks to pages within your site. You will use Document Relative links for the Cosmatic site.
- **HTTP address.** The URL of the Web site, which Dreamweaver uses to verify links. You will enter this URL in a later tutorial when you publish the Cosmatic site.
- **Case-sensitive links.** The option that makes all hyperlinks case sensitive (uppercase and lowercase letters are considered different letters). Linux Web servers are case sensitive, whereas Windows Web servers are not. Linux Web servers see index.html and Index. html as different files, whereas Windows Web servers see them as the same file. Check the Case-sensitive Links check box to avoid problems with case when you upload the site to the Web.
- **Cache: Enable cache.** The option that enables Dreamweaver to use a **cache**, a temporary local storage space, to speed up the processing time needed to update links when you move, rename, or delete a file. You'll usually leave this option checked.

You'll create a local site definition so you can view the Cosmatic site in Dreamweaver on your computer.

To create the local site definition for the Cosmatic site:

▶ **1.** Click **Site** on the menu bar, and then click **Manage Sites**. The Manage Sites dialog box opens. See Figure 1-9.

Manage Sites dialog box ◀ Figure 1-9

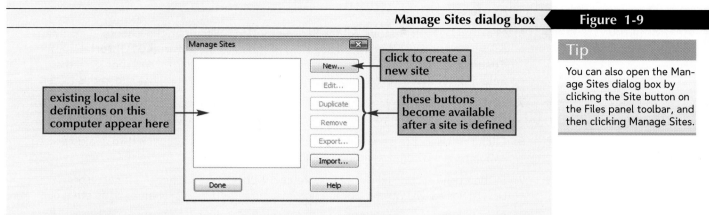

Tip

You can also open the Manage Sites dialog box by clicking the Site button on the Files panel toolbar, and then clicking Manage Sites.

▶ **2.** Click the **New** button, and then click **Site**. The Site Definition for Unnamed Site 1 dialog box opens.

▶ **3.** Click the **Advanced** tab, and then click **Local Info** in the Category box, if necessary. See Figure 1-10.

Site Definition for Unnamed Site 1 dialog box ◀ Figure 1-10

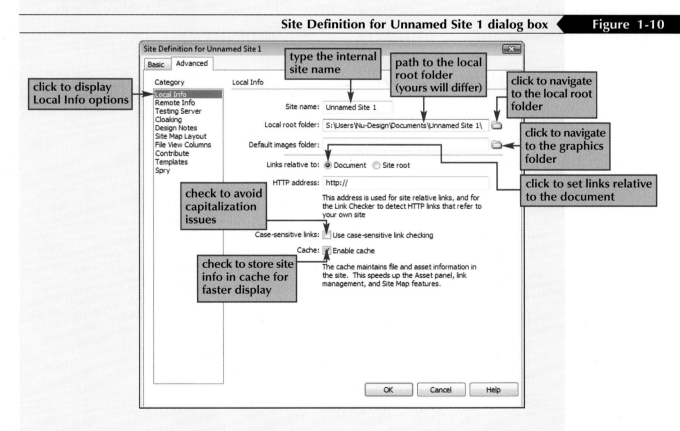

▶ **4.** Select the text in the Site name box, if necessary, and then type **Old Cosmatic**. Old Cosmatic is the name you will use to reference the site; this name is not used outside of Dreamweaver.

▶ 5. Click the **Local Root Folder Browse** button ▣ to open the Choose Local Root Folder for Site Old Cosmatic dialog box, navigate to the **Tutorial.01\Tutorial\Cosmatic** folder included with your Data Files (the location where the Cosmatic site is stored), and then click the **Select** button. The path to the Cosmatic site appears in the Local root folder box.

▶ 6. Click the **Default Images Folder Browse** button ▣ to open the Choose Local Images Folder for Site Old Cosmatic dialog box, navigate to the **Tutorial.01\Tutorial\ Cosmatic** folder if necessary, double-click the **graphics** folder, and then click the **Select** button. Dreamweaver will store all the graphics used in the site in this folder.

▶ 7. In the Links relative to section, click the **Document** option button, if necessary, to set the links relative to the document.

▶ 8. Click the **Use case-sensitive link checking** check box to check it to avoid capitalization issues when uploading the site to a Web server.

▶ 9. In the Cache section, click the **Enable cache** check box to check it, if necessary. Dreamweaver will quickly update links whenever you move, rename, or delete a file.

▶ 10. Click the **OK** button. The Site Definition dialog box closes, and the site name "Old Cosmatic" appears in the Manage Sites dialog box.

▶ 11. Click the **Done** button. The Manage Sites dialog box closes. Dreamweaver scans the existing files and creates the file list for the site, which is visible in the Files panel.

Trouble? If a dialog box opens with the message that the initial site cache will now be created, click the OK button.

Exploring the Dreamweaver Environment

Brian wants you to explore the Cosmatic site from within Dreamweaver. As you review the site, you will work with the Dreamweaver windows, panels, and toolbars.

Files Panel

The Files panel is located in the Files panel group. You use the Files panel to manage local and remote site files and folders. The name of the Web site that is currently selected appears in the Site button on the Files panel toolbar. After you create a local site definition on your current computer, the site name for that Web site is added to the menu—in this case, Old Cosmatic. The local root folder for the selected site appears in the lower portion of the Files panel. When you expand the root folder, a list of the folders and files in the local site appears. From the Files panel, you can view, move, copy, rename, delete, and open files and folders. You can also use the Files panel to transfer files to a remote site when you are ready to post the site to the Web. You will use these features of the Files panel when you begin working with the remote site.

Viewing the File List and Site Map in the Files Panel | Reference Window

- Click the View button on the Files panel toolbar, and then click Local view to view the file list.
- Click the Site button on the Files panel toolbar, and then click the Web site name.
- Click the Plus (+) button next to the Web site folder in the list.
- Click the View button on the Files panel toolbar, and then click Map View to view the site map.
- Click the Expand/Collapse button on the Files panel toolbar to view the file list and the site map simultaneously.
- Click the Expand/Collapse button on the Files panel toolbar again to collapse the view.

The Files panel also includes an **integrated file browser** that enables you to browse files that are located outside of the site. After you set up a remote site, you can select Remote View from the View menu, and a list of the files and folders in the remote site appears in the lower portion of the Files panel. You can expand the Files panel to fill the work area. When the Files panel is expanded, the lower portion of the panel is divided vertically into two panes so that you can display the local and remote views of the site simultaneously.

To view the file list of the local Cosmatic site in the Files panel:

1. Click the **View** button on the Files panel toolbar, and then click **Local view**, if necessary.

2. Click the **Site** button on the Files panel toolbar, and then click **Old Cosmatic**, if necessary. The Cosmatic site appears in the local files list below the Files panel toolbar.

3. Click the **Plus (+)** button [+] next to the Site - Old Cosmatic folder, if necessary. The graphics folder, the Library folder, and the Old Cosmatic Web page files appear in the list. See Figure 1-11.

Files panel with the site file list ◀ Figure 1-11

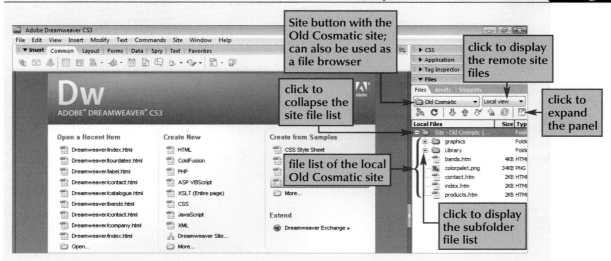

When a Web site is selected, the folders and pages in the local root folder of that site are displayed. Currently, the folders and pages in the local root folder of the Old Cosmatic site are visible. A folder icon precedes the folder name, whereas a Dreamweaver Web page icon precedes the Web page filenames. Each filename is followed by a **file extension**, which is used by Windows to determine the file type. The file extension for Web pages can be either .html or .htm. Depending on how your Web server is set up, you might be required to use one or the other for the entire site or for only the default page.

Another way to view the files and folders in a Web site is with the site map. A **site map** is a visual representation of how the pages in a Web site are interrelated. The Expand/Collapse button on the Files panel toolbar toggles the Files panel between a one-pane view and a two-pane view.

You'll view the site map for the Old Cosmatic site.

To view the Old Cosmatic site map alone and with the local file list:

▶ **1.** Click the **View** button on the Files panel toolbar, and then click **Map View**. The site map appears in the Files panel. See Figure 1-12.

| **Figure 1-12** | **Files panel with the site map** |

Tip

You might need to resize the Files panel to view the entire site map.

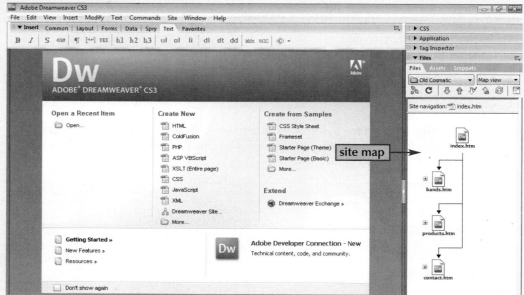

▶ **2.** Click the **Expand/Collapse** button ⊡ on the Files panel toolbar. The Files panel expands to fill the program window.

▶ **3.** Click the **Site Map** button ⬚▾ on the Files panel toolbar, and then click **Map and Files**. The site map (Map view) and the site list (Local view) are displayed simultaneously. See Figure 1-13.

Files panel with the file list and site map | Figure 1-13

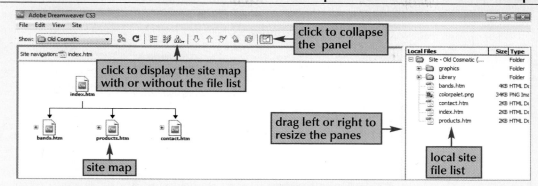

> **4.** Click the **Expand/Collapse** button 🗗 on the Files panel toolbar. The Files panel collapses to its original size.

> **5.** Click the **View** button on the Files panel toolbar, and then click **Local view** to return to Local view.

You can open any page in the Web site by double-clicking its filename in the file list or the site map. Each page opens in the Document window. You can open multiple pages at one time. Although there are other methods for opening Web pages in Dreamweaver, this method ensures that you always open the file from the local root folder (rather than from a backup copy or another location). You can move between the open pages by clicking the name of the page you want to make active. The page names of all of the open pages are located at the top of the Document window above the Document toolbar. The active page is displayed in the Document window, the name of the active page is displayed in the active tab, and the file path for the active page appears in brackets beside the software information in the title bar at the top of the Dreamweaver window.

You'll use the Files panel to open the Bands and Products pages.

To open the Bands and Products pages from the Files panel:

> **1.** Double-click **bands.htm** in the Files panel. The Bands page opens in the Document window to the left of the Files panel.

> **2.** Double-click **products.htm** in the Files panel. The Products page opens in the Document window and is the active page. See Figure 1-14.

Figure 1-14	Open Web pages

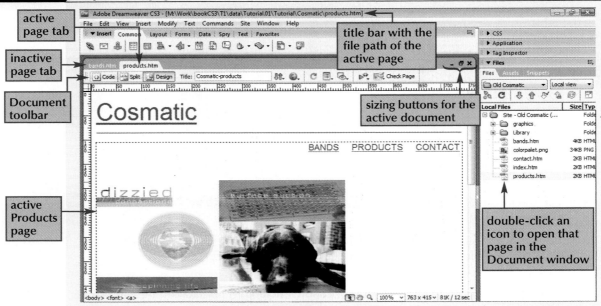

active page tab

inactive page tab

Document toolbar

active Products page

title bar with the file path of the active page

sizing buttons for the active document

double-click an icon to open that page in the Document window

▶ **3.** Click the **bands.htm** tab at the top of the Document window. The Bands page becomes the active page and appears in the Document window. The Bands page file path appears in the title bar at the top of the Dreamweaver window, and bands.htm is displayed in the active tab.

▶ **4.** Click the **Close** button ✖ on the Document window title bar. The Bands page closes, and the Products page is the active page.

▶ **5.** Click the **Close** button ✖ on the Document window title bar. The Products page closes.

Document Window

The **Document window** is the main workspace where you create and edit Web pages. You use tools from the various panels, toolbars, and inspectors to manipulate the page that is open in the Document window.

The Document toolbar, located below the active page tab, includes buttons for the most commonly used commands related to the Document window. It also includes a text box for entering the **page title**, which is the name you give a Web page that appears in the browser's title bar when the Web page is viewed in a browser window.

At the top of the Dreamweaver window, the title bar information for the active document appears beside the Dreamweaver information. The **title bar** information includes the file path in brackets. The file path ends with the **filename**, which is the name under which a Web page is saved. If an asterisk (*) appears after the file path outside of the brackets, it means that the page has been modified without being resaved. Usually, the page that opens by default when you visit a Web site has the filename index.htm, index.html, default.htm, or default.html. A Web server will display this page if the user has not requested a specific file in the URL.

The middle of the Document window is the workspace where you create and edit Web pages. You can display the information in the Document window in Design view, Code view, and Split view. The buttons that control the views are located on the Document toolbar.

- **Design view.** Displays the page as it will appear in a browser. Design view is the primary view used when you are designing and creating a Web page. In Design view, all of the HTML code is hidden so you can focus on how the finished product will look. When you view the home page of the Cosmatic site in Design view, it looks the same as it does in a browser.
- **Code view.** Displays the underlying HTML code that Dreamweaver automatically generates as you create and edit a page. You can also enter or edit HTML code in this window. This view is used primarily when you want to work directly with the HTML code.
- **Split view.** Splits the Document window into two panes: the upper pane shows the underlying code, and the lower pane shows the page as it will appear in the browser. You can easily move between the panes to either edit the HTML code or change the design using the Dreamweaver tools. This view is used primarily when you want to debug or troubleshoot a page.

You'll look at the home page of the Old Cosmatic site in the different views. The filename of the home page is index.htm, because it is the page that displays by default when the user has not requested a specific file in the URL.

To display the Old Cosmatic home page in different views:

▶ **1.** In the Files panel, double-click **index.htm**. The Cosmatic home page opens in the Document window workspace.

▶ **2.** Click the **Design** button on the Document toolbar, if necessary. The home page appears in Design view. See Figure 1-15.

Home page in Design view | **Figure 1-15**

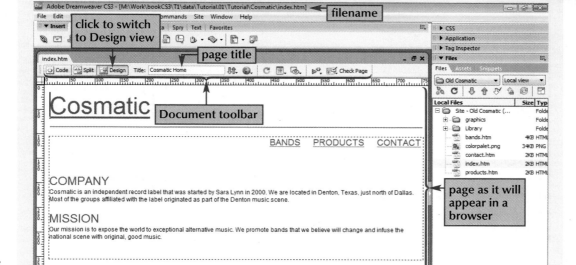

▶ **3.** Click the **Code** button on the Document toolbar. The HTML code for the home page appears in the Document window. See Figure 1-16.

| Figure 1-16 | Home page in Code view |

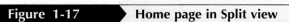

▶ **4.** Click the **Split** button on the Document toolbar. Both the code and the design of the home page appear in the Document window. See Figure 1-17.

| Figure 1-17 | Home page in Split view |

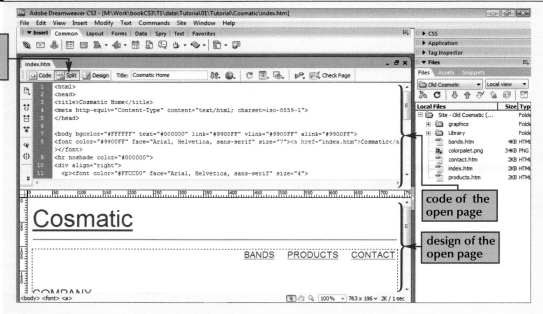

▶ **5.** Click the **Design** button on the Document toolbar. The home page returns to Design view.

▶ **6.** Click the **Close** button ☒ on the Document window title bar. The home page closes.

The **status bar**, located at the bottom of the Document window, displays details about the content in the Document window. The following items always appear in the status bar:

- **Tag Selector.** Displays all the HTML tags surrounding the current selection in the work area.
- **Select Tool.** Enables you to select text, graphics, and so on with the pointer. This is the default pointer tool.
- **Hand Tool.** Enables you to drag the active page up or down in the Document window. When the Hand tool is selected, the pointer becomes ⟨ᵐ⟩ .
- **Zoom Tool.** Enables you to magnify the active page and zoom in to the area you click. When the Zoom tool is selected, the pointer becomes a magnifying glass ⚲ . To zoom out, hold the Alt key as you click the active page.
- **Set Magnification.** Enables you to select the percentage of magnification at which the page will be displayed in the Document window from a list of preset values.
- **Window Size.** Displays the Document window's current dimensions in pixels. A **pixel**, which stands for picture element, is the smallest addressable unit on a display screen. The numbers change when you resize the Document window. You can set the window dimensions by manually resizing the window or by selecting one of the common monitor sizes from the menu. Before you change the window size, you must click the Maximize/Restore button to make the Document window sizable.
- **Document Size/Estimated Download Time.** Displays the size of the current page in kilobytes (K) and the approximate amount of time in seconds it would take to download the page over a modem transferring 56 kilobits per second (Kbps).

You'll review status bar items as you explore and modify the Bands page.

To use the status bar to modify the Bands page:

▶ **1.** Open the **bands.htm** page in the Document window.

▶ **2.** Drag to select the **Cosmatic logo** at the top of the Bands page. The status bar tag selector shows the HTML tags associated with the selected text. See Figure 1-18.

Figure 1-18   Status bar items

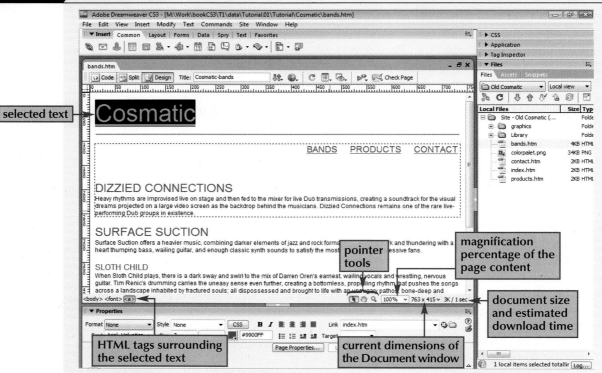

selected text

pointer tools

magnification percentage of the page content

document size and estimated download time

HTML tags surrounding the selected text

current dimensions of the Document window

Trouble? If you don't see the <font> tag or the <a> tag in the status bar, the tag isn't selected in the underlying code. Continue with Step 3.

3. Drag to select some of the text below the Cosmatic logo. Some of the following HTML tags appear in the tag selector: <body>, <div>, <p>, <font>, and <a>.

4. Click the **Restore** button ☐ on the Document window title bar. The Document window becomes sizable. See Figure 1-19.

Figure 1-19   Resized Document window

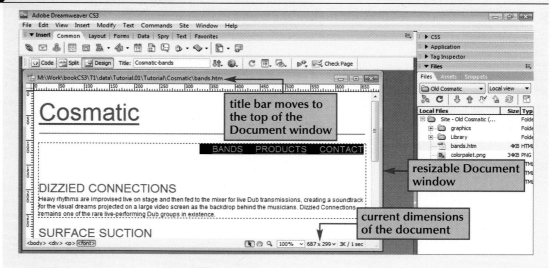

title bar moves to the top of the Document window

resizable Document window

current dimensions of the document

▶ **5.** Click the **Window Size** button on the status bar to display a menu of common monitor sizes, and then click **536 x 196**. The Document window reduces to approximately half its current size.

Trouble? If you don't see the status bar, you need to extend the Document window. Click the expand button at the bottom of the Document window. The status bar becomes visible. Click the collapse button below the Document window after you complete Step 6.

▶ **6.** Click the **Window Size** button on the status bar, and then click **955 x 600**. The Document window expands to fill most of the screen.

Trouble? If a dialog box opens with the message that the chosen size won't fit your current screen and that the screen size will be used, then your monitor size is smaller than 955 x 600. Click the OK button to resize the window to your screen size.

▶ **7.** Click the **Maximize** button on the Document window title bar. The Document window returns to its maximized state.

Trouble? If you can't see the Maximize/Restore button, click Window on the menu bar, click Tile Horizontally to have the Document window automatically fill the workspace, and then repeat Step 7.

▶ **8.** Click the **Set Magnification** button on the status bar to display the magnification options, and then click **50%**. The page content decreases to 50% magnification.

▶ **9.** Click the **Set Magnification** button on the status bar, and then click **100%**. The page returns to its original size.

▶ **10.** Click the **Zoom Tool** button on the status bar to change the pointer to ⊕, and then click anywhere in the Bands page. The page content is magnified.

▶ **11.** Press and hold the **Alt** key to change the pointer to ⊖, and then click anywhere in the Bands page. The page returns to its original magnification.

▶ **12.** Review the **Document Size/Estimated Download Time** for the Bands page.

▶ **13.** Close the Bands page.

Trouble? If a dialog box opens and prompts you to save changes, click the No button.

Property Inspector

The most frequently used tool is the **Property inspector**, a toolbar with buttons for examining or editing the attributes of any element that is currently selected on the page displayed in the Document window. A **page element** is either an object or text. The Property inspector buttons and options change to reflect the attributes of the selected element.

You'll use the Property inspector to explore the attributes of different objects in the Old Cosmatic site.

To use the Property inspector to explore object attributes in the Old Cosmatic site:

▶ 1. Open the **index.htm** page in the Document window. The home page appears in the Document window.

▶ 2. In the Document window, drag to select the text in the paragraph below the Company heading. The Property inspector attributes reflect the selected text. The attributes associated with text are similar to those in a word processing program, such as text size, color, styles (bold and italic), alignment, and indentation. See Figure 1-20.

Figure 1-20	Property inspector with text attributes

▶ 3. In the Document window, drag to select the **BANDS** link at the top of the page. The Property inspector attributes change to reflect the selected text and include the link information. See Figure 1-21.

Property inspector with text link attributes | Figure 1-21

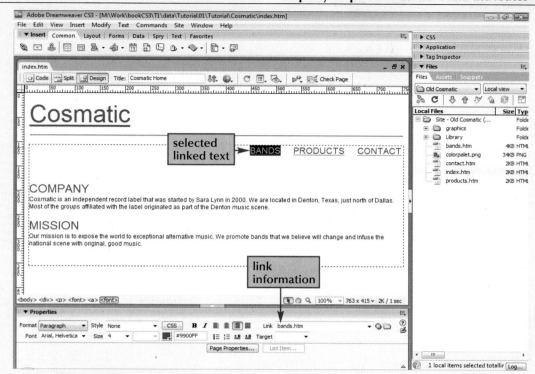

▶ **4.** Close the home page.

▶ **5.** Open the **products.htm** page in the Document window.

▶ **6.** In the Document window, click the **Dizzied Connections CD cover image**. The image is selected. The Property inspector displays attributes related to images, such as height and width, borders, and so on. See Figure 1-22.

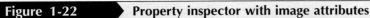

Figure 1-22 **Property inspector with image attributes**

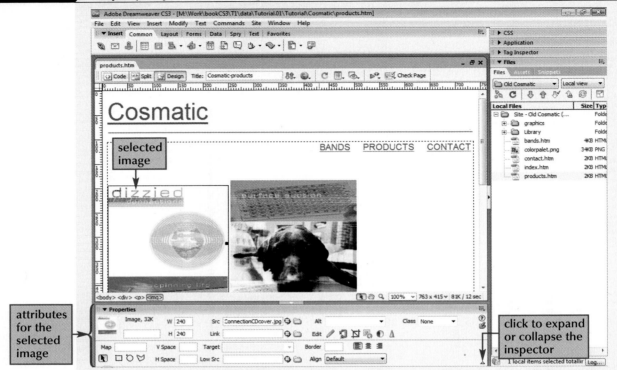

Trouble? If the Property inspector does not show a second row of attributes, you need to expand the Property inspector. Click the expander arrow in the lower-right corner of the Property inspector.

Insert Bar

In Dreamweaver, anything that you create or insert into a page is called an **object**. For example, tables, images, and links are objects. Whenever you want to create a new object, you use the Insert bar. The **Insert bar**, located directly below the menu bar, contains buttons that are used to create and insert objects. The buttons on the Insert bar are organized into tabbed categories. You click a Category tab to select that tab and display its buttons on the Insert bar below the selected tab. When you place the pointer over a button, a tooltip with the button name appears. Some buttons contain menus of additional buttons with common commands. Clicking a button on the Insert bar either enables you to insert or create the associated object or opens a menu containing additional, related buttons. For example, when you click the Image button, a menu of image-related buttons appears. An arrow at the right of a button indicates that the button opens a menu with additional options. Figure 1-23 describes the Insert bar categories and the tasks associated with each category.

Insert bar categories ◄ **Figure 1-23**

Category	Description of Tasks
Common	Create and insert the most frequently used objects, such as images, templates, media elements, and tables.
Layout	Draw and insert tables, div (division) tags, Spry elements, and frames as well as switch between Standard mode and Expanded Tables mode.
Forms	Create and insert form elements in pages that include interactive forms.
Data	Insert Spry data objects and other dynamic elements, such as record sets and repeated regions.
Spry	Insert Spry elements, including widgets and Spry data objects.
Text	Insert text and list formatting tags such as bold (b), unordered list (ul), and para- graph (p).
Favorites	Organize the most commonly used Insert bar buttons in one convenient location.

The Insert bar displays the Common category of buttons by default. You'll explore some of the categories on the Insert bar.

To explore the Insert bar categories:

▶ **1.** If the Insert bar categories are hidden, click the **Insert bar arrow**. The category tabs appear on the Insert bar.

▶ **2.** Click the **Common** tab on the Insert bar, if necessary. The buttons in the Common category appear on the Insert bar. See Figure 1-24.

Common category on the Insert bar ◄ **Figure 1-24**

selected category of Insert bar buttons; click a tab to select another category

click a button with an arrow to open a menu of buttons with related functionality

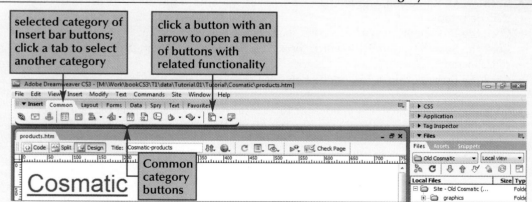

Common category buttons

▶ **3.** Point to each button to display a tooltip with its name.

▶ **4.** Click the **Images button arrow** on the Insert bar. The Images menu opens.

▶ **5.** Press the **Esc** key. The Images menu closes.

▶ **6.** Click the **Layout** tab on the Insert bar. The buttons for creating commonly used layout elements appear on the Insert bar.

▶ **7.** Point to each button to display a tooltip with its name.

▶ **8.** Click the **Forms** tab on the Insert bar. The buttons for creating a form and inserting form elements such as buttons, menus, check boxes, and images appear on the Insert bar.

▶ **9.** Point to each button to display a tooltip with its name.

▶ **10.** Click the **Common** tab on the Insert bar. The buttons in the Common category reappear on the Insert bar.

▶ **11.** Close the Products page.

Getting Help in Dreamweaver

As you develop a Web site, you might run into a question about the purpose of a certain feature or want to review the steps for completing a specific task. Dreamweaver has a comprehensive Help system that provides a variety of ways to get the information you need.

The Dreamweaver Help command opens the Adobe Help Viewer window, which provides three ways to access information about all of the Dreamweaver features. Contents arranges the information by subject categories, similar to the table of contents in a printed book. Index arranges the information alphabetically by topic. Search looks up information based on the keyword or phrase you enter. The selected Help topic appears in the right pane of the window and can include explanations, descriptions, figures, and links to related topics.

| Reference Window | **Getting Help in Dreamweaver** |

- Click Help on the menu bar, and then click Dreamweaver Help.
- Click the Contents link, and then click a topic or subtopic in the Contents list to display that Help topic.
- Click the Index link, click a letter, and then click a topic or subtopic in the Index list.
- Click the Search box, type keywords, press the Enter key, and then click a topic in the search results.
- Click the Close button in the Adobe Help Viewer window title bar.
  or
- Click the Help button in any window or toolbar (or right-click any panel tab, and then click Help on the context menu to open the Adobe Help Viewer window to a context-sensitive Help topic).
- Click the Close button in the Help Viewer window title bar.

You'll use the Dreamweaver Help to look up information about the Document window, the Insert bar, and the Property inspector.

To look up information in Dreamweaver Help:

▶ **1.** Open the **index.htm** page in the Document window.

▶ **2.** Click **Help** on the menu bar, and then click **Dreamweaver Help**. The Adobe Help Viewer window opens.

▶ **3.** Click the **Maximize** button on the Adobe Help Viewer window title bar, if necessary.

▶ **4.** Click the **Contents** link at the top of the left pane, if necessary.

▶ **5.** Click the **Plus (+)** button next to the Workspace link in the Contents list, and then click **Working in the Document window**. The Working in the Document window Help topic appears in the right pane of the Adobe Help Viewer window. The topic lists links to related topics. See Figure 1-25.

Tip

You can also press the F1 key to open the Adobe Help Viewer window.

Adobe Dreamweaver Help Contents ◀ **Figure 1-25**

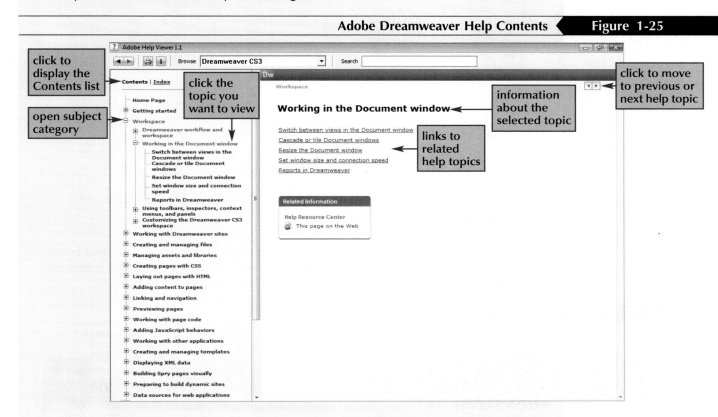

▶ **6.** Click the **Switch between views in the Document window** link, read the information, click the **Back** button on the Adobe Help Viewer window toolbar, and then repeat for each of the other links in the Working in the Document window topic.

▶ **7.** Click the **Index** link at the top of the left pane. An alphabetical list of Help topics appears in the left pane.

▶ **8.** Click the **I** link in the left pane to display a list of Help topics that begin with the letter I, click the **Insert bar** link, click **categories** under the Insert Bar heading in the list, and then click **Insert bar overview**. The selected Help topic appears in the right pane. See Figure 1-26.

Figure 1-26 ▶ **Adobe Dreamweaver Help Index**

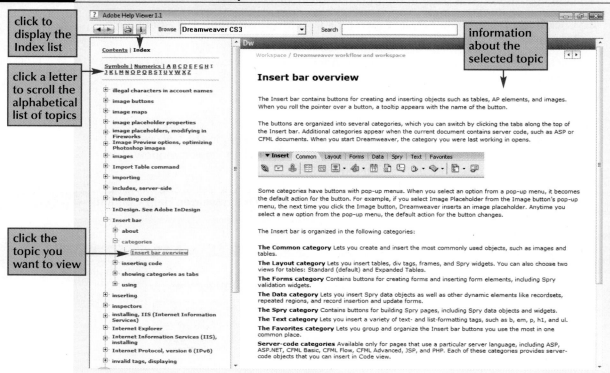

9. Read the information about using the Insert bar in each category.

10. Click in the **Search** box on the toolbar, type **Property inspector**, and then press the **Enter** key. A list of Help topics that contain the keywords "Property inspector" appears in the Adobe Help Viewer window. See Figure 1-27.

Figure 1-27 ▶ **Adobe Dreamweaver Help Search**

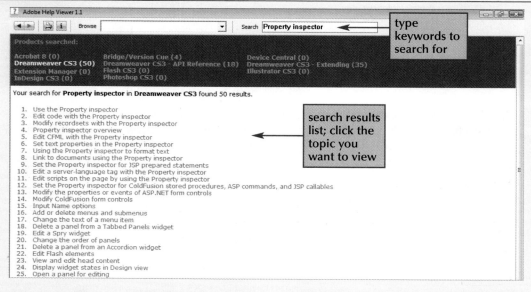

11. Click the **Use the Property inspector** link. The selected Help topic appears in the right pane.

▶ **12.** Read the information about using the Property inspector.

▶ **13.** Click the **Close** button ❌ on the Adobe Help Viewer window title bar. The Help window closes.

Another way to access Dreamweaver Help topics is by using context-sensitive help, which opens the Adobe Help Viewer window and displays the Help topic related to the feature you are using. You access context-sensitive Help by clicking the Help button in any dialog box or toolbar about which you have a question or by right-clicking any panel tab and then clicking Help.

You'll use context-sensitive Help to learn more about the text-formatting features of the Property inspector.

To use context-sensitive Help to learn about the text-formatting features of the Property inspector:

▶ **1.** Select the block of body text below the Company heading on the home page.

▶ **2.** Click the **Help** button ⑦ in the upper-right corner of the Property inspector. The Adobe Help Viewer window opens.

▶ **3.** Read the Help information about setting text properties in the Property inspector.

▶ **4.** Click the **Close** button ❌ on the Adobe Help Viewer window title bar. The Help window closes.

Adobe provides additional Dreamweaver product support and Help features on its Web site (*www.adobe.com*). You can also access the Dreamweaver Support section of the Adobe site by clicking Help Resources Online in the Help menu. The Web site provides you with the latest information on Dreamweaver, advice from experienced users, and advanced Help topics as well as examples, tips, and updates. You can also join a discussion group to converse with other Dreamweaver users.

Exiting Dreamweaver

When you are finished working, you need to close the Web site and exit the Dreamweaver program. The Exit command on the File menu exits Dreamweaver and closes all open windows. You can also use the Close command or the Close button on the Document window title bar to close each open window until the program exits. Dreamweaver prompts you to save any Web pages that you haven't yet saved. Because you haven't made any changes to the Old Cosmatic site, you can close any open pages without saving, and then exit the site.

To exit Dreamweaver:

▶ **1.** Click the **Close** button ❌ on the Document window title bar to close the home page.

▶ **2.** Click **File** on the menu bar, and then click **Exit**. Dreamweaver exits.

In this tutorial, you reviewed the existing Old Cosmatic site. After setting up the local site definition, you looked at the Old Cosmatic site and navigated its pages. In the process, you explored the Dreamweaver environment and the basic Dreamweaver tools and commands. In the next tutorial, you will begin planning the new Web site.

Review | **Session 1.2 Quick Check**

1. Do you need to know HTML to create a successful Web site in Dreamweaver? Why or why not?
2. True or False? If you move to another computer to work, you must re-create the site definition on that computer.
3. What is the difference between the local site and the remote site in Dreamweaver?
4. What is a site definition and where is it stored?
5. What is the local root folder?
6. Which window or panel do you use to manage local and remote site files?
7. Which view in the Document window displays only the underlying HTML code that Dreamweaver automatically generates as you create and edit a Web page?
8. Where would you turn for information about all of the Dreamweaver features?

Review | **Tutorial Summary**

In this tutorial, you learned about the Internet and the World Wide Web. You explored the relationship between Web servers and Web clients, and you opened and reviewed a Web site in a browser, examining the components of a basic Web page. You started Dreamweaver, arranged the work environment, and created the local site definition. You navigated a site, changed the page view in the Document window, and explored the Dreamweaver tool set, including the Files panel, the Document window, the Property inspector, and the Insert bar. Finally, you used the Help system to get additional information about Dreamweaver.

Key Terms

cache
content
Document window
domain name
Dreamweaver
encryption
file extension
File Transfer Protocol (FTP)
filename
graphic
home page
HTML (Hypertext Markup Language)
HTTP (Hypertext Transfer Protocol)
HTTPS (Hypertext Transfer Protocol Secure)
hyperlink (link)
Insert bar
integrated file browser

Internet
Internet service provider (ISP)
local root folder
local site definition
logo
machine name
menu bar
multiple document interface (MDI)
network
nonlinear
object
page element
page title
panel
panel group
pixel
Property inspector
protocol

server
site definition
site map
SMTP (Simple Mail Transfer Protocol)
status bar
title bar
top-level domain
Uniform Resource Locator (URL)
Web browser (browser)
Web client (client)
Web page
Web server
Web site
World Wide Web (WWW or Web)
WYSIWYG (What You See Is What You Get)

Practice	**Review Assignments**

Practice the skills you learned in the tutorial.

There are no Data Files needed for the Review Assignments.

Brian Lee is getting ready to have his team begin planning the new Cosmatic site. In preparation, he wants you to review the Web sites of bands that you like. While looking, keep your eyes open for possible improvements that could be incorporated into the new Cosmatic site.

1. Start your Web browser.
2. Type the URL for the Web site of a favorite band in the Address bar, and then press the Enter key. (*Hint:* If you don't know the URL for the band's Web site, try typing **www.thenameoftheband.com** in the Address bar, using the actual band name.)
3. Review the home page of the band's Web site to see what information is included and how the information is arranged. Write a few sentences describing your findings.
4. Use hyperlinks to explore the site. Look at how information is presented and whether you can move easily between sections.
5. Click the band's logo, if there is one. Notice whether the logo is a hotspot, and, if it is, where it takes you.
6. Repeat Steps 2 through 5 to explore the Web site for another band and review the information the site contains.
7. Compare the two sites that you explored. Write down your responses to the following questions:
   a. What are the similarities and the differences between the sites?
   b. Which features do you prefer? Why?
   c. Can any of the features from these sites be incorporated into the new Cosmatic site? If so, which features?
   d. How would the changes improve the Cosmatic site?
8. Close the browser window.
9. Start Dreamweaver.
10. Click Help on the menu bar, click Dreamweaver Help to open the Adobe Help Viewer window, and then click the Contents link, if necessary.
11. Click Workspace in the Contents list, read the information in the Help topics, and then click the right arrow button at the top of the overview to move to the next topic. (*Hint:* The left and right arrow buttons move you consecutively backward and forward through the Help topics.)
12. Read the next four Help topics, using the right arrow button to move to the consecutive pages, and then close the Adobe Help Viewer window.
13. List four things you learned about Dreamweaver.
14. Exit Dreamweaver. Submit the finished answers to your instructor, either in printed or electronic form, as requested.

| Research | | **Case Problem 1** |

Research existing Web sites in preparation for creating a Web site to present the data on the small rural communities in northern Vietnam.

There are no Data Files needed for this Case Problem.

World Anthropology Society Dr. Olivia Thompson is a well-respected social anthropologist and a member of the World Anthropology Society. She is currently living in Asia and collecting data on small rural communities in northern Vietnam. Because traditional communications are difficult, she has asked you to create a Web site that will enable her to share her ongoing research with colleagues and the grant funding committee to which she reports. She wants you to begin by reviewing existing Web sites that deal with social anthropology and northern Vietnam in preparation for designing her Web site. She also asks you to find out what image file formats are compatible with Dreamweaver.

1. Start your Web browser, type the URL for a search engine into the Address bar, and then press the Enter key to open the search engine. (Two popular search engines are *www.google.com* and *www.dogpile.com*.)

⊕ **EXPLORE**

2. Search for relevant Web sites by typing the term **social anthropology** into the search box and then clicking the Search button. The search engine displays a list of pages that contain the words in your search. (*Hint:* If too many unrelated choices appear, narrow the search by typing quotation marks around the keywords and clicking the Search button. If no matches appear, check your spelling and try again.)

3. Click the link for an appropriate page to open the Web site, and then explore the Web site, making notes about what information is included, how the material is organized, and what images are included.

4. Click the Back button on the browser toolbar until you return to the search engine results. Investigate a second Web site, taking notes about its content and organization.

5. Return to the search engine and search for Web sites related to **northern Vietnam**. Explore at least one Web site, taking notes about its content and organization.

6. Write a memo to Olivia giving a brief description of the sites' similarities and differences, and list features you would like to incorporate into the new Web site. Include the URL for each site you analyzed.

7. Close the browser window.

8. Start Dreamweaver, and then select the Designer workspace environment, if necessary.

9. Use Dreamweaver Help to find information about using images in a Web site. Use Search to locate the **About images** Help topic.

10. Read the About images topic to learn about the image file formats that Dreamweaver uses.

11. Add to your memo a brief explanation of which image file formats are compatible with Dreamweaver.

12. Exit Dreamweaver. Submit the finished memo to your instructor, either in printed or electronic form, as requested.

| Challenge | **Case Problem 2** |

Extend what you've learned to explore an art museum Web site from within Dreamweaver.

Data Files needed for this Case Problem: Museum\Dreamweaver\index.htm, Museum\Dreamweaver\contact.htm

Museum of Western Art   The Fort Worth Museum of Western Art has been a premier gallery for many years. As part of the museum's plan to further community education about Western art, Tika Hagge, the museum manager and curator, wants to expand the museum Web site. She has contracted C.J. Strittmatter to design and maintain the new site. You'll work with C.J. on the site. To start, you will review the museum's current Web site.

1. Start Dreamweaver, and then select the Designer workspace environment, if necessary.
2. Create a local site definition for the museum's Web site. Use **Old Museum of Western Art** as the site name, set the path to the **Tutorial.01\Case2\Museum\Dreamweaver** folder included with your Data Files as the local root folder, set the links relative to the document, use case-sensitive link checking, and enable cache.
3. Select Old Museum of Western Art in the Site list in the Files panel in Local view.
4. Expand the folder list, if necessary. How many pages are in the site?
5. Display the site map in the Files panel. How are the pages connected?

⊕**EXPLORE** 6. Click the Plus (+) button next to the contact.htm page. Notice the globe icon, which indicates a file on another site or a special link such as an e-mail link.

⊕**EXPLORE** 7. Expand the Files panel, and then display the page titles in the site map. (*Hint*: Click View on the Files panel menu bar, point to Site Map Options, and then click Show Page Titles.)

⊕**EXPLORE** 8. Display the filenames by turning off the Show Page Titles command, and then collapse the Files panel.

9. Right-click the Files panel group name, and then click Help on the context menu to open context-sensitive Help.
10. Read the Using the Files Panel Help topic, and then close the Adobe Help Viewer window.

⊕**EXPLORE** 11. Display the site map and the files list in the Files panel. (*Hint*: Expand the Files panel, click the Site Map button, and then select Map and Files to display both the site map and the file list.)

12. Collapse the Files panel, and then display only the local files list.
13. Open the site's home page (index.htm) from the Files panel, and then read the page's content.
14. Open the site's Contact page (contact.htm) from the Files panel, and then read the contents of the page.
15. Make the home page the active page.
16. Change the view to Split view.
17. Close all open pages, and then exit Dreamweaver. Submit the finished answers to your instructor, either in printed or electronic form, as requested.

Research	**Case Problem 3**

Find and review competing Web sites for a small, independent bookstore.

There are no Data Files needed for this Case Problem.

MORE Books   MORE Books is a small, independent bookstore in California that specializes in providing an outlet for fringe writings and alternative titles of all sorts. Natalie More started the company in 1988, using a public storage building as a storefront. Since then, MORE Books has grown and become a respected force in the world of underground literature. Natalie recently hired Mark Chapman to design and maintain a Web site for the company in hopes of expanding MORE's market through Internet exposure. Mark asks you to research the Web sites of other independent bookstores and distributors. Natalie has provided a list of some competitors: Seven Stories Press, Akashic Books, Soft Skull Press, and Verso. You'll use a search engine to find the Web sites of these competitors. Then you will investigate the sites you find.

1. Start your Web browser, type the URL for a search engine into the Address bar, and then press the Enter key to open the search engine. (Two popular search engines are *www.google.com* and *www.dogpile.com*.)

⊕ EXPLORE

2. Use a search engine to find the Web sites for the competing companies. Search for a competitor's Web site by typing the company's name in the search box, and then clicking the Search button. The search engine displays a list of pages that contain the words in your search.

3. Click the link for an appropriate page to open the Web site, and then explore the Web site, making notes about the site's design, what information is included, how the material is organized, and to whom the site would appeal.

4. Click the Back button on the browser toolbar until you return to the search engine results.

5. Repeat Steps 2 through 4 for each competitor.

6. Return to the search engine and search for Web sites for independent bookstores. Explore at least one Web site, taking notes about its content and organization.

7. Write a brief description of the sites' similarities and differences, listing both content and design features you would like to incorporate into the new Web site. Include the URL for each site.

8. Close the browser. Submit the finished description to your instructor, either in printed or electronic form, as requested.

Research	**Case Problem 4**

Find and review competing sushi restaurant Web sites and find information about basic HTML in preparation for creating a Web site for a newly opening sushi restaurant.

There are no Data Files needed for this Case Problem.

Sushi Ya-Ya   Sushi Ya-Ya is a small sushi restaurant that will be opening soon in the French Quarter of New Orleans. Charlie Lindahl, the store's owner, has decided that a Web site with online ordering features would help create publicity for the new restaurant and garner lunch sales by encouraging carry-out orders from local businesses. Charlie hired Mary O'Brien to create and design the site. You will assist Mary in building the site. Mary asks you to research what other sushi restaurants have done with their Web sites and to use Dreamweaver to find information about basic HTML.

1. Start your Web browser. Type the URL for a search engine into the Address bar, and then press the Enter key to open the search engine. (Two popular search engines are *www.google.com* and *www.dogpile.com*.)

EXPLORE

2. Use a search engine to find the Web sites for sushi restaurants. Search for sushi restaurant Web sites by typing the appropriate keywords in the search box, and then clicking the Search button. The search engine displays a list of pages that contain the words in your search.

3. Explore at least three sushi restaurant sites. For each site, write down the site's URL and any useful information about the site's content, organization, and design. (*Hint:* Use the Back button on the browser toolbar to return to the search results and link to a different restaurant.)

4. Write a brief description of the sites' similarities and differences, listing both content and design features you would like to incorporate into the new Sushi Ya-Ya Web site. Include the URL for each site.

5. Close your browser.

6. Start Dreamweaver, and then access Dreamweaver Help.

7. In the Adobe Help Viewer window, use Search to find topics about **Property inspector**.

8. Open the Edit code with the Property inspector topic, and read it.

9. Use Search to find topics about **formatting text**.

10. Open and read the About text formatting and CSS topic, click the Back button on the toolbar, and then open and read the About formatting text (CSS versus HTML) topic.

11. Close the Adobe Help Viewer window, and then exit Dreamweaver. Submit the finished description to your instructor, either in printed or electronic form, as requested.

Review | **Quick Check Answers**

Session 1.1

1. The Internet is the world's largest computer network used for communicating and exchanging information via computer.

2. The Web is a subset of the Internet with its own protocol (HTTP) and document structure (HTML).

3. A Web server is a specialized server that stores and distributes information to computers that are connected to the Internet. A Web client is a computer that an individual uses to access Internet information via a Web server.

4. A Web browser is the software installed on a client computer that allows users to view Web pages.

5. A URL is the unique address that Web browsers use to locate where a specific Web page is stored.

6. course.com

7. A hyperlink is a graphic, text, or a button with a hotspot that, when clicked, takes you to another related section on the same Web page, another Web page on the same site, or another Web site entirely.

8. The purpose of content is to effectively convey the Web site's intended message or information—usually with a combination of text, graphics, and possibly multimedia elements such as video, animation, or interactive content.

Session 1.2

1. No. However, some familiarity with HTML enables you to make the site work better, fix problems that arise, and create elements that are complex or impossible to create in Dreamweaver.

2. True.

3. The local site is stored on your computer and is the version you work on; the remote site is a copy of the local site that Dreamweaver posts to a publicly viewable space, such as a Web server.

4. A site definition is the information that tells Dreamweaver where to find the local and remote files for the Web site. It also defines other parameters that affect how the site is set up within Dreamweaver. It is stored in the Windows registry. If you move to another computer to work, you must re-create the site definition on that computer.

5. The local root folder is the location where you want to store all the files used by the local version of the Web site.

6. Files panel

7. Code view

8. Adobe Dreamweaver Help

Planning and Designing a Successful Web Site

Developing a Web Site Plan and Design

Case | Cosmatic

A professional Web site requires considerable amount of planning. Although planning might seem like a lot of work, it will help you avoid reworking site elements. In the end, planning will save you time and frustration. To create an effective Web site, you must have a clear idea of the site's goals; planning enables you to determine what you need from a Web site and how the site will meet those needs.

Brian Lee, the public relations and marketing director at Cosmatic, asks you to help plan the company's new Web site. First, you will determine site goals and identify the target audience. To do this, you will conduct market research and create end-user scenarios. Then, you will design the information architecture, create a flowchart and site structure, design the site navigation structure, and develop the aesthetic concept for the site. Finally, you will create the new site.

Starting Data Files

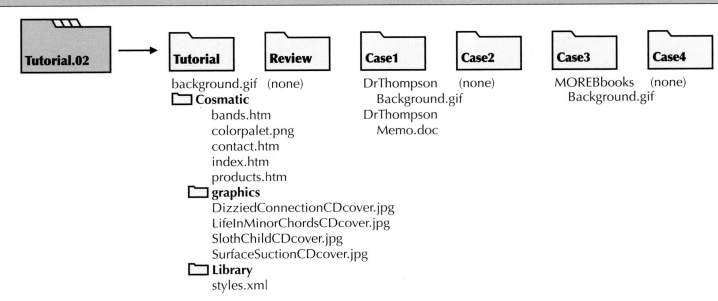

Tutorial.02 → Tutorial

| Tutorial | Review | Case1 | Case2 | Case3 | Case4 |

background.gif   (none)   DrThompson   (none)   MOREBbooks   (none)
Cosmatic   Background.gif   Background.gif
   bands.htm   DrThompson
   colorpalet.png   Memo.doc
   contact.htm
   index.htm
   products.htm
graphics
   DizziedConnectionCDcover.jpg
   LifeInMinorChordsCDcover.jpg
   SlothChildCDcover.jpg
   SurfaceSuctionCDcover.jpg
Library
   styles.xml

Session 2.1

Creating a Plan for a New Web Site

Whether you are part of an in-house Web team or an independent designer hired to create a Web site, the first order of business for designing a professional Web site is to determine the goals, the target audience, and the expectations for the site. You obtain this information from the **client**, the person or persons for whom you are creating the site. This process usually requires a series of meetings and a considerable amount of time.

These client meetings and initial time are a crucial part of the planning process, because it is impossible to design a Web site that will effectively meet the client's needs until you determine exactly what those needs are. You should explain clearly to the client what information you will need from him or her and what value his or her contribution will make to the final Web site.

There are many possible paths in any creative process. However, as you gain experience in planning, designing, and creating Web sites, you will find that some things work better than others. You will come up with your own ideas about the new Cosmatic site's goals, the target audience, and so on, and then compare them to those approved by Brian. You will then evaluate how your plan is similar to and different from the final Cosmatic site plan and consider the benefits and drawbacks of each plan.

> **Tip**
>
> To ensure a successful project and a satisfied client, make the client aware of what to expect and communicate effectively with the client throughout the process.

Reference Window | **Creating a Plan for a New Web Site**

- Determine the site goals.
- Identify the target audience.
- Conduct market research.
- Create end-user scenarios.

Determining Site Goals

The first question you should ask when you begin to plan a site is: What are the primary goals for the Web site? A Web site can have one goal or many goals. It is a good idea to brainstorm with the client, in this case Brian, and create a list of all of the goals you can think of for the site. For example, the goals of a commercial Web site might include the following:

- Provide information about a product
- Sell a product
- Increase brand recognition
- Provide help or operational instructions

This list is very general and could be expanded. The goal list for an actual site should be much more specific. For example, the first two bullets should state what the product is.

Developing an Effective List of Site Goals | InSight

The process for creating a strong list of site goals requires much thought. Keep in mind the following guidelines as you develop the list of site goals. First, write site goals in an active voice rather than passive. Second, use action verbs to help you select achievable goals rather than concepts. For example, brand recognition is a concept, not a goal; *increase* brand recognition is a goal. Action verbs include words such as *achieve*, *increase*, and *provide*. Third, think about the different aspects of the site. For example, in addition to selling products, you may want to provide reliable support. Finally, make a comprehensive list. Your final list should include no more than five goals.

After you have a list of possible site goals, review the list and place the goals in order of importance from most important to least important. For example, the commercial Web site goals might be reordered as follows:

- Sell a product
- Increase brand recognition
- Provide information about a product
- Provide help or operational instructions

Review your list. Combine goals if possible, and then reprioritize as needed. Some of the lower-priority goals might actually be part of higher-priority goals. For example, in some cases, providing help or operational instructions may be incorporated into the general goal of providing information about the product. There is a limit to the number of goals that a Web site can effectively achieve; therefore, you will probably want to focus on the first four or five goals. Remember that site goals are most effective if they are the result of collaboration with the client. After all, just as you are an expert on Web design, the client is an expert concerning his or her business.

Brian asks you to develop a list of goals for the new Cosmatic site. As you gain experience in designing Web sites, your ability to identify and articulate goals will continue to improve.

To create a list of goals for the new Cosmatic site:

▶ **1.** Write down at least 20 possible site goals.

▶ **2.** Review the list to be sure that all statements are in the active voice and use action verbs.

▶ **3.** Prioritize the goals in order of importance.

▶ **4.** Review your list, combining goals if possible and reprioritizing them if necessary.

▶ **5.** Review the top five goals. Think about what you want to accomplish with the site, and make sure that your list of goals will help achieve a successful site.

   Brian created a list of goals for the new Cosmatic site, and then he prioritized and combined them.

▶ **6.** Compare your list to Brian's goal list shown in Figure 2-1.

Figure 2-1 ▶ **Cosmatic Web site goals**

1. Enhance label identity.
2. Increase band recognition.
3. Promote band image.
4. Boost sales of CDs and promotional products.
5. Provide tour date information.
6. Provide information about individual band members.
7. Provide press information.
8. Create cross interest between bands with similar sounds.
9. Link to fan sites.
10. Produce a music library (long-term, not immediate).
11. Construct and link to individual band sites (long-term, not immediate).
12. Create a photo library for each band (long-term, not immediate).
13. Create other materials (such as Flash animations) to increase interest (long-term, not immediate).

You will use the site goals to make decisions about the site organization and structure. The site's primary goal is to enhance label identity—in other words, to make people aware of Cosmatic and to associate the label with certain types of bands. The site will be organized to emphasize the Cosmatic name and logo. The home page will include information about the label followed by band information. The label logo will appear at the top of every page, and the site navigation will be organized so that a "label information" category is included in the top level of the site.

The priority of the goals helps to determine the site's layout. If the first two goals were switched, and increased band recognition was the primary goal, the site structure might be organized differently. The band information could appear above the label information. The band logos could appear at the top of all of the pages instead of the label logo. The individual bands could be placed in their own categories in the top level of navigation. This is just one set of many possible changes.

When you start to examine the way that site goals can affect the structure of the final site, you can see just how important it is to carefully consider what you want to accomplish. Taking the time to establish goals and expectations from the very beginning will make a world of difference in the final site.

Identifying the Target Audience

Tip

The word *user* in user profile refers to the target user group, not an individual user.

The **target audience** for a Web site is the group of people whom you would *most* like to visit the site. You identify the target audience by creating a user profile. A **user profile** is the information that you gather from a list of questions, as shown in Figure 2-2. The user profile is a tool designed to help you determine the characteristics of the group of people you are trying to reach: the target audience.

General user profile questions ◀ Figure 2-2

1. **What is the age range of the user?** Sites can appeal to a range of ages. The age range will depend on the site goals. Generally, the group members are linked because they share a commonality such as a habit, a characteristic, or a developmental stage.

2. **What is the gender of the user?** Sites can be targeted to males only, females only, or males and females. Not all sites are targeted to a specific gender.

3. **What is the education level of the user?** Education level will be a range. Designate education level either by the current year in school (e.g., senior in high school) or the degree earned if out of school (e.g., associates degree).

4. **What is the economic situation of the user?** Economic situation refers to the annual income level of the user as well as other extenuating economic factors, such as parental support or student loans. For example, the user may be a student who has only a part-time job. As a student, the user may have a lower income bracket, earning only $20,000 a year, but extenuating economic factors, such as parental support and student loans, may affect the user's buying power. All of this information should factor into the user's economic situation.

5. **What is the geographic location of the user?** The site can be targeted at users in a specific city, a specific region, or a specific country.

6. **What is the primary language of the user?**

7. **What is the ethnic background of the user?** Most sites are targeted at a user group with diverse cross sections of ethnic backgrounds; however, sometimes ethnicity is a factor in your target audience. For example, Jet Magazine is targeted at African-American users.

8. **Are there other unifying characteristics that are relevant to the user?** If you know that the target group has a common characteristic that may be of use in designing the Web site, list it here. Unifying characteristics are useful if they are related to the topic of the Web site or if they could affect the goals of the site. For example, unifying characteristics might include things such as: target users have diabetes (for a diabetes disease-management site), target users ride dirt bikes (for a BMX motocross site), target users listen to club music (for an alternative music site), and so on.

Finding More Data to Create a User Profile | InSight

Other resources can help you create a user profile. If the client has an existing Web site, you might be able to obtain specific data about current visitors from usage logs and user registration data. Usage logs are exact records of every visit to the site; they include information such as the time and date of the visit, the visitor's ISP, pathway through the site, browser and operating system, and so on. Some sites require visitors to register by creating a user ID and providing personal information before being allowed access. You can analyze this registration information when it is available to further define the target audience.

Brian asks you to create a user profile that identifies the target audience of the Cosmatic site.

To identify the target audience for the new Cosmatic site:

▶ **1.** Answer the user profile questions listed in Figure 2-2.

▶ **2.** Review your answers to ensure that the target audience you identified reinforces the final site goals listed in Figure 2-1. If it does not, reevaluate your site goals or adjust your target audience so that the two are compatible.

▶ **3.** Compare your answers to the user profile questions to those compiled by Brian, as shown in Figure 2-3.

Figure 2-3 ▶ **User profile for the Cosmatic site**

1. Age: 18 to 29
2. Gender: male and female
3. Education level: late high school to college
4. Economic situation: students with expendable income from parental support/financial aid; recent college graduates entering the workplace
5. Geographic location: United States and Canada; the label has concentrated on signing bands from the Denton, Texas, area but wants to target a larger area with its Web site
6. Primary language: target user will speak/read English
7. Ethnic background: the Cosmatic site will not target a specific ethnic background
8. Other unifying characteristics: participation in the "indie" (independent) college music scene

Sometimes clients and designers are hesitant to identify the target audience, because they think it will limit the reach of the Web site. However, a very broad target audience can be even more restrictive than having a very narrow target audience. A Web site that must appeal to many different groups of people must be more generic in some ways. For example, if the new Cosmatic site is intended to appeal to an older audience (50 to 60 years of age) as well as to a college-aged audience (18 to 29 years of age), you can include only elements that will be attractive and communicate effectively with both age groups. You can see how this might limit some stylistic options such as graphics, wording, and color that would be available to a Web site with a target audience that includes only a college-aged group.

Some Web sites are intended to appeal to a broad target audience. Consider the Internal Revenue Service. The IRS site, *www.irs.gov,* is designed to be an informational site available to a diverse group of people. The site contains a huge amount of information about U.S. tax laws and tax preparation. Knowing that the target audience for the IRS site is broad and that the goal of the site is to dispense information, designers chose to create a text-based site, with very few graphic elements, that will be accessible to the broadest possible group of users. The IRS site is very effective at achieving its goals. However, this primarily text-based design would not be effective if the main goal was entertainment, because although rich in informational content, the site is not very entertaining.

InSight | **Creating a Web Site that Appeals to the Target Audience**

After you have identified a target audience, you can use the general information from the user profile as a basis to research and make more advanced decisions about user wants, needs, technical proficiencies, and so on. When used appropriately, the target audience information is a great tool for focusing a Web site to achieve the site goals. However, be careful not to get lost in stereotypes. It is easy to draw general conclusions about the target audience without backing up those assumptions with research. This can lead to a Web site that seems targeted to your intended audience but that, in fact, does not actually appeal to them. For example, we have all been sitting in front of the television when a commercial that is supposed to appeal to our gender and/or age group comes on the screen. Think about your reaction to a commercial that has the right look but underestimates your intelligence or misinterprets your styles, habits, and so on. Use the target audience information as a starting point for your research.

Conducting Market Research

Market research is the careful investigation and study of data about the target audience's preferences for a product or service. It also includes evaluating the products or services of competitors. The user profile provides information about your target audience. After you've created the user profile, you need to investigate the habits, interests, likes, and dislikes of that group of people as well as what Cosmatic's competitors are doing to attract them.

Advertising and design agencies spend a substantial amount of money subscribing to services that provide in-depth market analysis of products or services and their target audiences (such as *www.ipsos-asi.com* or *www.imarketinc.com*), but the average designer has to rely on his or her own research. You will look for information that will help you to build a Web site tailored to the target audience Cosmatic wants to attract. Technical information—such as the screen size and the speeds of the computer and Internet connection that the target audience uses—tells you the technical limitations of an effective site. Information on the spending habits of the target audience tells you the potential profitability of the Web site. Information on the interests of the target audience tells you what will appeal to the target audience and what elements you might include in the site to draw them in. Information about the culture and the customs of the target audience tells you what colors, symbols, fashions, styles, and so on will be effective in communicating with the target audience. Finally, information about competing Web sites tells you what the competition believes effectively attracts and communicates with the target audience.

The fastest way to obtain information about the habits, interests, and likes of a target audience is to use a search engine to locate Web sites with statistics and other data about the target audience's lifestyle and preferences. A **search engine** is a Web site whose primary function is to gather and report the information available on the Web related to specified keywords or phrases. Brian spent some time online and compiled the information shown in Figure 2-4.

Tip

Three common search engines are *www.google. com*, *www.yahoo.com*, and *www.dogpile.com*.

Cosmatic target audience information   Figure 2-4

- 90% of college students own computers.
- Student shoppers tend to go off-campus or online to find the most competitive pricing.
- 90% of students use online services on a daily basis. 52% use search engines to locate stores online. (Yahoo and Google are among the most frequently used.)
- College students spend an average of $480 online annually. Among the most commonly purchased items are music (46% of students buy their music online), books (37%), tickets for air travel (32%), concert and other event tickets (22%), and computer software (14%).
- 81% of college students downloaded music from the Internet in the last year.
- 42% of college freshmen and 91% of college seniors have and use credit cards.

You will look for additional information about the target audience for the Cosmatic site. Make sure that you note the source of the information and the URL of the Web page in case you need to refer to that source in the future.

To gather information on the Cosmatic target audience:

▶ 1. Start your Web browser, type **www.dogpile.com** in the Address bar, and then press the **Enter** key. The Dogpile home page opens.

   Trouble? Sometimes sites "go down" and cannot be accessed. If the Dogpile search engine is unavailable, you can try another search engine. Type **www.google.com** or the URL for your favorite search engine in the Address bar, and then press the Enter key.

▶ **2.** Type **market research student spending** into the box at the top of the page, and then click the **Go Fetch** button to start the search.

▶ **3.** Review the list of Web sites, click the link for a Web site that looks promising, and then explore that site.

▶ **4.** Write down all pertinent information. Make sure to include the source of the information and the URL of the Web page in case you need to refer to that source in the future. If the site contains no relevant statistics or information, continue with Step 5.

▶ **5.** Click the **Back** button ◉ on the browser toolbar to return to the search results.

▶ **6.** Repeat Steps 3 through 5 to gather information from other Web sites until you have documented at least five distinct facts about the spending habits of the target audience.

The information you have collected so far gives you an understanding of the target audience's habits and likes. Now, You will switch your focus from the habits of the target audience to what you can do with the Web site to attract the target audience. You will investigate Web sites that the target audience frequents as well as Web sites of Cosmatic competitors. You will have to make assumptions about which sites are popular with the target audience based on the information that you gathered about its habits and preferences. By exploring sites that are popular with the target audience and the sites of competitors, you can familiarize yourself with graphic styles to which the target audience is accustomed as well as the colors, symbols, fashions, styles, and slang terms that have been effective in communicating with the target audience.

While you are exploring competitor's Web sites, pay close attention to their designs. What colors do the sites use? How is the information laid out? What are the navigation systems like? Is there anything unique about the sites? What aspects of the sites might appeal to the target audience? How is the space used? Can you ascertain what the sites' goals might be? Is the content presented in straightforward language or in slang specific to the target audience? Is there a lot of text on each page, or is the text broken into smaller segments?

To explore other music Web sites:

▶ **1.** Type **www.mtv.com** in the Address bar, and then press the **Enter** key. The MTV home page opens.

▶ **2.** Navigate through the Web site, evaluating the colors, information layout, navigation system, use of space, content, language style (formal, conversational, slang, etc.), and so on.

▶ **3.** Record your findings and make notes about anything you feel is important about the site. Write a brief summary of your findings and notes.

▶ **4.** Repeat Steps 1 through 3 for **www.altpress.com**, the Web site for *Alternative Press Magazine*.

▶ **5.** Search for and explore at least two other sites that the target audience might frequent. For each site, write a brief summary of your findings.

▶ **6.** Look at the Web sites of two other music labels such as **www.fatwreck.com**, **www.4ad.com**, or **www.dischord.com**. What information do they include? Does the information change when the label is trying to target a different audience? For each site, write a brief summary of what you like and dislike about the site.

▶ **7.** Close your Web browser.

By this point, you should have a clear idea of the target audience, including the users' habits, interests, and so on. You should also have an understanding of what you can do with the Web site to attract the target audience. You will use this information to develop end-user scenarios.

Creating End-User Scenarios

End-user scenarios are imagined situations in which the target audience might access a Web site. End-user scenarios help you to envision actual conditions that various end users will experience while visiting the Web site. Scenarios enable you to visualize abstract target audience members as real people. By placing characters in realistic situations, you can get a better sense of the factors that might affect the users' experience with the Web site. You can then anticipate the end users' needs and build a Web site that incorporates these factors into its design.

Brian created two scenarios for the Cosmatic Web site, as shown in Figure 2-5. The scenarios provide insights that go beyond statistics and facts. For example, from Scenario 1, you learn that there is a good chance that the target audience will not have access to audio on the Web site; therefore, you can conclude that audio should not be a primary component.

End-user scenarios for the Cosmatic site | Figure 2-5

Scenario 1

Tim Roth is a junior at the University of North Texas in Denton, Texas. He is 21 and lives on campus in one of the older dorms. Tim has a computer, but the dorms are not equipped with high-speed Internet connections; therefore, when Tim wants to surf from his room, he must do it via a 56k modem. He does most of his surfing late at night in the computer science lab that has 24-hour access. Because the lab computers have no speakers, Tim can listen to sound only if he brings his headphones.

Tim is a fan of Surface Suction and attends the band's shows regularly. He visits the Cosmatic site frequently to check out new bands. The feature that he would most like to see added to the Cosmatic site is a regularly updated list of live shows. Tim's other favorite sites are the Rubber Gloves Rehearsal Studio Web site and The Good Records Web site.

Scenario 2

Sita Owanee, 26, is a recent graduate of Syracuse University's Art Media Studies MFA program. She is now living in New York City and is working as a graphic designer. Because Sita has just started her career and has little expendable income, she has access to the Web via only a 56k modem and a moderately equipped computer.

Sita has a passion for dub music. Dizzied Connections is one of her favorite bands. She discovered the Cosmatic Web site when Dizzied Connections moved to the label and has since become a regular visitor. She visits the site to keep up with Dizzied Connections and to see if Cosmatic has signed other bands with the same sound. Sita would most like to see an expanded section featuring her favorite band. Regularly updated news about the band would keep her interested in the site. Sita's other favorite sites include the Knitting Factory Web site and the Village Voice Web site.

Brian asks you to create a third scenario for the Cosmatic site.

To create an end-user scenario for the Cosmatic site:

▶ **1.** Review the Cosmatic site goals, user profile, and market research.

▶ **2.** Create a character who might visit the Cosmatic site. Give the character a name and attributes such as age, gender, location, and so on.

▶ **3.** Place the character in a situation where he or she is accessing the Web site. Write at least one paragraph describing the character's surroundings and the character's experience with the site.

Planning might seem time-consuming and difficult, but a few hours of advanced preparation will save you many hours of redesign work later. In the next session, you will work on the Cosmatic site's informational structure and aesthetic design.

Review | **Session 2.1 Quick Check**

1. True or False? Each Web site can have only one plan and design.
2. What is the purpose of listing site goals?
3. How many goals can a Web site achieve effectively?
4. What is a target audience for a Web site?
5. Why would you create a user profile?
6. What happens if you draw general conclusions about the target audience without backing up those conclusions with research?
7. Why would you conduct market research?
8. What are end-user scenarios?

Session 2.2

Creating Information Architecture

Creating an **information architecture** is the process of determining what you need a site to do and then constructing a framework that will allow you to accomplish those goals. It applies the principles of architectural design and library science to Web site design by providing a blueprint for Web page arrangement, Web site navigation, and page content organization. The basic process for creating the information architecture for a site is to construct information categories, draw a flowchart, and organize the available information into pages. You will work on the information architecture for the new Cosmatic site.

Creating Categories for Information

Categories provide structure for the information in a Web site and are used to create the main navigation system. The main **navigation system** is the interface that visitors use to move through a Web site. This interface appears on every page in the site. The main categories of a Web site are like the subject sections of a library or bookstore: fiction, poetry, reference material, and so on. They show the visitors what types of information are included in the Web site. The categories should be based on the site goals and the information gathered during the preliminary planning stages. When you create the Cosmatic categories, think about how the information should be organized to achieve the site goals, and then use what you learned from visiting other sites to create logical groupings of information.

Categories can be divided into subcategories, just like the fiction section in a library or bookstore might be divided into historical novels, mysteries, literature, science fiction, and so on. Subcategories should be arranged in hierarchical order, placing the most important subcategories first. After you know the major categories for the Cosmatic site, you can list all the subcategories that will fall under each category in a hierarchical order.

Developing an Efficient Navigation System   InSight

A Web site's navigation system should include a reasonable amount of categories and subcategories. Include no more than five main categories in a Web site so that the pages do not seem cluttered. Likewise, include no more than five subcategories for each main category, because fragmenting information into too many subcategories makes the Web site more difficult to navigate. For more complex sites, you can divide individual subcategories into third-level subcategories. Before creating third-level subcategories, make sure that enough information exists to warrant the breakdown. Visitors dislike having to link too far into a site to find relevant information. Third-level subcategories are appropriate only when a Web site is incredibly information intensive, such as a research site, and no other means effectively conveys the information.

The best way to present the major categories and the subcategories for a Web site is in a standard outline format. Brian created the outline shown in Figure 2-6 to show how the Cosmatic site content can be structured.

Cosmatic Web site categories   Figure 2-6

Cosmatic Web Site Category Outline

I. Home Page
   a. Label
      i. News
      ii. Mission statement
      iii. Company history
      iv. Employee biographies
   b. Bands
      i. Dizzied Connections
      ii. Sloth Child
      iii. Life in Minor Chords
   c. Catalogue
      i. CDs
      ii. Vinyl
   d. Tour Dates
      i. Tour schedules
      ii. Venues and ticket information
   e. Contact
      i. Company contact information
      ii. Directions
      iii. E-mail form

Brian asks you to create an alternate outline with another possible version of the categories and subcategories for the Cosmatic site.

To create an information category outline for the Cosmatic site:

▶ **1.** Review the site goals and your research, and then use that information to create a list of five categories of information for the Cosmatic site.

▶ **2.** Start an outline using the categories you listed in Step 1 as section headings.

▶ **3.** List all the subcategories that will be included in the first section of your outline, and then arrange them in hierarchical order.

▶ **4.** Break the subcategories into their respective subcategories, where applicable, and arrange them in hierarchical order.

▶ **5.** Repeat Steps 3 and 4 for each section of your outline.

▶ **6.** Compare your outline to Brian's outline, as shown in Figure 2-6.

Creating a Flowchart

Next, You will work on the flowchart for the Cosmatic site. A **flowchart** is a diagram of geometric shapes connected by lines that shows steps in sequence. The shapes represent steps, decision points, and dead ends. The lines represent the connection of steps. If steps must be followed in a particular order or direction, then arrows are attached to the lines. In Web design, a flowchart provides a visual representation of the hierarchical structure of the pages within the site. The shapes represent pages and the lines represent their connection.

You create a flowchart from the information category outline. The main categories become the major branches of the flowchart and the subcategories become the sub-branches. Most of the time, visitors can move between pages of a Web site in any direction, so arrows are usually not included. You can use shapes to designate different types of pages in the Web site. For example, all form pages can be hexagons whereas regular pages can be squares. A key or legend for deciphering what the shapes represent is often included in the flowchart. Figure 2-7 shows the flowchart that Brian created for the new site.

> **Tip**
>
> There is no widely recognized standard for the shapes used to designate different Web pages.

Figure 2-7 ▶ **Cosmatic Web site flowchart**

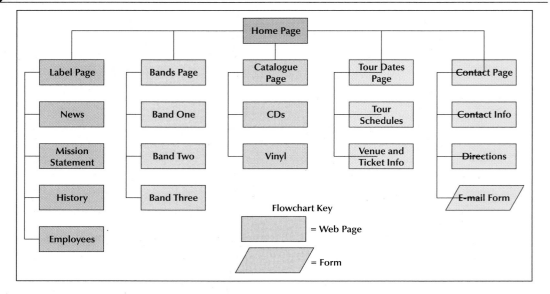

Brian asks you to create a flowchart using the outline that you created. You can create the flowchart using flowcharting software or sketch it using pen and paper.

To create a flowchart for the Cosmatic site:

▶ **1.** Draw a square at the top of the page and label it **Home Page**.

▶ **2.** Draw five squares in a horizontal row below the Home Page square for each of the main categories of your outline, and label each square with one category.

▶ **3.** Draw a line from each main category page to the home page to connect them.

▶ **4.** Repeat Steps 2 and 3 to add the subcategory pages below the category pages. Continue until all of the information from your outline is represented in the flowchart.

▶ **5.** Create a key for your flowchart by drawing and labeling the shapes you used.

▶ **6.** Compare your flowchart to the flowchart Brian created, as shown in Figure 2-7.

Gathering and Organizing Information

The next step in the process of creating an information architecture is to gather and organize all possible sources of information. The materials that you collect will be used to create the page content for the site. It is best to err on the side of excess at this stage, because the more raw materials you have to work with, the better job you can do once you actually start to create content.

Based on the site goals, the market research, the information outline, and the flowchart, you and Brian need information about the following:

- The company and the management team
- The bands and the band members
- The products (CDs and vinyl)

You will find this information in a variety of places. Much of the information you need can be found in promotional materials such as brochures, fliers, press releases, reviews, and articles. Gather all of the available graphic materials and any pertinent company documents such as the company's mission statement and employee biographies. Outside resources can also provide some information. Outside resources include reviews, articles, and other Web sites that reference the product or service. You will want a paper copy of all the information for ease of organization. After all the information is compiled and printed, you are ready to start organizing it.

> **Tip**
>
> Gathering information is often like detective work; use your instincts, follow leads, do research, and talk to others to gather as much information as you can.

Organizing Page Content Logically | InSight

Organizing the data lets you see exactly what you have gathered about each relevant topic. You need to sort the collected materials, piece by piece, into the categories and subcategories you established earlier. You may need to split some items, such as a brochure, into more than one category. Information that fits more than one category should be placed in the category that seems most appropriate. Review any information that is relevant but doesn't fit the planned pages. Try to find a place in the existing structure where the information might fit. You might also consider whether it warrants creating a separate section or a new page.

Next, you will create the aesthetic design for the site. After you have designed the aesthetic structure of the pages, you will create page content out of the materials that you have assembled and organized.

Designing a Web Site

The phrase "look and feel" is used to describe the overall impact of the external characteristics of a Web site. It refers to the way that all the elements of the site design interact to create an experience for the user. The look and feel is achieved from a mixture of many smaller choices including which colors, fonts, graphic style, and layout are selected for the design. To combine all these elements effectively, you start by creating a concept and metaphor for the site.

Reference Window | **Designing a Web Site**

- Create a site concept and metaphor.
- Consider accessibility issues.
- Select colors.
- Select fonts.
- Choose a graphic style and graphics.
- Sketch the layout.
- Check the design for logic.

Creating a Site Concept and Metaphor

A good concept is the basis for developing an aesthetically cohesive Web site. A **site concept** is a general underlying theme that unifies the various elements of a site and contributes to the site's look and feel. To develop a site concept, review some of the artwork and Web sites that appeal to the target audience and look for common underlying themes. Next, make a list of words that describe what you would like the site to convey. Try to think of words that will reinforce the site goals and words that will communicate something to the target audience. Finally, write down the concept.

After you have developed a site concept, you create a metaphor for the site. A **metaphor** is a comparison in which one object, concept, or idea is represented as another. For example, the expression "at that moment, time was molasses" and Shakespeare's famous observation that "all the world's a stage" are metaphors. The **site metaphor** should be a visual extension of the site concept, which reinforces the site message and the site goals. The metaphor helps to create a unified site design.

The metaphor you choose for your Web site does not have to be concretely represented in the site. For example, if the site concept is fluidity, the metaphor might be a river. The actual site does not need to be designed to look like a river, but instead could integrate elements that are commonly identified with rivers: a series of small, partially transparent, wavy lines in the page background; a flowing theme in the graphic design; and colors that are cool such as muted blues and silvers. The river metaphor is an instrument to focus the aesthetic choices.

For the new Cosmatic site, Brian came up with a list of words to describe the site: *hip, retro, logical, underground, alternative, minimalist,* and *intuitive.* Some words apply to a look that is popular with the target audience (hip, retro); other words apply to the flow of information (logical, intuitive). Next, he reviewed the CD cover art on the current Cosmatic site as well as the CD cover art of other bands in the same genre of music to get a feel for the artwork styles that are popular with the Cosmatic target audience. Finally, he decided on the site concept—appropriation of items from the past to create a new look—and the metaphor of "recycling." In later sections, you will see how the recycling metaphor helps to shape the site design by providing a foundation for color choice, font choice, graphics choice, and layout.

Brian asks you to develop another concept and metaphor for the new Cosmatic site.

To develop another concept and metaphor for the Cosmatic site:

▶ **1.** List at least five words that describe the site.

▶ **2.** Start your Web browser.

▶ **3.** Click **File** on the menu bar, click **Open** to access the Open dialog box, click the **Browse** button, navigate to the **Tutorial.02\Tutorial\Cosmatic** folder included with your Data Files, double-click **index.htm**, and then click the **OK** button. If necessary, click the **OK** button in the dialog box indicating that the Web page will open in a new window. The existing Cosmatic site opens in your Web browser.

▶ **4.** Click the **PRODUCTS** link, review the CD cover art on the Products page, and then close the Cosmatic site and your Web browser.

▶ **5.** Review other artwork that appeals to the target audience.

▶ **6.** Choose a site concept, and then write a short description of the concept and why you selected it.

▶ **7.** Choose a site metaphor, and then write a short description of the metaphor and why you selected it.

▶ **8.** Write a paragraph that explains how you could integrate the concept and the metaphor into the site.

Tip

If the menu bar is not visible, you can press the Ctrl+O keys to access the Open dialog box.

Considering Accessibility Issues

The Web is a public venue used by a variety of people, including people with disabilities. You will want to consider making your site accessible to them. With regard to Web design, **accessibility** refers to the quality and ease of use of a Web site by people who use assistive devices or people with disabilities. An **assistive device** is an apparatus that provides a disabled person with alternate means to experience electronic and information technologies. Some ways that you can enhance the accessibility of a Web site include providing alternate text descriptions for any graphics on the site that can be read by audio assistive devices and establishing basic text links in addition to graphical navigation structures.

Effective June 21, 2001, Section 508 of the federal Rehabilitation Act requires all United States federal government agencies, as well as public colleges and universities, to make their electronic and information technology accessible to people with disabilities. Although private companies are under no legal obligation to make their sites accessible, many try to ensure that their sites are at least partially in line with current federal guidelines. Because technologies change rapidly, the Web is the best source for current accessibility guidelines and accessibility-checking tools. You can find information about accessibility guidelines on the Section 508 Web site, *www.section508.gov*.

Adobe offers a number of tools to help you develop accessible Web sites, including templates and checking utilities. Search the Adobe Web site, *www.adobe.com,* using the keyword "accessibility" for information. You can also activate Accessibility dialog boxes within Dreamweaver so that every time you insert an object into a Web page, Dreamweaver prompts you for the information you need to add accessibility.

The World Wide Web Consortium (W3C) also provides information about accessibility technology, guidelines, tools, education and outreach, and research and development. It has created a Web Accessibility Initiative (WAI) whose mission is to promote usability of the Web for people with disabilities. For more information, go to the WAI Web site, *www.w3.org/WAI.*

For now, Brian wants to adjust the new Web site design for accessibility without changing the site's look and feel. This will make the site available to as wide an audience as possible while maintaining a look and feel that appeals to the target audience. Brian plans to implement basic accessibility modifications into the design for the new Web site, and then create a parallel site next year that will meet all the current accessibility guidelines.

Based on a review of the current guidelines, Brian has decided to include alternate text descriptions for graphics and graphic links. This alternate text can be "read" by audio assistive devices. Depending on the browser, this information will appear in place of a graphic or when the user points to an image or link. Brian wants to make the alternate text as descriptive as possible so that anyone can appreciate the site content even without seeing it.

Selecting Colors

Color is an interesting component of design because it affects the emotional response that a user has to the site. The colors you choose set the tone of the site. Before selecting colors for a Web site, You will need a basic understanding of how color applies to Web design.

Thee two major systems of color are subtractive and additive. The traditional **subtractive color system** uses cyan, magenta, and yellow as its primary colors; all other colors are created by mixing these primary colors. It is called the subtractive color system because new colors are created by adding pigment, such as ink and paint, and removing light. If the primary colors of the subtractive color system are combined in equal amounts, they make black—the absence of light. The **additive color system** uses red, green, and blue as its primary colors. This system is also called the **RGB system** for red, green, and blue. As with the subtractive color system, all other colors are created by combining these primary colors. It is called the additive color system because it works like a prism—new colors are created by adding varying amounts of light. If all of the primary colors of the additive system are combined in equal amounts, they create pure white light. Figure 2-8 shows how the primary colors red, green, and blue can be mixed in various combinations to create the secondary colors cyan, magenta, and yellow, and how the primary colors can be combined equally to create white.

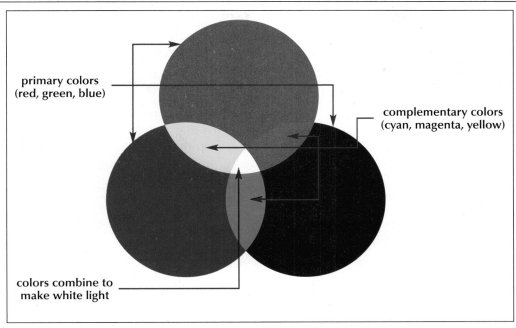

primary colors
(red, green, blue)

complementary colors
(cyan, magenta, yellow)

colors combine to
make white light

Web sites are a digital media designed to be viewed on monitors. A monitor combines hundreds of thousands of pixels (tiny dots of light that glow in different color intensities) to create images. Because monitors work with light, they use the additive RGB color system. When creating or saving graphics for the Web, you should use RGB color.

Color is a good tool for emphasizing information, such as differentiating headlines from body text, or for drawing the eye to a specific area of the page. Color can also be used to distinguish segments of the Web site. For example, you can use a different color for each major category.

Choosing a color palette can be difficult. There is no precise scientific method to ensure that you will choose the perfect colors. This is why most design teams include a graphic artist who is trained in color theory. However, even without extensive color training, you can select attractive and effective colors for a Web site. Keep in mind the following basic color concepts and strategies:

- **Keep it simple.** With color choice, more is definitely not better. Everyone has seen a Web site that looks as if it erupted from a rainbow. Too many competing colors cause the eye to race around the page, leaving the user dazed and confused.
- **Include three to six colors per site.** You will use these same colors for all of the site's elements including the text, background, links, logo, buttons, navigation bar, and graphics. Black and white count as colors when selecting a palette.
- **Consider the mood you want to create.** Colors create a mood. Studies have shown that colors have a psychological effect on people. For example, blue is calming, whereas red is hot or intense. Think about what your target audience might associate with a color when choosing a palette for a Web site.
- **Keep the target audience in mind.** Different cultures do not always have the same psychological associations with specific colors. For example, people in the United States associate white with purity and red with danger, whereas some countries associate white with death and red with marriage. If a Web site has a global or foreign target audience, you might need to research the customs and symbols of the target culture.

Tip

Photographic images may contain many thousands of colors. These do not count as part of the color palette.

One way to develop a color palette is to look to other works of art for inspiration. Think of what emotions and feelings you want to evoke with the Web site, and then find a painting, photograph, or other work of art that stirs those feelings in you. Evaluate the colors the artist used. Consider how the colors interact. Try to pinpoint colors that are causing the emotion. Consider how the color palette works with your metaphor. Think about how you might use that color palette in the Web site.

Brian chose the colors shown in Figure 2-9 for the new Cosmatic site. This color palette fits nicely into the recycling design metaphor because the varying shades of green, red, and yellow are reminiscent of colors popular in the early 1960s. In the site, all three colors will be used in the logo, green will be used in a strip across the top of the site, and yellow will be used in a smaller strip below the top strip. Font colors are discussed in the next section.

Figure 2-9 | **Color palette for the new Cosmatic Web site**

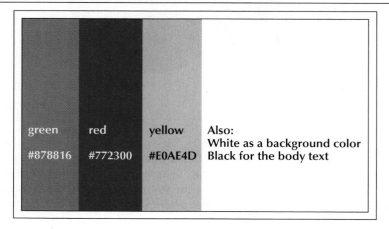

green	red	yellow	Also:
#878816	#772300	#E0AE4D	White as a background color Black for the body text

The figure refers to the colors by their generic color names as well as their hexadecimal color codes. Although color names such as green, red, and yellow are easy to remember and may have more meaning to most people, they can be unreliable when trying to communicate specific color values. One person might use the word *red* to refer to the generic red family of colors, another person might be referring to the specific color designated as red in the Web Safe Color Palette, and still another person might be referring to a red in a different color palette. The color names used in these tutorials are the generic color names.

The **Web Safe Color Palette** consists of 216 colors and provides Web designers a reliable color palette to work with. The Web Safe Color Palette was created when many computers could display only 256 colors at a time. Because current computers can display 16+ million colors and many designers have disregarded the Web Safe Color Palette, many of the colors currently in use in Web sites do not have reliable color names. All colors, however, have hexadecimal color codes, and all well-coded HTML uses hexadecimal color codes instead of color names.

Hexadecimal color codes are six-digit numbers in the form of #RRGGBB where RR is replaced by the hexadecimal color value for red, GG is replaced with the green value, and BB is replaced with the blue value. The specified amounts of each of these colors are mixed together by the system to create the color you specify. **Hexadecimal** is a number system that uses the digits 0 through 9 to represent the decimal values 0 through 9, plus the letters A through F to represent the decimal values 10 through 15. To ensure that the color you specify is understood by the browser and displayed properly, you will use the hexadecimal color codes to designate colors when you create the Cosmatic site. However, you do not need to know the hexadecimal color codes when you are selecting colors in Dreamweaver. Instead, you can click the color you want to use, and Dreamweaver will display the hexadecimal code for that color.

You will select a color palette that will work with the site metaphor you developed. You can use a graphic program (such as Adobe Photoshop, Adobe Fireworks, or Adobe Illustrator), crayons, markers, or colored paper to create your color palette.

To choose a color palette to complement your site metaphor:

▶ **1.** Envision a set of colors that will work with your site concept and metaphor.

▶ **2.** Look at works of art for inspiration.

▶ **3.** Think about the psychological associations of the colors. Do these fit with your site goals?

▶ **4.** Draw a series of rectangles side by side (one for each color in your palette), and then fill each rectangle with one color.

▶ **5.** Write a one-paragraph explanation of your color choice and how it reinforces the site concept and metaphor. Describe where and how you intend to use the colors in the site.

Selecting Fonts

Font refers to a set of letters, numbers, and symbols in a unified typeface. Font choice is important in creating an effective Web site, because a font conveys a wealth of subtle information and often creates an impression about the content before it is even read. Think about the different fonts that might be used on Web sites that present current news and events, Far East travel, and science fiction movies.

The three categories of typefaces are serif, sans serif, and mono. These categories are also referred to as **generic font families**. **Serif typefaces** are typefaces in which a delicate, horizontal line called a serif finishes the main strokes of each character; an example would be the horizontal bars at the top and bottom of an uppercase M. The most common serif typeface is Times New Roman. **Sans-serif typefaces** are those in which the serifs are absent. (*Sans* means "without" in French, so *sans serif* means "without serif.") The most common sans-serif typeface is Helvetica. A third category, mono, is sometimes used. *Mono* is short for *monospaced*. A **monospaced font** is one in which each letter takes exactly the same width in the line; for example, the letter *i* (a thin letter) takes the same amount of space as the letter *m*. A common monospaced font is `Courier`. Monospaced fonts are serif fonts, but they are considered a separate generic font family in Dreamweaver. Fonts that are not monospaced are **proportional fonts**, because each letter takes up a different width on the line proportional to the width of the letter. For example, the letter *i* takes less space than the letter *m*. Both the serif typeface Times New Roman and the sans-serif typeface Helvetica are proportional fonts.

A font must be installed on the end-user's computer for the page to be displayed using that font. If a font is not found on the client computer, the page will be displayed in the default font the end user has chosen for his or her browser. Dreamweaver arranges fonts into groups, which provide designers with the best chance for achieving the desired look for the page. Figure 2-10 lists the default Dreamweaver font groupings. Each group contains the most common names for the selected font; these include at least the most common PC name, the most common Mac name (when different), and the generic font family name. When you apply a font grouping to text, Dreamweaver places a CSS style that contains all three choices around the specified text, ensuring maximum potential for aesthetic continuity across all platforms and all computers. When a browser displays a page, it checks the user's computer for the first font in the group. If the computer doesn't have that font, the browser checks for the second font in the list, and then, if necessary, the third font.

Figure 2-10   **Default font groups in Dreamweaver**

> Arial, Helvetica, sans-serif
> Times New Roman, Times, serif
> Courier New, Courier, monospace
> Georgia, Times New Roman, Times, serif
> Verdana, Arial, Helvetica, sans-serif
> Geneva, Arial, Helvetica, sans-serif

Selecting a font also involves choosing a font color and size and sometimes a font style. **Font color** refers to the color that is applied to the font. The font color should be chosen from the colors you selected for the site's color palette. **Font size** refers to the size of the font. Font sizes can be relative or specific. Relative font sizes define font size in respect to the default font size that the end user has set for his or her browser. Relative font sizes range from xx small to xx large, where xx-small, x-small, and small are smaller than the browser's default font size; medium is equal to the browser's default font size; and large, x-large, and xx-large appear bigger than the browser's default font size. Relative font sizes are often used as part of accessible design because the end user controls the default size of the base font and can change the size at which the text is displayed in the browser. Specific font sizes are fixed sizes. Using fixed font sizes enables the designer to decide exactly how a page will display in a user's browser. Pixels work well as a unit for defining a specific font size, because the pixel unit is supported by major browsers. **Font style** refers to the stylistic attributes that are applied to the font. Stylistic attributes include bold, italic, and underline.

InSight | **Selecting Fonts When Designing a Web Site**

As you select fonts for a Web site, keep in mind the following strategies:

- **Less is more.** In general, you should use no more than two fonts in a Web site to give the site a consistent look. Select one font, one font size, and one font color for the general body text (although text links in the body text will be distinguished by a different color). You can choose a second font, size, and color for headings.
- **Convert headings to images.** Sometimes headings and logos are actually text that has been converted to an image in a graphics program. By converting text into an image, you have greater control over the look of the final site because you can choose a font that is not in the Dreamweaver font list and might not be found on every computer.
- **Consider what you are trying to convey.** Fonts create an impression about the content of the site. Different fonts are associated with specific types of content. For example, the titles of old horror movies usually appeared in a gothic font; therefore, that font is usually associated with horror movies. Choose fonts that support the concept and metaphor for your site.
- **Consider accessibility.** Visually impaired users of the Web site may have a hard time reading certain fonts or smaller sizes. Review accessibility Web sites to find guidelines about fonts and font size.

For the font of the general body text in the Cosmatic site, Brian decided to use black, 14 pixels, and Arial, Helvetica, sans-serif. Brian selected the Arial, Helvetica, sans-serif group because of its simplicity, which will help give the site a minimalist look. He used black text and the default font size because it is easy to read. The logo, headings, and site navigation categories will be graphics made from text using the Bauhaus Lt Bt font and a combination of the Web site palette colors. Brian selected the Bauhaus font, which was used prevalently on T-shirts and in advertising in the early 1960s, because it supports the site metaphor. Until the graphics are available, the font group for headings and subheadings will be Arial, Helvetica, sans-serif. Although it is not necessary, designers often choose to have links formatted in different colors, depending on their state. For example, Brian selected the following colors for links in the new Cosmatic site. A **text link**, a hyperlink that has not yet been clicked, will be green. An **active link**, a text hyperlink that is in the process of being clicked, will be red. A **visited link**, a text hyperlink that has been clicked, will be yellow. See Figure 2-11.

Font choices for the new Cosmatic site ◀ Figure 2-11

Page Headings will be:
font group: Arial, Helvetica, sans-serif; size: heading 1; color; red #772300

Subheadings will be:
font group: Arial, Helvetica, sans-serif; size: heading 2; color; red #772300

linked text will be:
font group: Arial, Helvetica, sans-serif; color; green #878816

active links will be:
font group: Arial, Helvetica, sans-serif; color; red #772300

visited links will be:
Font group: Arial, Helvetica, sans-serif; color; yellow #E0AE4D

body text will be:
Font group: Arial, Helvetica, sans-serif; size: 14 pixels; color; black #000000

You will select a set of fonts that will go with the concept and metaphor you developed for the Cosmatic site.

To choose fonts to complement your site concept and metaphor:

▶ **1.** Start your Web browser, review accessibility Web sites for information about font choice, and then exit your browser.

▶ **2.** Envision a font for the general body text that will work with the site concept and metaphor. Review the list in Figure 2-10 for a list of font grouping options.

▶ **3.** Choose a font color from your site color palette for the body text.

▶ **4.** Choose a color from your color palette for any text hyperlinks that will appear in the body text. Choose different colors for active links and visited links.

▶ **5.** Choose a font size for the body text.

▶ **6.** Choose a font, color, and size for the headings.

▶ **7.** Write a brief explanation of your font choices.

Choosing a Graphic Style and Graphics

The graphics in a Web site provide the personality of the site. Recall that graphics can include images, photographs, buttons, logos, and so on. **Graphic style** refers to the look of the graphic elements in the site. Designing a consistent look for all the graphics in a Web site is one of the keys to developing a cohesive, well-made site.

When selecting a graphic style, keep in mind the following strategies:

- **Be consistent.** If you use a cartoonish drawing for one button, then use cartoonish drawings for all the buttons. If you add a photographic image to the upper-right corner of one page, then consider adding photographic images to the upper-right corners of all the pages. Consistency in choosing graphics gives your site a cohesive look.
- **Design with purpose.** When you add a graphic to a page, ask yourself what the graphic adds to the page. Make sure that you have a reason for adding each graphic to the site.
- **Consider size.** Reduce all of the graphics to the smallest possible file size that you can get without sacrificing the quality of the image. The file size of each graphic contributes to the file size of the Web pages. The smaller you can keep the file size of the Web pages, the faster they will load in the user's browser. You will have to use a graphics program such as Adobe Photoshop or Adobe Fireworks to do this.
- **Consider the target audience.** Review the user profile and consider the technical capabilities of the target audience. Choose graphics that will not keep users from enjoying the site because the pages load too slowly.
- **Support your concept and metaphor.** Choose graphics that reinforce the concept and metaphor of the site. Visual symbols are very powerful tools for conveying information. Consider what each graphic adds to the site, and make sure that each graphic reinforces the site metaphor.

Based on the Cosmatic site goals, the CD cover art for the bands represented by the Cosmatic label, the color palette, the font choices, and the site metaphor, Brian selected a graphic style that mimics the flat, traditional, two-dimensional style prevalent in magazine advertisements during the 1950s and 1960s. Any graphics used in the site will be combined with processed industrial photographs to create a "hip," recycled look. By juxtaposing design styles and images from an earlier time with modern music and content, the site will deconstruct both the old and the new, creating a style and depth that should appeal to the target audience. Figure 2-12 shows the new Cosmatic logo as a sample of the graphic style that was chosen.

Figure 2-12 | **Sample of the graphic style for the new Cosmatic site**

You should make a list of the graphics that you want to include in the site. Include logos, buttons, illustrations, and so on.

You will choose a graphic style for the site concept that you selected for the new Cosmatic site.

To choose a graphic style and graphics to complement your site concept:

1. Review your concept and metaphor for the site, the user profile, and the research that you gathered about sites that appeal to the target audience.

2. Make a list of the graphics that you want to include in the site such as logos, buttons, and illustrations.

▶ **3.** Write a paragraph that describes the graphic style for your site. Explain how this graphic style supports your metaphor.

Sketching the Layout

With the colors, fonts, and graphic style in place, you can determine the site's layout. The term *layout* comes from traditional print design. **Layout** is the position of elements—in this case, on the computer screen. When creating the layout, you decide where in the Web pages to place the navigation system, text, logo, artwork, and so on. The layout should support the site goals and metaphor. It should be easy for a user to follow, and it should appeal to the target audience. Often, two or three effective layouts are possible. Initially, designers create rough sketches of possible layout designs. The client and design team then choose the sketch that they like best, and then create **comps** (comprehensive drawings) from the sketch. The comps are fully developed, detailed drawings that provide a complete preview of what the final design will look like.

> **Tip**
>
> Comps are also called **storyboards**.

Brian developed rough sketches of two possible layouts for the new Cosmatic site, as shown in Figure 2-13. The first sketch places the site navigation system at the top of the page, whereas the second sketch places the site navigation system along the left side of the page. Although both layouts are effective, Brian decided to go with Layout 1. The top navigation system makes better use of the available space and appears to flow better with the selected graphic style.

Layout sketches for the new Cosmatic site ◀ **Figure 2-13**

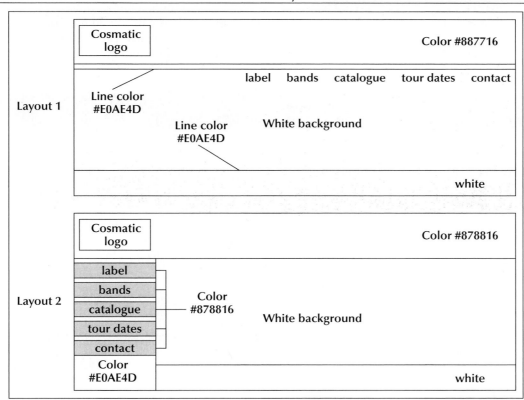

You will draw a rough sketch of a layout that will support the site metaphor that you have chosen.

To create a rough sketch of your site's layout:

▶ **1.** Draw a rough sketch of your site layout.

▶ **2.** Add objects to represent items that you cannot draw, and label them. For example, draw a square the size of a photograph you plan to include, and write a brief description of the photograph inside the square.

▶ **3.** Add labels to identify the colors of each section and the lines (for example, write "white background" across the background).

▶ **4.** Write a paragraph that explains why you selected this layout. Describe how the layout reinforces the site concept and metaphor and helps to achieve the site goals.

Checking the Design for Logic

The final step of designing a site is to check the design for logic. It is important for the end user to be able to navigate through the site easily. A Web site that is attractive to view but confusing to navigate is not well designed. When you check a design for logic, look at all of the elements of the site plan as though you were seeing them for the first time and answer the following questions:

- Is the navigation system easy to follow?
- Does the graphic style support the site metaphor?
- Do the individual elements flow together to create a consistent look for the site?

If you find problems or inconsistencies in any area, You will need to work through the steps that pertain to the trouble area again, addressing the problems as you go. Brian has checked the new Cosmatic site design and is satisfied that it is logical and consistent.

With the planning and design complete, you're ready to start building the site. You will do this in the next session.

Review | **Session 2.2 Quick Check**

---

1. What is information architecture?
2. What is the purpose of categories?
3. How is a flowchart used in Web design?
4. What is a site concept?
5. Why would you want to consider accessibility issues when creating a Web site?
6. What are the four color concepts and strategies?
7. True or False? Designing a consistent look for all the graphics in a Web site is one of the keys to developing a cohesive, well-made Web site.
8. What does the term *layout* mean?

Session 2.3

Creating a New Site

With the planning and design for the new Cosmatic site complete, you're ready to create the Web site. You create a new Web site in Dreamweaver by setting up the site definition. Remember that a site definition has two main parts: the local info and the remote info.

Creating a Local Site Definition

The process for creating the local site definition for a new site is the same as the process for creating one for an existing site. You need a site name and a local root folder to create the local site definition.

You will use "Cosmatic" as the site name to reference the site within Dreamweaver. Spaces and symbols (except hyphens and underscores) are not used in site names, folder names, or filenames because they can cause problems with some operating systems. You can capitalize the first letter of each word to make each site or filename more readable. To keep your local root folder organized, it's a good idea to set up additional folders before you begin working on a site and then save all the site files to the folders you designated for them as you go. The local root folder for the site will be named "Dreamweaver," which will be stored in a project folder named "Cosmatic" on the drive you select. Within the Dreamweaver folder, you will create a folder named "Graphics" so that you have a designated place within the local root folder to keep the copies of the graphics that you use in the site. This folder structure, Cosmatic\Dreamweaver\Graphics, keeps the Dreamweaver files separate from original, uncompressed artwork and working project files stored in the Cosmatic folder that you have not yet added to the site.

You will create the local site definition for the new Cosmatic site.

To create the local site definition for the Cosmatic site:

▶ 1. Start **Dreamweaver**, set the workspace environment to **Designer**, if it is not already set, and then close any pages that are open.

▶ 2. Click **Site** on the menu bar, and then click **Manage Sites**. The Manage Sites dialog box opens.

▶ 3. Click the **New** button, and then click **Site**. The Site Definition for Unnamed Site 1 dialog box opens.

▶ 4. Click the **Advanced** tab, if necessary, and then click **Local Info** in the Category box, if necessary.

▶ 5. Select the text in the Site name box, if necessary, and then type **Cosmatic**. Cosmatic is the name you will use to reference the site.

▶ 6. Click the **Browse** button 🗀 next to the Local root folder box to open the Choose Local Root Folder for Site Cosmatic dialog box, and then navigate to the location where you will store your Web site files.

   Trouble? If you are unsure of the location in which to store the Cosmatic site, ask your instructor or technical support person for help.

▶ 7. Click the **Create New Folder** button 🗀 in the Choose Local Root Folder for Site Cosmatic dialog box, type **Cosmatic** as the folder name, and then press the **Enter** key to name and open the Cosmatic folder. Filenames, folder names, and paths are often case sensitive. Make sure that you type the names exactly as shown in the steps.

▶ 8. Click the **Create New Folder** button 🗀 to create the new folder, type **Dreamweaver** as the folder name, and then press the **Enter** key to name and open the Dreamweaver folder.

▶ 9. Click the **Select** button to set the path for the local root folder. You can also type the path to the local root folder in the Local root folder box.

▶ 10. Click the **Browse** button 🗀 next to the Default images folder box. The Choose Local Images Folder for Site Cosmatic dialog box opens.

Tip

You can also type the path to the Graphics folder in the Default images folder box.

▶ **11.** Navigate to the **Cosmatic\Dreamweaver** folder (the local root folder), and then click the **Create New Folder** button 📄 . A new folder appears in the dialog box.

▶ **12.** Type **Graphics** as the folder name, and then press the **Enter** key. The folder is named and opened.

▶ **13.** Click the **Select** button to set the path for the default images folder.

▶ **14.** Click the **Document** option button.

▶ **15.** Click the **Use case-sensitive link checking** check box to check it.

▶ **16.** Click the **Enable cache** check box to check it, if necessary. The information for the local site definition is complete. See Figure 2-14.

Figure 2-14 ▶ **Local site definition for the new Cosmatic site**

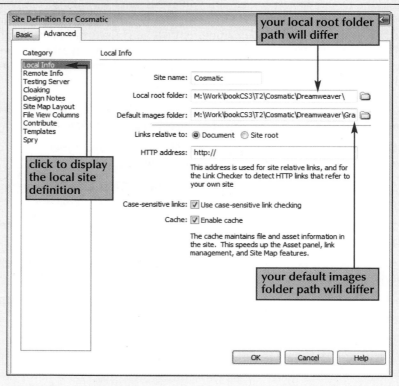

Sometimes Dreamweaver creates a folder in the local root folder named "_notes." You can ignore this folder, but do not delete it; this folder is necessary for Dreamweaver to display the site properly.

Creating a Remote Site Definition

Before you close the Site Definition dialog box, You will create the remote site definition. A **remote site definition** is the information stored on the computer that you are using that tells Dreamweaver where the remote server is located and how to connect to it. Creating a remote site definition enables you to put the Web site on a Web server so that it can be seen on the Web. Viewing a site in a browser on the Web enables you to verify that the features of your Web site work in the browser and when viewed by others over the Web. You set the remote site definition in much the same way as you do the local site definition.

Creating a Remote Site Definition for FTP Access | Reference Window

- Click Site on the menu bar, and then click Manage Sites.
- Click the site name in the list in the Manage Sites dialog box.
- Click the Edit button.
- Click the Advanced tab, if necessary, and then click Remote Info in the Category box.
- Click the Access button, and then click FTP.
- Type the FTP host address where the public version of your Web site will be hosted in the FTP host box.
- Type the host directory name in the Host directory box.
- Type your login name in the Login box.
- Type your password in the Password box, and then click the Save check box to check it if you want Dreamweaver to remember your password.
- Click the Use passive FTP check box to check it.
- Click the Maintain synchronization information check box to check it.
- Verify that the Enable file check in and check out check box is not checked.
- Click the OK button.
- Click the Done button.

First, you need to choose how you will access your Web server. Remote access is usually via FTP (File Transfer Protocol), although some larger organizations provide remote access through a local network. These tutorials use FTP in the remote site definition. The following list describes the FTP options you need to set:

- **FTP host.** The full name of the FTP host, which you will use to access the Web server where the public version of the site is stored. For example, the FTP host might be *www.domain.com* or *ftp.domain.com*. Do *not* include a protocol. (A common mistake is to precede the host name with a protocol, such as ftp:// or http://.) The FTP host name is available from your hosting provider.
- **Host directory.** The location where your Web site files are located on the Web server. For example, the host directory might be *public_html*. You often see more folders and files if you log on the host directory through FTP rather than with a Web browser; the Web folder is usually but not always a subfolder of your default FTP folder. The host directory is available from your hosting provider.
- **Login.** Your assigned login name.
- **Password.** Your assigned password. After you set the password, you can use the Test button to verify that you have entered the information correctly and that you can connect to the remote server.

Tip

Be careful when typing your login name and password, as they might be case sensitive.

- **Use passive FTP.** A server parameter. This information is available from your hosting provider. If you cannot obtain this information, leave the check box checked. If you have difficulties when you preview the site on the Web, reopen the Site Definition dialog box and uncheck the Use Passive FTP check box.
- **Use firewall.** This option is relevant only if your network includes a firewall that requires a password for outbound connections. (This is a rare occurrence, especially in schools, because most network firewalls are not set up to restrict outbound FTP connections.) A **firewall** is a hardware or software device that restricts access between the computer network and the Internet or between a computer and other computers (as with the built-in Microsoft Windows Vista firewall), protecting the computer behind the firewall.
- **Use Secure FTP (SFTP).** This option is relevant only if you are using secure FTP. This information is available from your hosting provider. If you cannot obtain this information, leave the check box unchecked.
- **Maintain synchronization information.** This option enables Dreamweaver to automatically synchronize your local and remote files. Be aware that if you check this option and the remote server time or your local computer time is not accurate, Dreamweaver may overwrite new files with old files.
- **Automatically upload files.** This option automatically uploads files to the remote server when you save a page. Do *not* check this check box.
- **Check in/out.** This option enables multiple users to access files on the Web site.

You will create a remote site definition so that you can preview the Cosmatic site on the Web. If you do not have access to FTP, you will not be able to create and preview the remote Web site.

To create the remote site definition for the Cosmatic site:

▶ 1. Click **Remote Info** in the Category box in the Site Definition for Cosmatic dialog box.

   Trouble? If you do not have access to an FTP host on a Web server, you cannot create a remote site definition using these steps. Your instructor might provide you with directions for creating a remote site definition using a local network. If you do not have access to an FTP host on a Web server, continue with Step 12 to save the local site definition.

▶ 2. Click the **Access** button, and then click **FTP**. Additional options appear in the dialog box. See Figure 2-15.

Remote site definition for FTP access Figure 2-15

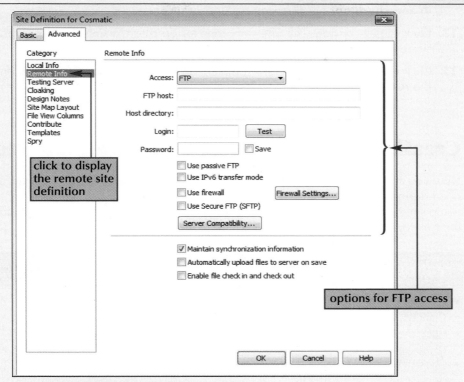

3. Click in the **FTP host** box, and then type the address to the FTP host, which enables you to connect to the server where the public version of your Web site will be hosted.

4. Press the **Tab** key to move the insertion point to the Host directory box, and then type the host directory name.

5. Press the **Tab** key to move the insertion point to the Login box, and then type your login or user name. Remember that the login ID is case sensitive on many systems.

6. Press the **Tab** key to move the insertion point to the Password box, and then type your password. Remember that the password is case sensitive on many systems.

7. Click the **Test** button. Dreamweaver tests the connection to ensure that you can connect to the remote server.

   Trouble? If the connection fails, you might have entered some of the information incorrectly. Verify the information you entered in Steps 3 through 6, and then repeat Step 7.

8. Click the **Save** check box to check it, if necessary. Dreamweaver will remember your password. If you are working on a public computer, remember to uncheck the Save check box before you end your work session.

9. Click the **Use passive FTP** check box to check it.

10. If your computer uses a firewall that restricts outbound connections, click the **Use firewall** check box to check it, and then enter the additional information. *Do not check the Use firewall check box if your computer uses a Windows or other computer-based software firewall.*

▶ **11.** Verify that the **Maintain synchronization information** check box is checked and that the **Automatically upload files to server on save** and the **Enable file check in and check out** check boxes are unchecked.

▶ **12.** Click the **OK** button. The Site Definition for Cosmatic dialog box closes, and the site definition is saved.

▶ **13.** Click the **Done** button to close the Manage Sites dialog box. The site definition for the new Cosmatic site is complete.

Creating and Saving Pages in a Defined Site

Now you can work on pages for the new Cosmatic site based on the flowchart developed during planning. Brian asks you to create, save, and set page titles for the new Cosmatic site home page and all the first-level Web pages: the Label page, the Bands page, the Catalogue page, the Tour Dates page, and the Contact page.

Reference Window | **Creating HTML Pages in a Site**

- Click File on the menu bar, and then click New.
- Click Blank Page in the category list, and then click HTML in the Page type box.
- Click the Create button.
  or
- Click HTML in the Create New list on the Start page.
  or
- In the Files panel, right-click the folder in which to create the file, and then click New File on the context menu.

Adding New Pages

After a site is defined, you can create the pages associated with the site. These pages will be located within the local root folder you specified in the local site definition—in this case, the Cosmatic\Dreamweaver folder. When you create a new page, you select a page category and then the type of page you want to create. You can create a page from scratch or you can use one of the prebuilt page designs that come with Dreamweaver. For now, you will create a simple HTML page. In later tutorials, you will learn about the other types of pages.

You will start by creating the home page for the new Cosmatic site.

To add a new page to the Cosmatic site:

▶ **1.** Click **File** on the menu bar, and then click **New**. The New Document dialog box opens.

▶ **2.** If necessary, click **Blank Page** in the category list, click **HTML** in the Page type box, and then click <**none**> in the Layout box. See Figure 2-16.

New Document dialog box | Figure 2-16

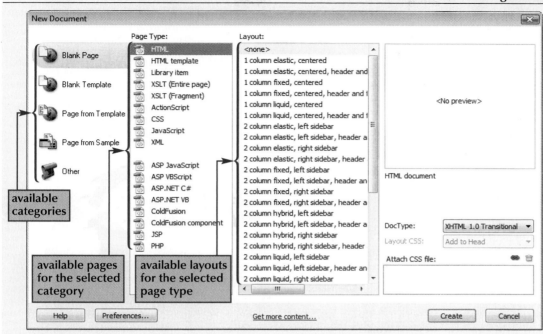

3. Click the **Create** button to create the page. The Untitled-1 page opens in the Document window. See Figure 2-17.

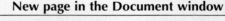

New page in the Document window | Figure 2-17

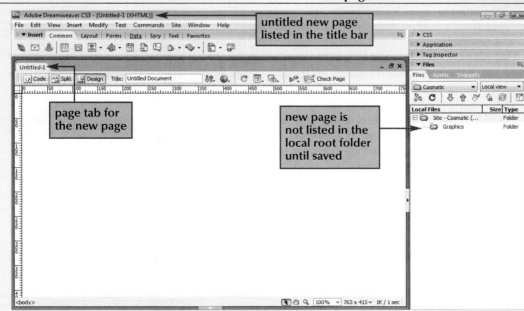

Trouble? If your Document window is restored down, you need to maximize it. Click the Maximize button on the Document window title bar.

Saving New Pages

After you create a page, you need to save it. It is important to save all the pages in the local root folder for the Web site. When you use the Save As command, the Save As dialog box opens to the local root folder for the site that is selected in the Files panel. This helps you to remember to save pages in the site's local root folder. When you save a page, you give the page a filename. Recall that the filename is the name under which a page is saved.

You will save the home page with the filename of index.html (or index.htm); remember that *index* must be all lowercase letters. You will use lowercase letters for all of the page filenames. It is important to keep the case of the filenames consistent, because some operating systems are case sensitive.

To save the home page:

▶ 1. Click **File** on the menu bar, and click **Save As**. The Save As dialog box opens.

▶ 2. Confirm that the dialog box is open to the site's local root folder: **Cosmatic\Dreamweaver**.

▶ 3. Select the text in the File name box, and then type **index.html**.

   Trouble? If your server requires .htm file extensions, then type **index.htm** in Step 3 and use .htm as the file extension whenever .html is used in these tutorials. If you are not sure which file extension to use, ask your instructor or technical support person.

▶ 4. Click the **Save** button. The new filename appears in the page tab at the top of the Document window, in the title bar, and in the Files panel. See Figure 2-18.

Figure 2-18 ▶ **Saved page in the Document window**

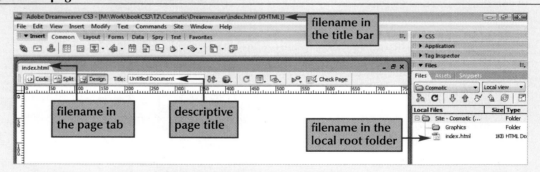

   Trouble? If you don't see the new file in the Files panel, the Files panel is probably set to Remote view. Click the View button on the Files panel toolbar, and then click Local View.

Setting Page Titles

Before you close the page, You will set the page title for the page. Recall that the page title is the name that appears in the browser title bar. You should use the name of the Web site and a descriptive word or phrase for each page so that users can quickly determine the overall page content.

You will enter "Cosmatic - Home" as the page title for the home page.

To add the page title for the home page:

▶ **1.** Select **Untitled Document** in the Title box on the Document toolbar.

▶ **2.** Type **Cosmatic - Home** in the Title box on the Document toolbar.

▶ **3.** Press the **Enter** key. The asterisks next to the filename in the title bar and in the page tab at the top of the Document window indicate that changes have been made to the page since the last time it was saved. See Figure 2-19.

Page title set for the home page | Figure 2-19

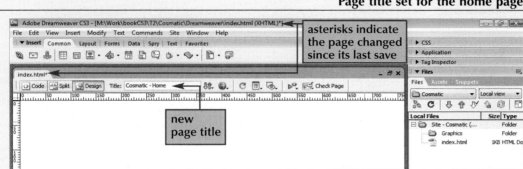

Resaving Pages

Dreamweaver has several built-in measures to help you keep your work safe. If you have not saved a page after you have edited it and you try to close the page or exit the program, Dreamweaver prompts you to save the changes you made to that page. If you use an element such as a graphic in a page, and that element is not yet part of the site, Dreamweaver saves a copy of the element in the local root folder. (Dreamweaver will automatically save a copy of each graphic you use in a page if you've created a default graphics folder. Otherwise, Dreamweaver will prompt you to save a copy of the graphic or element.) By including copies of all of the files associated with a site within its local root folder, you prevent a myriad of complications from occurring.

| **Saving Frequently** | | InSight |

It is important to save frequently—at least every 10 minutes—and whenever you have finished modifying a page. Also make sure that all pages in the Web site are saved before you preview the site. Anyone who has worked on a computer for any length of time can confirm that programs crash at the least opportune moment. Saving your work frequently prevents large losses.

You will resave the home page, and then You will close the page.

To resave and close the home page:

▶ **1.** Click **File** on the menu bar, and then click **Save**. The asterisks in the page tab and the Document window title bar disappear.

▶ **2.** Click the **Close Page** button ❌ on the Document window title bar. The home page closes.

You will use a similar process to create and save the remaining top-level pages for the new Cosmatic site. Rather than opening the New Document dialog box each time, You will use the HTML link on the Start page.

To create and save the remaining top-level pages:

▶ **1.** Click **HTML** in the Create New list on the Start page. A new Untitled page opens.

▶ **2.** Select **Untitled Document** in the Title box on the Document toolbar, type **Cosmatic - Bands**, and then press the **Enter** key. The title bar shows the new title for the page.

▶ **3.** Click **File** on the menu bar, and click **Save As**. The Save As dialog box opens.

▶ **4.** Type **bands.html** in the File name box, and then click the **Save** button. The page is saved and appears in the local root directory.

▶ **5.** Click the **Close Page** button ✖ on the Document window title bar. The page closes.

▶ **6.** Repeat Steps 1 through 5 for the remaining pages, using the following filenames and page titles:

Page Title | Filename
Cosmatic - Catalogue | **catalogue.html**
Cosmatic - Contact | **contact.html**
Cosmatic - Label | **label.html**
Cosmatic - Tourdates | **tourdates.html**

Reviewing HTML Tags

The most common language of the Web is Hypertext Markup Language (HTML), which provides instructions for how to structure Web pages for display. Because many types of computers are connected to the Web and people use different operating systems and software on their computers, Web pages are not tied to any specific software package. Instead, Web pages are created in a common markup language that is viewable by a variety of software packages, including Web browsers. HTML uses a series of tags to tell a browser what to do with the information on a Web page and how to display it.

Even though Dreamweaver provides a graphical interface for creating a Web site in HTML, a basic understanding of HTML is important to gain a true sense of what is going on. Web pages are text documents that include specific markup tags that tell a Web browser how to display the elements. Tags almost always appear in sets, and each tag is included within angle brackets: < and >. The opening tag tells a browser that a certain type of information follows. The opening tag also contains any parameters or attributes that are to be applied to that information. The closing tag always starts with a forward slash, /, which tells the browser that the type of information that had been started is now finished.

Some tags are required for every Web page. These tags—HTML, head, title, and body—are described in Figure 2-20.

Basic HTML tags ◄ **Figure 2-20**

Name	Opening Tag	Closing Tag	Description
HTML	<html>	</html>	Signify where the HTML coding begins and ends; usually appear at the beginning and ending of a Web page. Everything inside the <html> and </html> tags is HTML unless specifically denoted as something else by another type of tag.
head	<head>	</head>	Contain the page title, the descriptive information for the page, which is not seen in the browser, and programming scripts.
title	<title>	</title>	Surround the page title, which appears in the title bar of the browser window when a viewer opens that page.
body	<body>	</body>	Surround all the content or visible elements on the page. Include other tags to format the content. Also contain some scripts.

Many other tags appear within the body of a document to format the content. Other types of code, such as JavaScript and Cascading Styles, are often used within HTML to add further functionality and formatting to pages. For example, you might include Java-Script that adjusts the page to optimize display for the user's browser, and you can use Cascading Styles to format the display of text, graphics, page properties, and so on. You will see these additional tags as you continue to build the pages for the new Cosmatic site.

You will review the HTML tags that Dreamweaver generated when you created the Web pages.

To review HTML tags in the top-level pages of the Cosmatic site:

▶ 1. In the Files panel, double-click **index.html**. The home page opens in the Document window.

▶ 2. Click the **Code** button on the Document toolbar. The Document window displays the underlying HTML coding for the home page. See Figure 2-21. The line numbers are only for reference; the line numbers shown in the figure might not match the ones on your screen. Also, the lines of code on your screen might wrap differently than those in the figure.

HTML code for the home page ◄ **Figure 2-21**

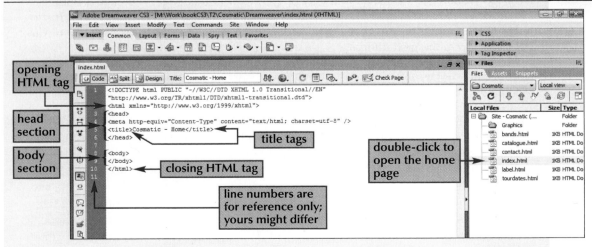

opening HTML tag

head section

body section

title tags

closing HTML tag

double-click to open the home page

line numbers are for reference only; yours might differ

> **Trouble?** If you cannot see all of the code, you may need to scroll the window. Drag the horizontal scroll box all the way to the left edge of the horizontal scroll bar.
>
> ▶ **3.** Click the **Close Page** button ☒ on the Document window title bar. The home page closes.

Although you will usually work in Design view, you can create and edit your pages in Code view. You will use Code view to change the page title for the Tour Dates page from "Cosmatic - Tourdates" to "Cosmatic - Tour Dates."

To edit the Tour Dates page in Code view:

▶ **1.** In the Files panel, double-click **tourdates.html** to open the Tour Dates page in the Document window, and then click the **Code** button on the Document toolbar, if necessary. The Tour Dates page is displayed in Code view.

▶ **2.** Locate the title tags in the Document window.

▶ **3.** Select the **Tourdates** text between the opening and closing title tags, and then type **Tour Dates**. The page title is updated. You will switch to Design view to review the change.

▶ **4.** Click the **Design** button on the Document toolbar. The Tour Dates page is displayed in Design view. The text in the Title box on the Document toolbar shows the revised page title, which you changed directly in the code.

▶ **5.** Click **File** on the menu bar, and then click **Save**. The change you made to the Tour Dates page is saved.

▶ **6.** Click the **Close Page** button ☒ on the Document window title bar. The Tour Dates page closes.

Setting Page Properties

After you have created a page, the next step is setting the basic page properties. **Page properties** are attributes that apply to an entire page rather than to only an element in the page. To set page properties, open the page for which you want to set page properties and then make the appropriate changes. You must resave the open page after changing the page properties to associate the new properties with that page. The page properties are broken into five categories: Appearance, Links, Headings, Title/Encoding, and Tracing Image. Page properties are created with Cascading Styles. You will learn more about Cascading Styles in the next tutorial.

The Appearance category includes general page properties such as the default text, background, and margin attributes. The different Appearance properties include the following:

• **Text settings.** The page font is the default font that is used to display page text. Remember that fonts can be displayed only if they are installed on the end-user's computer and that Dreamweaver groups fonts to ensure the highest possibility of successful display. The Page Font list contains the default Dreamweaver font group, as was shown in Figure 2-10. You will use the Arial, Helvetica, sans-serif group for the Cosmatic site. Size sets the default size for text in the page. You can select a specific or relative size from the list or you can type a different font size in the text box. If you select a specific size, you must also choose a unit. Pixels are the most frequently used unit for specific font size. You will use a variety of sizes in the Cosmaticsite. The text color sets the default color for text on the page. The initial default text color is black, which has the hexadecimal color code #000000. When you want to select a different color and do not know its hexadecimal color code, use the color picker toselect from a visual display and Dreamweaver will insert the hexadecimal color code. It is best to use the hexadecimal color code, if you know it, to ensure that you always use the exact same color each time you insert the color. Figure 2-22 shows the color picker in the Page Properties dialog box.

Page Properties dialog box with the color picker open ◀ **Figure 2-22**

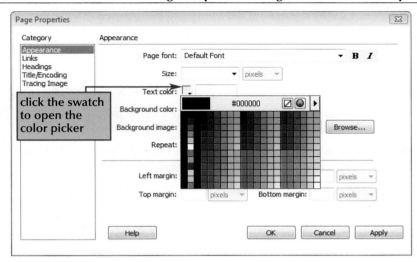

- **Background settings.** You can set the background color and the background image for the page. A Web page background can be an image, a color, or both. If both are used, the color will appear while the image is downloading, and then the image will cover up the color. If the image contains transparent pixels, then the background color will show through. The default background is no color, and most browsers display an absence of color as white. You will use white, which has the hexadecimal color code #FFFFFF, for the background color of the new Cosmatic site. You will also use a background image for the site.
- **Margin settings. Margins** are measurements that specify where page content is placed in the page. You can specify left, right, bottom, and top page margin spaces. The new Cosmatic site will have left and right margins of 5 and top and bottom margins of 0.

The Links category includes the page properties for hyperlinked text. You can select Same as Page Font from the Link Font list to use the page font for hyperlinked text, or you can select a different font group from the list if you want hyperlinked text to appear in another font. For the Cosmatic site, you will use the same font for links and text, and you will not set a size. You can set a default color for hyperlinked text in the page. If you do not specify a color for visited or active links, the browser's default colors will be used. The new Cosmatic site will use green for the links, yellow for the visited links, and red for the active links. The final attribute in the Links category is the Underline option. You can choose to always underline linked text, never underline linked text, show underline only on rollover, or hide underline on rollover. The Cosmatic site will use the Always Underline option.

The Headings category enables you to set font, font size, and font color attributes for the headings in your page. You will set two headings for the new Cosmatic site. The top-level heading, Heading 1, will be 30 pixels in size and red in color. The second-level heading, Heading 2, will be 20 pixels in size and red in color.

The Title/Encoding category enables you to set the page title and document encoding type. The page title can also be set from the Document window, as you did earlier. **Document encoding** specifies how the digital codes will display the characters in the Web page. Thedefault Western European setting is the setting for English and other Western European languages.

Finally, the Tracing Image category enables you to select an image as a guide for re-creating a design or mock-up that was originally created in a graphics program. For example, if you created a mock-up of your site in Adobe PhotoShop, you could import a copy of that mock-up into Dreamweaver as a tracing image. You could then use that image as a reference while re-creating the individual elements in Dreamweaver. The tracing image is visible only in Dreamweaver.

You will set the page properties for the pages you added to the new Cosmatic site.

To set the Appearance page properties for the home page:

1. In the Files panel, double-click **index.html**. The home page opens in the Document window.

2. Click **Modify** on the menu bar, and then click **Page Properties**. The Page Properties dialog box opens with the Appearance category selected.

3. Click the **Page font** arrow, and then click **Arial, Helvetica, sans-serif**.

4. Click the **Size** arrow, and then click **14**.

5. Click in the **Text color** text box, type **#000000** (the hexadecimal color code for black), and then press the **Tab** key. The color box changes to black to match the color code you just entered.

6. Click the **Background color** box to open the color picker, and then point to the **white swatch** in the color picker. The hexadecimal color code at the top of the color picker changes as you move the pointer over the color swatches.

7. Click the **white swatch** in the color picker to select white as the background color. The hexadecimal color code #FFFFFF appears in the Background color box.

8. Click the **Browse** button next to the Background image box to open the Select Image Source dialog box, navigate to the **Tutorial.02\Tutorial** folder included with your Data Files, and then double-click **background.gif**. The image is selected as the background image. A copy of the image is placed in the Graphics folder, and the file path appears in the Background image box.

9. Click in the **Left margin** box, and then type **5**.

10. Press the **Tab** key twice to move the insertion point to the Right margin box, and then type **5**.

11. Press the **Tab** key twice to move the insertion point to the Top margin box, and then type **0**.

12. Press the **Tab** key twice to move the insertion point to the Bottom margin box, and then type **0**. See Figure 2-23.

Completed Appearance category in the Page Properties dialog box ◀ **Figure 2-23**

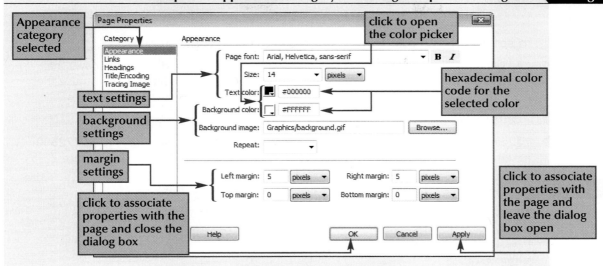

You've entered all the Appearance properties for the home page. Next, You will set the page properties for the Links category.

To set Links page properties for the home page:

▶ **1.** Click **Links** in the Category box. The Page Properties dialog box shows the settings for the Links category.

▶ **2.** Click in the **Link color** box, and then type **#878816** (the hexadecimal color code for green).

▶ **3.** Press the **Tab** key four times to move the insertion point to the Visited links box, and then type **#E0AE4D** (the hexadecimal color code for yellow).

▶ **4.** Press the **Tab** key twice to move the insertion point to the Active links box, and then type **#772300** (the hexadecimal color code for red). See Figure 2-24.

Completed Links category in the Page Properties dialog box ◀ **Figure 2-24**

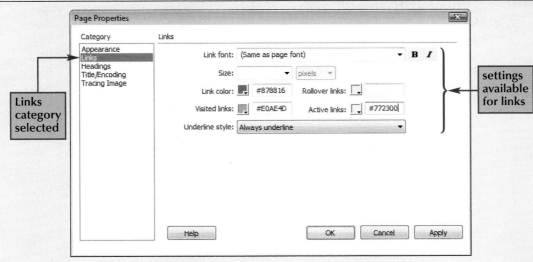

You've entered all the Links properties. You will set the page properties for the Heading 1 category.

To set Headings page properties for the home page:

▶ 1. Click **Headings** in the Category box. The Page Properties dialog box shows the settings for the Headings category. You will leave the heading font set to use the same fonts that you specified for the page font in the Appearance category.

▶ 2. Type **30** in the Heading 1 box.

▶ 3. Press the **Tab** key three times to move to the Heading 1 color box, type **#772300** (the hexadecimal color code for red), and then press the **Tab** key. See Figure 2-25.

| Figure 2-25 | Completed Headings category in the Page Properties dialog box |

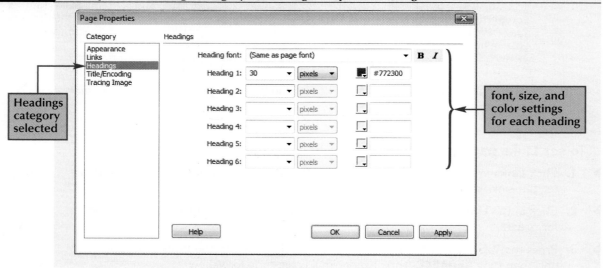

You've entered all the page properties for the home page. You will close the Page Properties dialog box, and then save and close the home page.

To save the page properties:

▶ 1. Click the **OK** button. The Page Properties dialog box closes, and the property settings are applied to the home page. See Figure 2-26.

Home page with the page properties set Figure 2-26

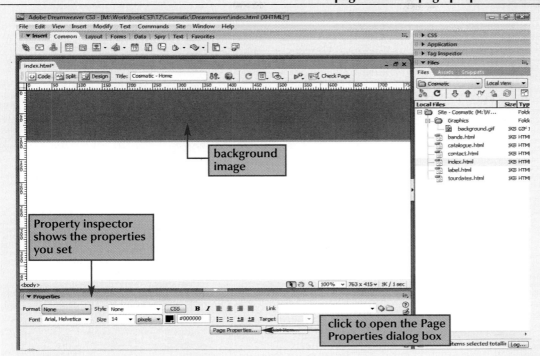

2. Click **File** on the menu bar, and then click **Save**. The page properties are saved with the page.

3. Click the **Close Page** button ✖ on the Document window title bar. The home page closes.

Next, You will set the page properties for the other pages you created for the new Cosmatic site: bands.html, catalogue.html, contact.html, label.html, and tourdates.html. You already saved the background.gif image in the Graphics folder when you set the page properties for the home page. You will use this same image as the background for the other pages.

To set the page properties for the remaining top-level pages:

1. In the Files panel, double-click **bands.html** to open the Bands page, and then, in the Property inspector, click the **Page Properties** button. The Page Properties dialog box opens with the Appearance category selected.

2. Click the **Page font** arrow, and then click **Arial, Helvetica, sans-serif**.

3. Click the **Size** arrow, and then click **14**.

4. Type **#000000** in the Text color box to change the text color to black.

5. Click the **Background color** box to open the color picker, and then click the **white swatch**. The hexadecimal color code #FFFFFF appears in the Background color box.

6. Click the **Browse** button next to the Background image box to open the Select Image Source dialog box, navigate to the **Cosmatic\Dreamweaver\Graphics** folder, and then double-click **background.gif**. You will use this same image for the background image on all of the pages.

▶ **7.** Type **5** in the Left margin box, type **5** in the Right margin box, type **0** in the Top margin box, and then type **0** in the Bottom margin box.

▶ **8.** Click **Links** in the Category box. The Page Properties dialog box shows the settings for the Links category.

▶ **9.** Type **#878816** (the hexadecimal color code for green) in the Link color box, type **#E0AE4D** (the hexadecimal color code for yellow) in the Visited links box, and then type **#772300** (the hexadecimal color code for red) in the Active links box.

▶ **10.** Click **Headings** in the Category box. The Page Properties dialog box shows the settings for the Headings category.

▶ **11.** Type **30** in the Heading 1 box, and then type **#772300** (the hexadecimal color code for red) in the Heading 1 color box.

▶ **12.** Click the **OK** button. The Page Properties dialog box closes, and the property settings are applied to the page.

▶ **13.** Click **File** on the menu bar, and then click **Save**. The page properties are saved with the page.

▶ **14.** Click the **Close Page** button ✖ on the Document window title bar to close the page.

▶ **15.** Repeat Steps 1 through 14 to set the page properties for the following pages: **catalogue.html**, **contact.html**, **label.html**, and **tourdates.html**.

You have finished creating the pages for the new Cosmatic site and setting the page properties. Now you will preview the site.

Previewing a Site in a Browser

Variations often exist in the way that different browsers display Web pages and even in the way that different versions of the same browser display Web pages. That is why after you have started building a Web site, you should preview it in all of the browsers that you are planning to support. Cosmatic plans to support both Internet Explorer and Firefox, the most commonly used browsers.

You can preview your Web site in any browser that is in the Dreamweaver Preview list. You might need to add a browser to the Preview list. You should designate the two browsers that you consider most important as the primary and secondary browsers. Dreamweaver defaults to the primary browser when you preview your work, and both the primary and secondary browsers have keyboard shortcuts.

To make a browser your primary browser, you check the Primary Browser check box when adding the browser to your list. To make a browser the secondary browser, you check the Secondary Browser check box. If you do not check either the Primary or Secondary check box, the browser will be added to the Preview in Browser list on the File menu, but it will not have a keyboard shortcut. These tutorials use Internet Explorer version 7 as the primary browser.

To add a browser to the Preview list:

▶ **1.** Click **File** on the menu bar, point to **Preview in Browser**, and then click **Edit Browser List**. The Preferences dialog box opens with Preview in Browser selected in the Category box. See Figure 2-27.

Preferences dialog box ◄ Figure 2-27

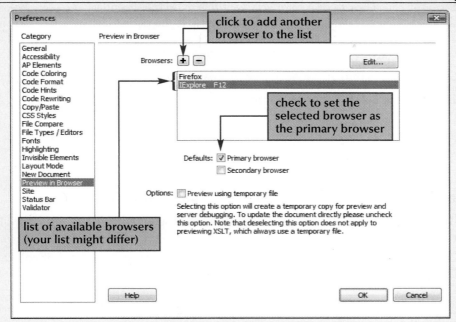

▶ **2.** Look for the browser that you use in the Browsers box. If the browser is listed, click the browser to select it, check the Primary browser or Secondary browser check box as needed, and then skip to Step 8. If the browser is not listed, continue with Step 3.

▶ **3.** If you need to add a browser, click the Browsers Plus (+) button ⊞. The Add Browser dialog box opens. See Figure 2-28.

Add Browser dialog box ◄ Figure 2-28

▶ **4.** Type the name of the browser you are adding in the Name box.

▶ **5.** Click the **Browse** button to open the Select Browser dialog box, navigate to the folder containing the browser that you want to add, click the browser program icon, and then click the **Open** button. The path to the file that you selected appears in the Application box.

Trouble? If you cannot find the browser program icon on the computer that you are using, ask your instructor or technical support person for help.

▶ **6.** Click the **Primary browser** check box to insert a check mark if you want Dreamweaver to default to this browser when you preview your work. Check the **Secondary browser** check box to check it if you want this to be the secondary browser choice that you can access when previewing your work. If you do not check either the Primary or Secondary check box, the browser will be added to the Preview in Browser list on the File menu, but it will not have a keyboard shortcut.

▶ **7.** Click the **OK** button in the Add Browser dialog box.

▶ **8.** Click the **OK** button in the Preferences dialog box.

Next, You will use the primary browser to preview the Web pages you created for the new Cosmatic site. You will start by previewing the home page.

To preview the top-level pages in the primary browser:

▶ **1.** In the Files panel, double-click **index.html**. The home page opens in the Document Window.

▶ **2.** Click **File** on the menu bar, point to **Preview in Browser**, and then click **IExplore** or the name of your browser. The browser opens with the home page. See Figure 2-29.

Figure 2-29	Home page previewed in Internet Explorer

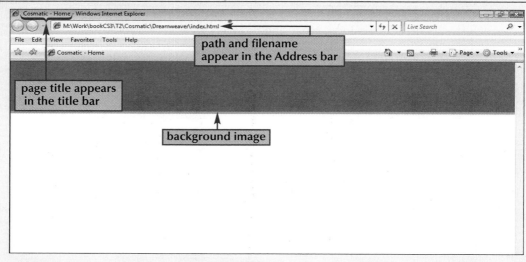

▶ **3.** Review the page. The background image is displayed, the page title appears in the title bar, and the filename is shown in the Address bar.

▶ **4.** Click the **Close** button ⊠ on the browser window title bar to close the browser window.

▶ **5.** Click the **Close Page** button ✖ on the Document window title bar to close the home page.

▶ **6.** Preview the other pages you created to verify that they all have the same background image and that their page titles appear in the title bar.

Uploading a Web Site to a Remote Location

After you have created pages in your Web site, you should upload the site to your remote location: either a Web server or your network server.

You upload a Web site to your server so that you can view the site over the Web as the end users will see it. Previewing the site from within Dreamweaver is a convenient way to check a site for problems as you work, but you should also upload the site periodically as you work on it, at least once each day, to make sure that it displays correctly. Sometimes the way a page previews from within Dreamweaver is different from the way it looks when it is viewed on the Web.

Uploading a Web Site to a Remote Location	Reference Window

- Click the Connects to Remote Host button on the Files panel toolbar.
- Select the files in the local root folder that you want to upload.
- Click the Put File(s) button on the Files panel toolbar.
- Click the Disconnects from Remote Host button on the Files panel toolbar.

All of the files that the remote version of a Web site will use must be located on the Web server. The first time you upload a site, you must include all the files and folders for the site, including the graphics located in the Graphics folder. From then on, you update the remote site by uploading only files that you have changed. When you upload a Web page or group of pages, Dreamweaver will prompt you to upload the dependent files. **Dependent files** are files, such as the graphics files, that are used in the Web page or pages. If you have not yet uploaded these files, or if you have modified them, you need to upload these dependent files. However, if you have already uploaded them and you have not modified them, it is not necessary to upload them again.

When you upload the pages to the remote server, be careful to use the Put File(s) button on the Files panel toolbar, not the Get File(s) button. The Get File(s) button downloads the files from the remote server to your local root folder, and you might overwrite the more current files in your local root folder.

You will upload the new Cosmatic site to the remote server so you can preview it on the Web.

To upload the Cosmatic site to your remote server:

► 1. Click the **Connects to Remote Host** button 🖳 on the Files panel toolbar. When Dreamweaver is connected to the remote host, you see a green light on the Connects to Remote Host button.

   Trouble? If you do not have access to a remote host, you cannot upload your site. Check with your instructor to see if he or she has alternate instructions. If not, skip to Step 9.

► 2. Click the **View** button on the Files panel toolbar, and then click **Local View**, if necessary.

► 3. Click the **Graphics** folder, press and hold the **Shift** key, and then click **tourdates.html** to select all of the files in the local file list. These are the files you want to upload to the server.

   Trouble? If all of the files in the local file list are not selected, your files are probably in a different order. Press and hold the Ctrl key as you click any files for the site that are not selected.

Tip

Press the Ctrl key as you select nonadjacent files; press the Shift key as you select adjacent files.

▶ **4.** Click the **Put File(s)** button ⬆ on the Files panel toolbar. A dialog box opens, prompting you to include dependent files. You have already selected all of the dependent files for the site—the Graphics folder—in addition to the pages.

▶ **5.** Click the **No** button.

▶ **6.** Click the **View** button on the Files panel toolbar, and then click **Remote View**. The Files panel switches to Remote view, and you see the list of files you uploaded to the remote server.

▶ **7.** Click the **Expand/Collapse** button 🖹 on the Files panel toolbar. The Files panel expands to display both the Remote and Local views. See Figure 2-30.

| Figure 2-30 | Files panel expanded with Remote view and Local view |

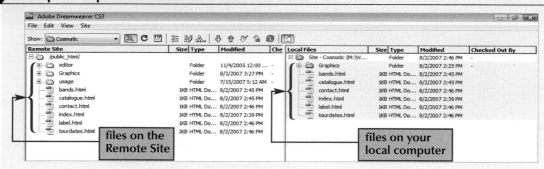

Trouble? If you see the site map, you need to show the site files. Click the Site Files button on the Files panel toolbar.

▶ **8.** Click the **Disconnects from Remote Host** button 🔌 on the Files panel toolbar, click the **Expand/Collapse** button 🖹 on the Files panel toolbar to collapse the Files panel, click the **View** button on the Files panel toolbar, and then click **Local View** to return to Local view.

If you are working on a public computer, continue with Step 9; otherwise, read but do not perform Steps 9 and 10.

▶ **9.** If you are working on a public computer, click **Site** on the menu bar, click **Manage Sites** to open the Manage Sites dialog box, make sure **Cosmatic** is selected in the list, and then click the **Edit** button. The Site Definition for Cosmatic dialog box opens.

▶ **10.** Click **Remote Info** in the Category box, click the **Save** check box to uncheck it, click the **OK** button, and then click the **Done** button in the Manage Sites dialog box. Now, the next person who uses the computer cannot use the remote site definition to log on to your account because the password will not be saved in the remote site definition when you close Dreamweaver.

Previewing a Remote Site on the Web

With the files are uploaded to the remote site, you and others can view them in a browser. You will explore the remote site using a browser to check if the page looks the same on the Web as it does in Dreamweaver. If you find differences, such as extra spaces, write them down and discuss them with your instructor. At this point, the only difference that you should see is in the site address. When you preview over the Web, the site will have an actual Web address instead of a file path.

To view the Cosmatic site from your remote location:

▶ **1.** Start your Web browser, type the URL of your remote site into the Address bar on the browser toolbar, and then press the **Enter** key. The index.html page of the Cosmatic site from the remote server loads in the browser window. See Figure 2-31.

Cosmatic home page viewed over the Web | **Figure 2-31**

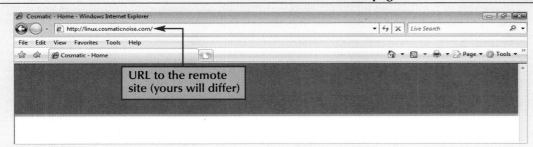

Trouble? If the browser window displays the list of files stored on the remote site, double-click the index.html file to open the home page.

Trouble? If the browser displays a warning that the listing was denied, type the base URL of the remote site, type "/" (a forward slash), and then type "index.html" into the Address bar in your browser's toolbar.

Trouble? If any pages or items are missing or do not display correctly, the files might have been corrupted during the upload process, or you might not have uploaded all the dependent files. Repeat the previous set of steps to upload all of the files to the remote location. If you still have problems with your remote site, you might need to edit the remote site definition and click the Use Passive FTP check box to uncheck it. If you still have problems and your remote server is a Windows server, using an outside FTP program to upload all the files to your remote server may solve the problem. Ask your instructor or technical support person for help.

▶ **2.** Click the **Close** button ![X] on the browser title bar to close the browser window.

You have finished creating the pages for the new Cosmatic site, setting the page properties for the home page, and previewing the page. In the next tutorial, You will add and format the text on each page.

Session 2.3 Quick Check | Review

1. What are the two main parts of the site definition?
2. What is the purpose of creating a remote site definition?
3. What happens when you click the New command on the File menu?
4. When should you save your work?
5. True or False? Web pages are created in a markup language that is viewable by only specific software packages.
6. Explain what page properties are.
7. What are two ways to preview a site you are creating?
8. What are dependent files?

Review | **Tutorial Summary**

In this tutorial, you planned the structure of a new Web site. You determined the site's goals, defined a target audience, and created an end-user profile. You researched the intended market and created end-user scenarios. You used this information to make preliminary decisions about the new site. Next, you created the information architecture for the new Web site, which included creating a flowchart and organizing information categories. Then, you designed the site by developing a site metaphor. You also established a color palette, a font set, a graphic style, and a layout design. Finally, you created the new site. You set up the site definition for both the local and remote information. You added all the top-level pages to the site, and then you reviewed the HTML tags that Dreamweaver created. You set the page properties for each page, and you previewed the site in a browser and on the Web.

Key Terms

accessibility	generic font families	sans-serif typeface
active link	graphic style	search engine
additive color system	hexadecimal	serif typeface
assistive device	hexadecimal color code	site concept
client	information architecture	site metaphor
comp	layout	storyboard
dependent file	margin	subtractive color system
document encoding	market research	target audience
end-user scenario	metaphor	text link
firewall	monospaced font	user profile
flowchart	navigation system	visited link
font	page properties	Web Safe Color Palette
font color	proportional font	
font size	remote site definition	
font style	RGB system	

Practice	Review Assignments

Practice the skills you learned in the tutorial.

There are no Data Files needed for the Review Assignments.

Web design teams often develop two or three Web site layouts and designs for a client, who then chooses one concept for development. The alternate design can have a different metaphor, can be based on reordered site goals, or can be geared for another target audience. Sara is considering expanding the Cosmatic label to include Texas Blues bands. Brian asks you to plan and design a Web site for a band lineup devoted to Texas Blues bands. Remember that a site devoted to Texas Blues music tends to appeal to a different audience than the Cosmatic alternative music site you just planned. Research this target audience, and then base your decisions for the Texas Blues site on that research.

1. Define a list of site goals for the Cosmatic Texas Blues site.
2. Research and identify the target audience for the alternate Cosmatic site.
3. Create a user profile for the Cosmatic Texas Blues site.
4. Conduct market research to gather information about Texas Blues music Web sites and other Web sites that cater to your target audience.
5. Develop two end-user scenarios for the Cosmatic Texas Blues site.
6. Create an information category outline arranged in hierarchical order for the Cosmatic Texas Blues site.
7. Create a flowchart for the Cosmatic Texas Blues site.
8. Develop a site concept and a metaphor for the alternate Cosmatic site.
9. Choose a color palette, fonts, and a graphic style for the Cosmatic Texas Blues site.
10. Create a rough sketch of the layout for the Cosmatic Texas Blues site.
11. Create a local site definition using **CosmaticBlues** as the site name. Use the Browse button to identify the local root folder as a **Dreamweaver** folder that you create within a folder named **CosmaticBlues** in the location where you are storing your Web site files. Create a folder named **Graphics** in the local root folder and select that folder as the default images folder. Use case-sensitive link checking, and enable cache.
12. Create a remote site definition using FTP access for the CosmaticBlues site.
13. Add the home page to the CosmaticBlues site, using **index.html** as the filename. Open the **index.html** page in the Document window, and then set an appropriate page title. In the Page Properties dialog box, set appropriate properties for the Appearance, Links, and Headings categories. Save the page.
14. Repeat Step 13 for all the first-level pages you need to add to the CosmaticBlues site, based on your site plan.
15. Review the HTML tags for the home page in Code view.
16. Preview the pages in your browser, looking for consistency in display. Each page should have the same background, and each page should have the page title that you assigned to it displayed in the browser title bar. Close the browser and any open pages.
17. Upload the site to your remote server, selecting all the files and the folder for upload.
18. Preview the pages on the Web, looking for consistency in display. Again, each page should have the same background and each page should have the page title that you assigned to it displayed in the browser title bar.
19. Submit the finished files to your instructor, either in printed or electronic form, as requested.

Research | **Case Problem 1**

Plan and design a Web site about the small rural communities of northern Vietnam.

Data Files needed for this Case Problem: DrThompsonMemo.doc, DrThompsonBackground.gif

World Anthropology Society To initiate the planning and design for the Web site you are creating for Dr. Thompson, you asked Dr. Thompson to provide you with a list of site goals, ideas on a target audience, and the material that she wants to include on the site. Dr. Thompson responded with a memo that outlines the decisions she made. You will use the information from the memo to plan the Web site. Dr. Thompson, however, did not provide all the requested information (a common occurrence when working with clients). You will use the information that was provided as a starting point. It will be necessary for you to research and make some decisions on your own.

1. Open the **DrThompsonMemo.doc** file located in the Tutorial.02\Case1 folder included with your Data Files in Microsoft Word or another word processing program, and then read the memo.
2. Review the goals that Dr. Thompson listed, and then create a list of site goals for the Web site. Consider the order of importance and wording.
3. Define a target audience and a user profile for the site. (*Hint:* Search online sources to learn more about the groups of people listed in the memo.)
4. Conduct market research. Find and review at least four Web sites that deal with the lesser-known areas of northern Vietnam, provide information on social anthropology, or are targeted at presenting research online.
5. Write a paragraph documenting the findings from your market research. Include the URLs of the Web sites that you visited as well as information about categories of information, graphic style, layout, and site metaphor.
6. Create three end-user scenarios for the site.
7. Develop an information category outline. Base the categories and hierarchy on the memo and your market research.
8. Create a flowchart for the site.
9. Develop a site concept and metaphor for the site. (Even sites that have minimal design can benefit from a site metaphor.)
10. Investigate usability guidelines that deal with text. Research these guidelines at *www.w3.org/WAI*. Write down your findings and use them when making font choices.
11. Design a color palette for the site. Write a paragraph explaining your choice.
12. Choose the fonts for the site. Write a paragraph explaining your choice.
13. Plan the graphic style of the site. Write a paragraph explaining your choice.
14. Create a rough sketch of the layout of the site. Write a paragraph explaining your choice.
15. Check the design for logic by reviewing the decisions that you have made. Make sure that your design reinforces the site goals and supports the site metaphor.
16. Create a local site definition, using **DrThompson** as the site name and **DrThompson\Dreamweaver** as the local root folder in the folder and location where you are storing your Web site. Create a folder named **Graphics** in the local root folder and select that folder as the default images folder. Use case-sensitive link checking and enable cache.
17. Create a remote site definition using FTP access for the DrThompson site.

18. Create an HTML page for the home page using **index.html** as the filename. Open the page in the Document window, and then enter **Dr. Olivia Thompson - Home** as the page title. In the Page Properties dialog box, set the background image to the **DrThompsonBackground.gif** file located in the Tutorial.02\Case1 folder included with your Data Files. (Remember to select this image from the Graphics folder for the other pages.) Set the background color to white, and set the text color to black. Save the page.

19. Repeat Step 18 to create the remaining top-level pages for the site, using the following filenames and page titles:

Filename	Page Title
contact.html	**Dr. Olivia Thompson - Contact**
cultural_cross_pollination.html	**Dr. Olivia Thompson - Cultural Cross-pollination**
linguistic_differences.html	**Dr. Olivia Thompson - Linguistic Differences**
dr_thompson.html	**Dr. Olivia Thompson**
rituals_and_practices.html	**Dr. Olivia Thompson - Rituals and Practices**

20. Preview the pages in your browser, looking for consistency in display. Each page should have the same background, and each page should have the page title that you assigned to it displayed in the browser title bar.

21. Review the HTML tags for the home page in Code view, and then close any open pages.

22. Upload the site to your remote server, selecting all the files and the folder for upload.

23. View the pages on the Web, looking for consistency in display. Again, each page should have the same background and each page should have the page title that you assigned to it displayed in the browser title bar.

24. Submit the finished files to your instructor, either in printed or electronic form, as requested.

Research | Case Problem 2

Plan and design a Web site for an art museum.

There are no Data Files needed for this Case Problem.

Museum of Western Art   C. J. Strittmatter asks you to work on the plan and design of the new Web site for the Fort Worth Museum of Western Art. To develop a feasible plan, You will need to conduct marketing research on other western art museum sites. In addition, C.J. asks you to research the current accessibility guidelines for using alternate text descriptions on graphics. You will then create the new site, add the home page and top-level pages to the site, and set page properties.

1. Define the goals for the site.
2. Define a target audience and a user profile for the site.
3. Conduct market research. Find and review at least four Web sites that deal with western art. (*Hint:* Use a search engine to search the keywords **western art**, **cowboy art**, and **Texas museums**.)
4. Write a paragraph documenting the findings from your market research. Include the URLs of the Web sites that you visited as well as information about categories of information, graphic style, layout, and site metaphor.
5. Create two end-user scenarios for the site.
6. Develop an information category outline for the site.
7. Create a flowchart for the site.

8. Develop a site concept and metaphor for the site. Write a paragraph explaining your choices.

⊕ EXPLORE

9. Investigate usability guidelines that deal with Alt text, which are messages that can be read by assistive devices. They are used with graphic buttons and so on to make the site more accessible. Research these guidelines at *www.w3.org/WAI*. Write down your findings to use when working on the site's graphics.

10. Design a color palette, choose the fonts, and select a graphic style for the site. Write a paragraph explaining your choices.

11. Create rough sketches of two layouts for the site. Write a paragraph explaining which layout you prefer and why.

12. Check the logical layout of the design you prefer by reviewing the decisions that you have made. Make sure that your design reinforces the site goals and supports the site metaphor.

13. Create a local site definition, using **Museum** as the site name and **Museum\Dreamweaver** as the folder and location where you are storing your Web sites as the local root folder. Create a folder named **Graphics** in the local root folder, and select that folder as the default images folder. Use case-sensitive link checking and enable cache.

14. Create a remote site definition using FTP access for the Museum site.

15. Create the home page for the Museum site using **index.html** as the filename and enter **Museum of Western Art - Home** as the page title.

16. Click the Page Properties button in the Property inspector. Set the page font to Times New Roman, Times, serif, set the size to medium, set the text color to #ECB888, and then set the background color to #CC6600. Set the links, visited links, and active links colors to #ECB888. Set heading 1 to size xx-large, and color #006666. Set heading 2 to size large and color #006666. Save the page.

17. Repeat Steps 15 and 16 to create the top-level pages for the Museum site, using the following filenames and page titles.

Filename	*Page Title*
art.html	**Museum of Western Art - Art**
artists.html	**Museum of Western Art - Artists**
location.html	**Museum of Western Art - Location**
museum.html	**Museum of Western Art - Museum**

18. Preview the pages in your browser, looking for consistency in display. Each page should have the same background, and each page should have the page title that you assigned to it displayed in the browser title bar.

19. Upload the site to your remote server. Remember to select all the files and the folder for upload.

20. View the pages on the Web, looking for consistency in display. Again, each page should have the same background and each page should have the page title that you assigned to it displayed in the browser title bar.

21. Submit the finished files to your instructor, either in printed or electronic form, as requested.

Research	Case Problem 3

Plan and design a Web site for small independent bookstore.

Data File needed for this Case Problem: MOREbooksBackground.gif

MORE Books   The Web design team is in the initial planning phase of designing the new MORE Books Web site. Using your research on MORE competitors, You will develop a plan for the new MORE Books site. You will then create the new site, add the home page and top-level pages to the site, and set the page properties.

1. Define a list of goals for the site.
2. Define a target audience and a user profile for the site.
3. Conduct market research as needed by visiting competitors' sites.
4. Compose two end-user scenarios for the site.
5. Develop an information category outline for the site.
6. Create a flowchart for the site.
7. Develop a site concept and metaphor for the site. Write a paragraph explaining your choices.
8. Design a color palette, choose the fonts, and select a graphic style for the site. Write a paragraph explaining your choices.
9. Create a rough sketch of the layout of the site. Write a paragraph explaining your choice.
10. Check the layout of the design for logic by reviewing the decisions that you have made. Make sure that your design reinforces the site goals and supports the site metaphor.
11. Create a local site definition, using **MOREbooks** as the site name and **MOREbooks\Dreamweaver** in the folder and location where you are storing your Web sites as the local root folder. Create a folder named **Graphics** in the local root folder, and select that folder as the default images folder. Use case sensitive link checking and enable cache.
12. Create a remote site definition using FTP access for the MORE Books site.
13. Create a new HTML page for the home page using **index.html** as the filename. Open the page in the Document window and set **MORE Books - Home** as the page title.
14. Set the following page properties. Set the page font to Arial, Helvetica, sans-serif, set the font size to 14 pixels, set the text color to #FFFFFF, and set the background image to the **MOREbooksBackground.gif** file located in the Tutorial.02\Case3 folder included with your Data Files. (Remember to select this image from the Graphics folder for the other pages.) Set the background color to #003366, set the left margin to 5, and set the right, top, and bottom margins to 0.
15. Set links, visited links, and active links color to #FFFFFF, set rollover links to #CCCFE6, and set the underline style to Show Underline Only on Rollover. Set heading 1 to size 40 pixels and color #FFFFFF. Set heading 2 to 20 pixels and color #FFFFFF. Save and close the page.

✛ EXPLORE 16. Right-click index.html in the Files panel, point to Edit, and then click Copy. Right-click a blank spot in the Files panel, point to Edit, and then click Paste. A page with the filename "Copy of index.html" appears in the list.

✛ EXPLORE 17. Right-click Copy of index.html in the Files pane, point to Edit, and then click Rename. Type **books.html** as the new filename, and then press the Enter key. The copied page is renamed as you can see in the file list.

18. Open the new page in the Document window, and then change the page title to a name that corresponds to the filename. Open the Page Properties dialog box to confirm that the page properties for the page are already set. Click the OK button, and then save and close the page.

19. Repeat Steps 16 through 18 to create the following pages: **company.html**, **contact.html**, and **links.html**.

20. Preview the pages in your browser, looking for consistency in display. Each page should have the same background, and each page should have the page title that you assigned to it displayed in the browser title bar.

21. Review the HTML tags for the home page in Code view, and then close any open pages.

22. Upload the site to the remote server. Remember to select all of the files and the folder for upload.

23. View the pages on the Web, looking for consistency in display. Each page should have the same background, and each page should display the page title you assigned it in the browser title bar.

24. Submit the finished files to your instructor, either in printed or electronic form, as requested.

| Create | | **Case Problem 4** |

Plan and design a Web site for a newly opening sushi restaurant. Then begin to create the site based on your plan.

There are no Data Files needed for this Case Problem.

Sushi Ya-Ya   Mary O'Brien asks you to develop a Web site plan and design to present to Charlie Lindahl, Sushi Ya-Ya's owner, at the next scheduled meeting. Because Sushi Ya-Ya is not yet open, there is no established customer base. You know that the client wants to attract the employees of local businesses for its lunch clientele. You will have to do further research to define the target audience as well as to develop content for the site, as the business has not yet generated any informational materials.

1. Research restaurant Web sites (sushi restaurants in particular) and the French Quarter in New Orleans. Make notes about your findings.

2. Construct a list of goals for the site.

3. Define a target audience and a user profile for the site.

4. Complete your market research. Review at least eight Web sites including restaurant sites, sites geared at your target audience, sites about New Orleans and the French Quarter, and sites about sushi.

5. Write a paragraph documenting the findings from your market research. Include the URLs of the Web sites that you visited.

6. Compose two end-user scenarios for the site.

7. Develop an information category outline for the site.

8. Create a flowchart for the site.

9. Develop a concept and metaphor for the site. Be creative, but make sure that your metaphor will support the site goals.

10. Design a color palette, choose the fonts, and select a graphic style for the site. Write a paragraph explaining your choices.

11. Create rough sketches of two layouts of the site. Write a paragraph explaining which layout you prefer and why.

12. Check the layout of the design you prefer for logic by reviewing the decisions that you have made. Make sure that your design reinforces the site goals and supports the site metaphor.

13. Create a local site definition, using **SushiYaYa** as the site name and **SushiYaYa\Dreamweaver** in the folder and location where you are storing your Web sites as the local root folder. Create a folder named **Graphics** in the local root folder and select that folder as the default images folder. Use case-sensitive link checking and enable cache.

14. Create a remote site definition using FTP access for the SushiYaYa site.

15. Create each of the first-level pages of the SushiYaYa site based on your site plan and flowchart. Name each page with a descriptive filename. Open each page in the Document window, and then set the appropriate page title, background, and colors in the Page Properties dialog box. Save each page.

16. Preview the pages in your browser, looking for consistency in display. Each page should have the same background, and each page should have the page title that you assigned to it displayed in the browser title bar.

17. Review the HTML tags for the home page in Code view, and then close any open pages.

18. Upload the site to the remote server. Remember to select all of the files and the folder for upload.

19. View the pages on the Web, looking for consistency in display. Again, each page should have the same background and each page should have the page title that you assigned to it displayed in the browser title bar.

20. Submit the finished files to your instructor, either in printed or electronic form, as requested.

Review | Quick Check Answers

Session 2.1

1. False; there are many possible paths in any creative process.
2. to make decisions about the site's organization and structure
3. four or five
4. the group of users that you would most like to visit the site
5. to help identify the target audience by determining the characteristics of the group of people you are trying to reach
6. You might create a Web site that seems targeted to the intended audience but that does not actually appeal to them.
7. to find out the target audience's preferences for a product or service; investigate the target audience's likes, dislikes, and interests; and evaluate competitors' products or services
8. imagined situations in which members of the target audience might access a Web site

Session 2.2

1. the process of determining what you want a site to do and then creating a framework that will allow you to accomplish those goals
2. to provide structure for the information in a Web site and are used to create the main navigation system

3. to provide a visual representation of the hierarchical structure of the pages within the site
4. a general underlying theme that runs through the site and is used as a unifying mechanism for various elements that contribute to the site's look and feel
5. because the Web is a publishing venue used by a variety of people, including people with disabilities
6. Keep it simple, include three to six colors per site, consider the mood you want to create, and keep in mind the target audience.
7. True
8. the position of elements—navigation system, text, logo, artwork, and so on—in a Web page

Session 2.3

1. local info and remote info
2. to put a Web site on a Web server so it can be seen on the Web, enabling you to verify that the Web site's features work in the browser and over the Web
3. The New Document dialog box opens.
4. at least every ten minutes and whenever you have finished modifying a page
5. False; HTML is a common markup language that is viewable by a variety of software packages, including Web browsers.
6. attributes that apply to an entire page rather than to an element on the page such as a page title, background, text and link colors, and margins
7. in a browser or on the Web
8. files that are used in the Web pages

Adding and Formatting Text with CSS Styles

Using the Property Inspector, CSS Styles, and HTML Tags

Case | Cosmatic

Sara Lynn, the president of Cosmatic, and Brian Lee, the public relations and marketing director, have approved the design plan for the new Cosmatic site. The next step is to add text to the Web site's pages and to format the text by adding the appropriate CSS styles, based on the design plan. Each page of the Cosmatic site will contain at least three text elements—the page heading, subheadings, and body text—as well as hyperlinks and so on. Formatting provides a way to distinguish between these different types of text. Dreamweaver created CSS styles for the page heading elements, body text, and hyperlinks when you set the page properties. You'll examine the code for those CSS styles, and you'll create additional CSS Styles in this tutorial.

In this tutorial, you will type text directly into a Web page and import text from text files. You will use the spelling checker and Find and Replace tools to correct typing and capitalization errors in the text. You will create hyperlinks to navigate among the pages in the site. You will create and apply different types of CSS styles to the text that you added. Finally, you will create an external style sheet and attach the external style sheet to all the Web pages to make the formatting consistent from one page to another and to enable you to easily add other styles in the future.

Starting Data Files

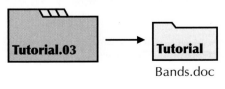

Tutorial	Review	Case1	Case2	Case3	Case4
Bands.doc	Catalogue.doc	DrThompson.doc	Artists.doc	Company.doc	SushiYa-YaContent.doc
	Contact.doc	Overview.doc	Location.doc	Home.doc	
	Label.doc	Thompson Contact.doc	Museum.doc	Links.doc	
			Welcome.doc	MOREContact.doc	

Session 3.1

Adding Text to a Web Page

Text is included in almost every Web page. In Dreamweaver, you can add text to a page simply by typing in the workspace of the Document window. This is a good method for adding small amounts of text or text that will be heavily formatted. You can also copy existing text from another file (whether a text document or a Web page) and paste it into the workspace of the Document window in Design view. This method is good for adding a great deal of text to a site; most word processing programs have better spelling- and grammar-checking features as well as a built-in thesaurus. However, errors—such as extra spaces, oddly positioned text, or misinterpreted symbols—sometimes appear in the Web page when text is imported from another program. Whenever you copy text from another source, it is important to read the text and correct any errors that were introduced.

Dreamweaver provides two commands for pasting items into a page: Paste and Paste Special. The Paste command places only the text from the other document without any of the formatting. The Paste Special command enables you to choose the level of formatting that will be retained with the pasted text. Most often, you'll use the Paste Special command.

InSight	**Communicating Effectively with Text Elements**

Almost every Web page includes text elements. In fact, text is the basis of most Web sites. To ensure maximum readability, the text you add to a Web page should be clearly written and free from spelling, punctuation, and grammatical errors. Well-written Web content is concise, effectively communicates the point, and is written with the end user in mind. By the time you are ready to add the content to a Web site, you will already have the information architecture, which will tell you what you need to include in each page. You will also have all the raw materials, including the text and the graphics, so that you are not composing on the fly. In addition, you will have set the page properties for the pages so that basic text formatting attributes are set.

Brian wants you to add text to the Bands page in the Cosmatic site. He has already typed the text into a Word document.

To add text to the Bands page:

▶ 1. Open the **Cosmatic** site that you modified in **Session 2.3**, click the **View** button on the Files panel toolbar, and then click **Local View**. If you are working on a different computer than you did in Session 2.3, you need to re-create the site definition (both the local info and the remote info) on this computer.

▶ 2. In the Files panel, double-click **bands.html** to open the Bands page in the Document window, and then click the **Design** button on the Document toolbar, if necessary, to switch to Design view.

▶ 3. Press the **Enter** key four times to move the insertion point below the colored portion of the page background, and then type **COSMATIC BANDS**. The text you typed appears in the Document window. See Figure 3-1.

Bands page with new text | Figure 3-1

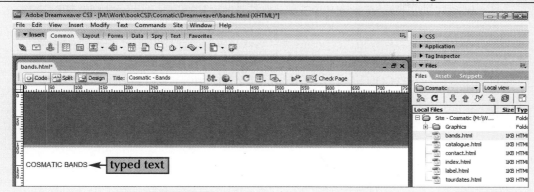

4. Open the **Bands.doc** file located in the **Tutorial.03\Tutorial** folder included with your Data Files in Word or another word processing program. This document contains the rest of the text you want to add to the Bands page. The paragraph headings are bold and the text is in the Times New Roman font.

5. Press the **Ctrl+A** keys to select all of the text in the document, press the **Ctrl+C** keys to copy the text to the Windows Clipboard, and then click the **Close** button ⊠ on the title bar of the program window to close the document and exit the word processing program.

6. Click the Document window to place the insertion point after the text you typed in the Bands page, if necessary, and then press the **Enter** key twice to move the insertion point down two lines.

7. Click **Edit** on the menu bar, and then click **Paste Special**. The Paste Special dialog box opens.

8. Click the **Text Only** option button, and then click the **OK** button. The text you copied from the Bands.doc document is pasted into the Bands page without any of the formatting. See Figure 3-2.

Text copied from the Bands document | Figure 3-2

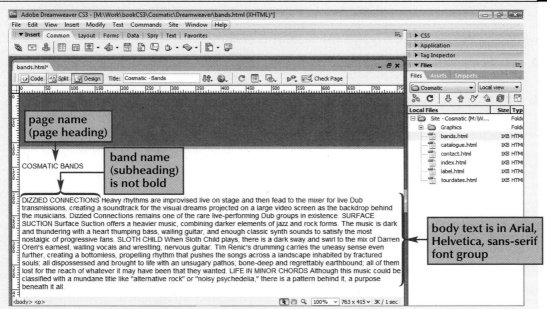

▶ **9.** Read the Bands page text, scrolling as needed. The paragraphs run together and the headings are no longer bold, as they were in the text document. The text is in the Arial, Helvetica, sans-serif font group that you selected when you set the page properties and not in the font from the text document.

Before you continue, you'll separate the text into paragraphs and save the page.

▶ **10.** Click to the left of the SURFACE SUCTION heading text, and then press the **Enter** key. The DIZZIED CONNECTIONS text is in a separate paragraph.

Tip

You can quickly save the page by pressing the Ctrl+S keys.

▶ **11.** Repeat Step 10 to create new paragraphs before the SLOTH CHILD and LIFE IN MINOR CHORDS headings.

▶ **12.** Click **File** on the menu bar, and then click **Save**. The page is saved.

Checking the Spelling in Web Pages

It is important to proofread all of the text that you add to Web pages, whether you typed it directly into the Web page or you copied it from another file. You cannot assume that text you receive from someone else has been proofed and corrected. You should also use the Dreamweaver built-in spelling checker to double-check for errors. You can choose to change or ignore one instance or all occurrences of any word that isn't found in the Dreamweaver built-in dictionary.

InSight	**Correcting All Spelling and Grammar Errors**

Errors in spelling and grammar can detract from the overall impression of a Web site. They can make the company, product, or service seem unprofessional. So be sure to use the spelling checker and proofread the text in all Web pages. Because no spelling checker is foolproof, proofread the pages carefully looking for errors that a spelling checker won't catch, such as incorrectly used homonyms (for example, there, their, and they're), a correctly spelled word that is wrong in context (such as from versus form), and missing words.

Brian asks you to check the spelling in the Bands page.

To check the Bands page for spelling errors:

▶ **1.** Scroll to the top of the Bands page, and then click to place the insertion point above the text.

▶ **2.** Click **Text** on the menu bar, and then click **Check Spelling**. The Check Spelling dialog box opens, displaying the first word that does not match any words in the built-in dictionary, in this case, the word "Cosmatic." The Check Spelling dialog box suggests that Cosmatic be corrected to "Cosmetic." See Figure 3-3.

Check Spelling dialog box ◄ Figure 3-3

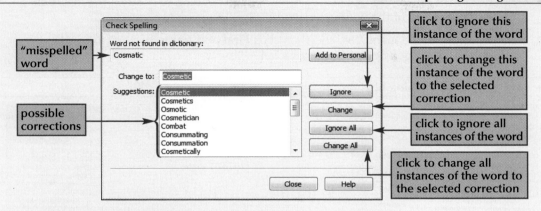

3. Click the **Ignore All** button to ignore every instance of Cosmatic in the page. The Check Spelling dialog box displays "fead"—the next word that does match any words in the built-in dictionary. The word should be "fed."

4. Click **fed** in the Suggestions box.

5. Click the **Change** button to replace the highlighted word with the selected word in the Suggestions box. The spelling checker stops at the next possible misspelled word it finds, "synth."

6. Read the sentence containing the highlighted word in the Document window. In this case, the word "synth" is an abbreviation for "synthesizer" and is not misspelled. Although the spelling checker does not recognize this abbreviation, it is a slang term that the target audience will recognize.

7. Click the **Ignore** button to leave the word as it is and continue checking the spelling.

8. Check the rest of the page, ignoring the remaining words that the spelling checker flags as misspelled. A dialog box opens indicating that the spelling check is complete.

9. Click the **OK** button.

10. Proofread the Bands page one last time, and then save the page.

Using the Find and Replace Tool

Like word processing programs, Dreamweaver has a Find and Replace tool that enables you to locate text or tags and then to replace the located elements with other text or tags. You can specify the area to search (Current Document, Open Documents, Entire Current Local Site, Selected Files in Site, Folder, or Selected Text) as well as the kind of search to perform. A Source Code search locates instances of the designated text string within the HTML source code. A Text search locates instances of the designated text string within the document text. A Text (Advanced) search enables you to further specify the parameters of the search. For example, you can set the search to locate instances of the designated text string within only a specified tag and so on. Finally, a Specific Tag search locates specific tags, attributes, and attribute values and enables you to replace each with a new tag, attribute, or attribute value.

You will use the Find and Replace tool to locate all of the instances of the word "Dub" in the Bands page and to replace it with the word "dub" (all in lowercase).

To find "Dub" and replace it with "dub":

▶ **1.** Click to the left of the COSMATIC BANDS page heading to position the insertion point at the top of the page.

▶ **2.** Click **Edit** on the menu bar, and then click **Find and Replace**. The Find and Replace dialog box opens. See Figure 3-4.

Figure 3-4 | **Find and Replace dialog box**

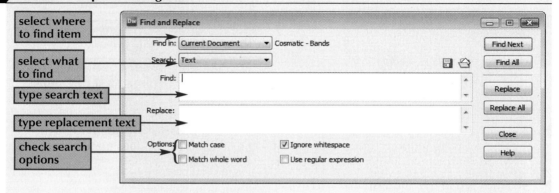

▶ **3.** Click the **Find in** button, click **Current Document**, and then, if necessary, click the **Search** button and click **Text**.

▶ **4.** Click in the **Find** box, and then type **Dub**. This is the word you want to search for.

▶ **5.** Click in the **Replace** box, and then type **dub**. This is the replacement word you want to use.

▶ **6.** Click the **Match case** check box to insert a check mark, and then make sure all of the other check boxes are unchecked. This instructs Dreamweaver to look for words with the exact capitalization as in the Find box and insert words with the exact capitalization as in the Replace box.

▶ **7.** Click the **Find Next** button. The first instance of the word *Dub* is selected in the Bands page. See Figure 3-5.

Figure 3-5 | **Completed Find and Replace dialog box**

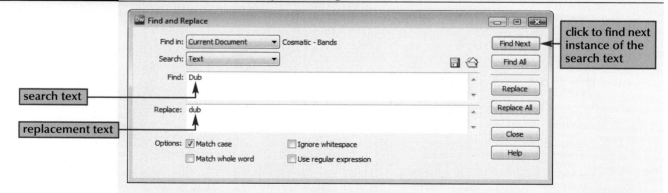

▶ **8.** Click the **Replace** button. The selected instance of *Dub* is replaced with *dub*, and then the next instance of *Dub* is selected. Rather than finding and replacing one instance of the search text at a time, you can replace all instances at one time.

▶ **9.** Click the **Replace All** button. The remaining instances of the text string in the page are replaced. The Results panel group expands to the Search panel and lists all instances where the search text was replaced in the page.

▶ **10.** Review the list in the Search panel, and then collapse the Results panel group.

Formatting Text Using the Property Inspector

The simplest way to format text in Dreamweaver is to select the text in the Document window and set the attributes for the text in the Property inspector. You can set the attributes for a single letter, a word, a line of text, or an entire block of text. The attributes for text formatting are similar to those you will find in a word processing program; however, when text is formatted in Dreamweaver, CSS styles that control the look and layout of the text are added behind the scenes. Text formatting attributes included in the Property inspector are format, font, style, size, color, emphasis, alignment, lists, and indents.

The format attributes are a list of standardized HTML tags used for text formatting. These include the paragraph tag and a variety of heading tags. When you select fonts, sizes, and colors for headings in the Page Properties dialog box, Dreamweaver creates CSS styles that customize the appearance of the heading tags in the Format list. In the Cosmatic site, selecting text and clicking the Heading 1 tag in the Format list will cause the selected text to be displayed in Arial, Helvetica, sans-serif; 30 pixels; and #772300 (red), which are the attributes you selected for the Heading 1 tag when you set the page properties. You did not select attributes for the other heading tags when you set the page properties. As a result, if you select text and click the Heading 2 or other heading tags, Dreamweaver will apply the default attributes for that tag to the selected text.

The font attributes are a list of the standard font groups available for use in Web pages. The default font group for the page is the font group that you selected for the page font in the Page Properties dialog box. The page font for the Cosmatic site is Arial, Helvetica, sans-serif. To select a different font group for a section of text, you simply select the text in the Document window and then choose the desired font group from the Font list in the Property inspector. If you do not select a font group in the Property inspector, the text will be displayed in the selected page font. The default font option displays the text in the default font of the end-user's browser. When a font group is selected, Dreamweaver creates a CSS style containing all the choices in the font group and places a tag containing the CSS style around the specified text. You can add fonts to the list, but you should use caution when doing this because a font must be installed on the end-user's computer to display the text in that font. If the font is not installed on the end-user's computer, the text will be displayed in the browser's default font.

The size attributes list shows available font sizes. You can select a specific or relative size from the list, or you can type a different font size in the box. If you select a specific size, you must also choose a unit selection. Pixels are the most frequently used unit for specific font size. The default size is the size that you selected in the Page Properties dialog box.

The font color attributes enable you to change the color of selected text. The default font color for a page is the color you selected in the Page Properties dialog box. To change the color of a selected block of text, you can type the hexadecimal color code into the color box or select a color with the color picker.

The buttons in the Property inspector enable you to change the emphasis of selected text with boldface and italics; apply left, center, or right alignment to a paragraph; turn paragraphs into items in an unordered (bulleted) or ordered (numbered) list; and apply or remove indents from paragraphs. You can also change the default text attributes for the page by clicking the Page Properties button in the Property inspector and changing the selections in the Page Properties dialog box.

Reference Window | **Formatting Text Using the Property Inspector**

- In the Document window, select the text that you want to format.
- In the Property inspector, click the Font arrow, and then click the font grouping you want.
- In the Property inspector, click the Size arrow, and then click the size you want.
- In the Property inspector, click in the color box and type the hexadecimal color code of the color you want (or click the color box and click a color swatch in the color picker).
- In the Property inspector, click the Bold button and/or the Italic button.
- In the Property inspector, click an alignment button.
- To create a text hyperlink, select the text, click the Browse for File button in the Property inspector, and then navigate to the file to which you want to link (or drag from the Point to File button in the Property inspector to the file to which to link, or type the external URL in the Link box).

You'll use the Property inspector to format the text in the Bands page.

To format the Bands page text with the Property inspector:

▶ 1. Select **COSMATIC BANDS** in the Document window, click the **Format** button in the Property inspector, and then click **Heading 1**. The page heading—COSMATIC BANDS—is formatted with the Heading 1 attributes you set in the page properties. See Figure 3-6.

| Figure 3-6 | **Property inspector for the formatted page name text** |

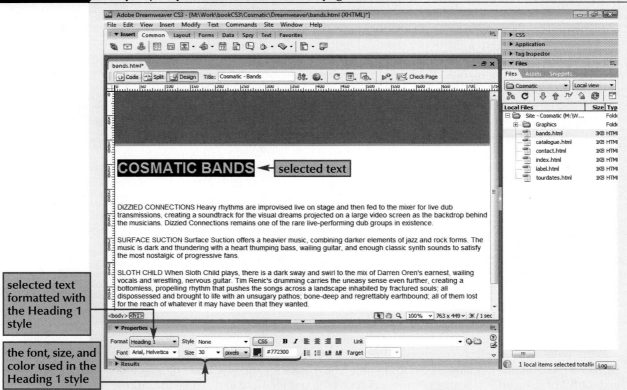

2. Place the insertion point after DIZZIED CONNECTIONS, and then press the **Enter** key. The text to the right of the heading moves to the next line in the page. You will format the band name as a subheading.

3. Select **DIZZIED CONNECTIONS**, click the **Format** button in the Property inspector, click **Heading 2**, and then press the **Right Arrow** key to deselect the text. The band name is formatted with the Heading 2 attributes. You did not set the Heading 2 attributes when you set the page properties, so the band name shows the tag's default formatting. See Figure 3-7.

Formatted page and band names ◄ **Figure 3-7**

Trouble? If the text in the paragraph above the DIZZIED CONNECTIONS heading text displays the heading attributes, the opening <h2> tag was placed before the affected text. Select the text you wanted to change, click the Split button on the Document toolbar, select the <h2> tag in the Code pane, drag the selected tag directly in front of the DIZZIED CONNECTIONS text, and then click the Design button on the Document toolbar.

4. Repeat Steps 2 and 3 to format the other three subheadings on the page: **SURFACE SUCTION**, **SLOTH CHILD**, and **LIFE IN MINOR CHORDS**.

5. Save the page.

Creating Text Hyperlinks

The Cosmatic site plan calls for text hyperlinks at the top of each page. Hyperlinks enable users to move between pages in a Web site and to connect to pages in other Web sites. For the Cosmatic site, you will create text hyperlinks for the main navigation system as called for in the site plan. First, you'll add the link text to one of the pages in the site and format it. Then, you'll create the hyperlinks. Finally, you will copy the links to the rest of the pages in the site.

Adding and Formatting Hyperlink Text

You'll insert the text for the hyperlinks—label, bands, catalogue, tour dates, and contact—on a blank line just below the colored part of the page background. You want to separate each word with two **nonbreaking spaces**, which are special, invisible characters used to create more than one space between text and other elements. In HTML, only one regular space appears between items no matter how many spaces you type using the Spacebar. Nonbreaking spaces enable you to separate items with more than one space between them.

After you insert the link text, you'll format it by setting the size and alignment. You won't set any colors for the link text because you specified them when you set the page properties.

To add and format the text for the navigation hyperlinks on the home page:

▶ 1. Click just below the colored portion of the background to position the insertion point, if necessary, and then press the **Shift+Enter** keys to move the insertion point down one line.

▶ 2. Type **label**, and then, on the Insert bar at the top of the Document window, click the **Text** tab, if necessary. The buttons in the Text category appear on the Insert bar.

▶ 3. On the Insert bar, click the **Characters button arrow** to open the Characters menu, click the **Non-Breaking Space** button ⬇ to insert a nonbreaking space, and then click the **Non-Breaking Space** button ⬇ again. Two nonbreaking spaces are inserted after the text.

You can also insert nonbreaking spaces using the keyboard. You'll use this method to enter the rest of the link text.

▶ 4. Type **bands**, and then press the **Ctrl+Shift+Spacebar** keys twice to insert two nonbreaking spaces.

▶ 5. Type **catalogue**, press the **Ctrl+Shift+Spacebar** keys twice, type **tour dates**, press the **Ctrl+Shift+Spacebar** keys twice, type **contact**, and then press the **Ctrl+Shift+Spacebar** keys twice. The text for each link is followed by two nonbreaking spaces. See Figure 3-8.

| Figure 3-8 | Link text typed in the Bands page |

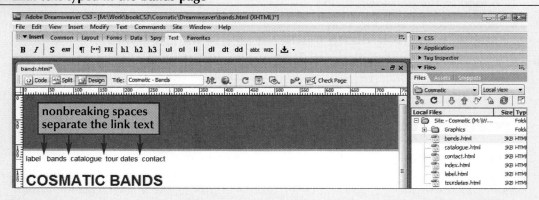

▶ 6. In the Property inspector, click the **Align Right** button ≡ . The link text moves to the right side of the page.

▶ 7. Save the Bands page.

Creating Links from Text

You can create text hyperlinks using the Property inspector to associate the text with a specific file or Web page. The first time you link to a file, you select the link text, then you use the Browse for File button or the Point to File button next to the Link box in the Property inspector to select the appropriate file. Dreamweaver will then create the link for you. (You can also type the URL into the Link box in the Property inspector, but if you mistype the URL or path, the link will not work.) If the page you link to is outside the local root folder, Dreamweaver prompts you to include a copy of the page in the site in the local root folder. Remember to keep all the elements you use in your site within the site's local root folder so that these elements will be accessible when you publish the site and Dreamweaver can manage the site and its elements for you.

After you link to a file, it appears in the Link list in the Property inspector. If you need to add another link to that file, first select the new link text, and then click the Link arrow and select the file from the list.

The two types of links are relative links and absolute links. Relative links can be relative to the document or to the site's root folder. **Document relative links** don't specify the entire URL of the Web page you are linking to; instead, they specify a path from the current page. You use document relative links when you are linking to pages within the site, because you can move the site to a different server location or different domain, and the links will still work. **Site root relative links** specify a path from the site root folder to the linked document. You can use site root relative links when you work on large sites with complex folder structures that change frequently. When you link to a page anywhere within the local root folder, Dreamweaver creates a relative link. The Web sites in these tutorials use document relative links.

When you link to a page in another site, you use an **absolute link**. An absolute link contains the complete URL of the page you are linking to, which includes the filename of the page to which you are linking, such as *http://www.domainname.com/filename.html*. You use an absolute link when you want to link to Web pages in other sites.

You'll create hyperlinks from the link text you just added. Each link connects to the appropriate existing Web page. The link text for the current page will not go anywhere, but formatting it as a link maintains consistency in the look of the navigation system text (for example, on the Contact page, you will link the link text "contact" to the Contact page). Also, when you copy the navigation system to other pages of the site, you will not have to create additional links. Remember that when you set the page properties, you designated various colors for four states of links (text links, rollover links, active links, and visited links).

To create hyperlinks from the navigation system text:

▶ **1.** Select **label** in the Bands page.

▶ **2.** In the Property inspector, click the **Browse for File** button 🗀 . The Select File dialog box opens. The Look in box lists folders and pages in the local root folder for the site that is currently selected in the Files panel.

▶ **3.** Click **label** in the Look in box. See Figure 3-9.

Figure 3-9 Select File dialog box

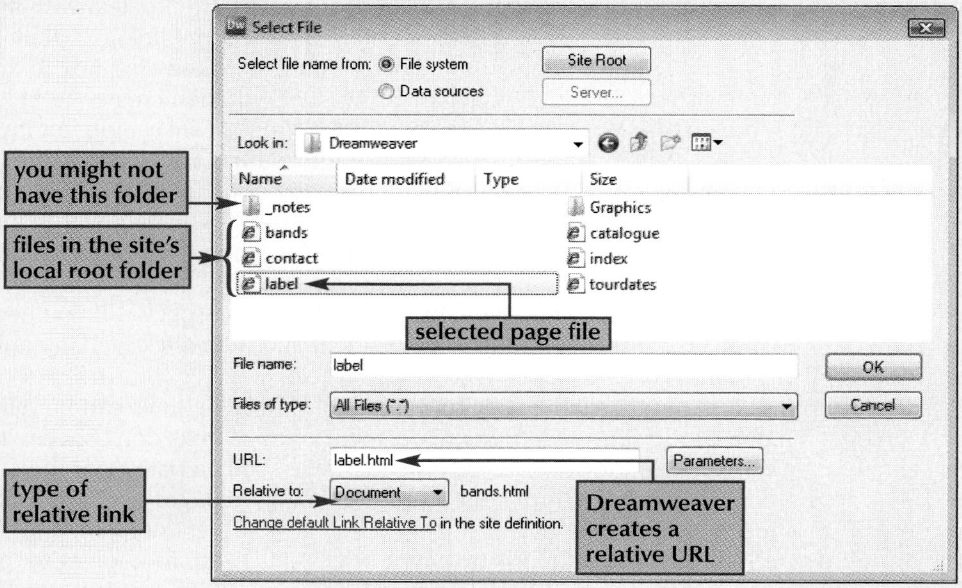

4. Click the **OK** button, and then press the **Right Arrow** key to deselect the text. The word "label" is a hyperlink to the Label page in the Cosmatic site. See Figure 3-10.

Figure 3-10 Label text converted to a hyperlink

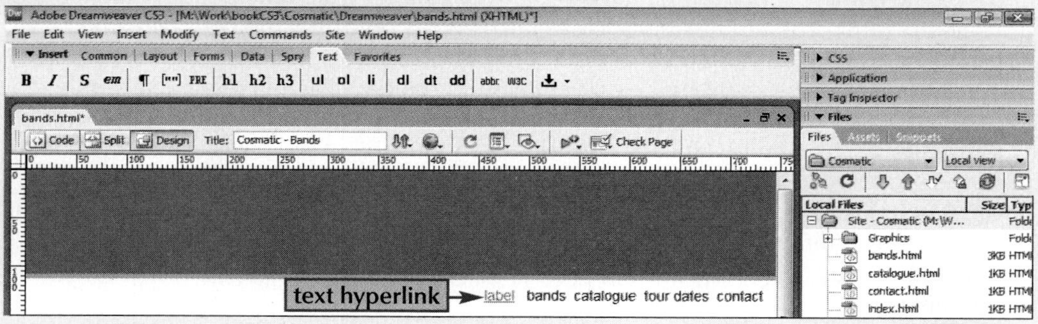

5. Select **bands** in the Document window, and then, in the Property inspector, click the **Point to File** button (do not release the mouse button) and drag the pointer to the **bands.html** file in the Files panel, as shown in Figure 3-11.

Hyperlink created with the Point to File button | Figure 3-11

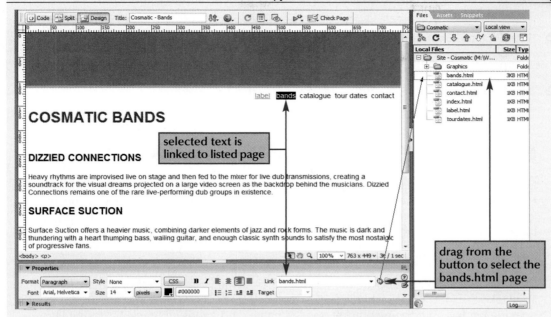

6. Release the mouse button. The word "bands" is linked to the Bands page.

7. Repeat Steps 5 and 6 to create hyperlinks for **catalogue**, **tour dates**, and **contact**, connecting each with its corresponding file. (For the tour dates link, make sure you select both words before you create the link.)

8. Save the Bands page, click **bands.html** in the Files panel to select it, and then preview the Bands page in your primary browser. See Figure 3-12.

Tip

You can quickly preview a page in your primary browser by pressing the F12 key.

Bands page previewed in a browser window | Figure 3-12

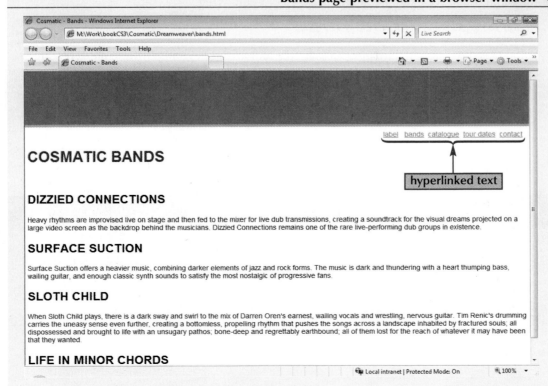

▶ **9.** Place the pointer over the **label** link. The pointer changes to ⬚.

▶ **10.** Click the **label** link. The Label page, which is blank, appears in the browser window.

▶ **11.** Click the **Back** button ⬅ on the browser toolbar. The Bands page appears in the browser window, and the label link text is yellow—the visited link color you specified earlier.

▶ **12.** Close the browser.

Exploring HTML Tags for Hyperlinks

Dreamweaver inserted HTML tags when you formatted text and created hyperlinks. HTML tags, whether they apply to text, hyperlinks, or other elements, follow a specific format. As you have seen, most HTML tags come in pairs with opening and closing tags that surround the text to which the tags is applied, as in the following example:

```
<tag>Some Text</tag>
```

Opening tags are placed before the text, or other element, to which they are applied. They take the form <tag>, where "tag" is replaced by the HTML tag you are using. An opening tag has an opening bracket, the tag name, and a closing bracket. Closing tags are placed after the text, or other element, to which they are applied, and take the form </tag>. Again, a closing tag has opening and closing brackets but also includes a forward slash inside the opening bracket before the tag name.

Tags can also be used together, or **nested**. With **nested tags**, one set of tags is placed around another set of tags so that both sets apply to the text they surround, such as:

```
<tag2><tag1>Some Text</tag1></tag2>
```

When working with nested tags, you must keep the opening and closing tags paired in the same order. For example, it would be incorrect to write:

```
<tag1><tag2>Some Text</tag1></tag2>
```

Some tags also contain attributes such as size, color, and alignment. These attributes are placed within the opening tag. Tag attributes are separated by a blank space, and the value of each attribute is usually placed in quotation marks, as shown in the example:

```
<tag color="x" size="x">Some Text</tag>
```

The specific tags depend on the applied formatting and the type of element. Some helpful reference sites for HTML tags include *www.w3.org*, *www.htmldog.com/reference/htmltags*, and *www.devx.com/projectcool/Article/19816*.

Reference Window | **Examining HTML Tags**

- Click the Code button or the Split button on the Document toolbar.
- If the lines of code do not wrap in the Document window, click the View Options button on the Document toolbar, and then click Word Wrap.
- Select the tag you want to examine in the Code pane, right-click the selected text, and then click Reference to display a description of the tag in the Reference panel.

Exploring HTML Tags that Apply to Hyperlinks

Hyperlinks are created in HTML with the **anchor tag**, which has the general format:

```
<a href="absolute or relative path">Link Text</a>
```

In this tag, "href" is short for hypertext reference, "absolute or relative path"—the URL or page for the link—is the value for href, and "Link Text" is the text on the Web page that users click to use the link. Absolute, document relative, and site root relative links have different path information in the href attribute. Figure 3-13 lists the anchor tag with the three types of links.

Anchor tags for absolute and relative links   Figure 3-13

Link	Anchor tag	Description
Absolute	**<a href="http://www.websitename.com">**Text link to a Web page outside current site**</a>**	Specifies the absolute or complete path to the linked page.
Document Relative	**<a href="anotherpage.htm">**Text link to another page within current site**</a>**	Specifies the location of the linked page relative to the current page. Commonly used.
Site Root Relative	**<a href="/subfolder/anotherpage.htm">**Text link to another page within current site**</a>**	Specifies the location of the linked page relative to the site's root folder. Used sometimes when sites have a lot of subfolders within the root folder and/or change frequently.

You can set the target attribute with an anchor tag. The **target** specifies where the link opens—in the current browser window or a new browser window. By default, the new page will open in the current browser window, replacing the page from which you linked. If you want the new page to replace the current page, you do not need to include a target attribute. If you want the linked page to open in a new browser window, you must specify "_blank" as the target attribute. The complete anchor tag for opening a page in a new browser window takes the following format:

```
<a href="absolute or relative path" target="_blank">Link Text</a>
```

Another anchor tag attribute is the name attribute. The name attribute associates a name with a specific, named location within a Web page. With the name attribute, you can link to the named location on the current page or another page, much like a bookmark. You use the anchor tag with the name attribute in the following format:

```
<a name="anchor_name">Some Text</a>
```

In this tag, "anchor_name" is the name you give the anchor, and "Some Text" is the text being named as the anchor. Anchor names are case sensitive. When you create a named anchor, Dreamweaver inserts an anchor icon into the Document window beside the text. The anchor icon is not visible in a browser window.

After a location on a page has a named anchor, you can create links to it from other locations in the same page or from other pages. For example, you can create an anchor to the selected page heading text named "top," type "back to the top" at the bottom of the page, and then create a link from that text to the "top" anchor. This enables the user to jump from the bottom to the top of the Web page by clicking the "back to the top" link. The format for an anchor tag that links to a named anchor on the same page is:

```
<a href="#anchor_name">Link Text</a>
```

If you are linking to a named anchor in a different page, you need to include the path and filename to the page containing the named anchor in the following general format:

```
<a href="absolute or relative path#anchor_name">Link Text</a>
```

The # symbol always precedes the anchor name when it is used in a link.

You'll look at the HTML for the hyperlinks you created in the Bands page.

To examine HTML tags for hyperlinks in the Bands page:

▶ **1.** In the Bands page, select the **contact** link, and then click the **Split** button on the Document toolbar. The page is in Split view.

▶ **2.** In the Code pane of the Document window, examine the anchor tag that surrounds the selected text. See Figure 3-14.

Figure 3-14 ▶ Anchor tag in the Bands page

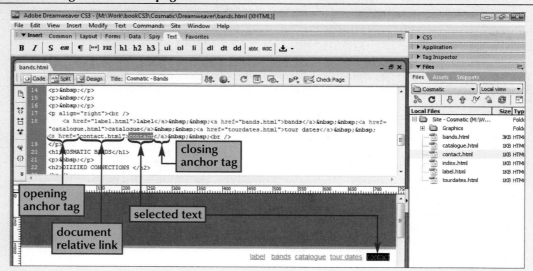

Trouble? If the lines of code do not wrap in the Document window, you need to turn on word wrap. Click the View Options button on the Document toolbar, and then click Word Wrap to check it.

▶ **3.** In the Code pane, select **a href=** (the entire opening anchor tag), right-click the selected tag, and then click **Reference**. The Reference panel in the Results panel group expands, displaying the O'Reilly HTML Reference description of the anchor tag.

▶ **4.** Read the description of the anchor tag.

▶ **5.** In the Reference panel, click the **Select Attribute** button, click **href**, read the description of the href attribute in the Reference panel, and then collapse the Results panel group.

▶ **6.** Click the **Design** button on the Document toolbar. The page appears in Design view.

So far, you have added text to a Web page, used the spelling checker and proofed the page, used the Find and Replace tool to change all instances of the capitalization of a word on the page, and then formatted text with the Property inspector. You also created text hyperlinks and reviewed the HTML tags used for the hyperlinks. In the next session, you'll work with Cascading Style Sheets.

Session 3.1 Quick Check | Review

1. What are two ways to add text to a page in Dreamweaver?
2. True or False? It is not necessary to read a page and look for errors if you use the spelling checker.
3. To format text, select the text in the Document window and select formatting options in the _____ .
4. _____ enable users to move between pages in a Web site and to connect to pages on other Web sites.
5. When you link to a page in the site's local root folder, what type of link is created by default?
6. What is the general format for the HTML code for the bold tag?
7. Which tag is used to create hyperlinks?

Session 3.2

Evolving HTML and CSS Standards

The way that HTML displays and formats text has evolved over time. Each evolutionary step has provided better control over the way text is formatted and displayed.

Recommended HTML Standards | InSight

The World Wide Web Consortium (W3C) publishes recommendations for HTML standards. As new versions of HTML are developed and then accepted, the W3C assigns version numbers to these standards (a lower number equals an earlier standard). New HTML versions contain new elements, tags, and updated methods of doing things. Tags that have been replaced in new versions of HTML are kept around for compatibility with older browsers. Older tags that are in the process of becoming obsolete are called **deprecated**. Because some people use older browsers that rely on the earlier versions of HTML, deprecated tags are phased out slowly. Specifications and standards change rapidly, so there is no easy way to predict exact adoption rates for newer standards and technologies. The W3C Web site (*www.w3c.org*) is a good reference for current trends and changes.

In the earliest days of the Web, designers had limited control over the way text was displayed in a browser. Text appeared in the default font and size set by the user's browser. The way it looked was also affected by the user's operating system. Designers had no font control within a Web page except for the six predefined heading tags that could be used to denote importance of text by changing the relative size of the headings. In HTML 2, bold, italic, and underline attributes were added. In HTML 3.2, another milestone in controlling the display of text was reached—the HTML font tag (or just font tag). The **font tag** allowed designers to designate in which font and relative font size the Web page should display (as long as the designated font was installed on the user's computer). Font tags were deprecated in HTML 4.01, and their functions were replaced and expanded upon by Cascading Style Sheets.

The current standard for creating Web pages is **eXtensible HyperText Markup Language (XHTML)**, which is basically a combination of HTML and XML. **XML (eXtensible Markup Language)** is a markup language that describes the structure of the data it contains. It provides a common and flexible method for applications and organizations to electronically exchange information. XML was created to describe or identify data, whereas HTML was designed to display data. The shift from HTML 4.01 to XHTML 1.0 continues the move toward separating style and content—XHTML structures the page content and CSS styles it for display. As an additional benefit, XHMTL more strictly defines the syntax and makes it easier to format the same content for display on various devices.

Exploring Cascading Style Sheets

Cascading Style Sheets were created as the answer to the limitations of HTML, and they are the current standard for layout and formatting in Web pages. A **Cascading Style Sheets (CSS)** is a collection of styles that is either inserted in the head of the HTML of a Web page and used throughout that page (an internal style sheet), or is attached as an external document and used throughout the entire Web site (an external style sheet). A **CSS style** is a rule that defines the appearance of an element in a Web page either by redefining an existing HTML tag or by creating a custom style (also called a class style or a custom style class). CSS styles define text appearance, position, and many other aspects of Web page layout. They allow you to specify more parameters of the design than earlier HTML specifications; for example, you can create custom list bullets.

Dreamweaver uses CSS styles by default to format page elements. When you defined the page properties for the Cosmatic site, Dreamweaver added CSS styles that control the appearance of the text placed in the page. For example, the text that you pasted in the Bands page is displayed in the Arial, Helvetica, sans-serif font group, which you defined as the page font when you set the page properties for the Bands page. You can also create CSS styles yourself.

A CSS style sheet provides a convenient way to store styles that can be defined in one location and then applied to content residing in many other locations. This ability to separate the look of the site from the content of the site enables the designer to more easily update the Web site's appearance. Designers can redefine an existing CSS style, and any content to which that style has been applied is updated to reflect the changes. This makes changing the font for all headings in a site or changing the color of body text on all the pages a simple task.

InSight | **Previewing Your Final Site**

Although CSS styles are the current standard for formatting the look and layout in Web pages, some limitations still exist. CSS styles were adopted as part of HTML 4 and are not fully compatible with older browsers. Be sure to preview the Web site in every browser and browser version you plan to support before making the site public. This is the best way to verify that all aspects of the site work and display as you expect.

Creating CSS Styles

You can create styles yourself using the CSS Styles panel located in the CSS panel group. When you create a CSS style, first you choose the type of style you want; then you choose the name, tag, or selector of the style; and finally, you choose the location of the style. The three types of CSS styles are redefined HTML tags, custom styles, and advanced. A **redefined HTML tag** is an existing HTML tag that you modify. You can change and remove existing attributes or add new attributes to any HTML tag to make the tag more useful. This is probably the most common type of CSS style. When you redefine an HTML tag, the modified CSS style is used in every instance of that tag. A **custom style** (also called a **custom style class**) is a style you create from scratch and apply to the element you have selected in the page. A custom style can be applied to any tag. The **advanced style** is used to redefine formatting for a group of tags or for all tags that contain a particular ID attribute. This type of style is most commonly used to customize the appearance of text links.

After you decide on a type of style, you choose a Name/Tag/Selector, depending on the type of style you selected. If you are redefining an HTML tag, you must select the tag that you want to modify. If you are creating a custom style class, you must type a name for the new style. If you are creating an advanced style, you must select the appropriate **selector**, the name of the style. In actuality, a selector can be a tag (if you are redefining an HTML tag), a period followed by a name you choose (if you are creating a custom style class), a combination of tags separated by commas, or a pseudoclass (if you are using an advanced style). When you create a new style, Dreamweaver refers to the name of the style as selector only when you create an advanced style.

Finally, you must select the location in which you will define the style. You can save the style you are creating in a new (external) style sheet file, in an existing external style sheet file, or only within the current document. When you save the file in the current document, Dreamweaver creates an **internal style sheet** that embeds (or inserts) the styles in the head of the current Web page and applies them only throughout that document. Creating an internal style sheet is useful because it enables you to update the look of all elements on which a style is used throughout the page. For example, if you wanted to change the look of all the subheadings in a page, you could change the subheading style instead of selecting and modifying each subheading individually. An **external style sheet** is a separate file that contains all the CSS styles used in a Web site. When you define styles in an external style sheet, you can use the styles in any page in the Web site to which you connect that style sheet. Editing a style in the external style sheet will update all instances in which that style is used throughout the site. This is the most powerful way to use styles.

Every CSS style (or rule) consists of two parts: the selector and the declaration. As mentioned above, the selector is the name of the style. The **declaration** defines the attributes that are included in the style. Once you select the type, the name (selector), and the location of the style, you can choose the various attributes to be included in the declaration for the style. The eight categories of attributes that you can combine to create a style are:

- **Type.** Font and type settings and attributes such as font family, font size, color, decoration, and weight. More type attribute choices are available here than in the Property inspector when text is selected.
- **Background.** A color or an image, fixed or scrolling, that can be placed behind a page element such as a block of text. CSS background attributes overlay the Web page background designated with the page properties and can be added behind any page element.
- **Block.** Spacing and alignment settings for tags and attributes. Examples include the spacing between words, letters, and lines of text; the horizontal and vertical alignment of text; and the indentation applied to the text.
- **Box.** Attributes that control the placement of elements in the page. When you select a letter, a word, a group of words, a graphic, or any other element, a selection box surrounds all the selected elements. Box attributes control the characteristics of the selection box, enabling you to set margins, padding, float settings, and so on.
- **Border.** The dimensions, color, and line styles of the borders of the selection box that surrounds elements.
- **List.** The number format or the bullet shape or image and its position used with ordered and unordered lists.
- **Positioning.** Attributes that determine how a tag or selected content is positioned in the page.

- **Extensions.** Attributes that control page breaks during printing, the appearance of the pointer when positioned over objects in the page, and special effects to objects. Most browsers do not support some extensions' attributes.

Modifying HTML Tags

The simplest way to create a CSS style is to redefine an existing HTML tag. Often, modifying an existing HTML tag can make it more useful. For example, The Heading 1 tag, <h1>, is an HTML tag that was introduced in an early version of HTML. It was created to give designers some control over the size at which text was displayed. Because designers did not have a lot of control over text size at the time, the format of the Heading 1 tag changes based on how each user's browser interprets the tag, making the heading's layout and appearance inconsistent and limited. However, when you set page properties, you selected size and color attributes for the Heading 1 tag, <h1>, and Dreamweaver created a style that customized the appearance of that tag. Customizing the existing Heading 1 tag gives you a consistency that the <h1> tag would otherwise lack and makes the tag useful.

Many designers prefer to redefine HTML tags when creating CSS styles because the tags are often automatically inserted and older browsers that don't support CSS styles will apply the standard formatting of the HTML tags. For example, Dreamweaver applies the paragraph tag whenever you press the Enter key. If you modify the paragraph tag, Dreamweaver automatically applies the new formatting attributes anywhere a paragraph tag is found in the Web page. A redefined HTML tag is applied in the same way that the tag would normally be applied.

When you create a CSS style to modify an HTML tag, Dreamweaver provides an extensive list of tags from which to choose. You can change and remove existing attributes or add new attributes to any tag. When you modify the attributes associated with a tag, the changes you make will apply to every instance of that tag.

Reference Window | Modifying an Existing HTML Tag

- Click the New CSS Rule button in the CSS Styles panel located in the CSS panel group.
- Click the Tag option button.
- Click the Tag arrow, and then click the tag you want to modify.
- Click the appropriate Define in option button.
- Click the OK button to open the CSS Rule Definition dialog box.
- Click a category in the Category box, and then set the options you want.
- Click the OK button.

Brian asks you to customize the look of the Heading 2 tag so that the subheadings in the Bands page will be displayed in accordance with the approved Cosmatic style: font—Arial, Helvetica, san-serif; size—20 pixels; color—red, #772300; and case—uppercase. You will not specify a font because the style uses the page font you selected when you defined the page properties for the Bands page.

Styles **inherit** the attributes of higher-level tags when those attributes are not also specified in the current style. Because the attribute that specifies the page font was defined in the body tag, which surrounds all the other tags that format content in a Web page, the specified font family applies to the Heading 2 tag by default, unless you specify another font for this tag when you create the style. If you do specify a font in the Heading 2 tag style, it will override what was specified in the body tag; text to which the Heading 2 tag is applied will display that font in the body tag. This happens because style sheets are **cascading**; if an attribute is defined in two styles that affect the same object, the style that is "closer" to the object in the code will override the value of the attribute in the tag that is farther away from the object in the code. The cascading effect of style sheets is very powerful because it enables you to create general styles that affect the entire page. You create additional styles only for items that are exceptions to the general style. From the CSS Styles panel, you can view the properties of a selected tag as well as the cascade of rules for a selected tag. This powerful tool enables you to see which styles are affecting the appearance of a selected tag so that you can create new styles without inadvertently affecting existing styles.

Brian wants the subheadings directly above the description paragraphs. Heading tags are block-level tags, which means that they always affect the entire block of text even if they are applied to only a few words in the block of text. Placing the heading tags directly above the paragraphs causes the paragraphs to be displayed with the heading formatting. You will change the Heading 2 tag style by selecting Inline from the Display list in the Block category of the CSS Rule Definition dialog box. This will enable you to place the subheadings directly above the paragraphs.

To modify the existing Heading 2 HTML tag:

▶ **1.** If you took a break after the previous session, make sure that the Cosmatic site is open, the bands.html page is open in the Document window, and the page is in Design view.

▶ **2.** In the CSS panel group, click the **Expand** arrow to open the CSS panel group, click the **CSS Styles** tab if necessary, and then click the **All** button if necessary. The CSS Styles panel lists the styles that Dreamweaver created. See Figure 3-15.

CSS Styles panel　　Figure 3-15

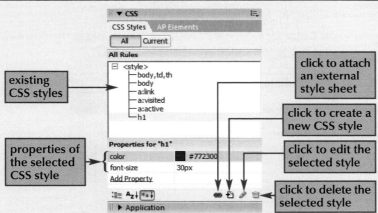

▶ **3.** In the CSS Styles panel, click the **New CSS Rule** button ⊞ . The New CSS Rule dialog box opens. See Figure 3-16.

Figure 3-16 **New CSS Rule dialog box**

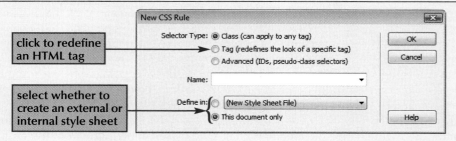

click to redefine an HTML tag

select whether to create an external or internal style sheet

4. Click the **Tag** option button in the Selector Type section. A list of tags appears in the Tag list.

5. Click the **Tag** arrow, and then click **h2**. This specifies that you'll modify the <h2> tag.

6. Click the **This document only** option button, if necessary. This creates an internal style sheet.

7. Click the **OK** button. The CSS Rule definition for h2 dialog box opens, and h2 appears in the CSS Styles panel.

8. In the Category box, click **Type**, if necessary.

9. Click in the **Size** box, type **20**, and then, if necessary, click the right **Size** button, and then click **pixels**.

10. Click the **Case** arrow, and then click **uppercase**.

11. Click in the right **Color** box, type **#772300**, and then press the **Tab** key. The specified color appears in the left Color box. See Figure 3-17.

Figure 3-17 **CSS Rule definition for h2 dialog box**

Tip

The hexadecimal color code must begin with # to display correctly when viewed outside of Dreamweaver.

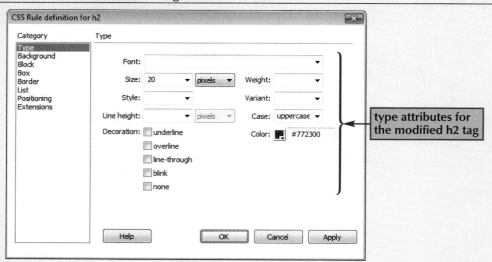

type attributes for the modified h2 tag

12. In the Category box, click **Block**, click the **Display** arrow, and then click **Inline**.

13. Click the **OK** button. The subheadings in the Bands page reflect the new style. In the CSS Styles panel, h2 is selected in the All Rules pane and its properties appear in the Properties pane. See Figure 3-18.

Heading 2 style modified ◄ **Figure 3-18**

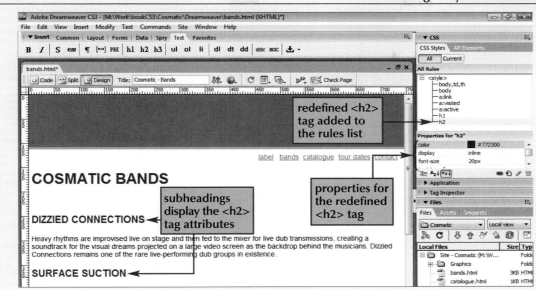

Now that you've created a style by modifying an existing tag, you'll remove the formatting from the paragraph text that follows each subheading in the Bands page.

To remove formatting from the paragraph text:

▶ **1.** Place the insertion point after the DIZZIED CONNECTIONS paragraph text, and then press the **Enter** key. The SURFACE SUCTION subheading moves down two lines.

▶ **2.** Place the insertion point before the DIZZIED CONNECTIONS paragraph text, click the **Format** button in the Property inspector, and then click **None**. The formatting is removed from the paragraph text, and the text moves to the same line as the subheading.

▶ **3.** Press the **Shift+Enter** keys to insert one line break. The paragraph text moves directly below the subheading. See Figure 3-19.

Paragraph text moved closer to subheading ◄ **Figure 3-19**

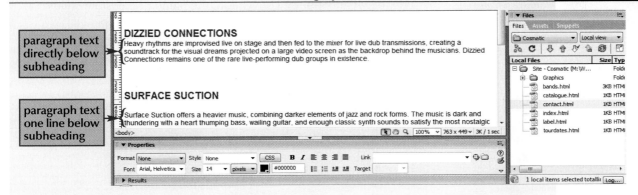

▶ **4.** Repeat Steps 1 through 3 to format the other subheadings and paragraph text in the page.

▶ **5.** Save the Bands page.

Creating and Applying Custom Style Classes

Modifying text attributes is not limited to redefining existing HTML tags. You can also create custom style classes, which are styles (or rules) you build from scratch and give a unique name. The process for creating a custom style class is similar to redefining an HTML tag except that you name the style and specify all the attributes you want the style to include.

Some designers prefer to create custom style classes instead of redefining existing tags (such as the heading tags) when they create styles for elements that will be used in a limited way or as an exception to the norm. For example, when you selected the page font in the Page Properties dialog box, Dreamweaver redefined the body tag to include the selected font group. This ensures that all of the text in the Web page displays in the selected font group, because the body tags are always included in the code for a Web page. If you decide to display a small section of text in a different font, a good way to do this would be to create a custom style and apply the custom style only to that text.

Reference Window | **Creating a Custom Style Class**

- Click the New CSS Rule button in the CSS Styles panel.
- Click the Class option button.
- Double-click in the Name box to select the text, and then type the name of the new custom style class.
- Click the appropriate Define in option button.
- Click the OK button to open the CSS Rule definition dialog box.
- Click a category in the Category box, and then set the options you want.
- Click the OK button.

Sara signed a new band to the Cosmatic label. Brian wants to use an alternate subheading style for new bands to promote them and draw attention to them in the Web site.

You will add the new band to the bottom of the Bands page, create a custom style class for the new band subheading, and then apply the custom style to the new heading text. You'll name the style .NewBandSub. By convention, the name of a custom style class always begins with a period, has no spaces, and cannot contain any special characters. In addition to a font, size, and color, you'll include a background color in the custom style class.

Tip

If you forget to begin a custom style name with a period, Dreamweaver will add the period for you.

To create a custom style class for the new band subheading:

▶ **1.** In the CSS Styles panel, click the **New CSS Rule** button 🖹 . The New CSS Rule dialog box opens.

▶ **2.** Click the **Class** option button in the Selector Type section.

▶ **3.** Double-click text in the Name box to select the text, if necessary, and then type **.NewBandSub** (including the period before the name).

▶ **4.** Click the **This document only** option button in the Define in section, if necessary, and then click the **OK** button. The CSS Rule Definition for .NewBandSub dialog box opens, and the name appears in the All Rules pane in the CSS Styles panel.

▶ **5.** In the Category box, click **Type**, if necessary.

▶ **6.** Type **20** in the Size box, and then click the **Size** button and click **pixels**, if necessary.

▶ **7.** Click the **Case** arrow, click **uppercase**, click in the right **Color** box, and then type **#878816**.

You will change the category so you can add the background color.

▶ **8.** In the Category box, click **Background**.

▶ **9.** Click in the right **Background Color** box, type **#E0AE4D**, and then click the **OK** button. The name of the new style is selected in the All Rules pane in the CSS Styles panel, and its properties appear in the Properties pane.

You must apply the custom style class to the text you want to format. When you create a new custom style class style, its name appears in the Style list in the Property inspector as well as in the All Rules pane in the CSS Styles panel. You apply the style to selected text by selecting the style from the Style list in the Property inspector. To help you remember what a style looks like, when possible, each style name in the Style list in the Property inspector is formatted with the attributes for that style.

You'll type the new band name, Lowbrow Theft, at the bottom of the Bands page, and then apply the .NewBandSub style to the name.

To apply the .NewBandSub custom style class to the new band name:

▶ **1.** Position the insertion point after the LIFE IN MINOR CHORDS paragraph text at the bottom of the Bands page, and then press the **Enter** key.

▶ **2.** Type **Lowbrow Theft**, and then press the **Shift+Enter** keys to insert one line break.

▶ **3.** Type **The newest band on the Cosmatic label. More info. coming soon**.

▶ **4.** Select **Lowbrow Theft**, click the **Style** arrow in the Property inspector, and then click **NewBandSub**. The style is applied to the text.

▶ **5.** Click in the heading to deselect the text. See Figure 3-20.

Figure 3-20 **Custom .NewBandSub style created and applied**

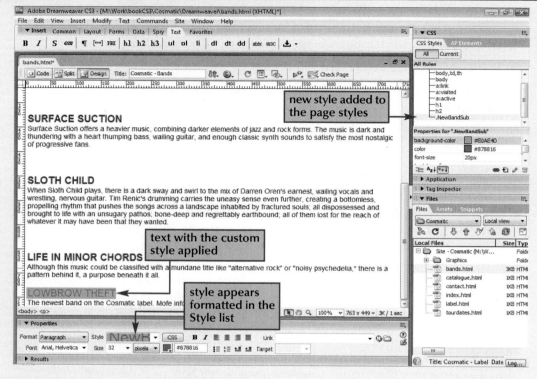

6. Save the Bands page, and then preview the page in a browser.

Using the Advanced Style to Customize Anchor Tag Pseudoclasses

When you set the page properties for the Cosmatic site, Dreamweaver created CSS styles to customize the appearance of hyperlinks for the site. You can also create these styles manually using the advanced style. When you create an advanced style, you redefine the formatting for a group of tags or for tags containing a specific id attribute. In this case, you would create a CSS style (or rule) for each part, or pseudoclass, of the <a> tag. According to style sheet standards, a **pseudoclass** is any class that is applied to entities other than HTML Specifications Standard tags. For example, the anchor tag <a> is broken into four pseudoclasses: a:link, a:hover, a:active, and a:visited. Each of these pseudoclasses controls a portion of the hyperlink functionality of the anchor tag. The a:link portion of the tag controls the way the link text looks before the link has been visited. The a:hover portion of the tag controls the way the link text looks while the pointer is over the link text. The a:active portion of the tag controls the way the link text looks as it is being clicked. The a:visited portion of the tag controls the way the link text looks after the link has been visited. You can use advanced styles to modify each part of the anchor tag in the same way that you redefined an existing HTML tag.

When you set the page properties for the Bands page, Dreamweaver created styles a:link, a:visited, and a:active pseudoclasses of the anchor tag. Now you will set the style for the a:hover pseudoclass.

When you define the parts of the anchor tag manually, you must define them in the order they appear in the CSS Selector list: a:link, a:visited, a:hover, a:active. The a:hover style must be placed after the a:link and a:visited styles so that they don't hide the color property of the a:hover style. Similarly, the a:active style must be placed after the a:hover style, or the a:active color property will display when a user both activates and hovers over the linked text. When you set the hyperlink attributes in the Page Properties dialog box, Dreamweaver creates the CSS styles for the pseudoclasses of the anchor tag and automatically places the styles in the correct order in the style sheet.

Using the Advanced Style for Hyperlinks | Reference Window

- Click the New CSS Rule button in the CSS Styles panel.
- Click the Advanced option button.
- Click the Selector arrow, and then click the selector you want to modify.
- Click the appropriate Define in option button.
- Click the OK button to open the CSS Rule definition dialog box.
- Click a category in the Category box, and then set the options you want.
- Click the OK button.

You'll finish customizing the appearance of the text links in the Bands page using the advanced type to create a style for the a:hover pseudoclass of the anchor tag. Dreamweaver inserts new styles just below the selected rule in the All Rules pane in the CSS Styles panel. If no rule is selected, then the new style is placed at the bottom of the All Rules pane. The a:hover selector must be placed before the a:active selector in the All Rules pane, so you'll select the a:visited rule before you click the New Rule button. The new a:hover rule you'll create will then appear above the a:active rule in the All Rules pane.

To customize the a:hover pseudoclass using the advanced type:

▶ **1.** In the All Rules pane of the CSS Styles panel, click the **a:visited** style in the style list to select it.

▶ **2.** In the CSS Styles panel, click the **New CSS Rule** button 🔁 . The New CSS Rule dialog box opens.

▶ **3.** Click the **Advanced** option button in the Selector Type section.

▶ **4.** Click the **Selector** arrow, and then click **a:hover**.

▶ **5.** Click the **This document only** option button in the Define in section, if necessary, and then click the **OK** button. The CSS Rule definition for a:hover dialog box opens and a:hover is added above a:active in the All Rules pane.

▶ **6.** In the Category box, click **Type**, if necessary.

▶ **7.** Type **#772300** in the right Color box, click the **None** check box in the Decoration section to check it, and then click the **OK** button. The a:hover style is customized for the Cosmatic site.

▶ **8.** Save the Bands page.

You'll preview the Bands page in a browser so that you can test the links.

To preview the customized text links in a browser:

▶ **1.** Preview the Bands page in a browser. The custom a:link style is visible.

▶ **2.** Point to the **catalogue** link. The hover style is visible. See Figure 3-21.

Figure 3-21 | **Bands page with customized link styles previewed in a browser**

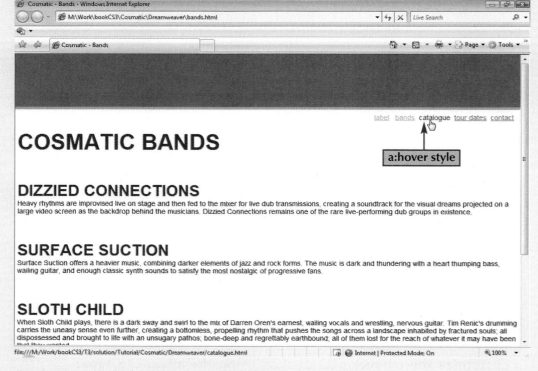

▶ **3.** Click the **catalogue** link. The Catalogue page opens in the browser.

▶ **4.** Click the **Back** button ⬅ on the browser toolbar. The Bands page reloads. The catalogue link is now yellow, which is the color you specified for the visited link formatting.

▶ **5.** Close the browser.

In this session, you created CSS styles in the Bands page by redefining an HTML tag, creating a custom style, and creating an advanced style. In the next session, you will export the styles from the Bands page to an external style sheet, create CSS styles in an external style sheet, and attach the external style sheet to the pages of the Cosmatic site.

Review | **Session 3.2 Quick Check**

1. What is a CSS style?

2. True or False? When you redefine a CSS style after it has been applied to text, the look of the content to which the style has been applied is also updated.

3. What is a CSS style that you create from scratch called?

4. True or False? You can save CSS styles in a style sheet that can be applied to all of the pages in a site.

5. How does modifying an HTML tag make it more useful?

6. When do some designers prefer to create custom style classes instead of redefining existing HTML tags?

7. With what letter or character do custom style class names start?

Session 3.3

Using External Style Sheets

Locating all of the styles for a Web site in one place is one of the greatest advantages of using CSS styles. An external style sheet enables you to separate the style of the Web site from the content of the Web site, enabling you to make sitewide stylistic changes by updating a single file. So far, you created and used styles within one document, or page, in the Cosmatic site. To use the styles you created throughout a site, they must be located in an external style sheet, a file that contains the CSS styles defined for a Web site. You can have as many external style sheets as you would like for a site, but it is usually easier to incorporate all styles into one external style sheet. You can either create a style in an external style sheet or you can move the styles you created within a Web page to an external style sheet.

> **Tip**
>
> An external style sheet has the file extension .css.

Moving Styles to an External Style Sheet

If you've already created styles in a specific document or page, you can move one or all of those styles to an external style sheet rather than re-create them. This enables you to use those styles throughout the Web site. To keep the files in a Web site organized, you should create a folder in the local root folder of the Web site, such as a folder named "Stylesheets," and then save the external style sheet file with a descriptive name such as "cosmatic_styles," within that folder. To move CSS styles to an external style sheet, the Web page where the styles are currently located must be open.

Moving Styles to a New External Style Sheet | Reference Window

- Open the Web page whose styles you want to move.
- In the CSS Styles panel, select the styles to move, right-click the selected styles, and then click Move CSS Rules.
- Click the A New Style Sheet option button, and then click the OK button.
- Navigate to the Stylesheets folder in the local root folder.
- Type a name for the style sheet in the File name box.
- Click the Save button.

You want to use the styles you created for the Bands page in all of the other pages in the Cosmatic site. You'll move those styles to an external style sheet that you'll store in a new folder named "Stylesheets" in the local root folder. When you move the styles from the Bands page, all of the styles from the Bands page, including the styles that Dreamweaver created when you set the page properties, are moved to the external style sheet. In this case, you will create the style sheet when you export the styles from the Bands page.

To move the styles from the Bands page to an external style sheet:

▶ **1.** If you took a break after the previous session, make sure that the Cosmatic site is open, the bands.html page is open in the Document window, and the page is in Design view.

▶ **2.** In the Files panel, select **bands.html**, if necessary.

▶ **3.** In the CSS Styles panel, select all of the styles, right-click the selected styles, and then click **Move CSS Rules** on the context menu. The Move To External Style Sheet dialog box opens.

▶ **4.** Click the **A New Style Sheet** option button, and then click the **OK** button. The Save Style Sheet File As dialog box opens.

You need to create a new folder in which to store the external style sheet.

▶ **5.** Verify that the Save in box displays the local root folder of your Cosmatic site (the Dreamweaver folder).

▶ **6.** Click the **Create New Folder** button 📝 on the dialog box toolbar. A new folder is created within the local root folder of your Cosmatic site and appears in the Save in list with the New Folder name selected.

▶ **7.** Type **Stylesheets**, and then press the **Enter** key. The new folder is renamed Stylesheets and opened. You'll save the external style sheet in this folder.

▶ **8.** Select any text in the File name box, and then type **cosmatic_styles**. The external style sheet has a descriptive name. See Figure 3-22.

Figure 3-22 ▶ **Save Style Sheet File As dialog box**

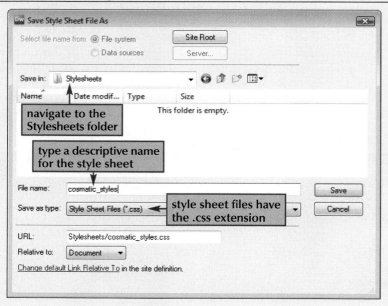

▶ **9.** Click the **Save** button. The external style sheet file is saved within the folder you created, and the cosmatic_styles.css page opens in the Document window.

▶ **10.** Click the **Refresh** button 🔁 on the Files panel toolbar to refresh the file list, if necessary, and then click the **Plus (+)** button ➕ next to the Stylesheets folder to display the cosmatic_styles.css file in the file list. See Figure 3-23.

External style sheet displayed in the Files panel | Figure 3-23

DIZZIED CONNECTIONS
Heavy rhythms are improvised live on stage and then fed to the mixer for live dub transmissions, creating a soundtrack for the visual dreams projected on a large video screen as the backdrop behind the musicians. Dizzied Connections remains one of the rare live-performing dub groups in existence.

SURFACE SUCTION

click to refresh the file list

external style sheet file stored in new folder

Deleting Styles from a Style Sheet

Styles moved to an external style sheet are automatically deleted from within the page. However, when you connect an existing style sheet to a page, you must move all of the styles from that page to the style sheet and then delete the styles from within the page. Otherwise, you will create multiple sets of styles with the same names, which can cause styles to conflict and lead to confusion.

Using multiple sets of styles negates the benefits of using style sheets, because you don't have one centralized set of styles that is easily updated and used throughout the site. Also, because style sheets are cascading, the styles in an internal style sheet will override styles in an external style sheet wherever a style conflict exists. And when an attribute is defined in the external style sheet but not in the internal style sheet, the attribute from the external style sheet will be displayed. You can see how this could get out of hand. This is why it is important to maintain an organized file structure and to keep all the styles for a Web site in one location. When you delete the styles from a page, the text returns to its default formatting and the background image disappears.

When you moved the styles from the Bands page to the external style sheet, the styles were automatically deleted from within that page. You'll delete all the styles located within the Label page so that you can attach the external style sheet to that page.

To delete all of the styles from within the Label page:

▶ 1. Open the **label.html** page in the Document window.

▶ 2. In the All Rules pane of the CSS Styles panel, click the **Minus (–)** button ⊟ next to <style>, if necessary, to close the style list.

▶ 3. In the All Rules pane of the CSS Styles panel, select **<style>** if necessary, right-click the selection, and then click **Delete** on the context menu. The styles are deleted from the page, "(no styles defined)" appears in the All Rules pane, and the formatting (including the background image) is removed from the page. See Figure 3-24.

Figure 3-24	**Label page without styles**

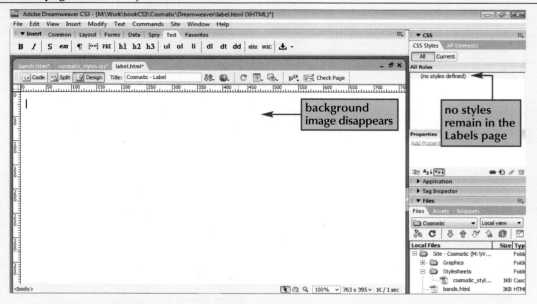

> **4.** Save the Label page.

You can also delete a single style if you are not going to use it in the site. Deleting styles that you are not using in a site helps to keep the site's files organized and lean. You delete a single style in the same way that you deleted all of the styles, except that you select only the style that you want to delete from the page. External style sheets are uploaded to the Web server along with the Web pages, graphics, and other files associated with the site. Deleting unused styles eliminates unnecessary materials from the site and reduces the size of the files.

Attaching a Style Sheet to Web Pages

When the styles for formatting a Web site are located in an external style sheet, you must attach the style sheet to each Web page you want to format with those styles. You can attach an existing style sheet to a Web page when you create it, or you can attach an existing style sheet to each page when you need the styles. (If you moved the styles from a page in the Web site to the external style sheet, the styles are automatically applied to the page content and the external style sheet is automatically attached to that page.)

Before you attach an external style sheet to a Web page, you must remove the current formatting. Otherwise, the older formatting might override the CSS style you apply or combine with the CSS style, causing the text to display differently than you had intended.

The process for applying a CSS style saved in an external style sheet is the same as the process for applying CSS styles created within a document. To apply a custom style, select the text to which you want to apply the style, and then click the style in the Property inspector. If the style is a modified HTML tag or an advanced type, apply the tag and the modified attributes of the tag are included.

Attaching an External Style Sheet to a Web Page | Reference Window

- Open the page in Design view.
- In the CSS Styles panel, click the Attach Style Sheet button.
- Click the Browse button, navigate to the folder within the local root folder that contains the style sheets, click the name of the style sheet that you want to attach to the Web page, and then click the OK button.
- Click the Link option button.
- Click the OK button.

Next, you'll attach the cosmatic_styles external style sheet to the Label page.

To attach the cosmatic_styles external style sheet to the Label page:

▶ **1.** In the CSS Styles panel, click the **Attach Style Sheet** button 📇 . The Attach External Style Sheet dialog box opens. See Figure 3-25.

Attach External Style Sheet dialog box ◀ Figure 3-25

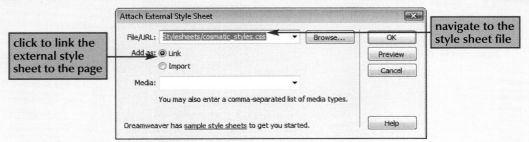

- click to link the external style sheet to the page
- navigate to the style sheet file

▶ **2.** If the style sheet file path is not in the File/URL box, click the **Browse** button, double-click the **Stylesheets** folder in the local root folder of your Cosmatic site, and then double-click **cosmatic_styles**. In the Attach External Style Sheet dialog box, Stylesheets/cosmatic_styles.css appears in the File/URL box.

▶ **3.** Click the **Link** option button, if necessary, and then click the **OK** button. The external style sheet is attached, and its name appears in the All Rules pane in the CSS Styles panel. Also, the styles in the external style sheet are applied to the Label page. See Figure 3-26.

External style sheet attached to the Label page ◀ Figure 3-26

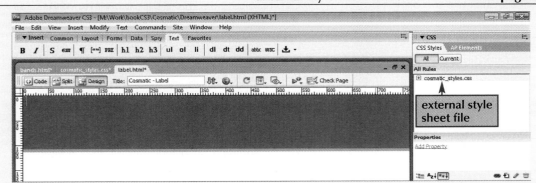

- external style sheet file

Tip

To move between multiple style sheets attached to a page, use the Plus (+) and Minus (–) buttons to open or close the desired style sheets.

▶ **4.** Click the **Plus (+)** button ⊞ beside the style sheet name to view the styles.

▶ **5.** Save and close the Label page, and then save the Bands page.

Creating a Style in an External Style Sheet

You can add new styles to an external style sheet at any time. The process of creating a style in an external style sheet is exactly the same as the process of creating a style in an internal style sheet. The only difference is that you choose the style sheet by name in the Define In list when you create the new style.

Reference Window | **Defining a Style in an External Style Sheet**

- In the CSS Styles panel, click the New CSS Rule button.
- Click the appropriate style selector type option button.
- Click in the Name, Tag, or Selector box, and then type a name for the new style.
- Click the top option button in the Define in section, and then select the style sheet name from the list.
- Click the OK button.
- In the Category box, click a category, and then set the options you want.
- Click the OK button.

You need to create a style for the copyright information that will appear as a footer at the bottom of each page. Because this style will be used on each page in the Cosmatic site, you'll define the new style in the cosmatic_styles.css external style sheet. When you add a new style to the style sheet, the style sheet will open in the Document window. You must save the style sheet to save the new style. You will examine the styles later.

To define the footer style in the external style sheet:

▶ **1.** In the CSS Styles panel, click the **New CSS Rule** button ⊞ . The New CSS Rule dialog box opens.

Trouble? If the buttons in the CSS Styles panel are not active, scroll to the top of the All Rules pane, click <style>, and then repeat Step 1.

▶ **2.** Click the **Class** option button, click in the **Name** box, and then type **.cosmatic_footer**.

▶ **3.** Click the top option button in the Define in section, make sure **cosmatic_styles.css** appears in the Define In box, and then click the **OK** button. The CSS Rule Definition for .cosmatic_footer in cosmatic_styles.css dialog box opens.

▶ **4.** In the Category box, click **Type**, if necessary, and then set the size to **10 pixels**.

▶ **5.** In the Category box, click **Block**, click the **Text Align** arrow, and then click **Center**.

▶ **6.** Click the **OK** button, and then, if necessary, click the **Plus (+)** button ⊞ beside the style sheet name to view the styles. The .cosmatic_footer style appears in the All Rules pane in the CSS Styles panel as well as in the Style list in the Property inspector. The cosmatic_styles.css page tab in the Document window includes an asterisk to indicate that the style sheet is not saved with the latest style you added.

The style was added to the style sheet. You must save the style sheet to save the changes.

7. Click the **cosmatic_styles.css** tab in the Document window, save the page, and then click the **bands.html** tab.

You'll add copyright text to the Bands page, and then apply the .cosmatic_footer style to it.

To add the copyright text and apply the footer style from the external style sheet:

1. Press the **Ctrl+End** keys to move the insertion point to the end of the text in the Bands page, and then press the **Enter** key twice. You'll type the copyright information in this location.

2. If necessary, click the **Text** tab on the Insert bar.

3. On the **Text** tab of the Insert bar, click the **Characters button arrow**, and then click the **Copyright** button ©. The copyright symbol (©) is inserted at the beginning of the line.

4. Press the **Right Arrow** key to deselect the copyright symbol, if necessary, and then press the **Spacebar** and type **Cosmatic, Inc. 2010**.

Next, you'll apply the .cosmatic_footer style to the copyright line.

5. Select the copyright symbol and text, click the **Style** arrow in the Property inspector, click **cosmatic_footer**, and then press the **Right Arrow** key to deselect the text. The style is applied to the text. See Figure 3-27.

Copyright text added to the Bands page | Figure 3-27

6. Save the Bands page.

Examining Code for CSS Styles

As you created and applied CSS styles to format the text in the Bands page and when Dreamweaver created styles in the other pages of the site, Dreamweaver added the appropriate HTML code within the head of each page. The **head** of a Web page is the portion of the HTML between the head tags. The actual code included within the head differs, based on whether you created an internal style sheet or an external style sheet.

When you create styles that apply only to the document in which you are working, the code for those styles is placed in the head of that page. If you attach an external style sheet to a Web page, a link tag to the style sheet is placed in the head of the HTML code for that page. The link tag allows the Web page to access the content of the external style sheet.

You will examine the HTML and CSS code in the head of the Bands page as well as the additional tags that appear throughout the Web page.

Viewing Code for Internal Style Sheets

When styles are defined in the current document only, the code is stored in an internal style sheet, which is also called an **embedded style sheet** because the styles are embedded (or placed) in the head of the Web page. The embedded styles can be used throughout the current Web page but not in any other page. The code usually takes the following format:

```
<style type="text/css">
<!--
name {
    attribute-name: attribute value;
    attribute2-name: attribute2 value;
}
-->
</style>
```

In this code, name is the style name, the HTML tag name, or the tag and pseudoclass name.

The style definitions (or rules) all appear inside the style tags, which are in the following format:

```
<style type="text/css">style definitions</style>
```

where type="text/css" indicates the format of the styles that will follow. Currently "text/css" is the only style type; however, the current HTML guidelines recommend that you include the style type to prevent problems if other style types are introduced in the future.

Nested within the style tag is the **comment tag**, which is in the following format:

```
<!-- style definitions -->
```

Comment tags hide the style definitions from older browsers that do not support CSS styles. Browsers tend to ignore tags that they do not understand. Browsers that do not understand CSS style tags will ignore the tags, but the content of the style tag (the style definitions) will be displayed in the Web page as text. To avoid this problem and prevent older browsers from displaying the style definitions in the Web page, comment tags are placed around the definitions.

Remember, every CSS style (or rule) consists of two parts: the selector and the declaration. The selector is the style name, and the declaration defines the attributes that are included in the style. The format for the style definition is:

```
name {
    attribute-name: attribute value;
    attribute2-name: attribute2 value;
}
```

In Dreamweaver, the selector and opening bracket are located on the first line of code for the style and are displayed in pink. You can tell by the style name whether the style is a custom style, a redefined tag, or an advanced style tag. When a custom style class is created, a period precedes the name of the new style (for example, .cosmatic_footer). If an existing tag is redefined, the tag name appears at the beginning of the style (for example, h1). If you use the advanced style, the tag name is followed by a colon and the pseudoclass (for example, a:active) or a number of tags separated by commas may appear if the advanced style is being created for a certain combination of tags. The style declaration is a series of attribute/value pairs. The attribute and value are separated by a colon and a space. Each attribute/value pair is displayed in blue on a separate line that ends with a semicolon and is indented under the selector. The closing bracket appears on a separate line after the final attribute/value pair and is displayed in pink. Styles follow this same format whether they are embedded within a page or located within an external style sheet.

You can view the embedded style sheet for a page by opening the page in the Document window and switching to Code view. You will open the Catalogue page and examine the internal style sheet code that Dreamweaver created when you defined the page properties.

To view the code for an internal style sheet for the Catalogue page:

▶ **1.** In the Files panel, double-click **catalogue.html** to open the Catalogue page in the Document window.

▶ **2.** Click the **Code** button on the Document toolbar, and then scroll to the top of the page, if necessary. The code for the Catalogue page appears in the Document window. See Figure 3-28.

Code for the internal style sheet in the Catalogue page — Figure 3-28

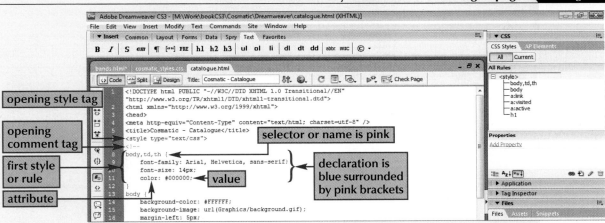

Trouble? If the code on your screen does not match the code in the figure, you do not have word wrap, line numbers, syntax coloring, and/or auto indent turned on. Click the View Options button on the Document toolbar, and then click Word Wrap, Line Numbers, Syntax Coloring, and/or Auto Indent to check each option as necessary.

▶ **3.** Examine the code associated with the styles. Locate the opening head tag, and then locate the opening style tag.

▶ **4.** Locate the opening comment tag, and then locate the first rule. Each rule starts with the selector (in pink) followed by the opening bracket. The declaration (in blue) is indented beneath the selector. Each attribute/value pair is on a separate line ending with a semicolon. The attribute is separated from the value by a colon and a space. The closing bracket (in pink) is on a separate line.

> **5.** Close the Catalogue page, and then make the Bands page active, if necessary.

Viewing Code for External Style Sheets

When an external style sheet is attached to a page, a link tag appears within the head of the Web page and the styles are located in the style sheet, not in the head of the Web page. External style sheets are also called **linked style sheets**. Link tags do not include a closing tag or any style content information; they only convey relationship information about the linked document.

Link tags appear in the following general format:

```
<link rel="stylesheet" href="stylesheeturl.css" type="text/css">
```

The first part of the tag, link, identifies the type of tag. The second part of the tag, rel=, indicates the relationship between the linked document and the Web page. The relationship itself appears within quotation marks; in this case, the relationship is "stylesheet," meaning that the linked document contains the CSS style for the page. Next, href="stylesheeturl.css" is the URL of the linked document. The URL appears within quotation marks. Finally, type= indicates the form of the content that will follow. MIME type is the standard for identifying content type on the Internet. The type also appears within quotation marks.

You'll look at the link to the external style sheet in the Bands page.

To view the code in the Bands page:

> **1.** Click the **Code** button on the Document toolbar, and then scroll to the top of the Bands page in the Document window.

> **2.** Locate the link tag in the head of the Bands page. See Figure 3-29.

Figure 3-29 | **Code for the external style sheet in the Bands page**

> **3.** Locate the closing head tag. Notice that no styles appear in the head of the Bands page.

When styles are located in an external style sheet, you must open the style sheet to view all of the code for the styles. If you know how to enter code manually, you can edit the styles for the page by changing the code in the style sheet. Style sheets open only in Code view; Split and Design views are not available options.

You will open the cosmatic_styles.css style sheet in the Document window and view the styles.

To view the cosmatic_styles.css external style sheet:

▶ 1. Click the **cosmatic_styles.css** tab in the Document window, and then scroll to the top of the page, if necessary. The external style sheet appears in the Document window. See Figure 3-30.

External style sheet page | Figure 3-30

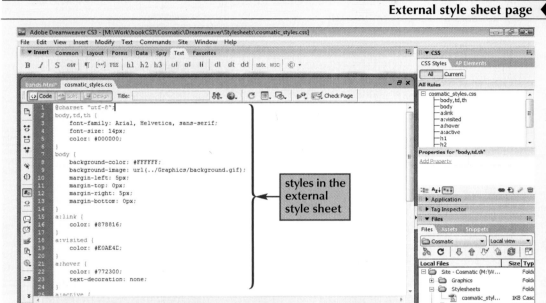

styles in the external style sheet

Trouble? If you don't see the cosmatic_styles.css tab in the Document window, the external style sheet is not displayed. Click the Plus (+) button next to the Stylesheets folder in the Files panel to display its content, and then double-click cosmatic_styles.css to open the external style sheet page.

▶ 2. Notice that the style format is the same as in the internal style sheet.

▶ 3. Close the cosmatic_styles.css page.

Viewing Style Tags

Whether styles are located in an internal or external style sheet, using CSS styles affects the code in the body of a Web page in the same way. When you use CSS styles to modify or customize HTML tags, you do not see any additional code in the body of the Web pages. The existing tags simply reference the new definitions, which are located either in the head of the Web page or in an external style sheet.

When you select text and apply a custom style class, Dreamweaver adds the attributes of that custom style class to the text by inserting additional code within the Web page in one of three ways:

- **Adding attributes to an existing tag.** When you apply a custom style class to text that is already surrounded by a tag, Dreamweaver adds the additional attributes of the custom style class to the existing tag. For example, if you apply a custom style class named "class_name" to a block of text that is already surrounded by a paragraph tag,<p>, Dreamweaver adds the attributes of the custom style to that paragraph tag in the following manner:

```
<p class="class_name">Content of text block</p>
```

where class="class_name" tells the browser to format the text according to the definition in the custom style class named "class_name." (The custom style class definition will be located either in the head of the Web page or in an external style sheet.)

- **Applying a custom style class to a block of text.** When you apply a custom style class to a block of text that is not already encompassed by a tag, Dreamweaver surrounds the entire block of text with the div tag that inserts the custom style attributes. The div tag appears in the general format:

  `<div class="class_name">`Content of text block**`</div>`**

- **Applying a custom style class to a text selection.** When you apply a custom style class to a selection smaller than a text block (such as a word, a phrase, or a portion of a text block), Dreamweaver surrounds the selection with a span tag that inserts the custom style attributes. The span tag appears in the following general format:

  `<span class="class_name">`Content of text selection**`</span>`**

You will view the subheadings and footer in the Bands page in Split view to examine the code that Dreamweaver inserted into the page.

To examine the Bands page in Split view:

1. Click the **Split** button on the Document toolbar, and then select **DIZZIED CONNECTIONS** in the Design pane. The text is also selected in the Code pane.

2. Examine the code around the selected text in the Code pane. The text is surrounded by the Heading 2 tag, <h2>. No extra code appears in the page because the <h2> tag simply references the style located in the style sheet and displays the text according to the defined rule. The rule's properties appear in the Property inspector. See Figure 3-31.

Figure 3-31	Code for a redefined HTML tag

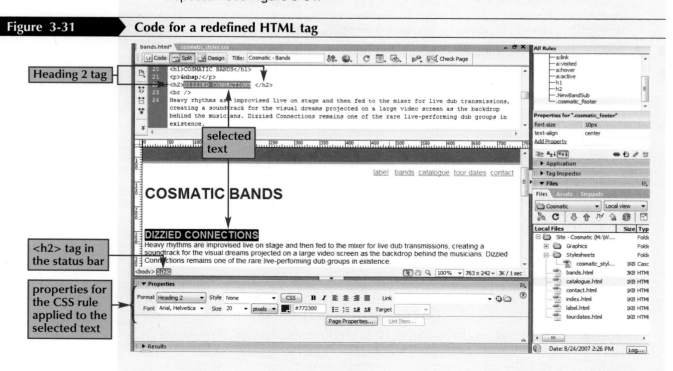

▶ **3.** Scroll to the bottom of the page in the Design pane, select **Lowbrow Theft**, and then examine the code surrounding the selected text in the Code pane. The custom style class information is inserted into a span tag, because the paragraph tag that surrounds the subheading also surrounds the following paragraph text, but the style is applied to only the heading. See Figure 3-32.

Custom style class applied with a span tag ◀ Figure 3-32

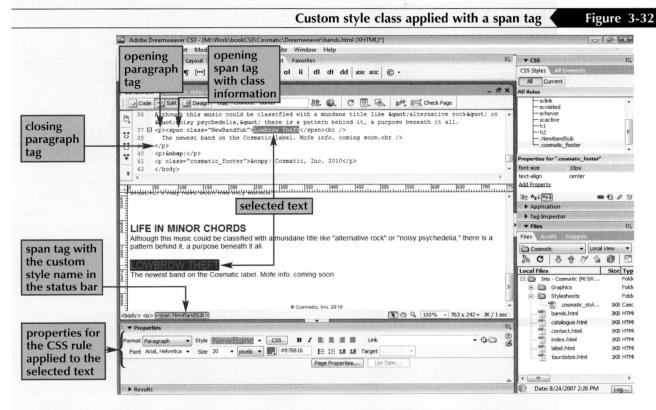

▶ **4.** Select the footer text in the Design pane and examine the code surrounding the selected text in the Code pane. The custom style class information is inserted into the paragraph tag this time because the paragraph tag is only surrounding the affected text. See Figure 3-33.

Figure 3-33 **Custom style class applied to the paragraph tag**

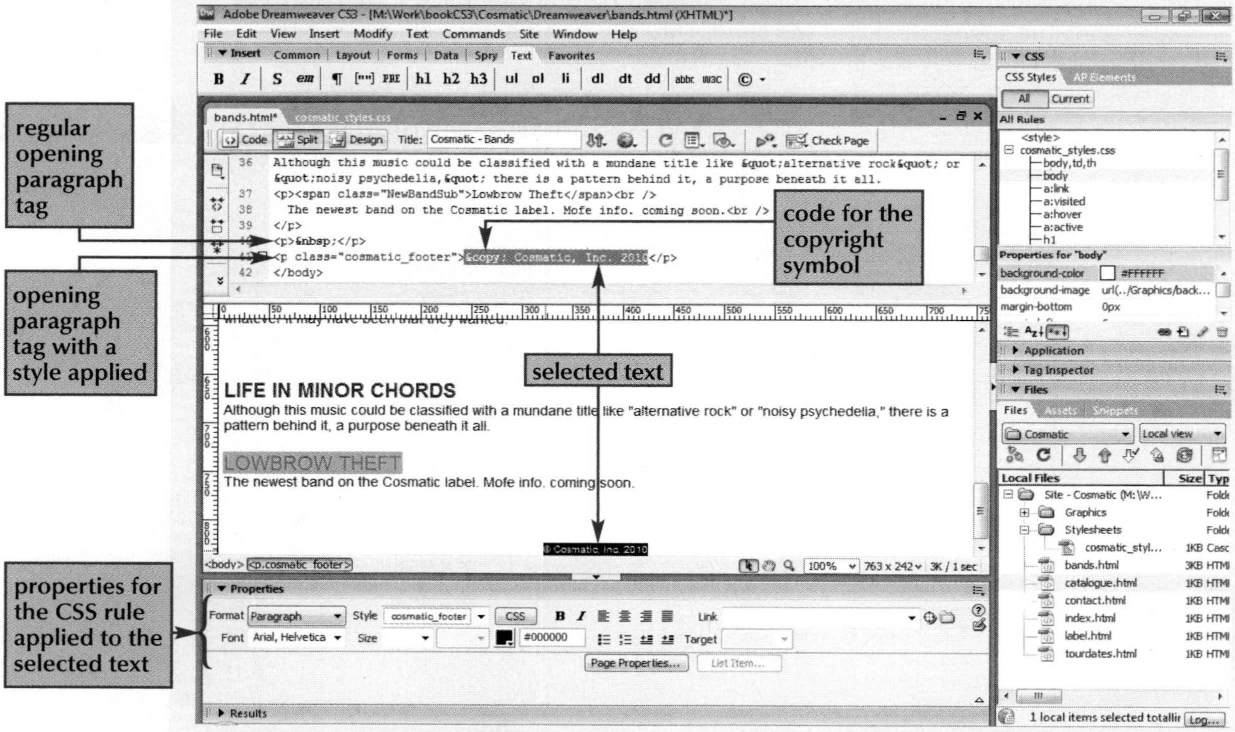

5. Click the **Design** button on the Document toolbar, and then scroll to the top of the page.

Editing CSS Styles

One of the most powerful aspects of CSS is the ability to edit styles. You edit a style by adding or removing formatting attributes from an existing style. When you edit a style, any element to which the style is applied is updated automatically to reflect the changes you made. This helps you to maintain a consistent look throughout a Web site, whether the site includes a few pages or many. It also enables you to control the look of an entire Web site from one centralized set of specifications. Dreamweaver includes several tools to help you manage and edit your styles including the CSS Rule Definition dialog box, the Properties pane in the CSS Styles panel, and the Property inspector.

Editing Styles in the CSS Rule Definition Dialog Box

You can edit styles in the CSS Rule Definition dialog box. This is the same dialog box that you used to create the definitions. The changes you make override the original style attribute selections. After you have selected attributes for the style, you can view the style in the page by clicking the Apply button in the CSS Rule Definition dialog box and viewing the page in the Document window.

Editing a Style

- Select the style that you want to edit in the All Rules pane in the CSS Styles panel.
- Right-click the name of the style, and then click Edit (or in the CSS Styles panel, click the style name, and then click the Edit CSS Style button).
- Make the changes in the CSS Rule definition dialog box.
- Click the OK button.

Brian wants the new band subheadings to be larger in size. He suggests making them 32 pixels. You will change the .NewBandSub style in the CSS Rule Definition dialog box.

To edit the .NewBandSub style:

1. In the All Rules pane of the CSS Styles panel, right-click the **.NewBandSub** style, and then click **Edit** on the context menu. The CSS Rule Definition for .NewBandSub in cosmatic_styles.css dialog box opens.

2. In the Category box, click **Type**.

3. In the Size box, double-click **20**, and then type **32** to replace the selected size value.

4. Click the **Apply** button. The new band subheading LOWBROW THEFT increases in size in the Bands page. See Figure 3-34.

Bands page with updated the .NewBandSub style ◄ Figure 3-34

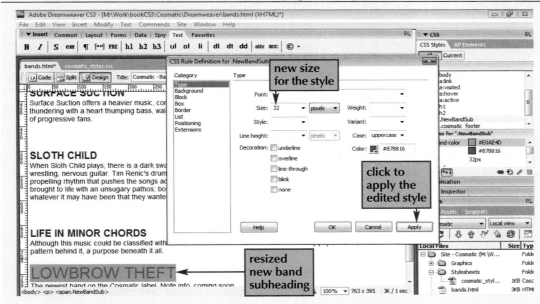

5. Click the **OK** button. The changes you made to the styles are accepted, and the external style sheet opens.

   You must save the external style sheet to save the style changes you made.

6. Save the cosmatic_styles page, and then close it.

7. Preview the Bands page in a browser, and then close the browser.

Tip

If an edited style was in an internal style sheet, you would save the page to save the changes to the style.

Editing Styles in the Properties Pane of the CSS Styles Panel

The CSS Styles panel is another tool that you can use to examine and edit CSS styles. When you select a page element in the Document window and click the Current button in the CSS Styles panel, the panel changes from All mode to Current mode and three panes display information about styles and properties for the selected page element. Because styles are inherited and cascading, several rules might contribute to the formatting of any particular element.

The Summary for Selection pane lists the properties for all rules that affect the formatting of the selected element. Properties are listed in hierarchical order; properties that are closer to the text appear at the bottom of the list. This is useful because styles sometimes inherit properties from higher-level styles, and when a property value is set in more than one style, the value located in the style closest to the element will override the value of the higher-level style. Viewing the properties in a hierarchical list enables you to see exactly which property takes precedence.

In About view, the Rules pane specifies which rule or cascade of rules affects the property selected in the Summary for Selection pane as well as the style sheet file in which that rule is saved. In Rules view, the Rules pane shows the cascade or hierarchy of all the rules that affect the selected element. You can switch between the Rules pane views by clicking the buttons in the Rules pane title bar.

The Properties pane enables you to edit CSS properties for the rule in which the property selected in the Summary for Selection pane is defined or the rule selected in the Rules pane. You can show only those properties that are set, you can display the properties in alphabetical order, or you can display the properties by category (such as font, background, and so on). You can switch between these views using the buttons in the lower-left corner of the Properties pane. Properties that have values are displayed in blue at the top of the list. When a property in another rule overrides the same property in the selected rule, the property in the selected rule has a red line through it. Property names are displayed in the left column, and values are displayed in the right column. You can change or add values by typing in the value column or by selecting a value from a list. Any changes you make in the Properties pane are immediately applied to the page, so you can see how that property affects the design. You must save the page and any relevant style sheets to save the changes.

Brian wants you to make the page head and subheadings larger. You will change the page heading size to 44 pixels and the subheading to 32 pixels. You will use the Properties pane in the CSS Styles panel to make the changes.

To edit styles using the Properties pane in the CSS Styles panel:

▶ 1. Collapse the **Files panel group**, and then, in the CSS Styles panel, click the **Current** button. The CSS Styles panel changes to Current Selection mode and displays the Summary for Selection pane, the Rules pane, and the Properties pane.

▶ 2. Select **COSMATIC BANDS** at the top of the Bands page. The Summary for Selection pane lists the properties that are set for the heading text; the color property is selected by default. The Rules pane is in About view and shows that the property selected in the Summary for Selection pane is located in the h1 rule. The Properties pane displays the properties set for the <h1> tag. You can edit a rule by changing the information in the bottom pane.

Trouble? If the Rules pane lists the rules pertaining to the selected property, the pane is in Rules view and you need to switch to About view. Click the Show Information About Selected Property button in the Rules pane title bar.

3. Drag the bottom border of each pane in the CSS Styles panel down until all of the text is visible. Dreamweaver uses the tag name as the style name for redefined HTML tags. See Figure 3-35.

CSS Styles panel in Current Selection mode | **Figure 3-35**

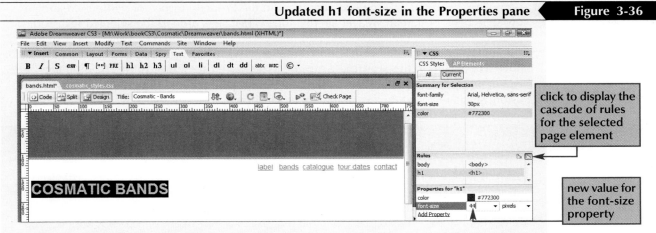

4. In the Rules pane title bar, click the **Show Cascade of Rules for Selected Tag** button ⬚. The cascade of rules that affect the selection are listed in the pane.

You'll use the Properties pane to change the font size for the heading to 44 pixels.

5. In the Properties pane, in the font-size value box, click **30px**. Arrows for the size and unit appear in the value column with 30 selected in the left list.

6. Type **44** to replace the selected size value in the left list. See Figure 3-36.

Updated h1 font-size in the Properties pane | **Figure 3-36**

7. Press the **Enter** key. The font size of the heading text increases in the Bands page.

You'll use the same process to edit the subheadings in the Bands page.

8. In the Bands page, select **DIZZIED CONNECTIONS**. The relevant rules and properties for the selected text appear in the CSS Styles panel with the properties set for the h2 style listed in the Properties pane.

9. Click **20px** in the font-size value list, type **32** to replace the selected size value, and then press the **Enter** key to accept the change. All of the subheadings with the h2 style change size.

▶ **10.** In the Rules pane, click the **body** rule to see how the properties from this tag affect the current selection. The color and font-size properties have black lines through them, because the color and font-size properties you set in the h2 style override the ones in this higher-level style. The font-family property has a value even though you did not select a font family in the h2 style, because the body tag affects all the elements in the body of your HTML code.

▶ **11.** Save the Bands page, click the **comsatic_styles.css** tab in the Document window, and then save and close the cosmatic_styles.css page.

▶ **12.** In the CSS Styles panel, click the **All** button, and then collapse the CSS panel group.

Changing Text Appearance in the Property Inspector

You can change the appearance of selected text with the Property inspector by applying an existing style to the text or changing attributes of the text. However, changing the attributes of selected text in the Property inspector does not edit the CSS styles applied to the selected text. Instead, it sometimes creates a new style that is applied only to the selected text. For example, if you selected CONNECTIONS in the DIZZIED CONNECTIONS subheading and changed the text color to blue (#0000FF) in the Property inspector, Dreamweaver would create a new style with the color attribute value of blue (#0000FF) and apply that style to the selected text. The text retains all the other styles applied to it as well as the new style. Dreamweaver saves the new style in an internal style sheet, not in the attached external style sheet with the rest of the styles for the site, and gives the new style a generic name (.style1, .style2, and so on). Although this is a simple way to modify the appearance of text, Dreamweaver creates a new style each time you modify text.

You can, however, change text alignment in the Property inspector without creating a new style because Dreamweaver simply adds HTML tags around the selected text. You can also indent text, create ordered and unordered lists, and bold or italicize text in this way. You will create styles (redefined HTML tags) to customize the HTML tags mentioned above as needed. In this way, these tags become more useful just as the Heading tags became more useful when you customized their appearance. In addition, you can create custom styles that specify any of the above attributes as part of the style.

| InSight | **Organizing Styles for a Site** |

Just as it is important to keep site files organized, it is important to keep styles organized. You should create a new style only when it is necessary. Also, you should limit the number of styles that are used in a site as much as possible to keep the style list manageable. If you are going to change the appearance of all the text to which an existing style is applied, you should edit the existing style. If you need a new style, you should create the style with the CSS Styles panel, and you should place the new style in the external style sheet so that you can use it throughout the site.

A good design practice is to use CSS styles for all Web page formatting, not just to define some display attributes. You should get in the habit of creating CSS styles for all formatting that you want to add to a site.

Exploring HTML Tags Used with Text

Several HTML tags are used with text. You worked with a few, such as the body tag <body> and the Heading 1 tag <h1>, when you created styles by modifying the existing tags. Now you will learn about some other tags that affect text. In addition, you will learn about some commonly used deprecated tags such as the font tag <font>.

Learning About Deprecated Tags | InSight

Deprecated tags such as the font tag are being phased out and Dreamweaver no longer uses them by default. However, the following are important reasons to learn about them:

1. You will most likely need to update older HTML pages. Familiarity with the version of HTML in which the older pages were created makes the task easier and more efficient.
2. Your target audience may include users of older browsers or technology. It is impossible for these people to reliably view HTML pages that use the latest specifications. (We all know people who have a five-year-old computer that they use but never update.)
3. Some new portable devices, specialized Web access tools, Web appliances and devices, and other programs are not compliant with the latest specifications and still rely on HTML 3.2 or earlier.
4. Some Web content management systems (for example, systems that dynamically create educational pages for online courses) do not support current formats.

The more you know about deprecated tags and older formats, the more versatile your skills will be. To become a professional Web designer, you need to possess the appropriate knowledge and skills as well as have the ability to solve problems and find solutions.

When you create Web pages in Design view, Dreamweaver places the appropriate HTML tags around the text for you. To see the HTML tags, you need to switch to either Code view or Split view. Some of the more common text tags are described in Figure 3-37.

Figure 3-37	Common HTML tags for text

Tag Name	Tag Description	Tag Sample	Browser Display
Font (deprecated)	Contains the font face grouping, font size, and font color properties. When you format text using the HTML mode in the Property inspector, Dreamweaver uses font tags to format the text.	**<fontcolor="#000000", size="3", font face="Arial, Helvetica, sans-serif">**Some text**</font>**	Some text
Italic	Adds italic style to text. Accessibility guidelines recommend that you use the emphasis tag instead of the italic tag, because the italic tag is used to create a visual presentation effect while the emphasis tag is used to indicate structural emphasis.	**<i>**Some text**</i>**	*Some text*
Emphasis	Adds structural meaning to text and is to be rendered differently from other body text to designate emphasis. When you use the Italic button, Dreamweaver places emphasis tags around the selected text, because accessibility guidelines recommend using the emphasis tag in place of the italic tag. Both Internet Explorer and Firefox italicize text that is surrounded by the emphasis tag.	****Some text****	*Some text*
Bold	Adds bold style to text. Accessibility guidelines recommend that you use the strong tag instead of the bold tag because the bold tag is used to create a visual presentation effect while the strong tag is used to indicate structural emphasis.	****Some text****	**Some text**
Strong	Adds structural meaning to text and is to be rendered differently from other body text to designate a stronger emphasis than the emphasis tag. When you use the Bold button, Dreamweaver places strong tags around the selected text because accessibility guidelines recommend using the strong tag in place of the bold tag. Both Internet Explorer and Firefox bold text that is surrounded by the strong tag.	****Some text****	**Some text**
Unordered List	Creates a list of bulleted items.	**<ul>** **<li>**Item1**</li>** **<li>**Item2**</li>** **</ul>**	• Item1 • Item2
Ordered List	Creates a list of numbered items.	**<ol>** **<li>**Item1**</li>** **<li>**Item2**</li>** **</ol>**	1. Item1 2. Item2
Paragraph	Designates a block of text that starts and ends with a break (a skipped line) and by default is left aligned with a ragged right edge. Dreamweaver places paragraph tags around blocks of text when you press the Enter key.	**<p>**Some text in a paragraph.**</p>** **<p>**Another paragraph.**</p>**	Some text in a paragraph. Another paragraph.
Blockquote	Usually indents text from both the left and right margins, and can be nested for deeper indents. Added in Dreamweaver with the Text Indent button; the Outdent button removes a blockquote tag.	<p>Introductory text</p> **<blockquote>**<p>Some text </p>**</blockquote>** <p>Closing text</p>	Introductory text Some text Closing text

Common HTML tags for text (continued) ◀ Figure 3-37

Tag Name	Tag Description	Tag Sample	Browser Display
Div	Divides a page into a series of blocks; for example, applying the Align attribute in the Property inspector sometimes creates a div tag with a value of left, center, or right to align the text.	**<div align="right">** Some text, a paragraph, or other element**</div>**	Some text, a paragraph, or other element
Pre	Preserves the exact formatting of a block of text when it is displayed in a Web page by rendering text in a fixed pitch font and by preserving the associated spacing with white space characters. For example, a poem with pre tags around it would maintain indents, multiple spaces between words, and new lines that would otherwise be discarded when it was rendered in a browser.	**<pre>** Some preformatted text might look like this. **</pre>**	Some preformatted text might look like this.
Break	Forces a line break on a page. Used singly without a closing tag because it does not surround text and add attributes. Add by pressing the Shift+Enter keys or clicking the Break button in the Characters list in the Text category on the Insert bar.	Some** **text	Some text
Nonbreaking space	Inserts a space that will be displayed by the browser. (Browsers will display only one regular space between items in a Web page, regardless of how many regular spaces are entered.) Use nonbreaking spaces when you want to add more than one visible space between items or when you want to ensure that a line does not break between items. The nonbreaking space is a special character (not a tag) that is often used like a tag to format text. Insert by pressing the Ctrl+Shift+Spacebar keys or by clicking the Non-Breaking Space button in the Characters list in the Text category on the Insert bar.	Some** **text	Some text
Basefont (deprecated)	Changes the attributes of the default font on which all the text contained in the Web page is based and overrides the default font settings in the user's browser. The basefont tag is placed in the head or body of the page and is used with the size attribute to change the size of the base font for the page. (When an absolute font size is used as the size value in the font tag, it overrides the basefont tag. When a relative font size is used as the size value in the font tag, it adds or subtracts from the size value you designate in the basefont tag.) This tag is used in conjunction with the font tag and does not apply to CSS styles.	**<basefont size="6">**Text at base font size	Text at base font size

You will examine the code for HTML tags that apply to text in the Bands page. You will also use the Reference panel in the Results panel group to gather additional information about some of the tags.

To examine the code for HTML tags that apply to text on the Bands page:

▶ 1. Click the **Code** button on the Document toolbar. The Bands page appears in Code view.

▶ 2. Scroll to the top of the page, locate the **body** tag, and then locate the first paragraph tag **<p>** below the body tag.

▶ 3. Right-click the paragraph tag **<p>**, and then click **Reference** on the context menu. The Results panel group opens to the Reference panel, which displays information about the paragraph tag. See Figure 3-38.

Figure 3-38 ▶ **Reference panel for selected HTML paragraph tag**

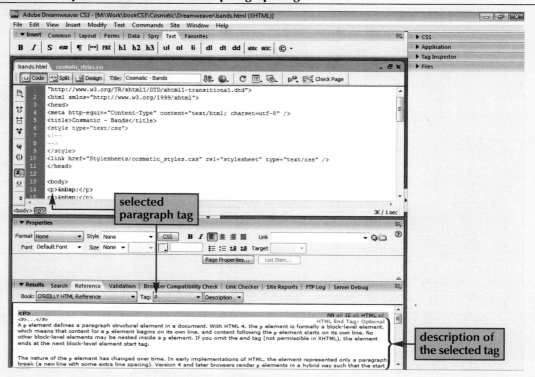

▶ 4. Read the information in the Reference panel, and then look at the code. There are four sets of paragraph tags. The top three sets of tags contain a nonbreaking space character and are included in the code to display blank lines. The fourth has an align attribute with a value of right. This tag surrounds the linked text that is displayed in the upper-right corner of the Bands page.

▶ 5. Select the entire fourth paragraph tag, including the text and anchor tags, and then click the **Split** button on the Document toolbar. The linked text is selected in the Design pane of the Document window.

▶ 6. In the Design pane, select the **COSMATIC BANDS** text. The text is also selected in the Code pane.

▶ **7.** In the Code pane, click in the opening **h1** tag before the selected text, right-click the selected tag, and then click **Reference** on the context menu. A description of the Heading 1 tag appears in the Reference panel. Read the description.

▶ **8.** In the Code pane, select the line break tag **
, right-click the selected tag, and then click **Reference on the context menu. Read the description of the <br /> tag.

▶ **9.** Examine the code for the rest of the page, using the Reference panel to learn about any tags that you do not recognize.

▶ **10.** Collapse the Results panel group, click the **Design** button on the Document toolbar, and then close the Bands page.

Formatting Text in HTML Mode

At times, you might work on Web sites that were created in an earlier version of HTML. It is not a good idea to add CSS styles to these sites. Instead, you can use HTML tags to format the pages. You can create the code manually in Code view, you can set the Dreamweaver preferences to use only HTML tags to format pages. To change Dreamweaver to HTML mode, you click Edit on the menu bar, click Preferences, and then uncheck the Use CSS Instead of HTML Tags check box in the Preferences dialog box. After the preference has been changed, formatting text using the Property inspector will add only HTML tags to the code of Web pages. Remember to change the preference back when you are finished.

The attributes and process for formatting text using the HTML font tag are not the same as the ones you have learned for formatting text using CSS styles. The following overview describes the properties associated with the font tag. To format text in HTML mode, you select the text in the Document window and set the properties for the selected text in the Property inspector. You can set the properties for a single letter, a word, a line of text, or an entire block of text. The properties for text formatting are similar to those in a word processing program; however, when text is formatted, HTML tags are added behind the scenes. Text formatting properties include format, font, font size, font color, emphasis, alignment, lists, and indents.

The format properties are a list of standardized HTML tags used for text formatting. These include the paragraph tag and a variety of heading tags.

The font attributes are a list of the fonts available for use. The Default Font option displays the text in the default font of the end-user's browser. To maintain greater control of the aesthetic look of a page, you can choose a font group from the list. When a font group is selected, Dreamweaver places a font tag containing all of the choices in the font group around the specified text. You can also add fonts to the list, but it is recommended that you use caution when doing this because a font must be installed on the end-user's computer to display the text in that font. If the font is not installed on the end-user's computer, the text will be displayed in the browser's default font.

The font-size properties are a list of available font sizes. Unlike word processing programs, HTML has no fixed font size. Instead, when you choose a font size from the list, you are choosing from a scalable range of sizes relative to a **base font size**. The default base font size is 3; however, you can set the base font size for the Web page to a different value by inserting a base font tag designating a different base font size into the head portion of a Web page. If you do not choose a value from the font size list, text will be displayed at the base font size you selected for that page. If you have not added a base font tag, the text will be a 3. If you have added a base font tag, the text will be displayed at the designated size.

When you choose a value from the font size list, Dreamweaver inserts a font size tag into the HTML of your page. The first seven choices in the font size list are absolute font sizes (1 to 7). **Absolute font sizes** are based on the standard default base size of 3. Sizes 1 and 2 are smaller than 3, while sizes 4 through 7 appear progressively larger than 3. If you choose an absolute font size, the font size tag will override the basefont tag, and the text you select will be displayed at the designated size regardless of the base font size. The remaining choices in the font size list are relative font sizes (–7 to +7). **Relative font sizes** add or subtract from the base font size. For example, a +2 value increases the base font size by two sizes, and a –2 value reduces the base font size by two sizes. Relative font sizes are the best choice because they ensure that text will be proportionately scaled in the browser window. For example, if you change the base font size for the page to the absolute size 4, a +2 value adds 2 sizes to size 4. If you later change the base font size for the page to the absolute size 3, the +2 value adds 2 sizes to size 3.

In addition to the font sizes that you create for a Web page, users can change the overall size of text that appears in their browser—essentially scaling the size that text appears in their browser. For example, a visually impaired user might set the browser text to Larger to increase the readability of text on Web pages.

The font color properties enable you to change the color of selected text. The default font color for a page is the color you selected in the Page Properties dialog box. To change the color of a selected block of text, you can type the hexadecimal color code into the color box or select a color with the color picker.

The buttons in the Property inspector enable you to change the emphasis of selected text with boldface and italics; apply a left, center, or right alignment to a paragraph; turn paragraphs into items in an unordered (bulleted) or ordered (numbered) list; and apply or remove indents from paragraphs.

Reference Window | **Formatting Text in HTML Mode**

- Click Edit on the menu bar, click Preferences, uncheck the Use CSS Instead of HTML Tags check box, and then click the OK button.
- Select the text you want to format in the Document window.
- To change the font, click the Font arrow in the Property inspector, and then click the font group you want.
- To change the font size, click the Size arrow in the Property inspector, and then click the size you want.
- To change the color, double-click in the right Text Color box in the Property inspector and type the hexadecimal color code of the color you want (or click the left Text Color box and click the color swatch you want using the color picker).
- To change the style, click the Bold button and/or Italic button in the Property inspector.
- To change the alignment, click one of the alignment buttons in the Property inspector.

Updating a Web Site on a Remote Server

As a final review of your work, you'll post the updated files for the Cosmatic site to your remote server. Because you have already uploaded the entire site, you need to upload only the files that you have changed to update the remote site. This includes the Bands and Label pages and the external style sheet located in the Stylesheets folder.

Uploading a Site to the Remote Server | Reference Window

- Click the Connects to Remote Host button on the Files panel toolbar.
- Click the View button on the Files panel toolbar, and then click Local View.
- Press and hold the Ctrl key, and then click all of the files and folders on the local site that have been modified or added.
- Click the Put File(s) button on the Files panel toolbar.
- Click the No button in the dialog box that opens and prompts you to include dependent files.
- Click the View button on the Files panel toolbar, and then click Remote View.
- Click the Disconnects from Remote Host button on the Files panel toolbar.

You will upload the modified pages and new dependent files in the Cosmatic site to the remote server. Then you'll preview the site on the Web.

To upload the updated pages of the Cosmatic site to your remote server:

▶ 1. Expand the **Files** panel group, and then click the **Connects to Remote Host** button on the Files panel toolbar. Dreamweaver connects to the remote host.

▶ 2. On the Files panel toolbar, click the **View** button, and then click **Local View**.

▶ 3. In the Files panel, click the **Stylesheets** folder, press and hold the **Ctrl** key, click **bands.html**, click **label.html**, and then release the Ctrl key.

▶ 4. On the Files panel toolbar, click the **Put File(s)** button 🔼 .

▶ 5. Click the **No** button when prompted to include dependent files. You already selected the new dependent file for the site when you selected the Stylesheets folder.

▶ 6. On the Files panel toolbar, click the **View** button, and then click **Remote View**. A copy of the Stylesheets folder and the updated files appear in the remote file list in the Files panel.

▶ 7. On the Files panel toolbar, click the **Disconnects from Remote Host** button 🔍 .

▶ 8. On the Files panel toolbar, click the **View** button, and then click **Local View**.

Next, you'll preview the updated site in a browser. The site will include all of the new styles and text that you added to the local version.

To preview the updated site in a browser:

▶ 1. Start your Web browser, type the URL of your remote site into the Address bar on the browser toolbar, and then press the **Enter** key. The home page opens in the browser window.

▶ 2. Select **index.html** in the Address bar, type **bands.html**, and then press the **Enter** key. The Bands page opens in the browser window.

▶ 3. Read the text on the Bands page and examine the text to ensure that the formatting is displayed correctly.

▶ 4. Close the browser.

In this session, you exported the styles from the Bands page to an external style sheet, created CSS styles in an external style sheet, and attached the external style sheet to a page of the Cosmatic site.

Review | **Session 3.3 Quick Check**

1. What is the file extension for an external style sheet?
2. True or False? You can apply CSS styles that you create in one Web page to text on another Web page in the same site.
3. Why is it a good idea to delete unneeded styles from a style sheet?
4. Why do you need to remove the current formatting from text in a Web page before attaching an external style sheet?
5. True or False? You cannot add new styles to an external style sheet.
6. What happens when you edit a CSS style?
7. Why is an internal style sheet also called an embedded style sheet?
8. True or False? A link tag has a closing tag.

Review | **Tutorial Summary**

In this tutorial, you learned how to add text to a page. You explored basic formatting techniques and learned to use the spelling checker and find and replace tools. You created Cascading Style Sheets, and you used CSS styles to modify an existing HTML tag, to create a custom style class, and to customize the appearance of text links. You examined the styles in an internal style sheet, moved styles to an external style sheet, and attached an external style sheet to Web pages. You edited existing styles, examined the code for CSS styles, and learned about HTML tags that are associated with text. Finally, you uploaded the modified site to your remote Web server.

Key Terms

absolute font size	declaration	linked style sheet
absolute link	deprecated	nest
advanced style	document relative link	nested tags
anchor tag	embedded style sheet	nonbreaking space
base font size	eXtensible HyperText Markup	pseudoclass
cascading	Language (XHTML)	redefined HTML tag
Cascading Style Sheets (CSS)	external style sheet	relative font size
comment tag	font tag	selector
CSS style	head	site root relative link
custom style (custom style	inherit	target
class)	internal style sheet	XML (eXtensible Markup
		Language)

Practice	**Review Assignments**

Practice the skills you learned in the tutorial.

Data Files needed for the Review Assignments: Contact.doc, Catalogue.doc, Label.doc

Brian wants you to continue adding and formatting the text in the Cosmatic site. You'll open each page, delete the internal styles that were added, and then attach each page to the external style sheet. You will add text to the Contact, Company, Catalogue, and Label pages. You will add a navigation system to these pages by creating hyperlinks. You'll use existing CSS styles and create new styles to format the text you added, including a third-tier subheading style.

1. Open the **Cosmatic** site that you modified in **Tutorial 3**, switch to Local view, if necessary, and then open the **catalogue.html** page in the Document window in Design view.

2. Expand the CSS Styles panel, click the All button, click the Minus (–) button next to the style in the CSS Styles panel list to collapse the list, select <style>, if necessary, right-click the selection, and then click Delete on the context menu. The page is blank and "(no styles defined)" appears in the CSS Styles panel.

3. Click the Attach Style Sheet button, browse to the Stylesheets/cosmatic_styles.css page, if necessary, and then click the OK button to attach the external style sheet to the page. The background image is visible in the Document window.

4. Open the **bands.html** page, place the insertion point at the top of the page, press and hold the Shift key, click after the contact text link, click Edit on the menu bar, click Copy, and then close the Bands page.

5. Place the insertion point at the top of the Catalogue page, click Edit on the menu bar, and then click Paste. The formatted text links are pasted into the page. (*Hint:* If you cannot see the links, place the insertion point at the top of the page, and then press the Enter key. The links are the same color as the background image.)

6. Open the **Catalogue.doc** document located in the Tutorial.03\Review folder included with your Data Files in a word processing program, select all the text in the document, copy the selected text to the Windows Clipboard, and then close the document.

7. Place the insertion point after "contact" in the Catalogue page, press the Enter key, click Edit on the menu bar, click Paste Special, click the first Text With Structure (Paragraphs, Lists, Tables, etc.) option button, and then click the OK button to paste the text into the page.

8. Select "Cosmatic Catalogue," click the Format button in the Property inspector, and then click Heading 1. (*Hint:* If the formatting is applied to additional text, click Edit on the menu bar and click Undo Text Format to undo the last step, switch to Code view, place paragraph tags around the heading text, switch to Design view and select the text, and then apply the Heading 1 style.)

9. Select "CDs," click the Format button in the Property inspector, click Heading 2 to apply the style to the selected text, and repeat the process to apply the Heading 2 style to "VINYL." (*Hint:* If the formatting is applied to additional text, click Edit on the menu bar and click Undo Text Format to undo the last step, switch to Code view, place paragraph tags around the subheading text, switch to Design view and select the text, and then apply the Heading 2 style.)

10. Edit the Heading 1 style. Select the page heading in the Document window, select the h1 style in the All Rules pane in the CSS Styles panel, click the Show List View button at the bottom of the panel, click in the value column for the Text-transform property to display value options, and then click Uppercase to accept the change. The style sheet opens, and the page heading is in uppercase in the Catalogue page.

11. Create a third-tier subheading CSS style to apply to the band names and CD titles. Click the New CSS Rule button in the CSS Styles panel, click the Tag option button, click h3 in the Tag list, click the top Define in option button, select cosmatic_styles.css in the Define In list, if necessary, and then click the OK button.

12. In the CSS Rule definition dialog box, click Type in the Category box, change the size to 14 pixels, change the color to #878816, click the Background in the Category box, change the background color to #E0AE4D, click the Block in the Category box, click Inline from the Display list, and then click the OK button.

13. In the Catalogue page, select "Dizzied Connections: Spinning Life," and then click Heading 3 in the Format list in the Property inspector. (*Hint:* If the formatting is applied to additional text, click Edit on the menu bar, click Undo Text Format to undo the last step, switch to Code view, place paragraph tags around the text, switch to Design view and select the text, and then apply the Heading 3 style.)

14. Apply the Heading 3 style to the other band names and CD titles: "Surface Suction: Black Lab"; "Sloth Child: Them Apples"; and "life in minor chords: i believe in ferries."

15. Switch to Split view. In the Code pane, move the opening paragraph tag at the beginning of each numbered list to the end of that list directly before the closing paragraph tag, type a line break tag **
** at the beginning of each list, and then switch to Design view. Each list is directly below its list heading.

16. Scroll to the bottom of the page, insert a blank line, switch the Insert bar to the Text category, click the Copyright button in the Characters list, press the Right Arrow key if necessary, press the Spacebar, and then type **Cosmatic, Inc. 2010**. Select the copyright line you just typed, and apply the cosmatic_footer style from the Style list in the Property inspector.

17. Save the style sheet, save the Catalogue page, preview the page in a browser, and then close the page and the style sheet.

18. Open the **contact.html** page in the Document window, and then repeat Steps 2 through 7 for the Contact page, using the **Contact.doc** document located in the Tutorial.03\Review folder included with your Data Files in Step 6.

19. Apply the Heading 1 style to the page heading, apply the Heading 2 style to "Contact" and "Directions," and then move the corresponding paragraph text to the line directly below each subheading. If necessary, switch to Code view, place a break tag **
** to the right of each closing h2 tag, and then move the opening paragraph tag to the end of the paragraph text under each subheading. Save and close the page.

20. Open the **label.html** page in the Document window, and then repeat Steps 4 through 7 for the Label page, using the **Label.doc** document located in the Tutorial.03\Review folder included with your Data Files in Step 6.

21. Apply the Heading 1 style to "COSMATIC LABEL" using the Property inspector. Apply the Heading 2 style to "News - HEY, look what they're saying!!!"; "Mission"; "History"; and "Employees." Apply the Heading 3 style to the following employee names: Sara Lynn, Enya Allie, Mark Salza, and Brian Lee.

22. Delete the blank lines below the Mission and History subheadings and below each employee name by moving the opening paragraph tag to the end of each block of text and then adding a line break tag after the subheading or employee name.

23. Scroll to the bottom of the page, insert a blank line, switch the Insert bar to the Text category, click the Copyright button in the Characters list, press the Right Arrow key if necessary, press the Spacebar, and then type **Cosmatic, Inc. 2010**. Select the copyright line you just typed, and apply the cosmatic_footer style from the Style list in the Property inspector.

24. Save the Label page, preview the page in a browser, and then close the page.

25. Open the **tourdates.html** page, repeat Steps 2 through 5 for the Tour Dates page, and then save and close the Tour Dates page.

26. Upload the pages you modified and the updated style sheet to the remote site. Click the Connects to Remote Host button on the Files panel toolbar, switch to Local view, press the Ctrl key as you click the Stylesheets folder, catalogue.html, contact.html, label.html, and tourdates.html in the Local Files list, click the Put File(s) button on the Files panel toolbar, click the No button when prompted to upload dependent files, and then click the Disconnects from Remote Host button on the Files panel toolbar.

27. Open a browser, type the URL for the remote Cosmatic site into the Address bar on the browser toolbar, and then press the Enter key.

28. Navigate through the Cosmatic site using the text links to open the other pages in the site.

29. Submit the finished files to your instructor, either in printed or electronic form, as requested.

| Apply | **Case Problem 1** |

Add and format text links and page content for a Web site about the small rural communities of northern Vietnam.

Data Files needed for this Case Problem: Overview.doc, ThompsonContact.doc, DrThompson.doc

World Anthropology Society   Dr. Olivia Thompson has asked you to create a simple navigation system and to add text to the Web site you are creating to present her research about the small rural communities of northern Vietnam. Because her research is in process and she is in one of the remote villages for the next two weeks, you'll add text stating that the research is in process. Dr. Thompson wants minimal text formatting in the site so that her research will be accessible to the widest possible audience. Some of her colleagues also live and work in remote areas and have access only to outdated computer systems.

1. Open the **DrThompson** site you created in **Tutorial 2**, **Case 1**, and then open the **index.html** page in the Document window.

2. Move the insertion point below the color band at the top of the home page by pressing the Shift+Enter keys four times, type **Dr. Olivia Thompson**, insert three nonbreaking spaces, type **Linguistic Differences**, insert three nonbreaking spaces, type **Cultural Cross-pollination**, insert three nonbreaking spaces, type **Rituals and Practices**, insert three nonbreaking spaces, type **Contact Information**, and then insert three nonbreaking spaces.

3. Use the Property inspector to create hyperlinks between each phrase you typed (Dr. Olivia Thompson, Linguistic Differences, Cultural Cross-pollination, Rituals and Practices, and Contact Information) and its corresponding page (dr_thompson.html, linguistic_differences.html, cultural_cross_pollination.html, rituals_and_practices.html, and contact.html).

4. Place the insertion point at the top of the page, select the blank lines and all the links, click Edit on the menu bar, and then click Copy to copy the links from the page.

5. Save the home page, preview it in a browser, and then close the browser and the page.

6. Open the **contact.html** page in the Document window, move the insertion point to the top of the page, click Edit on the menu bar, and then click Paste to copy the links onto the page.

7. Save the Contact page, preview the page in a browser, and then close the browser and the page.

8. Repeat Steps 6 and 7 to copy the links to each page in the site: cultural_cross_pollination.html; linguistic_differences.html; dr_thompson.html; and rituals_and_practices.html.

9. Open the **index.html** page in the Document window.

10. Copy the text in the **Overview.doc** document located in the Tutorial.03\Case1 folder included with your Data Files, and then paste the text below the links on the home page. (*Hint:* Use the Paste Special command on the Edit menu.)

11. Apply the Heading 1 style to the Brief History and Overview heading using the Property inspector, and then save and close the page.

12. Open the **contact.html** page, copy the text from the **ThompsonContact.doc** document located in the Tutorial.03\Case1 folder included with your Data Files, and then paste the text below the links on the Contact page.

13. Apply the Heading 1 style to the Contact Information heading using the Property inspector, and then save and close the page.

14. Open the **dr_thompson.html** page, copy the text from the **DrThompson.doc** document located in the Tutorial.03\Case1 folder included with your Data Files, and then paste the text below the links on the Dr. Thompson page.

15. Select all the contact information at the top of the Dr. Thompson page from the name through the e-mail address, and then use the Property inspector to format the text as bold and with center alignment.

16. Select the following text, and then use the Property inspector to format the text with boldface: Higher Education, Academic Appointments, Editorial Work, Publications: Books, and Grants and Awards. Save and close the page.

17. Open the **cultural_cross_pollination.html** page, move the insertion point below the text links at the top of the page, type **Cultural Cross-pollination**, apply the Heading 1 style to the Cultural Cross-pollination heading using the Property inspector, and then save and close the page.

18. Open the **linguistic_differences.html** page, move the insertion point below the text links, type **Linguistic Differences**, apply the Heading 1 style to the Linguistic Differences heading using the Property inspector, and then save and close the page.

19. Open the **rituals_and_practices.html** page, move the insertion point below the text links, type **Rituals and Practices**, apply the Heading 1 style to the Rituals and Practices heading using the Property inspector, and then save and close the page.

20. Open the **dr_thompson.html** page, and switch to Split view. Select the first link and review the code. Select the bold text and find the strong tag and align attribute in the paragraph tag. Select the strong tag, right-click the selected tag, and then click Reference in the context menu. Read about the strong tag in the Reference panel, and then close the page.

21. Connect to your remote server, select the Graphics folder and all of the pages in the Local Files list, and then upload them to the remote folder.

22. View the remote DrThompson site in a browser. Test all of the links and read the text on each page.

23. Submit the finished files to your instructor, either in printed or electronic form, as requested.

Challenge | Case Problem 2

Add and format text links, create an external style sheet, and apply styles to text you add to a Web site for an art museum.

Data Files needed for this Case Problem: Welcome.doc, Museum.doc, Artists.doc, Location.doc

Museum of Western Art   C. J. Strittmatter asks you to add text to the Web site you are creating for the Museum of Western Art. He also asks you to create a navigation system on all of the pages and add a horizontal rule to each page. You'll create an external style sheet and create CSS styles for the site. You will delete the styles from the pages of the site and attach the external style sheet to the pages, and then you will use these styles to format the text. Finally, you'll upload the site to a remote location and preview it.

1. Open the **Museum** site you created in **Tutorial 2**, **Case 2**, and then open the **index.html** page in the Document window.

2. Move the styles from the home page to an external style sheet named **museum_styles.css** stored in a new folder named **Stylesheets** in the local root folder for the site, and then save and close the page.

3. Attach the external style sheet to the page, and then save and close the page.

4. Open each of the following pages, delete the styles from the page, attach the external style sheet to the page, and then save and close the page: **art.html**, **artists.html**, **location.html**, and **museum.html**.

5. Open the **index.html** page, type **The Museum of Western Art** at the top of the page, apply the Heading 1 style to the text, select the text and create a hyperlink from the text to the index.html page. (You will copy the linked text to the other pages in the site and you want it to have the same formatting in all the pages.)

⊕ **EXPLORE**   6. Double-click the h1 style in the CSS Styles panel to open the CSS Rule definition for h1 in museum_styles.css dialog box. In the Border category, uncheck the Same for All check boxes in the Style, Width, and Color sections. Click Solid in the Bottom list in the Style section, click Thin in the Bottom list in the Width section, type **#006666** in the Bottom box in the Color section, and then click the OK button. A horizontal line appears in the home page.

⊕ **EXPLORE**   7. Select the a:link style in the All Rules pane in the CSS Styles panel to display the properties for a:link in the Properties pane. Change the Text-decoration value to None to remove the underline from the a:link style. Repeat this process for the a:visited style to remove the underline from the style. The underline disappears from the text in the home page.

8. Move the insertion point directly below the horizontal line, and type the following text for the menu bar links with three nonbreaking spaces after each word: **Museum**, **Art**, **Artists**, and **Location**.

9. Create a custom style to format the menu bar text; name the style **.menustyle** and save it in the museum_styles.css style sheet. In the Type category, select Bold from the Weight list; in the Block category, select Right from the Text Align list, select Block from the Display list (styles must be applied to block level tags for the align attribute to work), and then click the OK button. Select the menu bar link text and apply the new .menustyle from the Property inspector.

10. Create a hyperlink between each word (Museum, Art, Artists, and Location) and its corresponding page (museum.html, art.html, artists.html, and location.html).

11. Save the page, save and close the museum_styles.css page, and then preview the page in a browser.

⊕ **EXPLORE**   12. Switch to Code view, select all the code between the body tags, copy the content from the home page, and then switch to Design view.

⊕ EXPLORE

13. Open the **art.html** page, switch to Code view, place the insertion point to the right of the opening body tag, press the Enter key, and then paste the code from the home page into the Art page.

14. Switch to Design view to view the copied content in page, and then save and close the page.

15. Repeat Steps 13 and 14 for the following pages: **artists.html**, **location.html**, and **museum.html**.

16. Copy the text from the **Welcome.doc** document located in the Tutorial.03\Case2 folder included with your Data Files, and then paste it below the links in the home page.

17. Edit the h2 style in the CSS Styles panel to set the size to xx-large in the Type category.

18. Apply the Heading 2 style to the WELCOME text, save and close the page, and then save and close the style sheet.

19. Open the **museum.html** page, copy the text from the **Museum.doc** document located in the Tutorial.03\Case2 folder included with your Data Files, paste the text with structure in the Museum page below the links, and apply the Heading 2 tag to THE MUSEUM heading, and then save and close the page.

20. Open the **artists.html** page, copy the text from the **Artists.doc** document located in the Tutorial.03\Case2 folder included with your Data Files, paste the text with structure in the Artists page below the links, apply the Heading 2 tag to THE ARTISTS heading.

21. Create a custom style for the subheadings named **.sub_headings** and then add the style to the external style sheet. In the Type category, set the size to x-large and set the color to #006666.

22. Place the insertion point after "Fredric Remington," press the Delete key to move the following paragraph onto the Fredric Remington line, and then press the Shift+Enter keys to move the text directly below the subheading.

23. Apply the .sub_headings style to the Fredric Remington subheading using the Property inspector. The style is applied only to the selected text; you do not need to add line breaks or move paragraph tags because the style you created is applied using a span tag.

24. Repeat Steps 22 and 23 for the Charles M. Russell subheading, and then save and close the page and the style sheet.

25. Open the **location.html** page, copy the text from the **Location.doc** document located in the Tutorial.03\Case2 folder included with your Data Files, paste the text with structure in the Location page below the links, apply the Heading 2 tag to THE LOCATION heading, apply the .sub_headings style to the HOURS: and LOCATION: subheadings, and then save and close the page.

26. Connect to your remote server, upload the Graphics folder, the Stylesheets folder, and all of the pages to the remote server, and then disconnect from the remote server.

27. View the remote Museum site in a browser. Visit each page of the site, read the text, and test each link. Remember to click the logo text.

28. Click View on the browser's menu bar, point to Text Size, and then click Largest. The text in the page changes size because you used a relative font size in the page. Using a relative font size helps to make a page more accessible to users with disabilities. Click View on the menu bar, point to Text Size, and then click Medium. (*Hint*: If the menu bar is hidden, press the Alt key to display it. If you are using a different browser, use the appropriate commands and options to change the text size.)

29. Submit the finished files to your instructor, either in printed or electronic form, as requested.

Create an external style sheet, and then create, edit, and apply new CSS styles to text you add to a Web site for an independent bookstore.

Data Files needed for this Case Problem: Home.doc, Company.doc, MOREContact.doc, Links.doc

MORE Books   With a plan and design in place for the MORE Books Web site, you're ready to add and format the text for the site. Natalie More, the CEO of MORE Books, has already written the text for the site. You need to create an external style sheet, export the existing styles from the home page, delete the CSS styles from the pages of the site, and attach the style sheet to the pages. You will also edit the existing CSS styles and create new styles as needed. Finally, you will add and format the text on the pages.

1. Open the **MOREbooks** site you created in **Tutorial 2**, **Case 3**, and then open the **index.html** page.
2. Move the styles from the home page to an external style sheet named **more_styles.css** stored in a new folder named **Stylesheets** in the local root folder for the site. View the new folder in the Files panel, clicking the Refresh button, if necessary.
3. Save and close the style sheet, and then save and close the page.
4. Open the **books.html** page, delete the styles from the page, attach the more_styles.css style sheet to the page, and then save and close the page. Repeat this process for the **company.html**, **contact.html**, and **links.html** pages.
   ⊕ **EXPLORE**
5. Open the **more_styles.css** style sheet. Create a custom style class with the name **.more_headings** and defined in this document only because you are in the more_styles.css external style sheet. In the CSS Rule Definition dialog box, click Type in the Category box, change the size to 55 pixels, and then change the case to Uppercase.
6. Create a custom style class named **.more_sub_headings** defined in this document only. In the CSS Rule Definition dialog box, click Type in the Category box, change the size to 18 pixels, change the case to uppercase, and change the decoration to underline.
7. Create a custom style class named **.more_book_titles** defined in this document only. In the CSS Rule Definition dialog box, click Type in the Category box, change the style to Italic, and then change the color to #FFCC00.
8. Save and close the style sheet.
   ⊕ **EXPLORE**
9. Open the **index.html** page, type **MOREbooks on the edge**, select MORE, and then apply the .more_headings style from the Style list in the Property inspector. (The style is only applied to the selected text because the style is applied with a span tag.)
10. Select the MOREbooks on the edge text, and then use the Property inspector to create a hyperlink to the home page.
11. Move the insertion point one line below the horizontal line, and then type the following words separated by three nonbreaking spaces between each word: **company**; **books**; **links**; and **contact**. (*Hint*: To move the insertion point down one line instead of two lines, press the Shift+Enter keys instead of just the Enter key.)
12. Use the Property inspector to create a hyperlink between each word (company, books, links, and contact) and its respective page (company.html, books.html, links.html, and contact.html).
    ⊕ **EXPLORE**
13. Select all of the text on the page, click Edit on the menu bar, click Copy to copy the selected text, and then save and close the page.

⊕ **EXPLORE**

14. Open each of the following pages, click Edit on the menu bar, click Paste to paste the copied text at the top of the page, and then save and close the page: **company.html**, **books.html**, **contact.html**, and **links.html**.

15. Preview the site in a browser and test the links to make sure that they work.

16. Copy the text in the **Home.doc** document located in the Tutorial.03\Case3 folder included with your Data Files, open the **index.html** page, move the insertion point below the text links, and then paste the text with structure into the page.

17. Apply the .more_sub_headings style to the MORE featured book list subheading and the News subheading, apply the .more_book_titles style to each book title on the page, and then save and close the page.

18. Open the **books.html** page, move the insertion point directly below the text links, type **Coming Soon**, apply the .more_sub_headings style to the text you typed, and then save and close the page.

19. Copy the text in the **Company.doc** document located in the Tutorial.03\Case3 folder included with your Data Files, open the **company.html** page, move the insertion point below the text links, paste the text with structure into the page, apply the .more_sub_headings style to the Mission and Staff subheadings, and then save and close the page.

20. Copy the text in the **MOREContact.doc** document located in the Tutorial.03\Case3 folder included with your Data Files, open the **contact.html** page, move the insertion point below the text links, paste the text with structure into the page, apply the .more_sub_headings style to the Contact subheading, and then save and close the page.

21. Copy the text in the **Links.doc** document located in the Tutorial.03\Case3 folder included with your Data Files, open the **links.html** page, move the insertion point below the text links, paste the text with structure into the page, and then apply the .more_sub_headings style to the Links subheading.

⊕ **EXPLORE**

22. Select Ludlow Press, type **http://www.ludlowpress.com** in the Link box in the Property inspector to create an absolute link to that Web site, and then delete the URL located beside Ludlow Press in the Document window. (*Hint:* Include *http://* when you type the link because it is an offsite hyperlink.) Repeat for the rest of the links using the URLs listed in the page.

23. Select Ludlow Press, switch to Split view, examine the code for an absolute link, switch to Design view, and then save and close the page.

24. Connect to your remote server, upload the Graphics folder, the Stylesheets folder, and the pages to the remote server, and then disconnect from the remote server.

25. View the remote site in a browser. Read each page of the site, check each link, and visit each page to make sure everything uploaded correctly.

26. Submit the finished files to your instructor, either in printed or electronic form, as requested.

Create	Case Problem 4

Create a navigation system, and then create and apply CSS styles to text in a Web site for a newly opening sushi restaurant.

Data File needed for this Case Problem: SushiYa-YaContent.doc

Sushi Ya-Ya Mary O'Brien wants you to start working on the navigation system and the styles for the Sushi Ya-Ya site. She asks you to create CSS styles, add appropriate text to the Web site, and then format the text you added. You'll view the code, upload the modified pages to the remote site, and then preview the remote site.

1. Open the **SushiYaYa** site you created in **Tutorial 2**, **Case 4**, and then open the **index.html** page.
2. Move the styles from the home page to an external style sheet named **sushiyaya_styles.css** stored in a new folder named **Stylesheets** in the local root folder for the site.
3. Open each page in the site, delete the styles from the page, attach the style sheet to the page, and then save and close the page.

⊕ **EXPLORE**
4. Open the **index.html** page and review the styles that Dreamweaver created. Make a list of additional styles you need to create. (*Hint:* Look at the styles that were needed for the Cosmatic site and for the sites in the other Case Problems.)
5. Create the rest of the styles that you will need for the site based on the list you created in Step 4. Remember to save the style sheet.
6. Create the navigation system for the home page. Remember to create links to all the other pages in the SushiYaYa site.
7. Copy the links from the home page to the other pages.

⊕ **EXPLORE**
8. Preview the site in a browser, testing the links to be sure that they work.
9. Copy the text in the **SushiYa-YaContent.doc** document located in the Tutorial.03\Case4 folder included with your Data Files throughout the pages in the site as appropriate.
10. Apply appropriate styles to the text you added to the pages, creating additional styles as needed. Save and close the pages.
11. Upload the SushiYaYa site to your remote server, and then test the remote site in a browser.
12. Submit the finished files to your instructor, either in printed or electronic form, as requested.

Review	Quick Check Answers

Session 3.1

1. You can type in the Document window, or you can copy and paste text from another document.
2. False; you should proofread a page for incorrectly used words that are spelled correctly.
3. Property inspector
4. hyperlinks or links
5. a relative link
6. Some Text
7. anchor

Session 3.2

1. a rule that defines the appearance of an element in a Web page by redefining an existing HTML tag or by creating a custom style

2. True
3. custom style class
4. True; in an external style sheet
5. by giving you more control over the appearance of a Web page because it controls the way elements appear in the end-user's browser rather than allowing the browser to interpret the tag in the default manner
6. when they are creating a style that will apply to only a few items, or a style that will be an exception to the norm
7. a period

Session 3.3

1. .css
2. True; you must first export the styles to an external style sheet.
3. to help keep them uncluttered and streamlined
4. because the older formatting might override the CSS style you apply or it might combine with the CSS style, causing the text to display differently than you had intended
5. False; you can add new styles to an external style sheet.
6. Any element to which the style is applied is updated automatically to reflect the changes.
7. because the styles are embedded in the head of the Web page
8. False; a link tag does not have a closing tag.

Organizing Page Content and Layout

Working with Graphics, Rollovers, and Tables

Case | Cosmatic

Sara Lynn, the president of Cosmatic, hired an artist to design a new graphic logo for Cosmatic. She wants this logo added to each page in the Cosmatic site and linked to the site's home page. To match the style of the new logo, the artist created graphics to replace the existing text links in the navigation system. Brian Lee, public relations and marketing director, wants you to add tables containing the regional tour date information to the Tour Dates page as well as add a map with links to the tables. He also wants you to create a table in the Catalogue page in which to place the cover graphics and song lists. In addition, after meeting with Sara, Brian wants to add a page to the Web site to promote new releases.

To accomplish this, you will add the new Cosmatic logo to all of the pages in the site and then format it. You will add a map of the United States in the Tour Dates page and link each region of the map to a table listing its corresponding tour dates. You will replace the text links with the new graphics. Then you will add tables in the Tour Dates page, listing the tour dates for each region. Finally, you will create a new page that describes one of the label's bands; you'll use a table to hold the content, and then create a link from the home page to the new promotional page.

Starting Data Files

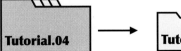

Tutorial	Review	Case1
CosmaticLogo.gif	DCcd300.jpg	WASlogo.jpg
CosmaticLogoRollover.gif	LIMCcd300.jpg	
SurfaceSuctionCDcover.jpg	SCcd300.jpg	
tabledata.csv	SScd300.jpg	
USmap.gif		

Case2	Case3	Case4
MuseumLogo.gif	Punch.jpg	SushiYaYaLogo.gif
MuseumLogoOver.gif	PunchSmall.jpg	SushiYaYaLogoOver.gif
	MORElogo.jpg	TikkaRollTuna.gif
	MORElogoOver.jpg	

Session 4.1

Understanding Graphics and Compression

The Cosmatic site plan calls for a graphic logo to be included in each page. The logo will increase the brand recognition of Cosmatic, which is a major goal of the site. Because the logo was designed with the site metaphor in mind, it will enhance the intended look and feel of the site. The site plan also calls for adding graphics of the CD cover art to the Catalogue page to help promote the bands and to sell products, two additional goals of the site. Like the logo, these graphics have a look that is appealing to the target audience; they will further extend the site metaphor and add to the cohesive look of the site. Other graphics will be added as needed to carry the look and feel of the site throughout the pages.

Because graphics files are usually large, the graphics you add to a Web site are stored in compressed file formats. **Compression** shrinks the graphic's file size by using different types of encoding to remove redundant or less-important information. The smaller the graphic's file size, the faster the graphic will load in a browser.

InSight	**Using Graphics Effectively**

Graphics can make a Web site more interesting and provide valuable information. For example, maps and graphs can summarize information more succinctly and intuitively than a written description. As a society, we are accustomed to distilling information from images. Therefore, the graphics you add to a Web site should enhance the feel you are trying to create and provide users with visual clues about the page content and/or the site's intended message. Most importantly, the graphics you add to a Web site should reinforce the goals of the Web site. When choosing graphics for a Web site, consider what each graphic will add to the page. Will it supply information or reinforce the page content? Will it aid the user in navigating through the Web site? Will it help the page to maintain the look of the site? If the graphic does not add anything to the page, it should not be used.

Graphics you choose to add to a site should be an appropriate file size. When deciding what file size a graphic should be, you must consider the total file size of all the graphics in the Web page and the connection speed that the target audience will have. If you are going to include only one graphic in a page, the file size of that graphic can be larger. If you are going to include several graphics in a page, the size of each graphic will contribute to the amount of time it takes a user's browser to download the page. In this case, you might want to make the file size of each graphic smaller. In addition, if the target audience is using dial-up service to connect to the Internet, it will take them longer to download graphic-intensive pages, so you might consider keeping the graphics to a minimum or choosing graphics with small file sizes. Finally, you should consider the importance of the graphic when looking at file size. A user will be more willing to wait for a page to download if the page is interesting and provides content that the user is looking for.

Figure 4-1 lists the approximate times it takes to download files of various sizes over a standard 56 kb/s (kilobits per second) dial-up connection, a DSL connection, and a cable modem connection.

Approximate download times for files of different sizes ◀ Figure 4-1

Connection Type*	Size of Page (in kilobytes)				
	10 kB	50 kB	100 kB	200 kB	400 kB
Dial-up 56 kb/s (approx. 5 kB/s)	2 seconds	10 seconds	20 seconds	40 seconds	80 seconds
DSL 1.5 mb/sec (approx. 160 kB/s)	< 1 second	< 1 second	< 1 second	1.25 seconds	2.5 seconds
Cable modem 3 mb/s (approx. 380 kB/s)	< 1 second	< 1 second	< 1 second	1 second	1.1 seconds

*Speeds shown in their common forms of kilobit (kb) for dial-up and megabit (mb) for DSL and cable, and then converted to kilobyte (kB) for comparison with Web pages.

Current versions of Internet Explorer and Firefox can universally display three graphics file formats: GIF, JPEG, and PNG. All three formats compress graphic files but in different ways. If you want to use graphic images that are in another format, you will need to use a graphics processing program such as Adobe Photoshop, Adobe ImageReady, or Adobe Fireworks to convert them to GIF, JPEG, or PNG.

Using GIF

GIF (Graphics Interchange Format) was invented by the CompuServe Company to provide its customers with a means to exchange graphics files online. Unisys, which now owns the patent on the type of compression used in GIFs, requires that software producing GIFs license the GIF patent. However, graphics compressed as GIFs can be used free of charge. Files saved as GIF images have the file extension *.gif*. The GIF format is usually used on images that have large areas of flat, or nongradient, color. **Nongradient** refers to color that is one shade and does not vary with subtle darkening or lightening. Many line-drawn graphics and nonphotographic images use GIF. GIF supports a palette of up to 256 colors, one of which can be used for single-color transparency. GIF transparency is usually used to create a clear background for graphics. For example, if you want an image to appear on a Web site without its background, you can make the background transparent so that the color of the Web page or the background image behind it is visible. In GIF format, greater compression (and therefore smaller file size) is achieved by further limiting the graphic's color palette. This means that the fewer colors used in a GIF image, the smaller the file size. You need to find a balance between how colorful an image you want to use and how fast the target audience can load the image.

The new Cosmatic logo that will appear in each page of the Web site is shown in Figure 4-2. Brian compressed the new logo using GIF because it is comprised of flat colors and has a transparent background. The transparent background enables the logo to be laid over the background of the Web pages seamlessly. The logo file size is 6 K.

Cosmatic logo as a GIF image ◀ Figure 4-2

logo uses flat colors, like a line drawing

logo corners are rounded, but the transparent background is rectangular

Using JPEG

A committee from the Joint Photographic Experts Group created the **JPEG** format to digitize photographic images. Files saved as JPEG images have the file extension *.jpg*. The JPEG format is usually used on photographic images and graphics that have many gradient colors. The JPEG format can support millions of colors but not transparency.

JPEG is a **lossy** compression format, which means that it discards (or loses) information to compress an image. Because it was designed for photographic images, JPEG discards the information that is less perceptible to the human eye, such as the fine details in the background of a photograph. As an image is further compressed, additional information is discarded, the blurry spots increase in size and the image becomes less and less sharp. So, as with a GIF image, you must make a tradeoff between the image quality and the file size (or download time).

The CD covers for the Bands page will be JPEG images because each CD cover contains photographic images, which will be compressed more effectively in this format. Figure 4-3 shows the surface suction: black lab CD cover as a JPEG image.

Figure 4-3	CD cover as a JPEG image

CD cover is 50 K

photographic elements and layers of varying color make this graphic perfect for JPEG compression

Using PNG

PNG (Portable Network Graphics), a graphic compression format, was created by a group of designers who were frustrated by the limitations of existing compression formats. PNG files use the file extension *.png*. PNG supports up to 48-bit true color or 16-bit grayscale. It uses **lossless** compression, so no information is discarded when the file is compressed. It also supports **variable transparency**, the ability to make the background of the image transparent at different amounts; for example, a background can fade (using gradient shades of color) from a dark color to transparent. Generally, PNG compresses files 5% to 25% better than GIF. For transmission of photographic style images, JPEG is still a better choice because the file size of a photographic style image compressed with JPEG is usually smaller than the file size of a photographic style image compressed with PNG. The biggest drawback of the PNG format is that variable transparency usually does not display correctly in Internet Explorer 6 and earlier versions. Internet Explorer 7 has strong but not full support of variable transparency of PNGs. If you are considering using a PNG with variable transparency, test the page in the browser to insure that it displays correctly.

Figure 4-4 shows a graphic from the Dizzied Connections CD cover saved in the PNG format. Because the graphic has gradient colors fading to transparency, the image is a perfect example of variable transparency.

CD cover graphic as a PNG image | **Figure 4-4**

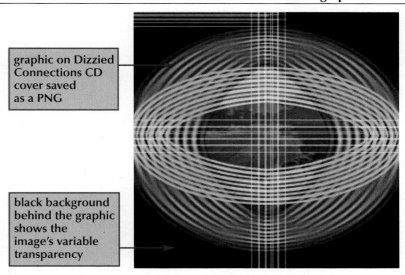

graphic on Dizzied Connections CD cover saved as a PNG

black background behind the graphic shows the image's variable transparency

Adding Graphics to Web Pages

You can add graphics to a Web site using Dreamweaver with the Insert bar or the Assets panel. The first time you place a graphic in the site, you use the Insert bar to place the graphic in the page. When you add a graphic to a Web site, the best place to store it is in the Graphics folder within the site's local root folder so that Dreamweaver always knows where to locate the image file. You need to include only one copy of each graphic in the Graphics folder, even when you plan to use the same image in several pages. After a graphic is stored in the local root folder, it appears in the Assets panel. Then you can use either method to insert that graphic into the pages.

When you place a graphic in a page, you are actually placing an image tag, <img>, in the page. The image tag tells the page to display the graphic, which you placed in the Graphics folder, at that spot in the Web page. When the same graphic appears multiple times in a site, Dreamweaver retrieves the graphic from the Graphics folder and displays it in the various pages. If you decide to change a graphic in the site, you can simply replace the old graphic with a new one in the Graphics folder, and each page that contains an image tag for the old graphic then displays the new one.

Reference Window | **Adding a Graphic to a Web Page**

- On the Common tab of the Insert bar, click the Image button in the Images list.
- Select the file to insert in the Select Image Source dialog box.
- Click the OK button.
  or
- Click the Assets tab in the Files panel group.
- Click the Images button on the Assets panel toolbar.
- Click the file you want to insert, and then click the Insert button in the Assets panel (or drag the image or its filename from the Assets panel to its position in the page).

You can set the Dreamweaver preferences to select Adobe Photoshop or Adobe Fireworks as an external image editor for each image file type (.jpg, .gif, .png). After you select an external editor for a file type, you can open a selected image in the external image editor, edit and save the image, and then view the changes in Dreamweaver in the Document window. Appendix A covers how to use Adobe Photoshop to edit images in Web pages.

InSight | **Using Graphics Effectively**

Graphics are an integral part of Web pages. Before you add graphics to a site, make sure that each graphic is saved at the proper size for insertion into the pages. Do not resize a graphic after it has been added to a Web page unless you use an external editor because the graphic is included in the page at its original size and then resized on the user's computer. This can make the Web page load much more slowly. Also, each graphic should be compressed to the smallest possible file size you can achieve without losing image quality. Be sure to retain the original uncompressed graphics in addition to the compressed Web versions because you might need to return to the original version to create another variation of the graphic in the future. A compressed graphic cannot be returned to its original resolution. It is also a good idea to use descriptive and meaningful names for the graphic files. Logical naming structures will save you time in later identifying the files.

Using the Insert Bar to Add Graphics

The new Cosmatic logo is a GIF graphic that you will include in the upper-left corner of every page in the Cosmatic site. When you insert a graphic, you move the insertion point to the location where you want the image to appear in the page and then place the image. If the image is not already stored within the site, Dreamweaver copies the file to the Graphics folder within the local root folder to ensure that the correct image is always available.

A selected graphic is surrounded by a black box with squares in the corners. The squares are **resize handles**. If you drag a resize handle, it enlarges or shrinks the selected object. To select an object such as a graphic, you can click it. When you click another area of the page, the graphic is deselected.

Brian asks you to add the redesigned Cosmatic logo to the site. You'll start with the home page. Before you add the graphic, you'll attach the style sheet to the home page.

To add a graphic to the home page using the Insert bar:

▶ **1.** Open the **Cosmatic** site that you modified in the **Tutorial 3 Review Assignments**, and then open the **index.html** page in the Document window in Design view. The home page opens with the insertion point in the upper-left corner.

   Trouble? If you did not complete the Tutorial 3 Review Assignments, you can still complete the steps in the tutorial. Open the Cosmatic site that you modified in Tutorial 3. If you are not completing the Review Assignments, the Cosmatic site shown in the tutorials might show additional content and pages that your Cosmatic site does not have. You will be able to complete all the tutorial steps.

▶ **2.** Expand the **CSS panel group**, click the **CSS Styles** tab, if necessary, delete the styles from the page, and then attach the **cosmatic_styles.css** style sheet to the page.

▶ **3.** Collapse any open panel groups, and then expand the **Files panel group**.

▶ **4.** On the **Common** tab of the Insert bar, click the **Images button arrow** ▣ ·, and then click the **Image** button ▣ . The Select Image Source dialog box opens.

▶ **5.** Navigate to the **Tutorial.04\Tutorial** folder included with your Data Files, and then click the **CosmaticLogo.gif** graphic file. The Image Preview box shows the graphic and lists its specifications.

▶ **6.** Click the **OK** button. A copy of the Cosmatic logo image is saved in the Graphics folder in the site's local root folder. The image appears in the page and is selected.

   Trouble? If the Image Tag Accessibility Attributes dialog box opens, the Accessibility dialog boxes are activated on your computer. The dialog box prompts you to enter alternate text descriptions for users viewing the site with assistive devices. You don't want to add alt text right now. Click the Cancel button to close the dialog box. To avoid seeing this and similar dialog boxes as you complete the steps in these tutorials, click Edit on the menu bar, click Preferences to open the Preferences dialog box, click Accessibility in the Category box, uncheck all of the check boxes indented in the Show Attributes When Inserting list, and then click the OK button.

▶ **7.** In the Files panel, click the **Plus (+)** button ⊞ next to the Graphics folder to view the folder's contents. See Figure 4-5.

Figure 4-5	Cosmatic logo in the home page

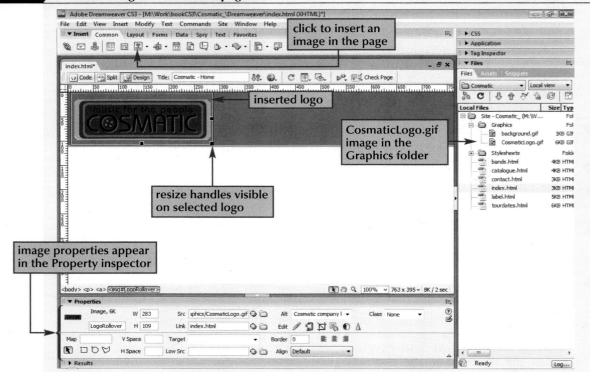

Trouble? If you don't see the CosmaticLogo.gif file in the Graphics folder, click the Refresh button on the Files panel toolbar to refresh the list.

▶ **8.** Click in a blank area of the Document window. The logo is deselected.

▶ **9.** Save and close the home page.

You'll repeat this process to insert the logo in the Label page, except that you'll use the GIF image saved in the Graphics folder.

To add the logo from the Graphics folder in the Label page:

▶ **1.** Open the **label.html** page in the Document window.

▶ **2.** In the **Common** category on the Insert bar, click the **Image** button 🖳 in the Images list. The Select Image Source dialog box opens.

▶ **3.** Navigate to the **Graphics** folder in the local root folder, click **CosmaticLogo.gif**, and then click the **OK** button. The Cosmatic logo appears in the upper-left corner of the Label page and the text moves down. You will adjust the position of the text later.

▶ **4.** Save and close the Label page.

Using the Assets Panel to Insert Graphics

Another way to add graphics to Web pages is to use the Assets panel. In Dreamweaver, **assets** are the images, colors, URLs, Flash, Shockwave, movies, scripts, templates, and library items that you use throughout a site. The Assets panel is used to manage these assets. The Assets panel helps you keep track of the assets in the site by listing them all in one place. After a graphic is stored in the site's local root folder, you can use the Assets panel to place the graphic in other pages. When you display images in the Assets panel, the graphic image appears in the upper pane and the graphic's filename, type, size, and location appear in the lower pane.

You'll open the Assets panel.

To open the Assets panel:

▶ **1.** In the Files panel group, click the **Assets** tab. The Assets panel opens.

▶ **2.** Click the **Images** button [▣] on the Assets panel toolbar, if necessary, and then click the **Site** option button at the top of the Assets panel, if necessary. The images in the Cosmatic site are listed in the Assets panel.

▶ **3.** In the Images list in the Assets panel, click **CosmaticLogo.gif**. The selected image appears in the top pane of the Assets panel. See Figure 4-6.

Images in the Assets panel ◄ **Figure 4-6**

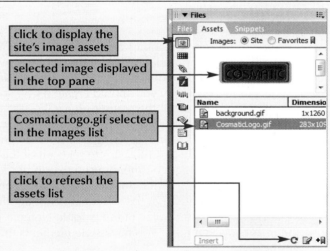

click to display the site's image assets

selected image displayed in the top pane

CosmaticLogo.gif selected in the Images list

click to refresh the assets list

Trouble? If you don't see the CosmaticLogo.gif file in the Assets panel, click the Refresh button at the bottom of the Assets panel. If you see additional files in the list, right-click any of the files, and then click Recreate Site List on the context menu.

You'll use the Assets panel to place the Cosmatic logo in the remaining pages of the Cosmatic site.

To insert the Cosmatic logo using the Assets panel:

▶ **1.** Click the **Files** tab in the Files panel group to display the Files panel, and then double-click **bands.html** to open the page in the Document window. The insertion point is positioned in the upper-left corner of the Bands page.

▶ **2.** Click the **Assets** tab in the Files panel group to open the Assets panel, click **CosmaticLogo.gif** in the Images list, and then click the **Insert** button at the bottom of the Assets panel. The logo is inserted in the Bands page and the text moves down.

▶ **3.** Save and close the Bands page.

▶ **4.** Switch to the **Files** panel, and then open the **catalogue.html** page in the Document window.

▶ **5.** Switch to the **Assets** panel, and then drag the **CosmaticLogo.gif** image from the top pane in the Assets panel to the upper-left corner of the Catalogue page in the Document window.

▶ **6.** Save and close the Catalogue page.

▶ **7.** Insert the Cosmatic logo from the Assets panel in the **contact.html** and **tourdates.html** pages, using either method, and then save and close each page.

Formatting Graphics Using CSS Styles and the Property Inspector

You can change some attributes of inserted graphics by formatting them. You format graphics either by creating a CSS style and applying it to the graphic or by selecting the graphic and setting its attributes in the Property inspector. If you plan to add the same attributes to multiple graphics in the Web site, you should create a CSS style that contains the attributes you want, to ensure that all the graphics have the same formatting. Also, with a CSS style, you can easily change and update the formatting for all of the graphics in the site. The process for creating and applying CSS styles to graphics is the same as the process for creating and applying CSS styles to text. All of the same categories of attributes are available. CSS styles are commonly used to add borders to graphics; define the border style, width, and color; add margins or padding to graphics; and align or position graphics. If you define an attribute in the style that is not applicable to a graphic element, such as a font group, the display of the graphic element is not affected. You can also redefine the image tag, <img>, if you have style elements that you want to apply to all of the images in a site.

| InSight | | **Naming Custom Styles** |

When creating custom styles, be sure to use naming strategies that enable you to identify the styles by the ways they will be used rather than by their attributes. For example, you don't want a style that makes subheadings pink and bold to be named *blueskinny* because the original style made the subheading text blue and narrow. A better name for the style would be *subheadings*. Remember, the beauty of CSS is that you can quickly and easily change the look of styles over time. Use meaningful names that will not become outdated.

Brian wants you to create a CSS style for the Cosmatic logo.

To create and apply a CSS style to the logo:

▶ 1. Switch to the **Files** panel, open the **index.html** page in the Document window, and then expand the **CSS Styles** panel.

▶ 2. In the CSS Styles panel, click the **New CSS Rule** button [⊞], and then create a **custom style class** with the name **.logostyle** defined in the **cosmatic_styles.css** style sheet.

▶ 3. In the CSS Rule definition dialog box, click **Box** in the Category box, click the **Same For All** check box in the Margin section to remove the check mark, and then type **5** in the Right and Left boxes. This setting creates a 5 pixel margin on either side of the logo.

▶ 4. Click **Border** in the Category box, click the **Same For All** check box to insert a check mark in the Width section, if necessary, and then type **0** in the Top box. This setting ensures that the logo does not have a border.

▶ 5. Click the **OK** button. The .logostyle rule is added to the site's style sheet and is ready to be applied to the logo.

▶ 6. Click the **Cosmatic logo** to select it in the home page, click the **Class** arrow in the Property inspector, and then click **logostyle**. The style is applied to the logo, which moves 5 pixels to the right. See Figure 4-7.

Formatted Cosmatic logo in the home page ◀ Figure 4-7

▶ 7. Save and close the page, and then save and close the style sheet.

▶ 8. Open each page in the site (**bands.html**, **catalogue.html**, **contact.html**, **label.html**, and **tourdates.html**), repeat Step 6 to apply the new CSS style to the logo, and then save and close each page.

If you are formatting only one graphic, you can either create a CSS style or you can set the attributes for that graphic in the Property inspector. When a graphic is selected in the Document window, the Property inspector displays a small picture of the graphic and the graphic's attributes. The Property inspector includes the following graphic attributes:

- **Image.** A descriptive name of the image. The image name is used in some advanced forms of programming to allow you to tell Dreamweaver or the browser what to do with the image. The name does not have to be the same as the filename, but it should enable you to identify the image. The image name must begin with a letter or an underscore; the rest of the name can contain letters and numbers, but it cannot contain any spaces or symbols. You cannot name an image with a CSS style. You must name the image in the Property inspector or by typing the information directly into the code.
- **W (Width)** and **H (Height).** The horizontal and vertical dimensions of the graphic in pixels. You can resize the image by changing the values or dragging a resize handle on the selected image in the Document window. However, if you resize a graphic in Dreamweaver, the Web site will load more slowly, because Dreamweaver must transmit the original graphic to the end-user's computer and then resize the image on the client computer. Also, resizing an image larger than its original size will degrade the image quality. Instead, you should use an external image processing program to resize a graphic, or you should resample the graphic after you adjust its width or height. You will learn about resampling in the next section.
- **Reset image to original size.** After you have changed the width or height of an image, the Reset Image to Original Size button appears between the W and H boxes. Clicking the button restores the selected image to its original dimensions.
- **Src (Image source file).** The graphic's file path (which includes the filename). The file path will either be relative or absolute, depending on what you selected when you inserted the graphic. A relative path is used most commonly, because the path will still work even if you change the site's URL or move its root directory. You can replace an image by entering the path to the new source image file, clicking the Browse for File button and navigating to the new image, or by dragging the Point to File button to the new file. You can also double-click the image in the Document window and enter the new path information in the Select Image Source dialog box.
- **Alt (Alternate).** Text that appears in place of the graphic when the page is opened in a browser that displays only text or is set to download images manually. In some browsers, the Alt text also appears in a tooltip when the pointer is positioned over the graphic. You should add an Alt message that describes the image to all graphics. This is extremely helpful for individuals who have visual disabilities and rely on screen readers to verbally communicate the graphic information. You cannot set the Alt description of an image with a CSS style. You must do this in the Property inspector or by typing the information directly into the code.
- **Class.** A list of the CSS styles you created that you can apply to a selected graphic. Any text attributes defined in the style do not affect the graphic's display.
- **V Space** and **H Space.** The blank space, in pixels, that appears vertically along the top and bottom of the image or horizontally along the left and right sides of the image.
- **Low Src (Low-resolution image source file).** The path (including the filename) to a low-resolution image that displays while the high-resolution image is downloading. This enables users with slow connections to see something while they wait for the high-resolution image to load. It is not necessary to use a low-resolution image.

- **Border.** A rectangular group of lines that surrounds a graphic. The width of the lines is measured in pixels. A border of 0 pixels (the default) is equivalent to no visible border. If there is no value in the Border box, it will default to the user's browser setting. For most browsers, this is equivalent to 0. If the image is linked, then the border is the link color you specified in the page properties; otherwise, the border is the text color of the paragraph around the image.
- **Align.** The alignment of the graphic to text adjacent on the page. Default uses the browser's default alignment setting, which is usually baseline. The **baseline** is the imaginary line on which the text is sitting. Baseline and Bottom align the bottom of the graphic to the baseline of the text. Top aligns the top of the graphic to the top of the tallest item, whether an image or text, in the same line. Middle aligns the middle of the graphic to the baseline of the text. TextTop aligns the top of the graphic to the top of the tallest character in the text line. Absolute Middle aligns the middle of the graphic to the middle of the text line. Absolute Bottom aligns the bottom of the graphic to the bottom of the lowest character in the text line, for example, with the bottom of a lowercase *g*. Left aligns the left edge of the graphic at the left margin and wraps text around its right side. Right aligns the right edge of the graphic at the right margin and wraps text around its left side.

The Property inspector expands to show all of the available graphic attributes or collapses to show only the most common ones. You'll enter alternate text in the Property inspector for the Cosmatic logo.

To add Alt text to Cosmatic logo graphic:

▶ **1.** Open the **index.html** page in the Document window, and then click the **Expander arrow** ▽ on the Property inspector to display all the attributes, if necessary.

▶ **2.** Click the **Cosmatic logo**. The logo is selected, and resize handles appear around the selected image.

▶ **3.** In the Property inspector, click in the **Alt** box, type **Cosmatic company logo, link to home page**, and then press the **Tab** key. The Alt text is entered for the logo.

▶ **4.** Save the page, and then preview the page in a browser.

▶ **5.** Place the pointer over the Cosmatic logo, but do not click. The Alt text description appears in the browser window. See Figure 4-8.

Alt text description for the Cosmatic logo previewed in browser Figure 4-8

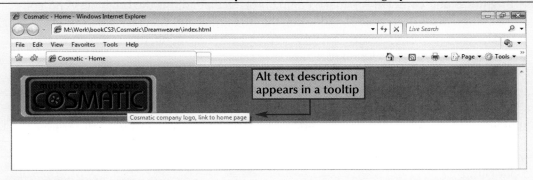

▶ **6.** Read the Alt text description, close the browser, and then close the page.

▶ **7.** Repeat Steps 1 through 6 for the rest of the pages in the site: **bands.html**, **catalogue.html**, **contact.html**, **label.html**, and **tourdates.html**.

Editing Graphics from Within Dreamweaver

You can change the appearance of a graphic by editing it. Unlike formatting, which changes the way the graphic is displayed by defining values for attributes such as borders, alignment, and spacing, editing a graphic is the process of changing and manipulating the actual image. Because you must often adjust graphics while you work on a Web page, Dreamweaver includes some basic graphics editing components such as edit, optimize, crop, resample, brightness and contrast, and sharpen. You can use these editing components even if a graphics editing program is not installed on your computer.

- **Edit.** The option to set Adobe Photoshop or Adobe Fireworks as the external image editor for each image file type (.jpg, .gif, .png). You can then open a selected image in the external image editor, edit and save the image, and then view the edited image in Dreamweaver in the Document window. Appendix A covers how to edit Web page images in Adobe Photoshop.
- **Optimize.** The option to compress or convert for best display, all or part of an Adobe Photoshop file (.pdf) in a Web page for display on the Web in the Image Preview window. The Image Preview window opens when you insert the image or when you click the Optimize button.
- **Crop.** An image editing process that reduces the area of a graphic by deleting unwanted outer areas. For example, you might want to **crop** the surrounding area and other people from a photograph of your family at an amusement park to emphasize your family. When you click the Crop button, a dark filter with a clear center appears over the graphic. You select the area of the graphic to keep in the page by dragging the resize handles of the inner clear area. You can crop only rectangular areas. Clicking the Crop button a second time removes any areas of the graphic that are covered by the dark filter.
- **Resample.** An image editing process that adds or subtracts pixels from a resized graphic. Remember, when you resize a graphic, the graphic's file size does not change. **Resampling** a graphic reduces its file size and improves its image quality at the new size and shape. Only bitmap graphics (JPEGs and GIFs) can be resampled. Because resampling changes the file size of the actual graphic, it can create some problems. For example, if you used the same graphic in more than one location in a site, every instance of the graphic will have the new, smaller file size. Instances of the graphic that were not resized smaller will probably display poorly because the smaller file size reduces the quality at the larger width and height.
- **Brightness and contrast.** An image editing process that adjusts the brightness and contrast of the pixels in a graphic. Adjusting the Brightness and Contrast sliders in the Brightness/Contrast dialog box enables you to lighten a graphic that is too dark or darken a graphic that is too light.
- **Sharpen.** An image editing process that increases contrast of a graphic's edges to improve definition. You can adjust the sharpness of a blurry image to make it clearer.

When you edit a graphic, the actual graphic is altered and the edits cannot be undone. It is a good idea to keep a copy of the original graphic outside the local root folder so that you can reinsert the original graphic in the page if you dislike the edited version. All of the original graphics used in the Cosmatic site are included with your Data Files.

Brian wants you to edit and insert the Surface Suction CD cover graphic in the Catalogue page.

To edit the cover graphic in the Catalogue page:

▶ 1. Open the **catalogue.html** page in the Document window, click to the left of the Surface Suction: Black Lab subheading to position the insertion point to the left of the subheading (you might need to scroll to see the subheading), press the **Shift+Enter** keys, and then press the **Up Arrow** key to move the insertion point to the blank line.

▶ 2. On the **Common** tab of the Insert bar, click the **Image** button 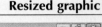 in the Images list, navigate to the **Tutorial.04\Tutorial** folder included with your Data Files, click the **SurfaceSuctionCDcover.jpg** graphic, and then click the **OK** button. The graphic is inserted in the page above the Surface Suction: Black Lab subheading. The file size of the graphic appears to the right of the graphic's picture in the Property inspector.

▶ 3. Drag the graphic's lower-right resize handle until **200** appears in both the W and H boxes in the Property inspector. The graphic is resized but the graphic's file size hasn't changed. The Reset Image to Original Size button appears between the W and H boxes so you can return the image to its original settings. See Figure 4-9.

Resized graphic ◀ Figure 4-9

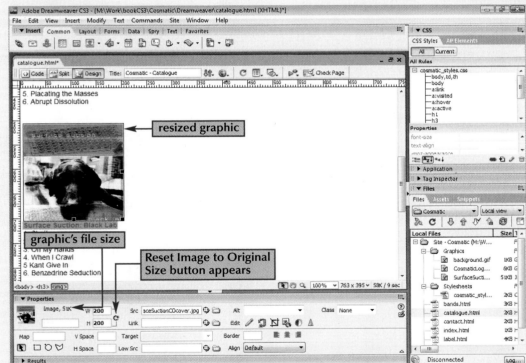

▶ 4. In the Property inspector, click the **Reset Image to Original Size** button ⟳ . The graphic returns to its original size.

▶ 5. Double-click the graphic. The Select Image Source dialog box opens and the image width, height, and file size appear below the graphic in the Image Preview box.

   Trouble? If the graphic does not appear in the Image Preview box, click SurfaceSuctionCDcover.jpg in the list of filenames to select it.

6. Click the **Cancel** button to close the Select Image Source dialog box, type **300** in the W and H boxes in the Property inspector, and then double-click the graphic. The graphic's original width, height, and file size are still displayed at the bottom of the Image Preview box, because visually resizing an image does not change its dimensions or file size in the Graphics folder. (Remember that if you include a visually resized graphic in a page, the original graphic will be loaded in the user's browser and then resized on the client computer, which slows down the Web page.)

Tip

You can undo any resampling, cropping, brightness/ contrast changes, and sharpening by pressing the Ctrl+Z keys.

7. Click the **Cancel** button in the Select Image Source dialog box, click the **Resample** button 🖼 in the Property inspector, and then click the **OK** button in the dialog box that warns that the resampling action will permanently alter the selected graphic. The graphic's new file size appears in the Property inspector.

8. Double-click the graphic. The new width, height, and file size appear below the Image Preview box. Resampling a graphic reduces the file size of the actual graphic in the Graphics folder. See Figure 4-10.

Figure 4-10 | **Resampled graphic**

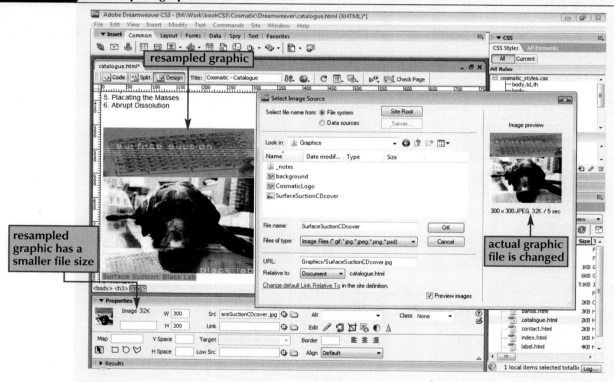

9. Click the **Cancel** button to close the dialog box, click the **Crop** button 🔲 in the Property inspector, and then click the **OK** button in the dialog box that warns that the cropping action will permanently alter the selected graphic. A filter appears around the edges of the graphic, and resize handles appear around the clear inner square.

10. Drag the resize handles so that only the dog's face remains in the clear inner area. See Figure 4-11.

Graphic being cropped | Figure 4-11

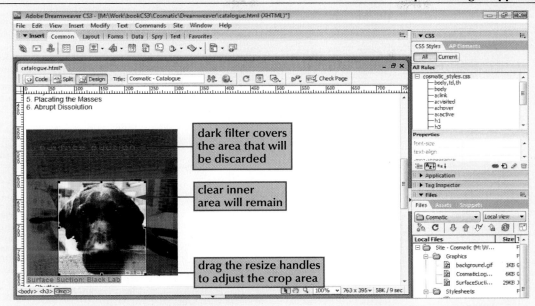

11. Press the **Enter** key. The graphic is cropped, and the new width, height, and file size appear in the Property inspector.

12. In the Property inspector, click the **Brightness and Contrast** button ◑ , and then click the **OK** button in the dialog box that warns that the action will permanently alter the selected graphic. The Brightness/Contrast dialog box opens.

13. Drag the **Brightness** slider to the right until 50 appears in the box, and then drag the **Contrast** slider to the left until −40 appears in the box. The graphic is lighter, and the contrast between colors is decreased. See Figure 4-12.

Brightness/Contrast dialog box | Figure 4-12

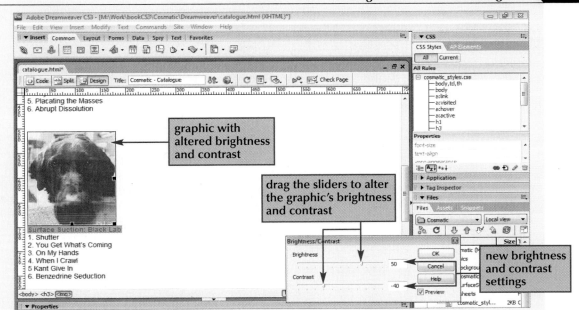

▶ **14.** Click the **OK** button. The Brightness/Contrast dialog box closes, and the changes are applied.

▶ **15.** In the Property inspector, click the **Sharpen** button ⬜, and then click the **OK** button in the dialog box that warns that the action will permanently alter the selected graphic.

▶ **16.** Drag the **Sharpen** slider to the right until 10 appears in the box. See Figure 4-13.

Figure 4-13 ▶ **Sharpen dialog box**

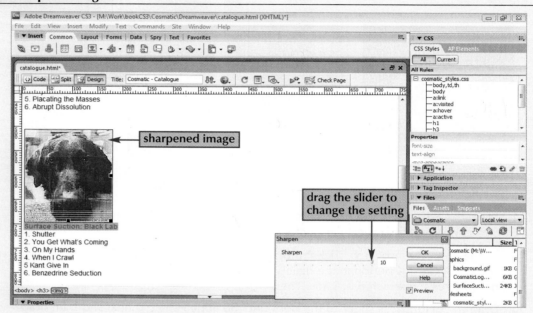

▶ **17.** Click the **OK** button to close the dialog box and accept the changes, and then save and close the page.

Creating Graphic Hyperlinks

Another common use of graphics is as hyperlinks. You can create a link for an entire image, or you can divide the image into smaller sections and create a link for each of those sections.

Linking an Image

The process for creating a graphic hyperlink is similar to the process for creating a text hyperlink. You select the graphic in the Document window, and then use the Browse to File button or the Point to File button in the Property inspector to create the link to the page you want. After you have created a link to a page, you can select it as the link for a selected graphic using the Link box in the Property inspector. When a graphic is linked, the border appears as a rectangle around the graphic in the color you set for links in the page properties (unless the border is 0 pixels).

You will create a graphic link from the Cosmatic logo to the home page. You won't see a rectangle around the graphic, because you set the border of the Cosmatic logo to 0 in the .logostyle style. Using a logo as a link to the home page of a site is a common convention that the Cosmatic target audience should be familiar with. You'll start by creating the link in all of the pages in the site except the home page. Because creating the link does not affect the appearance of the logo graphic, you won't create a link from the logo on the home page to itself.

To create a graphic link from the logo to the home page:

▶ 1. Open the **label.html** page in the Document window.

▶ 2. Click the **Cosmatic logo** to select it.

▶ 3. In the Property inspector, next to the Link box, click the **Browse for File** button 🗀, and then double-click **index.html** in the Select File dialog box. The link information appears in the Link box in the Property inspector.

▶ 4. Save and close the page.

▶ 5. Open each of the following pages, and repeat Steps 2 through 4 to create a graphic hyperlink from the logo to the home page: **bands.html**, **catalogue.html**, **contact.html**, and **tourdates.html**.

Tip

You can also use the Point to File button in the Property inspector to link the selected graphic to a page.

Creating an Image Map

In addition to creating a link from an entire image, you can create multiple links from different areas of an image. An **image map** is a graphic that is divided into invisible regions, or hotspots. A **hotspot** is an area of an image that you can click to cause an action such as loading another Web page. Image maps are useful when you want to link parts of an image to different pieces of information. In a music site, for example, each touring region on a map could be a hotspot so that when a user clicks a particular region, the corresponding tour dates appear on the screen.

Creating an Image Map | Reference Window

- Select the image.
- In the Property inspector, type a name in the Map box.
- For each hotspot, click the rectangular, oval, or polygonal hotspot tool in the Property inspector, and then drag over the image in the Document window to create a rectangular or oval hotspot or click at various points to create a polygonal hotspot.
- For each hotspot, type alternate text in the Alt box in the Property inspector.

You can create three types of hotspots: rectangular, oval, and polygonal. After the hotspots are created in the image, you create separate links for each hotspot. When a hotspot is selected, the Property inspector displays the hotspot and pointer tools and the hotspot attributes, which include:

- **Link.** The Web page or file that opens when the hotspot is clicked. You can type a URL or path and filename into the Link box, or you can use the Browse for File button to navigate to the page to which you want to link.
- **Target.** The frame or window in which the linked Web page will open. This option is available only after you specify a link for the hotspot.

- **Alt (Alternative).** The alternate text description for each link.
- **Map.** A descriptive name of the image map. The Map box appears when a hotspot is selected. You do not have to name image maps; however, some advanced coding requires that objects be named so they may be referenced. If you do not name the image map after you create the first hotspot, Dreamweaver assigns the name *Map* to the first image map, *Map2* to the second image map, and so forth. Map names must begin with a letter or underscore, and they can contain letters and numbers but not spaces or symbols.

Brian asks you to delete the empty lines between the Cosmatic logo and the site navigation text links in all the pages, add a map graphic to the Tour Dates page, and then use the graphic to create an image map.

To delete blank lines in the Web pages:

1. Open the **tourdates.html** page in the Document window, position the insertion point before the navigation links, and then click the **Split** button on the Document toolbar. See Figure 4-14.

Figure 4-14

Tour Dates page in Split view

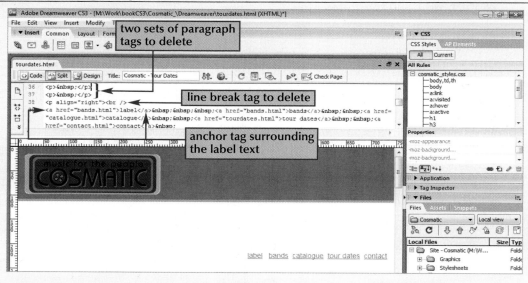

You'll delete the line break tag from the Code pane.

2. In the Code pane, select the line break tag <br /> that precedes the anchor tag surrounding the label text, and then delete it from the code.

3. Locate the paragraph tag with the align attribute in it (do not delete this tag), select the two sets of paragraph tags directly above it, and then delete those tags from the page.

4. Click in the Design pane to view the changes, click the **Design** button on the Document toolbar to return to Design view, and then save and close the page.

5. Repeat Steps 1 through 4 for the following pages: **bands.html**, **catalogue.html**, **contact.html**, and **label.html**.

Tip

You can also click the Refresh button in the CSS Styles panel or press the F5 key to update the code changes.

Next, you'll add the map graphic to the Tour Dates page.

To insert the map graphic in the Tour Dates page:

▶ **1.** Open the **tourdates.html** page in the Document window, move the insertion point after the link text, and then press the **Enter** key.

▶ **2.** If the insertion point remains at the right of the screen, in the Property inspector, click the **Align Right** button ▤ . The insertion point is repositioned at the left of the screen.

▶ **3.** Type **TOUR DATES**, click the **Format** button in the Property inspector, click **Heading 1** to apply the style to the text.

▶ **4.** Deselect the text, if necessary, and then press the **Enter** key twice to move the insertion point down two lines.

▶ **5.** On the **Common** tab of the Insert bar, click the **Image** button ▣ in the Images list. The Select Image Source dialog box opens.

▶ **6.** Navigate to the **Tutorial.04\Tutorial** folder included with your Data Files, and then double-click **USmap.gif**. A copy of the USmap.gif graphic is saved in the Graphics folder and the graphic appears in the page.

▶ **7.** In the Document window, click the **map** graphic to select it, if necessary, and then, in the Property inspector, click the **Align Center** button ▤ . The map is centered on the page.

▶ **8.** In the Property inspector, click in the **Alt** box, and then type **US map with links to tour dates by region**. The alternate text description is entered for the map graphic.

Next, you'll add hotspots to the map, which turns the graphic into an image map. You want to create a hotspot for the West Coast, Central, and East Coast regions on the map. You'll use a polygon hotspot so you can outline the irregular shape of each region.

To create the image map from the tour map:

▶ **1.** In the Property inspector, click in the **Image** box to the right of the map image, and then type **USmapIM**.

▶ **2.** In the Property inspector, click the **Polygon Hotspot Tool** button ▽ . The pointer changes to ✛ in the Document window.

▶ **3.** In the Document window, click the upper-left corner of the West Coast region. The first point of the hotspot is added to the page. See Figure 4-15.

Figure 4-15 First point of the polygon hotspot inserted for the West Coast region

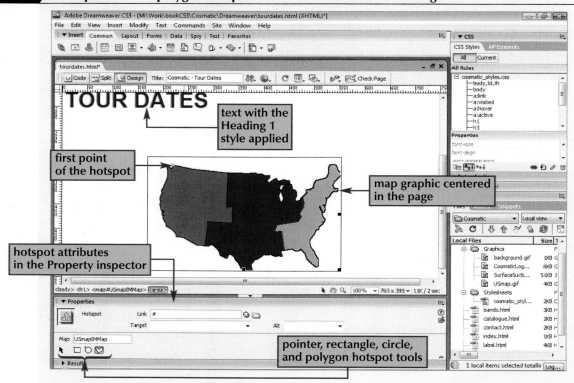

Trouble? If a dialog box opens prompting you to enter alt text for the hotspot, click the OK button here and each time you create a hotspot. You'll add the alt text after you create the hotspot.

4. Continue to click around the perimeter of the West Coast region to add the hotspot border. Dreamweaver created a map name by adding "Map" to the image name you entered earlier. See Figure 4-16.

Figure 4-16 Completed West Coast hotspot

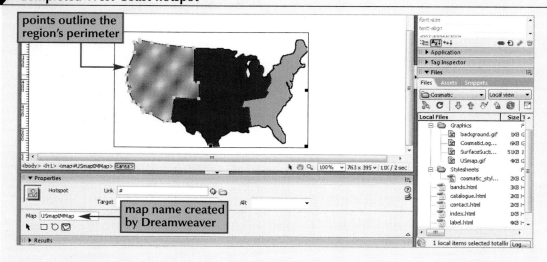

If any parts of the hotspot are not aligned correctly to the region's perimeter, you can use the Pointer Hotspot Tool to drag the appropriate points to realign the hotspot.

5. In the Property inspector, click the **Pointer Hotspot Tool** button ▶ , and then drag a point on the hotspot to adjust its position, if necessary.

6. In the Property inspector, click in the **Alt** box, and then type **Link to West Coast tour dates**. The alternate text is entered for the hotspot.

7. In the Document window, click anywhere outside the hotspot but inside the graphic border to deselect the hotspot.

8. Repeat Steps 2 through 7 to create the hotspots for the Central and East Coast regions of the map. Use the name of each region in the Alt text for the corresponding hotspot. Make sure you click the **Pointer Hotspot Tool** button ▶ in the Property inspector before you click to deselect the hotspot.

9. Save and close the page.

Tip

You can move or resize a hotspot using the Pointer Hotspot Tool. If the hotspot is a polygon, you can move the individual points as well.

In the Review Assignments, you will link the regional hotspots to the text they reference.

Creating Rollovers

A **rollover** is an image that changes when the pointer moves across it. In actuality, a rollover enables two seemingly stacked graphics—the original graphic and the rollover graphic—to swap places during a specified browser action, such as a mouseover, and then to swap back during another specified browser action, such as when the pointer is moved off the images. The two graphics must be the same size.

Inserting Rollovers

You can insert rollover buttons that change when the user points to them and that link the user to another page when the button is clicked. When you use the Rollover Image button to create rollovers, Dreamweaver does more than just create code to make the images swap. After you fill in the requested information in the Insert Rollover Image dialog box, Dreamweaver creates all the code to make four separate things happen:

1. The graphics preload when the Web page is loaded so that they are in place when the browser action (such as a mouseover) occurs.
2. The graphics swap places when the pointer is placed over the graphic.
3. The graphics swap places again when the pointer is moved off of the graphic.
4. If a URL is specified in the When Clicked, Go To URL box of the Insert Rollover Image dialog box, the user is hyperlinked to the new page when the graphic is clicked.

Technically, a rollover is a JavaScript behavior. **JavaScript** is a scripting language that works with HTML. A JavaScript behavior is a set of JavaScript instructions that tell the browser to do specified things. After you enter the image name, the original image source file, the rollover image source file, and a URL, if appropriate, Dreamweaver adds the JavaScript for you.

The image name is the name that appears in the Property inspector when one of the rollover graphics is highlighted. The image name does not replace the filename of either graphic you designate. The image name must begin with a letter or an underscore and cannot have any spaces or special characters. Use a descriptive name that includes the word *rollover* to remind you that a graphic has rollover behaviors attached to it. Unless the word *rollover* appears in the image name, you cannot tell that a graphic has rollover behaviors attached to it without looking at the code or previewing the page in a browser.

Reference Window | **Inserting a Rollover**

- On the Common tab of the Insert bar, click the Rollover Image button in the Images list.
- Type a name for the rollover image in the Image Name box.
- Click the Original Image Browse button, navigate to the file you want to insert as the original image, and then double-click the image.
- Click the Rollover Image Browse button, navigate to the file you want to insert as the rollover image, and then double-click the image.
- Click the Preload Rollover Image check box to check it.
- Type alternate text for the image in the Alternate Text box.
- Click the When Clicked, Go To URL Browse button, navigate to the page to which you want to link, and then double-click the filename.
- Click the OK button in the Insert Rollover Image dialog box.

You'll create a rollover for the Cosmatic logo in the Bands page. Then, you'll replace the existing logo in each page of the Web site with the new rollover.

To insert a rollover for the logo in the Bands page:

▶ 1. Open the **bands.html** page in the Document window, click the **Cosmatic logo** to select it, and then press the **Delete** key. The logo image is deleted from the Bands page, and the text moves up in the page. (The link text might not be visible because it is the same color as the top stripe in the background.)

▶ 2. On the **Common** tab of the Insert bar, click the **Images button arrow** 🖼️ ▾ , and then click the **Rollover Image** button 🖼️ . The Insert Rollover Image dialog box opens.

▶ 3. In the Image Name box, type **LogoRollover**. Remember, graphic names cannot include spaces. Whenever you see the name in the Property inspector, you'll be reminded that the image has rollover behaviors.

▶ 4. Click the Original Image **Browse** button, navigate to the **Graphics** folder in the local root folder of your Cosmatic site, if necessary, and then double-click **CosmaticLogo**. The path to the CosmaticLogo.gif graphic appears in the Original Image box.

▶ 5. Click the Rollover Image **Browse** button, navigate to the **Tutorial.04\Tutorial** folder included with your Data Files, and then double-click **CosmaticLogoRollover.gif**. A copy of the CosmaticLogoRollover.gif graphic is saved in the Graphics folder in the site's local root folder, and the path to the graphic appears in the Rollover Image box.

▶ 6. Click the **Preload Rollover Image** check box to insert a check mark, if necessary. Both graphics will load with the Web page.

▶ 7. Click in the **Alternate Text** box, and then type **Cosmatic company logo, link to home page**.

▶ 8. Click the When Clicked, Go To URL **Browse** button, and then double-click **index.html** in the local root folder of the Cosmatic site. The index.html page is added to the When Clicked, Go To URL box.

▶ 9. Click the **OK** button. The Insert Rollover Image dialog box closes, and the rollover image is added to the Bands page.

▶ **10.** Press the **Right Arrow** key to position the insertion point to the right of the logo, and then click the **Cosmatic logo** to select the logo rollover. No information in the Property inspector identifies this graphic as a rollover except its name, which appears in the Image box. See Figure 4-17.

Rollover in the Bands page ◀ **Figure 4-17**

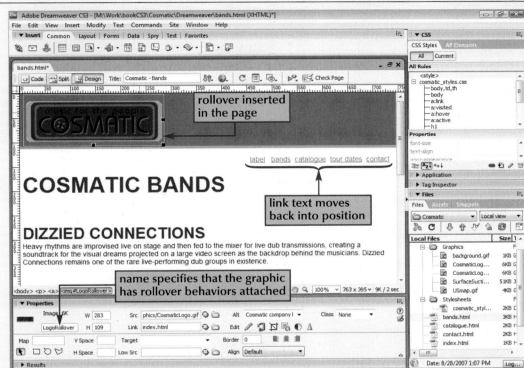

You'll view the page in a browser and test the rollover.

▶ **11.** Save the page, preview the page in a browser, and then point to the **Cosmatic logo**. The rollover image appears in the browser. See Figure 4-18.

Figure 4-18 **Rollover previewed in a browser**

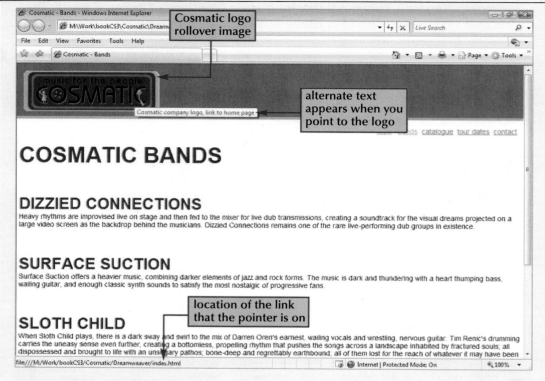

Trouble? If the Information Bar appears at the top of the browser window explaining that Internet Explorer has restricted content, you need to allow the blocked content. Click the Information Bar, and then click Allow Blocked Content to view the rollover functionality. If necessary, allow the blocked content any time you preview pages in the browser.

▶ **12.** Click the **Cosmatic logo** to open the home page, and then close the browser.

You want the same logo rollover to appear in all the other pages of the Cosmatic site. Rather than inserting the rollover in each page, you can copy it from the Bands page, and then paste it in the other pages. If necessary, allow the blocked content any time you preview pages in the browser.

To copy and paste the Cosmatic logo rollover:

▶ **1.** Click the **Cosmatic logo** in the Bands page to select it.

▶ **2.** Click **Edit** on the menu bar, and then click **Copy**.

Tip

You can also press the Ctrl+C keys to copy the selected graphic and press the Ctrl+V keys to paste it.

▶ **3.** Close the Bands page.

▶ **4.** Open the **catalogue.html** page in the Document window.

▶ **5.** Select the **Cosmatic logo**, and then press the **Delete** key. The logo is deleted from the page.

▶ **6.** Click **Edit** on the menu bar, and then click **Paste**. The logo rollover is inserted in the page.

Because the new logo looks exactly the same as the graphic you just deleted, you'll verify that it is the rollover graphic.

▶ **7.** Click the **Cosmatic logo** to select it, and then verify that **LogoRollover** appears in the Image box of the Property inspector.

▶ **8.** Save and close the page.

▶ **9.** Open each of the following pages in the site, and then repeat Steps 5 through 8: **contact.html**, **index.html**, **label.html**, and **tourdates.html**.

Editing a Rollover

You can modify a rollover by changing the original graphic, changing the rollover graphic, or by editing the code of the rollover. For example, you might need to replace a graphic with an updated design, or you might decide to open the linked page in a new browser window. You can edit a rollover graphic in three ways:

- Delete the original graphic and insert a new rollover using the Rollover Image button. This deletes all the code, as well as the graphic, so you can create a new rollover from scratch.
- Replace the original graphic or the rollover graphic with a new one, leaving the attached code unchanged. To replace the original graphic, select the graphic and then select a new source file in the Property inspector. To replace the rollover graphic, select the graphic, open the Behaviors panel in the Tag Inspector panel group, double-click onMouseOver in the behaviors list, and then select a new source file for the rollover graphic.
- Edit the code for the rollover graphic in Code view if you know JavaScript, or edit the behaviors in the Behaviors panel.

For now, you'll leave the original and rollover images. In this session, you added graphics to the pages, and then you formatted and edited the graphics. You created graphic hyperlinks, an image map, and rollovers. In the next session, you'll work with tables.

Session 4.1 Quick Check | Review

1. What are the three graphic formats that browsers can display?
2. What is the best graphic file format to use for photographs?
3. Why would you use the Assets panel?
4. What is an image map?
5. What is a hotspot?
6. What is a rollover?

Session 4.2

Creating Tables

In the early days of the Web, text and images were aligned to the left of the page. Designers soon discovered that they could use tables to provide a vertical and horizontal structure for the content of a Web page. This provided more flexibility in arranging the content and elements in the Web page. Tables are used in Web pages to simplify the presentation of data as well as to increase layout options, both of which aid in Web page design.

Tables are grid structures that are divided into rows and columns. **Rows** cross the table horizontally, whereas **columns** cross the table vertically. The container created by the intersection of a row and a column is called a **cell**. The four lines that mark the edges of a cell are called **borders**. Borders can be invisible or visible lines of a width that you select. When the borders of the cells of a table are set to 0, the borders still exist but are invisible. The use of tables with invisible borders to place text and images in a Web page presented designers with new options for laying out Web page content. Today, designers also use CSS styles to position and arrange content and other elements in a Web page. CSS styles are beneficial because they separate the content from the style and layout of a page, they load faster than tables, and they are read more easily by devices such as screen readers that aid visually impaired people in viewing Web sites. However, CSS styles are not well supported by older (4.0 and earlier) browsers and, in some instances, it is cumbersome to lay out a page using CSS styles. It is important to learn how to use tables for layout because you will encounter them frequently.

Reference Window | Inserting a Table

- On the Common tab of the Insert bar, click the Table button.
- Type the number of rows in the Rows box.
- Type the number of columns in the Columns box.
- Type a percentage value in the Table width box, click the Table width arrow, and then click percent.
- Type a border width in the Border thickness box (type 0 if you do not want the table structure to appear on the Web page).
- Click the OK button.

Inserting a Table

You can quickly insert a table in a Web page by selecting where to insert the table and its parameters. Dreamweaver then inserts the HTML code for the table. The table parameters that you can specify are:

- **Rows.** The number of rows for the table. You can also add rows to the table later.
- **Columns.** The number of columns for the table. You can also add columns to the table later.
- **Table width.** The horizontal dimension of the table specified either in pixels or as a percentage of the width of the browser window. Specifying the table width in pixels creates a table that has a somewhat fixed width—the table will still expand as needed to fit the content, but it will not change size when the browser window is resized. Specifying the table width as a percentage creates a table that adjusts in size as the Web page is resized in the browser window. Initially, all the cells have equal widths; however, you can adjust the height and width of cells, rows, and columns. Be aware that changing the width of a cell changes the width of all the cells in the column, and changing the height of a cell changes the height of all the cells in the row.
- **Border thickness.** The size of the table border in pixels. A border of 0 creates an invisible table. When no value is specified, most browsers display the table as if the thickness were set to 1. It is a good idea to specify a border thickness to ensure that the table is displayed correctly. By default, the borders of an invisible table are visible within Dreamweaver so you can see the table structure, making the table easier to work with. You must preview the page in a browser to see what the table content will look like without borders.

- **Cell padding.** The amount of empty space, measured in pixels, maintained between the border of a cell and the cell's content. When no cell padding is specified, most browsers display the table as if the cell padding were set to 1. In most cases, this is fine; however, it is a good idea to specify a cell padding to ensure that the table is always displayed correctly.
- **Cell spacing.** The width of the cell walls measured in pixels. If you set the border to 0, then the table still will be invisible no matter what you set the cell spacing to. When no cell spacing is specified, most browsers display the table as if the cell spacing were set to 2. In most cases, this is fine; however, you should specify a cell spacing to ensure that the table is always displayed correctly.
- **Header.** The row and columns of a table that contain heading information (also called header cells). There are four possible header options: None specifies no heading cells, Left makes the first column of cells heading cells, Top makes the first row of cells heading cells, and Both makes both the first row and the first column of cells heading cells. Designating heading cells enables users who rely on screen readers to more easily make sense of the table information.
- **Caption.** A table title that is displayed outside of the table. The optional caption can aid users who rely on assistive devices.
- **Align caption.** Designates the alignment of the caption in relation to the table.
- **Summary.** A description of the table. Assistive devices read the summary, but the text is not displayed in the page.

You'll create a table to hold the West Coast region tour dates in the Tour Dates page.

To insert a table for the West Coast region tour dates in the Tour Dates page:

1. If you took a break after the previous session, make sure that the Cosmatic site is open, the Files panel is expanded, and the CSS Styles panel is expanded.

2. Open the **tourdates.html** page in the Document window, click to the right of the U.S. map, and then press the **Enter** key to move the insertion point below the map.

3. On the **Common** tab of the Insert bar, click the **Table** button 🔳 . The Table dialog box opens. You'll set the table parameters.

4. Type **14** in the Rows box, press the **Tab** key, and then type **3** in the Columns box, if necessary. The table will have 14 rows and 3 columns.

5. Press the **Tab** key, type **75** in the Table width box, click the **Table width** button, and then click **percent**. The table will resize in the browser window to be 75% of the available space.

6. Press the **Tab** key, and then type **0** in the Border thickness box. The table borders will be invisible.

7. Press the **Tab** key, and then type **1** in the Cell padding box. One pixel of space will be maintained between the cell border and its content.

8. Press the **Tab** key, and then type **2** in the Cell spacing box. The cell walls will be 2 pixels.

9. Click **Top** in the Header area. The first row of cells in the table will be heading cells.

10. Press the **Tab** key four times until the insertion point is in the Summary box, and then type **Cosmatic bands, west coast tour dates**. Assistive devices will be able to read the summary text, but it will not appear in the browser window. See Figure 4-19.

Tip

The Table button is also available on the Layout tab of the Insert bar.

Figure 4-19 | **Completed Table dialog box**

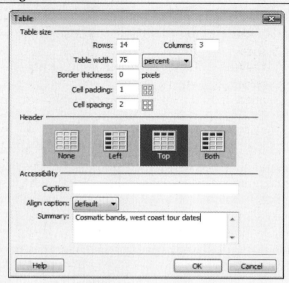

▶ **11.** Click the **OK** button. The table appears in the Document window and is selected. You might need to scroll down to see the entire table. See Figure 4-20.

Figure 4-20 | **Selected table in the Tour Dates page**

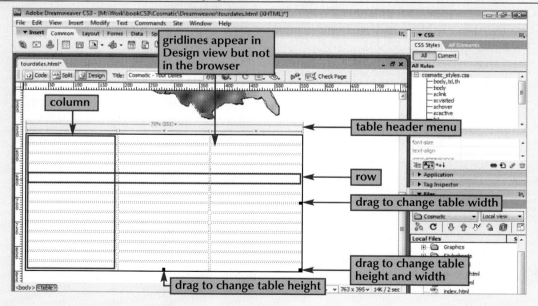

▶ **12.** Save the Tour Dates page.

When you create a table, Dreamweaver inserts a nonbreaking space in each cell. Some browsers collapse cells that are empty, destroying the table structure. The nonbreaking space is invisible, but it keeps the cells from collapsing. To view a nonbreaking space, you must be in Code view or Split view.

You will view the nonbreaking space in the first cell of the table in the Tour Dates page.

To view the nonbreaking space in the Tour Dates table:

▶ 1. Click in the upper-left cell of the table in the Tour Dates page. The insertion point is placed in the cell.

▶ 2. Click the **Split** button on the Document toolbar. Notice the nonbreaking space ( ) to the right of the insertion point in the Code pane.

▶ 3. Click the **Design** button on the Document toolbar.

Adding Content to Cells and Importing Tabular Data

To add text to a cell, you simply click in the cell and type. Pressing the Enter key adds another paragraph within the cell. You can also copy data between cells using the standard Copy and Paste commands. When you type or paste text into a cell, the text wraps within the cell to fit the width you defined. If you check the No Wrap check box in the Property inspector, the cell will expand to fit the text when the page is viewed in a browser but remain wrapped when viewed in Dreamweaver. In addition, you can import data stored in a spreadsheet into a table.

Keyboard commands help you move through the table. To move the insertion point to the next adjacent cell, press the Tab key. Pressing the Tab key in the last cell of the table adds a new row to the table. Press the Shift+Tab keys to move the insertion point to the previous cell. You also can use the arrow keys to move the insertion point to an adjacent cell.

In addition to text, you can insert graphics into table cells the same way you insert them into a page. When a graphic is inserted into a cell, the cell's column width and row height expand as needed to accommodate the graphic.

Reusing Content to Reinforce Marketing | InSight

The same content is often used in many contexts, including printed brochures, promotional letters and advertisements, and the Web site, to reinforce the message you want to convey. This reusing of material helps to create a specific branding and identity for the business or product. Rather than retyping content that is already available in another file, possibly introducing errors into the text, you can copy that text from its original source and paste it into the Web pages. When you want to place data stored in a spreadsheet or a table into a table in a Web page, you can save the data in a delimited format (such as comma, tab, semicolon, colon, or other delimited format) and then import the data into the table. Comma delimited format inserts commas between pieces of data to indicate how data should be divided into table cells. Most spreadsheet programs and programs that create tables will let you save the tabular data in comma delimited (.csv) format.

The Cosmatic tour schedules are stored in spreadsheets. Brian saved the data as a comma delimited file and wants you to import the West Coast tour schedule in the Tour Dates page.

To enter and import text into the Tour Dates table:

▶ 1. Click in the upper-left cell in the table, type **West Coast Tour Dates**, and then press the **Tab** key. The text you typed is entered in the first cell in the table, and the active cell is the second cell in the first row.

You could continue to type all of the tour dates information, but it's faster to import the data from the comma delimited file.

Tip

You can also drag to select all of the cells in the table.

▶ **2.** Click in the upper-left cell in the table, press and hold the **Shift** key as you click in the lower-right cell, and then release the Shift key. All of the cells in the table are selected. You'll import the tabular data into the selected cells.

▶ **3.** Click **File** on the menu bar, point to **Import**, and then click **Tabular Data**. The Import Tabular Data dialog box opens.

▶ **4.** Click the Data file **Browse** button, navigate to the **Tutorial.04\Tutorial** folder included with your Data Files, and then double-click the **tabledata.csv** file.

▶ **5.** Click the **Delimiter** button, and then click **Comma**.

▶ **6.** In the Table width section, click the **Set to** option button, type **75** in the Set to box, and then make sure **Percent** appears as the unit.

▶ **7.** Type **1** in the Cell padding box, type **2** in the Cell spacing box, select **Bold** in the Format top row list, and then type **0** in the Border box. These settings match the table parameters you used when you created the table. See Figure 4-21.

Figure 4-21 ▶ **Import Tabular Data dialog box**

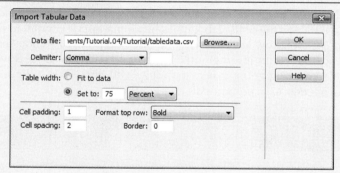

▶ **8.** Click the **OK** button. The data from the document is entered in the table. See Figure 4-22.

Figure 4-22 ▶ **Table with imported content**

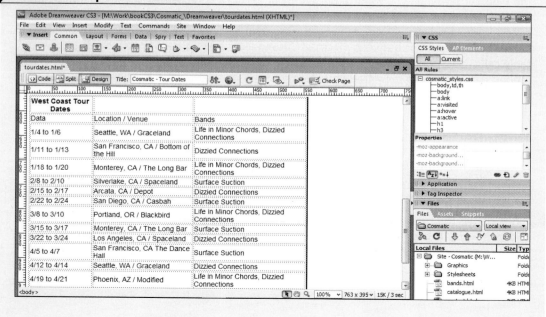

▶ **9.** Save the Tour Dates page.

All of the text formatting options can also be applied to text in a table. Text formatting attributes are available in the Property inspector when you select a cell, a row, or a column. You can also create CSS styles for table text.

Selecting Tables and Table Elements

You often need to modify a table and its elements to fit a particular Web page layout or specific content. To work with a table or table element, you must select it. You can select a table cell, a row, a column, or the table itself. Anytime the table or a table element is selected, the table header menu appears at the top of the table. You can switch to Expanded Table mode, which increases the width of the cell walls, to more easily select various table elements.

Selecting a Table

When you want to change attributes that affect the entire table, the whole table must be selected. When the entire table is selected, a bold black line surrounds the table, and resize handles appear on the left side, in the lower-right corner, and at the bottom of the table. The attributes in the Property inspector also change to reflect the entire table.

You'll use two methods to deselect and then select the table in the Tour Dates page.

To select the table in the Tour Dates page:

▶ **1.** Click the **Layout** tab on the Insert bar. The table is currently displayed in Standard mode.

▶ **2.** Click outside the table to deselect the table.

▶ **3.** Right-click the table, point to **Table** on the context menu, and then click **Select Table**. The table is selected, and the table properties appear in the Property inspector. See Figure 4-23.

Figure 4-23   **Table selected in the Tour Dates page**

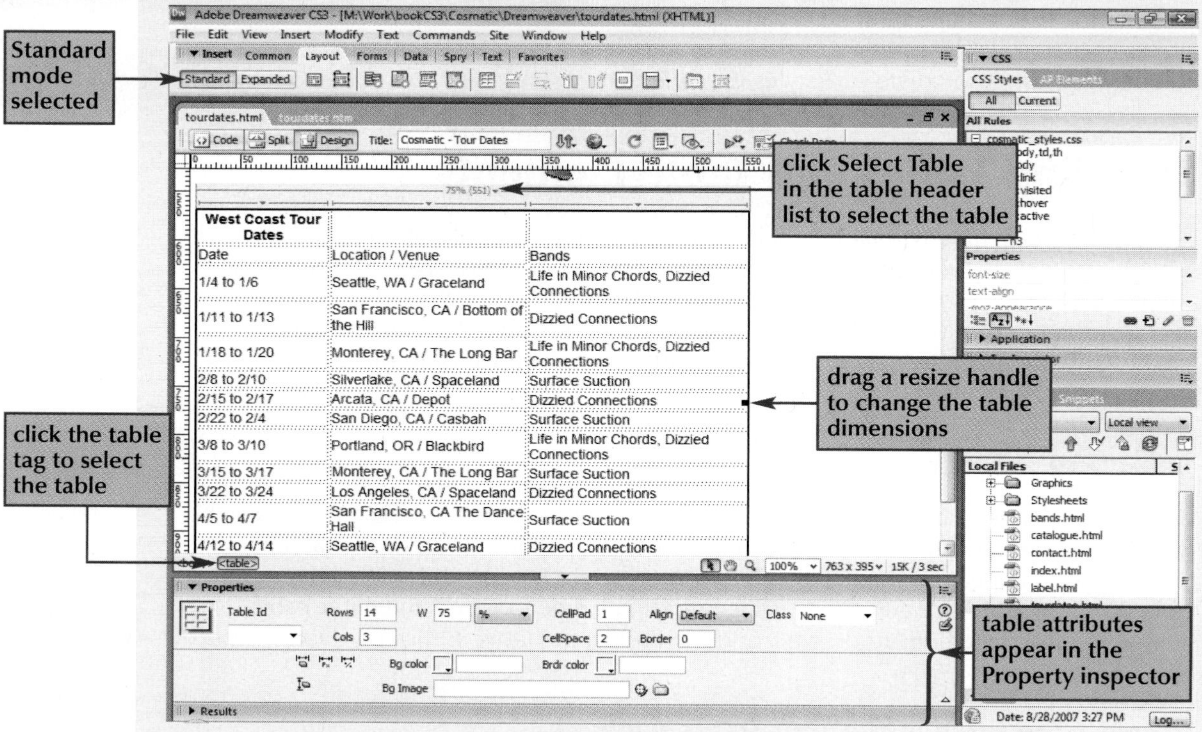

Standard mode selected

click Select Table in the table header list to select the table

drag a resize handle to change the table dimensions

click the table tag to select the table

table attributes appear in the Property inspector

▶ **4.** Click anywhere in the Document window outside the table to deselect it.

▶ **5.** Position the pointer over the upper-left corner of the table to change the pointer to ⌖⊞ , and then click. The entire table is selected.

Selecting a Table Cell

You must select a cell to adjust its attributes. The borders of a selected cell are bold black. Any content in the cell is selected as well. Clicking in a cell displays the cell properties in the Property inspector but does not select the cell. You can also select multiple cells. The borders of all the selected cells are bold black, and any content within the selected cells is also selected.

You'll select a single cell and a group of cells in the table in the Tour Dates page.

To select cells in the tour dates table:

Tip

To select a group of cells, press and hold the Ctrl key as you click in each cell.

▶ **1.** Press and hold the **Ctrl** key, click the cell at the upper-left corner of the table, and then release the **Ctrl** key. The cell is selected. See Figure 4-24.

Cell selected in the table ◀ **Figure 4-24**

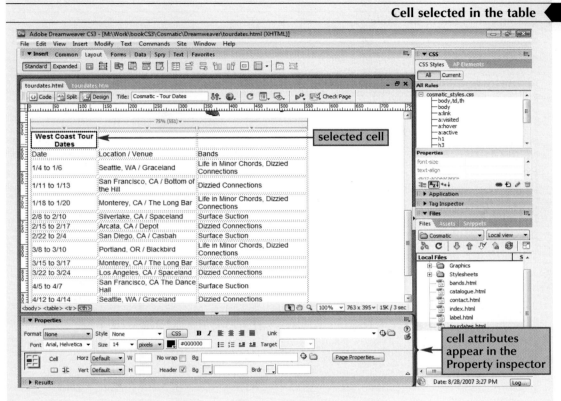

selected cell

cell attributes appear in the Property inspector

▶ **2.** Drag across the three cells in the top row until their borders are bold black. The three cells are selected.

▶ **3.** Click outside the table to deselect the cells.

Selecting Columns and Rows

You can use the mouse to select one or more columns or rows. The borders of all the cells in the selected column or row are bold. You can also tell that a column or row is selected because the word *Column* or *Row* appears in the Property inspector alongside an icon showing a highlighted column or row in a table. Selecting all the cells in a row or column is the same as selecting the row or column.

You'll select the third column in the table in the Tour Dates page, and then you'll select the second row of cells.

To select a row and a column in the tour dates table:

▶ **1.** Click in the table, click the **arrow** button above the top border of the third column of the table, and then click **Select Column**. The third column of the table is selected. See Figure 4-25.

| Figure 4-25 | Column selected in the table |

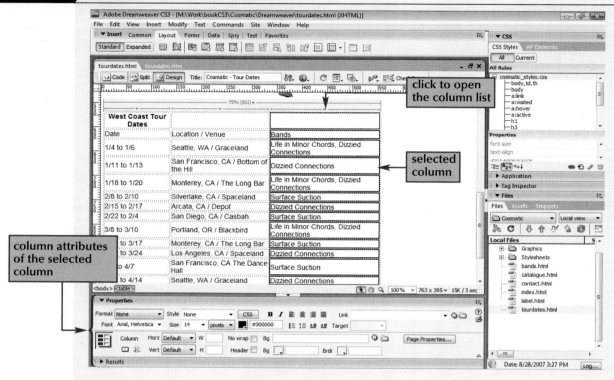

▶ **2.** Point outside the left border of the second row of the table. The pointer changes to ➡ .

▶ **3.** Click the mouse button. The second row of the table is selected.

▶ **4.** Click outside the table to deselect the row.

Tip

To select multiple columns or rows, drag across additional columns or rows.

Using Expanded Tables Mode

If you are having difficulty selecting a table element, you can use Expanded Tables mode. **Expanded Tables mode** temporarily adds cell padding and spacing to all of the tables in the page so that you can more easily select table elements and more precisely position the pointer inside cells. Tables in Expanded Tables mode might not be positioned precisely in the page because of the additional cell padding and spacing. Be sure that you return to Standard mode before you check the final page layout. You select tables and table elements in Expanded Tables mode in the same way you do in Standard mode.

You'll switch to Expanded Tables mode, and then select various table elements. When you are finished, you'll return to Standard mode.

To select elements of the tour dates table in Expanded Tables mode:

▶ 1. On the **Layout** tab of the Insert bar, click the **Expanded** button, and then click the **OK** button in the Getting Started in Expanded Tables Mode dialog box, if necessary. The page changes to Expanded Tables mode.

▶ 2. Click the left corner of the table. The table is selected and takes up more space in the page. See Figure 4-26.

Table selected in Expanded Tables mode ◀ | **Figure 4-26**

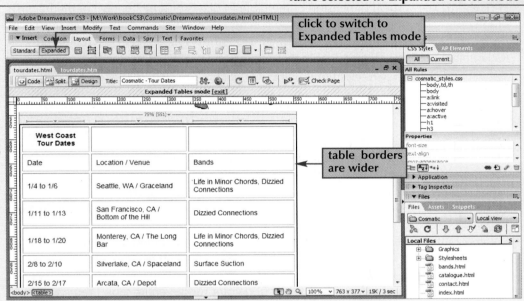

▶ 3. Click the **arrow** button above the first column, and then click **Select Column** to select the column.

▶ 4. Click outside of the table to deselect it, and then select the third row of the table. Notice that it is easier to select table elements when the borders are wider.

▶ 5. On the **Layout** tab of the Insert bar, click the **Standard** button. The page returns to Standard mode.

Working with the Entire Table

After a table is selected, you can change the attributes of the table, resize the table, move the table, or delete the table.

Modifying Table Attributes

You can change the attributes of an existing table in the Property inspector, you can create a CSS style with the table attributes you want to use, or you can create a CSS style to modify the <table> tag to change the attributes of all the tables in the site. When the entire table is selected, the Property inspector includes the attributes from the Table dialog box: rows, columns, width, border, cell padding, and cell spacing. It also includes the following additional formatting attributes:

- **Table ID.** A unique descriptive name for the table. The table name helps you to distinguish between multiple tables in a Web page. Also, some programming languages use the name to refer to the table. The Table ID must begin with a letter or underscore and can contain letters and numbers but not spaces or symbols.
- **H (Height).** The vertical dimension of the table in pixels or a percentage of the height of the browser window. Most of the time it is not necessary to specify a table height. If no Height value is entered, the cells remain at their default heights. Specifying the table height in pixels creates a table that has a somewhat fixed height (the table will still expand to fit the content, but it will not change size when the browser window is resized). Specifying the table height as a percentage creates a table that will adjust in size as the Web page is resized in the browser window.
- **Align.** The position of the table within the Web page. Table alignment can be the browser's default alignment, left, right, or center.
- **Clear row heights** and **Clear column widths.** Buttons that remove all row height and column width settings from the table.
- **Convert table widths to pixels** and **Convert table heights to pixels.** Buttons that change the table width or table height from a percentage to its current width or height in pixels.
- **Convert table widths to percent** and **Convert table heights to percent.** Buttons that change the current table width or height from pixels to a percentage of the browser window.
- **Bg color (Background color).** The background color for the entire table. You specify a color by typing its hexadecimal color code in the Bg color box or by selecting the color with the color picker. If a background color is not specified, the Web page background is seen through the table.
- **Brdr color (Border color).** The border color for the entire table. You can specify a color in the Brdr Color box or with the color picker.
- **Bg image (Background image).** The background image for the table. You can type the file path and filename in the Bg Image box, or you can use the Browse for File button or Point to File button to select a graphic file to use as the background image.

You'll name the table in the Tour Dates page and align the table to the center of the page.

InSight | **Previewing Tables in Different Browsers**

Differences occur in the way that browsers handle tables, such as the differences in the way browsers display table border color. Some versions of Firefox do not display the table border color correctly. Because of differences like this, it is very important to preview Web pages that use tables in all of the different browsers that you intend to support. If you find problems in the way a browser displays the tables you have created, you can look at sites such as *www.blooberry.com* as well as support sites from browser manufacturers such as *www.microsoft.com* and *www.firefox.com* to research issues and fixes for specific browsers and browser versions.

To change the tour dates table attributes:

▶ **1.** Select the table in the Tour Dates page.

▶ **2.** In the Property inspector, type **WestCoastTourDates** in the Table Id box.

▶ **3.** In the Property inspector, click the **Align** button, and then click **Center**. The table is centered in the page.

▶ **4.** In the Property inspector, double-click in the **CellPad** box, type **0**, double-click in the **CellSpace** box, type **0**, and then press the **Enter** key. The cell padding and cell spacing tighten up. See Figure 4-27.

Table with modified attributes ◀ **Figure 4-27**

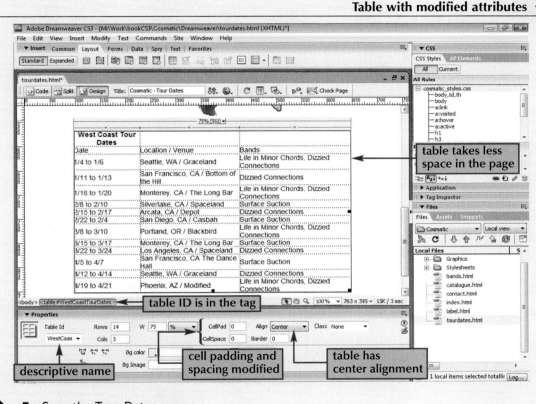

▶ **5.** Save the Tour Dates page.

Resizing and Moving a Table

Sometimes you know how you want a table to look on a page, but you don't know the exact dimensions to create that look. When a table is selected, you can adjust its size (height and width) and position it manually from within the Document window. As you drag the lower-right corner of the table, a dotted border indicates the resized table's new dimensions. The new width and height values are entered in the Property inspector. The values are calculated in the unit (percentage or pixels) specified for the attribute. If no height value was specified previously, the new value is in pixels. You can move a table on the page by cutting and pasting the table or by dragging the table to the new location.

You will adjust the size and location of the table in the Tour Dates page.

To resize and move a table:

▶ 1. If the rulers are not visible, click **View** on the menu bar, point to **Rulers**, and then click **Show**.

▶ 2. If the rulers' units are not set to pixels, click **View** on the menu bar, point to **Rulers**, and then click **Pixels**.

▶ 3. Click a **resize handle** on the table to make the Document window active and keep the table selected, and then point to the lower-right corner of the selected table. The pointer changes to ⬋ .

▶ 4. Press and hold the left mouse button, drag down and to the right about **200 pixels**, but do not release the mouse button. A dotted border shows the new dimensions of the table. See Figure 4-28.

Figure 4-28 ▶ Table being resized

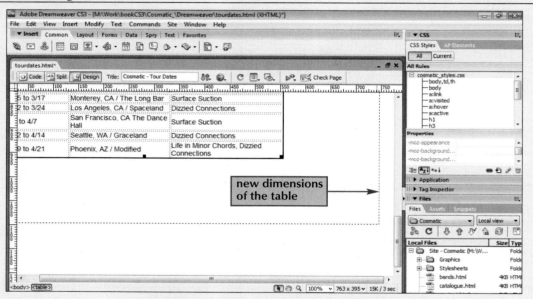

Trouble? If the exact numbers on your screen differ from those in Figure 4-28 (in other words, if the table is in a different position relative to the measurements on the rulers), then your screen size is different than the one shown in the figure. Continue with Step 5.

▶ 5. Release the mouse button. The Width changes to a different percentage in the Property inspector, reflecting the larger table size. The table doesn't need to be this large, so you'll try a smaller size.

▶ 6. Drag the lower-right corner of the table up and to the left about **300 pixels** to reduce the table size. The new Width percentage values appear in the Property inspector, reflecting the smaller table size.

The text is difficult to read in the smaller table, so you'll return to the original table size by resetting the values in the Property inspector.

▶ 7. In the Property inspector, double-click in the **W** box, type **75**, press the **Enter** key, and then make sure **%** is still selected. The table returns to its original size.

Next, you'll move the table to another location.

▶ **8.** Click **View** on the menu bar, point to **Rulers**, and then click **Show**. The rulers are hidden.

▶ **9.** Position the pointer in the upper-left corner of the selected table. The pointer changes to ⊞.

    Trouble? If you have difficulty getting the pointer to change to the correct shape, switch to Expanded Tables mode, perform Steps 9 through 11, and then return to Standard mode.

▶ **10.** Press and hold the left mouse button, and then drag the table above the map. The table moves to the new location.

    Trouble? If there is no blank line between the page heading and the map, release the mouse button when the indicator line is to the left of the map.

    The original position is more appropriate, so you'll move the table back to that location.

▶ **11.** Drag the table to its original position below the map, and then save the Tour Dates page.

    Trouble? If the window won't scroll when you try to reposition the table, move the pointer near the vertical scroll bar as you drag.

Deleting a Table

Sometimes you'll need to remove a table from a Web page. To delete a table, simply select the table and then press the Delete key. The table, as well as any content in the table, is deleted from the page.

Working with Table Cells

You can customize tables by modifying individual cells or groups of cells. When a cell or a group of cells is selected, you can change its attributes in the Property inspector, including modifying the formatting attributes of the cell content and changing the cell properties.

Modifying Cell Formatting and Layout

Cells have a different set of attributes than tables. You can change the attributes of a selected cell, and the attributes of any content within the cell, in the Property inspector. Cell attributes include text formatting, because within a table, content can be contained only in cells.

    You can format the content of an entire table by selecting all the cells in the table and then changing the text formatting attributes. Text formatting attributes are not available when you select the table itself, because the HTML code for text formatting is in the tags for the individual cells and rows, not in the code for the table itself. This setup allows for formatting variations within cells and makes tables more flexible.

    In addition to the familiar text formatting attributes, you can use the following options in the Property inspector to change the cell's layout attributes:

- **Merges selected cells using spans.** Joins all selected cells into one cell. This button is active only if more than one cell is selected.
- **Splits cell into rows or columns.** Divides a single cell into multiple rows or columns. This button is active only when a single cell is selected.
- **Horz (Horizontal).** The horizontal alignment options for the cell's content. Content can be aligned to the browser's default setting, left, right, or center.

- **Vert (Vertical).** The vertical alignment options for the cell's content. Content can be aligned to the browser's default setting, top, middle, bottom, or baseline.
- **No wrap.** Enables or disables word wrapping. Word wrapping enables a cell to expand horizontally and vertically to accommodate added content. If the No wrap check box is checked, the cell will expand only horizontally to accommodate the added content.
- **Header.** Formats the selected cell or rows as a table header. By default, the content of header cells is bold and centered; however, you can redefine the header cell tag with CSS styles to create a custom look.
- **Bg (Background image).** The background image for a cell, column, or row. You can type the file path and filename of the background image or browse to select the background image. If no image is specified, the Web page background is seen through the cell. The background image for a cell takes precedence over the background color for the cell. Also, the background image for a cell takes precedence over a background image or color for the table.
- **Bg (Background color).** The background color for the selected cells. You can specify a color by typing its hexadecimal color code in the Bg box or by selecting the color with the color picker. If no color is specified, the Web page background is seen through the cell. The background color for a cell takes precedence over the background image or color for the table.
- **Brdr (Border color).** The color of the cell border. You can type a hexadecimal color code in the Brdr box or select a color with the color picker. If the cell borders for the table are set to 0, the border is not seen.

When a single cell is selected, the word *Cell* and an icon of a table with a selected cell appear in the lower-left corner of the Property inspector. You can then verify that you have selected the correct element before you begin to adjust the attributes.

You'll merge the cells in the top row of the table and then make the new cell a header cell.

To merge the top row and make the new cell a header cell:

▶ **1.** Select the three cells in the top row of the table in the Tour Dates page.

▶ **2.** In the Property Inspector, click the **Merges Selected Cells Using Spans** button ▣ . The three cells are combined into one, and the text moves to the center of the table because this is a header cell. See Figure 4-29.

Three header cells merged into one header cell ◀ **Figure 4-29**

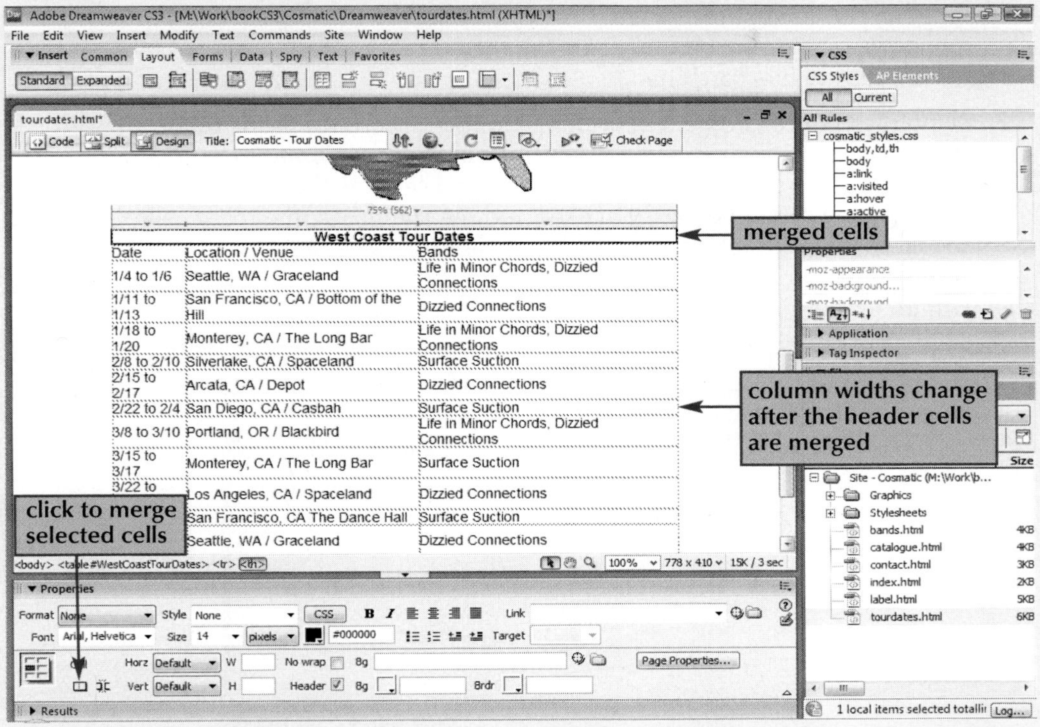

Trouble? If the header row is not formatted, you need to reapply the style to the text. In the Property inspector, click the Header check box to insert a check mark.

▶ **3.** Save the Tour Dates page.

Adjusting the Row Span and Column Span of Cells

You can adjust the height and width of individual cells of a table. **Row span** is the height of the cell measured in rows. **Column span** is the width of the cell measured in columns. You can change the row and column spans by increments of one. For example, increasing a cell's row span makes the selected cell span the height of two rows of the table. If you increase the row span of a cell twice, the cell becomes three rows high. Decreasing the row span removes one increment. If a cell is only one row high, decreasing the row span does not work. Adjusting column span works the same way. Increasing the column span of a cell makes the selected cell span the width of two columns of the table. If you increase the column span of a cell twice, it becomes three columns wide. Decreasing the column span removes one increment. If a cell is only one column wide, decreasing the column span does not work.

You'll adjust the row span and the column span of cells in the table in the Tour Dates page.

To adjust row span and column span of cells in the tour dates table:

▶ 1. Right-click the cell in the first column and the second row of the table, point to **Table** on the context menu, and then click **Increase Row Span**. The cell's height spans two table rows. (Actually, the cell merges with the one below it and the content of both cells is combined.)

▶ 2. Right-click the cell in the first column and the second row of the table, point to **Table** on the context menu, and then click **Increase Column Span**. The cell's width spans two table columns. Because the merged cell was the height of two cells in the adjoining column before you executed the command, the three cells merged and all of the cell content was combined. See Figure 4-30.

Figure 4-30 ▶ **Cell with increased row and column spans**

merged cell ▶

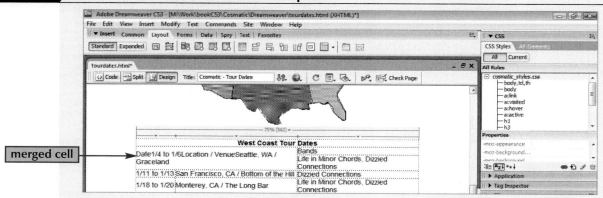

The cell doesn't need to have a different height or width, so you'll decrease the row span and the column span.

▶ 3. Right-click the cell in the first column and the second row of the table, point to **Table** on the context menu, and then click **Decrease Row Span**.

▶ 4. Right-click the cell in the first column and the second row of the table, point to **Table** on the context menu, and then click **Decrease Column Span**. The cell's height and width return to their original settings, but all the text is still in one cell.

▶ 5. Right-click the cell in the first column and the third row of the table, point to **Table**, and then click **Decrease Column Span**. The cell's height and width return to their original settings.

▶ 6. Select **1/4 to 1/6** in the cell in the first column and the second row, press the **Ctrl+X** keys to cut the selected text, click in the first cell in the third row in the table, and then press the **Ctrl+V** keys to paste the cut text.

▶ 7. Select **Location / Venue** from the first cell in the second row, and drag the selected text into the cell in the second column and second row of the table.

▶ 8. Use either method to move **Seattle, WA / Graceland** from the first cell in the second row into the cell in the second column and third row of the table. The text is in the correct cells again.

▶ 9. Save the Tour Dates page.

Tip

You can also restore the table to its original state by pressing the Ctrl+Z keys until all the changes are undone.

Working with Rows and Columns

Table rows and columns provide the vertical and horizontal structure for the content of the table as well as for the content of some Web pages. When a row or column is selected, you can change its attributes and resize, add, or delete the entire row or column. Selecting all of the cells in a row or column is the same as selecting the row or column.

Modifying Rows and Columns

The attribute options available for rows and columns are the same as those for cells. When you modify attributes while a row or column is selected, the changes apply to all of the cells in the selected row or column. Before you change attributes, you should verify that the correct element is selected by looking in the Property inspector.

You want to change the second row of the table to a header row.

To change row attributes in the tour dates table:

▶ **1.** Select the second row of the table.

▶ **2.** In the Property inspector, click the **Header** check box to insert a check mark. The content of each cell in the row is centered and in boldface.

▶ **3.** Save the Tour Dates page.

Resizing Columns and Rows

When a table is created, columns are all of equal width and rows are all the default height. You can adjust the width of a selected column by typing a new value in the W (Width) box or by dragging a column's left or right border to the desired position. When you adjust a column width manually, Dreamweaver calculates the width you selected. You can adjust the height of a selected row by typing a new height value into the H (Height) box or by dragging the row's top or bottom border to the desired position. When you adjust a row height manually, Dreamweaver calculates the height you selected. You can press the Shift key as you drag a row or column border to retain the other row or column sizes.

You'll resize the columns in the table to better fit the content.

To resize columns in the tour dates table:

▶ **1.** Position the pointer on the right border of the first column. The pointer changes to ╫.

▶ **2.** Drag the border so that the content in the first column appears on only one line, if necessary. When you increase the first column's width, the second column width decreases, causing the text in some cells to wrap to fill two lines. See Figure 4-31.

Figure 4-31 ▶ **Resizing a table column**

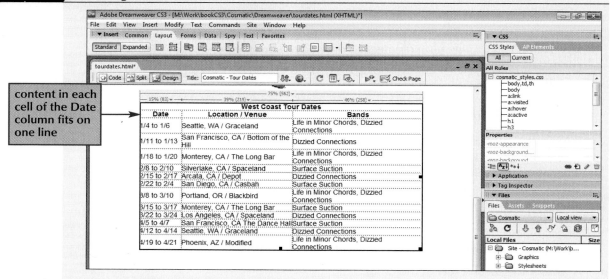

content in each
cell of the Date
column fits on
one line

▶ **3.** Point to the right border of the second column, and then drag the border so that the content in the cell in the fourth row from the top fills one line, if necessary.

▶ **4.** Point to the right border of the third column, and then hold the **Shift** key as you drag the border so that the content in the cell in the third row from the top fills only one line.

▶ **5.** Save the Tour Dates page.

Adding and Deleting Columns and Rows

As you work, you might find you need more or fewer columns and rows in a table. To insert a column, you select a cell or a column and use the Insert Column command. A new column of the same width as the selected cell or column is inserted to the left of the selection. To insert a row, you select a cell or a row and use the Insert Row command. The new row is added above the selected cell or row. You can also add a new row at the end of the table by clicking in the last cell of the table and pressing the Tab key. You can add multiple columns or rows by using the Insert Rows or Columns command; when you click this command, a dialog box opens and you set the number of columns or rows you want to insert and where you want to insert them relative to the selection.

If you need to remove extra columns or rows, you can select the column or row and then use the Delete Column or Delete Row command. Be aware that all of the content in that column or row is also deleted. You can also press the Delete key to remove a selected column or row and all of its content.

Brian tells you that the shows in Phoenix on 4/19 to 4/21 have been postponed. He asks you to delete the row with that information from the table.

To delete the row with the Phoenix tour dates:

▶ **1.** Select the last row of the table.

▶ **2.** Right-click the selected row, point to **Table** on the context menu, and then click **Delete Row**. The row and all its content are removed from the table.

▶ **3.** If necessary, delete any extra blank rows from the table.

▶ **4.** Save the Tour Dates page.

Using CSS to Format a Table

The correct way to format tables is with CSS styles. Although some formatting options such as background color, border color, and background image are available in the Property inspector when table elements are selected, these table formatting options are deprecated in the current version of XHTML. The proper way to format tables is by creating a series of CSS styles and applying those styles to the table elements. You can apply styles to the entire table, rows, columns, cells, and even the table content.

Brian asks you to create two row styles for the West Coast Tour Dates table. You will apply these styles to alternating rows of the table.

To format a table with CSS styles:

▶ **1.** In the CSS Styles panel, click the **New CSS Rule** button 🔳 . The New CSS Rule dialog box opens.

▶ **2.** Click the **Class** option button, type **.row** in the Name box, define the rule in the **cosmatic_styles.css** style sheet, and then click the **OK** button. The new rule is added to the Cosmatic styles.

▶ **3.** Click **Background** in the Category box, type **#878816** in the Background Color box, and then click the **OK** button. The background color of the table is added to the style.

You'll apply the new .row style to the tour dates table.

▶ **4.** Select the first row of the West Coast Tour Dates table, press and hold the **Ctrl** key as you select every other row in the table, and then release the **Ctrl** key. Alternating rows in the table are selected.

▶ **5.** In the Property inspector, click the **Style** arrow, click **row**, and then press the **Right Arrow** key. The rows are deselected and the .row style is applied to the rows. See Figure 4-32.

Figure 4-32   **Table with alternating rows formatted**

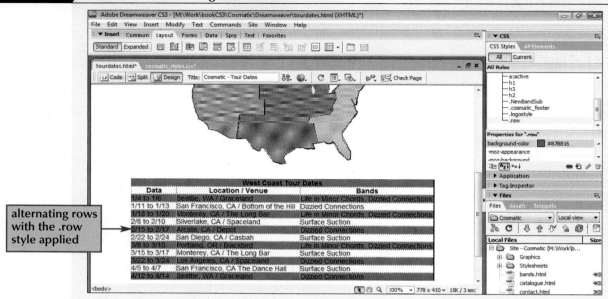

alternating rows with the .row style applied

▶ **6.** In the CSS Styles panel, click the **New CSS Rule** button ⊞ . The New CSS Rule dialog box opens. You'll create a style to apply to the alternate rows in the table.

▶ **7.** Click the **Class** option button, type **.row_alt** in the Name box, define the rule in the **cosmatic_styles.css** page, and then click the **OK** button.

▶ **8.** Click **Background** in the Category box, type **#E0AE4D** in the Background Color box, and then click the **OK** button.

▶ **9.** Select the second row of the West Coast Tour Dates table, press the **Ctrl** key as you select every other row, release the **Ctrl** key, select **row_alt** in the Style list in the Property inspector, and then press the **Right Arrow** key to deselect the rows. Alternating rows of the table are formatted with the new style. See Figure 4-33.

Figure 4-33   **Table with new format attributes applied**

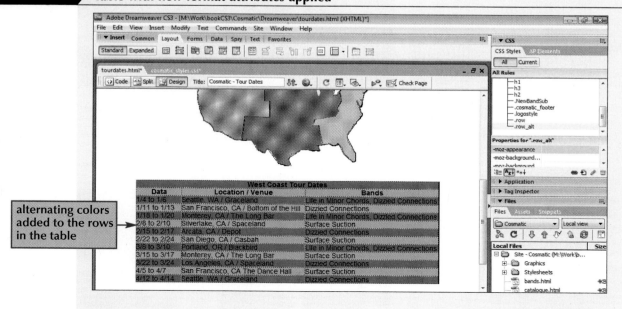

alternating colors added to the rows in the table

▶ **10.** Save and close the cosmatic_styles.css page, save the tourdates.html page, preview the page in a browser, and then close the Tour Dates page.

Exploring the HTML Code of Tables

Four types of tags are associated with tables: table tags, table row tags, header cell tags, and cell tags. Although you can select columns of cells, no HTML tags exist to define columns. All of the tags associated with tables are **bracketing tags**, which consist of an opening tag and a closing tag that bracket the content to which they are applied. The tags' parameters are explained in the following list:

- **Table tags.** A set of table tags that surrounds every table. Table tags take the form:

```
<table attribute1="value" attribute2="value">tags defining table
rows and cells</table>
```

If you apply attributes to the entire table (when the table is selected), the parameters for those attributes appear in the opening table tag.

- **Table row tags.** A set of row tags surrounds every row. An opening table row tag always appears after the opening table tag, because every table must have at least one row. Table row tags take the form:

```
<tr>all the tags for the cells in the row</tr>
```

If you apply attributes to a row of cells, the parameters for those attributes usually appear in the tags for the cells, not in the tag for the row.

- **Cell tags.** A set of cell tags surrounds every cell (except those cells you designate as header cells). Cell tags are nested inside the row tags. Every table must have at least one cell. Cell tags take the form:

```
<td attribute1="value" attribute2="value">text in the cell</td>
```

Every cell in the table has its own set of cell tags (unless it is a header cell), and any attributes applied to the cell are contained in the opening cell tag. Attributes that you apply to columns appear in the cell tags for each cell in the column. If you check the Apply All Attributes to TD Tags Instead of TR Tags check box in the Format Table dialog box, then the row attributes you apply will appear in the cell tags as well.

- **Header cell tags.** A set of header cell tags surrounds every cell that you designate as a header cell by checking the Header Cell check box in the Property inspector while the cell is selected. Like regular cell tags, header cell tags are nested between the row tags. Header cell tags take the form:

```
<th attribute1="value" attribute2="value">text in the cell</th>
```

Every header cell in the table has its own set of header cell tags, and any attributes applied to the cell are contained in the opening tag.

A table may seem complex; however, all table code can be broken down into the four types of tags described above.

Figure 4-34 shows the table in the Tour Dates page in Code view.

Figure 4-34 Table tags in Code view

opening table tag with table attributes

opening table heading cell in row 1

three table heading cells in row 2

three regular cells in the other rows

table row tags for the first row

closing table tag

```
46  <table width="75%" border="0" align="center" cellpadding="0" cellspacing="0" id=
    "WestCoastTourDates">
47    <tr class="row">
48      <th colspan="3">West Coast Tour Dates</th>
49    </tr>
50    <tr class="row_alt">
51      <th width="15%">Data</th>
52      <th width="41%">Location / Venue</th>
53      <th width="44%">Bands</th>
54    </tr>
55    <tr class="row">
56      <td>1/4 to 1/6</td>
57      <td>Seattle, WA / Graceland</td>
58      <td>Life in Minor Chords, Dizzied Connections</td>
59    </tr>
60    <tr class="row_alt">
61      <td>1/11 to 1/13</td>
62      <td>San Francisco, CA / Bottom of the Hill</td>
63      <td>Dizzied Connections</td>
64    </tr>
65    <tr class="row">
66      <td>1/18 to 1/20</td>
67      <td>Monterey, CA / The Long Bar</td>
68      <td>Life in Minor Chords, Dizzied Connections</td>
69    </tr>
70    <tr class="row_alt">
71      <td>2/8 to 2/10</td>
72      <td>Silverlake, CA / Spaceland</td>
73      <td>Surface Suction</td>
74    </tr>
75    <tr class="row">
76      <td>2/15 to 2/17</td>
77      <td>Arcata, CA / Depot</td>
78      <td>Dizzied Connections</td>
79    </tr>
80    <tr class="row_alt">
81      <td>2/22 to 2/24</td>
82      <td>San Diego, CA / Casbah</td>
83      <td>Surface Suction</td>
84    </tr>
85    <tr class="row">
86      <td>3/8 to 3/10</td>
87      <td>Portland, OR / Blackbird</td>
88      <td>Life in Minor Chords, Dizzied Connections</td>
89    </tr>
90    <tr class="row_alt">
91      <td>3/15 to 3/17</td>
92      <td>Monterey, CA / The Long Bar</td>
93      <td>Surface Suction</td>
94    </tr>
95    <tr class="row">
96      <td>3/22 to 3/24</td>
97      <td>Los Angeles, CA / Spaceland</td>
98      <td>Dizzied Connections</td>
99    </tr>
100   <tr class="row_alt">
101     <td>4/5 to 4/7</td>
102     <td>San Francisco, CA The Dance Hall</td>
103     <td>Surface Suction</td>
104   </tr>
105   <tr class="row">
106     <td>4/12 to 4/14</td>
107     <td>Seattle, WA / Graceland</td>
108     <td>Dizzied Connections</td>
109   </tr>
110 </table>
111 <p> </p>
112 <h1 align="center"><br />
113 </h1>
114 </body>
115 </html>
116
```

In this session, you created a table, added content, and formatted the table in both Standard mode and Extended Tables mode. In the next session, you'll work with a layout table in Layout mode.

Session 4.2 Quick Check | Review

1. What is a table cell?
2. True or False? Table borders can be invisible.
3. Explain the difference between cell padding and cell spacing.
4. Explain what pressing the Tab key does when you are entering data into a table.
5. Describe what happens when you merge two cells.
6. What is the opening HTML tag for a table row?
7. What is the opening HTML tag for a table cell?

Session 4.3

Planning a Table in Layout Mode

Designers most often use CSS to provide structure for the layout of Web pages. However, you still need to understand and know how to use tables for layout because many existing Web sites are structured with tables and you will likely encounter them at some point. Also, if you are creating a site for older browsers or other devices that do not fully support CSS functionality, you might need to use tables to structure the page layout.

To make it easier to create tables for Web page layout, you can switch to Layout mode, which enables you to draw table cells and tables directly in an empty Web page. Drawing individual cells is the most common way of working in Layout mode. When you draw a cell in the page, Dreamweaver adds a table that fills the page and additional cells that hold your cell in position. The cells you draw are transparent with blue outlines; the cells Dreamweaver creates are translucent gray with white outlines. When you add additional cells, Dreamweaver modifies the cells it created to hold all your cells in place. This method is far more convenient than creating a table in Standard mode and then merging and splitting the cells yourself.

You can also draw tables in Layout mode. In an empty page, the table is positioned in the upper-left corner of the page. When you draw cells in the table, Dreamweaver creates additional cells to hold yours in place. Additional layout tables created outside the original table will be flush with the lower-left corner of the top table. You cannot leave space between layout tables because they provide structure for the page, and leaving spaces between tables makes their position less stable.

If you want to add rows and columns that do not align with the structure of the rows and columns you already created, you can draw another table inside an existing table. Another option is to draw a table that surrounds an existing layout table to create a **nested table**. The inside table is the nested table. You cannot draw a nested table inside a cell you created; you can only draw a nested table inside a cell that Dreamweaver created to hold your cells in place.

After you created tables in Layout mode, you can add, resize, and adjust the elements on the page. You cannot create a table in Layout mode if the Web page already contains any content. However, you can adjust and resize existing tables even after content has been added to the page. You can switch back and forth between Standard mode and Layout mode when you are working on tables. Any table selected in Standard mode is considered a regular table, and any table selected in Layout mode is considered a layout table. This is true regardless of the view in which the table was created.

InSight | **Planning a Table**

It is a good idea to sketch the tables for the layout of a Web page before you start to create them. Just like planning the Web site, planning the placement of the cells and tables on the page will help you avoid reworking the page elements, saving you time and frustration in the end. Planning the page layout enables you to determine where to place the cells and tables on the page so that the information can be conveyed effectively.

Brian wants you to add a new page titled "What's Hot" to the Cosmatic site to promote new CD releases. A link from the home page of the site, when clicked, will load the What's Hot page in a new browser window. The What's Hot page will use tables for structure. It will not have a navigation system because it is a pop-up promotion instead of a regular page in the site. Figure 4-35 shows a sketch of the layout for the new page.

Figure 4-35 | **Sketch of the layout for the new What's Hot page**

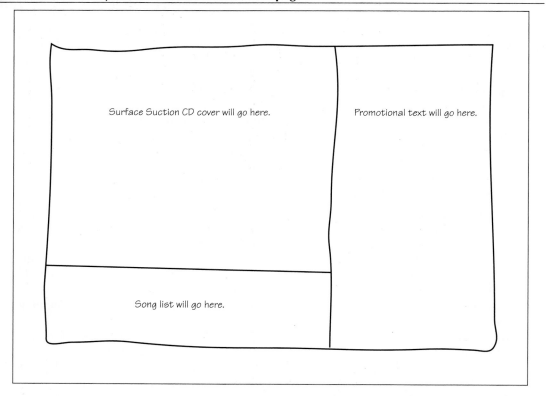

Surface Suction CD cover will go here.

Promotional text will go here.

Song list will go here.

You'll start by creating the What's Hot page, adding a page heading, and attaching the external style sheet to the page.

To create the What's Hot page and attach the Cosmatic style sheet:

1. If you took a break after the previous session, make sure that the Cosmatic site is open.

2. In the Create New list on the Start page, click **HTML**. A new page opens in the Document window.

3. Type **Cosmatic - What's Hot** in the Title box on the Document toolbar, and then press the **Enter** key.

4. Click **File** menu on the menu bar, click **Save As** to open the Save As dialog box, navigate to the local root folder of your Cosmatic site, type **whatshot.html** in the File Name box, and then click the **Save** button. The whatshot.html page is saved to the local root folder and appears in the Files panel.

5. In the CSS Styles panel, click the **Attach Style Sheet** button. The Attach External Style Sheet dialog box opens.

6. If necessary, click the **Browse** button, navigate to the **Stylesheets** folder in the local root folder of your Cosmatic site, and then double-click the **cosmatic_styles.css** external style sheet.

7. Click the **OK** button, and then save the What's Hot page.

Tip

To create a new page, you can also click File on the menu bar, click New, click Blank Page in the category list, click HTML in the Page Type list, and then click the Create button.

Creating a Table in Layout Mode

You'll create a layout table for the What's Hot page in Layout mode. In Layout mode, you create a table either by drawing a cell and having Dreamweaver create a table around it or by drawing a table and populating it with cells.

Creating a Table in Layout Mode | Reference Window

- Click View on the menu bar, point to Table Mode, and then click Layout Mode.
- On the Layout tab of the Insert bar, click the Draw Layout Cell button, and then drag on the page to draw a table cell.
- On the Layout tab of the Insert bar, click the Draw Layout Table button, and then drag on the page to draw a table.

You'll start by switching to Layout mode.

To switch the What's Hot page to Layout mode:

1. Click the **Layout** tab on the Insert bar, if necessary. The Standard button is selected.

2. Click **View** on the menu bar, point to **Table Mode**, and then click **Layout Mode**. The Document window is in Layout mode, as indicated by the light blue-gray bar with the words *Layout mode [exit]* at the top of the Document window.

   Trouble? If the Getting Started in Layout Mode dialog box opens, click the OK button.

3. If the rulers are not displayed, click **View** on the menu bar, point to **Rulers**, and then click **Show**.

4. If the ruler units are not in pixels, click **View** on the menu bar, point to **Rulers**, and then click **Pixels**.

Drawing Cells in Layout Mode

You can use the Draw Layout Cell button on the Layout tab of the Insert bar to create a table or to add cells to an existing table (even if you drew the table in Standard mode). A cell cannot exist outside a table. If you draw a cell before you have drawn a table or if you draw a cell outside a table, Dreamweaver creates a table around the cell to fill the Document window. The number and placement of cells created to fill this table depend on the size of the Document window. Cells you create have a white background; additional cells that Dreamweaver creates to maintain the structure are gray. Cells cannot overlap.

As you draw a cell, its measurements, in pixels, appear on the status bar. You can use these measurements or the rulers at the top and left of the Document window to help you draw accurately sized cells.

You'll draw a cell in Layout mode in the What's Hot page. This cell will be used to position the CD cover graphic.

To draw a cell for the CD cover graphic in Layout mode:

▶ **1.** On the **Layout** tab of the Insert bar, click the **Draw Layout Cell** button ▦ . The pointer changes to ┼ .

▶ **2.** Click in the upper-left corner of the What's Hot page, and drag down diagonally to draw a square cell approximately **230 pixels** by **230 pixels**, but do not release the mouse button. You can use the rulers to help you measure, or you can use the pixel measurements in the status bar as a guide. See Figure 4-36.

Figure 4-36 ▶	Table cell being drawn in Layout mode

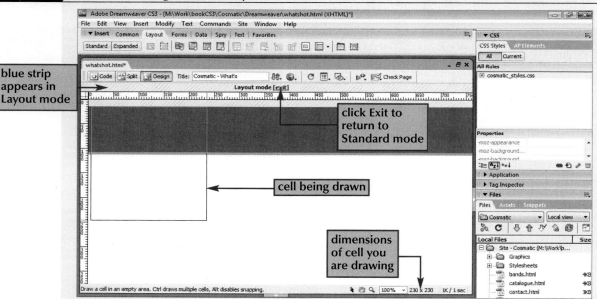

▶ **3.** Release the mouse button. The transparent cell you drew and any gray structure cells that Dreamweaver drew appear in a table that fills the Document window. The cell's outline is red when the pointer is over it and blue when the pointer is elsewhere on the screen. See Figure 4-37.

Cell drawn in Layout mode ◄ **Figure 4-37**

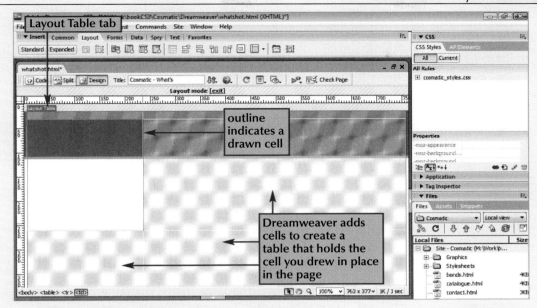

4. In the lower-right corner of the Property inspector, click the **Collapse arrow** button △ to collapse the Property inspector to two rows. The gray cells that Dreamweaver drew expand to fill the resized Document window.

5. In the Property inspector, click the **Expander arrow** button ▽ to expand the Property inspector to its full size. The gray cells return to their original size.

Drawing a Table in Layout Mode

You can use the Draw Layout Table button to draw a table in the same way that you drew a cell. After you draw a table, you need to add cells. You can add more than one table to a page; you can even add a nested table within a table by simply drawing it there. Nested tables are beneficial because each table retains its own attributes. However, some older browsers have difficulty displaying nested tables properly, so consider your target audience before you create a complex table structure for a page layout.

Brian asks you to create an additional table in the What's Hot page to hold the promotional text.

To create another table in the What's Hot page in Layout mode:

1. On the **Layout** tab of the Insert bar, click the **Draw Layout Table** button 🔲 .

2. To the right of the existing cell (and inside the existing table), drag to draw a table that is approximately **230 pixels** by **230 pixels**. The green outline indicates a table in Layout mode. See Figure 4-38.

Figure 4-38 ▸ **Nested table in Layout mode**

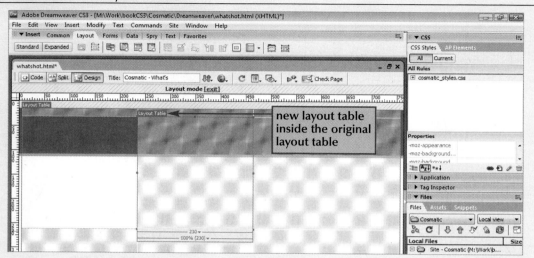

3. On the **Layout** tab of the Insert bar, click the **Draw Layout Cell** button ⬚ , and then draw one cell in the new table that is the same size as the table. The cell you create has a blue outline. See Figure 4-39.

Figure 4-39 ▸ **Nested table and cell in Layout mode**

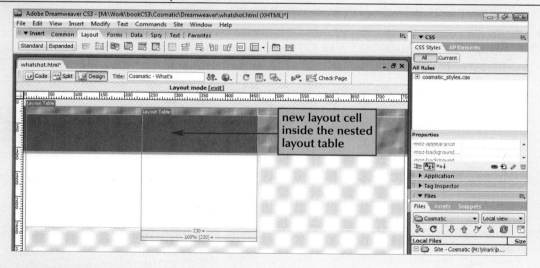

4. Save the What's Hot page.

Selecting Tables and Cells in Layout Mode

After you create a table, you can work with it in Layout mode in much the same way you work with tables in Standard mode. Just like Standard mode, before you can move, size, and format tables or cells, they must be selected.

Selecting Tables in Layout Mode

You select tables in Layout mode by clicking anywhere in them. You can also click the Layout Table tab at the upper-left corner of the table. To select a table that is completely filled with a cell, you must click the Layout Table tab. After you select a table, the table border changes from a dotted green line to a solid green line, and green resize handles surround the table. Also, an image of a table and the words *Layout Table* appear in the upper-left corner of the Property inspector to indicate that a table in Layout mode is selected. You need to select a table to make any other changes to it.

You'll select the tables in the What's Hot page in Layout mode.

To select the tables in the What's Hot page in Layout mode:

1. Click anywhere in the outer table. The resize handles appear and the outer table is selected.

2. Click the **Layout Table** tab at the top of the nested table. The resize handles appear, and the nested table is selected, as indicated in the Property inspector. See Figure 4-40.

Selected nested table in Layout mode | **Figure 4-40**

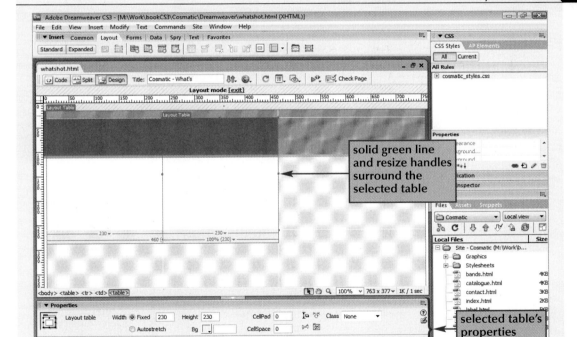

Selecting Cells in Layout Mode

You can also select cells in Layout mode. When the pointer is positioned over the border of an unselected cell that you created, the border changes from a dotted blue line to a solid red line. You select a cell in Layout mode by clicking the cell's border. When a cell is selected, the perimeter changes to a solid blue line and resize handles appear. Also, an image of a cell and the words *Layout Cell* appear in the Property inspector. Cells in Layout mode can be **active**—ready to accept input—but not selected. When a cell in Layout mode is active, the cell border is a solid blue line and the insertion point blinks inside the cell, but no resize handles appear.

You will select a cell on the layout table in the What's Hot page.

To select a cell in the layout table in the What's Hot page in Layout mode:

▶ 1. Point to the perimeter of the left cell. The cell perimeter turns red.

▶ 2. Click the red cell perimeter. The cell is selected. The perimeter of the selected cell changes to a solid blue line and its resize handles are visible. See Figure 4-41.

| Figure 4-41 | Selected cell in Layout mode |

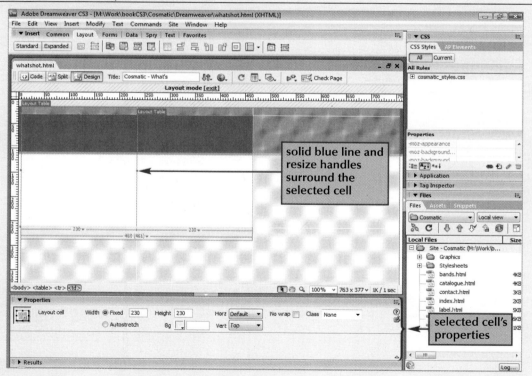

▶ 3. Select the right cell, position the pointer inside the cell, and then click. The resize handles disappear and the cell is active but not selected.

Working with Tables in Layout Mode

After a table or cell in Layout mode is selected, you can change its attributes, resize it, move it, or delete it.

Resizing Tables in Layout Mode

Once a table has been selected in Layout mode, you can drag the table's resize handles to change its size. Nested tables can be moved freely within the outer table. A nested table cannot overlap a cell that you drew in Layout mode, but it can overlap the gray cells that Dreamweaver drew to hold the cells that you created in place. Tables in Layout mode can also be resized by changing the attributes in the Property inspector while the table is selected.

You'll resize the tables in the What's Hot page.

To move and resize the tables in the What's Hot page in Layout mode:

▶ **1.** Click the upper-left **Layout Table** tab twice to select the outer table.

▶ **2.** Drag the right **resize handle** to the right until the width of the table is approximately **815 pixels**. (Remember to use the rulers.) You will need to scroll to see the entire page.

▶ **3.** Click the **Collapse arrow** ▼ in the Property inspector title bar to collapse the Property inspector entirely, and then drag the bottom **resize handle** until the table is approximately **500 pixels** high.

▶ **4.** Click the **Layout Table** tab at the top of the nested table twice, and then drag the table tab down to move the nested table below the first layout cell you drew. See Figure 4-42.

| Nested layout table repositioned in the page | Figure 4-42 |

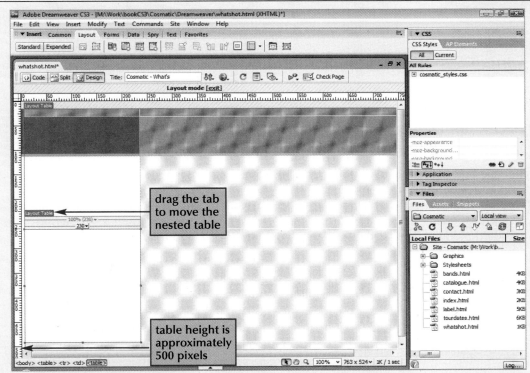

▶ **5.** Scroll to the bottom of the Document window, click the bottom (green) border of the outer table to select the outer table, and then drag the bottom **resize handle** of the outer table up so that the bottom of the outer table is flush with the bottom of the table you just moved.

▶ **6.** Drag the **Layout Table** tab of the nested table back to its original position, and then drag the bottom **resize handle** of the nested table down to meet the bottom of the outer table (so that the nested table is approximately **500 pixels** high). See Figure 4-43.

Figure 4-43 **Resized tables in Layout mode**

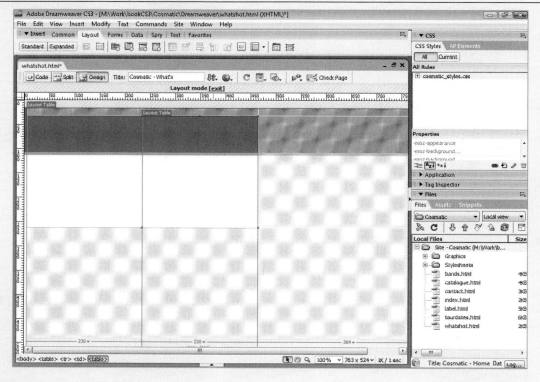

▶ **7.** Save the page.

Modifying Table Attributes in Layout Mode

You can add formatting to customize tables either by changing their attributes in the Property inspector or by applying CSS styles to the table. The attributes are visible in the Property inspector when a table is selected in Layout mode. The attributes in the Property inspector for tables selected in Layout mode are similar to those for tables selected in Standard mode except for the Autostretch option, Border, and Border Color. Table attributes in Layout mode include:

• **Width.** The horizontal dimension of the table. The two types of widths in Layout mode are fixed and autostretch. Fixed width is a numeric value, specified in pixels, that does not change when you add content to the cell, and it applies to the entire table. You can enter a fixed width in the Property inspector. Autostretch sets the width of one column to resize automatically with the width of the browser window. Only one column in each table can be set to autostretch. To create a table that autostretches, you select the Autostretch option in the Property inspector and then designate which column you want to autostretch. The default option is fixed width, which you establish when you drag to create the table.

- **Height.** The vertical dimension of the table in pixels. Dreamweaver calculates the height when you draw the table and displays it in the Height box. You can modify this by typing a new value in the Height box.
- **Bg (background color).** The background color for the table. You enter the hexadecimal color code in the Bg box or use the color picker to select a color. If a background color is not specified, the Web page background is seen through the table.
- **CellPad (cell padding).** The amount of empty space, measured in pixels, maintained between the border of a cell and the cell's content. When you don't specify cell padding, most browsers display the table as if the cell padding were set to 1.
- **CellSpace (cell spacing).** The width of the invisible cell walls, measured in pixels. If the border is set to 0, then the table structure will be invisible despite thick walls. When you don't specify cell spacing, most browsers display the table as if the cell spacing were set to 2.
- **Clear row heights.** Removes the height settings for all the cells in a selected table. If there are no cells in the selected table when you clear row heights, the table will collapse completely.
- **Make cell widths consistent.** Resets the widths of the fixed-width cells in the selected table to match the cell content when the cell content is wider than the fixed width.
- **Remove all spacers.** Removes all of the spacer images from the selected layout table. A **spacer image** is a one-pixel transparent image that is inserted into the fixed-width columns in a table created in Layout mode that contains an autostretch column to maintain the widths of the fixed-width columns.
- **Remove nesting.** Deletes a selected nested table and adds the cells and their content to the parent table.

Tables that are used for layout are often designated as autostretch to enable the Web page content to adjust to the size of the user's browser window. When you format a table as autostretch, you are prompted to create and use a spacer image. The spacer image maintains a minimum width for the fixed-width columns in a table with an autostretch column. Without spacer images, the fixed-width columns in a table with an autostretch column might disappear in Design view. The first time you choose autostretch in a Web site, you can choose to have Dreamweaver create a spacer image file, select an existing graphic file as the spacer image, or not use spacer images in autostretch tables. Usually, you want Dreamweaver to create a spacer image. When prompted, store the spacer image Dreamweaver creates in the Graphics folder for the site.

When a column in a table is set to autostretch in Layout mode, a double set of wavy lines appears at the top of the column. When a column in a table has a fixed width, in Layout mode the numeric value of the width appears at the top of the column in the Document window. The sum of the values of the column widths of the table equals the width of the table.

Brian asks you to set the attributes for the outer table in the What's Hot page. You will change the table to an autostretch table so that the table contents can scale in the user's browser window. You will have Dreamweaver create a spacer image and place it in the Graphics folder in the site's local root folder. You will also change the height of the table to accommodate the graphic and text that you will place in the table.

To set attributes for the What's Hot page table in Layout mode:

▶ 1. Scroll to the top of the Document window, if necessary, click the **Layout Table** tab of the outer table twice to select the outer table, and then expand the Property inspector.

▶ **2.** Click the **Autostretch** option button in the Property inspector to set the width of the selected table to autostretch. The Choose Spacer Image dialog box opens because you have not yet set autostretch options for this site.

Trouble? If the Choose Spacer Image dialog box does not open, continue with Step 4.

▶ **3.** Click the **Create a Spacer Image File** option button, if necessary, click the **OK** button, navigate to the **Graphics** folder within the local root folder of your Cosmatic site, and then click the **Save** button. Dreamweaver continues to use the spacer image you selected for all the layout tables in the site; you specify the spacer image only once.

▶ **4.** In the Property inspector, double-click in the **Height** box, type **650**, and then press the **Enter** key.

▶ **5.** Save the page.

Deleting a Layout Table

You might need to delete a table in Layout mode. To delete a table, you select the table and press the Delete key, just as you would delete a table in Standard mode. If you want to delete a nested table, including the cells and content in the nested table, you select the nested table and press the Delete key. If you want to delete a nested table but add the cells and content from the nested table to the outer table, you first select the nested table and then click the Remove Nesting button in the Property inspector.

You'll delete the nested table from the What's Hot page, but you'll add the cells and content to the outer table.

To delete the nested table from the What's Hot page in Layout mode:

▶ **1.** Select the nested table in the What's Hot page.

▶ **2.** In the Property inspector, click the **Remove Nesting** button 🖾 . The nested table structure is deleted from the page, and the cell is added to the outside table. See Figure 4-44.

Figure 4-44 **Nested table deleted in Layout mode**

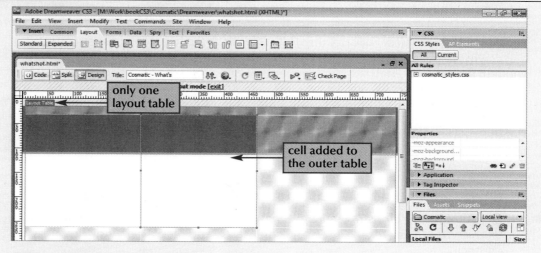

▶ **3.** Save the What's Hot page.

Working with Cells in Layout Mode

Working with cells in Layout mode is similar to working with cells in Standard mode. Once a cell is selected, the cell can be moved, sized, formatted, or deleted.

Moving and Resizing Cells in Layout Mode

When a cell is selected in Layout mode, you can move it by clicking the blue border between the resize handles and dragging the cell to the desired location. When the cell is placed in a new location within a table in Layout mode, Dreamweaver creates all the additional cells necessary to hold the selected cell in place. To resize a cell, you drag a blue resize handle to the desired dimensions, or you select the cell and specify the desired dimensions in the Property inspector.

You'll move and resize the cells in the table in the What's Hot page.

To resize and move cells in the What's Hot page in Layout mode:

▶ 1. Select the left cell, drag the top resize handle to the top of the table, if necessary, and then drag the bottom resize handle until the cell is approximately **425 pixels** in height.

▶ 2. Select the right cell in the table and drag the top resize handle to the top of the table, if necessary, and then drag the bottom resize handle until the cell is approximately **220 pixels** in height.

▶ 3. Click the right edge of the right cell between the blue resize handles, and then drag the cell below the left cell.

▶ 4. Select the bottom cell, and then drag the resize handle at the bottom of the selected cell down to the bottom of the table, if necessary.

▶ 5. Select the top cell, and then drag the right resize handle to the right until the cell is approximately **425 pixels** in width.

▶ 6. On the **Layout** tab of the Insert bar, click the **Draw Layout Cell** button 🖻 , and then draw a third cell to the right of the upper-left cell that fills the gray space on the right side of the table.

▶ 7. Collapse the Property inspector to better see the table. See Figure 4-45.

Figure 4-45 | **New cell added to the table in Layout mode**

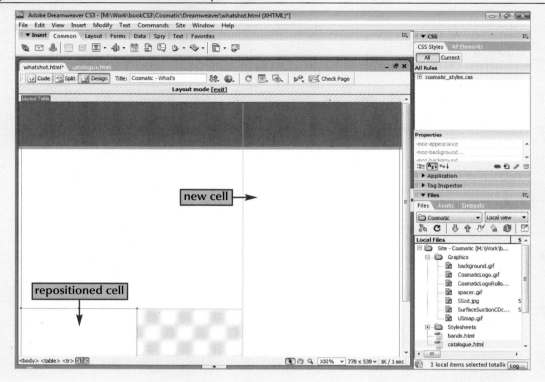

Modifying Cell Attributes in Layout Mode

When a cell is selected in Layout mode, the formatting attributes for the cell that are associated with the Layout mode are visible in the Property inspector. You can change the attributes of a selected cell in the Property inspector, or you can add CSS styles to the selected cell. Cell attributes in Layout mode include:

- **Width.** The horizontal dimension of the cell. In Layout mode, a cell, like a table, can be fixed width or autostretch width.
- **Height.** The vertical dimension of the cell in pixels. You can change the value in the Height box. If you do not change it, the cell remains the height that it was drawn.
- **Bg (background color).** The background color for the cell. You can enter the hexadecimal color code in the Bg box or use the color picker to select a color. If a background color is not specified, the Web page background is seen through the table.
- **Horz (horizontal).** The horizontal alignment of the cell's content. Content can be aligned to the browser's default setting, left, right, or center.
- **Vert (vertical).** The vertical alignment of the content of the cell. Content can be aligned to the browser's default setting, top, middle, bottom, or baseline.
- **No wrap.** The option to enable or disable word wrap within the cell.

You can switch back and forth between Standard mode and Layout mode as you work with cells. Any cell selected in Standard mode is considered a regular cell, and any cell selected in Layout mode is considered a layout cell. This is true regardless of the mode in which the cell was created. To modify attributes such as border and border color, you must be in Standard mode. To modify attributes such as autostretch, you must be in Layout mode.

You'll set the attributes for the layout cells in the What's Hot page.

To set the attributes of cells in the What's Hot page in Layout mode:

▶ **1.** Expand the Property inspector, and then select the cell in the lower-left corner of the table.

▶ **2.** In the Property inspector, click the **Fixed** option button, if necessary, double-click in the **Width** box, type **400**, and then press the **Enter** key. The cell resizes to 400 pixels wide.

▶ **3.** Select the cell again, if necessary, click the **Horz** button, and then click **Center** to change the horizontal alignment to center.

▶ **4.** Click the **Vert** button, and then click **Top** to change the vertical alignment to top.

▶ **5.** Select the cell in the upper-left corner of the table.

▶ **6.** In the Property inspector, click the **Fixed** option button, if necessary, double-click in the **Width** box, type **400**, press the **Tab** key to move to the Height box, type **400**, and then press the **Enter** key.

▶ **7.** Change the horizontal alignment to **Left** and the vertical alignment to **Bottom**.

▶ **8.** Select the right cell, and then drag the left **resize handle** to the left until the cell is flush with the other cells in the table.

Trouble? If the lower-left cell resized wider than 400 pixels, preventing you from widening the tall cell on the right, select the bottom cell, double-click in the Width box, type 400, press the Enter key, and then try Step 8 again.

▶ **9.** In the Property inspector, click the **Autostretch** option button, and then change the horizontal alignment to **Center** and the vertical alignment to **Default**. See Figure 4-46.

Modified cells in Layout mode **Figure 4-46**

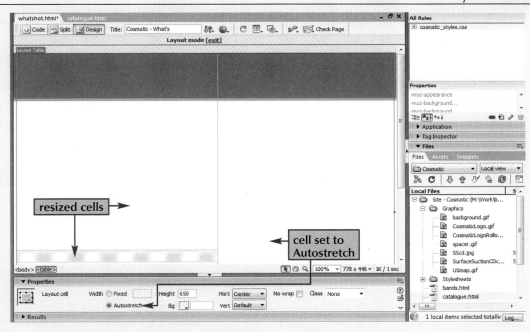

▶ **10.** Click **View** on the menu bar, point to **Rulers**, and then click **Show** to hide the rulers.

▶ **11.** Save the What's Hot page.

Adding Content to Cells in Layout Mode

You can add content to cells in either Layout mode or Standard mode. Adding content to a cell in Layout mode is just like adding content to a cell in Standard mode. Just click in the cell and start typing. To add a graphic to a cell in Layout mode, click in the cell and use the Image button in the Images list on the Common tab of the Insert bar to select the desired graphic.

Brian wants you to place a graphic of a CD cover in the upper-left cell and a song list in the lower-left cell. You will type the promotional text in the right cell of the table.

To add content to cells in the What's Hot page in Layout mode:

▶ **1.** Click in the upper-left cell of the table. The insertion point is in the lower-left corner of the cell.

▶ **2.** Click the **Common** tab on the Insert bar, click the **Images button arrow** , click the **Image** button , and then insert the **SurfaceSuctionCDcover.jpg** graphic located in the **Tutorial.04\Tutorial** folder included with your Data Files. A dialog box warns that the file already exists in the Graphics folder and asks whether you want to overwrite the file.

▶ **3.** Click the **Yes** button to replace the copy of the graphic that you edited earlier. The new copy is saved in the Graphics folder in the local root folder of the Cosmatic site.

The new graphic will also be visible in the Catalogue page.

▶ **4.** Open the **catalogue.html** page in the Document window, and then scroll, if necessary, to see the graphic. The graphic was updated in the Catalogue page. Although the graphic was resized smaller in the Catalogue page, the file size is the same as the graphic in the Graphics folder because you replaced the graphic that you edited with a copy of the original graphic.

▶ **5.** Select the **Surface Suction: Black Lab CD title** and **song list**, click **Edit** on the menu bar, click **Copy**, and then close the page.

▶ **6.** Click in the lower-left cell of the table in the What's Hot page, press the **Enter** key, click **Edit** on the menu bar, and then click **Paste**. The song list is entered in the cell.

▶ **7.** Click in the cell on the right side of the table, and then type **Black Lab: The latest release from Surface Suction**.

▶ **8.** Select the text you just typed, click the **Format** button in the Property inspector, and then click **Heading 1**. The text is formatted with the Heading 1 style.

▶ **9.** Press the **Right Arrow** key, press the **Enter** key to skip a line, and then type **Available at record stores in your area**.

▶ **10.** Select the text you just typed, click the **Style** arrow in the Property inspector, and then click **NewBandSub**. The new text is formatted with the new band subheading style.

▶ **11.** Save the What's Hot page, and then preview the page in a browser. See Figure 4-47.

What's Hot page previewed in browser ◀ Figure 4-47

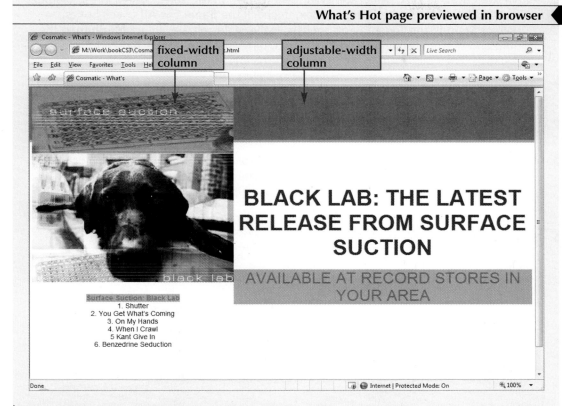

▶ **12.** Drag the lower-right corner of the browser window to resize the window larger and then smaller so that the text on the right rewraps as you resize the window. The right column has an adjustable width, whereas the left column has a fixed width.

> **Trouble?** If your browser window is maximized, click the Restore button in the browser window title bar, and then try Step 12 again.

▶ **13.** Close the browser, and then close the What's Hot page.

Finally, you will add a text hyperlink to the home page that opens the What's Hot page in a new window. You can specify where a linked Web page will open by defining a target for the linked page. Recall that a target is the page or browser window in which a linked Web page will open.

To add a targeted link to the What's Hot page:

▶ **1.** Open the **index.html** page in the Document window.

▶ **2.** Click **Exit** in the blue bar at the top of the Document window to return to Standard mode.

▶ **3.** Place the pointer to the right of the logo, press the **Enter** key seven times, and then type **What's Hot at Cosmatic**.

▶ **4.** In the CSS Styles panel, click the **New CSS Rule** button and create a new custom style class named **WithLines** in the **cosmatic_styles.css** style sheet.

▶ **5.** Click **Type** in the Category box, if necessary, set the size to **18 pixels**, click **Block** in the Category box, select **Center** in the Text Align list, select **Block** in the Display list, click **Border** in the Category box, uncheck the **Same For All** check boxes, select **Solid** in the Top and Bottom lists in the Style column, select **Medium** in the Top and Bottom lists in the Width column, type **#772300** in the Top and Bottom boxes in the Color column, and then click the **OK** button.

▶ **6.** Select the text you just typed, click the **Style** arrow in the Property inspector, and then click **WithLines**. The new style is applied to the text.

▶ **7.** In the Property inspector, drag the link **Point to File** button ⊚ to **whatshot.html** in the Files panel to create a link.

▶ **8.** In the Property inspector, click the **Target** arrow, click **_blank**, and then click in the Document window to deselect the text. The linked page will open in a new browser window when the link is clicked. See Figure 4-48.

| Figure 4-48 | Targeted link created for the What's Hot page |

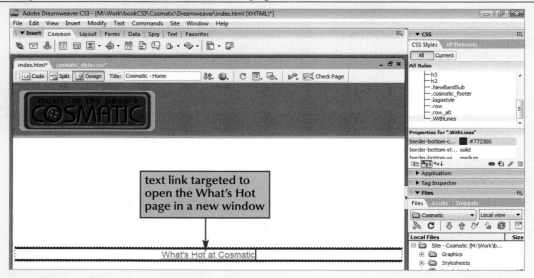

Trouble? If the Target box is inactive, click anywhere in the Document window to deselect the link text, and then select the line again.

▶ **9.** Save the home page, and then save and close the style sheet.

▶ **10.** Preview the home page in a browser, and then click the **What's Hot** link. A new browser window opens displaying the What's Hot page.

▶ **11.** Close the browser, close the home page, and then collapse the CSS panel group.

Updating the Web Site on the Remote Server

As a final review of the changes you made to the Cosmatic site, you'll update the files on the remote server and review the pages over the Web. You need to upload every page of the site because you have made changes to every page. When you upload the pages, you will also need to include the dependent files so that the new graphics and new CSS styles are uploaded to the remote server. Then you'll preview the site on the Web.

To upload the updated Cosmatic site to your remote server:

▶ **1.** Click the **Connects to Remote Host** button 🔗 on the Files panel toolbar to connect to the remote host.

▶ **2.** Click the **View** button on the Files panel toolbar, and then click **Local View**.

▶ **3.** Select **bands.html**, **catalogue.html**, **contact.html**, **index.html**, **label.html**, **tourdates.html**, and the **whatshot.html** files in the Local file list, and then click the **Put File(s)** button ⬆ on the Files panel toolbar.

▶ **4.** Click the **Yes** button when asked if you want to include dependent files, because you have not yet uploaded the new dependent files for the site.

▶ **5.** Click the **View** button on the Files panel toolbar, and then click **Remote View**.

▶ **6.** Double-click the **Graphics** folder in the Remote file list in the Files panel. Copies of the new graphic files (CosmaticLogoRollover.gif, spacer.gif, SurfaceSuctionCDcover.jpg, and USmap.gif) are uploaded to the remote site.

▶ **7.** Click the **Disconnects from Remote Host** button 🔗 on the Files panel toolbar, click the **View** button on the Files panel toolbar, and then click **Local View**.

▶ **8.** Close the Cosmatic site.

Next, you'll preview the updated site in a browser. The site will include all of the new styles and text that you added to your local version.

To preview the updated Cosmatic site in a browser:

▶ **1.** Open your browser, type the URL of your remote site in the Address bar on the browser toolbar, and then press the **Enter** key. The home page opens in the browser window.

▶ **2.** Click at the end of the URL in the Address bar, type **/** if there is not already one at the end of the URL, type **label.html**, and then press the **Enter** key to make sure that the Label page was successfully uploaded.

   Trouble? If the new CSS styles that you created do not appear in your browser window, click the Refresh button on the browser window toolbar.

▶ **3.** Move the pointer over the **Cosmatic logo** in the Label page to see the rollover graphic, and then click the **logo** to return to the home page.

▶ **4.** Click the **Back** button ⬅ on the browser toolbar to return to the Label page, click the **bands** link to make sure that the page was successfully uploaded, and then move the pointer over the **Cosmatic logo**.

▶ **5.** Click the **catalogue** link to make sure that the page was successfully uploaded, and then move the pointer over the **Cosmatic logo**.

▶ **6.** Click the **tour dates** link to make sure that the page was successfully uploaded, and then move the pointer over the **Cosmatic logo**.

▶ **7.** Click the **contact** link to make sure that the page was successfully uploaded, and then move the pointer over the **Cosmatic logo**.

▶ **8.** Click the **What's Hot at Cosmatic** link to make sure that the page was successfully uploaded, and then examine the What's Hot page.

▶ **9.** Close the browser.

In this session, you created a pop-up page for the Cosmatic site. You used layout tables to add the content.

Review | **Session 4.3 Quick Check**

1. What is a nested table?
2. Why is it good to plan the page layout when you are using tables?
3. True or False? A cell cannot exist outside a table.
4. What does Dreamweaver do automatically if you draw a cell in Layout mode before you draw a table?
5. Can you resize a cell by dragging its resize handles when it is active in Layout mode?
6. What is a spacer image?

Review | **Tutorial Summary**

In this tutorial, you learned about the different types of graphics you can use in a Web site. You added a graphic to each page and formatted it. You created a link to the graphic, you created an image map, and you inserted a rollover object for the graphic. You inserted tables in Standard mode, and then selected, modified, moved, resized, and deleted a table and table elements. You explored the HTML tags associated with tables. You worked in Layout mode, drawing layout cells and layout tables, and then selecting, sizing, moving, and modifying them. You also added content to the layout table. Finally, you updated the files on the Web and previewed the remote Web site.

Key Terms

active	GIF (Graphics Interchange Format)	PNG (Portable Network Graphics)
asset		
baseline	hotspot	resample
border	image map	resize handles
bracketing tags	JavaScript	rollover
cell	JPEG (Joint Photographic Experts Group)	row
column		row span
column span	lossless	spacer image
compression	lossy	table
crop	nested table	variable transparency
Expanded Tables mode	nongradient	

Practice	Review Assignments

Practice the skills you learned in the tutorial.

Data Files needed for the Review Assignments: DCcd300.jpg, SScd300.jpg, SCcd300.jpg, LIMCcd300.jpg

Brian wants you to create a variety of tables in the other pages of the Cosmatic site to insert content and organize the layout. You'll create tables in Standard mode for Central tour dates and East Coast tour dates in the Tour Dates page. Then, you'll hyperlink the hotspots on the map to the appropriate tables. For the Catalogue page, you'll delete the resized graphic from the page, create a table in Standard mode, insert graphics of the CD covers as well as text of the CD titles and song lists, and then you will edit the graphics.

1. Open the **Cosmatic** site that you modified in this tutorial, and then open the **tourdates.html** page in the Document window.
2. Select the West Coast Tour Dates table, change its width to 80%, select all the cells in the table, and then click the Align Center button in the Property inspector.
3. Click below the West Coast Tour Dates table in the Tour Dates page, and then click the Table button on the Common tab of the Insert bar. Create a table in Standard mode with 13 rows, 3 columns, table width 80 percent, 0 border thickness, 0 cell padding, and 0 cell spacing. Click Top in the Header area, if necessary, and then type **Cosmatic bands, central U.S. tour dates** in the Summary box.
4. Enter **CentralUSTourDates** in the Table ID box in the Property inspector.
5. Merge the top row of cells in the table.
6. Make the top two rows of the table header cells. (*Hint:* Check the Header check box.)
7. Type **Central U.S. Tour Dates** in the top row.
8. Select the table, and then center align the table, using the Align list in the Property inspector. (*Hint:* If you have trouble selecting the table, switch to Expanded Tables mode.)
9. Adjust the widths of the columns so they are the same as the column widths in the West Coast table.
10. Type the information from the following table into the three columns in the Central U.S. Tour Dates table.

Date	Location / Venue	Band
1/4 to 1/6	Cleveland, OH / Grog Shop	Surface Suction
1/11 to 1/13	Chicago, IL / Abbey Pub	Surface Suction
2/8 to 2/10	Minneapolis, MN / 9th Street Entry	Surface Suction
2/15 to 2/17	Iowa City, IA / Gabe's Oasis	Surface Suction
2/22 to 2/24	Lawrence, KS / Bottleneck	Surface Suction
3/15 to 3/17	Denton, TX / Rubber Gloves	Surface Suction
3/22 to 3/24	Austin, TX / Emo's	Surface Suction
4/12 to 4/14	Houston, TX / Sidecar Pub	Surface Suction

11. Apply the row style to the first, third, fifth, seventh, and ninth rows and then apply the row_alt style to the even-numbered rows in the table.
12. Select the empty cells and delete them.

13. Repeat Steps 3 through 12 to create a third table, typing **Cosmatic bands, east coast tour dates** in the Summary box, typing **EastCoastTourDates** in the Table ID box, typing **East Coast Tour Dates** in the top row, and using the following information.

Date	Location / Venue	Band
1/4 to 1/6	Atlanta, GA / Echo Lounge	Sloth Child
1/11 to 1/13	Carbord, NC / Room Four	Sloth Child
2/8 to 2/10	Baltimore, MD / Ottobar	Sloth Child
2/15 to 2/17	Washington, DC / Black Cat	Sloth Child
2/22 to 2/24	Philadelphia, PA / Unitarian Church	Sloth Child
3/15 to 3/17	Cambridge, MA / Middle East	Sloth Child
3/22 to 3/24	New York, NY / Bowery Ballroom	Sloth Child
4/13 to 4/14	New York, NY / Knitting Factory	Sloth Child

14. Select all of the cells in the Central U.S. Tour Dates and East Coast Tour Dates tables, and then center align all of the text in the table.

15. Create a named anchor for the West Coast Tour Dates table. Click to the right of the text in the first row of the first table, and then click the Named Anchor button on the Common tab of the Insert bar. In the Named Anchor dialog box, type **westcoast** in the Anchor Name box, and then click the OK button.

16. Repeat Step 15 to create a named anchor for the Central U.S. Tour Dates table named **central** and for the East Coast Tour Dates table named **eastcoast**.

17. Add a link from each hotspot to a named anchor. Click the left hotspot on the U.S. map and enter **#westcoast** in the Link box in the Property inspector; click the middle hotspot on the map and enter **#central** in the Link box; and then click the right hotspot and enter **#eastcoast** in the Link box.

18. Save the page, and then test the links to the anchors by previewing the page in a browser and clicking each hotspot on the map. (*Hint:* If each table does not move to the top of the window when you click the appropriate hotspot, you may not have enough blank lines at the end of your Web page. Open the page in the Document window and add extra lines to the end of the page by pressing the Enter key.) Close the page when you are finished.

19. Open the **catalogue.html** page in the Document window, insert a table below the CDS heading that has 4 rows, 2 columns, 75% table width, 0 border thickness, 4 cell padding, 0 cell spacing, and no header cells. Center align the table.

20. Select "Dizzied Connections: Spinning Life" and the song list below it, cut the selected text, and then paste the text into the first cell in the second row of the table.

21. Delete the Surface Suction CD cover from the page, select "Surface Suction: Black Lab" and the song list below it, cut the selected text, and then paste the text into the second cell in the second row of the table. (*Hint:* If you have difficulty selecting the right column, switch to Expanded Tables mode.)

22. Select "Sloth Child: Them Apples" and the song list below it, cut the selected text, and then paste the text into the first cell in the fourth row of the table.

23. Select "life in minor chords: i believe in ferries" and the song list below it, cut the selected text, and then paste the text into the second cell in the fourth row of the table.

24. Insert the following images located in the Tutorial.04\Review folder included with your Data Files in the specified location in the table: **DCcd300.jpg** in the first cell in the first row, **SScd300.jpg** in the second cell in the first row, **SCcd300.jpg** in the first cell in the third row, and **LIMCcd300.jpg** in the second cell in the third row.

25. Select each cell with text, and then select Center in the Horz list and Top in the Vert list. (*Hint:* To see all the cell formatting options, expand the Property inspector.)

26. Increase the Dizzied Connections CD cover sharpness by 1. Decrease the Life in Minor Chords CD cover brightness by 10 and increase its contrast by 20.

27. Select each row with graphics in it, and then select Center in the Horz list and Bottom in the Vert list in the Property inspector.

28. Make sure the table width is 75% in the W box in the Property inspector. (Sometimes the width changes when you add graphics.)

29. Save the page, preview the page in a browser, scroll to the bottom of the page to see if the paragraph below the VINYL heading appears inside the green bar, and then close the browser. If necessary, click below the table, scroll down to see the entire green bar, and then press the Delete key as many times as necessary to move up a paragraph so that it is all inside the green bar when previewed in a browser.

30. Copy the copyright line from the Catalogue page, paste the text at the bottom of the home page, the Contact page, and the Tour Dates page, apply the cosmatic_footer style, and then save and close each page.

31. Connect to your remote server, upload the site, and then preview the site over the Web.

32. Submit the finished files to your instructor, either in printed or electronic form, as requested.

| Apply | Case Problem 1 |

Add a hyperlinked logo and create tables to insert page content for a Web site about the small rural communities of northern Vietnam.

Data File needed for this Case Problem: WASlogo.jpg

World Anthropology Society   As you continue working on Dr. Olivia Thompson's Web site, you'll add the World Anthropology Society logo to every page of the site and create a hyperlink from the logo to Dr. Thompson's home page. Then, you'll create a table to contain the information in each area of research and put placeholder text in the tables while the research is being completed.

1. Open the **DrThompson** site you modified in **Tutorial 3**, **Case 1**, and then open the **index.html** page in the Document window.

2. In the upper left-corner of the page, using the Image button in the Images list on the Common tab of the Insert bar, insert the logo graphic **WASlogo.jpg** located in the Tutorial.04\Case1 folder included with your Data Files.

3. Delete spaces after the logo graphic as needed so that the links are in their original positions, and then save and close the page.

4. For each of the rest of the pages in the site, open the page, insert the logo, create a hyperlink from the logo to the home page, delete extra spaces after the logo, and then save and close the page: **contact.html**, **cultural_cross_pollination.html**, **linguistic_differences.html**, **dr_thompson.html**, and **rituals_and_practices.html**.

5. Open the **linguistic_differences.html** page, click to the right of the Linguistic Differences heading, and then press the Enter key to position the insertion point below the heading.

6. Insert a table that has 3 rows, 1 column, 100% table width, 0 border thickness, 0 cell padding, 0 cell spacing, no header cells, and no summary, caption, or table ID because the table is being used for layout rather than to display information.

7. Left align the table, select the top cell, and type **#910C26** in the second Bg (Background Color) box.

8. Copy the Linguistic Differences heading, and then paste the text into the top cell of the table. (*Hint:* You may need to reapply the Heading 1 tag.)

9. Delete the old heading text and any extra spaces, click in the second cell and type **Research in process, check back soon.**, and then press the Enter key twice to add blank lines.

10. Click in the bottom cell, type © **Dr. Olivia Thompson, World Anthropology Society, 2010.**, and then horizontally center the text.

11. Copy the table, save and close the page, open the **cultural_cross_pollination.html** page, select the current heading, paste the table in the Cultural Cross-pollination page in place of the current heading, replace the text in the top cell with **Cultural Cross-pollination**, and then save and close the page.

12. Open the **rituals_and_practices.html** page, select the current heading, paste the table in the Rituals and Practices page in place of the current heading, replace the text in the top cell with **Rituals and Practices**, and then save the page.

13. Preview the site in a browser, and then close the browser and the page.

14. Upload the site to your remote server, and then preview the site over the Web, checking the links and pages to ensure the upload was successful.

15. Submit the finished files to your instructor, either in printed or electronic form, as requested.

| Apply | **Case Problem 2** |

Add a logo rollover and move the navigation links into a table you create in a Web site for an art museum.

Data Files needed for this Case Problem: MuseumLogo.gif, MuseumLogoOver.gif

Museum of Western Art C. J. Strittmatter asks you to use the new graphics that the art department has provided to create a rollover image out of the new Museum of Western Art logo, and then to replace the text logo in each page of the site with the new logo rollover, which will link to the home page. In addition, you will add a table in the home page and move the navigation links into the table. Then, you'll copy the new navigation table to the other pages of the site.

1. Open the **Museum** site that you modified in **Tutorial 3**, **Case 2**, and then open the **index.html** page in the Document window.

2. Delete the text logo at the top of the page.

3. Insert a rollover image with **MuseumLogoRollover** as the image name. For the original image, use **MuseumLogo.gif** located in the Tutorial.04\Case2 folder included with your Data Files. For the rollover image, use **MuseumLogoOver.gif** located in the Tutorial.04\Case2 folder included with your Data Files. Enter **Museum of Western Art Logo with link to the home page** as the alternate text, and use the index.html page for the URL to go to when clicked.

4. Save the page, preview the page in a browser, place the pointer over the rollover image to see the image change and view the alternate text in the tooltip.

5. Copy the rollover image, and then paste it in place of the text logo in the **art.html**, **artists.html**, **location.html**, and **museum.html** pages.

6. Save each page, preview each page in a browser, testing the new logo, and then close each page.

7. Open the **index.html** page in the Document window, position the insertion point to the right of the navigation text and insert a table with 4 rows, 1 column, 100 pixels table width, 1 pixel border thickness, 0 cell spacing, 0 cell padding, no header cells, no caption and **Site navigation** as the summary.

8. Select the table, if necessary, align the table to the right in the Property inspector (the table moves to the right above the Welcome text). Create a new style named **.navtable** in the **museum_styles.css** style sheet. In the Background category, type **#006666** in the Background Color box. In the Border category, check the Same For All check boxes, select solid from the Style list, select thin from the Width list and type **#ECB888** in the Color box. Apply the .navtable style to the selected table.

9. Copy the Museum text link into the first cell, copy the Art text link into the second cell, copy the Artists text link into the third cell, and then copy the Location text link into the fourth cell. Delete the original text links from the page and any extra lines between the table and the horizontal line.

10. In the CSS Styles panel, select .menustyle in the All Rules pane. In the Properties pane, select Center in the Text-Align list.

⊕ **EXPLORE**

11. In the CSS Styles panel, select h2 in the All Rules pane. In the Properties pane, set the font size to 42 pixels, click Normal in the Font-Weight list, and click Right in the Text-Align list. (*Hint:* Use Add Properties to add properties to the list.)

12. Position the insertion point before the heading text, and then insert line breaks as needed to move the text to below the table. (*Hint:* Press the Shift+Enter keys to move the insertion point down one line.)

13. Save and close the style sheet, save the home page, and then preview it in a browser.

14. Copy and paste the table into the **art.html**, **artists.html**, **location.html**, and **museum.html** pages to the right of the navigation text. Delete the old navigation text and any extra spaces from each page, position the insertion point before the heading text, and then insert line breaks as needed to move the text to below the table. Save each page.

15. Preview the site in a browser, and then close the browser and any open pages.

16. Upload the site to your remote server, and then preview the site over the Web, checking the links and pages to ensure the upload was successful.

17. Submit the finished files to your instructor, either in printed or electronic form, as requested.

Challenge	**Case Problem 3**

Add a rollover logo graphic and insert page content into tables you create in a Web site for an independent bookstore.

Data Files needed for this Case Problem: MORElogo.jpg, MORElogoOver.jpg, PunchSmall.jpg, Punch.jpg

MORE Books   Mark Chapman asks you to add a new logo graphic to the MORE books site and to create a rollover image out of it, linking users back to the home page. You'll create a two-cell table in the home page, and add the book list to one cell and a new book cover graphic in the other cell of the table.

1. Open the **MOREbooks** site you modified in **Tutorial 3**, **Case 3**, and then open the **index.html** page in the Document window.

2. Delete the text logo at the top of the home page.

3. Insert a new logo with a rollover. Name the image **MORElogoRollover**, use **MORElogo.jpg** located in the Tutorial.04\Case3 folder included with your Data Files for the original image, use **MORElogoOver.jpg** located in the Tutorial.04\Case3 folder included with your Data Files for the rollover image, type **MORE logo with link to home page** as the alternate text, and then browse to the index.html page in the When Clicked, Go To URL box.

4. Save the page, and then preview the page in a browser.

⊕ **EXPLORE**   5. Copy the logo to the **books.html**, **company.html**, **contact.html**, and **links.html** pages to replace the text logos on those pages. Save the pages as you go and preview the site when you are finished to ensure that the rollover images are working.

6. Open the **index.html** page, position the insertion point directly before the MORE FEATURED BOOK LIST heading, and insert a table with 1 row, 2 columns, 100% table width, 0 border thickness, 0 cell spacing, 0 cell padding, no header cells, and no summary, caption, or table ID because the table is being used for layout rather than to display information.

⊕ **EXPLORE**   7. Select the MORE FEATURED BOOK LIST heading and the following list of books and authors, drag the selected text into the left cell of the table, and then delete any blank lines from the page.

8. Drag the right border of the first cell to the left until it is directly beside the longest line of content in the cell, position the insertion point in the right cell, type **Featured Book**, and then apply the .more_sub_headings style to the text.

9. Select the left cell, click Top from the Vert list in the Property inspector, select the right cell, and then click Top in the Vert list in the Property inspector.

10. Place the insertion point after the text in the right cell, press the Shift+Enter keys to create a new line, and then insert in the cell **PunchSmall.jpg** located in the Tutorial.04\Case3 folder included with your Data Files. Save and close the page.

11. Create a new page saved as **featuredbook.html** in the site's local root folder. Type **MORE Books - Featured Book** as the page title, expand the CSS Styles panel, and attach the page to the more_styles.css style sheet.

12. Switch to Layout mode, and, in the left corner of the page just below the white horizontal line, draw a layout cell that is 250 pixels wide by 350 pixels high. Insert **Punch.jpg** located in the Tutorial.04\Case3 folder included with your Data Files in the cell and resize the cell to the same size as the graphic. (*Hint:* You'll need to switch to the Common category on the Insert bar to insert the image.)

13. Directly below the first layout cell, draw a second cell the same width as the first cell and 85 pixels high. (*Hint:* If you can't draw the second cell 85 pixels high, increase the size of the outer table to at least 435 pixels high.)

14. To the right of the first layout cell (just below the white horizontal line), draw a third layout cell the combined height of the first two cells and 525 pixels wide.

15. Select the table, and then click the Autostretch option button in the Property inspector. If necessary, create a spacer image in the Graphics folder in the local root folder for the MOREbooks site.

⊕ EXPLORE
16. In the lower-left cell, type **Punch by Kelly Moore**, select "Punch," and then apply the .more_book_titles CSS style.

17. In the right cell, type: **"A wacky, eccentric collection of female voices searching for meaning in a world gone awry. Punch is a hilarious romp." - Melissa Thurman, Voice.**

18. Select the cell, and then click Middle in the Vert list in the Property inspector.

19. Increase the graphic's sharpness by 2 and its brightness by 22. Save and close the page.

20. Open the **index.html** page, and link the book cover graphic and the "Featured Book" text to the Featured Book page targeted to open in a new browser window (_blank).

21. Select the graphic, and then center align it.

22. Save the page, and then preview the site in a browser.

23. Upload the site to your remote server, and then preview the site over the Web.

24. Submit the finished files to your instructor, either in printed or electronic form, as requested.

| Create | **Case Problem 4** |

Add a rollover graphic and create tables in Layout mode to enter content for a new page in a Web site for a newly opening sushi restaurant.

Data Files needed for this Case Problem: SushiYaYaLogo.gif, SushiYaYaLogoOver.gif, TikkaRollTuna.gif

Sushi Ya-Ya   Mary O'Brien asks you to add graphics and tables to the Sushi Ya-Ya site. You'll add the new Sushi Ya-Ya logo, with a rollover and link to the home page, to every page of the site. Then, you'll create a Specials button in the home page. Finally, you'll create a new Specials page. You will create tables in Layout mode to structure the new page.

1. Open the **Sushi Ya-Ya** site that you modified in **Tutorial 3**, **Case 4**, and then open the **index.html** page in the Document window.

2. Delete the text logo if there is one.

3. Add a graphic logo with a rollover (either the one provided by the design team or one that you created yourself) to the top of each page in the site. You can insert the logo into the home page, and then copy the logo and the functionality to the other pages of the site. Use the **SushiYaYaLogo.gif** located in the Tutorial.04\Case4 folder included with your Data Files as the original image, and the **SushiYaYaLogoOver.gif** located in the Tutorial.04\Case4 folder included with your Data Files as the rollover image (or use your own graphics). Add alternate text and a link to the home page.

4. Create a new page with the page title **Sushi Ya-Ya - Specials** saved as **specials.html** in the site's local root folder, attach the external style sheet to the page, and then save the page.

5. Design a layout for the Specials page. The special is the Tikka roll. The page will contain a graphic of the roll (use the **TikkaRollTuna.gif** located in the Tutorial.04\Case4 folder included with your Data Files or create your own graphic), the name of the special ("Tikka Roll"), a description of the special ("The Tikka Roll combines spicy tuna and rice wrapped in a seaweed roll."), and the price ("$3.00").

6. Based on your layout, create a table in Layout mode to hold the content, and then place the content in the page. Edit the graphic as needed to fit the page layout.

7. Create a specials link in the home page of the Sushi Ya-Ya site. You can use the graphic you used in the Specials page as well as text. You might want to create a table to hold the link in place on the page, and you might want to create a style for the graphic that creates borders in a desired color to frame the graphic. Target the link to open the Specials page in a new browser window.

8. Save your changes, and then preview the site in a browser.

9. Upload the site to your remote server, and then preview the site over the Web, checking all the links and the added page.

10. Submit the finished files to your instructor, either in printed or electronic form, as requested.

Review | **Quick Check Answers**

Session 4.1

1. GIF, JPEG, and PNG
2. JPEG
3. You can use the Assets panel to manage the assets of your site.
4. An image map is a graphic that is divided into hotspots.
5. A hotspot is an area of an image map that you can click to cause an action to occur.
6. A rollover is an image that changes when the pointer moves across it.

Session 4.2

1. A table cell is the intersection of a row and a column in the table.
2. True.
3. Cell padding is the amount of empty space maintained between the border of a cell and the cell's content. Cell spacing is the width of the cell walls.
4. Pressing the Tab key moves the insertion point to the next cell to the right or, if the insertion point is in the last cell in a row, to the first cell in the next row. If the insertion point is in the last cell in the table, pressing the Tab key inserts a new row and moves the insertion point to the first cell in the new row.
5. The content is merged into one cell and the new cell is the width and the height of the two original cells put together.
6. <tr>
7. <td>

Session 4.3

1. A nested table is a table inside another table.
2. To avoid reworking the page elements once you have placed them on the page
3. True.
4. Dreamweaver inserts the rest of the cells and a table to hold the cell you drew.
5. No. When a cell is active, it is ready to accept input. A cell must be selected and the resize handles visible in order to resize it by dragging the resize handles.
6. A spacer image is a 1-pixel transparent image that is inserted into the fixed-width columns in a table that contains an autostretch column.

Objectives

Session 5.1
- Insert a navigation bar
- Copy a navigation bar to other pages
- Modify a navigation bar

Session 5.2
- Understand frames and framesets
- Create a Web page with frames
- Adjust frame properties and attributes

Session 5.3
- Add content to frames
- Create hyperlinks with targets
- Explore the HTML behind frames, framesets, and targets

Adding Shared Site Elements

Creating a Navigation Bar and Using Frames

Case | Cosmatic

As you add pages to a Web site, the additional content needs to be organized in a way that is easy for users to navigate and understand, as well as catch their eye. You organized some of the content in the Cosmatic site using tables. Now you'll add pages that are organized with frames and that use the navigation bar object.

Brian Lee, public relations and marketing director at Cosmatic, wants you to replace the text navigation system in the Cosmatic site with a navigation bar that uses a series of rollover elements for the navigation links. Each rollover element includes a graphic for the four states of each element to provide users additional information, such as which page of the site is currently open. Also, the graphic elements will add to the look and feel of the site.

Brian also wants you to create a Web page to promote the band Life in Minor Chords (fulfilling one of the site goals). You'll add links to the new page from the band's name in the Bands page and from the CD cover graphic in the Catalogue page. You will use frames when you design the new page.

Starting Data Files

Tutorial.05 →

Tutorial
LIMCmainframetext.doc
bands.gif through
tourdatesOWD.gif
(30 GIF files)
LifeBanner.jpg
☐ FrameTest
bands.html
☐ Graphics
☐ Stylesheets

Review
DCbanner.jpg through
DCtoursUp.jpg
(12 JPEG files)

Case1
WAScontactinformationDown.gif
through
WASritualsandpracticesUp.gif
(10 GIF files)

Case2
AmongTheLedHorses.html
TheLoveCall.html
TheLucklessHunter.html
TheRiderlessHorse.html
AmongTheLedHorsesBig.jpg
through
RiderlessHorseSmall.jpg
(8 JPEG files)

Case3
PunchAuthorBioOver.gif
through
PunchPressUp.gif
(6 GIF files)
featured_author_bio.html
featured_excerpt.html

Case4
SushiDescriptions.doc
SushiCaliforniaRoll.gif
through
SushiTunaHandRoll.gif
(9 GIF files)

Session 5.1

Creating a Navigation Bar Object

The ways to add navigation to a Web site increase as you learn more advanced Web design techniques. You added text hyperlinks to enable the user to move between Web pages in the Cosmatic site. You defined CSS styles to customize the look of the various states of the hyperlink tags. You also created a rollover button for the Cosmatic site logo. Now you will replace the text links with a navigation bar.

Reference Window | **Creating a Navigation Bar**

- On the Common tab of the Insert bar, click the Navigation Bar button in the Images list.
- Type a name for the first navigation bar element in the Element name box.
- Click each image's Browse button to navigate to the image to display for that element.
- Type alternate text in the Alternate text box.
- Click the When clicked, Go to URL Browse button, and then navigate to the file to which you want to link the element.
- Click the In button, and then select the target window for the link.
- Click the Preload images check box to check it.
- If this element represents the current page, click the Show "Down image" initially check box to check it; otherwise, leave it unchecked.
- Click the Insert arrow, and then select the orientation of the navigation bar.
- Click the Use tables check box to check it.
- For each element you want to add to the navigation bar, click the Add Item button above the Nav bar elements list, and then enter the element's information.
- Click the OK button.

Tip

In this tutorial, the term *navigation bar* refers to the specific Dreamweaver navigation bar object.

In general, any navigation or menu system in a Web page can be referred to as a navigation bar. In Dreamweaver, however, the **navigation bar** is a series of rollover graphics that change state when specific browser actions occur, such as when the pointer is placed over a graphic. The rollover graphics are held in place in the Web page by a container such as a table. Each rollover is called an **element** and can have up to four states. The **Up state** refers to the element before the user clicks it. The **Over state** refers to the element when the pointer is positioned over the Up graphic. The **Down state** refers to the element after it has been clicked. The **Over While Down state** refers to the element when the pointer is placed over the Down graphic.

Understanding Navigation Bar Components | InSight

Understanding the components used in the navigation bar will help you comprehend what the navigation bar does. The navigation bar uses hyperlinks, rollovers, and tables. The information you already know about these items helps you to better understand how the navigation bar works. When you use the navigation bar, several things happen:

- As with a rollover, the graphics in a navigation bar preload when the Web page is loaded, if the preload option is selected, so that they are in place when the browser action occurs.
- A series of navigation bar elements is defined. (Each element is similar to a rollover button with a set of up to four state images.)
- The navigation bar is placed within a table in the Web page if the Use Table check box is checked; otherwise, the elements are placed directly in the Web page. The navigation bar is best placed in a table, which keeps the elements in their proper positions in the page.
- If you set a URL for each element, users will jump to the new page when they click an element, just like when they click a text link.

You will open a sample of the Bands page in the Cosmatic site with a navigation bar inserted in the page so you can explore its elements. (You will not be able to jump to the other pages of the site.)

To examine a navigation bar in the sample Bands page:

▶ **1.** Start your browser.

▶ **2.** Click **File** on the menu bar, and then click **Open**. The Open dialog box opens.

▶ **3.** Click the **Browse** button, navigate to the **Tutorial.05\Tutorial** folder included with your Data Files, double-click **bands.html**, and then click the **OK** button. The Bands page with a navigation bar opens in the browser window. See Figure 5-1.

Tip

You can also press the Ctrl+O keys to access the Open dialog box.

Navigation bar with elements in the Up and Down states ◀ Figure 5-1

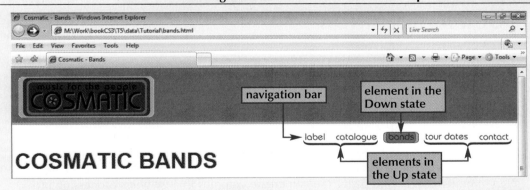

Trouble? If an Internet Explorer dialog box opens to indicate that the Bands page needs to open in a new browser window, click the OK button.

Graphics were created for each link in the navigation bar. The bands element is in the Down state because the Bands page is currently visible in the browser. The other elements—label, catalogue, tour dates, and contact—are in the Up state.

▶ **4.** Move the pointer over the **bands** element, but do not click. The element changes to the Over While Down state to indicate that the link cannot be clicked because you are currently on that page. See Figure 5-2.

Figure 5-2 **Navigation bar with the bands element in the Over While Down state**

Trouble? If the bands element does not change to the Over While Down state, you probably need to allow blocked content. Click the Information Bar, click Allow Blocked Content on the shortcut menu, click the Yes button in the Security Warning dialog box, and then repeat Step 4.

▶ **5.** Move the pointer over the **label** element. The element changes to the Over state. See Figure 5-3.

Figure 5-3 **Navigation bar with the label element in the Over state**

▶ **6.** Close the browser.

Inserting a Navigation Bar

Before you create a navigation bar, you need graphics to use for each state of the elements. The graphics must be saved in one of the Web-safe formats (GIF, JPEG, or PNG) to be used in a Web page. You can create graphics in a graphics processing program such as Adobe Photoshop, Adobe Fireworks, or Adobe Illustrator. When you add an image to the navigation bar, you should place a copy of it in the Graphics folder within the site's local root folder, just as you have done when adding other graphics to the site. To create a navigation bar, you'll enter the following information:

• **Nav bar elements.** The list of elements included in the navigation bar. After you have created elements, you can add, delete, or reorder them.
• **Element name.** The name of each element added to the navigation bar. Element names must start with a letter or an underscore, and they can contain only letters and numbers (no spaces or symbols).When you rename an element, its name will change in the Nav bar elements list.

- **Up image.** The graphic that appears when the element is in the Up state. You can type the path to the image or browse to select the image. You must include a graphic for the Up image for the navigation bar to work. The other states are optional.
- **Over image.** The graphic that appears when the element is in the optional Over state. You can type the path to the image or browse to select the image.
- **Down image.** The graphic that appears when the element is in the optional Down state. You can type the path to the image or browse to select the image.
- **Over while down image.** The graphic that appears when the element is in the optional Over While Down state to provide users a visual cue that the button cannot be clicked from that particular part of the Web site. For example, if the navigation bar includes an Over while down image that grays out the bands element in the Bands page of the Cosmatic site, the image becomes gray when a user points to the bands element in the navigation bar, indicating that the Bands page is already displayed and that link cannot be clicked. You can type the path to the image or browse to select the image.
- **Alternate text.** Text that appears in place of the image in browsers that display only text. This text will be read by screen readers and will appear in tooltips.
- **When clicked, Go to URL.** The URL or file path to which you want the element to hyperlink, along with the window or frame in which you want the new URL to appear (frames are explored later in this tutorial). The Main Window option opens the new Web page in the existing browser window.
- **Options.** Options that affect the entire navigation bar, not each individual element. The Preload Images option enables the browser to download all of the graphics in the navigation bar when the page is loaded. If you don't preload images, users might experience a delay before the Over image appears when they move the mouse over a button. The Show "Down image" initially option enables Dreamweaver to display the element in its Down state (rather than its default Up state) when the page is loaded. (The element's Up state is displayed by default when a page is loaded.) This feature is used to indicate which page of the Web site is displayed. For example, you'll show the Down state of the label element in the navigation bar in the Label page of the Cosmatic site; when the Label page is loaded in the browser, the user knows the Label page is open because the label element in the navigation bar is in the Down state.
- **Insert.** The orientation of the navigation bar—horizontal or vertical. This option applies to the entire navigation bar. After you create a horizontal or vertical navigation bar, you cannot change this setting.
- **Use tables.** The option to use tables to keep the navigation bar elements in place. This option applies to the entire navigation bar. It is a good idea to create navigation bars with tables.

> **Tip**
>
> To switch the orientation of a navigation bar, you must delete the existing navigation bar and create a new one.

Brian asks you to upgrade the navigation system for the Cosmatic site by deleting the current text links and creating a navigation bar in each page of the site. When you create the new navigation bar in the first page, you will include a graphic for each state of each element and store a copy of each graphic in the Graphics folder within the site's local root folder.

You'll start by creating the navigation bar in the Label page.

To turn on the rulers and delete text links:

▶ **1.** Open the **Cosmatic** site that you modified in the **Tutorial 4 Review Assignments**, and then open the **label.html** page in the Document window.

▶ **2.** Click the **Design** button on the Document toolbar, if necessary.

3. Click **View** on the menu bar, point to **Rulers**, and then click **Show** to display the rulers in the Document window, if necessary. The rulers will help as you place the navigation bar and heading text in the page.

4. Drag to select the link text for the current navigation system, and then press the **Delete** key. The text links disappear from the page.

Next, you'll create a graphic-based navigation bar. Brian supplied the graphics you should use for each element in the four states.

To create the navigation bar in the Label page:

1. On the **Common** tab of the Insert bar, click the **Images button arrow** 🖼 ▾ , and then click the **Navigation Bar** button 🖥 . The Insert Navigation Bar dialog box opens. See Figure 5-4.

Figure 5-4
Insert Navigation Bar dialog box

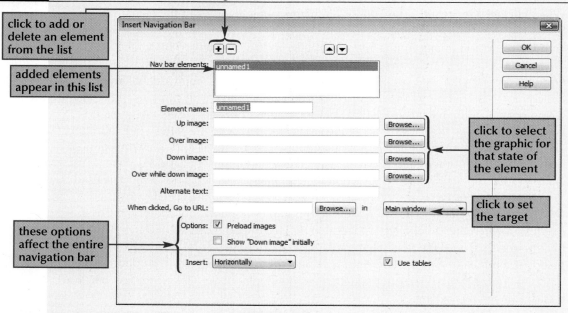

2. Type **Label** in the Element name box.

Tip

You can also type the paths and filenames of the graphics in the image boxes.

3. Click the Up image **Browse** button to open the Select Image Source dialog box, navigate to the **Tutorial.05\Tutorial** folder included with your Data Files, and then double-click **label.gif**. A copy of the label.gif graphic is placed in the site's Graphics folder, and the file path appears in the Up image box.

You'll repeat this process to insert the images for the Over, Down, and Over While Down states.

4. Click the Over image **Browse** button, and then double-click **labelOver.gif** located in the **Tutorial.05\Tutorial** folder included with your Data Files.

5. Click the Down image **Browse** button, and then double-click **labelDown.gif** located in the **Tutorial.05\Tutorial** folder included with your Data Files.

6. Click the Over while down image **Browse** button, and then double-click **labelOWD.gif** located in the **Tutorial.05\Tutorial** folder included with your Data Files.

▶ **7.** Click in the **Alternate text** box, and then type **label**. This text will appear in the tooltip and be read by screen readers.

▶ **8.** Click the When clicked, Go to URL **Browse** button, and then double-click **label.html** in the local root folder of your Cosmatic site. The Label page will open in the browser window when the label element is clicked.

▶ **9.** If necessary, click the **In** button, and then click **Main window**. The Label page will open in the current browser window.

▶ **10.** Click the **Preload images** check box to check it, if necessary. All of the graphics in the navigation bar will preload.

You want to show the Down image initially for the label link to give a visual cue to the user that this is the currently displayed page of the Cosmatic site.

▶ **11.** Click the **Show "Down image" initially** check box to check it. An asterisk appears next to the element name in the Nav bar elements box to indicate that the Down image (rather than the Up image) will be displayed initially in the page.

▶ **12.** If necessary, click the **Insert** button, and then click **Horizontally**. The navigation bar will display horizontally to match the design plan.

▶ **13.** Click the **Use tables** check box to check it, if necessary. The navigation bar will be inserted as a table. You've entered all the information for the first element. See Figure 5-5.

Completed label element information ◀ **Figure 5-5**

You'll repeat the same process to add the elements for the other pages in the Cosmatic site.

To add the other page elements to the navigation bar:

▶ 1. In the Insert Navigation Bar dialog box, click the **Add Item** button ⊞ above the Nav bar elements box. The boxes and options are cleared so you can add the next element, and the next element name, currently *unnamed1*, appears in the Nav Bar Elements box.

▶ 2. Type **Bands** in the Element name box.

▶ 3. Browse to the **Tutorial.05\Tutorial** folder included with your Data Files to insert the following graphics for each state.

Element	Graphic
Up image	bands.gif
Over image	bandsOver.gif
Down image	bandsDown.gif
Over while down image	bandsOWD.gif

▶ 4. Type **bands** in the Alternate Text box.

▶ 5. Click the When clicked, Go to URL **Browse** button, and then double-click **bands.html** in the local root folder of your Cosmatic site.

▶ 6. If necessary, click the **In** button, and then click **Main window**.

▶ 7. Verify that the **Show "Down image" initially** check box is unchecked.

You do not need to change the Preload Images, Insert, or Use tables attributes, because you already set them when you set the attributes for the first element. If you change these options, the entire navigation bar is affected. You'll follow the same procedure to create the elements for the Catalogue, Tour Dates, and Contact pages.

▶ 8. Repeat Steps 1 through 7 for the **catalogue** element, the **tour dates** element, and the **contact** element, using the following files located in the **Tutorial.05\Tutorial** folder included with your Data Files for the graphics. For the tour dates element, use **TourDates** (no space) as the element name.

Element name	Catalogue	TourDates	Contact
Up image	catalogue.gif	tourdates.gif	contact.gif
Over image	catalogueOver.gif	tourdatesOver.gif	contactOver.gif
Down image	catalogueDown.gif	tourdatesDown.gif	contactDown.gif
Over while down image	catalogueOWD.gif	tourdatesOWD.gif	contactOWD.gif
Alternate text	catalogue	tour dates	contact
URL	catalogue.html	tourdates.html	contact.html

▶ 9. Click the **OK** button, and then select the table, if necessary. The navigation bar is inserted in the Label page in a table and the table is selected. The label link is in the Down state to indicate that you are viewing the Label page. See Figure 5-6.

Figure 5-6 ▶ **Label page with the unformatted navigation bar**

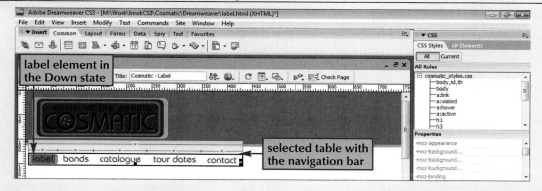

Trouble? If the page heading appears on two lines, you need to add a paragraph return after the navigation bar table. Click to the right of the navigation bar table, and then press the Enter key.

You want the navigation bar to be aligned along the right edge of the page. You'll make this change, and then test the navigation bar in a browser.

To format and test the navigation bar:

▶ **1.** In the Property inspector, click the **Align** button, and then click **Right**. The selected navigation bar moves to the right side of the page, and the table is still selected.

▶ **2.** Click a blank part of the Document window to deselect the table. See Figure 5-7.

Label page with the formatted navigation bar ◀ Figure 5-7

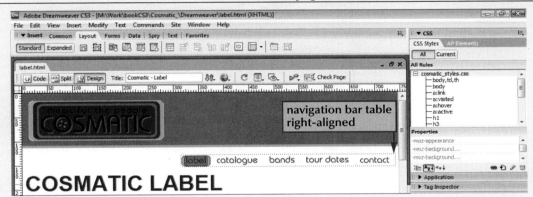

▶ **3.** Save the page, and then preview it in a browser.

▶ **4.** In the browser window, move the pointer over the **label** link to see how the link changes.

▶ **5.** Move the pointer over the other links to see how they change.

▶ **6.** Click the **tour dates** link. The image briefly changes after the link is clicked but before the Tour Dates page opens.

▶ **7.** Close the browser, and then close the Label page.

Reusing Graphics in a Web Site   InSight

When you create the navigation bar in the other pages of the Web site, you do not want to add more copies of the navigation bar graphics to the Web site, which will increase the size of the site unnecessarily. Instead, you should browse to the Graphics folder located within the site's local root folder and use the graphics that you placed there. Reusing graphics keeps the Web site lean. Also, if you decide later to change the look of the navigation bar, you have to replace only one set of images instead of a set for each page.

You need to add a navigation bar to each of the other pages in the Cosmatic site. After you have added the navigation bar to each page, you'll align the navigation bar and heading text so that they are in the same location in each page.

To create the navigation bar in the Bands page:

▶ 1. Open the **bands.html** page in the Document window, and then delete the text links at the top of the page.

▶ 2. On the **Common** tab on the Insert bar, click the **Navigation Bar** button 🖳 in the **Images** list.

▶ 3. Create the following elements, using the graphics files located in the **Graphics** folder within the local root folder of your Cosmatic site.

Element	Label	Bands	Catalogue	Tour Dates	Contact
Element name	Label	Bands	Catalogue	TourDates	Contact
Up image	label.gif	bands.gif	catalogue.gif	tourdates.gif	contact.gif
Over image	labelOver.gif	bandsOver.gif	catalogueOver.gif	tourdatesOver.gif	contactOver.gif
Down image	labelDown.gif	bandsDown.gif	catalogueDown.gif	tourdatesDown.gif	contactDown.gif
Over while down image	labelOWD.gif	bandsOWD.gif	catalogueOWD.gif	tourdatesOWD.gif	contactOWD.giv
Alternate text	label	bands	catalogue	tour dates	contact
URL	label.html	bands.html	catalogue.html	tourdates.html	contact.html
Show "Down image" initially	unchecked	checked	unchecked	unchecked	unchecked

▶ 4. Make sure the **Preload images** check box is checked, **Horizontally** is selected in the Insert list, and the **Use tables** check box is checked.

▶ 5. Click the **OK** button. The navigation bar appears in the Bands page with the bands element showing the Down state.

▶ 6. Right-align the navigation bar, and then make sure that it is located one line below the top border of the page with the heading text just below it.

▶ 7. Save the page and then preview the page in a browser.

▶ 8. Test the links, and then close the browser.

Copying a Navigation Bar

You could continue to create the navigation bar for each page manually, but a faster method is to copy an existing navigation bar and then modify the appropriate elements for that page. When you copy the navigation bar to a new page, Dreamweaver cannot automatically determine which element should be displayed in the Down state, so you must change these elements yourself. You will copy the navigation bar to the remaining pages in the Cosmatic site, and then change the navigation bar to display the element that represents the current page in the Down state.

To copy the navigation bar to the rest of the Cosmatic pages:

▶ 1. Select the navigation bar table in the Bands page, click **Edit** on the menu bar, click **Copy**, and then close the page.

▶ 2. Open the **catalogue.html** page, delete the link text, click **Edit** on the menu bar, and then click **Paste**. The navigation bar table is pasted in the Catalogue page.

Trouble? If the Image Description (Alt Text) dialog box opens, some elements do not have alternate text. For any image missing a description, click in the Description column and type the appropriate alternate text, and then click the OK button.

Tip

You can also press the Ctrl+C keys to copy the navigation bar and press the Ctrl+V keys to paste it.

3. If necessary, right-align the navigation bar and position it one line below the top border of the page with the heading text just below it.

Next, you will modify the navigation bar by changing the bands element to show the Up state initially and changing the catalogue element (the element that represents the current page) to show the Down state initially.

4. Click **Modify** on the menu bar, and then click **Navigation Bar**. The Modify Navigation Bar dialog box opens.

5. Click **Bands*** in the Nav bar elements box, and then click the **Show "Down image" initially** check box to uncheck it.

6. Click **Catalogue** (the element for the current page) in the Nav bar elements box, and then click the **Show "Down image" initially** check box to check it. See Figure 5-8.

Modify Navigation Bar dialog box   Figure 5-8

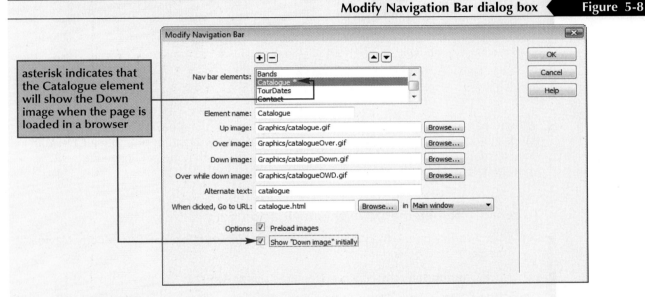

asterisk indicates that the Catalogue element will show the Down image when the page is loaded in a browser

7. Click the **OK** button. The navigation bar in the page is modified to display the current page in the Down state.

8. Save the page, preview the page in a browser, test the navigation bar, and then close the browser and the page.

9. Repeat Steps 2 through 8 for the **contact.html** and **tourdates.html** pages, changing the element that represents the current page to show the Down image initially.

10. Open the **index.html** page, click to the right of the logo image, press the **Enter** key, click **Edit** on the menu bar, and then click **Paste**. The navigation bar is pasted in the home page.

When you modify the navigation bar in the home page, you will not designate an element to show the Down image initially, because no element in the navigation bar represents the home page.

11. Click **Modify** on the menu bar, click **Navigation Bar**, click **Bands*** in the Nav bar elements list, click the **Show "Down image" initially** check box to uncheck it, and then click the **OK** button.

▶ **12.** Save the page, preview the page in a browser, test the navigation bar, and then close the browser.

Modifying the Navigation Bar

As a Web site grows and changes, you will undoubtedly need to modify the navigation bar. You might need to add new elements, delete current elements, reorder existing elements, change the graphics associated with the various states of the elements, and update the URLs to which elements are hyperlinked. Remember, you cannot change the horizontal or vertical orientation of an existing navigation bar. To change the orientation of the navigation bar, you must delete the current navigation bar and create a new one.

Reference Window | **Modifying a Navigation Bar**

- Click Modify on the menu bar, and then click Navigation Bar.
- In the Nav bar elements box, click the element you want to modify.
- Change the options as needed.
- Click the OK button.

Brian has decided that placing the catalogue element of the navigation bar before the bands element is more effective and better achieves the site goal of promoting CDs. You need to modify the navigation bar in the Cosmatic site so that the catalogue element appears before the bands element.

To reorder the elements in the navigation bar:

▶ **1.** Click **Modify** on the menu bar, and then click **Navigation Bar**. The Modify Navigation Bar dialog box opens.

▶ **2.** Click **Catalogue** in the Nav bar elements box to select it.

▶ **3.** Click the **Move Item Up In List** button ▲ above the Nav bar elements box so that the element is second in the list. See Figure 5-9.

Figure 5-9 ▶ **Elements reordered in the Modify Navigation Bar dialog box**

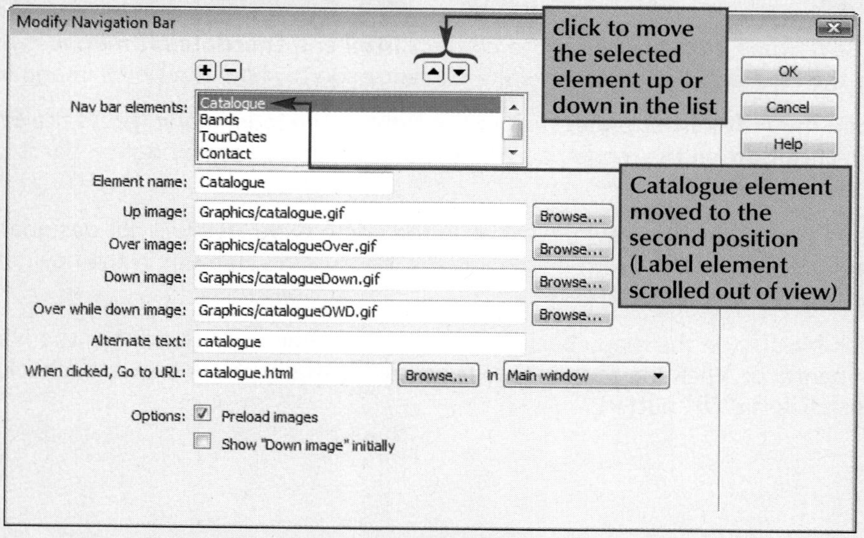

▶ **4.** Click the **OK** button. The elements are reordered in the navigation bar.

▶ **5.** Click outside the navigation bar to deselect it. See Figure 5-10.

Home page with reordered navigation bar elements ◀ **Figure 5-10**

▶ **6.** Save and close the page.

▶ **7.** Repeat Steps 1 through 6 for the **bands.html**, **catalogue.html**, **contact.html**, **label.html**, and **tourdates.html** pages.

▶ **8.** Starting with the home page, preview all the pages in the Cosmatic site in a browser, and then close the browser and any open pages.

So far, you have created and modified the navigation bar in each page of the Cosmatic site. In the next session, you will create frames and framesets.

Session 5.1 Quick Check | Review

1. What is a navigation bar?
2. How many states can each element in a navigation bar have?
3. In which state is a navigation bar element when the pointer is positioned over the element before the graphic has been clicked?
4. Where should you store the graphics used in navigation bar elements?
5. True or False? When you copy a navigation bar from one page to another, Dreamweaver automatically adjusts the elements so that the element for the link to the page in which you are pasting shows the Down state.
6. What property of a navigation bar cannot be changed after the navigation bar has been created?

Session 5.2

Understanding Frames and Framesets

Frames divide one Web page into multiple HTML documents. Each frame contains a single HTML document with its own content and, if necessary, its own scroll bars. A Web page with frames is held together by a frameset. A **frameset** is a separate HTML document that defines the structure and properties of a Web page with frames. The frameset page is not displayed in the browser; its only function is to store the information abouthow the frames will display in the Web page and to provide the browser with that information when the page is loaded. Every frame must be contained in a frameset. When you create frames in Dreamweaver, code to display NoFrames content is automatically added to the code of the frameset page. **NoFrames content** is the content shown by browsers that cannot display frames to provide information for users who cannot view the frames. You will learn more about NoFrames content when you add content to frames.

In the past, frames were used to allow Web authors to update page content without having to reload the fixed navigation, header, and footer elements of the page. As connection speeds have increased and new technologies have emerged, frames have been replaced by the following methods:

1. Reloading all page elements, because fast connections and caching eliminates most of the associated delay.
2. Iframes, which enable individually updateable content to be placed within a page.
3. Ajax, which enables updating of specific page content and form submission without reloading the entire page.

Although these approaches have eliminated the need for traditional framesets in current design, you still need to understand frames so that you can edit or redesign existing sites that rely on them.

InSight | **Deciding When to Continue Using Frames**

Frames have a bad reputation, primarily because many sites made poor use of them. In addition, the use of frames has some definite drawbacks. You should be aware of the following problems associated with frames:

- Too many frames in a page fragments that page and makes it difficult to read. When frames were first introduced, many designers placed so many frames in their pages that users found the sites confusing and difficult to follow. Be sure to use a reasonable number of frames in a page.
- Frames run more slowly in Internet Explorer earlier than version 5.5 because older versions open an additional, invisible browser window for each frame in the page, which uses processing power and makes things slower. If you are supporting very old browsers, you should not use frames.
- Frames make it difficult for users to bookmark specific content, because bookmarks mark the initial state of the frameset. Any changes to page content due to a clicked navigation element or a link are usually not reflected when the bookmark is loaded. This can frustrate users who want to come back to a particular place in a site.
- Frames can make it difficult for search engines to list the site.

When you see frames in a site, ask yourself why the frames were used and what they add to the site. Continue to use frames only when they contribute to the overall site design.

When a site includes a frameset and frames, it is important that they are coded correctly. Some common mistakes include targeting a link to open in the wrong frame and miscoding so that multiple instances of the same frame open within one Web page. You will learn the correct way to create frames in this session.

Before you start using frames, you will explore a Web page that uses frames. The sample Web page was used during planning stages to develop the Life in Minor Chords frame layout. The frame borders are visible so that you can see the location of the frames. Also, one of the sample links is targeted to open in the wrong frame. Experiencing the effects of a mistargeted link will help you recognize the mistake when you work with frames. The sample Web page contains text placeholders where the final artwork, navigation bar, and content will be. Designers often use text placeholders to help lay out Web pages while the art and content are being created. In the final version of the page, the Life in Minor Chords logo art will be substituted for the text in the top frame, a navigation bar will be created for the left frame, finalized content will be added to content frames, and the frame borders will be invisible.

To explore the sample frames page in a browser:

1. Start your browser.

2. Click **File** on the menu bar, click **Open**, click the **Browse** button, navigate to the **Tutorial.05\Tutorial\FrameTest\Dreamweaver** folder included with your Data Files, double-click **LIMCFrameSet.htm**, and then click the **OK** button. The sample page with frames loads in the browser window. See Figure 5-11.

Sample Web page with frames **Figure 5-11**

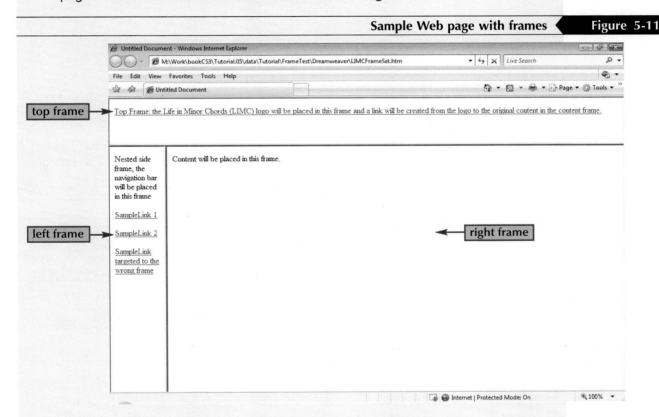

Trouble? If an Internet Explorer dialog box opens to indicate that the page needs to open in a new browser window, click the OK button.

These are the frames that you will create for the Life in Minor Chords page. The top frame is where the logo will be placed, the left frame will contain the navigation bar, and the right frame will display the changing page content.

3. Read all the text in the page, and then click the **SampleLink 1** link. The content in the main content frame (the right frame) changes. See Figure 5-12.

Figure 5-12 Content changed in the right frame

4. Click the **Top Frame** link in the top frame. The text that was originally in the content frame reappears.

5. Click the **SampleLink targeted to the wrong frame** link in the left frame. The new content replaces the navigation text, making it impossible to navigate through the page, which is a very common mistake. See Figure 5-13.

Figure 5-13 Sample frames page with a mistargeted link

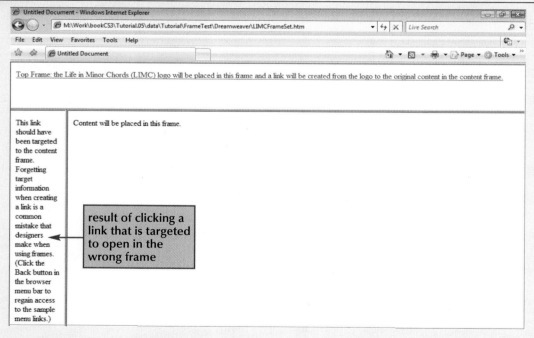

6. Click the **Back** button on the browser toolbar to return to the navigation links in the left frame.

▶ **7.** Close the browser.

Creating a Web Page that Uses Frames

To better understand how frames work, you will create a new page in the Cosmatic site for the band Life in Minor Chords that has three frames. The top frame will contain an HTML document with the band logo, a frame at the left of the page will contain an HTML document with the navigation bar for the page, and a frame at the right of the page will contain one of the many HTML documents with content. When a user clicks a different link, the HTML document with the requested information will appear in the content frame in the page; the other two frames in the page will remain the same.

Initially, each Web page can be thought of as one frame. You can then create more frames in any page. There are many ways to add frames to a Web page. You can split the page into frames, you can drag the borders of a page to create frames, you can insert frames, or you can use predefined framesets. No matter which method you use to create frames, you need to set Dreamweaver so that frame borders are visible. To view the frame borders after you have made them visible, the page must be in Design view.

| **Creating a Web Page with Frames** | | Reference Window |

- Open the page in which you want to create frames.
- Click View on the menu bar, point to Visual Aids, and then click Frame Borders.
- Click Modify on the menu bar, point to Frameset, and then click a Split Frame command.
  or
- Drag a frame border.
  or
- On the Layout tab of the Insert bar, click the Frames button, and then click a predefined frameset.

You'll display the frame borders for the home page.

To view frame borders for the home page in Dreamweaver:

▶ **1.** If you took a break after the previous session, make sure that the Cosmatic site is open.

▶ **2.** Open the **index.html** page in the Document window.

▶ **3.** Click **View** on the menu bar, point to **Visual Aids**, and then click **Frame Borders**. A gray frame border surrounds each frame in the page. In this case, only one frame border appears around the entire page because you haven't yet created any frames. See Figure 5-14.

Tip

Each time you close and reopen a page, you need to redisplay the frame borders to make them visible.

Figure 5-14 ▸ **Home page with the frame border visible**

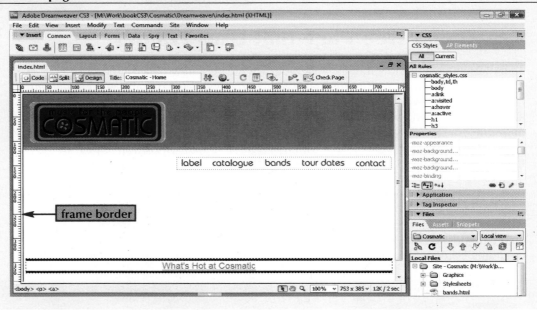

Creating Frames by Splitting a Web Page

You can create frames in a Web page by splitting the page. When you split a page, the Document window divides into two frames—either vertically (left and right) or horizontally (top and bottom). The Web page properties and any content move into the specified frame (left, right, top, or bottom). You can continue to split the page by selecting and splitting a frame until you have achieved the desired number of frames. The four ways to split a page are:

- **Split Frame Left.** Splits the page vertically into two frames, and moves the Web page properties and any content into the left frame.
- **Split Frame Right.** Splits the page vertically into two frames, and moves the Web page properties and any content into the right frame.
- **Split Frame Up.** Splits the page horizontally into two frames, and moves the Web page properties and any content into the top frame.
- **Split Frame Down.** Splits the page horizontally into two frames, and moves the Web page properties and any content into the bottom frame.

You'll create frames in the home page to become familiar with the way frames affect the content of Web pages.

To split the home page into frames:

▸ 1. Click **Modify** on the menu bar, point to **Frameset**, and then click **Split Frame Left**. The home page splits into two vertical frames with the content in the left frame and nothing in the right frame. The left frame also has its own scroll bar. See Figure 5-15.

Home page with two vertical frames ◄ Figure 5-15

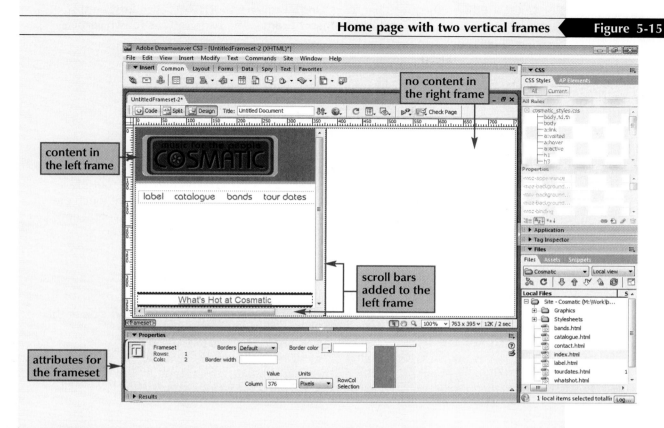

2. Click in the left frame. The left frame becomes active.

3. Click **Modify** on the menu bar, point to **Frameset**, and then click **Split Frame Up**. The left frame splits into two horizontal frames with the content in the upper frame. See Figure 5-16.

Home page split into three frames ◄ Figure 5-16

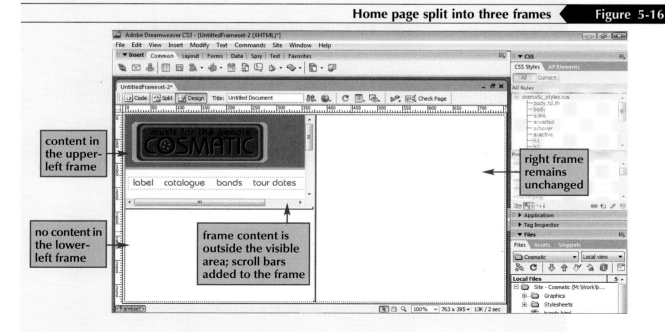

▶ **4.** Click **Edit** on the menu bar, click **Undo Convert to XHTML**, click **Edit** on the menu bar, and then click **Undo Insert Frame**. The page returns to two vertical frames.

▶ **5.** Press the **Ctrl+Z** keys twice. The page returns to one frame.

Creating Frames by Dragging Borders

When frame borders are visible, you can create frames in a page by dragging the frame borders at the perimeter of the Web page up, down, left, or right. If a Web page already has frames, you can create additional frames by dragging the borders of the outside frames away from the edges of the page. Dragging frame borders that do not touch the edge of the Web page resize the frames. Be careful; the frame (and any content it contains) is deleted if you drag the frame border back to the Web page perimeter.

You'll create frames by dragging the borders of the home page.

To create frames in the home page by dragging borders:

▶ **1.** Position the pointer over the **left frame border** (all the way on the left side of the screen). The pointer changes to ⟷ .

▶ **2.** Drag the **border** to the right approximately one-third of the way to the center of the page to create two vertical frames. Use the rulers to help you, if necessary. The Web page content and settings (such as the page background) are in the larger right frame. See Figure 5-17.

Figure 5-17 | **Home page with uneven vertical frames**

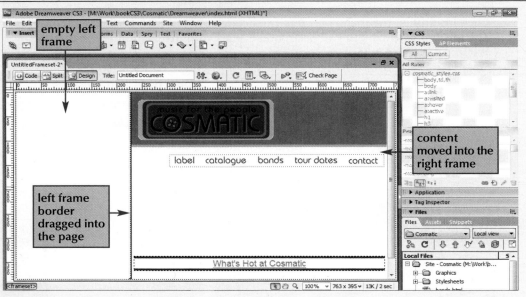

▶ **3.** Position the pointer over the **top frame border** to change the pointer to ↕ , and then drag the **border** down approximately one-third of the way toward the center of the page to create horizontal frames. The content moves into the lower-right frame. See Figure 5-18.

Home page with four frames | Figure 5-18

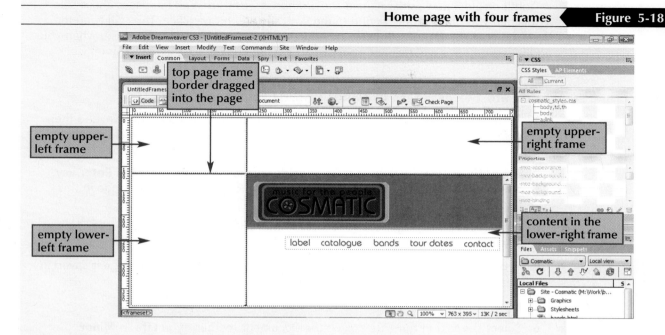

> **4.** Press the **Ctrl+Z** keys to undo the horizontal frames.
>
> You'll use the mouse to remove the left frame.

> **5.** Drag the **vertical frame border** left to the edge of the Document window. The empty left frame disappears.
>
> **Trouble?** If a dialog box opens prompting you to save the index.html page, you dragged the frame border to the right. Click the No button to delete the page content without saving, click Edit on the menu bar, click Undo Delete Frame to reverse the deletion, and then repeat Step 5, being careful to drag the frame border to the left.

> **6.** Close the home page without saving changes.

Using a Predefined Frameset

You can select from several predefined framesets to add frames to Web pages. These framesets create commonly used frame layouts. Using them can save you the time of creating each frame yourself. In addition to creating simple left, right, top, and bottom frames, there are also predefined framesets for more complex layouts that split a page into three or four frames of different sizes. Some of these more complex predefined framesets include nested framesets. A **nested frameset** is a frameset that is inside another frameset. The frameset that holds the nested frameset is called the **parent frameset**.

After you have inserted a predefined frameset, you can resize the frames by dragging any frame border inside the Web page. Remember, dragging a frame border from the perimeter of the Web page will add frames.

You will create a new section of the Web site devoted to the Life in Minor Chords band. This section will have its own look that will distinguish it from the rest of the site, because it will function as the Life in Minor Chords Web site and should create a specific look that will be identified with the band. Brian asks you to use frames for this part of the site.

You'll create a new folder named *LifeInMinorChords* so that all the pages and assets associated with this unique section of the Web site are in one place. This will keep the Web site organized. You will name the new page *limc_content1.html* because, when you add frames to the page, this will become the default content for the main frame.

To create the new Life in Minor Chords folder and page:

▶ 1. In the Files panel, right-click the local root folder for your Cosmatic site, and then click **New Folder** on the context menu. An untitled new folder appears in the Files panel.

▶ 2. Type **LifeInMinorChords** as the new folder name, and then press the **Enter** key. The new folder is renamed with descriptive name. You'll save a new page in this folder.

▶ 3. In the Files panel, right-click the **LifeInMinorChords** folder, and then click **New File** on the context menu. An untitled HTML file is created in the folder.

Tip

You can also click HTML in the Create New section on the Start page to create a new page.

▶ 4. Type **limc_content1.html**, and then press the **Enter** key. The new page is saved in the LifeInMinorChords folder.

▶ 5. Open the **limc_content.html** page in the Document window.

▶ 6. Select the text in the Title box on the Document toolbar, type **Life in Minor Chords - content 1 frame**, and then press the **Enter** key. Page titles will help you identify the individual frames; users will see only the title of the frameset in the browser window title bar.

▶ 7. Type **Content 1 frame** in the Document window to help identify the page. See Figure 5-19.

Figure 5-19 ▶ **New limc_content1.html page**

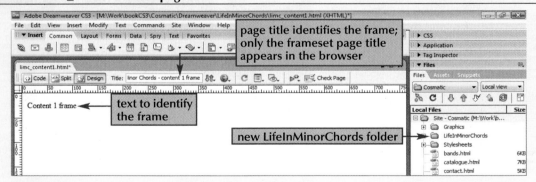

▶ 8. Save the limc_content1.html page.

After the page is created, you can add the predefined frameset.

To add the predefined frameset to the limc_content1.html page:

▶ 1. On the **Layout** tab of the Insert bar, click the **Frames button arrow** ▤ ▾. Buttons for the 13 predefined framesets appear.

▶ 2. Click **Top and Nested Left Frames** button ▤ . The page is split into three frames, and the content of the page appears in the lower-right frame. See Figure 5-20.

Page with top and nested left frames ◀ **Figure 5-20**

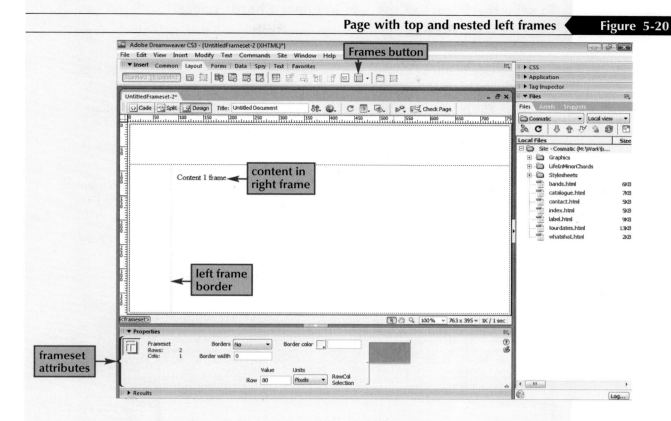

Trouble? If the Frame Tag Accessibility Attributes dialog box opens, the Accessibility preferences are set to prompt you to specify frame titles. Click the Cancel button to close the dialog box whenever it opens as you create frames in this tutorial.

Selecting and Saving Frames

You must save the frames you created before you begin working on the page. Each frame contains a separate HTML document, so you must select and save the document in each frame individually. You select a frame when you want to add content to the HTML document in that frame or when you want to save the HTML document in that frame. After you select the frame, you can save it.

Saving a Frame	Reference Window

- Select the frame in the Document window or in the Frames panel.
- Click File on the menu bar, and then click Save Frame.
- Type a filename in the File name box.
- Click the Save button.

You will save the top and left frames that you created for the Life in Minor Chords page. You will add a page title and identifying text when you save each frame. (You saved the HTML document in the right frame when you created the page, so you do not need to save it again.)

To save the frames in the Life in Minor Chords page:

▶ 1. Click in the **top frame** to make that frame active, and then type **LIMC - top frame**. The content appears in the frame.

▶ 2. Type **Life in Minor Chords top frame** in the Title box on the Document toolbar, and then press the **Enter** key.

▶ 3. Click **File** on the menu bar, and then click **Save Frame**. The Save As dialog box opens.

▶ 4. If necessary, navigate to your site's local root folder, and then double-click the **LifeInMinorChords** folder to open it.

▶ 5. Type **limc_top_frame.html** in the File name box, and then click the **Save** button. The new HTML document appears in the LifeInMinorChords folder in the Files panel and the filename appears in the Document window title bar.

▶ 6. In the Files panel, click the **Plus (+)** button ⊞ next to the LifeInMinorChords folder to display the files stored in that folder. See Figure 5-21.

Figure 5-21 | **Modified top frame**

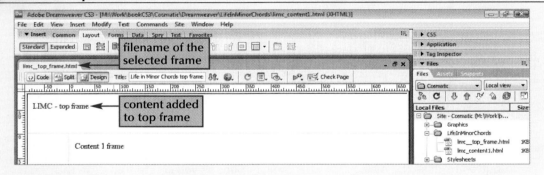

You'll repeat this process to save the left frame.

▶ 7. Click in the **left frame** in the Document window to make that frame active, type **LIMC - left frame** to add the content, type **Life in Minor Chords - left frame** in the Title box on the Document toolbar, and then press the **Enter** key.

▶ 8. Click **File** on the menu bar, click **Save Frame**, and then save the frame in the **LifeInMinorChords** folder with the filename **limc_left_frame.html**.

Selecting and Saving the Frameset

After you have saved the HTML document in each frame of the page, you must save the frameset. The frameset is a separate page that contains all the information about how the frames will display in the Web page and what HTML documents will initially be loaded into each frame. (When you adjust the size of a frame, the attributes of a frame, or the attributes of the frameset, that information is stored in the frameset page.) In addition, the frameset page title appears in the browser window title bar whenever any of the frames included in the frameset are displayed.

You select the frameset from the Document window by selecting the outer border of the page. (The frame borders must be visible to select the frameset in the Document window.) When the frameset is selected, a dotted line is visible inside the border of one frame or all the frames in the Document window and the frameset properties appear in the Property inspector.

Saving a Frameset | Reference Window

- Select the frameset in the Document window or in the Frames panel.
- Click File on the menu bar, and then click Save Frameset.
- Type a filename in the File name box.
- Click the Save button.

You'll select the frameset you created for the LIMC page and save it.

To select and save the frameset for the LIMC page:

▶ **1.** Make sure the frame borders are visible, and then click the **border** that surrounds the entire page in the Document window. The frameset is selected. See Figure 5-22.

Selected frameset ◀ **Figure 5-22**

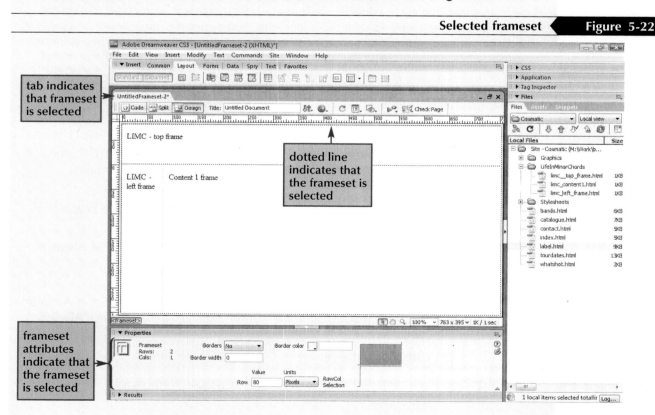

▶ **2.** Type **Cosmatic - Life in Minor Chords** in the Title box on the Document toolbar, and then press the **Enter** key.

Tip

You can save any changes you make to the frames or frameset by clicking the Save All command on the File menu.

▶ 3. Click **File** on the menu bar, and then click **Save Frameset**. The Save As dialog box opens.

▶ 4. Save the frameset in the **LifeInMinorChords** folder as **limc_frameset.html**. The frameset filename will appear in the browser window title bar. These tutorials use *frameset* in the filename to avoid confusion, but this is not usually considered good practice in Web site design because it is meaningless to users.

▶ 5. Preview in a browser the four pages that you created and stored in the LifeInMinorChords folder, and then close the browser and the pages.

If you want to work on or view the Web page that contains the frames, you open the frameset page, because it contains all of the instructions for creating the frames. You can also open each frame individually in the Document window by selecting that page in the Files panel.

Adjusting Page Properties for Frames

You can adjust page properties and attributes for each HTML document in a saved frame or frameset. Because each frame contains a separate HTML document, you must set page properties and attributes for each frame separately, or you can create an external style sheet with styles that set the desired attributes and then connect each HTML document to the external style sheet. As with other elements, you adjust the attributes of any page content by selecting the content and adjusting the attributes in the Property inspector or by creating additional styles in the style sheet and applying those styles to the content.

You will set the page properties for the limc_top_frame.html page. This is the HTML document that is displayed in the top frame of the limc_frameset.

To set page properties for the top frame:

▶ 1. Open the **limc_top_frame.html** page in the Document window. The HTML document for the top frame of the limc_frameset page is open in the Document window.

▶ 2. In the Property inspector, click the **Page Properties** button. The Page Properties dialog box opens with the Appearance category displayed.

▶ 3. Click **Arial, Helvetica, sans-serif** in the Page font list, set the Size to **14 pixels**, type **#666666** in the Text color box, type **#A1CEF4** in the Background color box, and then type **0** in the margin boxes.

▶ 4. Click **Links** in the Category box, type **#FFFFFF** in the Link color, Rollover links, and Active links boxes, type **#CCCCCC** in the Visited links box, and then click **Always underline** in the Underline style list, if necessary.

▶ 5. Click the **OK** button, and then save the page. See Figure 5-23.

Page properties set for the top frame page | Figure 5-23

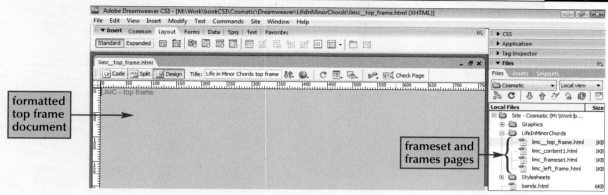

You will move the styles from the limc_top_frame.html page to an external style sheet, and then delete the styles from the page.

To move the limc_top_frame.html page properties to an external style sheet:

▶ 1. Click the **Code** button on the Document toolbar, place the pointer in the first style, right-click the style, point to **CSS Styles** on the context menu, and then click **Move CSS Rules**. The Move To External Style Sheet dialog box opens.

▶ 2. Click the **A New Style Sheet** option button, and then click the **OK** button. The Save Style Sheet File As dialog box opens.

▶ 3. Navigate to the **Stylesheets** folder in your Cosmatic site's local root folder, type **limc_styles.css** in the File name box, and then click the **Save** button. The new style sheet is created and saved in the Stylesheets folder. The selected style is moved to the new style sheet, and the remaining styles in the limc_top_frame.html page are selected.

▶ 4. Right-click the selected styles, point to **CSS Styles** on the context menu, click **Move CSS Rules**. The Move To External Style Sheet dialog box opens.

▶ 5. Click the **Style Sheet** arrow, click **limc_styles.css** in the list, and then click the **OK** button. The remaining styles move to the external style sheet.

▶ 6. Click the **Design** button on the Document toolbar, and then save and close the limc_top_frame.html and limc_styles.css pages.

You'll attach the external style sheet to all of the HTML documents that are displayed in the frames of the limc_frameset page.

Tip

You can also click Text on the menu bar, point to CSS Styles, and then click Move CSS Rules to open the Move To External Style Sheet dialog box.

To attach the limc_styles.css external style sheet to all the pages in the LIMC frameset:

▶ 1. Open the **limc_frameset.html** page in the Document window. The HTML document in the top frame is formatted with the styles you just created. See Figure 5-24.

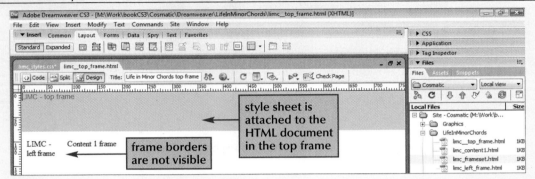

▶ 2. Click **View** on the menu bar, point to **Visual Aids**, and then click **Frame Borders**, if necessary. The frame borders are visible. See Figure 5-25.

Figure 5-25 ▶ Frame borders displayed in the frameset

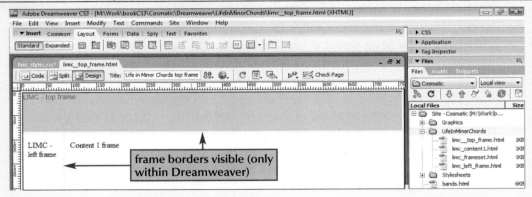

▶ 3. In the Document window, click in the **left frame** to select it.

▶ 4. Expand the **CSS Styles panel**, click the **Attach Style Sheet** button [icon], and then attach the **limc_styles.css** style sheet to the page.

▶ 5. In the Document window, click in the **right frame** to select it.

▶ 6. In the CSS Styles panel, click the **Attach Style Sheet** button [icon], and then attach the **limc_styles.css** style sheet to the page.

▶ 7. Click the **gray border** around the page to select the frameset, click **File** on the menu bar, and then click **Save All**. All of the changes you made to the frames are saved. See Figure 5-26.

Formatted frameset | Figure 5-26

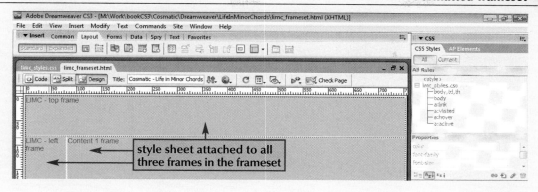

Adjusting Frame and Frameset Attributes

You set and adjust attributes for each frameset and frame individually. This enables you to customize the way each frame is displayed in the browser. For example, you can make the borders of one frame visible and make the borders of other frames invisible. To adjust the attributes of a frame or frameset, you must first open the frameset page and then select the frame or frameset you want to modify in the Frames panel. The Frames panel enables you to select and adjust the frame and frameset information that is contained in the frameset page. Remember, the frameset contains all of the instructions for creating the frames, and the individual HTML pages contain the content that appears in the frames. When you select a frame in the Document window, you are actually selecting the HTML document contained in that frame (because the frameset page is not actually displayed). Selecting the frameset in the Document window is the same as selecting the frameset from the Frames panel, but it only provides you with access to the main frameset information (not the elements in the frameset page). When you select a frame or frameset from the Frames panel, you are selecting the information within the frameset page that pertains to the selected item.

You will open the Frames panel, and then select the frames and the framesets in the limc_frameset.html page.

To select frames and framesets in the limc_frameset.html in the Frames panel:

▶ **1.** Click **Window** on the menu bar, and then click **Frames**. The Frames panel opens below the Files panel group.

▶ **2.** In the Frames panel, click the **topFrame** box. The top frame is selected in the Document window, and its attributes appear in the Property inspector. See Figure 5-27.

Figure 5-27

Top frame selected in the Frames panel

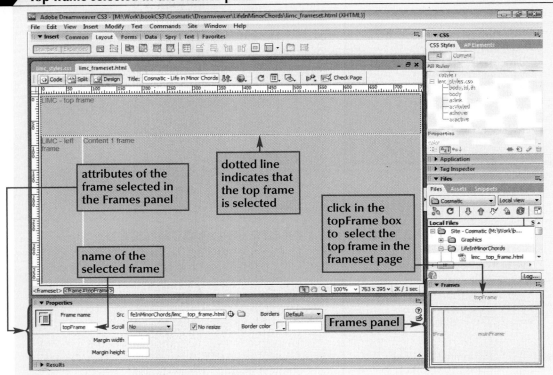

3. In the Document window, click the **top frame**. The attributes for the HTML document in the top frame appear in the Property inspector.

4. In the Frames panel, click the **leftFrame** box. The left frame is selected within the frameset, and its attributes appear in the Property inspector.

5. In the Frames panel, click the **outermost border**. The limc_frameset is selected and the frameset attributes appear in the Property inspector.

Adjusting Frame Attributes

You adjust the attributes of frames by selecting the frame in the Frames panel and changing its attributes in the Property inspector. Frame attributes include:

- **Frame name.** A descriptive name you give the frame. The frame name appears in the Frames panel and in the Property inspector when the frame is selected. The name is also used for hyperlink targets, so the name must begin with a letter and cannot include spaces or special characters. Also, the frameset uses these names as a reference to know where to load the file.
- **Src (Source).** The filename of the page that appears in the frame. If you already saved the frame, that filename appears in this box.

- **Borders.** The option to turn on the frame's borders so that they can be seen in the browser (Yes), turn off the frame's borders so that they are invisible in the browser (No), or default to the frameset settings (Default). The frame border setting overrides the frameset border setting. However, the border can be turned off only if all adjacent frames borders are also set to No or if all adjacent frames are set to Default and the frameset is set to No.
- **Scroll.** The option to display scroll bars when the frame content does not fit within the frame. Yes displays the scroll bars. No hides the scroll bars. Auto displays scroll bars if they are needed. Default leaves the decision up to the user's browser default, which is usually Auto.
- **No resize.** The option to prevent users from resizing a frame by dragging its borders. Checking this option does not restrict you from resizing the frame within the Document window.
- **Border color.** The color of the frame's border entered as a hexadecimal color code or selected with the color picker. The frame border color overrides any frameset border color. This attribute does not display correctly in all browsers.
- **Margin width.** The amount of space, in pixels, between the frame content and the left and right borders.
- **Margin height.** The amount of space, in pixels, between the frame content and the top and bottom borders.

You will set the frame attributes for the frames in the limc_frameset.html page.

To set the attributes for the frames in the LIMC frameset:

1. In the Frames panel, click the **topFrame** box.
2. In the Property inspector, type **LIMCtop** in the Frame name box, press the **Enter** key, and then verify that **limc_top_frame.html** appears in the Src box. The top frame in the Frames panel is named LIMCtop.
3. In the Property inspector, click the **Borders** button and then click **No**.
4. In the Property inspector, click the **Scroll** button and click **No**, if necessary.
5. In the Property inspector, click the **No resize** check box to check it, if necessary.
6. In the Property inspector, type **0** in the Margin width box, and then type **0** in the Margin height box. See Figure 5-28.

Tip

Save all the pages that make up the frameset so Dreamweaver can create relative file paths. If a full file path appears, save the page and replace with the relative path so it links and displays correctly on the remote site.

Top frame attributes set | Figure 5-28

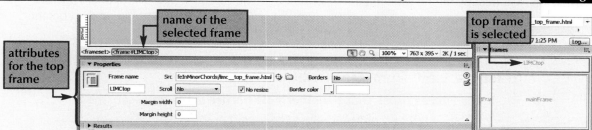

7. In the Frames panel, click the **leftFrame** box.
8. In the Property inspector, type **LIMCleft** in the Frame name box, press the **Enter** key, and then verify that **limc_left_frame.html** appears in the Src box.

▶ 9. If necessary, in the Property inspector, click the **Borders** button and click **No**, click the **Scroll** button and click **No**, click the **No resize** check box to check it, type **0** in the Margin width box, and then type **0** in the Margin height box.

▶ 10. In the Frames panel, click the **mainFrame** (right frame).

▶ 11. In the Property inspector, type **LIMCcontent** in the Frame name box, press the **Enter** key, and then verify that **limc_content1.html** appears in the Src box.

▶ 12. If necessary, in the Property inspector, click the **Borders** button and click **No**, click the **Scroll** button and click **Auto**, click the **No resize** check box to check it, type **0** in the Margin width box, and then type **0** in the Margin height box.

▶ 13. Click **File** on the menu bar, and then click **Save All**.

Adjusting Frameset Attributes

Frameset attributes are adjusted in the same way that frame attributes are adjusted: by selecting the frameset in the Frames panel and changing its attributes in the Property inspector. When you use nested framesets (such as the lower frame of the LIMC page, which is divided into a nested left frame and right frame), Dreamweaver inserts additional framesets within the code of the main frameset page to designate the nested frames. In addition to selecting and setting the attributes of the main frameset for the page, you can select and set attributes for the nested framesets.

Frameset attributes include two of the same attributes available for frames: borders and border color. You can also set the border width and the frame size in the frameset attributes. Border width, measured in pixels, affects all the borders within the frameset. The frame size is set separately for each frame within the frameset. Rows and columns can be sized as Pixels, Percent, or Relative. Pixels size the row or column to the specified pixel value. Percent sizes the row or column as a percentage of the entire browser window. Frames in the selected rows or columns will expand and shrink as the browser window is resized to maintain the specified percentage of the window area. Relative places an asterisk in the code for size. The asterisk means "take up all remaining space in the browser window." If you enter a specific relative value, it has no effect unless more than one row or column is set to relative. If more than one row or column is set to relative and a value is specified, the value specifies what portion of available space will be designated for each row or column. For example, if two rows are set to relative and have the same numeric value (1, 2, 3, etc.), then each will occupy half of the available space. However, if one column value is 1 and the other column value is 2 (totaling 3 units of measure), then the second column will be twice the width of the first, and together they will occupy all the available browser space. If you do not set the width of at least one row to Relative, users with smaller monitors may need to scroll to read all the content.

You'll set the frameset attributes for the new page.

To set the LIMC frameset attributes:

▶ 1. In the Frames panel, click the **outermost border** of the frameset. The Property inspector shows the frameset attributes.

▶ 2. If necessary, in the Property inspector, click the **Borders** button and click **No**, and then type **0** in the Border width box.

▶ 3. In the Property inspector, click the **top box** in the RowCol Selection box, type **130** in the Row Value box, and then, if necessary, click the **Units** button and click **Pixels**.

4. In the Property inspector, click the **bottom box** in the RowCol Selection box, and then, if necessary, type **1** in the Value box, click the **Units** button, and click **Relative**.

    Next, you will set the attributes for the nested frameset.

5. In the Frames panel, click the **nested frameset border**. The nested frameset includes the lower-left and lower-right frames. See Figure 5-29.

Nested frameset selected ◄ **Figure 5-29**

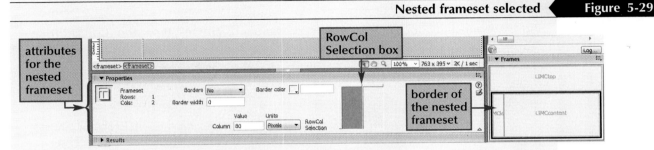

6. If necessary, in the Property inspector, click the **Borders** button and click **No**, and then type **0** in the Border width box.

7. In the Property inspector, click the **left column** in the RowCol Selection box, type **100** in the Column Value box, and then, if necessary, click the **Units** button and click **Pixels**.

8. In the Property inspector, click the **right column** in the RowCol Selection box, and then, if necessary, type **1** in the Column Value box, click the **Units** button, and click **Relative**.

9. Click **File** on the menu bar, and then click **Save All**. The changes are saved.

10. Preview the page in a browser. See Figure 5-30.

Frameset page previewed in a browser ◄ **Figure 5-30**

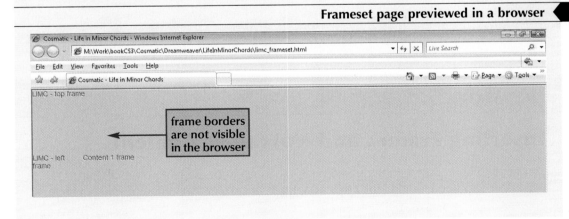

InSight | **Troubleshooting Frames in Existing Web Sites**

Although frames are not currently used when designing and creating new Web sites, you might encounter frames when maintaining or updating an existing site that uses them. As you work with these existing frame pages, you might encounter problems and issues not discussed in this tutorial. When you need to troubleshoot problems that arise with existing frame pages, it is a good idea to have a list of resources that you can reference to find information about "known problems." Some useful Web sources for frame information include:

http://dorward.me.uk/www/frames
http://webdesign.about.com/od/framesprosandcons/Frames_Pros_and_Cons.htm

You can find additional resources by typing "problems with frames" into your favorite search engine. Be aware that not all information posted on the Web is accurate or current. Check your sources and use reliable sites.

In this session, you created a new Web page with frames for the Life in Minor Chords band, set the properties for the HTML documents that are displayed in the frames, set attributes for the frames, and set attributes for the framesets. In the next session, you'll add content to the frames.

Review | **Session 5.2 Quick Check**

1. What are frames?
2. When a Web page contains frames, what can each frame contain?
3. What is a frameset?
4. Why does Dreamweaver create NoFrames content when you create frames?
5. True or False? The only way to create frames on a page in Dreamweaver is to use one of the preset frames by clicking a button in the Frames list on the Layout tab of the Insert bar.
6. What is a nested frameset?
7. Why do you need to save a frameset?

Session 5.3

Inserting Frames and NoFrames Content

You need to add content to the frames that you created for the Life in Minor Chords page. You also need to add NoFrames content for browsers that cannot display frames.

Adding Content to Frames

There are several ways to place content in a frame. You can open the frameset page, select the HTML document in a frame, and create the content in the frame using the same techniques that you would use to insert content into a Web page that does not contain frames. You can open the HTML document in the Document window and create the content in the regular way. (When you open the frameset, the content will be displayed.) You can also select a Web page you already created as the Source for the selected frame in the Property inspector. The existing Web page will open in the selected frame by default whenever the frameset page is opened. If the frameset is open, you must resaveeach frame every time that you make a change within that frame. Remember, you canuse the Save All command on the File menu to save all of the open frames and the frameset at once.

Brian asks you to add the content to the frames of the Life in Minor Chords page. You'll insert a graphic of the Life in Minor Chords logo with background artwork taken from the band's latest CD in the top frame of the new Web page. Then you'll insert and format text in the main frame of the Web page.

To insert the logo graphic into the top frame:

▶ **1.** If you took a break after the previous session, make sure your Cosmatic site is open, the limc_frameset.html page is open in the Document window, and the frame borders are displayed.

▶ **2.** In the Document window, click in the **top frame** to make the frame active, and then delete the text in the frame. You will insert the logo graphic into this frame.

▶ **3.** On the **Common** tab of the Insert bar, click the **Images button arrow** , and then click the **Image** button . The Select Image Source dialog box opens.

▶ **4.** Navigate to the **Tutorial.05\Tutorial** folder included with your Data Files, and then double-click **LifeBanner.jpg**. The logo graphic is added in the top frame of the page. See Figure 5-31.

Frameset page with content in the top frame ◀ **Figure 5-31**

▶ **5.** Click **File** on the menu bar, and then click **Save Frame**.

▶ **6.** Close the frameset page, and then close the limc_styles.css page.

Next, you'll open the HTML document displayed in the right frame of the frameset page and add the text content to the document. Then you will format the text. Brian supplied the text in a Word document, so you can copy and paste the content rather than retyping it.

To paste text into the right frame content:

▶ 1. Open the **LIMCmainframetext.doc** document located in the **Tutorial\Tutorial.05** folder included with your Data Files in Word or another word processing program, copy the entire document, and then close the document and word processing program.

▶ 2. Open the **limc_content1.html** page in the Document window, select all of the text, click **Edit** on the menu bar, and then click **Paste**. The text you copied appears in the Document window.

▶ 3. In the CSS Styles panel, click the **New CSS Rule** button 🔁, and then create a custom style class for the heading text named **.limc_heading** defined in the **limc_styles.css** style sheet. The CSS Rule Definition for limc_heading dialog box opens.

▶ 4. In the Type category, set the size to **28 pixels**, set the case to **Lowercase**, set the color to **#FFFFFF**, and then click the **OK** button. The .limc_heading style is created.

▶ 5. In the Document window, select the heading text, and then, in the Property inspector, click the **Style** arrow and click **limc_heading**. The style is applied to the heading.

▶ 6. In the Document window, select the last two paragraphs of the body text beginning with "Sure we've sold out..." and ending with "...makes us authentic.", and then, in the Property inspector, click the **Text Indent** button ⊉≣. The text in the limc_content1.html page is formatted.

▶ 7. Save and close the limc_content1.html page, and then save and close the limc_styles.css style sheet.

▶ 8. Open the **limc_frameset.html** page in the Document window. The new content appears in the right frame. See Figure 5-32.

Figure 5-32 ▶ **Frameset page with content in the main frame**

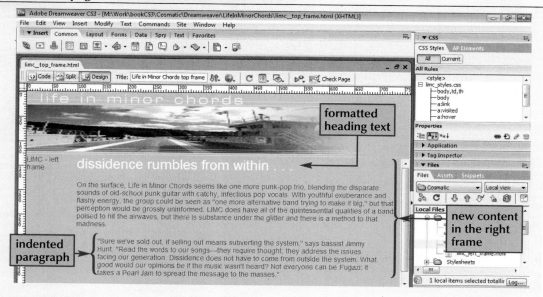

▶ 9. Preview the page in a browser, and then close the browser.

Adding NoFrames Content

The NoFrames code is automatically added to the HTML code for the frameset page when you create frames in Dreamweaver. You add NoFrames content just as you add content to any other frame or Web page. The content appears in place of the regular Web page when a user's browser does not support frames. (Frames are not supported in some devices, such as PDAs, that support limited Web browsing.)

| **Adding Appropriate NoFrames Content** | InSight |

The NoFrames content should be simple text that explains that the page users are attempting to view has frames and cannot be seen by their browser. The text should also provide a brief explanation of the purpose of the page, links to alternate pages where users can locate information, or contact information so that users have another way to get the information they were trying to obtain from the Web page.

| **Adding NoFrames Content** | Reference Window |

- Open the frameset page in the Document window.
- Click Modify on the menu bar, point to Frameset, and then click Edit NoFrames Content.
- Type the content you want to appear in browsers that cannot display frames.
- Add a link to the home page.
- Click File on the menu bar, and then click Save All.

You'll add content to the NoFrames code for the LIMC frameset page. The text will provide users with a link to the main Cosmatic site so they can get more information about Life in Minor Chords or Cosmatic.

To add NoFrames content to the frameset page:

▶ 1. Click **Modify** on the menu bar, point to **Frameset**, and then click **Edit NoFrames Content**.

▶ 2. Type **This Web page uses frames. Click here for more information about the band Life in Minor Chords or about the Cosmatic label.**

You'll link the word *here* to the home page of the Cosmatic site.

▶ 3. Select the word **here**.

▶ 4. In the Property inspector, click the **Browse for File** button 📁, navigate to the site's local root folder, and then double-click **index.html**. The word *here* is linked to the home page.

▶ 5. Double-click the word **here** in the NoFrames content. The path to the home page appears in the Link box. See Figure 5-33.

Figure 5-33   **NoFrames content added**

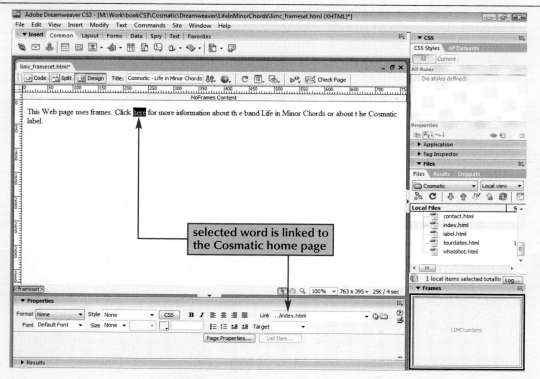

You will switch back to the frameset page.

▶ **6.** Click **Modify** on the menu bar, point to **Frameset**, and then click **Edit NoFrames Content** to toggle back to the frameset page.

▶ **7.** Click **File** on the menu bar, and then click **Save All**. The frameset page is saved with the NoFrames content.

▶ **8.** Close the page.

Using Hyperlinks with Frames

When you click a hyperlink in a Web page, the linked page usually replaces the current page in the browser window. In a frames page, where one Web page contains more than one HTML page, you don't always want the linked page to replace the HTML page in the same frame. For example, consider the common practice of creating a navigation bar in a frame at the left or top of a page. When a user clicks an element in the navigation bar, the linked page opens in the main frame of the Web page (rather than replacing the navigation bar). You can change where a Web page will open by modifying the target for the linked page. The target can specify the browser window as well as the frame in which the linked Web page will open. Figure 5-34 describes the target options.

Target options | Figure 5-34

Target Option	Description
_blank	Opens the link in a new browser window and leaves the current window open.
_parent	Opens the link in the parent frameset if you are using nested framesets.
_self	Opens the new page in the same frame as the link. If there are no frames, self replaces the old page with the new page. This is the default target.
_top	Replaces all the frames and the content of the current Web page with the content of the new page.
named frames	Opens the new page in the frame you select. The names you gave each frame appear at the end of the Target list.

Brian wants you to create targeted hyperlinks for the frames in the Life in Minor Chords page. The navigation bar will appear in the nested left frame and target the links to the LIMCcontent frame. Another team member is working on the content for the additional pages, so you'll create placeholder pages for that content. Also, you'll create a link from the Lifebanner.gif to the limc_content1.html page and target the link to the LIMCcontent frame. This will provide the illusion that the user is linking to the home page of the LIMC site when the logo is clicked, because the content that displayed when the page was originally loaded will reappear.

You'll start by creating the placeholder pages for the targets.

To create the placeholder pages:

▶ 1. Click **HTML** in the Create New section in the Start page. A new HTML page opens.

▶ 2. Save the page in the **LifeInMinorChords** folder in the site's local root folder with the filename **limc_content_history.html**.

▶ 3. Type **LIMC - History** in the Title box on the Document toolbar, and then press the **Enter** key.

▶ 4. In the CSS Styles panel, click the **Attach Style Sheet** button 🖼, and then attach the **limc_styles.css** style sheet to the page.

▶ 5. In the Document window, type **LIMC History**, select the text you typed, and then, in the Property inspector, click the **Style** arrow and click **limc_heading**. The style is applied to the heading text, which changes to all lowercase.

▶ 6. Press the **Right Arrow** key to deselect the text. See Figure 5-35.

Tip

You can also right-click the document, point to CSS Styles and then click Attach Style Sheet to attach the style sheet to the page.

Figure 5-35 | **Life in Minor Chords history page**

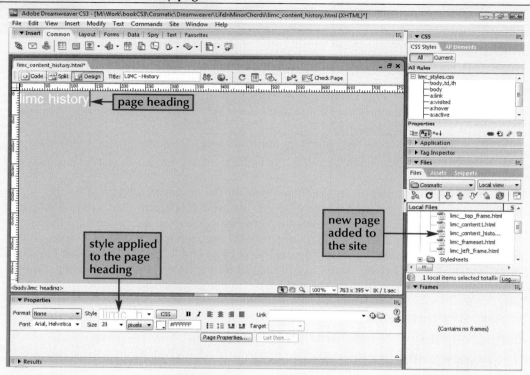

7. Save and close the page.

You'll repeat this process for each placeholder HTML document you need to create.

8. Repeat Steps 1 through 7 to create the following the pages.

Filename	Title	Page heading
limc_content_members.html	LIMC - Members	LIMC Members
limc_content_cds.html	LIMC - CDs	LIMC CDs
limc_content_tours.html	LIMC - Tours	LIMC Tours
limc_content_photos.html	LIMC - Photos	LIMC Photos

Next, you'll insert the navigation bar in the nested left frame of the limc_frameset.html page. Each element in the navigation bar will display graphics. For each element, you'll specify the linked page and the target frame. (You will add alternate text for each element in the Review Assignments.)

To create the navigation bar with targeted links:

1. Open the **limc_frameset.html** page in the Document window, click **View** on the menu bar, point to **Visual Aids**, and then click **Frame Borders** to make the frame borders visible.

2. Click in the **lower-left frame** to make it active, select the text in the frame, and then press the **Delete** key. The lower-left frame is active and empty.

3. On the **Common** tab of the Insert bar, click the **Images button arrow** 🖼 ▾, and then click the **Navigation Bar** button 🖳 . The Insert Navigation Bar dialog box opens.

▶ **4.** Create the first element using the following name and images. The Down image is the same as the Over image, so select the Over image in the Graphics folder for the Down image.

Element name	LIMChistory
Up image	Tutorial.05\Tutorial\LIMChistory.gif
Over image	Tutorial.05\Tutorial\LIMChistoryOVER.gif
Down image	Cosmatic\Graphics\LIMChistoryOVER.gif
When clicked, Go to URL	limc_content_history.html (in the LifeInMinorChords folder in the local root folder)
Target in	LIMCcontent (the name of the target frame)
Preload images	checked
Insert	Vertically
Use tables	checked

The Insert Navigation Bar dialog box contains all of the information for the LIMChistory element. You did not check the Show "Down image" initially check box, because you are using the same navigation bar for every content frame. You'll add the next navigation bar element, which is LIMCmembers.

▶ **5.** In the Insert Navigation Bar dialog box, click the **Add Item** button ⊞.

▶ **6.** Create the second element using the following name and images. Remember, you do not need to change the Preload images, Insert, or Use tables options for each element.

Element name	LIMCmembers
Up image	Tutorial.05\Tutorial\LIMCmembers.gif
Over image	Tutorial.05\Tutorial\LIMCmembersOVER.gif
Down image	Cosmatic\Graphics\LIMCmembersOVER.gif
When clicked, Go to URL	limc_content_members.html (in the LifeInMinorChords folder in the local root folder)
Target in	LIMCcontent

▶ **7.** In the Insert Navigation Bar dialog box, click the **Add Item** button ⊞, and then create the third element using the following name and images.

Element name	LIMCcds
Up image	Tutorial.05\Tutorial\LIMCcds.gif
Over image	Tutorial.05\Tutorial\LIMCcdsOVER.gif
Down image	Cosmatic\Graphics\LIMCcdsOVER.gif
When clicked, Go to URL	limc_content_cds.html (in the LifeInMinorChords folder in the local root folder)
Target in	LIMCcontent

▶ **8.** In the Insert Navigation Bar dialog box, click the **Add Item** button ⊞, and then create the fourth element using the following name and images.

Element name	LIMCtours
Up image	Tutorial.05\Tutorial\LIMCtours.gif
Over image	Tutorial.05\Tutorial\LIMCtoursOVER.gif
Down image	Cosmatic\Graphics\LIMCtoursOVER.gif
When clicked, Go to URL	limc_content_tours.html (in the LifeInMinorChords folder in the local root folder)
Target in	LIMCcontent

9. In the Insert Navigation Bar dialog box, click the **Add Item** button ⊞, and then create the fifth element using the following name and images.

Element name	LIMCphotos
Up image	Tutorial.05\Tutorial\LIMCphotos.gif
Over image	Tutorial.05\Tutorial\LIMCphotosOVER.gif
Down image	Cosmatic\Graphics\LIMCphotosOVER.gif
When clicked, Go to URL	limc_content_photos.html (in the LifeInMinorChords folder in the local root folder)
Target in	LIMCcontent

All of the elements for the navigation bar are created with the appropriate names, graphics, linked pages, and target frames.

10. In the Insert Navigation Bar dialog box, click the **OK** button. The navigation bar appears in the nested lower-left frame. See Figure 5-36.

Figure 5-36 ▶ **Navigation bar in the nested lower-left frame**

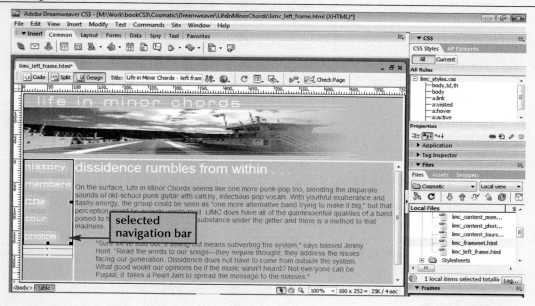

11. Click **File** on the menu bar, click **Save All**, preview the page in a browser, and then close the browser.

You'll use the Property inspector to create the targeted link from the logo in the top frame to the HTML document that was originally displayed in the LIMCcontent frame. You'll target the link to open in the LIMCcontent frame.

To create a targeted link from the logo using the Property inspector:

1. In the Document window, click the **logo graphic** in the top frame to select it.

2. In the Property inspector, click the **Browse for File** button 📁 next to the Link box, and then double-click the **limc_content1.html** page in the **LifeInMinorChords** folder in the site's local root folder.

3. In the Property inspector, click the **Target** arrow, and then click **LIMCcontent**. See Figure 5-37.

Target information for the top frame ◣ **Figure 5-37**

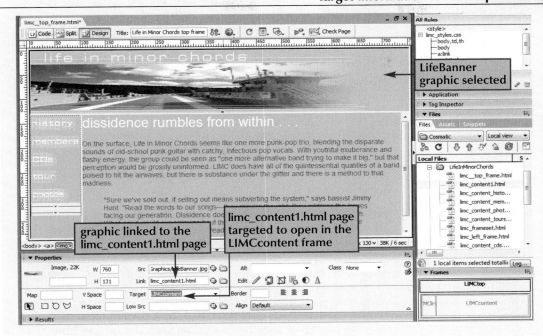

▶ **4.** In the Document window, click the **LifeBanner** graphic to select it.

▶ **5.** In the Property inspector, type **0** in the Border box, and then press the **Enter** key. No border appears around the graphic.

▶ **6.** Click **File** on the menu bar, and then click **Save All**. All of the changes you made to the frameset are saved. You'll test the navigation bar.

▶ **7.** Preview the page in a browser, click each link in the navigation bar, and then click the banner graphic link in the top frame. See Figure 5-38.

Completed limc_frameset.html page previewed in a browser ◣ **Figure 5-38**

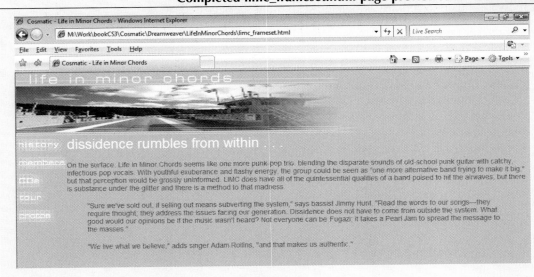

▶ **8.** Close the browser, and then close the page.

You'll add links from the Bands page and the Catalogue page to the limc_frameset.html page targeted to open in a new browser window so that the limc_frameset page does not replace the open page. This enables the user to easily return to the main Cosmatic site.

To create additional targeted links using the Property inspector:

▶ 1. Open the **bands.html** page in the Document window, and then select the **Life In Minor Chords** subheading text.

▶ 2. In the Property inspector, click the **Browse for File** button 📁, and then double-click **limc_frameset.html** in the **LifeInMinorChords** folder in the site's local root folder.

▶ 3. In the Property inspector, click the **Target** arrow, and then click **_blank** to open the link in a new browser window.

▶ 4. Save the page, preview the page in a browser, and then click the **LIFE IN MINOR CHORDS** link. The Life in Minor Chords page opens in a new browser window.

▶ 5. Close the browser, and then close the page.

▶ 6. Open the **catalogue.html** page in the Document window, select the **Life in Minor Chords CD cover** graphic, and then link the CD cover to the **limc_frameset.html** page targeted to open in a new browser window.

▶ 7. Save the page, preview the page in a browser, and then click the **Life in Minor Chords CD cover** graphic. The linked page opens in a new browser window.

▶ 8. Close the browser, and then close the page.

Tip

You can also drag the Point to File button from the Property inspector to the appropriate file in the Files panel to create the link.

Reviewing HTML Frame Tags and Targets

When you use frames in a Web page, all the frame tags associated with the Web page are in the frameset page. Additional content pages are simply regular Web pages that are targeted to open in one of the frames. The following three tags, described below and shown in Figure 5-39, are associated with frameset pages:

- **Frameset tags.** A set of frameset tags surround the frameset and, if nested frames are used, additional sets of frameset tags surround the nested frames within the parent frameset. The opening frameset tag contains the values for the frameset attributes.
- **Frame tag.** A frame tag is inserted between the opening and closing frameset tags for each frame in the frameset. There is no closing frame tag, making this one of the few HTML tags that is not in a pair. The frame tag contains the values for the frame attributes.
- **Noframes tags.** The noframes tags are inserted after the closing frameset tag. They surround content that is seen by browsers that do not support frames.

HTML frame tags Figure 5-39

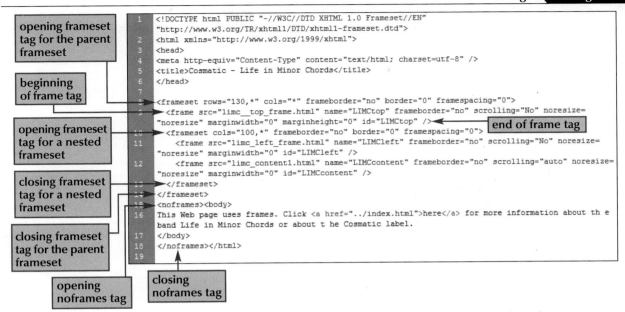

When you set a target for a hyperlink, the target information is added to the HTML code for the hyperlink in the following format:

```
<a href="theURL" target="value">Linked text or graphic</a>
```

where the target value options are the same Target options listed in the Property inspector: _blank, _parent, _self, _top, and named frames. Sometimes the code for a page can be very long. You can hide code you don't want to review by collapsing selected portions of the code or collapsing a full tag in Code view.

You will examine the code of the limc_frameset page and review the frameset, frame, and noframes tags—as well as the hyperlink tags with target information inserted into them.

To examine the HTML code in the LIMC frameset page:

▶ **1.** Open the **limc_frameset.html** page in the Document window, and then, in the Frames panel, select the frameset.

▶ **2.** Click the **Code** button on the Document toolbar. The code for the limc_frameset.html page appears in the Document window. The parent frameset tags and everything between them are highlighted. See Figure 5-40.

Figure 5-40 **Code for the limc_frameset.html page**

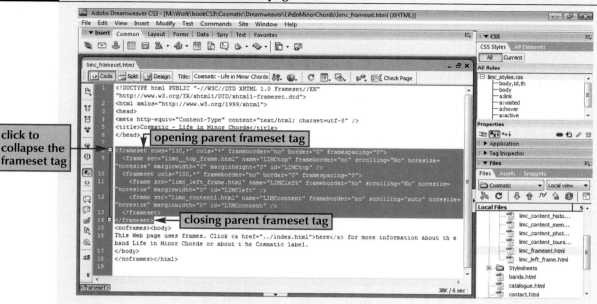

Trouble? If your screen does not match the screen shown in Figure 5-40, click the Design button on the Document toolbar, select the outermost frame in the Frames panel, and then repeat Step 2.

3. Locate the opening frameset tag and examine the frameset attributes and their values.

4. Click the **Collapse Full Tag** button on the Coding toolbar to hide the frameset coding.

5. Click the **Plus (+)** button to redisplay the frameset code.

6. Right-click the opening frameset tag, click **Reference** on the context menu, and then read the reference information in the Reference panel of the Results panel group.

7. Locate the closing frameset tag.

8. Find the nested frameset, and then locate the first frame in the nested frameset.

9. Examine the frame attributes and their values in the first frame.

10. Right-click the frame tag, click **Reference** on the context menu, and then read the reference information in the Reference panel.

11. Click the **Design** button on the Document toolbar, and then close the page.

12. Collapse the Frames panel group and the Reference panel group, and then expand the Files panel group, if necessary.

Tip

You can hide selected lines of code or a tag by clicking the Collapse Selection button on the Coding toolbar. To redisplay the code, you can click the Expand All button on the Coding toolbar.

Updating the Web Site on the Remote Server

As a final review of the changes you made to the Cosmatic site, you'll update the files on the remote server and review the pages over the Web. You need to upload every page in the site as well as the new Life in Minor Chords pages because you modified all of them. When you upload the pages, you will include dependent files so that the new graphic-sand new CSS styles are uploaded to the remote server.

To upload the modified Cosmatic site to your remote server:

▶ 1. Click the **Connects to Remote Host** button ⌗ on the Files panel toolbar.

▶ 2. Click the **View** button on the Files panel toolbar, and then click **Local View**.

▶ 3. Select the **Site-Cosmatic** root folder in the Local View list, and then click the **Put File(s)** button ⬆ on the Files panel toolbar.

▶ 4. Click the **Yes** button when asked if you want to Put the entire site.

▶ 5. Click the **Disconnects from Remote Host** button ⌗ on the Files panel toolbar.

▶ 6. Click the **View** button on the Files panel toolbar, and then click **Local View**.

You'll preview the updated site in a browser. The site will include all the new styles and text that you added to the local version of the site.

To preview the updated Cosmatic site in a browser:

▶ 1. Start your browser, type the URL of your remote site in the Address bar on the browser toolbar, and then press the **Enter** key. The home page opens.

▶ 2. Click the **catalogue** link, click the **Life in Minor Chords CD cover** to open the Life in Minor Chords page in a new browser window, and then close the new browser window that opened.

▶ 3. Click the **bands** link in the Catalogue page, and then click the **LIFE IN MINOR CHORDS** subheading to open the Life in Minor Chords page in a new browser window.

▶ 4. In the Life in Minor Chords page, click the **history**, **members**, **CDs**, **tour**, and **photos** links to make sure that each link is appropriately targeted and that all of the HTML documents were uploaded.

▶ 5. Click the **graphic** at the top of the Life in Minor Chords page to redisplay the original information that appeared on the page when it was opened, and then close the Life in Minor Chords browser window.

▶ 6. On the home page, click the **label** link, click the **tour dates** link, click the **contact** link, and then click the **Cosmatic** logo to return to the home page.

▶ 7. Click the **What's Hot at Cosmatic** link.

▶ 8. Close the browser.

In this session, you added content to the frames you created, and then you reviewed the HTML associated with frames and targets.

Review | **Session 5.3 Quick Check**

---

1. Name two ways to insert content into a frame.
2. True or False? You can add NoFrames content to a frameset page.
3. What is typically added as NoFrames content for a frameset?
4. Why is it common practice to target a navigation bar to a specific frame?
5. True or False? A link cannot be targeted to open in a different frame in the page.
6. What are three HTML tags associated with frameset pages?

Review | **Tutorial Summary**

In this tutorial, you worked on shared site elements. You inserted a navigation bar in a Web site, copied the navigation bar to all of the pages in the site, and then modified the navigation bar. Then you learned about frames and framesets. You used several techniques to create frames. You saved the frames page and then set page properties and attributes for frames and framesets. You added content to the HTML documents in the frames, and then you created hyperlinks and targeted the links to specific frames. Finally, you explored the HTML behind frames and targets.

Key Terms

Down state	navigation bar	Over While Down state
element	nested frameset	parent frameset
frame	NoFrames content	Up state
frameset	Over state	

Practice		Review Assignments

Practice the skills you learned in the tutorial.

Data Files needed for the Review Assignments: DCbanner.jpg, DCbottombanner.jpg, DCcdsUp.jpg, DCcdsOver.jpg, DChistoryUp.jpg, DChistoryOver.jpg, DCmembersUp. jpg, DCmembersOver.jpg, DCphotosUp.jpg, DCphotosOver.jpg, DCtoursUp.jpg, DCtoursOver.jpg

Brian asks you to create a Web page for Dizzied Connections similar to the one you created for Life in Minor Chords. You will create a page with a navigation bar and frames. The Dizzied Connections page uses colors and a style similar to the Cosmatic site, so you will attach the cosmatic_styles.css style sheet to all of the HTML documents to format the page. Because you do not want the background image from the Cosmatic site to appear in each frame of the Dizzied Connections page, you will create an additional custom style and apply the style to the body tag in each document. When the page is complete, you'll link the new page to the band name in the Bands page. After all of the changes are complete, you'll upload the Cosmatic site to the Web server.

1. Open the **Cosmatic** site that you modified in this tutorial, right-click the local root folder for your Cosmatic site in the Files panel, click New Folder on the context menu, and then name the new folder **DizziedConnections**.

2. Right-click the DizziedConnections folder in the Files panel, click New File on the context menu to create a new page in the DizziedConnections folder, and then name the page **dc_content.html**.

3. Open the **dc_content.html** page in the Document window, click in the page in the Document window, and then on the Layout tab of the Insert bar, click the Top and Bottom Frames button in the Frames list to insert frames into the page.

4. Click in the top frame, and then save the frame in the DizziedConnections folder in the local root folder of the Cosmatic site as **dc_top_frame.html**.

5. Click in the bottom frame, and then save the frame in the DizziedConnections folder in the local root folder of the Cosmatic site as **dc_bottom_frame.html**.

6. Select the frameset, change the title to **Cosmatic - Dizzied Connections**, and then save the frameset in the DizziedConnections folder as **dc_frameset.html**.

7. Click in the top frame, and then attach the cosmatic_styles.css style sheet. Attach the cosmatic_styles.css style sheet to the documents in the middle and bottom frames.

8. Click in the top frame, change the title to **DC - top frame**, create a new custom style class rule named **.dc_body** that is defined in the cosmatic_styles.css style sheet. In the Background category, set the background color to #FFFFFF, and set the background image to None.

9. Click in the top frame if necessary, click the <body> tag on the status bar to select it, and use the Style list in the Property inspector to apply .dc_body style. The top frame displays a white background.

10. In the top frame, insert the **DCbanner.jpg** graphic located in the Tutorial.05\Review folder included with your Data Files.

11. In the CSS Styles panel, select the .dc_body style in the All Rules pane, scroll to the margin-left attribute in the Properties pane, and then change the margin-left value to 0.

12. Save and close the cosmatic_styles.css style sheet.

13. Select the graphic, create a hyperlink to the dc_content.html page, and then target the link to mainFrame in the Target list in the Property inspector. Save all the frames and the frameset.

14. Click in the middle frame, change the title to **DC - content**, click the <body> tag to select it, then apply the dc_body style to the body tag. The tag in the status bar changes to <body.dc body> and the background changes to white.

15. Type **dizzied connections . . .** in the middle frame, and then, in the Property inspector, format the text you just typed as Heading 2.

16. Click in the bottom frame, and then change the title to **DC - bottom frame**.

17. Create a new custom style class named **.dc_bottomframe** and defined in the cosmatic_styles.css style sheet. In the Background category, insert the **DCbottombanner.jpg** graphic located in the Tutorial.05\Review folder included with your Data Files as the background image, set the horizontal position to Left, and then set the vertical position to Top.

18. Click in the bottom frame, select the body tag in the status bar, and then apply the dc_bottomframe style to the body tag. The background graphic is displayed.

19. Save all the frames and the frameset, and then close the page and the style sheet.

20. Create a new HTML page, and save the new page as **dc_cds.html** in the DizziedConnections folder in the local root folder. Attach the cosmatic_styles.css style sheet to the page, apply the dc_body style to the body tag in the page, change the page title to **DC - CDs**, type **Dizzied Connections – CDs . . .** in the page, apply the Heading 2 tag, and then save and close the page.

21. Repeat Step 20 to create the following pages: **dc_history.html**, **dc_members.html**, **dc_photos.html**, and **dc_tours.html**. Make sure you change the page title for each page and type appropriate heading text on each page (for example, for the dc_history page, type **Dizzied Connections - History . . .**).

22. Open the **dc_frameset.html** page in the Document window, click at the top of the bottom frame, and then insert a navigation bar. (*Hint:* View the frame borders, if necessary.)

23. Create the first element in the navigation bar using the following name and images. (*Hint:* The Down image is the same as the Up image, so for the Down image, select the Up image you stored in the Graphics folder.)

Element name	DCcds
Up image	Tutorial.05\Review\DCcdsUp.jpg
Over image	Tutorial.05\Review\DCcdsOver.jpg
Down image	Cosmatic\Dreamweaver\Graphics\DCcdsUp.jpg
Alternate text	Dizzied Connections CDs
When clicked, Go to URL	dc_cds.html (in the DizziedConnections folder in the local root folder)
Target in	mainFrame
Preload images	checked
Insert	Horizontally
Use tables	checked

24. Add a new element to the navigation bar, using the following name and images.

Element name	DChistory
Up image	Tutorial.05\Review\DChistoryUp.jpg
Over image	Tutorial.05\Review\DChistoryOver.jpg
Down image	Cosmatic\Dreamweaver\Graphics\DChistoryUp.jpg
Alternate text	Dizzied Connections History
When clicked, Go to URL	dc_history.html (in the DizziedConnections folder in the local root folder)
Target in	mainFrame

25. Add a third element to the navigation bar using the following name and images.

Element name	DCmembers
Up image	Tutorial.05\Review\DCmembersUp.jpg
Over image	Tutorial.05\Review\DCmembersOver.jpg
Down image	Cosmatic\Dreamweaver\Graphics\ DCmembersUp.jpg
Alternate text	Dizzied Connections Members
When clicked, Go to URL	dc_members.html (in the DizziedConnections folder in the local root folder)
Target in	mainFrame

26. Add a fourth element to the navigation bar using the following name and images.

Element name	DCphotos
Up image	Tutorial.05\Review\DCphotosUp.jpg
Over image	Tutorial.05\Review\DCphotosOver.jpg
Down image	Cosmatic\Dreamweaver\Graphics\DCphotosUp.jpg
Alternate text	Dizzied Connections Photos
When clicked, Go to URL	dc_photos.html (in the DizziedConnections folder in the local root folder)
Target in	mainFrame

27. Add a fifth element to the navigation bar using the following name and images.

Element name	DCtours
Up image	Tutorial.05\Review\DCtoursUp.jpg
Over image	Tutorial.05\Review\DCtoursOver.jpg
Down image	Cosmatic\Dreamweaver\Graphics\DCtoursUp.jpg
Alternate text	Dizzied Connections Tours
When clicked, Go to URL	dc_tours.html (in the DizziedConnections folder in the local root folder)
Target in	mainFrame

28. Click the OK button, click the Save All command on the File menu, preview the dc_frameset page in a browser, and then close the page.

29. Open the **limc_left_frame.html** page in the Document window, modify the navigation bar to include alternate text for each element by clicking the element in the Nav bar element box and typing **Life in Minor Chords -** followed by the name of the element in the Alternate text box (for example, the LIMChistory element has the alternate text **Life in Minor Chords - History**). Save and close the page.

30. Open the **catalogue.html** page in the Document window, select the Dizzied Connections CD cover graphic, and create a link to the dc_frameset.html page, targeting the link to open in a new browser window (_blank), and then save and close the page.

31. Open the **bands.html** page in the Document window, select the Dizzied Connections subheading, and create a link to the dc_frameset.html page, targeting the link to open in a new browser window, and then save the page.

32. Preview the site in a browser, test the new links, and then close the browser and the page.

33. Upload the site to your remote server, and then preview the site over the Web.

34. Submit the finished files to your instructor, either in printed or electronic form, as requested.

Apply	**Case Problem 1**

Create a navigation bar for a Web site about the small rural communities of northern Vietnam.

Data Files needed for this Case Problem: WASdrthompsonUP.gif, WASdrthompsonDown.gif, WASlinguisticdifferencesUp.gif, WASlinguisticdifferencesDown.gif, WASculturalcrosspollinationUp.gif, WASculturalcrosspollinationDown.gif, WASritualsandpracticesUp.gif, WASritualsandpracticesDown.gif, WAScontactinformationUp.gif, WAScontactinformationDown.gif

World Anthropology Society Dr. Olivia Thompson wants you to create a navigation bar for the site. An artist has already created the graphic elements that you will need. You will create the navigation bar in the home page of the site; then you will copy it to the other pages of the site. You will modify the navigation bar in these pages so the element that represents the selected page appears in the Down state when the page is loaded into a browser window.

1. Open the **DrThompson** site that you modified in **Tutorial 4**, **Case 1**, and then open the **index.html** page in the Document window.
2. Delete the text links, place the insertion point below the red stripes, and then insert a navigation bar.
3. Create the first element using the following name and images. The Down image is the same as the Over image, so use the Over image stored in the Graphics folder for the Down image. (*Hint:* To save time, you can copy the text from the Over image box and paste it into the Down image box.)

Element name	WASdrthompson
Up image	Tutorial.05\Case1\WASdrthompsonUp.gif
Over image	Tutorial.05\Case1\WASdrthompsonDown.gif
Down image	DrThompson\Dreamweaver\Graphics\ WASdrthompsonDown.gif
When clicked, Go to URL	dr_thompson.html
Target in	Main window
Preload images	checked
Insert	Horizontally
Use tables	checked

4. Add a second element to the navigation bar using the following name and images.

Element name	WASlinguisticdifferences
Up image	Tutorial.05\Case1\WASlinguisticdifferencesUp.gif
Over image	Tutorial.05\Case1\WASlinguisticdifferencesDown.gif
Down image	DrThompson\Dreamweaver\Graphics\ WASlinguisticdifferencesDown.gif
When clicked, Go to URL	linguistic_differences.html
Target in	Main window

5. Add the third element using the following name and images.

Element name	WASculturalcrosspollination
Up image	Tutorial.05\Case1\ WASculturalcrosspollinationUp.gif
Over image	Tutorial.05\Case1\ WASculturalcrosspollinationDown.gif
Down image	DrThompson\Dreamweaver\Graphics\ WASculturalcrosspollinationDown.gif
When clicked, Go to URL	cultural_cross_pollination.html
Target in	Main window

6. Add the fourth element using the following name and images.

Element name	WASritualsandpractices
Up image	Tutorial.05\Case1\WASritualsandpracticesUp.gif
Over image	Tutorial.05\Case1\WASritualsandpracticesDown.gif
Down image	DrThompson\Dreamweaver\Graphics\WASritualsandpracticesDown.gif
When clicked, Go to URL	rituals_and_practices.html
Target in	Main window

7. Add the fifth element using the following name and images.

Element name	WAScontactinformation
Up image	Tutorial.05\Case1\WAScontactinformationUp.gif
Over image	Tutorial.05\Case1\WAScontactinformationDown.gif
Down image	DrThompson\Dreamweaver\Graphics\WAScontactinformationDown.gif
When clicked, Go to URL	contact.html
Target in	Main window

8. Add appropriate alternate text to each element in the navigation bar.
9. Save the page, and then preview the page in a browser.
10. Select the navigation bar table, and then use the Property inspector to change the width to 100% and the background color to #000000.
11. Copy the navigation bar table in the Document window, and then save and close the page. (*Hint:* You can switch to Extended Tables mode, if necessary to select the table.)
12. Open the **dr_thompson.html** page in the Document window, delete the link text, paste the navigation bar into the page, delete any extra spaces that were added above or below the navigation bar, and then save the page.

⊕ EXPLORE 13. Modify the navigation bar to have the WASdrthompson element show the Down image initially. The navigation bar shows the Down image of the WASdrthompson element. Save and close the page.

14. Repeat Steps 12 and 13 for the **linguistic_differences.html** page, the **cultural_cross_pollination.html** page, the **rituals_and_practices.html** page, and the **contact.html** page using the element that corresponds to the page as the Down image.
15. Preview the pages in a browser, clicking each link to test it, and then close the browser.
16. Upload the site to your remote server, and then preview the site over the Web.
17. Submit the finished files to your instructor, either in printed or electronic form, as requested.

Create a frames page with small graphics of paintings that link to larger graphics in a Web site for an art museum.

Data Files needed for this Case Problem: LoveCallSmall.jpg, AmongTheLedHorsesSmall.jpg, LucklessHunterSmall.jpg, RiderlessHorseSmall.jpg, AmongTheLedHorses.html, TheRiderlessHorse.html, TheLoveCall.html, TheLucklessHunter.html, AmongTheLedHorsesBig.jpg, RiderlessHorseBig.jpg, LoveCallBig.jpg, LucklessHunterBig.jpg

Museum of Western Art   C. J. Strittmatter asks you to create a page for the artist Fredric Remington. The page will contain small graphics of some of the artist's more famous paintings. When the user clicks a painting, the page will display a larger version of the painting as well as a detailed description. You'll use frames for the new page and link the page to the artist's name in the Artists page. Another designer has created content pages that you'll add to the site to complete the Fredric Remington page.

1. Open the **Museum** site that you modified in **Tutorial 4**, **Case 2**, and then create a new folder named **Remington** in the site's local root folder.

2. Create a new page in the Remington folder named **remington_content.html**, and then open the page.

3. Attach the museum_styles.css style sheet to the page, change the page title to **Museum of Western Art - Remington Content frame**, and then save and close the page.

4. Repeat Steps 2 and 3 to create and format a new page named **remington_top.html** with an appropriate page title.

5. Open the **remington_content.html** page in the Document window, add a top frame to the page, and then save the frameset in the Remington folder with the name **remington_frameset.html**.

6. Select the top frame, and then link the Src box in the Property inspector to the remington_top.html page in the Remington folder to load that page in the top frame when the page is displayed in a browser.

7. Select the frameset, change the page title to **Museum of Western Art - Remington**, and then save the frameset.

8. Select the bottom frame. The Src box in the Property inspector displays the remington_content.html page, which is the page that will load in the bottom frame when the page is displayed in the browser.

9. In the bottom frame, type **Click any of the Fredric Remington paintings to view a larger version and a detailed description.**

10. In the top frame, type **The Art of Fredric Remington**, and then apply the Heading 1 style to the text.

11. Press the Right Arrow key, press the Enter key, and then create a table in the top frame with 1 row, 4 columns, a cell padding of 5, no header cells, no caption, and no summary. Select the table, and then center-align it.

12. In the first cell in the table, insert the graphic file **LoveCallSmall.jpg** located in the Tutorial.05\Case2 folder included with your Data Files. Drag the right border of the cell snug against the graphic (there is a cell padding of 5 pixels, so the border will remain 5 pixels from the edge of the graphic). Select the graphic and align the graphic to Middle in the Property inspector.

13. In the second cell in the table, insert the graphic file **AmongTheLedHorsesSmall.jpg** located in the Tutorial.05\Case2 folder included with your Data Files. Resize the cell horizontally snug against the graphic. Select the graphic and align the graphic to Middle in the Property inspector.

14. In the third cell in the table, insert the graphic file **LucklessHunterSmall.jpg** located in the Tutorial.05\Case2 folder included with your Data Files. Resize the cell horizontally snug against the graphic. Select the graphic and align the graphic to Middle in the Property inspector.

15. In the fourth cell in the table, insert the graphic file **RiderlessHorseSmall.jpg** located in the Tutorial.05\Case2 folder included with your Data Files. Select the graphic and align the graphic to Middle in the Property inspector. Save all the frames and the frameset.

◆ **EXPLORE**   16. Drag the lower border of the frame down to resize the frame until you can see the entire table and the page heading in the top frame. The bottom frame might almost disappear from view if the Document window is small.

◆ **EXPLORE**   17. Copy the following pages from the Tutorial.05\Case2 folder included with your Data Files and paste them in the Remington folder: **AmongTheLedHorses.html**, **TheRiderlessHorse.html**, **TheLoveCall.html**, and **TheLucklessHunter.html**. (*Hint:* To copy the pages, display the site list in the Files panel, navigate to the Tutorial.05\Case2 folder included with your Data Files, select the files you want to copy, right-click the selected files, point to Edit, click Copy on the context menu, navigate to the Museum site local root folder, right-click the Remington folder in the Files panel, point to Edit, and then click Paste on the context menu.)

18. Open the **AmongTheLedHorses.html** page in the Document window, click in the left column of the table, and insert the **AmongTheLedHorsesBig.jpg** graphic located in the Tutorial.05\Case2 folder included with your Data Files in the cell, and then save and close the page.

19. Repeat Step 18 for the **TheRiderlessHorse.html** page, the **TheLoveCall.html page**, and the **TheLucklessHunter.html** page using the corresponding big graphic for each page (**RiderlessHorseBig.jpg**, **LoveCallBig.jpg**, and **LucklessHunterBig.jpg**).

◆ **EXPLORE**   20. Select the small **LoveCallSmall.jpg** graphic in the first cell of the table in the top frame of the remington_frameset.html page and link it to the TheLoveCall.html page. Target the link to open in mainFrame (the bottom frame of the page) in the Property inspector.

21. Repeat Step 21 for the AmongTheLedHorses, LucklessHunter, and RiderlessHorse graphics.

22. Create a custom style class named **.image_border** defined in the museum_styles.css style sheet. In the Border category, check the Same for All check boxes, if necessary, set the top style to Solid, set the top width to Thin, and then set the top color to #ECB888.

23. Apply the image_border the style to each of the following graphics: **LoveCallSmall.jpg**, **AmongTheLedHorsesSmall.jpg**, **LucklessHunterSmall.jpg**, and **RiderlessHorseSmall.jpg**. (*Hint:* Click the Class arrow in the Property inspector.) Click the Save All command on the File menu, and then close the page.

24. Open the **artists.html** page in the Document window, link the Fredric Remington heading text to the remington_frameset.html page. Target the link to open in a new browser window, and then save the page.

25. Preview the page in a browser, click the Fredric Remington link, click the links in the Remington page to test them, and then close the browser and the page.

26. Upload the site to your remote server, and then preview the site over the Web.

27. Submit the finished files to your instructor, either in printed or electronic form, as requested.

Challenge | Case Problem 3

Create a navigation bar and add frames to the Featured Books page in a Web site for an independent bookstore.

Data Files needed for this Case Problem: featured_author_bio.html, featured_excerpt.html, PunchAuthorBioUp.gif, PunchAuthorBioOver.gif, PunchExcerptUp.gif, PunchExcerptOver.gif, PunchPressUp.gif, PunchPressOver.gif

MORE Books   The Featured Books page has generated so much response that Mark Chapman wants to add more information to the page. You'll add frames to the existing Featured Books page and expand it to include an author bio, an excerpt from the book, and a navigation bar.

1. Open the **MOREbooks** site that you modified in **Tutorial 4**, **Case 3**, and then open the **featuredbook.html** page in the Document window.

2. Press the Left Arrow key to move the pointer to the left of the table, and then insert a top frame and a nested left frame into the page. The content moves to the lower-right frame.

3. Click in the top frame, change the page title to **Featured - top**, and then attach the more_styles.css style sheet to the HTML document.

4. Create a new custom style class named **.featured_body** and defined in the more_styles.css style sheet; in the Background category, change the background color to #003366 and set the background image to None. Select the body tag in the status bar and apply the new style.

5. Save the frame as **featured_top.html** in the site's local root folder, and then save and close the style sheet.

6. Click in the left frame, change the page title to **Featured - left**, attach the more_styles.css style sheet, and then apply the .featured_body style to the body tag. Save the frame as **featured_left.html** in the site's local root folder.

7. Select the frameset, and then, in the Property inspector, click Yes in the Borders list, set the Border width to 1, set the Border color to #FFFFFF, and change the page title to **Featured book - frameset**. Repeat for the nested frameset.

⊕ **EXPLORE**　8. Select the right frame, and then, in the Property inspector, click Auto in the Scroll list to enable the frame to display its own scroll bar when the frame content extends beyond the borders.

⊕ **EXPLORE**　9. Click in the right frame, switch to Code view, locate the opening body tag (<body>), place the pointer after the word body and before the closing bracket, press the Spacebar, and then type **class="featured_body"**. (*Hint:* The entire tag will read: <body class="featured_body">.) Switch to Design view. The new body style is visible in the frame.

10. Save the frameset in the site's local root folder with the filename **featured_frameset.html**.

⊕ **EXPLORE**　11. Copy the **featured_author_bio.html** page and the **featured_excerpt.html** page located in the Tutorial.05\Case3 folder included with your Data Files, and paste them in the root folder of the MOREbooks site. (*Hint:* To copy the pages, display the site list in the Files panel, navigate to the Tutorial.05\Case3 folder included with your Data Files, select both files you want to copy, right-click the selected files, point to Edit, click Copy on the context menu, navigate back to the MOREbooks site local root folder, right-click in the Files panel, point to Edit, and then click Paste on the context menu.)

⊕ **EXPLORE**　12. Insert a vertical navigation bar in the left frame.

13. Create the first element in the navigation bar using the following name and images. The Down image is the same as the Up image, so select the Up image stored in the Graphics folder for the Down image. (*Hint:* To save time, you can copy the text from the Up image box and paste it into the Down image box.)

Element name	AuthorBio
Up image	Tutorial.05\Case3\PunchAuthorBioUp.gif
Over image	Tutorial.05\Case3\PunchAuthorBioOver.gif
Down image	MOREbooks\Dreamweaver\Graphics\PunchAuthorBioUp.gif
When clicked, Go to URL	featured_author_bio.html
Target in	mainFrame
Preload images	checked
Use tables	checked

14. Create the second element in the navigation bar using the following name and images.

Element name	Excerpt
Up image	Tutorial.05\Case3\PunchExcerptUp.gif
Over image	Tutorial.05\Case3\PunchExcerptOver.gif
Down image	MOREbooks\Dreamweaver\Graphics\PunchExcerptUp.gif
When clicked, Go to URL	featured_excerpt.html
Target in	mainFrame

15. Create the third element in the navigation bar using the following name and images.

Element name	Press
Up image	Tutorial.05\Cases\PunchPressUp.gif
Over image	Tutorial.05\Cases\PunchPressOver.gif
Down image	MOREbooks\Dreamweaver\Graphics\PunchPressUp.gif
When clicked, Go to URL	featuredbook.html (this is the page that was originally in the frame)
Target in	mainFrame

16. Add appropriate alternate text for each element.

 EXPLORE

17. Adjust the width of the left frame so that the entire image is visible. (*Hint:* Drag the right border of the frame.)

18. Create a new custom style class named **.featured_heading** and defined in the more_styles.css style sheet. In the Type category, set the size to 50 pixels and set the color to #CCCC33.

19. Type **PUNCH by Kelly Moore** in the top frame, and then apply the featured_heading style to the text.

20. Save all the frames and the frameset, close all open pages, and then open and preview the featured_frameset.html page in a browser, testing the links and reading all the text, and then close the browser and the page.

21. Open the **index.html** page in the Document window, link the Featured Book text to featured_frameset.html in the Property inspector, and then verify that the link is still targeted to _blank so that the page opens in a new browser window.

22. Select the featured book graphic and change the link to featured_frameset.html; verify that the link is still targeted to _blank.

23. Save the page, preview the page in a browser, test the Featured Book links, and then close the browser and the page.

24. Upload the site to your remote server, and then preview the site over the Web.

25. Submit the finished files to your instructor, either in printed or electronic form, as requested.

| Create | **Case Problem 4** |

Create a navigation bar and a frames page showing different types of sushi in a Web site for a newly opening sushi restaurant.

Data Files needed for this Case Problem: SushiCompanyUp.gif, SushiCompanyOver.gif, SushiMenuUp.gif, SushiMenuOver.gif, SushiContactUp.gif, SushiContactOver.gif, SushiCaliforniaRoll.gif, SushiTunaHandRoll.gif, SushiSalmon.gif, SushiDescriptions.doc

Sushi Ya-Ya Mary O'Brien asks you to create a navigation bar for the Sushi Ya-Ya site and then to create a new page in the site. The new page will provide pictures of some common types of sushi. When a user clicks each picture, information about the sushi type shown in the picture will be displayed. You'll use frames for this page.

1. Open the **SushiYa-Ya** site that you modified in **Tutorial 4**, **Case 4**, and then open the **index.html** page in the Document window.

2. Delete the link text, place the pointer to the left of the logo, and then create a table with 1 row, 2 columns, and 5 pixels of cell padding.

3. Drag the SushiYa-Ya logo into the left column, and then adjust the width of the column snug against the outer border of the graphic.

⊕ EXPLORE

4. In the right column of the table, insert a horizontal navigation bar with the following elements (as well as elements needed to reflect any additional pages in your SushiYa-Ya site): company, menu, and contact. Use the **SushiCompanyUp.gif**, **SushiCompanyOver.gif**, **SushiMenuUp.gif**, **SushiMenuOver.gif**, **SushiContactUp.gif**, and **SushiContactOver.gif** images located in the Tutorial.05\Case4 folder included with your Data Files to create the elements in your navigation bar, or create your own graphics. Use the Over image as the Down image. Add appropriate alternate text, and link each element to its corresponding page. (If your site does not include pages that correspond to the navigation bar elements, rename existing pages or create new ones.)

5. Right-align the navigation bar table, resize the outer table as needed to accommodate the graphics, and then delete any spaces that were introduced into the page by the creation of the table. The horizontal blue line is deleted from the page.

6. Select the outer table and apply the logo style. The horizontal blue line reappears. Save the page.

7. Copy the entire top table including the logo and navigation bar to the **company.html** page, the **menu.html** page, and the **contact.html** page (as well as to any other pages in your SushiYa-Ya site). Modify the table in each page so that the navigation bar element that represents the selected page is in the Down state when the page is displayed in a browser window. Save and close any open pages.

8. Create a new page, add top and bottom frames to the page so that the page contains three frames, change the title of each frame and the frameset, and then save everything with an appropriate name. (*Hint:* The frameset name should be **sushi_descriptions_frameset.html**.)

9. Attach the Sushi Ya-Ya style sheet to each frame.

10. Type **Sushi Descriptions** in the top frame, and then apply the heading style.

11. Create a table with 1 row and 3 columns in the middle frame. Set the borders of the table to 1 and the border color to black, then place the **SushiCaliforniaRoll.gif** graphic in the first column, the **SushiTunaHandRoll.gif** in the second column, and the **SushiSalmon.gif** graphic in the third column. (The files are located in the Tutorial.05\Case4 folder included with your Data Files.)

12. Adjust the column widths so that the columns are flush against the sides of the graphics, center-align the table, select the frameset, select the middle column in the RowCol Selection box in the Property inspector, type **90** in the Row Value box, and then select pixels for the Row Units.

13. In the bottom frame, type **Click on the sushi picture to view the name and description.**

14. Save all the frames and the frameset.

15. Create three new pages named **tuna_hand_roll.html**, **california_roll.html**, and **salmon.html** and saved in the site's local root folder. For each page, enter an appropriate page title, and then attach the style sheet.

16. Open the **SushiDescriptions.doc** document located in the Tutorial.05\Case4 folder included with your Data Files in Word or another word processing program, copy the name and description of each type of sushi into its respective page, click at the end of the description you pasted, press the Enter key, format the text using CSS styles, and then save the page.

17. Click each sushi graphic, create a link to the appropriate description page, and then target the link to the bottom frame. Save all the frames and the frameset.

18. Open the **menu.html** page, and then type **Sushi Descriptions** below the horizontal line. (If you do not have a menu page, create one.)

19. Apply the subheadings style to the text, create a link to the sushi_descriptions_frameset.html page, and then target the link to open in a new browser window.

20. Save the page, preview the page in a browser, testing the new link and the links on the Sushi Descriptions page, and then close the browser and the page.

21. Upload the site to your remote server, and then preview the site over the Web.

22. Submit the finished files to your instructor, either in printed or electronic form, as requested.

Review | Quick Check Answers

Session 5.1

1. a page element that consists of a series of rollover graphics that change state when specific browser actions occur, such as when the user places the pointer over a graphic
2. four
3. Over state
4. in the Graphics folder in the site's local root folder
5. False; you must manually adjust which image shows in the Down state initially.
6. the vertical or horizontal orientation of the navigation bar

Session 5.2

1. Frames divide a Web page into multiple documents.
2. a single HTML document with its own content and scroll bars

3. a separate HTML document that defines the structure and properties of a Web page with frames

4. NoFrames content is added to the frameset so that you can provide information for browsers that cannot view frames.

5. False; you can also drag the frame border or use the Frameset options on the Modify menu.

6. a frame that is inside another frameset

7. because the frameset is a separate page that contains all of the information about how the frames will display in the Web page and which HTML document initially will be loaded into each frame

Session 5.3

1. You can open the frameset page, select the HTML document in a frame, and create the content in the frame using the same techniques that you would use to insert content into a Web page that is not part of a frameset. You can open the HTML document in the Document window and create the content in the regular way. You can select a Web page you have already created as the Source in the Property inspector when the frame properties are selected so that page will open in the selected frame whenever the frames page is opened.

2. True.

3. Typical content is text that explains that the page users are attempting to view uses frames and cannot be seen by their browser. The text should include a brief explanation of the purpose of the page, links to alternate pages where users can locate information, or contact information.

4. so that the linked page opens in the main frame of the Web page rather than replacing the navigation bar, and the navigation bar remains on the user's screen

5. False; a link can be targeted to open in a different frame in the page.

6. frameset tags, frame tags, and noframes tags

Creating Dynamic Pages

Using CSS to Lay Out Pages and Add Behaviors

Case | Cosmatic

Sara Lynn, president of Cosmatic, likes the general look of the pages in the new Web site, but she wants to add a small information box about the Dizzied Connections band to the home page. Brian Lee, public relations and marketing director, decides to use CSS to create a more interesting display of the information. Sara also wants a page for Sloth Child with a link from the home page to that page. Brian suggests making the Sloth Child page a dynamic page so that the user can point to or click items on the page to change the page in the user's browser. Sara gives Brian the go-ahead. You'll modify the home page, and then create the Sloth Child page.

Starting Data Files

Tutorial.06 → **Tutorial**

nu_randomZen.txt
SC2.jpg
SC3.jpg
SC4.jpg
SCWebPageImage.jpg
SSCD200.jpg

Review

(none)

Case1

WASetiquette_terms.gif
WASetiquetteButton.gif

Case2

AFigureOfTheNight.jpg
AQuietDayInUtica.jpg
BuffaloRunners.jpg
CowpunchingSometimes.jpg
DeerInForest.jpg
IndiansHuntingBuffalo.jpg
TheBucker.jpg
TheCowPuncher.jpg

Case3

BookCoverBasketSm.gif
BookCoverQueenSm.jpg
BookCoverStopGapSm.jpg

Case4

WasabiChili.jpg
WasabiCold.gif
WasabiHotWings.jpg
WasabiLowRiseJeans.jpg
WasabiLukeWarm.gif
WasabiOnFire.gif
WasabiOriginal.gif
WasabiPicture.gif
WasabiPictureSmall.gif
WasabiToasty.gif
WasabiWasabi.gif

Session 6.1

Laying Out Pages with CSS

CSS page layout is the current standard for laying out professional Web pages. This method of page layout uses Cascading Style Sheets rather than HTML tables or frames to structure content in a page. CSS page layout enables you to create both fixed width and flexible width pages, as you have done with tables and frames, but with more precision and leaner code. (Flexible width CSS pages are often referred to as fluid pages because they enable the content to move to fill the user's browser window regardless of the size of the screen.) In CSS page layout, the div tag is commonly placed around content, images, and so on to structure and position the content in the page. The **div tag** creates a transparent container you place in a Web page to hold content. As with any other tag, you can add CSS styles to a div tag.

In this tutorial, you create Web pages that use CSS layout, and you explore the two methods for inserting and positioning divs in a page: relative positioning and absolute positioning. You also examine prebuilt CSS layout pages.

Exploring Prebuilt CSS Layout Pages

The prebuilt CSS layout pages in Dreamweaver provide designers with files for building commonly used CSS page layouts. These pages are not templates; they are more like the basic architecture from which you can create your own designs. There are many discrepancies in the way that browsers interpret and display CSS layout. These pages are helpful tools for designers because they contain the fixes that enable the content to display similarly across the most common browsers. According to Adobe, these layouts render correctly in the following browsers: Firefox (Windows and Macintosh) 1.0, 1.5, and 2.0; Internet Explorer (Windows) 5.5, 6.0, 7.0; Opera (Windows and Macintosh) 8.0, 9.0; and Safari 2.0. Without cross-browser fixes in place, creating CSS layout can be a frustrating process.

You will examine one of the prebuilt CSS layout pages. The page contains div tags, a list of CSS styles, and placeholder content. By selecting and replacing placeholder content, and by editing the existing CSS styles and creating new styles, you can create your own Web pages using the prebuilt pages as a starting point. You can also move the styles to a style sheet and use them in all of the pages of your site.

To view the prebuilt CSS layout pages:

▶ 1. Click **File** on the menu bar, and then click **New**. The New Document dialog box opens.

▶ 2. Click **Blank Page**, if necessary, and then, in the Page Type box, click **HTML**. The prebuilt CSS layout pages are listed the Layout box.

▶ 3. Click **1 column elastic, centered**. An image of a page with that layout appears at the right of the dialog box. See Figure 6-1.

New Document dialog box ◀ Figure 6-1

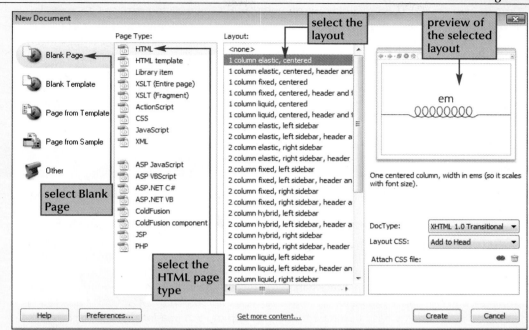

4. Click **1 column fixed, centered, header and footer**, and then click the **Create** button. A new page that contains div tags, a list of CSS styles, and placeholder content appears in the Document window. See Figure 6-2.

Prebuilt CSS page with placeholder content ◀ Figure 6-2

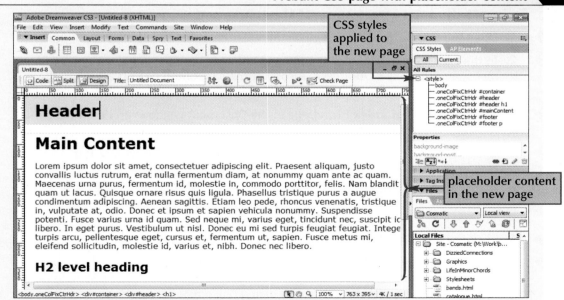

5. Scroll the page to view its placeholder content and structure, and then close the page without saving it.

Formatting a Page with Divs That Use Relative Positioning

You can also create a CSS page layout on your own. One way to create a CSS page layout is to insert divs into a page, create CSS styles to format the divs, and then place content into the div. When inserting div tags for layout, the page will display div tags inserted higher in the page code above div tags that are inserted lower in the page code. To position the div content at the right or left of the browser window, you will create a CSS style that uses the Float and Padding attributes in the Box category. Recall that Float sets which side of an object other elements such as text or divs will float around and Padding adds space between the content of an element and its border.

| InSight | | **Planning the CSS Layout** |

Before you begin creating a CSS layout, you should spend time planning the pages of your site. After your plan is in place, you can determine what CSS elements your pages require. For example, most pages need a common heading style as well as one or two subheading styles. When you create styles, remember to use names that refer to the way each style is used rather than its characteristics, because as Web sites evolve, the characteristics of each style might change. For example, if you name a subheading style as *blue_medium* to reflect the text color, and then later change the look of the site so that subheading text is red, the CSS style name will no longer make sense. After you know what CSS styles you need for a site, and you have developed a flexible naming schema for the styles, you can create the styles and place them all in an external style sheet.

You will copy the home page, and then create a CSS layout by inserting div tags into the new page.

To insert div tags into a copy of the home page:

▶ 1. Open the **Cosmatic** site that you modified in the **Tutorial 5 Review Assignments**.

▶ 2. In the Files panel, right-click the **index.html** page, point to **Edit** on the context menu, and then click **Duplicate**. A copy of the index.html page is added to the Cosmatic site.

Tip

You can also select a page in the Files panel, and then press the Ctrl+D keys to duplicate the selected page.

▶ 3. Open the **Copy of index.html** page in the Document window, and then click in the page below the navigation bar.

▶ 4. Click the **Layout** tab on the Insert bar, and then click the **Insert Div Tag** button 🔲 . The Insert Div Tag dialog box opens.

▶ 5. If necessary, click the **Insert** button, and then click **At Insertion Point**.

You will create a new style to apply to the div.

▶ 6. Click the **New CSS Style** button. The New CSS Rule dialog box opens.

▶ 7. Click the **Class** option button, type **right** in the Name box, make sure the style is defined in **cosmatic_styles.css**, and then click the **OK** button. The CSS Rule Definition for .right in cosmatic_styles.css dialog box opens.

▶ 8. Click **Box** in the Category box, click **right** in the Float list, type **5** in the Padding Top box, select **Pixels** if necessary, click the **Same For All** check box to check it, if necessary, and then click the **OK** button. The right style is created.

▶ 9. Click the **OK** button in the Insert Div Tag dialog box. The div tag is added to the code and the div placeholder text is added to the page. See Figure 6-3.

Div added to the home page Figure 6-3

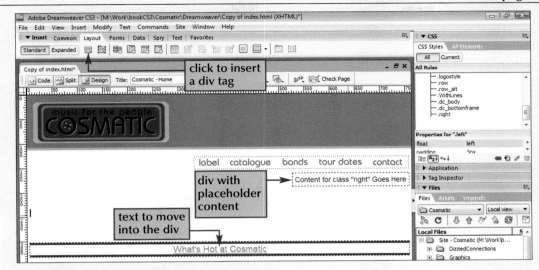

Next, you will copy the What's Hot text into the new div.

To add the What's Hot text to the div:

▶ **1.** Click the dotted line surrounding the What's Hot text. The area is selected, including the text and lines.

▶ **2.** Press the **Ctrl+C** keys to copy the text, and then press the **Delete** key to delete the text and lines from the page.

▶ **3.** In the div, select the **Content for class "right" Goes Here** text, and then press the **Ctrl+V** keys to paste the text and lines into the div. See Figure 6-4.

Div with the What's Hot text Figure 6-4

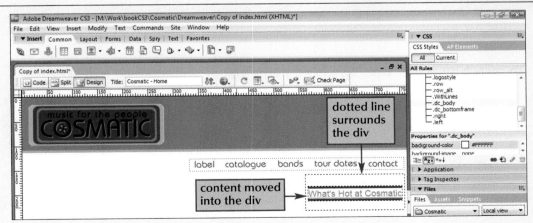

▶ **4.** Click the dotted line around the What's Hot text (not the dotted line around the div) to select it, and then press the **Right Arrow** key to deselect the text and move the insertion point to the right of the text.

▶ **5.** Press the **Shift+Enter** keys to move the insertion point to the next line within the div.

▶ **6.** Click the **Common** tab on the Insert bar, click the **Images button arrow** 🖼 ▾ , and then click the **Image** button 🖼 to insert an image into the div.

▶ **7.** Navigate to the **Graphics** folder within your local root folder, click **SScd300.jpg**, and then click the **OK** button. The image is inserted in the div. See Figure 6-5.

Figure 6-5 ▸ **Div with text and image**

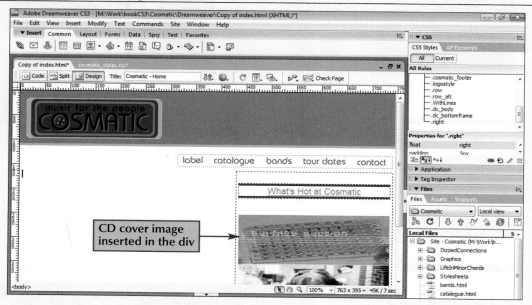

Trouble? If the Image Tag Accessibility Attributes dialog box opens, the prompt is active for your installation of Dreamweaver. Click the Cancel button to close the dialog box without adding alternate text here and any other time it opens in this tutorial.

Trouble? If the SScd300.jpg image file is not in the Graphics folder, you probably did not complete the Tutorial 4 Review Assignments. Browse to the Tutorial.04/Review folder included with your Data Files, click SScd300.jpg, and then click the OK button.

You will add another div tag to the page.

To insert a second div tag in the home page:

▶ **1.** Click the dotted border of the div to select it, and then press the **Right Arrow** key to deselect the div in the page. The insertion point is to the right of the div in the page (and lower in the code of the page).

▶ **2.** Click the **Layout** tab on the Insert bar, and then click the **Insert Div Tag** button 🖾 . The Insert Div Tag dialog box opens.

▶ **3.** If necessary, click the **Insert** button, and then click **At Insertion Point**.

▶ **4.** Click the **OK** button. The new div appears in the page.

▶ **5.** In the div, select the placeholder text, if necessary, type **Temporary text for band number one content.** (including the period), and then press the **Right Arrow** key to move the insertion point to the line below the div. See Figure 6-6.

Second div added to the home page | **Figure 6-6**

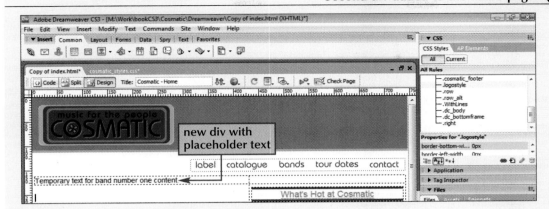

6. Save the Copy of index.html page, save and close the cosmatic_styles.css page, and then preview the Copy of index.html page in a browser. See Figure 6-7.

Home page with divs previewed in a browser | **Figure 6-7**

7. Drag the right edge of the browser window to the left. The text layout changes width as the browser window resizes. See Figure 6-8.

Figure 6-8 **Home page in a resized browser window**

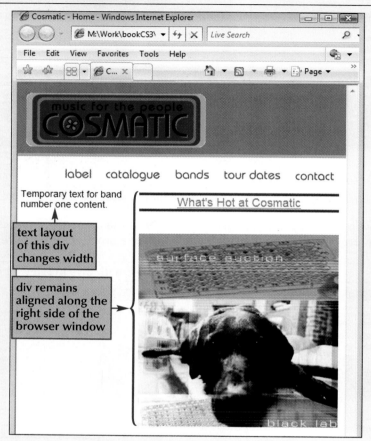

8. Close the browser, and then close the page.

Using Absolutely Positioned Div Tags

With **absolute positioning (AP)**, div tags can be positioned anywhere on the screen with great accuracy and reliability, and they remain in place relative to the top and left margins of the page regardless of how a user resizes the browser window. Unlike tables and frames, **AP divs** (absolutely positioned divs) can be stacked on top of one another so that their content overlaps. They can be animated, made visible or invisible, and have their stacking order (the order in which they overlap) changed. You can also use CSS styles to customize the display attributes of an AP div just like with a regular div tag.

Brian wants you to add a new section to the Cosmatic home page. The new section will contain two text links and a graphic link to the What's Hot page. This content is designed to promote the new release that appears in the What's Hot page. He wants you to use an AP div to place the new content so it maintains a consistent position in the page.

Inserting AP Divs

You draw an AP div in a page in Design view. The borders of each AP div you draw are visible in the Dreamweaver environment to make them easier to work with. The borders do not appear in the browser window.

You will draw an AP div in the home page. The AP div will contain a link to the What's Hot page.

To draw an AP div in the home page:

▶ **1.** Open the **index.html** page in the Document window.

▶ **2.** If the rulers are not visible, click **View** on the menu bar, point to **Rulers**, and then click **Show**.

▶ **3.** If the units on the ruler are not pixels, right-click the ruler, and then click **Pixels**.

▶ **4.** On the **Layout** tab of the Insert bar, click the **Draw AP Div** button 🖻. The pointer changes to ╋.

▶ **5.** Position the pointer approximately **50 pixels** below the navigation bar in the home page, and then drag to draw an AP div approximately the width of the navigation bar and **100 pixels** high. The rectangular AP div appears in blue below the navigation bar when you release the mouse button. See Figure 6-9.

Tip

You can also press the Ctrl+Alt+R keys to show or hide the rulers.

AP div drawn in the home page ◀ **Figure 6-9**

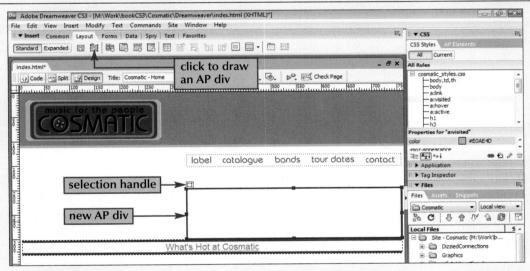

Trouble? If your AP div is in a slightly different location, has more space below it, or is not selected, you'll select, resize and move the AP div in the next section. Just continue with Step 6.

▶ **6.** Click in a blank area of the Document window, and then save the page.

Selecting, Resizing, and Moving an AP Div

As with other container objects, such as tables, an AP div can be active or selected. When an AP div is active, its border is visible and a selection handle appears in the upper-left corner. You must select the div before you can reposition or resize it. When an AP div is selected, resize handles appear all around it and a selection handle appears in the upper-left corner. You can use the resize handles to change the dimensions of the AP div to fit the content that you enter. If the page contains multiple AP divs on top of one another, the selected AP div temporarily becomes the top item so that you can work with its contents.

You might also want to reorder or move AP divs. Each AP div is positioned in a page using x, y, and z coordinates, much like graphs. The x and y coordinates correspond to the AP div's Left and Top positions, respectively. Left and Top refer to the distance from the left and the top of the page; if the AP div is nested inside another AP div, Left and Top refer to the distance from the left and the top of the parent AP div. When you view an AP div in a browser window, it remains in the exact same place, even when the browser window is resized. The z coordinate—also called the **z-index number**—determines the stacking order (the order in which the AP div is stacked in the user's browser window when more than one AP div is used in a page). When AP divs overlap, the higher-numbered AP divs are at the front of the stack and are seen in front of those that have lower numbers. If a top AP div has transparent areas, AP divs stacked below it are visible in those areas. The areas of the top AP div that contain text, background color, or images obscure any AP divs stacked below it.

Reference Window | **Working with AP Divs**

- To make an AP div active, click in the AP div.
- To select an AP div, click the edge of the AP div in the Document window when its border is visible (or click the selection handle when the AP div is active, or in the AP Elements panel, located in the CSS panel group, click the name of the AP div).
- To resize an AP div, drag any resize handle until the AP div is the desired size (or enter exact height and width values in the Property inspector).
- To move an AP div, drag the AP div by its selection handle to the desired location (or press the arrow keys to shift the selected AP div one pixel at a time to the desired location, or enter Left, Top, and z-index numbers in the Property inspector).

The rulers and guides enable you to more easily place elements in a specific position in the page. Rulers, which you have already used, provide markings in pixels, inches, or centimeters that help you to position elements in the page. **Guides** are lines that you drag from the horizontal and vertical rulers into the Document window to help you place and align objects, such as AP divs, in a page. You can drag multiple guides into the page, move visible guides to new positions in the page, or drag unneeded guides from the Document window back to the ruler to remove the guide from sight. Guides are visible only within the Dreamweaver environment.

You want to reposition the AP div from below the navigation bar to the right. You'll use guides to help you position the AP div.

To select, resize, and move the AP div in the home page using guides:

▶ **1.** In the Document window, place the pointer over the border of the AP div. The border becomes red. See Figure 6-10.

AP div drawn in the home page ◀ Figure 6-10

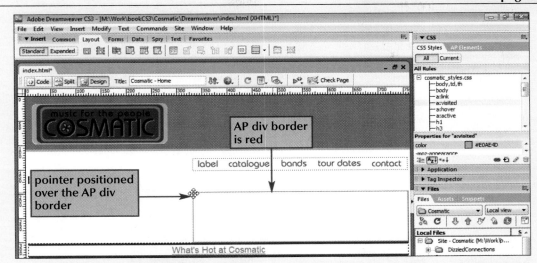

2. Click the **red border** of the AP div. The AP div is selected, which you can see because resize handles surround it, its border is blue, and its selection handle appears. The AP div's width and height values appear in the Property inspector in the W and H boxes. See Figure 6-11.

AP div selected in the home page ◀ Figure 6-11

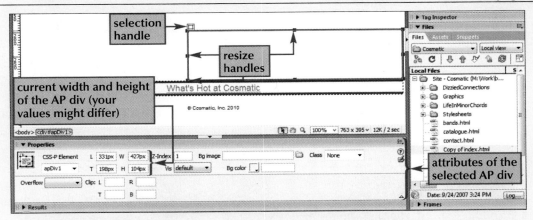

3. Drag from the vertical ruler to the **520 pixel** mark on the horizontal ruler (the tool-tip shows 520.00 px), and then release the mouse button. (If you cannot get the exact location, just drag to the closest mark possible.) A vertical guide appears in the page over the AP div and other elements.

4. Drag the middle-right resize handle of the AP div to the guide, as shown in Figure 6-12. In the Property inspector, the W value changes as you drag the AP div border.

Figure 6-12 ▶ **AP div being resized**

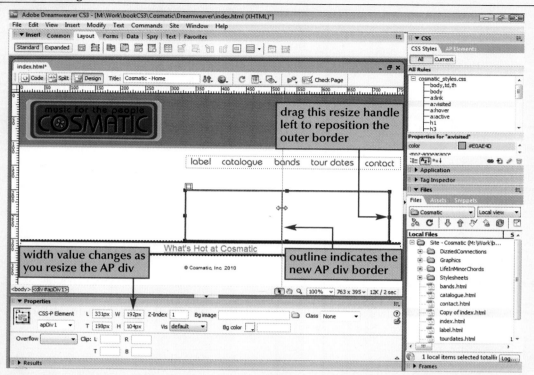

5. Release the mouse button. The right border of the AP div is adjusted. See Figure 6-13.

Figure 6-13 ▶ **AP div resized**

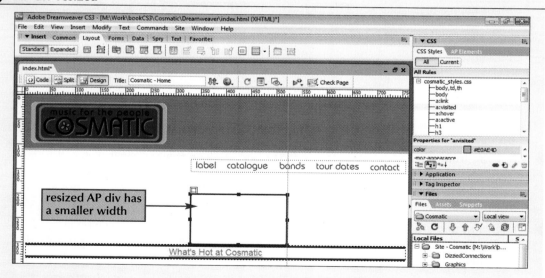

6. Drag the guide to the right so that it is even with the right edge of the navigation bar.

7. Position the pointer over the AP div selection handle. The pointer changes to ⊕ .

You will drag the AP div to a new position. The value in the L (left) box in the Property inspector changes as you drag the AP div.

8. Drag the AP div selection handle to the right so that the right edge of the AP div snaps to the guide, which aligns the AP div with the right edge of the navigation bar above it, as shown in Figure 6-14.

AP div being repositioned ◄ **Figure 6-14**

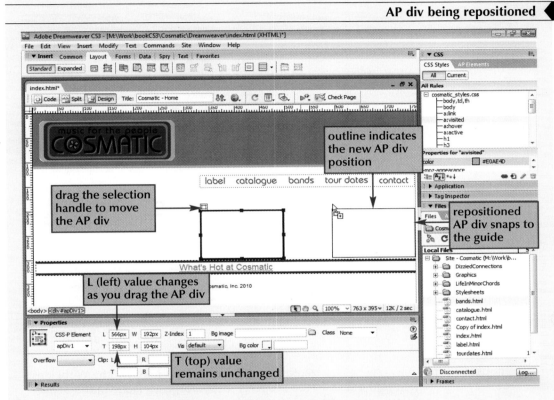

9. Release the mouse button. The AP div is repositioned.

10. Click in the Document window to deselect the AP div, and then save the page.

Adding Content to an AP Div

An AP div can contain almost any type of content, including text, graphics, forms, multimedia content, tables, and other divs. AP divs cannot contain frames, but you can place an AP div within a frame. You add content to an AP div using the same methods you use to insert content directly into a Web page. You can also move existing content from the page to an AP div by dragging it. Similar to layout cells, AP divs need to be active to accept content. To enter text into an AP div, for example, you need to first click inside of it to make it active.

Brian wants text and the Surface Suction CD cover graphic added to the AP div in the home page. This new content will draw attention to the What's Hot page. He also wants a user to be able to click anywhere in the AP div to open the What's Hot page in a new browser window. You'll add content to the AP div you created in the home page and then create hyperlinks to the What's Hot page.

To add content to the AP div in the home page:

▶ **1.** In the home page, select the **What's Hot at Cosmatic** text, drag the selected text into the AP div, and then click outside of the AP div to deselect it. The AP div might expand to fit the inserted text. See Figure 6-15.

Figure 6-15 AP div with text content

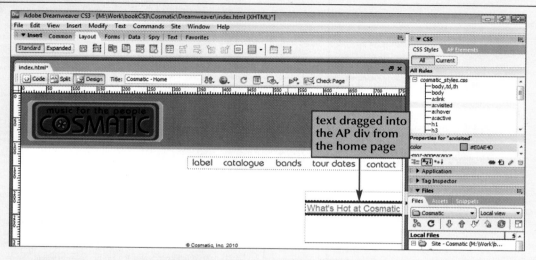

Trouble? If a copy of the lines above and below the What's Hot at Cosmatic text remain in the page, you need to delete them. Position the pointer in the lines, and then press the Backspace key to delete the extra lines.

▶ **2.** In the AP div, click to the right of the text, and then press the **Enter** key to move the insertion point down one line in the AP div. You'll insert the CD cover graphic on this line.

Trouble? If the new line has horizontal lines at the top and bottom, the WithLines CSS style is applied to the line. In the Property inspector, click None in the Style list, and then continue with Step 3.

▶ **3.** Click the **Common** tab on the Insert bar, click the **Image** button 🖼 in the **Images** list, navigate to the **Tutorial.06\Tutorial** folder included with your Data Files, and then double-click **SSCD200.jpg**. The Surface Suction CD cover is added to the AP div. The AP div width expands to accommodate the new content, although the width of the text content remains unchanged. See Figure 6-16.

AP div with text and image content ◀ Figure 6-16

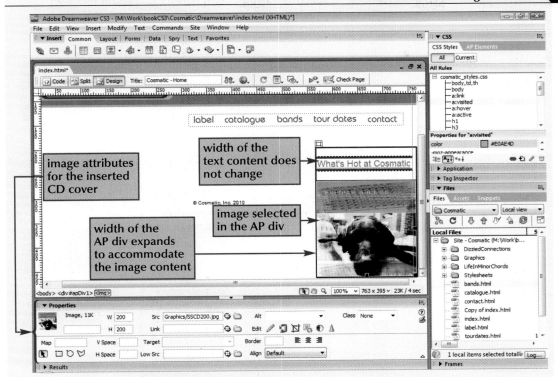

Trouble? If the footer changes format and has lines above and below it, then it picked up the WithLines styles from the What's Hot at Cosmatic text. Select the footer text, click the Format arrow in the Property inspector, click cosmatic_footer, click the CD cover image in the AP div, and then continue with Step 4.

4. Press the **Right Arrow** key to deselect the graphic, press the **Enter** key to move the insertion point down one line in the AP div, and then type **What's Hot** below the graphic.

5. In the Document window, click above the copyright line to deselect the graphic and position the insertion point, and then press the **Enter** key eight times to move the copyright line below the AP div into an attractive position in the page.

Because the right border of the AP div expanded automatically, the width value in the Property inspector still reflects the old width. This is why the top What's Hot text does not extend all the way to the right border of the expanded AP div. You will update the AP div width, format the text you typed, and then create links from the text and the graphic to the What's Hot page.

To update the width, format text, and create links from the AP div:

▶ **1.** Click the AP div border, and then click a right resize handle to extend the width. The width is updated in the Property inspector and the top What's Hot text extends to the right edge of the AP div. See Figure 6-17.

Figure 6-17 ▶ **AP div width updated in the Property inspector**

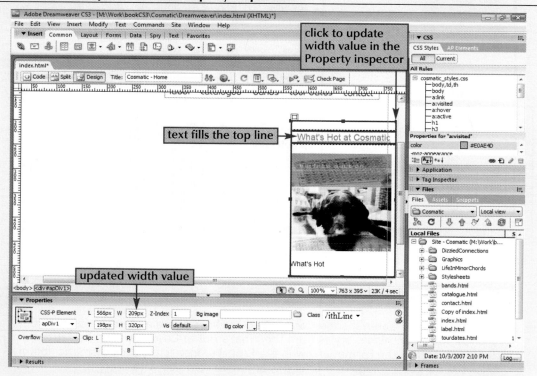

You'll format the text at the bottom of the AP div and then link the formatted text to the What's Hot page.

▶ **2.** In the Document window, select the **What's Hot** text at the bottom of the AP div.

▶ **3.** In the Property inspector, click the **Style** arrow, and then click **WithLines**. The selected text is reformatted to match the text at the top of the AP div.

▶ **4.** In the Property inspector, create a link from the formatted text to the **whatshot.html** page, and then click the **Target** arrow and click **_blank**. When a user clicks the link, the What's Hot page will open in a new browser window. You do not need to create the link for the text at the top of the AP div because it is already linked.

You'll center the graphic in the AP div, and then link the graphic to the What's Hot page.

▶ **5.** In the AP div, click the graphic to select it, and then, in the Property inspector, click the **Align Center** button 🖹 . The graphic aligns to the center of the AP div.

▶ **6.** In the Property inspector, create a link from the selected graphic to the **whatshot.html** page, and then click the **Target** arrow, and click **_blank**. See Figure 6-18.

Attributes for the selected graphic in the AP div | **Figure 6-18**

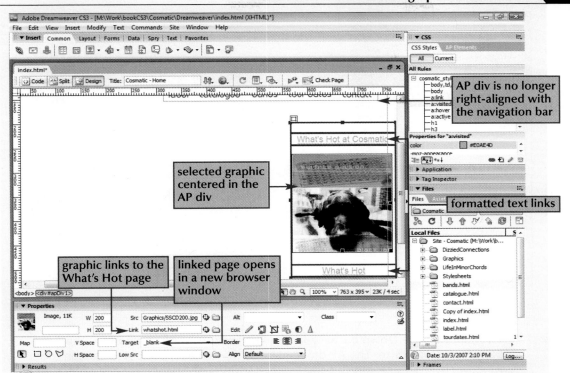

All three items in the AP div are linked to the What's Hot page; when a user clicks any of the links, the What's Hot page will open in a new browser window. You'll align the right edge of the AP div with the right edge of the navigation bar.

▶ **7.** Drag the guide to the **755 pixel** mark on the horizontal ruler.

   Trouble? If 755 pixel mark on the horizontal ruler is not visible, you can hide all the panel groups to extend your view. Collapse the side panel groups, complete Steps 7 through 9, and then expand the side panel groups.

▶ **8.** Click the AP div selection handle, and then press the **Left Arrow** or **Right Arrow** key until the right border of the AP div is aligned on the guide. If the Document window is opened to 787 × 405, the right border of the AP div is aligned with the right border of the navigation bar.

▶ **9.** Click outside the AP div to deselect it, and then save the page.

   The content in the AP div is complete. You'll preview the page in a browser to test the links.

To preview the home page containing the AP div:

▶ **1.** Preview the home page in a browser, and then click the **Maximize** button [▣] on the browser window title bar to maximize the browser window. The position of the AP div is absolute; it will remain in the same location regardless of the size of the browser window. The position of the navigation bar is relative; it will always align to the right of the window, regardless of the browser window size. See Figure 6-19.

Figure 6-19 Home page previewed in a browser

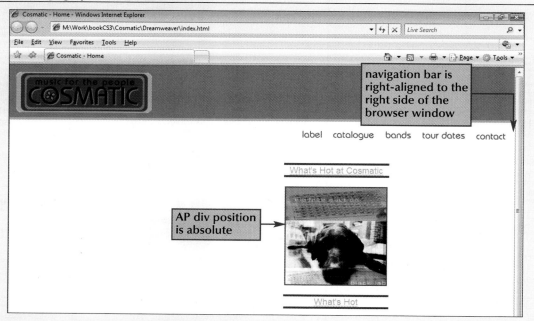

2. Click the **Restore Down** button on the browser window title bar. The window decreases in size. The AP div remains in the same location even though the window changed size, but the navigation bar shifts position to remain right-aligned in the window. See Figure 6-20.

Figure 6-20 Home page in a restored down browser window

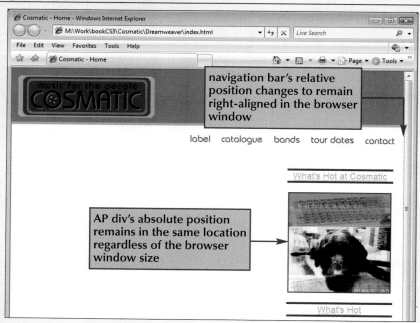

Trouble? If the browser window did not change size, then drag the lower-right corner of the browser window up and left to decrease its size.

▶ **3.** Click the top **What's Hot** link. The What's Hot page opens in a new browser window.

▶ **4.** Close the What's Hot window, and then click the **graphic**. The What's Hot page again opens in a new browser window.

▶ **5.** Close the What's Hot window, and then click the bottom **What's Hot** link to reopen the What's Hot page.

▶ **6.** Close the browser.

Adjusting AP Div Attributes

Sometimes it is necessary to change the attributes of an AP div tag. You can change the attributes for a selected AP div in the Property inspector, or you can create a CSS style with the desired attribute values and attach that style to one or more AP divs that you want to have the same attributes. To adjust the attributes in the Property inspector, the AP div must be selected. When the AP div is selected, the Property inspector includes the following attributes:

- **CSS-P Element ID.** A unique name for that AP div. The ID name cannot contain any spaces or symbols because it will be used in HTML code to refer to the AP div. If you don't specify a name, Dreamweaver assigns the name *apDiv1* to the first AP div you draw, *apDiv2* to the second, and so on.
- **L (Left)** and **T (Top).** The horizontal (L) and vertical (T) positions of the AP div measured in pixels from the left margin and the top margin. If the AP div is nested within another AP div, the values reference the distance from the left and top edge of the parent AP div instead of the page margin. As you have seen, these numbers adjust automatically to reflect the AP div's position in the page when you drag the AP div.
- **W (Width)** and **H (Height).** The horizontal (W) and vertical (H) dimensions of the AP div. If you delete the width, the AP div will scale with the browser window.
- **Z-Index.** A number that indicates the AP div's stacking order. AP divs with higher numbers are stacked in front of AP divs with lower numbers.
- **Vis (Visibility).** The visibility options that specify whether the AP div is visible when the Web page is loaded. If the AP div is hidden when the page is loaded, different actions by the user can make it visible. The Default option uses the browser's default visibility, which is usually visible. The Inherit option, which is the default for most browsers, sets the same visibility property as the parent AP div of a nested AP div. The Visible option displays the AP div content when the page is loaded. The Hidden option hides the AP div content when the page is loaded.
- **Bg Image (Background Image).** The path to the background image file for the AP div. If no image is specified, the Web page background is seen through the AP div.
- **Bg Color (Background Color).** The hexadecimal color code for the background color of the AP div. You can type the code in the Bg Color box or select a color with the color picker. If no color is specified, the AP div is transparent and the Web page background is seen through the AP div.
- **Class.** A list of the styles you created. You can select a style to apply to the AP div.

- **Overflow.** The options for how the AP div will appear in a browser window if its content exceeds its specified size. The Visible option expands the AP div to display the overflow content. The Hidden option maintains the AP div's size and prevents the overflow text from being displayed in the browser. The Scroll option adds scroll bars to the AP div (whether or not they are needed) in Internet Explorer and behaves as the Auto option in FireFox. The Auto option displays scroll bars for the AP div in the browser only if the content overflows. Overflow options are not supported in all browsers.
- **Clip.** The portion of the AP div that will be visible in a browser. If you specify L (left), R (right), T (top), and B (bottom) Clip values, only the portion of the AP div in the Clip area appears in the browser. Clip does not work correctly in all browsers.

You need to name the AP div that you created in the home page. Because the content of the AP div you created might overflow the AP div's boundaries, you also need to adjust the Overflow attribute.

To adjust the AP div's attributes in the Property inspector:

1. In the Document window, click the AP div border to select the AP div.

2. In the Property inspector, double-click in the **CSS-P Element ID** box, and then type **WhatsHot** (do not type an apostrophe before the s).

3. In the Property inspector, Click the **Overflow** button, and then click **Visible**. The AP div will expand to display any overflow content.

4. Save the page.

You'll create a CSS style to add a colored medium-width double line around the AP div. Because these attributes will be saved in a style, you can quickly apply them to other elements you create in the Cosmatic site.

To create the CSS style:

1. In the CSS Styles panel, click the **New CSS Rule** button 🗗 , and then create a custom style class named **.whats_hot** and defined in the **cosmatic_styles.css** style sheet.

2. Click **Border** in the Category box, click **Double** in the Style Top list, click **Medium** in the Width Top list, and then type **#E0AE40** in the Color Top box.

3. Make sure that the Style, Width, and Color **Same For All** check boxes are checked, and then click the **OK** button.

4. Select the **WhatsHot** AP div, click the **Class** arrow in the Property inspector, and then click the **whats_hot** style. The style is applied to the WhatsHot AP div.

5. Click in the Document window to deselect the WhatsHot AP div. See Figure 6-21.

   Trouble? If the bottom border overlaps the image, you need to manually adjust the AP div height. Select the image in the WhatsHot AP div and view its width and height values in the Property inspector. Select the AP div and then in the Property inspector enter these same width and height values.

AP div with the whats_hot CSS style applied ◄ Figure 6-21

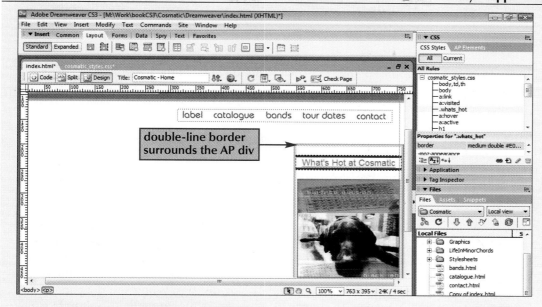

6. Save the page, and then save and close the style sheet.

7. Preview the home page in a browser. The double lines around the AP div are visible.

8. Close the browser.

Examining the Code for AP Div Tags

Remember that a div tag is a generic block-level HTML tag that can be used for many things; you have examined the div tag in an earlier tutorial. When you create an AP div, Dreamweaver places an ID selector in the head of the page that defines the type of positioning, the AP div's left and top coordinates, the width and height, the overflow value, and the z-index number. An **ID selector** is a custom style class that is used only one time. The ID selector style is used because AP div positioning is usually unique to that particular AP div, and you do not want to clutter a style sheet with a lot of styles that will be used only one time. The ID selector name is the same as the CSS-P Element ID entered in the Property inspector. When you create additional CSS styles to apply only to a particular AP div tag, you select its ID selector from the Selector list, and then Dreamweaver places the additional CSS rules in the selected ID selector. ID selectors are defined in the head of the page in which they are located, which helps keeps the page organized.

When you view the code for the WhatsHot AP div in the home page, you see its ID selector in the internal style sheet in the head of the page. The following code shows the ID selector (the exact measurements of your AP div might be slightly different):

```
<style type="text/css">
<!--
#WhatsHot {
     position:absolute;
     left:542px;
     top:198px;
     width:214px;
```

```
        height:100px;
        z-index:1;
        overflow: visible;
}
-->
</style>
```

The following code for the AP div tag is placed in the body of the page:

```
<div class="whats_hot" id="WhatsHot">
        <p class="WithLines"><a href="whatshot.html" target="_blank">
        What's Hot at Cosmatic</a></p>
        <p align="center"><a href="whatshot.html" target="_blank">
        <img src="Graphics/SSCD200.jpg" width="200" height="200" />
        </a></p>
        <p class="WithLines"><a href="whatshot.html" target="_blank">
        What's Hot</a></p>
</div>
```

The CSS-P Element ID (or the ID selector) that you assigned in the Property inspector is placed in the opening div tag, as shown in the first line of the code. In the code, id is the attribute name, and everything to the right of the equal sign in the quotation marks is the value. The div tag also references the external whats_hot style that you created. The AP div content appears between the opening and closing div tags. When you drag an AP div tag to a new position or when you change its attributes in the Property inspector, Dreamweaver updates the ID selector style.

InSight | Creating AP Div Positioning Styles

It is sometimes useful to create external styles to define the AP div positioning; for instance, if you plan to use the same positioning for multiple AP divs. If you create a site that enables users to choose from a variety of looks for the display of the pages (depending on which style sheet is attached to the page), creating external styles for the AP divs enables you to change the location of the AP divs in each style sheet to accommodate the corresponding look. You can also use this technique to create pages that display differently in different types of devices such as phones. There are many other reasons to create external styles to define the AP div positioning. When you drag an AP div whose positioning is defined externally to a new position in the page, the style is updated with the new positioning coordinates in the same way that an ID selector style would be. This can cause problems if you have attached more than one AP div to the style and want to reposition only one AP div. As you can see, both methods of AP div positioning have drawbacks and benefits. However, because Dreamweaver automatically places AP div positioning styles in the head of the page, this tutorial uses that method.

You'll examine the HTML code for the WhatsHot AP div in the home page.

To examine the HTML code for the WhatsHot AP div:

▶ **1.** Select the **WhatsHot** AP div in the home page, and then click the **Split** button on the Document toolbar. The home page is in Split view with the AP div tag code found in the body of the page selected.

▶ **2.** Scroll the top pane and drag the bottom border of the top pane to resize the top pane, if necessary, until all of the AP div code is visible, and then identify the ID selector style. See Figure 6-22.

AP div in Split view ◄ **Figure 6-22**

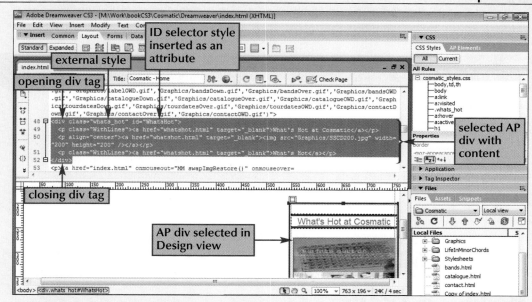

3. Locate the content of the WhatsHot AP div in the Code pane (refer to Figure 6-22). The WithLines style is attached to the text in the AP div.

4. Locate the three anchor **<a>** tags that link the top text, the graphic, and the bottom text to the whatshot.html page.

5. Locate the **<img>** tag.

6. Click the **Code** button on the Document toolbar. The home page is in Code view.

7. Scroll to the head of the page to view the internal style sheet, and then review the ID selector style for the AP div you created. See Figure 6-23.

Code for the AP div's ID selector style ◄ **Figure 6-23**

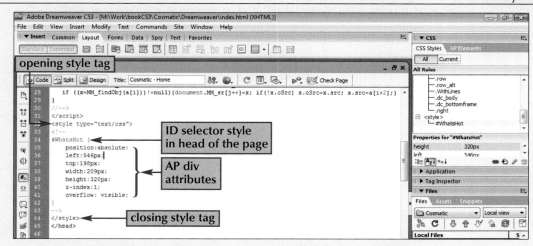

8. Click the **Design** button on the Document toolbar. The home page returns to Design view.

So far, you have created a page that uses relatively positioned divs, drawn an AP div in a page, inserted content in the AP div, adjusted its attributes, and examined its code. In the next session, you will create multiple AP div tags, including a nested AP div, and you will adjust the stacking order of the AP divs.

| Review | | Session 6.1 Quick Check |

1. What is a div tag?
2. What does the AP in AP div tag stand for?
3. Are div tags part of CSS styles?
4. Describe two ways to select an AP div.
5. What is the *z*-index number?
6. Describe the Visibility attribute of AP divs.

Session 6.2

Modifying AP Divs

Designing Web pages using AP divs gives you precise control over the placement of the content in your pages. After you have added an AP div to a page, you will most likely need to modify it. You can change the stacking order of AP divs, you can align them to each other or to an invisible grid, and you can nest one AP div inside another.

Adjusting Stacking Order

One benefit of using AP divs in a Web page is that they can be stacked or overlapped. Think of each AP div as a clear acetate sheet such as those used for overhead projectors. You can stack one on top of another and still see the bottom AP div through any transparent portions of the top AP div. If the top AP div does not have any transparent portions, the bottom AP div is hidden from view. Stacking enables you to create more sophisticated and interesting layout designs. Also, because AP divs can be animated, stacking enables you to create interesting user interactions. For example, you could stack two AP divs that contained text so that the back AP div is hidden by the front AP div and then animate the AP divs to switch their stacking order when the user clicks a button. This brings the back AP div to the front so that its text is visible.

Each new AP div you create is assigned the next consecutive *z*-index number—the first AP div you create is 1, the second is 2, and so on. On the screen, AP divs with higher *z*-index numbers appear in front of those with lower *z*-index numbers. You can change the stacking order by changing the *z*-index number. For example, an AP div with the *z*-index number of 2 appears behind an AP div with a *z*-index number of 3. If you change the first AP div to a *z*-index number of 4, then it will appear in front of the second AP div when they are stacked. You can set more than one AP div with the same *z*-index number to make them appear at the same time. You can change stacking order of AP divs by typing a new *z*-index number in the Property inspector or dragging an AP div to a new position in the AP Elements panel.

Keeping Up with CSS Developments | InSight

Designers are constantly pushing the limits of what can be done with CSS and how it can be used to lay out Web pages. New techniques of using CSS are being developed all the time. At Web sites such as *www.csszengarden.com*, designers contribute CSS page layouts that they have created, demonstrating new and innovative ways to use CSS. Visit sites like this regularly to remain up-to-date with the latest innovations.

Brian wants to add a Dizzied Connections section to the home page. You will create a second AP div in the home page for this content.

To create a new AP div in the home page:

▶ **1.** If you took a break after the previous session, make sure that the Cosmatic site is open and the index.html page is open in the Document window in Design view.

▶ **2.** Drag the guide in the home page to the right edge of the navigation bar, select the **WhatsHot** AP div, and then press the **Left Arrow** key until the right side of the WhatsHot AP div is aligned with the guide.

▶ **3.** Drag a guide from the horizontal ruler to **50 pixels** below the navigation bar, and then drag the vertical guide in the page to the left edge of the navigation bar.

▶ **4.** Click the **Layout** tab on the Insert bar, and then click the **Draw AP Div** button 🖼 .

▶ **5.** Draw a new AP div in the home page approximately **250 pixels** wide and **100 pixels** high, starting where the two guides intersect. The new AP div overlaps the WhatsHot AP div. See Figure 6-24.

Second AP div drawn in the home page ◀ Figure 6-24

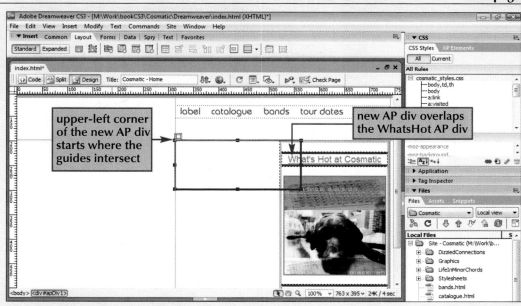

Trouble? If you cannot draw the new AP div in front of the WhatsHot AP div, the Prevent Overlaps check box in the AP Elements panel is probably checked. Expand the CSS panel group, click the AP Elements tab to display the AP Elements panel, click the Prevent Overlaps check box in the panel to uncheck it, click the selection handle to select the AP div you just drew, press the Delete key, and then repeat Steps 4 and 5.

Trouble? If the AP div is not positioned or sized correctly, you need to move or resize it. Click the AP div's selection handle to select the AP div, and then drag the AP div to the correct position or drag a resize handle to resize it.

▶ 6. Click in the new AP div to make it active, type **Dizzied Connections**, press the **Enter** key to move the insertion point to a new line, and then type **Information about the band will be here soon.** (including the period).

▶ 7. Select **Dizzied Connections**, click the **Format** button in the Property inspector, click **Heading 2**, and then deselect the text. Both lines of text overlap the first AP div. See Figure 6-25.

| **Figure 6-25** | **Formatted text in the second AP div** |

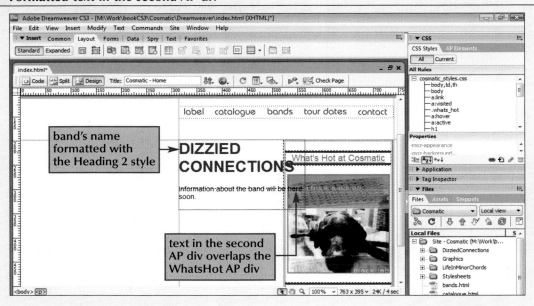

You'll expand the AP Elements panel, name the new AP div in the Property inspector, and then look at the stacking order in the AP Elements panel. Dreamweaver gives a generic name to each new AP div—the first unnamed AP div is *apDiv1*, the second is *apDiv2*, and so on. After you rename first AP div you create, the next AP div you create is named *apDiv1*.

To adjust the stacking order of the AP divs in the home page:

▶ 1. In the CSS panel group, click the **AP Elements** tab. The AP Elements panel expands. See Figure 6-26.

AP Elements panel ◄ Figure 6-26

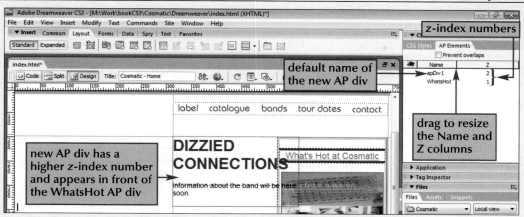

Tip

To display more characters in the Name column of the AP Elements panel, drag the border between the Name and Z column headings.

You will rename the new AP div.

▶ **2.** Click the border of the new AP div to select it, double-click **apDiv1** in the CSS-P Element box in the Property inspector to select the text, type **DizziedConnections**, and then press the **Enter** key. The ID name changes in the AP Elements panel.

AP divs appear in the AP Elements panel in their current stacking order. The DizziedConnections AP div has a z-index of 2, which means that it is in front of the WhatsHot AP div, which has a z-index of 1. This is evident in the Document window.

▶ **3.** In the AP Elements panel, drag **DizziedConnections** AP div below the WhatsHot AP div, but do not release the mouse button, as shown in Figure 6-27.

Stacking order being changed in the AP Elements panel ◄ Figure 6-27

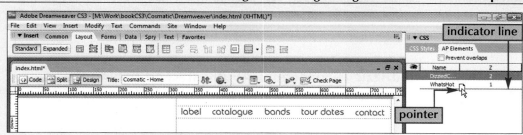

▶ **4.** Release the mouse button when the indicator line is below the WhatsHot AP div. When you reposition an AP div in the AP Elements panel, the z-index numbers are automatically updated to correspond to the new stacking order. The WhatsHot AP div is stacked in front of the DizziedConnections AP div in the Document window, obscuring the text in the DizziedConnections AP div. The border of the DizziedConnections AP div remains visible through the WhatsHot AP div because the DizziedConnections AP div is still selected. See Figure 6-28.

Figure 6-28	AP div stacking order changed

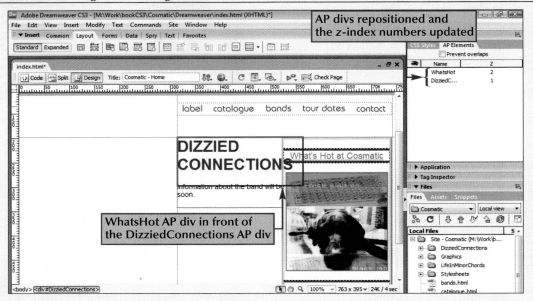

5. Save the page, and then preview it in a browser. Some of the text in the Dizzied-Connections AP div is hidden behind the WhatsHot AP div.

6. Close the browser.

You'll reposition the DizziedConnections AP div in the Document window so that the content in both AP divs is visible. The DizziedConnections AP div is stacked behind the WhatsHot AP div. When you select the back AP div or make the back AP div active, the back AP div temporarily moves to the front so that you can modify it. The z-index number in the Property inspector and in the AP Elements panel remains unchanged.

To work with the DizziedConnections AP div stacked behind the WhatsHot AP div:

1. In the Document window, click in the **DizziedConnections** AP div to make it active, and then click the **selection handle** to select it. The DizziedConnections AP div moves to the front. Although the DizziedConnections AP div appears in front of the WhatsHot AP div in the Document window, the z-index number in the Property inspector and in the AP Elements panel remains 1.

2. In the Document window, click a blank area outside the DizziedConnections AP div. The DizziedConnections AP div again appears behind the WhatsHot AP div, and the portion of the border behind the WhatsHot AP div appears as a dashed line.

3. In the Document window, drag the vertical guide **50 pixels** to the left, select the **DizziedConnections** AP div, and then drag it to the guide so that the text is no longer obscured by the WhatsHot AP div. See Figure 6-29.

DizziedConnections AP div repositioned in the home page ◀ Figure 6-29

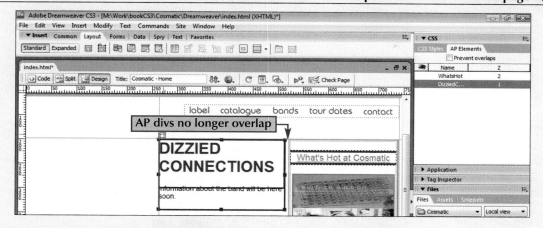

4. Click in a blank area of the Document window, and then save the page.

Aligning AP Divs

You have dragged AP divs around the page to reposition them, using the rulers and guides to help you place them in the page. In some pages, you might want to align the elements so that the page looks tidy. You can align AP divs to the left, right, top, or bottom of another AP div. To align them, you select one AP div, press and hold the Shift key, and then click any other AP div you want to align. The last AP div that you select will remain stationary and the other AP divs will align to it. The Left Align command aligns the left borders of selected AP divs to the horizontal position of the left border of the last AP div you select. The Right Align command aligns the right borders of selected AP divs to the horizontal position of the right border of the last AP div you select. The Top Align command aligns the top borders of the selected AP divs to the vertical position of the top border of the last AP div you select. Finally, the Bottom Align command aligns the bottom borders of the selected AP divs to the vertical position of the bottom border of the last AP div you select.

Brian asks you to align the tops of the two AP divs in the home page.

To align AP divs using the Align commands:

1. Select the **DizziedConnections** AP div, press and hold the **Shift** key, click the **WhatsHot** AP div, and then release the **Shift** key. The two AP divs are selected. The Property inspector indicates that multiple CSS-P Elements are selected. The resize handles for the WhatsHot AP div are solid, indicating that this AP div will remain stationary and any other selected AP divs will align with it.

2. Click **Modify** on the menu bar, point to **Arrange**, and then click **Align Top**. The selected AP divs align their tops at the horizontal position of the top of the WhatsHot AP div, if they weren't already aligned. See Figure 6-30.

> **Tip**
>
> You can also press the Shift key as you click AP divs in the AP Elements panel to select them.

Figure 6-30	AP divs top-aligned

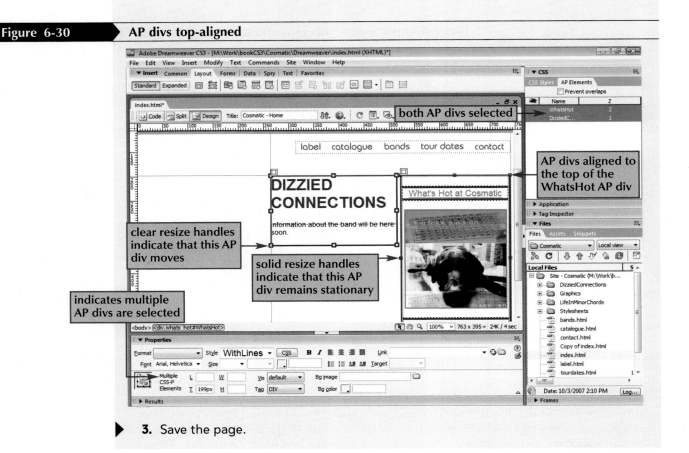

3. Save the page.

Positioning Elements Using the Grid

In addition to the Align commands, you can also use the grid to help you adjust the position of elements in a Web page. The **grid** is a series of parallel horizontal and vertical lines that overlap to create equal-sized squares in the background of the Document window. The grid, like guides, helps you position or resize AP divs or other objects. The default is for the grid to be hidden, but you can display it as needed. You can also change the size of the grid squares to align elements more precisely by adjusting the grid's line spacing in the Grid Settings dialog box. You can also use the Grid Settings dialog box to change the grid's appearance.

You will use the grid to position the elements in the home page.

To align the AP divs in the home page using the grid:

Tip

You can also press the Ctrl+Alt+G keys to show or hide the grid.

1. With both AP divs still selected, click **View** on the menu bar, point to **Grid**, and then click **Show Grid**. Grid lines appear in the background of the Document window, creating 50-pixel squares.

2. Move the guides well out of the way to prevent the AP divs from snapping to the guides, and then press the **Arrow** keys to nudge the AP divs to align the left edge of the DizziedConnections AP div with a grid line and the base of the word "Dizzied" with a grid line. The two AP divs move together because they are both selected. See Figure 6-31.

DizziedConnections AP div aligned to the grid Figure 6-31

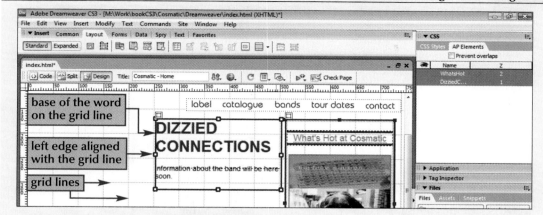

▶ **3.** Click **View** on the menu bar, point to **Grid**, and then click **Show Grid** to hide the grid lines.

▶ **4.** Click in the Document window outside the selected AP divs to deselect them, and then save the page.

Creating Nested AP Divs

You might want two or more AP divs to move together, which you can do by nesting AP divs. A **nested AP div** is an AP div contained within an outer (parent) AP div similar to nested tables and nested frames. With AP divs, however, nesting does not refer to the AP divs' physical positions but instead to the underlying code. This means that the nested AP div does not have to touch its on-screen parent to be nested. The nested AP div is indented under the parent in the AP Elements panel. Nesting is used to group AP divs. When AP divs are nested, if you move the parent, the nested AP div will move with it. This is because the position of the nested AP div is relative to the left and top borders of the parent rather than to the left and top borders of the page. A nested AP div also shares other attributes with its parent.

Brian asks you to create a new AP div that will contain information about Sloth Child. You'll nest this AP div with the DizziedConnections AP div.

To nest and unnest the SlothChild AP div:

▶ **1.** Drag the vertical guide flush with the left side of the DizziedConnections AP div.

▶ **2.** Draw a **100-pixel-square** AP div below and flush left with the DizziedConnections AP div in the home page. See Figure 6-32.

Figure 6-32 | **Third AP div drawn in the home page**

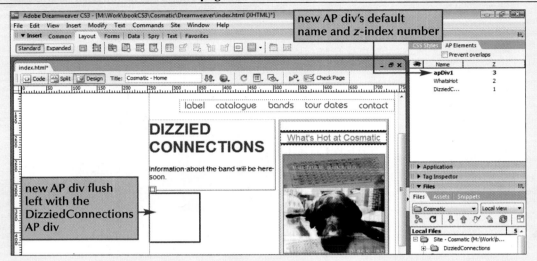

3. Click in the new AP div to make it active, if necessary, type **Sloth Child** in the AP div, and then press the **Enter** key. The placeholder content helps you distinguish this AP div from the others.

Tip

You can also rename an element by double-clicking its name in the AP Elements panel, typing the new name, and then pressing the Enter key.

4. Click the **selection handle** on the new AP div to select it, double-click **apDiv1** in the CSS-P Element ID box in the Property inspector, type **SlothChild**, and then press the **Enter** key. The new AP div is renamed.

5. Press and hold the **Ctrl** key, and then, in the AP Elements panel, drag the **SlothChild** AP div over the DizziedConnections AP div, and then release the mouse button and the **Ctrl** key. See Figure 6-33.

Figure 6-33 | **Nested SlothChild AP div repositioned**

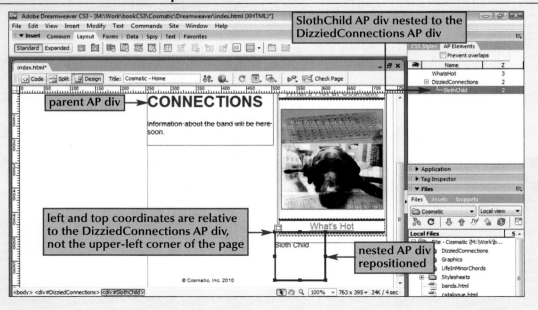

The SlothChild AP div is indented under the DizziedConnections AP div in the AP Elements panel. The SlothChild AP div shifts to the bottom of the page in the Document window because its position is relative to the top and left of the Dizzied-Connections AP div, not to the top and left of the page.

▶ **6.** In the AP Elements panel, drag the **SlothChild** AP div to the top of the list to unnest it. The SlothChild AP div moves back to below the DizziedConnections AP div.

▶ **7.** Save and close the page, and then collapse the CSS panel group.

So far, you have created multiple AP divs in the home page, changed the stacking order of the AP divs, aligned AP divs, and nested and unnested the AP divs. In the next session, you will add behaviors to the AP divs to allow users to interact with them.

Session 6.2 Quick Check | Review

1. True or False? AP divs can be overlapped.
2. Do AP divs with higher z-index numbers appear in front of, or behind, AP divs with lower z-index numbers?
3. When you align AP divs, to which AP div will the other align?
4. In Dreamweaver, what is the grid?
5. Does a nested AP div need to be positioned inside of its parent?
6. How do you unnest an AP div?

Session 6.3

Understanding Behaviors

In Dreamweaver, a **behavior** is code added to a Web page that enables users to interact with various elements in the Web page, to alter the Web page in different ways, or to cause tasks to be performed. For example, in a Web page with two AP divs, you could stack the two AP divs and then create a behavior that switches their stacking order when the user clicks a button. The word *behavior* is an Adobe convention for describing inter-active functions in multimedia programs that are managed by the program and accessed through an authoring interface, in this case the Behaviors panel.

A behavior is like a mathematical equation that consists of three elements: *object + event = action*. An **object** is the element in the Web page to which the behavior is attached, such as a graphic or an AP div. An event has two components: the user event and the event handler. The **user event** is what the user does to trigger the action. Common user events are moving the pointer over an object (mouseover), clicking an object, and so on. The **event handler** is the code used to refer to the event. For example, the code used to refer to a mouseover is onMouseOver. The **action** is what you want to happen when the event is performed on the object.

Dreamweaver provides three ways to insert behavior functionality into Web pages: the preset behavior tools, the Behaviors panel, and custom scripting. Figure 6-34 explains each method.

Figure 6-34 ▶ **Methods of inserting behaviors in Dreamweaver**

Tool	Description	You...	Dreamweaver...
Preset behavior tools	You use buttons located throughout Dreamweaver to perform common tasks.	Enter requested information, for example, which graphic you want to use, in the dialog box, if necessary.	Writes the behavior and inserts it for you automatically.
Behaviors panel	You choose the event handler and action for a behavior from a prewritten list.	Select the elements of the behavior from drop-down lists.	Writes the code and inserts it into the page.
Custom scripting	You write your own code (usually JavaScript) in the Document window in Code view or click the Script button in the Script list on the Common tab of the Insert bar.	Write the code and insert in the page; your code then appears as a custom script in the Behaviors panel.	

Using a preset behavior tool is the easiest way to insert behaviors into Web pages. Preset behavior tools are buttons that perform common tasks for you and insert the behaviors into a page automatically. They are located throughout Dreamweaver. You have already used many of the preset behavior tools, including the Rollover button and the Navigation Bar button. When you use the Rollover button, Dreamweaver inserts a swap image behavior and a preload behavior as you insert the rollover images. The swap image behavior consists of the action (the images being swapped) triggered by a user event (the user moving the mouse to place the pointer over the image). The image is the object. The preload behavior consists of the action (the image being downloaded) triggered by a user event (the user loading the Web page into a browser window). The Web page is the object. When you select an object in the document window and open the Behaviors panel, the behaviors that Dreamweaver inserted for you appear in the list.

Reference Window | **Adding the Show-Hide Elements Prewritten Behavior**

- Select the AP div image or hotspot to which you want to add the behavior.
- In the Behaviors panel, click the Add Behavior button, point to Show Events For, and then click the desired browser choice.
- In the Behaviors panel, click the Add Behavior button, and then click Show-Hide Elements.
- Click each AP div that you want to react to the user event, and then click the Show button to show the AP div or click the Hide button to hide the AP div.
- Click the OK button.

You can use the Behaviors panel to create more customized behaviors. When you use the Behaviors panel to create behaviors, you select an object, and then you select from lists of prewritten actions and event handlers, which Dreamweaver combines to create the behavior. Dreamweaver will allow you to choose only actions that work with the object you have selected, and it will allow you to choose only event handlers that go with the action you selected. For example, if you select text as the object, you cannot select swap image as the action. You can also limit the behavior list options by HTML version, browser version, or browser brand and version. In general, the more complex behaviors require newer browsers, whereas simpler behaviors work with very old browsers.

If your target audience includes users of very old browsers, you might need to create an alternate site that does not use behaviors. Some discrepancy exists in the way that different browsers interpret JavaScript, so you need to test pages that use behaviors extensively in all the browsers you intend to support. In addition, some users turn off JavaScript in their browsers so that pop-up ads on Web sites cannot run. This means that some users with newer browsers will still not be able to access Web sites that use behaviors. Therefore, even if your target audience does not include users of older browsers, you should consider providing links to alternate pages or an alternate site for anyone whose browser has difficulty running JavaScript. Or, you should alert users that they must enable JavaScript to view the site.

You can add the advanced functionality of behaviors to a Web page by writing your own code (usually JavaScript) in the Script dialog box or in the Document window in Code view. When you write the code yourself, the code you create is not actually considered a behavior, because it is not added to the reusable prewritten choice lists in the Behaviors panel. Instead, the code you write is considered a custom script and will appear in the Behaviors panel when you select the object to which it is attached.

Adding Behaviors Using the Behaviors Panel

The Behaviors panel is like a sophisticated menu for ordering behaviors. First, you choose an object in the page, and then you select a target browser brand and version. The Behaviors panel displays only actions that are compatible with the selected object and browser. You then choose an action from the list in the Behaviors panel. You can select only the actions that are available for use with the object you selected; actions that are not available for use with the selected object are dimmed. If you don't choose any object, the actions listed are available for the page itself. After you have selected an action, Dreamweaver provides a list of possible events—with the most common event associated with that action selected by default. You choose an event from that list. Based on your selections, Dreamweaver creates the behavior and inserts the code.

Sara and Brian like the way the Life in Minor Chords page looks in the site, and they ask you to create an interactive page for Sloth Child that uses AP divs and behaviors to show or hide the various AP divs, depending on what the user points to. You'll start by creating the new page.

To create the new Sloth Child page:

▶ **1.** If you took a break after the previous session, make sure that the Cosmatic site is open.

▶ **2.** Create a new folder named **SlothChild** within the site's local root folder, create a new, blank page, and then save the new page in the SlothChild folder with the filename **sloth_child.html**.

3. Open the **sloth_child.html** page, if necessary, change the page title to **Cosmatic - Sloth Child**, and then modify the page properties as follows (you will not create an external style sheet because the Sloth Child styles will be used only within this page):

Property	Attribute
Page font	**Arial, Helvetica, sans-serif**
Size	**14 pixels**
Text color	**#FFFFFF**
Background color	**#000000**
Margins	**0**
Color for all links	**#FFFFFF**
Link underline style	**Always Underline**

4. Save the page.

You'll add four AP divs to the new Sloth Child page. For each AP div, you'll set the properties, insert an image, and then adjust its position in the page.

To add AP divs to the Sloth Child page:

1. In the middle of the Document window, draw an AP div that is approximately **300 pixels** wide and **150 pixels** high.

2. Select the AP div, if necessary. See Figure 6-35.

Figure 6-35	First AP div drawn in the Sloth Child page

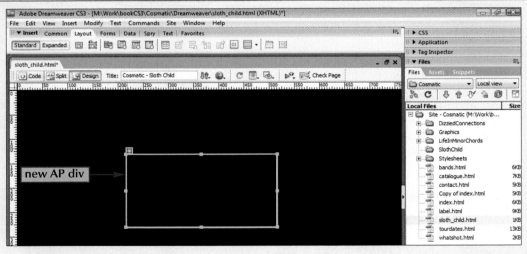

3. In the Property inspector, type **background** in the CSS-P Element ID box, click the **Vis** button, and then click **Visible**.

4. Click in the AP div. The background AP div is active, and you can enter content—in this case, a graphic.

5. Click the **Common** tab on the Insert bar, click the **Image** button in the **Images** list, browse to the **Tutorial.06\Tutorial** folder included with your Data Files, and then double-click **SCWebPageImage.jpg**. The AP div expands to accommodate the inserted image, which includes the words *sloth child* in the upper-left corner and a photo above the words *try an apple* in the lower-right corner.

6. Scroll to the upper-left corner of the Document window, click the **selection handle** to select the background AP div instead of the graphic, and then drag the **selection handle** to the upper-left corner of the page. See Figure 6-36.

Graphic added to the background AP div   Figure 6-36

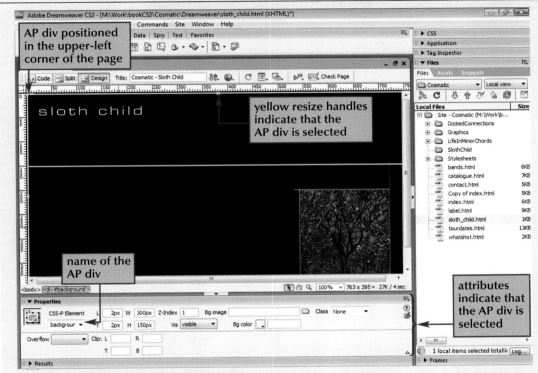

Trouble? If you have difficulty positioning the background AP div in the upper-left corner of the page, press the Arrow keys to nudge the selected AP div into position.

Next, you'll draw hotspots on the graphic in the background AP div.

To draw hotspots on the graphic in the background AP div:

1. Click in the background AP div to select the graphic. The graphic is selected when "Image" appears in the upper-left corner of the Property inspector, the <img> tag is selected in the status bar, and black resize handles appear around the graphic (you might need to scroll to see the resize handles). See Figure 6-37.

Figure 6-37
Selected graphic in the background AP div

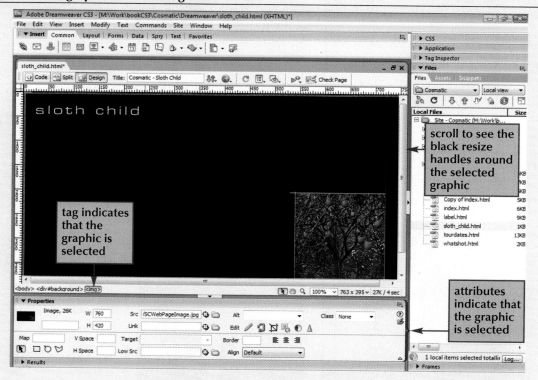

▶ **2.** Expand the Property inspector, if necessary, and then click the **Oval Hotspot Tool** button 🔘 in the Property inspector.

You'll draw three oval hotspots on the photo.

Tip

To turn off prompts, click Edit on the menu bar, click Preferences, click Accessibility, uncheck the items in the Show Attributes When Inserting check boxes, and then click the OK button.

▶ **3.** Draw the an oval hotspot over the rightmost apple about one-third of the way down the photo, and then click the **OK** button if a dialog box opens, prompting you to enter alternate text for the hotspot.

▶ **4.** Draw an oval hotspot over the apple at the upper-center of the tree, and then click the **OK** button if the dialog box opens prompting you to enter alternate text for the hotspot.

▶ **5.** Draw an oval hotspot over the centermost apple on the apple tree, and then click the **OK** button if the dialog box opens prompting you to enter alternate text for the hotspot. See Figure 6-38.

Hotspots added to the graphic in the background AP div | Figure 6-38

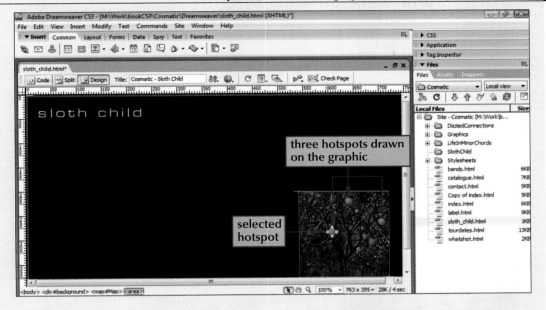

Trouble? If the hotspots on your graphic are in the wrong position, you need to reposition them. Click the Pointer Hotspot Tool button in the Property inspector, and then drag each hotspot to the position that matches the hotspot placement shown in Figure 6-38.

6. In the Property inspector, click the **Rectangular Hotspot Tool** button ▢ , draw a rectangular hotspot over the Sloth Child band name in the upper-left corner of the AP div, and then click the **OK** button if the dialog box opens prompting you to enter alternate text for the hotspot.

You will draw four additional AP divs in the Sloth Child page, and then modify their attributes so that they are hidden. You will later attach behaviors to make them visible when a user event occurs.

To draw additional AP divs in the Sloth Child page and modify their attributes:

1. Expand the **CSS panel group**, and then click the **AP Elements** tab. The AP Elements panel is displayed.

2. Drag a guide from the horizontal ruler to about **25 pixels** below the band name, and then drag a guide from the vertical ruler to the left edge of the letter *s* in sloth child.

3. Draw an AP div starting where the guides intersect that has the same width as the band name and a height of **100 pixels**.

4. Select the new AP div, and then, in the Property inspector, type **SC2** in the CSS_P Element ID box, click the **Vis** button, and click **Hidden**.

Tip

You can also click the eye icon in the AP Elements panel to show or hide an AP div.

▶ **5.** Click in the **SC2** AP div to make it active, and then, on the **Common** tab of the Insert bar, use the **Images** button 🖼 in the **Images** list to insert the **SC2.jpg** graphic located in the **Tutorial.06\Tutorial** folder included with your Data Files. The AP div expands to accommodate the inserted graphic.

Trouble? If you can't see the new AP div in the Document window, you clicked outside the borders and the Hidden attribute became effective. In the AP Elements panel, click SC2 to select the AP div and make its borders visible in the Document window.

▶ **6.** Create a link from the graphic in the SC2 AP div to the **bands.html** page, type **0** in the Border box, and then press the **Enter** key. See Figure 6-39.

Figure 6-39 ▸ **SC2 AP div added to the Sloth Child page**

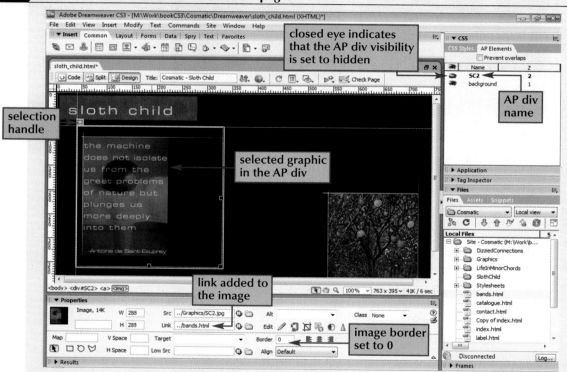

▶ **7.** Click in the **background** AP div outside the SC2 AP div. The SC2 AP div disappears because its visibility is set to Hidden.

▶ **8.** Drag the horizontal guide to the top of the hotspot over the band name sloth child, and then drag the vertical guide to the right edge of the hotspot over the band name.

▶ **9.** Starting where the guides intersect, draw a third AP div that is approximately **250 pixels** wide and **100 pixels** high, and then repeat Steps 4 through 6 to change its CSS_P Element ID to **SC3**, change its visibility to click **Hidden**, insert the **SC3.jpg** graphic located in the **Tutorial.06\Tutorial** folder, create a link from the graphic to the **index.html** page, and change the graphic's border to **0**.

▶ **10.** Reposition the SC3 AP div, if necessary, so that no part of the image overlaps the sloth child band name or the apple tree photograph. See Figure 6-40.

SC3 AP div added to the Sloth Child page | Figure 6-40

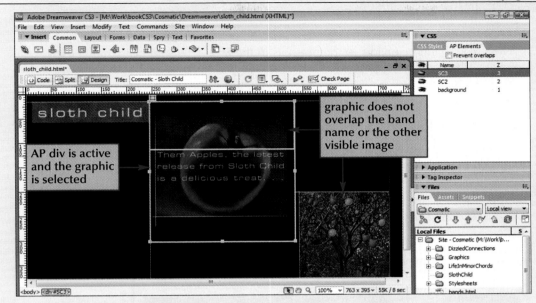

▶ **11.** Click in the background AP div outside the two hidden AP divs, and then repeat Steps 4 through 6 to draw a fourth AP div to the left of the apple tree image that is approximately **250 pixels** wide and **100 pixels** high, change its CSS_P Element ID to **SC4**, change its visibility to **Hidden**, insert the **SC4.jpg** graphic located in the **Tutorial.06\Tutorial** folder, create a link from the graphic to the **catalogue.html** page, and then change the graphic's border to **0**.

▶ **12.** Reposition the SC4 AP div, if necessary, so that its left border starts about **225 pixels** from the left margin, the image does not overlap the apple tree photograph, and the bottom of the image (not necessarily the bottom of the SC4 AP div) aligns with the bottom of the apple tree photograph. Use the guides to help you position the image. See Figure 6-41.

SC4 AP div added to the Sloth Child page | Figure 6-41

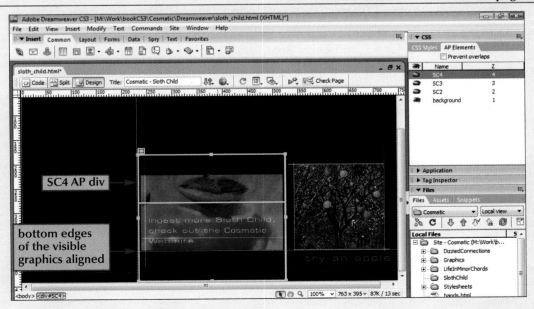

▶ **13.** Click in a blank area of the Document window. Only the first AP div that you drew is visible.

▶ **14.** Save the page.

Next, you'll add behaviors to the hotspots in the SC2 AP div so that when a user points to a hotspot, the appropriate hidden AP div will become visible in the page in the browser window.

To add behaviors to the hotspots:

▶ **1.** Collapse the **Files panel group**, expand the **Tag Inspector panel group**, and then click the **Behaviors** tab. The Behaviors panel is displayed. See Figure 6-42.

Figure 6-42 ▶ **Behaviors panel displayed**

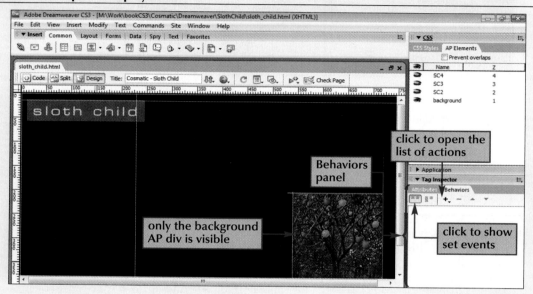

▶ **2.** In the Document window, click the hotspot over the rightmost apple. The selected hotspot is the object to which you want to apply the behavior.

▶ **3.** In the Behaviors panel, click the **Add Behavior** button ⊞, point to **Show Events For**, and then click **4.0 and Later Browsers**.

▶ **4.** In the Behaviors panel, click the **Add Behavior** button , and then click **Show-Hide Elements** (the action). The Show-Hide Elements dialog box opens.

You want the first hidden AP div, SC2, to become visible when the user event occurs, and you do not want either of the other two AP divs to be visible when this happens. You can set the AP div visibility in the Show-Hide Elements dialog box.

▶ **5.** Click **div "SC2"** in the Elements box, and then click the **Show** button.

If either of the other two AP divs whose Visibility attribute is set to Hidden is visible when the user event occurs, you want it to be hidden.

▶ **6.** Click **div "SC3"** in the Elements box, click the **Hide** button, click **div "SC4"** in the Elements box, and then click the **Hide** button. You do not need to make a selection for the background AP div because it never changes; that is, it is always visible. See Figure 6-43.

Show-Hide Elements dialog box ◄ **Figure 6-43**

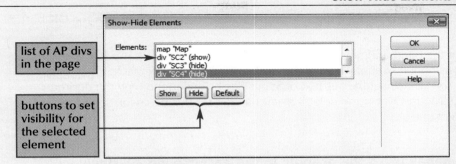

7. Click the **OK** button. The dialog box closes and the first behavior is added to the list in the Behaviors panel. The event handler onMouseOver is associated automatically with this behavior because it is the most frequently chosen event handler for this action. See Figure 6-44.

Behavior added to the selected hotspot ◄ **Figure 6-44**

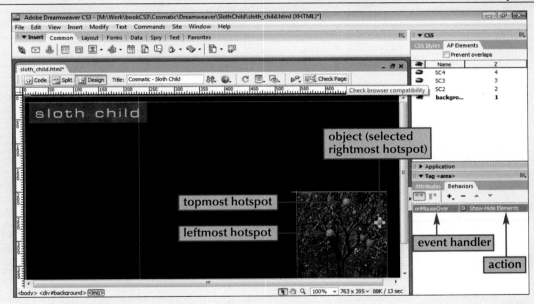

You'll repeat the same process to add the Show-Hide behavior to the other apple hotspots. Each hotspot will show a different AP div and make the remaining AP divs hide.

To add behaviors to the other apple hotspots:

▶ 1. Select the hotspot over the leftmost apple. No behaviors are listed in the Behaviors panel because the Behaviors panel displays only behaviors attached to the selected object; you have not yet created a behavior for the selected hotspot.

▶ 2. In the Behaviors panel, click the **Add Behavior** button ☐ , and then click **Show-Hide Elements**. The Show-Hide Elements dialog box opens.

▶ 3. Show the **SC3** AP div, hide the **SC2** and **SC4** AP divs, and then click the **OK** button.

▶ 4. Select the topmost hotspot.

▶ **5.** In the Behaviors panel, click the **Add Behavior** button ⊞ , and then click **Show-Hide Elements**. The Show-Hide Elements dialog box opens.

▶ **6.** Hide the **SC2** and **SC3** AP divs, show the **SC4** AP div, and then click the **OK** button.

You want the band and album name to appear in the browser status bar when the pointer is positioned over any part of the background image. The background graphic is the object. You will select the Set Text of Status Bar behavior and type the desired message. OnMouseOver is the default event handler for this behavior, so you do not need to select one.

To add a behavior to the graphic in the background AP div:

▶ **1.** Click in the Document window to select the image in the background AP div.

▶ **2.** In the Behaviors panel, click the **Add Behavior** button ⊞ , point to **Set Text**, and then click **Set Text of Status Bar**. The Set Text of Status Bar dialog box opens.

▶ **3.** Type **sloth child: try an apple**, and then click the **OK** button. The behavior is added to the graphic in the background AP div.

▶ **4.** Save the page.

You must preview a page that includes behaviors in a browser to verify that the behaviors work. You'll preview the Sloth Child page in your browser and then test the behaviors you added to the hotspots and the graphic in the background AP div.

To test the behaviors in the Sloth Child page in a browser:

▶ **1.** Preview the Sloth Child page in a browser, and then maximize the browser window, if necessary.

▶ **2.** Position the pointer anywhere in the window except on one of the hotspots in the apple photograph. The pointer changes to 🖑 and the status bar shows the band and album name (sloth child: try an apple).

▶ **3.** Position the pointer over the rightmost hotspot on the apple photograph. The image in the SC2 AP div appears, and the status bar shows the file path. The AP div will remain visible until the pointer moves over another hotspot. See Figure 6-45.

Hidden AP div previewed in a browser ◄ Figure 6-45

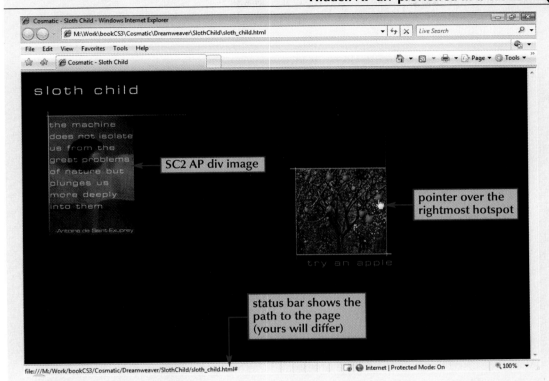

4. Position the pointer over the visible AP div, and then read the text. The pointer changes to 🖑 because the graphic is linked to the Bands page.

5. Click the graphic. The Bands page appears in the browser window.

6. Click the **Back** button 🔙 on the browser toolbar to return to the Sloth Child page.

7. Position the pointer over the centermost hotspot on the apple photograph. The image in the SC2 AP div is hidden, and the image in the SC3 AP div appears.

8. Read the text, and then click the **graphic**. The Cosmatic home page appears in the browser window.

9. Click the **Back** button 🔙 on the browser toolbar to return to the Sloth Child page.

10. Position the pointer over the topmost hotspot on the apple photograph. The image in the SC4 AP div appears, and the image in the SC3 AP div is hidden.

11. Read the text, and then click the **graphic**. The Catalogue page appears in the browser window.

12. Close the browser.

Adding an E-Mail Link to a Page

An **e-mail link** is a link in a browser window that a user can click to start his or her default e-mail program and open a blank message window with the e-mail address specified in the e-mail link already entered in the To field. The process of adding an e-mail link is similar to the process of adding a hyperlink. A user can click the e-mail link when viewing the Web page in a browser window. If no e-mail program is installed on the user's computer, the e-mail link will not work.

You'll create an e-mail link from the band name to a general information e-mail address at Cosmatic.

To add the e-mail link to a hotspot in the Sloth Child page:

▶ 1. Click the rectangular hotspot over the band name. The Property inspector changes to show that a hotspot is selected.

▶ 2. In the Property inspector, double-click the **Link** box, type **mailto:info@cosmaticnoise.com** (make sure that there are no spaces), and then press the **Enter** key.

▶ 3. Save the page, and then preview the page in a browser.

▶ 4. Click the **Sloth Child logo** to test the e-mail link, and then close the browser and the message window.

Trouble? If clicking the link does not open a message window in an e-mail program, your computer might not have a default e-mail program installed and configured. Close the browser and continue with the tutorial.

Adding a Custom Script to a Page

When you used the Rollover Image button and the Navigation Bar button on the Common tab of the Insert bar, you used the preset behavior tools to insert behaviors. In the Sloth Child page, you added behaviors to the hotspots using the Behaviors panel. Now you will add a custom script written by another programmer to the Sloth Child page.

InSight | **Writing Custom JavaScripts**

If you know JavaScript, you can write your own scripts. You can also find scripts that other people have written and posted for public use. However, you'll often need to fine-tune scripts that you use in Web pages, so it is a good idea to learn at least enough JavaScript so that you can debug a page. Some good basic JavaScript resources include:

- *www.webreference.com/programming/javascript/index.html*
- *www.javascript.com*
- *javascript.internet.com.*

The script you are adding will cause one of three quotations to appear randomly in the page when the page is loaded in a browser window, which will provide the illusion that the page has a continuous source of fresh content.

To add a custom script to the Sloth Child page:

▶ 1. On the **Common** tab of the Insert bar, click the **Script button arrow** 🖘 ▾, and then click the **Script** button 🖘 . The Script dialog box opens. You will enter the custom script.

▶ 2. Click the **Type** button, and then click **Text/javascript**, if necessary.

▶ 3. Start **Notepad**, open the **nu_randomZen.txt** file located in the **Tutorial.06\Tutorial** folder included with your Data Files, copy the contents of the file, exit Notepad, and then paste the text into the Content box in the Script dialog box. See Figure 6-46.

Script dialog box ◄ **Figure 6-46**

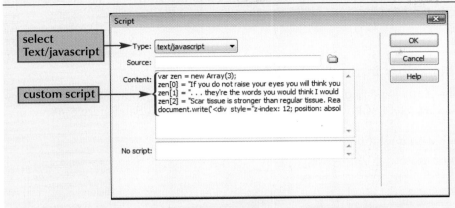

4. Click the **OK** button. This script creates the custom action of displaying one of the three quotations included in the script. The action occurs when the page is loaded in the browser window (this is the event). The event handler is automatically onLoad. (The Sloth Child page is the object.)

Trouble? If a dialog box opens, indicating that you won't see this element unless Invisible Elements are displayed, you might need to display Invisible Elements. Click the OK button to close the dialog box, click View on the menu bar, point to Visual Aids, and then click Invisible Elements, if necessary, to check the option.

5. Click the **Code** button on the Document toolbar. The Document window switches to Code view, showing the script code you just copied. See Figure 6-47.

Sloth Child page in Code view ◄ **Figure 6-47**

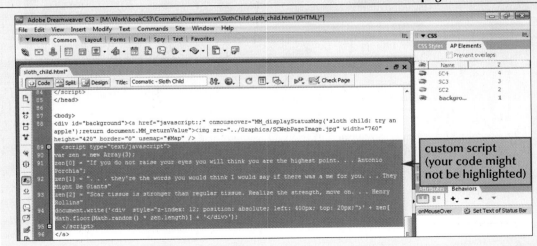

Trouble? If the script was inserted on a different line in your page, you don't need to make any changes. The script will work correctly. Continue with Step 6.

6. Click the **Design** button on the Document toolbar.

7. Save the page.

Now that you are finished adding scripts and behaviors to the page, you need to test the behaviors again. It is important to continue testing all of the scripts each time you add a new one to the page, because new behaviors can affect the behaviors that are already in the page.

To test the behaviors in the Sloth Child page:

▶ **1.** Preview the Sloth Child page in a browser. One of the three quotations that the script added appears when the page is loaded in the window. See Figure 6-48.

Figure 6-48 ▶ **Sloth Child page with quotation in the browser window**

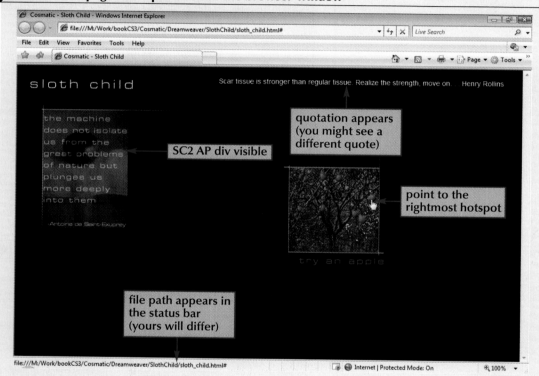

▶ **2.** Position the pointer anywhere in the window except on the band name or on one of the apple hotspots. The pointer changes to 🖑 and the status bar shows the band and album name.

▶ **3.** Position the pointer over the rightmost hotspot on the apple tree photograph. The graphic image in the SC2 AP div appears, and the status bar changes to reflect the file path.

▶ **4.** Click the **graphic** in the SC2 AP div. The Bands page opens.

▶ **5.** Click the **Back** button 🔙 on the browser toolbar. The Sloth Child page is reloaded, the SC2 AP div is hidden, and a different quotation appears in the page.

Trouble? If the quotation doesn't change, you might need to refresh the page to see a new quotation. Click the Refresh button on the browser toolbar, or click at the end of the URL in the Address bar, and then press the Enter key.

▶ **6.** Point to the leftmost hotspot on the apple tree photograph. The graphic image in the SC3 AP div appears. See Figure 6-49.

Image visible from the SC3 AP div ◀ Figure 6-49

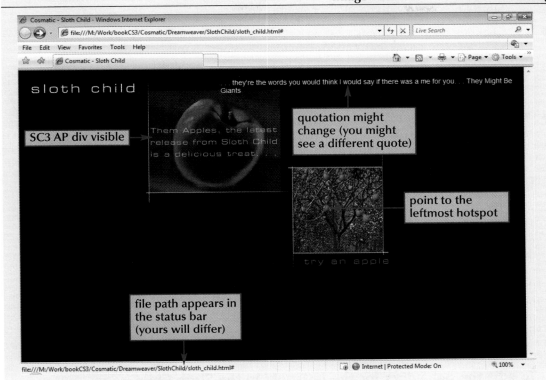

7. Point to the topmost hotspot on the apple tree photograph. The graphic image in the SC4 AP div appears and the image in the SC3 AP div is hidden. See Figure 6-50.

Image visible from the SC4 AP div ◀ Figure 6-50

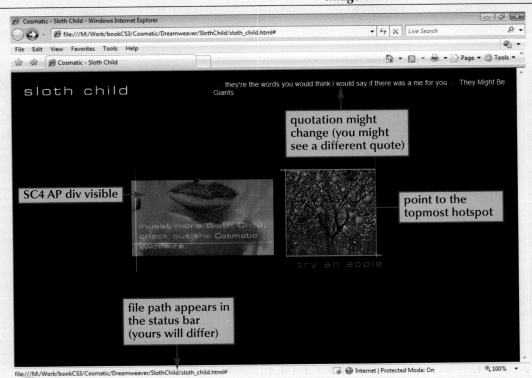

▶ **8.** Click the **graphic** in the SC4 AP div to open the Catalogue page in the browser window, and then click the **Back** button 🔙 on the browser toolbar to reload the Sloth Child page with no AP divs visible.

▶ **9.** Click the band name hotspot. The default e-mail program starts, and a new message window opens with "info@cosmaticnoise.com" in the To field.

Trouble? If a new e-mail message window did not open, then your computer is probably not configured with a default e-mail program. Close any dialog boxes and windows that open and continue with Step 10.

▶ **10.** Close the message window, if necessary, and then close the browser.

Editing and Deleting Behaviors

After a behavior has been created, you can change the event handler associated with the behavior or you can delete the behavior. If you want to change the action, you need to delete the old behavior, select the object, and then attach the new behavior. You can do this in the Behaviors panel.

Brian wants you to see whether a different event handler would be a better choice for the apple hotspots. You will edit one of the behaviors associated with the rightmost hotspot on the apple tree photograph. You will also delete the behavior that displays a message in the status bar, because it makes the pointer seem like it is positioned over a link even though it isn't.

To edit the behaviors for the hotspots in the Sloth Child page:

▶ **1.** Select the rightmost hotspot on the apple tree photograph. The behavior is listed and selected in the Behaviors panel.

▶ **2.** In the Behaviors panel, click the behavior, and then click the **Events** arrow. The events that are supported by 4.0 and later browsers and the Show-Hide Elements action are listed: onClick, onDblClick, onMouseOut, and onMouseOver.

▶ **3.** Click **onClick**. The behavior's event is changed so that the action will occur when the user clicks this hotspot.

▶ **4.** Click anywhere in the Document window to select the image in the background AP div. The Set Text of Status Bar action appears in the Behaviors panel.

▶ **5.** In the Behaviors panel, click the behavior, if necessary, to select it, and then click the **Remove Event** button ⊟ . The selected behavior is deleted.

▶ **6.** Save the page, preview the page in a browser, and position the pointer anywhere in the window except over a hotspot. The status bar no longer displays "sloth child: try an apple."

▶ **7.** Click the rightmost hotspot on the apple tree photograph. The image in the SC2 AP div appears, and a blue border is visible around the background image. See Figure 6-51.

Tip

Small changes in code sometimes affect the page display, so be sure to check modified pages you modify in a browser.

Edited behavior for the SC2 AP div | Figure 6-51

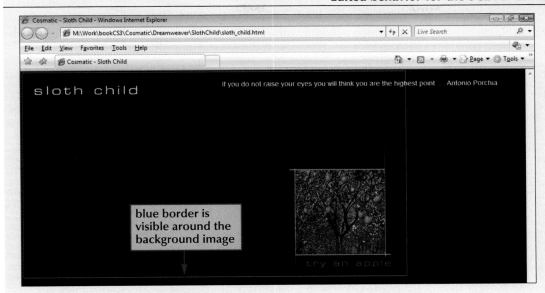

Brian decides that it is better if the user simply points at the apple hotspots, and he wants you to remove the blue border around the background image.

8. Close the browser, click the rightmost hotspot on the apple tree photograph, click the behavior in the Behaviors panel to select it, click the **Events** arrow, and then click **onMouseOver**. The event is changed back to mouseover.

9. Click the background graphic to select it, and then, in the Property inspector, type **0** in the Border box.

10. Save the page, preview the page in a browser, test the mouseovers and links, and then close the browser and the page.

The Sloth Child page is complete. You will add a link to this page in the Review Assignments.

Updating the Web Site on the Remote Server

As a final review of the changes you made to the Cosmatic site, you'll update the files on your remote server and review the pages over the Internet. You will upload the pages and files of the site that have changed or been added. These include the Graphics folder, the SlothChild folder, and the index.html page. Then you'll preview the site on the Web.

To upload the Cosmatic site to your remote server:

1. Collapse the **CSS panel group** and the **Tag panel group**, and then click the **Connects to Remote Host** button on the Files panel toolbar.

2. If necessary, click the **View** button on the Files panel toolbar, and then click **Local View**.

3. Select the **SlothChild** folder and the **index.html** page in the Local View list, and then click the **Put File(s)** button on the Files panel toolbar.

Trouble? If you cannot select only the files you want, click the Minus (–) button next to the SlothChild folder to collapse the file list in the folder, press and hold the Ctrl key, and then click the folders and files you want to upload.

▶ **4.** Click the **Yes** button when asked if you want to include dependent files, because you have not selected the new dependent file for the site yet.

▶ **5.** Click the **Disconnects from Remote Host** button 🔌 on the Files panel toolbar.

▶ **6.** Click the **View** button on the Files panel toolbar, and then click **Local View**.

You will preview the updated site in a browser. The site will include all the new features and pages that you added to the local version.

To preview the updated Cosmatic site in a browser:

▶ **1.** Start your browser, type the URL of your remote site in the Address bar on the browser toolbar, and then press the **Enter** key.

▶ **2.** Click the top **What's Hot** link to open the What's Hot page in a new browser window, and then close the new browser window that opened.

▶ **3.** Repeat Step 2 for the graphic in the WhatsHot AP div and for the bottom **What's Hot** link.

▶ **4.** Click in the **Address** box in the browser window, press the **Right Arrow** key to position the insertion point at the end of the current URL, press the **Backspace** key to delete /index.html if necessary, type **/SlothChild/sloth_child.html**, and then press the **Enter** key. The Sloth Child page opens in the same browser window.

▶ **5.** Point to each of the three hotspots on the apple photograph to test the behaviors.

▶ **6.** Click the band name to open a new e-mail message window, and then close the message window.

Trouble? If a new e-mail message window does not open, then your computer might not be configured with a default e-mail program. Close any dialog boxes and windows that open, and continue with Step 7.

▶ **7.** Close the browser.

Sara and Brian are pleased with the latest changes you made to the Cosmatic site. It has a nice look and useful functionality.

Review | **Session 6.3 Quick Check**

1. What is a behavior?

2. What is an event?

3. What is an action?

4. Are all behaviors selected and assigned in the Behaviors panel?

5. True or False? You cannot change the action associated with a behavior.

6. What is a custom script?

Tutorial Summary | Review

In this tutorial, you created an alternate home page and inserted divs that use relative positioning to lay out a page. You drew AP divs in a Web page. You selected, moved, resized, and added content to AP divs. You also adjusted the AP divs' attributes. You adjusted their stacking order. You aligned the AP divs and created nested AP divs. You also reviewed the HTML code involved with AP divs. Finally, you added behaviors to a Web page, and then you edited and deleted behaviors.

Key Terms

absolute positioning (AP)	e-mail link	nested AP div
action	event handler	object
AP div	grid	user event
behavior	guides	z-index number
div tag	ID selector	

Practice the skills you learned in the tutorial.

There are no Data Files needed for the Review Assignments.

Brian asks you to complete the home page for the new Cosmatic site. You'll move, resize, and align the AP divs that you have already created and fill them with content. Then you will create new AP divs and fill them with content. Finally, you will create links from the content to the other pages of the site.

1. Open the **Cosmatic** site that you modified in this tutorial, open the **index.html** page in the Document window, expand the AP Elements panel, and then select the WhatsHot AP div and move the AP div to the right until its right side is aligned to the right side of the tables surrounding the navigation bar. (*Hint:* Use the guides to help you.)

2. Select the DizziedConnections AP div and then move it so that its left border is approximately 10 pixels from the left page border. (*Hint:* Use the guides to help you position the AP div.)

3. Hold down the Shift key and select the WhatsHot AP div to select both AP divs.

4. Click Modify on the menu bar, point to Arrange, and then click Align Top to align the top border of the two AP divs. Because the WhatsHot AP div was selected last, the DizziedConnections AP div aligns to it.

5. Drag the right resize handle of the DizziedConnections AP div to the right, leaving approximately 10 pixels between it and the left border of the WhatsHot AP div.

6. Click after "Dizzied Connections," press the Spacebar, and then type **Heads West**.

7. Select the text "Information about the band will be here soon." and then type **The boys have packed up their toys and are heading to the West Coast to play for a while. Check out the tour dates to see if they'll be stopping by your hometown.**

8. Select "Dizzied Connections Heads West," create a link from the selected text to the dc_frameset.html page in the DizziedConnections folder, and set the target to _blank.

9. Link the words "tour dates" to the tourdates.html page.

10. Select the h2 style in the All Rules pane in the CSS Styles panel, edit the style by changing the font weight to Normal and the font size to 26 pixels. The heading text in the DizziedConnections AP div changes size and weight to match the edited h2 style, and the Dizzied Connections heading text is in one line at the top of the AP div. If the heading text is more than one line, expand the AP div width slightly to move all of the heading text into the top line.

11. If the DizziedConnections AP div is longer than the text inside of it, select it, and then drag the bottom resize handle up to resize the AP div to a smaller size. If the AP div will not resize, click in the blank line at the bottom of the AP div, press the Backspace key as many times as necessary to move the insertion point so that it is positioned immediately after the end of the last sentence, and then resize the AP div.

12. Use the Align command to align the SlothChild and DizziedConnections AP divs to the left border of the DizziedConnections AP div. (*Hint:* Select the SlothChild AP div first. If the Dizzied Connections AP div moves, you selected it first; click Edit on the menu bar, click Undo Align, and then try again.)

13. Select only the SlothChild AP div, and then press the Arrow keys to nudge the AP div until the top border is about 20 pixels from the bottom of the text in the Dizzied-Connections AP div.

14. Select the words "Sloth Child" and apply the Heading 2 tag from the Format list in the Property inspector, link the selected text to the sloth_child.html file in the Sloth-Child folder, and then set the target to _blank.

15. Select the SlothChild AP div, and then enter **195px** in the Width box in the Property inspector to change the width of the AP div.

16. Click below the Sloth Child heading, and then type **The new release is shaking things up. Check out the catalogue to see what the buzz is all about.**

17. Link the word "catalogue" to the catalogue.html page.

18. Draw another AP div approximately 15 pixels to the right of the SlothChild AP div. Make it the same height as the SlothChild AP div, and extend the AP div to the right until its right border aligns with the right border of the DizziedConnections AP div above it. (Use the guides to help you with the alignment.)

19. Select the new AP div, name it **LIMC**, type **Life in Minor Chords** in the new AP div, press the Enter key, select the text you typed, and then apply the Heading 2 style from the Format list in the Property inspector. Adjust the width of the AP div, if necessary, to fit the heading on one line.

20. Move the insertion point below the Life in Minor Chords heading, and then type **If you are an LIMC fan, keep checking their Web site over the next few weeks! The new look is in place and we are adding more every day.**

21. Drag the bottom border of the AP div up so that it just fits to the text, if necessary.

22. Select the heading text, link it to the limc_frameset.html page in the LifeInMinorChords folder, and then set the target to _blank.

23. Align the top border of the LIMC AP div to the top border of the SlothChild AP div.

24. Select the DizziedConnections, SlothChild, LIMC, and WhatsHot AP divs, and then press the Up Arrow key to nudge them up to approximately 20 pixels below the navigation bar, if necessary.

25. Save the page, save and close the cosmatic_styles.css page, preview the page in a browser, test the new links, close the browser, and then close the page.

26. Upload the changed pages to your remote server, and then preview the site over the Web.

27. Submit the finished files to your instructor, either in printed or electronic form, as requested.

| Apply | **Case Problem 1** |

Create a new page with AP divs for a Web site about the small rural communities of northern Vietnam.

Data Files needed for this Case Problem: WASetiquette_terms.gif, WASetiquetteButton.gif

World Anthropology Society   Dr. Olivia Thompson has developed a short list of etiquette tips about Vietnamese culture that she wants to include in her Web site. New staff members as well as visitors to the camp can review these tips, so that they can avoid offending the native people. To do this, you will use divs in a new page. You will also create an AP div beside the logo in the home page with a link to the new page.

1. Open the **DrThompson** site that you modified in **Tutorial 5**, **Case 1**, and in the Files panel, duplicate the linguistic_differences.html page in the site's local root folder. (*Hint:* Right-click the page, point to Edit on the context menu, and then click Duplicate.)

2. Rename the copied page **etiquette_tips.html**, update the links, open the new page in the Document window, and then change the page title to **Dr. Olivia Thompson - Etiquette Tips**.

3. Draw an AP div approximately 500 pixels wide and 25 pixels high at the bottom of the page, and then enter **Footer** as the CSS-P Element ID.

4. Copy the footer information from the table, paste it into the Footer AP div, resize the Footer AP div to be the same width as the footer, and then position the Footer AP div approximately 200 pixels below the table at the bottom of the page.

5. Delete the entire Linguistic Differences table and the navigation bar from the page. Everything below the logo and above the Footer AP div is removed from the page.

6. Approximately 20 pixels below the lowest horizontal line and 10 pixels from the left edge of the window, draw a square AP div approximately 100 pixels by 100 pixels, and then enter **EtiquetteTermsList** as the CSS-P Element ID.

7. Insert the **WASetiquette_terms.gif** graphic located in the Tutorial.06\Case1 folder included with your Data Files in the EtiquetteTermsList AP div, and then drag the borders of the AP div to fit snugly against the borders of the graphic, if necessary.

8. About 20 pixels to the right of the EtiquetteTermsList AP div, draw an AP div that is approximately 400 pixels wide and the same height as the EtiquetteTermsList AP div, enter **OpeningText** as the CSS-P Element ID, and then type the following text into the AP div: **As we continue our stay in this amazing country, we are always seeking to develop a deeper understanding of the people and their culture. We have provided some insights here. I hope they will help make your transition to productive team member a smooth one!**

9. Align the top of the OpeningText AP div with the top of the EtiquetteTermsList AP div.

10. Hide the OpeningText AP div from view. (*Hint:* Display the closed eye icon for the AP div in the AP Elements panel.)

11. To the right of the EtiquetteTermsList AP div, draw an AP div approximately the same size and in the same position as the OpeningText AP div. (It is okay to overlap the hidden OpeningText AP div.) Enter **Appointments** as the CSS-P Element ID, and then type the following text in the AP div: **Vietnamese often do not take appointment times literally. Sometimes they will purposely arrive late so that they do not appear overly eager.**

⊕ EXPLORE   12. Align the Appointments AP div with the top and left border of the OpeningText AP div. (*Hint:* Because the OpeningText AP div is invisible, select the AP div in the AP Elements panel. The hidden AP div will become visible while it is selected and will return to its hidden state when it is not selected.)

13. Hide the Appointments AP div.

14. Repeat Steps 11 through 13, entering **Invitations** as the CSS-P Element ID, and then typing the following text in the AP div: **In Vietnamese culture, the person who extends an invitation is also expected to pay the bill.**

15. Repeat Steps 11 through 13, entering **Gifts** as the CSS-P Element ID, and then typing the following text in the AP div: **Often the giver of a gift will discount the item, even though it may be of great value. The recipient, however, is expected to display significant gratitude. This gratitude sometimes lasts a lifetime. Some Vietnamese are reluctant to accept gifts because of the burden of gratitude. Vietnamese may refuse a gift on the first offer, even if they intend to accept it, so as not to appear greedy.**

16. Click the closed eye icon next to the OpeningText AP div in the AP Elements panel to make the OpeningText AP div visible.

17. Select the EtiquetteTermsList graphic, and then use the Rectangular Hotspot Tool in the Property inspector to draw hotspots over each of the three terms in the list.

18. Display the Behaviors panel in the Tag Inspector panel group. (You may see a behavior in the list, depending on where the insertion point is in the page.)

19. Select the top hotspot, click the Add Behavior button in the Behaviors panel, click Show-Hide Elements, and then set the AP divs visibility to show the Footer, EtiquetteTermsList, and Appointments AP divs and to hide the others.

20. Select the middle hotspot, and then set the AP divs visibility in the Show-Hide Elements dialog box to show the Footer, EtiquetteTermsList, and Invitations AP divs and to hide the others.

21. Select the bottom hotspot, and then set the AP divs visibility in the Show-Hide Elements dialog box to show the Footer, EtiquetteTermsList, and Gifts AP divs and to hide the others.

22. Select the Footer AP div, and then move the AP div until the top is positioned at approximately 350 pixels. (*Hint:* You can press the Up Arrow key to shift the vertical position without affecting its horizontal position.)

23. Save the page, preview the page in a browser, test each of the hotspots, and then close the browser and the page.

24. Open the **index.html** page, and then draw an AP div that is 100 pixels wide and 75 pixels high in the colored banner at the top of the home page positioned above the Cultural Cross-Pollination link in the navigation bar.

25. Insert the **WASetiquetteButton.gif** graphic located in the Tutorial.06\Case1 folder included with your Data Files into the AP div, resize the AP div so that it fits snugly around the graphic, and then use the Arrow keys to nudge the AP div so the graphic is completely within the colored bar.

26. Link the graphic to the etiquette_tips.html page, and then target the link to open the page in a new browser window.

27. Save the page, preview the page in a browser window, test the Etiquette Tips link, and then close the browser and the page.

28. Upload the site to the remote server, and then preview the site over the Web.

29. Submit the finished files to your instructor, either in printed or electronic form, as requested.

Apply		Case Problem 2

Add AP divs with graphics and behaviors to display related information when a user moves the pointer over the painting in a Web site for an art museum.

Data Files needed for this Case Problem: AQuietDayInUtica.jpg, BuffaloRunners.jpg, CowpunchingSometimes.jpg, IndiansHuntingBuffalo.jpg, AFigureOfTheNight.jpg, TheBucker.jpg, TheCowPuncher.jpg, DeerInForest.jpg

Museum of Western Art C. J. Strittmatter asks you to add the art to the Art page of the museum's Web site. Because the museum has so many paintings, C.J. wants to feature a few paintings at a time from the collection. You'll use AP divs to add paintings to the page. You'll create an additional AP div for painting information, attach the Set Text for Container behavior to each painting graphic, and then set the text in the new painting information AP div. You'll use onMouseDown as the event handler, which will cause the painting information AP div to update with information associated with the painting that the user mouses over.

1. Open the **Museum** site that you modified in **Tutorial 5**, **Case 2**, and then open the **art.html** page.

2. Draw an AP div approximately 150 pixels wide and 100 pixels high, and then drag the AP div approximately 10 pixels from the left border of the page and approximately 10 pixels below the bottom of the heading text (ART) located at the right of the page. (*Hint:* Use the grid or guides to help you position the AP div.)

3. Insert the **AQuietDayInUtica.jpg** graphic located in the Tutorial.06\Case2 folder included with your Data Files into the AP div, drag the borders so that the AP div fits snugly around the graphic, and then enter **UticaPic** as the CSS-P Element ID.

4. Select the graphic, and then apply the image_border style from the Class list in the Property inspector.

5. Repeat Steps 2 through 4 to add seven more AP divs. Draw each new AP div approximately 20 pixels to the right of the previous one to create four AP divs in the row; then draw the other four AP divs in a second row approximately 20 pixels below the bottom border of the top row. Use the following list to add graphics to the AP divs and to name the AP divs.

Graphic	CSS-P Element ID
BuffaloRunners.jpg	BuffaloPic
CowpunchingSometimes.jpg	CowPic
IndiansHuntingBuffalo.jpg	IndianPic
AFigureOfTheNight.jpg	FigurePic
TheBucker.jpg	BuckerPic
TheCowPuncher.jpg	PuncherPic
DeerInForest.jpg	DeerPic

6. Select all of the graphics in the top row, top-align them to fine-tune the horizontal alignment of the graphics, and then repeat for the graphics in the second row.

7. Select the two graphics in the first column, left-align them to fine-tune the alignment of the graphics in the first column, and then do the same for the graphics in the other three columns.

8. Draw a new AP div centered above the four columns of paintings and with its top border aligned with the top border of the table that holds the menu bar. Make the AP div approximately 250 pixels wide and 100 pixels high. (*Hint:* After the AP div is drawn, the center resize handles should be visually aligned with the center space between the four columns of paintings.)

9. Name the new AP div **PaintingID**, and then apply the image_border style from the Class list in the Property inspector.

10. Place the insertion point inside the PaintingID AP div, type **Click on each painting to view additional information.**, and then apply the menustyle style to the text. (The text you typed will be displayed in the AP div until the user mouses over a painting.)

11. Select the **AQuietDayInUtica.jpg** graphic, click the Add Behavior button in the Behaviors panel, point to the Show Events For list, click 4.0 and Later Browsers, click the Add Behavior button, point to Set Text, and then click Set Text of Container.

⊕ EXPLORE 12. In the Set Text of Container dialog box, click div "PaintingID" in the Container list, and then type the following HTML code in the New HTML box that tells the browser how to display the text as well as the text to display. (*Hint:* You can press the Enter key at the end of each line to keep the lines organized as they are here, or you can type all of the text on one line; either way the text will display correctly.)

```
<span class="menustyle">
A Quiet Day in Utica<br>
Charles M. Russell<br>
1907<br>
Oil on canvas<br>
</span>
```

13. Click the OK button, and then save the page and preview the page in a browser. The text you typed directly into the PaintingID AP div is displayed when the page is initially loaded. Click the UticaPic AP div; the image changes to the text you typed in Step 12. Notice that the code you typed is not displayed. Close the browser window. (*Hint:* If you made a mistake when you typed the text in Step 12, click the graphic to display the behavior in the Behaviors panel, double-click the Set Text of Container action to open the Set Text of Container dialog box with the text you typed displayed, correct the text, click the OK button, and then save and preview the page in a browser again.)

14. Repeat Steps 11 through 13 to add the Set Text of Container behavior to each painting, using the following text for each painting:

Graphic	AP Div Text
BuffaloRunners.jpg	PaintingID <span class="menustyle">Buffalo Runners-Big Horn Basin Frederic Remington 1909 Oil on canvas </span>
CowpunchingSometimes.jpg	PaintingID <span class="menustyle">Cow Punching Sometimes Spells Trouble Charles M. Russell 1889 Oil on canvas </span>
IndiansHuntingBuffalo.jpg	PaintingID <span class="menustyle">Indians Hunting Buffalo (Wild Men's Meat; Buffalo Hunt) Charles M. Russell 1894 Oil on canvas </span>
AFigureOfTheNight.jpg	PaintingID <span class="menustyle">A Figure of the Night (The Sentinel) Frederic Remington 1908 Oil on canvas </span>
TheBucker.jpg	PaintingID <span class="menustyle">The Bucker Charles M. Russell 1904 Pencil, watercolor, and gouache on paper </span>
TheCowPuncher.jpg	PaintingID <span class="menustyle">The Cow Puncher Frederic Remington 1901 Oil (black and white) on canvas </span>
DeerInForest.jpg	PaintingID <span class="menustyle">Deer in Forest (White Tailed Deer) Charles M. Russell 1917 Oil on canvas </span>

15. Save the page, preview the page in a browser, test the behaviors by clicking each painting, and then close the browser and the page.

16. Upload the site to the remote server, and then preview the site over the Web.

17. Submit the finished files to your instructor, either in printed or electronic form, as requested.

Apply	**Case Problem 3**

Add AP divs with graphics and behaviors to display related information when a user mouses over a book cover in a Web site for an independent bookstore.

Data Files needed for this Case Problem: BookCoverQueenSm.jpg, BookCoverBasketSm.gif, BookCoverStopGapSm.jpg

MORE Books   Mark Chapman asks you to add book covers to the Books page in the MORE Books site using AP divs. He also wants you to add behaviors to create some interactivity in the site. You'll add behaviors so that when a user points to a book cover, information about the book will appear at the bottom of the screen.

1. Open the **MOREbooks** site that you modified in **Tutorial 5**, **Case 3**, and then open the **books.html** page.

2. Select the Coming Soon text, type **MORE Books**, and then apply the more_sub_headings style to the text. The text appears in all uppercase because of the attributes of the applied style.

3. Draw a 150-pixel square AP div at the left of the page 10 pixels below the text that you just typed, enter **PunchCover** as the CSS-P Element ID, insert the **BookCoverPunchSmall.jpg** graphic located in the Graphics folder in the site's local root folder into the AP div, change the graphic's border to 1, and then resize the AP div to fit snugly around the graphic.

4. Draw an AP div to the right of the PunchCover AP div approximately the same size as the PunchCover AP div, enter **QueenCover** as the CSS-P Element ID, insert the **BookCoverQueenSm.jpg** graphic located in the Tutorial.06\Case3 folder included with your Data Files, change the graphics border to 1, and then resize the AP div to fit snugly around the graphic.

5. Repeat Step 4 for the **BookCoverBasketSm.gif** and the **BookCoverStopGapSm.jpg** graphics located in the Tutorial.06\Case3 folder included with your Data Files, entering **BasketCover** and **StopGapCover** for the CSS-P Element IDs, respectively.

6. Adjust the horizontal spacing of the AP divs as needed so there are 15 pixels between each, and then align the tops of the AP divs.

7. Draw an AP div approximately 25 pixels below the book covers that extends from the middle of the first book cover to the middle of the fourth book cover and is approximately 100 pixels high, and then enter **PunchText** as the CSS-P Element ID.

8. Type the following text into the AP div, pressing the Enter key only after the first line:
   Punch by Kelly Moore
   Punch is a wacky, eclectic collection of monologues that give voice to the psyche of the modern woman with stories that range from heroic to tragic to just plain goofy.

9. Apply the more_book_titles style to the book title, and then hide the AP div in the AP Elements panel.

10. Repeat Steps 7 through 9 for each of the remaining book titles, using the following CSS-P Element IDs and text:

CSS-P Element ID	AP Div Text
QueenText	Queen of Chimeras by Sajanya BaRae
	Queen of Chimeras is the story of Sheila Helt, a woman who is part misfit and part mystic. It is a story for every woman who has dared to follow her own path and stumbled a bit along the way.

BasketText	Basket Dropping 101 by Tika
	A story for those who are strong at heart, this book is an edgy, graphic, and perversely hilarious account of life through the eyes of a young woman struggling to find dignity in poverty and to create her place in the world.
StopGapText	Stop Gap by Kim Flores
	Stop Gap is an investigation of the effects of the new global economy on the exploited workers in Third World countries. Kim Flores uses her background in economics, sociology, and international business to shed light on the complex problems associated with globalization, and to suggest practical, real-world solutions.

11. In the AP Elements panel, select all of the text AP divs, and then align them to the top and to the left.

12. Select the graphic in the PunchCover AP div, expand the Behaviors panel, and then add the Show-Hide Elements behavior.

13. In the Show-Hide Elements dialog box, show the PunchText AP div, hide the Queen-Text, BasketText, and StopGapText AP divs (do not set the BookCover AP divs to Show or Hide because they never change), click the OK button, and then change the event handler to onMouseOver in the Behaviors panel, if necessary. (*Hint:* In the Behaviors panel, select onMouseOver from the events list. If onMouseOver does not appear in the list, click the New Behavior button, click Show Events, click HTML 4.01 to check it, and then select onMouseOver from the events list.)

14. Repeat Step 13 for the graphics in the QueenCover, BasketCover, and StopGapCover AP divs using the corresponding text AP div as the AP div to show each time.

15. Position the insertion point in the Document window to the right of the text "MORE BOOKS," type **(Place your mouse over a book cover to view a description.)**, select the text you just typed, and then remove the CSS style applied to it. (*Hint:* Click None in the Style list in the Property inspector.)

16. Save the page, preview the page in a browser, move the mouse over each book cover to show the hidden AP divs, and then close the browser and close the page.

17. Upload the site to the remote server, and then preview the site over the Web.

18. Submit the finished files to your instructor, either in printed or electronic form, as requested.

Create	**Case Problem 4**

Add a new page that uses AP divs with graphics and behaviors to display the spiciness of selected food items in a Web site for a newly opening sushi restaurant.

Data Files needed for this Case Problem: WasabiChili.jpg, WasabiHotWings.jpg, WasabiLowRiseJeans.jpg, WasabiPicture.gif, WasabiOriginal.gif, WasabiCold.gif, WasabiLukeWarm.gif, WasabiToasty.gif, WasabiOnFire.gif, WasabiWasabi.gif, WasabiPictureSmall.gif

Sushi Ya-Ya Mary O'Brien asks you to create a How Hot Is Wasabi page for the Sushi Ya-Ya site. The page will use AP divs and behaviors to create an interactive thermometer that will "measure" the hotness of different objects. You will place graphics of a pepper, a plate of hot wings, low-rise jeans, and wasabi in AP divs at the bottom of the page. You will place a graphic of a thermometer in an AP div above them. You will include alternate thermometer graphics in hidden AP divs. The alternate graphics will show the thermometer with the temperature at various levels. You will then use the Show-Hide Elements behavior to show various hotness levels when each graphic is selected. Finally, you will create a link from the home page to the How Hot Is Wasabi page.

1. Open the **SushiYa-Ya** site that you modified in **Tutorial 5**, **Case 4**, duplicate the menu.html page in the local root folder of the site, and then rename the copied page **wasabi.html**.

2. Open the **wasabi.html** page, and then delete the Sushi Descriptions text, the coming soon text, and the navigation bar.

3. Type **How Hot Is Wasabi?** below the horizontal line, and then apply the heading style that you created to the text.

4. Draw an AP div 20 pixels from the left border of the page and 10 pixels below the heading text, enter **ChiliPic** as the CSS-P Element ID, insert the **WasabiChili.jpg** graphic located in the Tutorial.06\Case4 folder included with your Data Files, apply the imageborders style to the graphic, and then fit the AP div to the graphic.

5. Draw an AP div 20 pixels below the ChiliPic AP div, enter **HotWingsPic** as the CSS-P Element ID, insert the **WasabiHotWings.jpg** graphic located in the Tutorial.06\Case4 folder included with your Data Files, apply the imageborders style to the graphic, and then fit the AP div to the graphic.

6. Draw an AP div at the right of the page, across from the ChiliPic AP div and starting at approximately 500 pixels, enter **JeansPic** as the CSS-P Element ID, insert the **WasabiLowRiseJeans.jpg** graphic located in the Tutorial.06\Case4 folder included with your Data Files, apply the imageborders style to the graphic, and then fit the AP div to the graphic.

7. Draw an AP div 20 pixels below the JeansPic AP div, enter **WasabiPic** as the ID, insert the **WasabiPicture.gif** graphic located in the Tutorial.06\Case4 folder included with your Data Files, apply the imageborders style to the graphic, and then fit the AP div to the graphic.

8. Align the top border of the top row of graphics, and then align the top border of the bottom row of graphics.

9. Draw an AP div in the center of the page, enter **ThermoOriginal** as the CSS-P Element ID, and then insert the **WasabiOriginal.gif** graphic located in the Tutorial.06\Case4 folder included with your Data Files.

10. Draw an AP div in the center of the page, enter **ThermoCold** as the CSS-P Element ID, insert the **WasabiCold.gif** graphic located in the Tutorial.06\Case4 folder included with your Data Files, and then hide the AP div.

11. Repeat Step 10 to create AP divs with each of the following graphics:

Graphic	**CSS-P Element ID**
WasabiLukeWarm.gif	ThermoLukeWarm
WasabiToasty.gif	ThermoToasty
WasabiOnFire.gif	ThermoOnFire1
WasabiWasabi.gif	ThermoWasabi

12. Select the ThermoOriginal, ThermoCold, ThermoLukeWarm, ThermoToasty, ThermoOnFire1, and ThermoWasabi AP divs in the AP Elements panel, and then align them top and left.

13. Reposition all of the selected Thermo graphics in the page, if necessary, so that they are centered between the other graphics.

⊕ EXPLORE

14. Select the ThermoOriginal AP div in the AP Elements panel, click the closed eye icon to open it, and then change the z-index number to 5, if necessary. The ThermoOriginal AP div moves to the number 5 position in the stacking order.

15. Select the graphic in ChiliPic AP div, add the Show-Hide Elements behavior, and then show the ThermoOnFire1 AP div, hide the ThermoToasty, ThermoLukeWarm, ThermoCold, and ThermoWasabi AP divs, and do nothing to the ThermoOriginal, ChiliPic, HotWingsPic, JeansPic, and WasabiPic AP divs.

16. In the Behaviors panel, select the event, and then click Show Events For 4.0 and Later Browsers for (onClick). (*Hint:* In the Behaviors panel, select onClick from the events list. If onClick does not appear in the list, click the New Behavior button, click Show Events, click HTML 4.01 to check it, and then select onClick from the events list.)

17. Select the graphic in the HotWingsPic AP div, add the Show-Hide Elements behavior, and then show the ThermoToasty AP div, hide the ThermoOnFire1, ThermoLukeWarm, ThermoCold, and ThermoWasabi AP divs, and do nothing to the ThermoOriginal, ChiliPic, HotWingsPic, JeansPic, and WasabiPic AP divs.

18. In the Behaviors panel, select the event, and set the event handler to onClick.

19. Select the graphic in the JeansPic AP div, add the Show-Hide Elements behavior, and then show the ThermoCold AP divs, hide the ThermoOnFire1, ThermoToasty, ThermoLukeWarm, and ThermoWasabi AP divs, and do nothing to the ThermoOriginal, ChiliPic, HotWingsPic, JeansPic, and WasabiPic AP divs.

20. In the Behaviors panel, select the event, and then set the event handler to onClick.

21. Select the WasabiPic AP div, add the Show-Hide Elements behavior, and then show the ThermoWasabi AP div, hide the ThermoOnFire1, ThermoToasty, ThermoLukeWarm, and ThermoCold AP divs, and do nothing to the ThermoOriginal, ChiliPic, HotWingsPic, JeansPic, and WasabiPic AP divs.

22. In the Behaviors panel, select the event, and then set the action to onClick.

23. Save the page, preview the page in a browser, click each graphic, and then close the browser.

24. Open the **index.html** page, click in the cell that contains the heading text, and then split the cell into two columns. (*Hint:* Right-click the cell, point to Table, and then click Split Cell.) Select the heading text, and move it to the center cell.

25. Click in the new left cell, insert the **WasabiPictureSmall.gif** graphic located in the Tutorial.06\Case4 folder included with your Data Files, apply the imageborders style, and then click in a blank part of the cell to deselect the graphic. In the Property inspector, click Center in the Horz list, click Top in the Vert list, and then press the Enter key. (*Hint:* If the title moves to the left cell, select it, and then drag it to the middle cell.)

26. Type **How Hot Is Wasabi???**, apply the sub_headings style, place the pointer before "Wasabi???," and then press the Shift+Enter keys to create a line break.

27. Select the Wasabi graphic, create a link to the wasabi.html page, and then target the link to open in another window. Select the text, link it to the wasabi.html page, and target the link to open in a new browser window. Move the right border of the first cell to the left, and the left border of the last cell to the right until all of the heading text appears on one line.

28. Save the page, preview the page in a browser, click the Wasabi graphic and text, and then close the browser.

29. Upload the site to the remote server, preview the site over the Web, and test all the new links.

30. Submit the finished files to your instructor, either in printed or electronic form, as requested.

Session 6.1

1. a transparent container you place in a Web page to hold different types of content
2. absolute positioning
3. Yes; div tags use CSS styles to define the positions of the content elements within the opening and closing div tags.
4. Click the edge of the div, or click the selection handle if the div is active.
5. It determines the order in which the AP div is stacked in the user's browser window when more than one AP div is used in a page; higher-numbered AP divs are at the front of the stack and are seen in front of AP divs with lower numbers.
6. The Visibility attribute indicates whether the AP div is visible when the Web page is loaded; if an AP div is hidden when the page is loaded, actions taken by the user can make it visible.

Session 6.2

1. True.
2. in front of
3. the last AP div selected, as indicated by black selection handles
4. a series of parallel horizontal and vertical lines that overlap to create equal squares in the background of the Document window to provide a guide for positioning or resizing elements
5. No; in fact, it does not need to even be touching its parent AP div.
6. To unnest an AP div, select it in the AP Elements list and drag it to a new position in the list.

Session 6.3

1. code that is added to a Web page that enables users to interact with various elements in the Web page, to alter the Web page in different ways, or to cause tasks to be performed
2. An event is comprised of a user event and an event handler. The user event is what the user does to trigger the action; the event handler is the code used to refer to the event.
3. what happens when an event is performed on an object
4. No; preset behaviors are available in different areas of the Dreamweaver environment, such as the rollover behavior; you can also write code for new behaviors.
5. False. If you want to change the action, you need to delete the old behavior, select the object, and then attach the new behavior.
6. code you write (usually in JavaScript) in Code view

Creating Animations

Adding a Timeline

Case | Cosmatic

Sara Lynn, president of Cosmatic, wants some animated elements added to the Cosmatic site. She believes these animated elements will increase interest for the site's target audience. Brian Lee, public relations and marketing director, thinks a good place to add the animation that Sara wants is in the Tour Dates page. He asks you to create an interactive component for the map in the Tour Dates page. You will animate the route each band will take during its tour. Then you will create a button for each band so that when the user clicks the button, the route for that band will animate.

You'll use AP divs to add the animated elements to the Web site. Then you will use behaviors with the animated AP divs to add sophistication and advanced functionality to the site.

Starting Data Files

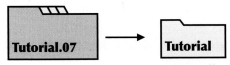

Tutorial.07 → **Tutorial**

BusSmall.gif
Central1.gif
  through
  Central15.gif
East1.gif
  through
  East13.gif
SCbusButtonOver.gif
SCbusButtonUp.gif
SSbusButtonOver.gif
SSbusButtonUp.gif

Review

DCbusButtonOver.gif
DCbusButtonUp.gif
Dizzied1.gif
  through
  Dizzied12.gif

Case1

WASetiquetteButton2.gif

Case2

SlideShowBG.gif

Case3

(none)

Case4

Wasabi2.gif

Session 7.1

Understanding Animation

Adding animated elements to a Web site can create interest and interactivity. **Animation** is a series of graphics or images that appear to move over time. Think about a flip book with a series of pictures. The picture changes slightly on each page. When you flip the pages of the book quickly, the image appears to move. You can create animation in a Web page that uses a similar process.

InSight		**Planning Animations for a Web Site**

Before you add animation to the pages in a Web site, it is important to plan which elements will be animated. You should consider what each animation will add to the page, and include only those animations that support the underlying site goals and provide the user with useful information. Also, you should avoid adding too much animation to a page, which can distract users from the main message or information. We have all seen sites that look as though a cartoon has exploded across the pages. Avoid overloading the user with unnecessary distractions by limiting the number of animated elements that are included in a page and in the site. You should not include more than one animated element in a page unless you have a compelling reason for doing so, and you should not include more than three or four animations in the site.

Exploring the Timelines Panel

You use the Timelines panel to create animations in Dreamweaver. The Timelines panel enables you to create animation by using dynamic HTML code and AP divs to change AP div position, change the source of an image, or automatically call behaviors without using Flash, ActiveX, Java, or any other plug-in application.

You will open the Timelines panel and explore the options for adding animation to Web pages.

To open the Timelines panel:

▶ 1. Open the **Cosmatic** site that you modified in the **Tutorial 6 Review Assignments**, and then open the **tourdates.html** page in the Document window.

▶ 2. Click **Window** on the menu bar, and click **Timelines**. The Timelines panel opens below the Property inspector and the Results panel.

▶ 3. Collapse the Property inspector. See Figure 7-1.

Tip

You can also press the Alt+F9 keys to open and close the Timelines panel.

Timelines panel expanded | Figure 7-1

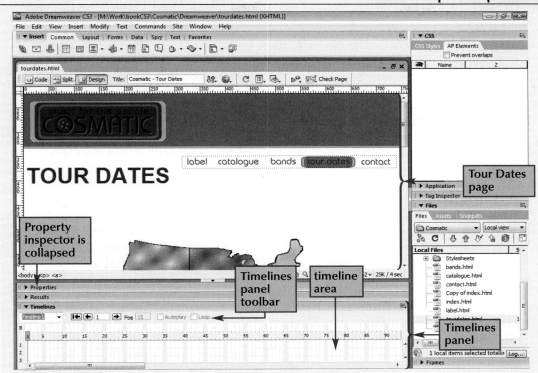

Each element of the timeline controls a different aspect of the animation. If you have used animation software, such as Adobe Flash or Adobe Director, or video editing software such as Adobe Premier, the timeline might look somewhat familiar because most time-based software have some similar components. If you have never used a program that enabled you to move objects over time, the next sections introduce the Timelines panel. Figure 7-2 identifies all of the components in the Timelines panel.

Components of the Timelines panel | Figure 7-2

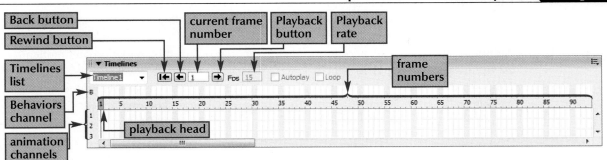

The Timelines panel consists of a toolbar with buttons that control various aspects of the animation and the timeline area where you create your animation.

The timeline area is divided into frames vertically and into channels horizontally (each frame is in a different column, and each channel is in a different row). In the timeline, frames are not the same as the frames that you used earlier to divide an HTML page to display more than one HTML document. Timeline **frames** are the units of temporal measurement used in animation. (In film, a frame is one section of the film strip; in traditional animation, a frame is one cell of animation.) As you move to the right on the timeline, the animation progresses in time. Frame numbers are visible in the second row of the timeline to help you keep track of what frame you are in.

The **playback head** (the red bar) indicates which frame of the animation is visible in the Document window. You can move forward and backward in the timeline by dragging the playback head. The length of an animation is determined by the number of frames included in the animation and by the speed at which those frames play in the user's browser. The default setting for the **playback rate**, the speed of an animation, in Dreamweaver is 15 frames per second (Fps), which is generally a good average rate. Be aware that there is no way to guarantee the playback rate on a user's computer, because browsers always play every frame of the animation even if they cannot attain the specified playback rate. This means that an animation will run slower on a slow machine and faster on a fast machine, but the fastest it will ever run is the playback rate you specify. To ensure that you achieve the look that you want, it is a good idea to test animations on a variety of computers.

The **Behaviors channel**, the row above the frame numbers, is where you insert any behaviors that will be called from a certain frame in the timeline. The Behaviors channel is discussed in Session 7.2.

The numbered rows below the frame numbers are the animation channels. **Animation channels** are the rows in which objects are animated. If you are animating more than one object (an AP div or an image) at a time, you use a different animation channel for each object. Unlike other time-based software, the vertical position of a row within the timeline has nothing to do with the z-index number (or stacking order) of the object within the Web page.

The Timelines panel toolbar includes the following:

- **Timelines.** Displays the selected timeline when more than one timeline is added to a Web page.
- **Rewind.** Moves the playback head to the first frame of the timeline.
- **Back.** Rewinds the timeline one frame at a time.
- **Current frame number.** Displays the number of the current frame of animation.
- **Playback.** Advances the timeline one frame at a time. Holding down the Playback button plays the entire timeline.
- **Autoplay.** Attaches a behavior to the Web page that makes the animation automatically start playing when the Web page is loaded into a user's browser.
- **Loop.** Attaches a behavior to the Web page that makes the animation continue to loop as long as the page is loaded in the user's browser window. **Looping** restarts the animation from the first frame after the last frame is played.

You'll use the Timelines panel to add an AP div to the timeline.

Creating a Timeline

The first step in creating an animation is to create a timeline for the AP div you want to animate. The image or text that you want to animate must be in an AP div in the Web page before you can add it to the Timelines panel.

Adding AP Divs to the Timelines Panel | Reference Window

- Open the Timelines panel.
- In the Document window, select the AP div.
- Drag the selected AP div from the Document window to the desired position in the Timelines panel.

Brian wants you to create an animated tour path for the Sloth Child band over the U.S. map in the Tour Dates page. You will insert the U.S. map graphic into an AP div in the Tour Dates page. Then, you'll create another AP div over the U.S. map and insert a graphic. Placing the AP div and graphic over the hotspots on the U.S. map will not inhibit the functionality of the hotspots; they will work through the AP div. The map will be the first in a series of graphics that you will add to the Tour Dates page to create an animated path for the Sloth Child tour.

To move the map graphic into a new AP div in the Tour Dates page:

▶ 1. Click the **Layout** tab on the Insert bar, click the **Draw AP Div** button 📰 , and then draw a new AP div to the left of the U.S. map.

▶ 2. Select the **map graphic** and the **hotspots** by pressing the **Shift** key as you click each hotspot, drag the selected map graphic into the new AP div, and then resize the AP div to fit snugly against the graphic.

▶ 3. Select the **AP div**, drag the selected AP div to **20 pixels** below the page heading, and then align the selected AP div to the center of the West Coast tour dates table. You can use the rulers and guides to help you.

▶ 4. If necessary, position the pointer above the table, and then press the **Enter** key until the table is **50 pixels** below the U.S. map graphic.

▶ 5. Collapse the Property inspector, expand the **CSS panel group**, and then click the **AP Elements** tab to open the AP Elements panel.

▶ 6. In the AP Elements panel, double-click **apDiv1** in the Name column, type **USmap**, and then press the **Enter** key to rename the AP div. The U.S. map is in the USmap AP div positioned in the Tour Dates page. See Figure 7-3.

USmap AP div centered in the Tour Dates page ◀ Figure 7-3

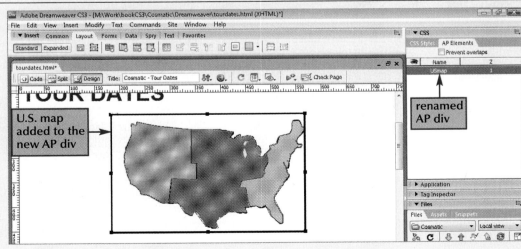

You'll create a new AP div over the USmap AP div named "East1," and then insert a graphic marking the first stop on the tour to the new AP div. The first tour stop image will be displayed over the U.S. map because the z-index number of the East1 AP div is higher than the z-index number of the USmap AP div.

To create the East1 AP div in the Tour Dates page:

▶ **1.** On the **Layout** tab on the Insert bar, click the **Draw AP Div** button 📄 , and then draw a small AP div over the U.S. map in the Document window.

▶ **2.** In the AP Elements panel, rename the new AP div as **East1**.

▶ **3.** Click in the East1 AP div to make it active, click the **Common** tab on the Insert bar, and then click the **Image** button 📷 in the **Images** list to insert the **East1.gif** graphic located in the **Tutorial.07\Tutorial** folder included with your Data Files. A graphic with one small, black dot appears in the East1 AP div, which might expand to fit the graphic.

Trouble? If the graphic is not in the East1 AP div, then it was added into the Tour Dates page. Drag the graphic into the East1 AP div.

Trouble? If the Image Tag Accessibility Attributes dialog box opens, prompting you to add alternate text for the image, this prompt is not disabled in your installation of Dreamweaver. Click the Cancel button to close the dialog box without adding alternate text here and whenever it appears in this tutorial.

▶ **4.** Resize the East1 AP div to fit snugly against the edges of the graphic. Although only one small, black dot appears, the graphic has approximately the same dimensions as the U.S. map.

Trouble? If you cannot locate the edges of the graphic, the graphic image is not selected. Select the graphic to view its dimensions, select the AP div, and then drag the edges of the AP div to fit snugly around the graphic image or change its dimensions in the Property inspector.

▶ **5.** Center the East1 AP div over the map. See Figure 7-4.

| Figure 7-4 | **East1 AP div centered on the U.S. map** |

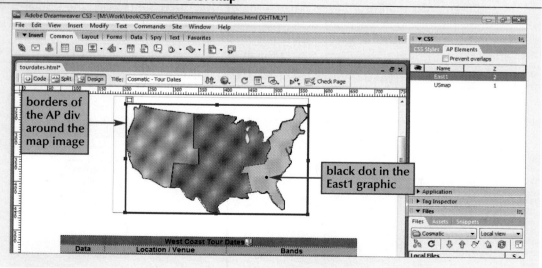

You'll drag the East1 AP div into the Timelines panel to create an animation bar from the AP div.

To add the East1 AP div to the Timelines panel:

▶ **1.** Drag the **East1** AP div from the Document window into **frame 1** in **animation channel 1** in the Timelines panel. A line with a white circle at each end and the word "East1" appears in the first channel in the Timelines panel, indicating that an animation bar has been created. A dialog box opens, explaining the capabilities of the Timelines panel.

Trouble? If the animation bar does not appear in the Timelines panel, you might be trying to drag the AP div from the AP Elements panel. Drag the AP div from the Tour Dates page to frame 1 in animation channel 1 in the Timelines panel.

Trouble? If the dialog box doesn't open, the message was turned off for your installation of Dreamweaver. Compare your Timelines panel with Figure 7-5, and then continue with Step 3.

▶ **2.** Click the **OK** button. See Figure 7-5.

| Timelines panel with the East1 layer animation bar | Figure 7-5 |

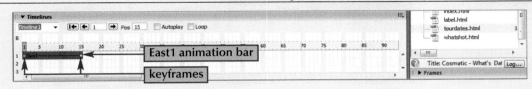

▶ **3.** Save the Tour Dates page.

When you drag an AP div to the Timelines panel, an animation bar and keyframes are added for the AP div. An **animation bar** is the purple line that appears in the channel to which the AP div is added. By default, the animation bar is 15 frames. The AP div name appears at the left of the animation bar and can be used to identify it. If you have not named the AP div, the default AP div name appears at the left of the timeline. The white circles in the first and last frames of the animation bar are keyframes. A **keyframe** is a frame in a timeline where an event occurs. Every timeline has at least two keyframes—one placed at the first frame and one placed at the last frame of the animation bar.

Next, you will add the other graphics that you will use in the animation to the timeline. For each, you'll create an AP div over the U.S. map, insert a graphic into the AP div, resize the AP div to fit snugly around the graphic, align the AP div with the East1 AP div, rename the AP div in the AP Elements panel, and then add the new AP div to an animation channel of the timeline. Each graphic has the same width and height. When the graphics are stacked and aligned, the points along the tour path connect. To ensure that the points of the tour path align correctly, you need to fit the AP div snugly against the graphic before aligning the AP divs. When the stack of aligned AP divs is positioned correctly over the U.S. map, the tour path will appear over the correct portion of the map. For this reason, it is important that the borders of the East1 AP div fit along the edges of the U.S. map and that the other AP divs are then aligned to the top and left of the East1 AP div. You'll use the guides to help align the AP divs accurately.

To add the remaining graphics for the East tour path to the timeline:

▶ **1.** Drag guides from the horizontal and vertical rulers to the top and left borders of the East1 AP div. You will use these guides to align additional AP divs.

▶ **2.** Draw a new AP div over the U.S. map, aligning the top and left edges of the new AP div to the guides.

▶ **3.** Insert the **East2.gif** graphic located in the **Tutorial.07\Tutorial** folder included with your Data Files into the new AP div.

▶ **4.** Resize the AP div as needed to fit snugly against the borders of the graphic. (Remember, you must select the graphic to see the edges of the graphic.)

▶ **5.** In the AP Elements panel, rename the new AP div as **East2**. See Figure 7-6.

Figure 7-6 | **East2 AP div with graphic**

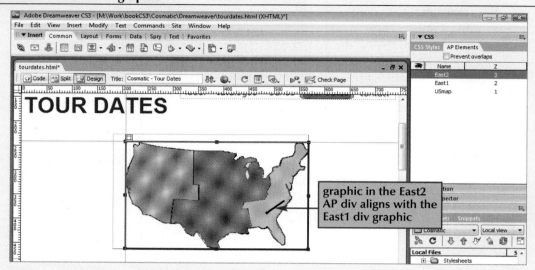

Trouble? If the lines in the two AP divs in your page do not touch as shown in Figure 7-6, make sure the East1 and East2 AP divs are sized to fit snugly to the borders of the graphics you inserted in each AP div, and then left-align and top-align the AP divs.

▶ **6.** In the Document window, select the **East2** AP div, drag the selected AP div to **animation channel 2** in the Timelines panel, and then click the **OK** button in the dialog box that opens. The East2 AP div is added to channel 2 of the timeline and an animation bar is created.

▶ **7.** Repeat Steps 2 through 6 to add the following graphics to the timeline (use the name of each graphic for the AP div name and add each graphic to the next animation channel): **East3.gif**, **East4.gif**, **East5.gif**, **East6.gif**, **East7.gif**, **East8.gif**, **East9.gif**, **East10.gif**, **East11.gif**, **East12.gif**, and **East13.gif**. All the graphics for the tour path animation are added to the timeline. See Figure 7-7.

East Coast tour path animation graphics added to page and timeline ◀ Figure 7-7

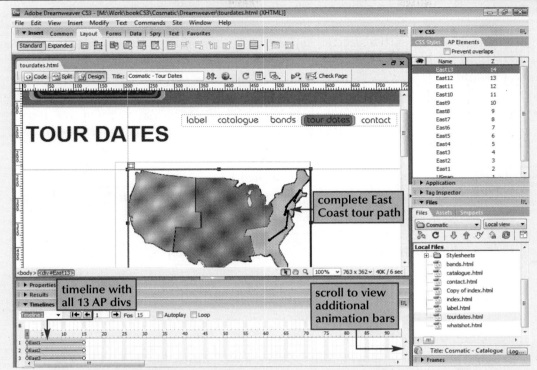

8. In the Timelines panel, drag the vertical scroll bar to view all of the animation bars.

9. Save the Tour Dates page.

Tip

You can also drag the panel border up to view additional animation bars.

Moving and Resizing Animation Bars

You can move an animation bar to another animation channel or to another location within the same animation channel. You can also resize an animation bar to include more or fewer frames.

Moving an Animation Bar

Moving an animation bar to another channel does not affect the AP div's stacking order. At times, however, you might need to move an animation bar to another animation channel. Consider the following example: Two animation bars are in the same animation channel, but now you want to add more frames to the first animation bar. You can move one of the animation bars to another animation channel so that you can add more frames to the first animation bar without changing the frame in which the second animation bar starts.

You'll move the East2 through East13 animation bars to animation channel 1.

To move all the animation bars in the Timelines panel to the first animation channel:

▶ **1.** In the Timelines panel, click the **East2** animation bar anywhere between its keyframes but not on its keyframes. (If you select a keyframe, the animation bar will not move and only the selected keyframe will move either to the left or to the right.) The East2 animation bar is selected and is a darker purple color.

Trouble? If only a keyframe is a darker purple color, you selected a keyframe and not the animation bar. Click the animation bar, being sure not to click a keyframe.

▶ **2.** Drag the **East2** animation bar to the right of the East1 animation bar in animation channel 1. Both the East1 and East2 animation bars are in animation channel 1. See Figure 7-8.

Figure 7-8 ▶ **East2 animation bar moved to animation channel 1**

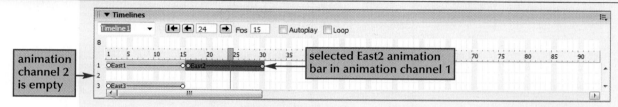

▶ **3.** Select the **East3** animation bar, and then move it to the right of the East2 animation bar in animation channel 1.

▶ **4.** Select and move the **East4**, **East5**, **East6**, **East7**, **East8**, **East9**, **East10**, **East11**, **East12**, and **East13** animation bars to the end of animation channel 1, scrolling as needed. All of the animation bars are in animation channel 1. See Figure 7-9.

Figure 7-9 ▶ **Animation bars in animation channel 1**

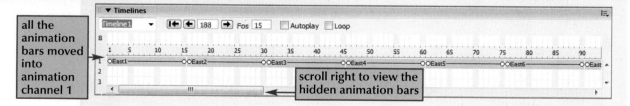

▶ **5.** Drag the horizontal scroll bar right to view all the animation bars.

Tip

To move multiple animation bars, hold down the Shift key as you click each animation bar to select it, and then drag the selected animation bars to the new location.

In addition to moving an animation bar to another channel, you can also reposition an animation bar within the same animation channel. The horizontal position within the channel determines when that animation bar plays within the timeline. Often, when creating an animation, you will want each AP div to start and end at different times within the animation. One way to do this is to move the opening frame of the animation bar to the frame in which you want the AP div to appear.

You'll move the East13 animation bar to the right so that it starts on frame 190 of the timeline.

To move an animation bar within an animation channel:

▶ **1.** In the Timelines panel, select the **East13** animation bar, and then drag it to the right until the first frame of the animation bar is in **frame 190** of the timeline. The number in the Current Frame Number box is the frame that the red playback head is over, not the frame number in which the animation bar begins. The playback head is in the middle of the animation bar because you cannot move the animation bar by selecting the first frame, which is a keyframe. See Figure 7-10.

East13 animation bar repositioned within animation channel 1 | **Figure 7-10**

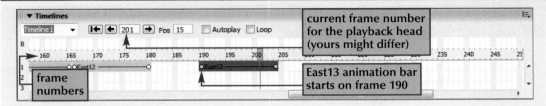

▶ **2.** Drag the **East13** animation bar so its first frame begins in **frame 181**. The East13 animation bar is repositioned.

Resizing an Animation Bar

You can resize, or change the length of, an animation bar in the animation channel. Lengthening the animation bar increases the duration of the animation by adding more frames, whereas shortening the animation bar decreases the duration of the animation by reducing the number of frames. Longer timelines enable you to create more complex actions as well as more gradual and fluid movements. Although the number of frames over which an animation occurs is one component in the speed of the animation, it is not the only component. Remember that the frame rate of the timeline also affects the speed of the animation. When you change the number of frames within an animation bar, any additional keyframes in the animation bar are spaced proportionately through the timeline so that all of the events in the animation are shortened or lengthened proportionately to preserve the animation.

You'll increase the length of the East13 animation bar to 30 frames.

To increase the duration of the East13 animation bar:

▶ **1.** In the Timelines panel, click the ending keyframe of the East13 animation bar to select it.

▶ **2.** Drag the selected ending keyframe to **frame 210** in animation channel 1. See Figure 7-11.

Tip

You can resize an animation bar by selecting and dragging the keyframe at either end of the bar to a new position within the animation channel.

East13 animation bar resized | **Figure 7-11**

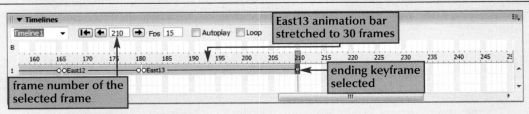

▶ **3.** Drag the selected ending keyframe to **frame 195** in animation channel 1 to decrease the animation bar to its original size of 15 frames.

▶ **4.** Save the Tour Dates page.

In this session, you learned about animation and the Timelines panel. Then you added AP divs to the timeline, moved animation bars, and changed the duration of animation bars. In the next session, you will insert keyframes into an animation bar, adjust the visibility and the size of AP divs, and then preview the animation in a browser.

Review | Session 7.1 Quick Check

1. What is animation?
2. What are the four timeline actions?
3. What are the numbered columns in the Timelines panel called?
4. What is the default frame rate of a timeline?
5. What are the white bullets at the beginning and end of an animation bar?
6. What effect does increasing the duration of an animation bar have on the animation?

Session 7.2

Adding Keyframes to an Animation Bar

Keyframes are where you input instructions for an animation. You can think of keyframes as the control frames of an animation. You need a keyframe in each frame of the timeline where something happens. For example, if you are moving an AP div, you need a keyframe each time the movement changes direction, stops, or starts. If you are changing the visibility of an AP div, you need a keyframe each time the AP div is hidden or displayed.

Reference Window | Adding Keyframes to an Animation Bar

- In the Timelines panel, select the animation bar to which you want to add a keyframe.
- Click in the frame to which you want to add the keyframe.
- Right-click the selected frame, and then click Add Keyframe on the context menu.

You want to create the illusion of movement in the animation path in the Tour Dates page. You can accomplish this by adjusting the visibility of the animation bars to hidden and then setting them to become visible one at a time. To do this, you must add an additional keyframe to each animation bar. You'll start by adding a keyframe to the second frame of the East1 animation bar, which is the frame in which you want to input instructions.

To add a keyframe to the East1 animation bar:

▶ **1.** If you took a break after the previous session, make sure that the Cosmatic site is open, the tourdates.html page is open in the Document window, the Property inspector is collapsed, and the Timelines panel is open.

▶ **2.** In the Timelines panel, click **frame 2** of the East1 animation bar. The East1 animation bar is selected, the red playback head is positioned over the second frame, and the frame number appears in the Current Frame Number box. See Figure 7-12.

Selected East1 animation bar | **Figure 7-12**

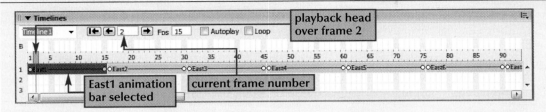

▶ **3.** Right-click **frame 2** of the East1 animation bar, and then click **Add Keyframe** on the context menu. A white circle, indicating the presence of a keyframe, appears in the second frame of the animation bar. See Figure 7-13.

Keyframe added to the East1 animation bar | **Figure 7-13**

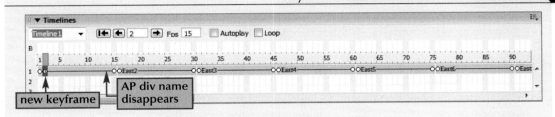

When you add a keyframe to an animation bar, the AP div name disappears if the added keyframe is in a frame in which the name appears. You can still tell which AP div is being used by selecting the animation bar in the Timelines panel; the AP div is then also selected in the AP Elements panel. You can also select the animation bar by selecting the appropriate AP div in the AP Elements panel.

Creating an Animation

You create animation by doing one of three types of things. You can change AP div position. You can change the source of an image. Or, you can automatically call behaviors without using Flash, ActiveX, Java, or any other plug-in application. The following list of **timeline actions** are used to change AP div properties over time:

- **Show or hide an AP div.** Switches the visibility of an AP div between three states: Visible, Hidden, or Default.
- **Change the z-index or stacking order.** Changes the order in which AP divs are stacked on the page by adjusting the z-index number of the AP div.
- **Move an AP div.** Repositions an AP div by changing its X and Y coordinates.
- **Resize an AP div.** Adjusts the width and height dimensions of an AP div.

In addition to changing AP div properties, you can also change the image source with the timeline. Changing the image source enables you to perform image rollovers within a timeline without using added JavaScript. (Image Source is the only image property that a timeline can change directly.)

You will use all four timeline actions to create animations.

Adjusting AP Div Visibility

Changing the visibility of AP divs is one of the easiest ways to create an animation. The Timelines panel enables you to change the visibility of an AP div between visible and hidden over time. For example, you can place an AP div with hidden visibility in a page and then change that AP div to visible at a designated frame in the timeline, causing the AP div to appear on screen at a specific moment. The change in visibility is not gradual, like a fade; it occurs immediately when the timeline encounters the keyframe with instructions to change the AP div's visibility. The three visibility attributes are the same as the regular AP div visibility attributes: Visible, Hidden, and Default. The AP Elements panel includes a column that shows the selected visibility attribute for each AP div.

InSight		**Choosing How to Accomplish a Task**

There are many ways to accomplish any task. Part of a professional designer's job is to assess the situation and decide which path provides the best way to accomplish that goal. For example, you have used the timeline to change the visibility of objects over time. You can also do this using Spry elements (which you will learn to use later in another tutorial), or you could write a JavaScript to cause the action. Some factors to consider when making a decision on how to accomplish a task include:

- How long will it take to accomplish the task using each technique or technology? For example, if you need to learn JavaScript, then another method will likely be faster.
- What techniques or technologies do you already have in the site? For example, if you are currently using JavaScript, you might want to continue using it for consistency.

As your experience increases, it becomes easier to assess situations and to make informed decisions.

You will animate the AP divs you added to the timeline by changing the visibility of each AP div. First, you will add a keyframe to the second frame of each animation bar. Then, you will set the visibility of the AP div to hidden in the first keyframe in each animation bar. Finally, you will set the visibility of the second keyframe to visible. Because the animation bars are positioned one after another in the timeline, this will create the illusion that the tour path is being drawn over time.

To change visibility of the East1 AP div in the timeline:

▶ **1.** Click the first keyframe in the East1 animation bar. The keyframe is selected and the playback head is positioned over the selected keyframe. See Figure 7-14.

Figure 7-14	**Selected first keyframe**

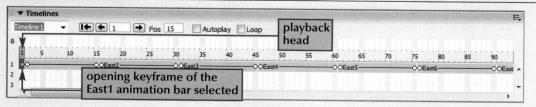

▶ **2.** In the AP Elements panel, click the **visibility column** to the left of the East1 name until the closed eye icon ![eye icon] appears. The first keyframe of the East1 AP div is set to a hidden visibility. See Figure 7-15.

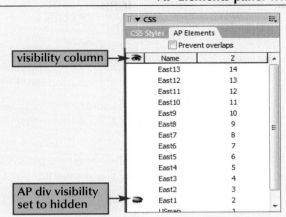

visibility column

AP div visibility set to hidden

Tip

You can also set the selected keyframe's visibility in the Property inspector by clicking the Vis button.

3. In the Timelines panel, select the second keyframe in the East1 animation bar, and then, in the AP Elements panel, click the **visibility column** until the open eye icon 👁 appears. The second keyframe of the East1 AP div is set to visible and will remain visible through the remaining frames of the timeline.

You'll repeat this process to add a new keyframe to each of the remaining animation bars and set the visibility for the first and second keyframes of the animation bar. You'll start with the East2 animation bar.

To add keyframes and set visibility for the remaining animation bars:

1. In the Timelines panel, select **frame 17** (the second frame) in the East2 animation bar.

2. Right-click the selected frame, and then click **Add Keyframe** on the context menu. A new keyframe is added to the animation bar.

3. Select the first keyframe in the animation bar, and then, in the AP Elements panel, set the visibility to **hidden**.

4. Select the second keyframe in the animation bar, and then, in the AP Elements panel, set the visibility to **visible**.

5. Repeat Steps 1 through 4 to add a keyframe to and set the visibility of the first two keyframes for each of the following animation bars: **East3**, **East4**, **East5**, **East6**, **East7**, **East8**, **East9**, **East10**, **East11**, **East12**, and **East13**.

6. Save the Tour Dates page.

Previewing a Timeline

Dreamweaver has two ways to preview a timeline. You can drag the playback head across the timeline in the Timelines panel while viewing the animation in the Document window, or you can click and hold the Playback button on the Timelines panel toolbar while viewing the animation in the Document window. Dragging the playback head enables you to review a piece of an animation quickly. However, when you drag the playback head, you control the playback rate. You need to use the Playback button to preview the playback speed as well as the animation. You'll use both methods to preview the timeline on which you have been working within Dreamweaver.

You'll start by previewing the timeline within Dreamweaver.

To preview the timeline within Dreamweaver:

▶ **1.** Scroll until the U.S. map is visible in the Document window, if necessary.

▶ **2.** In the Timelines panel, drag the **playback head** across the timeline from frame 1 to frame 195 while viewing the animation in the Document window. The animation plays at the speed you drag.

▶ **3.** Click and hold the **Playback** button ⏩ on the Timelines panel toolbar while viewing the animation in the Document window. The animation plays at the default frame rate, 15 frames per second.

To preview a timeline within a browser window, you must add a behavior to the Web page that instructs the browser to play the timeline. The simplest way to do this is to check the Autoplay check box on the Timelines panel toolbar. When you check the Autoplay check box, Dreamweaver inserts the Autoplay behavior into the code of the Web page. The Autoplay behavior tells the browser to play the timeline as soon as the page is finished loading. Because the behavior is added to the page and not to the timeline or an object in the timeline, the behavior will not appear in the Behaviors channel in the Timelines panel. You will learn other ways to start a timeline when you add behaviors to timelines.

You'll add the Autoplay behavior to the Web page, and then preview the Tour Dates page in a browser window.

To add the AutoPlay behavior and preview the timeline in a browser:

▶ **1.** In the Timelines panel, click the **Autoplay** check box on the Timelines panel toolbar to insert a check mark. A dialog box opens with an explanation that the Play Timeline action is being added to the Web page.

   Trouble? If the dialog box doesn't open, the message has been disabled for your installation of Dreamweaver. The Autoplay behavior is inserted into the code for the Tour Dates page. Continue with Step 3.

▶ **2.** Click the **OK** button to confirm that you want to add the action to the Tour Dates page. The Autoplay behavior is inserted into the code for the Tour Dates page.

▶ **3.** Expand the **Tag Inspector panel group**, click the **Behaviors** tab to display the Behaviors panel, and then click the **body tag** in the status bar. The Play Timeline behavior appears in the Behaviors panel. See Figure 7-16.

Play Timeline behavior added to the Tour Dates page | Figure 7-16

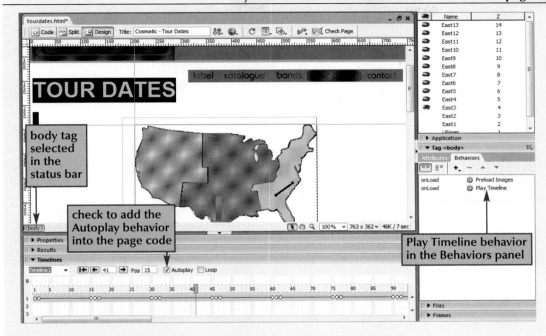

4. Save the Tour Dates page, and then preview the page in a browser, allowing blocked content if necessary here and throughout the tutorial. The timeline runs in the browser window. See Figure 7-17.

Timeline running in a browser | Figure 7-17

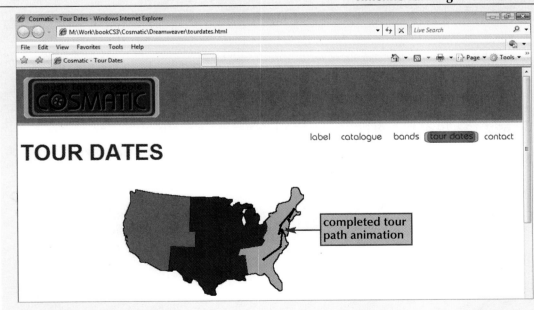

5. Close the browser.

As you create an animation, you should preview it in Dreamweaver as well as in a browser. Previewing a timeline in Dreamweaver is helpful because it enables you to see what you are creating while you are working. Because the animation can run differently in a browser, it is important to also preview the animation in any browser your target audience might use. In addition, you should test a finished animation on a number of computers after you have posted the animation, so that you can get an accurate view of the playback speed over the Internet and on different computers. Testing the animation helps to ensure that as many viewers as possible see the animation as you intended them to see it.

Adjusting AP Div Stacking Order in the Timeline

You adjust the z-index number of AP divs to change their stacking order. You can change the order in which AP divs are stacked during a timeline so that the AP divs appear stacked in different orders. For example, you might have one AP div jump in front of another AP div. Unlike most other time-based software, the channel in which the animation bar for the AP div appears has no effect on the stacking order. Like changes in visibility, the change in stacking order occurs immediately when the timeline encounters a keyframe with instructions to change the z-index number of an AP div.

Reference Window | **Adjusting AP Div Timeline Stacking Order**

- In the Timelines panel, select the keyframe in which you want the stacking order to change in the animation bar.
- In the AP Elements panel, type the desired z-index number in the Z column, and then press the Enter key.

Brian wants you to add a graphic of a tour bus that will eventually move along the tour path you already created. You'll add the new AP div with the bus graphic to the timeline, and then adjust the stacking order.

To add the tour bus graphic to the animation timeline:

▶ 1. Draw a new AP div over the U.S. map that is approximately **20 x 20 pixels**.

▶ 2. In the new AP div, insert the **BusSmall.gif** graphic located in the **Tutorial.07\Tutorial** folder included with your Data Files.

▶ 3. Drag the borders of the AP div to fit snugly around the graphic, and then move the AP div to position the bus over the lowest point on the tour path. See Figure 7-18.

Bus graphic in the Tour Dates page | Figure 7-18

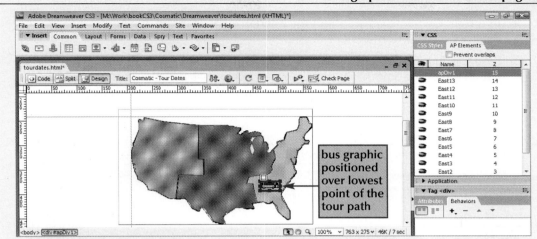

bus graphic
positioned
over lowest
point of the
tour path

4. In the AP Elements panel, rename the new AP div as **Bus**.

5. Drag the **Bus** AP div from the Document window to **frame 1** in **animation channel 2** in the Timelines panel, and then click the **OK** button in the dialog box to add it to the timeline.

6. Save the Tour Dates page, and then preview the page in a browser. The bus graphic covers the path in the other AP divs. See Figure 7-19.

Animation previewed in a browser | Figure 7-19

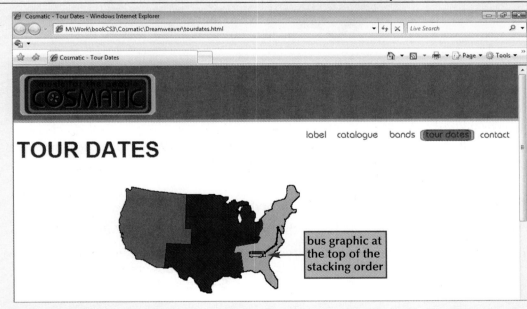

TOUR DATES

label   catalogue   bands   (tour dates)   contact

bus graphic at
the top of the
stacking order

7. Close the browser.

You'll change the stacking order of the Bus AP div in the ending keyframe of the Bus animation bar. You want the Bus AP div to move behind the other AP divs of the animation in the last keyframe, enabling the user to see the path over the bus.

To adjust the AP div stacking order in the Timelines panel:

▶ **1.** In the Timelines panel, select the ending keyframe in the Bus animation bar.

▶ **2.** In the AP Elements panel, select the z-index number of the Bus AP div, type **2**, and then press the **Enter** key.

▶ **3.** Save the Tour Dates page, and then preview the page in a browser. The bus starts out on top of the animation, and then the path moves over the bus. This is because the stacking order of the Bus AP div changes in the keyframe on frame 15 of the animation. See Figure 7-20.

Tip

You can also enter the appropriate stacking order number in the Z-Index box in the Property inspector.

Figure 7-20	Changed stacking order of the AP divs in the timeline

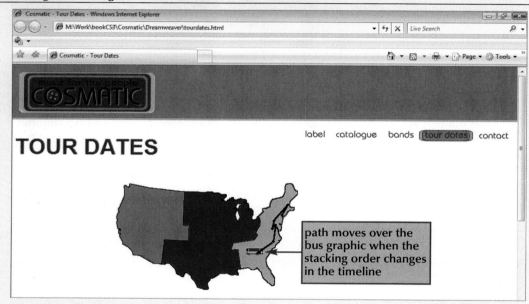

path moves over the bus graphic when the stacking order changes in the timeline

▶ **4.** Close the browser.

You can also see the change in AP div position from within Dreamweaver after you deselect the AP div. A selected AP div remains at the top of the stacking order in Dreamweaver so that you can work on it. You'll deselect the Bus AP div, and then view the changed stacking order from within Dreamweaver.

To view the change in the stacking order:

▶ **1.** Click the page background beside the map to deselect the Bus AP div.

▶ **2.** In the Timelines panel, drag the playback head to **frame 1**. The Bus AP div has a z-index number of 15 in the AP Elements panel and the Bus graphic is the top AP div in the animation in the Document window. See Figure 7-21.

Frame 1 stacking order **Figure 7-21**

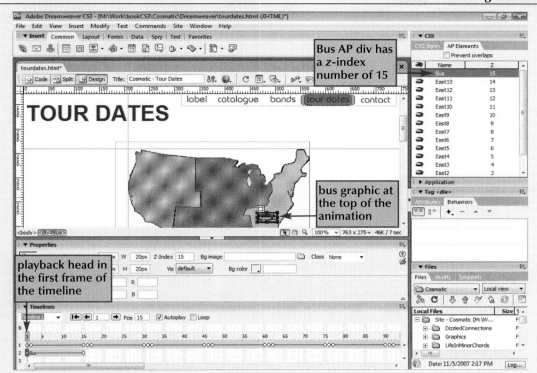

Trouble? If the *z*-index number in the AP Elements panel is 2, but the bus graphic is the top AP div in the animation in the Document window, don't worry. As long as the stacking order of the bus graphic changes when you view the animation, everything is working correctly.

3. In the Timelines panel, drag the playback head to **frame 15**. The Bus AP div has a *z*-index number of 2 in the AP Elements panel and the tour path is over the Bus graphic in the Document window. See Figure 7-22.

| Figure 7-22 | **Frame 15 stacking order** |

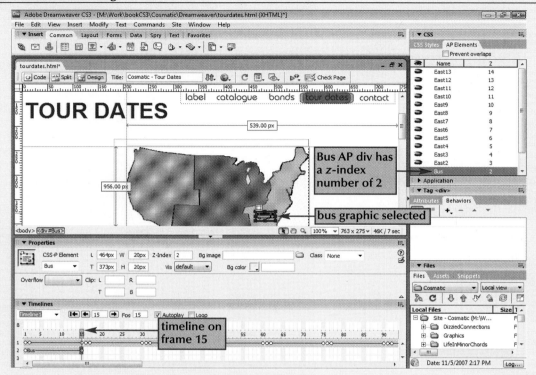

Trouble? If the *z*-index number in the AP Elements panel is 15, the stacking order might not be functioning correctly in your installation of Dreamweaver. Continue with Step 4.

You'll select the ending keyframe for the Bus animation bar and change the *z*-index number back to its original *z*-index number.

▶ **4.** In the Timelines panel, select the ending keyframe in the Bus animation bar.

▶ **5.** In the AP Elements panel, select the *z*-index number, type **15**, and then press the **Enter** key.

▶ **6.** Save the Tour Dates page.

Moving an AP Div in the Timelines Panel

Moving an AP div is another way to add animation to a page. The timeline enables you to move an AP div from one position in the page to another position in the page over a period of time. This technique is sometimes used in Web pages to fly headings into the page.

You move an AP div by selecting a keyframe and changing the position of the AP div. Unlike stacking order and visibility, the AP div will not jump to the new position when the playback head crosses the keyframe that contains instructions to change the position. Instead, Dreamweaver moves the AP div from its initial position to the new position during the intermediary frames, and the AP div arrives at its new position as the playback head reaches the new keyframe. Consider the following example: An AP div is at the left edge of the screen in the first keyframe of the animation bar. You set a second keyframe in the tenth frame of the animation bar. Then you select the second keyframe and move the AP div to the middle of the screen. When you play the timeline, the AP div will move one-tenth of the way to its new position in each frame, arriving at the middle of the screen on the tenth frame of the timeline. Adding more frames between keyframes will make the motion slower and smoother.

Brian asks you to move the bus along the Sloth Child tour path in the Tour Dates page.

To move the Bus AP div in the Timelines panel:

▶ 1. In the Timelines panel, select the ending keyframe in the Bus animation bar, and then drag the ending keyframe to the right until the Bus animation bar is **195 frames** long. The Bus animation bar ends on the same frame as the East13 animation bar.

▶ 2. Click **frame 45** in the Bus animation bar. The Bus animation bar is selected and the playback head is over frame 45.

▶ 3. Right-click the selected frame, and then click **Add Keyframe** on the context menu. A new keyframe is added to frame 45 in the Bus animation bar.

   Trouble? If the keyframe is inserted into the wrong frame, you need to reposition it. Drag the keyframe in the Bus animation bar to frame 45.

▶ 4. Select the new keyframe, if necessary, and then drag the **Bus** AP div in the Document window over the second point on the tour path. See Figure 7-23.

Bus moved to the second point on the animation path | Figure 7-23

▶ 5. Save the Tour Dates page, preview the page in a browser to test the first step of the bus animation, and then close the browser. (When the bus reaches the second point on the tour path, it moves backward because the Bus AP div was set to that position in the first and final keyframes when you added the AP div to the timeline. The backward movement will stop when you set the final keyframe of the animation bar to its new position in Step 8.)

You will continue to add new keyframes and move the bus along the tour path.

▶ **6.** Add a new keyframe to **frame 75** in the Bus animation bar, select the keyframe, and then drag the **Bus** AP div in the Document window over the third point on the tour path.

▶ **7.** Add keyframes at **frames 105**, **135**, and **165**, dragging the **Bus** AP div to the next point on the tour path after you create each new keyframe.

▶ **8.** Select the ending keyframe in frame 195 in the Bus animation bar, and then drag the **Bus** AP div to the final point on the tour path. See Figure 7-24.

Figure 7-24 ▶ **Bus in final position in the animation path**

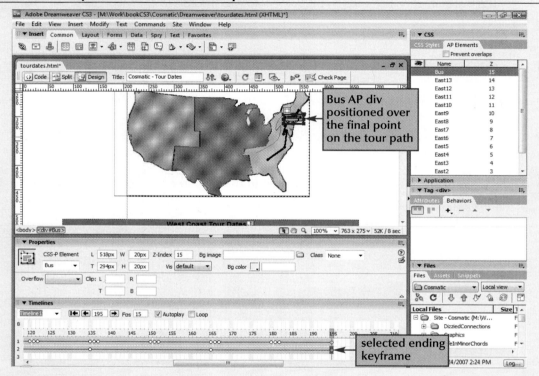

▶ **9.** Save the Tour Dates page, preview the page in a browser to view the animation, and then close the browser.

Resizing an AP Div Over Time

Changing the dimensions of an AP div over a period of time is another way to add animation to a page. For example, you can set the background color of an AP div to red and then set the AP div to a larger size in the ending keyframe of an animation bar. As the timeline progresses, the AP div increases in size and the red square appears to grow in size. Adding a background color to the AP div enables you to see it change dimensions over time. To see the AP div shrink or grow, the AP div's overflow must be set to Hidden in the Property inspector. Resizing an AP div does not change the dimensions of images in the AP div, but it reduces the amount of the images that are visible in the AP div as the AP div becomes smaller.

Brian wants you to add a colored square that grows in size behind the U.S. map. To do this, you'll add a new AP div to the page, change the background color of the AP div, add the AP div to the timeline, and then resize the AP div.

To create and resize an AP div in the Tour Dates page:

▶ **1.** Draw a **50 x 50 pixel** AP div at the center of the map.

▶ **2.** Select the new AP div, expand the **Property inspector**, change the background color to **#772300**, and then collapse the Property inspector.

▶ **3.** In the AP Elements panel, rename the AP div as **BackgroundSquare** and change the z-index number of the AP div to **0**.

▶ **4.** In the AP Elements panel, select the **BackgroundSquare** AP div, and then drag the selected AP div from the Document window to **frame 1** in **animation channel 3** in the Timelines panel.

▶ **5.** Click the **OK** button in the dialog box that opens, and then drag the ending keyframe in the BackgroundSquare animation bar to **frame 100**. The ending keyframe is selected.

▶ **6.** Drag the resize handles of the BackgroundSquare AP div until the AP div is about **20 pixels** larger than the map on every side; use guides as needed to help you resize the AP div accurately. Changing the size of the AP div in the ending keyframe will cause the AP div to grow from its original size in frame 1 to its new size in frame 100 while the timeline is playing.

▶ **7.** Click an empty space in the page to deselect the AP div. The colored square appears behind the map. See Figure 7-25.

Tour Dates page with a background square ◀ Figure 7-25

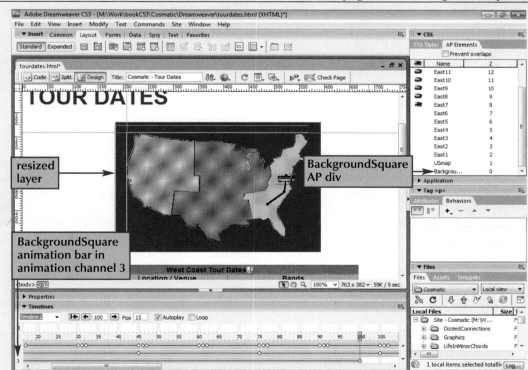

▶ **8.** Save the Tour Dates page, and then preview the page in a browser. The square grows from its original size in frame 1 to its ending size in frame 100, and then remains that size for the duration of the animation. Because the square is behind the other AP divs, you see the square growing only where another graphic is not covering it.

▶ **9.** Close the browser.

Deleting an Animation Bar

It is easy to get carried away with animation. Too much can make it difficult for a viewer to focus on the intended message. Remember to consider what each animated element adds to the page. If you decide that you don't need a specific element, you can easily delete its animation bar.

After previewing the Tour Dates page with the background square, Brian and the rest of the team decide that the growing square makes the page too busy. Brian asks you to delete the background square.

To delete the BackgroundSquare animation bar from the timeline:

▶ **1.** In the Timelines panel, select the **BackgroundSquare** animation bar.

Tip

You can also delete the animation bar by deleting its AP div from the page.

▶ **2.** Press the **Delete** key. The BackgroundSquare animation bar is removed from the timeline, but the new AP div is still in the page.

▶ **3.** In the AP Elements panel, select the **BackgroundSquare** AP div, and then press the **Delete** key. The new AP div is removed from the page.

▶ **4.** Save the Tour Dates page.

In this session, you added keyframes to an animation bar. You explored all the timeline actions, including adjusting AP div stacking order, moving AP divs, resizing AP divs, and changing AP div visibility. You previewed a timeline in a browser and deleted an animation bar from the timeline. In the next session, you will add behaviors to timelines and add multiple timelines to a page.

Review | **Session 7.2 Quick Check**

1. Where do you input instructions for an animation?
2. What are the four AP div actions that you can perform in a timeline?
3. How can you preview a timeline in a browser?
4. How do you change the stacking order of AP divs in a timeline?
5. True or False? Changing the dimensions of an AP div will change the dimensions of an image in that AP div.
6. True or False? Once you add an animation to an AP div, you cannot delete it.

Session 7.3

Starting a Timeline with a Button

Timelines can start when the page is loaded in a browser by using the Autoplay behavior, or they can be started by user interaction such as when a user clicks a button.

| **Using Buttons to Start Animations** | | InSight |

Buttons are a good way to start a timeline because they enable the user to choose when the animation begins and they enable you to tie the animation to a decision. For example, you can pose a question and have the user click a button to indicate his or her answer. The animation that plays is then based on the user's selection.

You start a timeline with a button by adding a behavior to the button that triggers the timeline to begin playing. Using buttons and timelines together enables you to add interesting interactivity to Web pages, because the user's choices affect what is displayed in the page. For example, you can create interactive demonstrations, drop-down menus, animated tabs, and so on.

Brian wants you to add a button (rollover image) to the left of the U.S. map that, when clicked, will start the Sloth Child tour path animation. First, you will add a rollover image to the page.

To add a rollover image button to the Tour Dates page:

▶ **1.** If you took a break after the previous session, make sure that the Cosmatic site is open, the tourdates.html page is open in the Document window, the Property inspector is collapsed, and the Timelines panel, the AP Elements panel, and the Behaviors panel are open.

▶ **2.** In the Tour Dates page, click below the TOUR DATES heading and to the left of the U.S. map. You want to place the rollover image in this location.

▶ **3.** On the **Common** tab of the Insert bar, click the **Images button arrow** 🖼 ⏷ , and then click the **Rollover Image** button 🖼 . The Insert Rollover Image dialog box opens.

▶ **4.** In the Image Name box, type **SCbusRollover**.

▶ **5.** Click the Original Image **Browse** button, and then double-click the **SCbusButtonUp.gif** graphic located in the **Tutorial.07\Tutorial** folder included with your Data Files.

▶ **6.** Click the Rollover Image **Browse** button, and then double-click the **SCbusButtonOver.gif** graphic located in the **Tutorial.07\Tutorial** folder included with your Data Files.

▶ **7.** Click the **Preload Rollover Image** check box to check it, if necessary.

▶ **8.** Click the **OK** button. The SCbusRollover button is added to the page.

▶ **9.** Press the **Right Arrow** key to deselect the SCbusRollover button. See Figure 7-26.

Figure 7-26 ▸ Rollover button added to the Tour Dates page

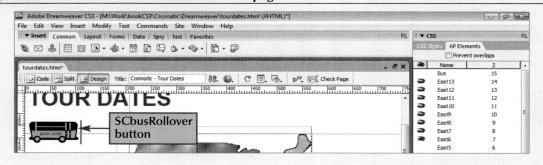

Next, you will add the Play Timeline behavior to the rollover image, which will enable the user to start the timeline animation.

To add the Play Timeline behavior to the SCbusRollover button:

▸ **1.** In the Document window, click the **SCbusRollover** button to select it. The Swap Image Restore and the Swap Image behaviors already appear in the Behaviors panel. Remember, these behaviors are added to create the button rollover.

▸ **2.** In the Behaviors panel, click the **Add Behavior** button ➕ , point to **Timeline**, and then click **Play Timeline**. The Play Timeline dialog box opens so you can add the Play Timeline behavior to the SCbusButtonUp.gif graphic. See Figure 7-27.

Figure 7-27 ▸ Play Timeline dialog box

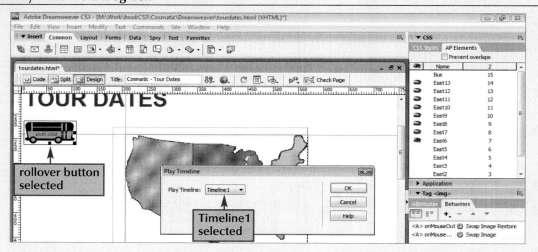

▸ **3.** If necessary, click the **Play Timeline** button, and then click **Timeline1**. You must select the timeline to which the behavior will be added. Because you can add multiple time-lines to a page, you must specify which timeline you want the button to play.

▸ **4.** Click the **OK** button. The Play Timeline behavior is added to the end of the list in the Behaviors panel.

The Play Timeline behavior sometimes has the event set to onLoad, which would cause the timeline to play when the SCbusRollover image is loaded into the browser. Because you want the timeline to start playing when the button is clicked instead of when the button is loaded, you'll change the event to onMouseDown, if necessary.

To change the event:

▶ 1. In the Behaviors panel, make sure the **Play Timeline** behavior is selected.

▶ 2. If onMouseDown is not already selected as the event, click the **Events** arrow, and then click **onMouseDown**. The event is onMouseDown. See Figure 7-28.

Behaviors panel with the Play Timeline behavior | **Figure 7-28**

event set to onMouseDown

Play Timeline behavior added to the SCbusRollover

▶ 3. Click the **Autoplay** check box on the Timelines panel toolbar to uncheck the check box. The Autoplay behavior is removed from the page so that the timeline will not play automatically when the page is loaded.

▶ 4. Save the Tour Dates page, and then preview the page in a browser.

▶ 5. Click the **Sloth Child tour bus** button to play the animation, and then close the browser.

Adding Behaviors to the Behaviors Channel

You can add many of the behaviors from the Behaviors panel list within a timeline. Placing behaviors in a timeline enables you to make things that are not necessarily triggered by user interaction (such as a mouse click) happen over time within a Web page. You can do something simple such as reset the timeline to frame 1 after the animation has ended so that the timeline can run again. You can also do something a little more complex, such as a timed pop-up window, by creating a Click To Begin button that starts a timeline with a behavior in frame 1 that makes a window open and a behavior in frame 200 that makes the window close.

Adding Behaviors to the Behaviors Channel | Reference Window

- In the Timelines panel, in the Behaviors channel, select the frame to which you want to add the behavior.
- In the Behaviors panel, select the desired behavior from the behaviors list, and then set any required parameters.

Brian asks you to add four behaviors in three frames of the timeline in the Tour Dates page to make the animation a little more useful. He wants you to do the following:

- In frame 1, add a Show-Hide Elements behavior, and hide all of the AP divs in the timeline. This will make the animation invisible in the first frame, which will be helpful when more tour paths and buttons are added to the page.
- In frame 2, add a Show-Hide Elements behavior, and show the East1 and Bus AP Elements. This will enable the user to see these AP divs as the animation begins. The other AP divs will become visible as the timeline passes the keyframes that change their visibility.
- In frame 215, add a Stop Timeline behavior and a Go To Timeline Frame 1 behavior. This will enable the completed animation to remain visible for 20 frames and then disappear as the timeline resets to frame 1. Right now, after the button has been pressed and the timeline has run, the AP divs remain visible.

Adding these behaviors will end the timeline after the animation is complete and reset the timeline, enabling the user to press the button and run the animation again.

To add the Show-Hide Elements behavior to frame 1 of the timeline:

▶ **1.** In the Timelines panel, click **frame 1** in the Behaviors channel.

▶ **2.** In the Behaviors panel, click the **Add Behavior** button ⊞ , and then click **Show-Hide Elements**. The Show-Hide Elements dialog box opens.

▶ **3.** In the Elements box, click **div "Bus"**, and then click the **Hide** button. The word "(hide)" appears beside the selected AP div to indicate that this AP div will be hidden in frame 1. See Figure 7-29.

Figure 7-29 ▶ **Show-Hide Elements dialog box**

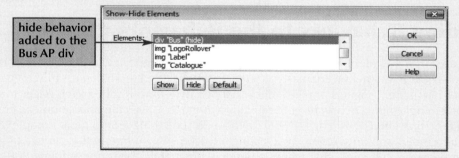

▶ **4.** Repeat Step 3 to hide all 13 of the East AP divs (**div "East13"** through **div "East1"**). Do not place anything beside div "USmap" or any other elements in the list because they should remain visible.

▶ **5.** Click the **OK** button. The dialog box closes and the behavior is added to the frame. See Figure 7-30.

Behavior added to frame1 of the timeline ◀ Figure 7-30

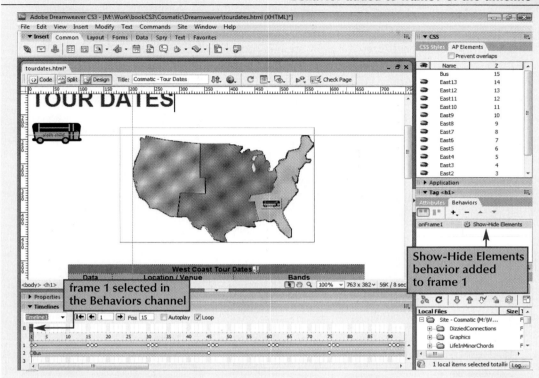

You will use the same process to add a Show-Hide Elements behavior to frame 2 of the timeline. For this frame, you want to show both the Bus AP div and the East1 AP div.

To add a Show-Hide Elements behavior to frame 2 of the timeline:

▶ **1.** In the Timelines panel, click **frame 2** in the Behaviors channel.

▶ **2.** In the Behaviors panel, click the **Add Behavior** button ⊞ , and then click **Show-Hide Elements**. The Show-Hide Elements dialog box opens.

▶ **3.** In the Elements box, click **div "Bus"**, and then click the **Show** button.

▶ **4.** In the Elements box, click **div "East1"**, and then click the **Show** button.

▶ **5.** Click the **OK** button. The Show-Hide Elements behavior is added to the second frame of the timeline.

Next, you'll add two behaviors to frame 215 of the timeline—the Stop behavior and the Go To Frame behavior.

To add the Stop and Go To Frame behaviors to frame 215 of the timeline:

▶ **1.** In the Timelines panel, click **frame 215** in the Behaviors channel.

▶ **2.** In the Behaviors panel, click the **Add Behavior** button ⊞ , point to **Timeline**, and then click **Stop Timeline**. The Stop Timeline dialog box opens.

▶ **3.** Click the **Stop Timeline** button, and then click **Timeline1**.

▶ **4.** Click the **OK** button. The Stop Timeline behavior is added to the frame.

5. In the Behaviors panel, click the **Add Behavior** button ➕ , point to **Timeline**, and then click **Go To Timeline Frame**. The Go To Timeline Frame dialog box opens.

6. In the Go to Frame box, type **1**, if necessary, and then click the **OK** button. The Go To Timeline Frame behavior is added to the frame. This behavior will reset the timeline to frame 1 after the animation is completed. See Figure 7-31.

| Figure 7-31 | Behaviors added to frame 215 of the timeline |

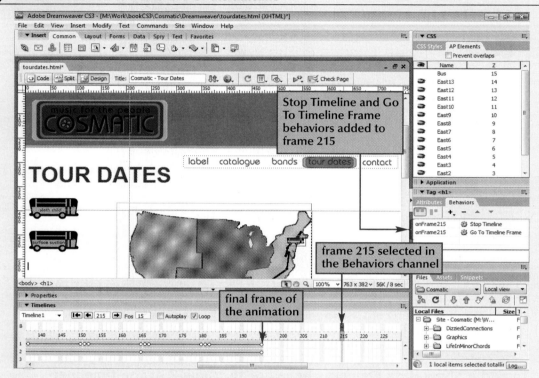

7. Save the page, and then preview the page in a browser.

8. Click the **Sloth Child tour bus** button to view the animation. The animation pauses after it is complete, and then resets to the first frame of the timeline.

9. Click the **Sloth Child tour bus** button again to confirm that the behaviors are working properly.

10. Close the browser.

Creating Multiple Timelines

You can create more complex interactions in a Web page by adding multiple timelines in the same page. For example, you might add a second tour path to the U.S. map in the Tour Dates page. By creating each animation in a separate timeline, you can control the animations independently.

You add additional timelines to a page in the same way that you added the first timeline to the page. You do not need to add new copies of images that are already included in your site to use those images in another timeline. You can use the same objects in more than one timeline.

When you have multiple timelines in a page, all of the timelines can run at the same time, or you can use behaviors to make one timeline start another timeline and so on. When using multiple timelines in one page, each timeline should be fairly simple so that the page will be able to run at a reasonable speed. The more movement that occurs at one time in a page, the more processing power it takes to run the animation at the desired frame rate. Too much movement can cause the user's computer to run slowly.

Brian wants you to add a tour path animation for the Surface Suction band to the Tour Dates page. This timeline will have an animated tour path and an animated tour bus just like the Sloth Child animation. You will create this animation in another timeline. Then, you will add a rollover image button to the page, add a behavior that starts the new timeline with the button, and add behaviors to the new timeline.

To create a second timeline in the Tour Dates page:

▶ 1. In the Timelines panel, right-click a blank frame, and then click **Add Timeline** on the context menu. A second timeline is added to the Tour Dates page.

You want the second timeline to be named "Timeline2."

▶ 2. In the Timelines panel, if the second timeline is not already named "Timeline2," select the default timeline name in the Timelines box, type **Timeline2**, and then press the **Enter** key. The timeline is renamed. See Figure 7-32.

Tip

You can also click Modify on the menu bar, point to Timeline, and then click Add Timeline to create another timeline.

Timeline2 in the Tour Dates page | Figure 7-32

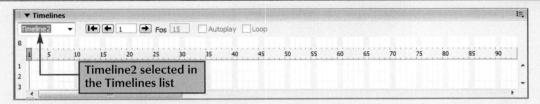

▶ 3. Click the **Timelines** arrow on the Timelines panel toolbar, and then click **Timeline1**. The first timeline appears.

▶ 4. Click the **Timelines** arrow on the Timelines panel toolbar, and then click **Timeline2** to return to Timeline2.

You will add AP divs and graphics for the tour path animation for Surface Suction to Timeline2.

To add the Central AP divs to Timeline2:

▶ 1. Select the **East1** AP div, and then drag horizontal and vertical guides to align to the top and left borders of the AP div, if necessary (which also aligns the guides to the top and left of the U.S. map). Remove any unused guides from the page.

▶ 2. Draw a new AP div over the U.S. map, aligning the top and left borders of the new AP div to the guides.

▶ 3. Insert the **Central1.gif** graphic located in the **Tutorial.07\Tutorial** folder included with your Data Files into the new AP div. A graphic with a small, black dot appears in the map.

4. Resize the AP div as needed to fit snugly against the borders of the graphic that you inserted in the AP div, and then left-align and top-align the AP divs as needed.

5. In the AP Elements panel, rename the new AP div as **Central1**.

6. In the Timelines panel, drag the **Central1** AP div to **animation channel 1** of Timeline2 (make sure that Timeline2 is selected in the Timelines list), and then click the **OK** button to close the dialog box, if necessary.

7. Repeat Steps 2 through 6 to create the remaining 14 Central AP divs with their corresponding graphics (**Central2.gif** through **Central15.gif**), using the graphic name for the AP div name and placing the animation bar for each new AP div to the right of the animation bars already placed in the animation channel. See Figure 7-33.

Figure 7-33 ▶ **AP divs added to Timeline2**

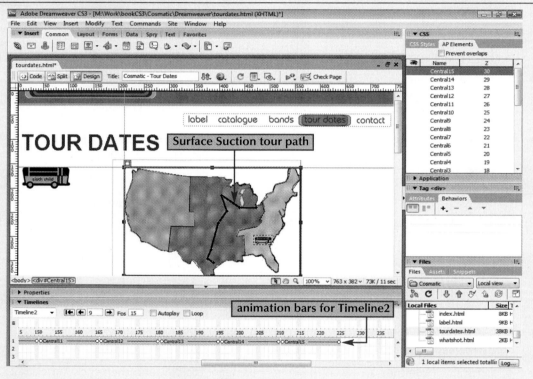

You'll add the Bus AP div to animation channel 2 of Timeline2, and drag the last frame of the Bus animation bar to frame 225. Then you'll create keyframes in the Bus animation bar and animate the bus like you did in the first timeline.

To add the Bus AP div to Timeline2 and animate the AP div:

1. In the AP Elements panel, select the **Bus** AP div.

2. In the Document window, move the Bus over the first point (Central1) in the Surface Suction tour path (the northeasternmost point in the map).

3. Drag the **Bus** AP div to **frame 1** in **animation channel 2** in Timeline2, and then click the **OK** button in the dialog box.

4. Drag the ending keyframe of the Bus animation bar to **frame 225**.

5. Select the opening keyframe in the Bus animation bar in Timeline2, and then, in the AP Elements panel, change the z-index number of the Bus AP div to **32**.

▶ **6.** Select the ending keyframe in the Bus animation bar in Timeline2, and then, in the AP Elements panel, change the z-index number of the Bus AP div to **32**. The Bus AP div is now the top AP div in Timeline2.

▶ **7.** In the Timelines panel, select **frame 45** of the Bus animation bar, right-click the selected frame, and then click **Add Keyframe** on the context menu. A new keyframe is added to the animation bar.

▶ **8.** Select the new keyframe, and then move the bus to the second point on the Surface Suction tour path.

▶ **9.** Place keyframes in **frames 75**, **105**, **135**, **165**, and **195** of the Bus animation bar, moving the **Bus** AP div to the next point on the tour path at each keyframe.

▶ **10.** Select the ending keyframe in frame 225 of the Bus animation bar, and then move the **Bus** AP div to the final point (Central15) on the tour path (the southernmost point in the map). See Figure 7-34.

Animated Bus AP div in Timeline2 ◄ Figure 7-34

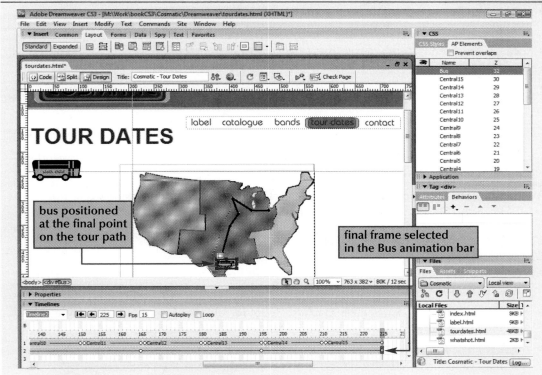

Now that the tour path is animated, you'll add a keyframe to the second frame of each animation bar in channel 1 and then change the visibility of each AP div to hide in frame 1 of the animation bar and be visible in frame 2 of the animation bar.

To change the visibility of each AP div in Timeline2:

▶ **1.** In the Timelines panel, select **frame 2** in the Central1 animation bar, and then add a keyframe.

▶ **2.** In the AP Elements panel, click the **visibility column** of the Central1 AP div until the open eye icon 👁 appears. The visibility of the animation bar is set to visible in frame 2.

▶ **3.** In the Timelines panel, select **frame 1** in the Central1 animation bar, and then, in the AP Elements panel, click the **visibility column** of the Central1 AP div until the closed eye icon 👁 appears. The visibility of the animation bar is set to hidden in frame 1.

▶ **4.** Repeat Steps 1 through 3 to set the visibility for the following animation bars: **Central2**, **Central3**, **Central4**, **Central5**, **Central6**, **Central7**, **Central8**, **Central9**, **Central10**, **Central11**, **Central12**, **Central13**, **Central14**, and **Central15**. All of the animation bars will be hidden until the animation plays the second frame.

You have added the animated Surface Suction tour path to the Tour Dates page. Next, you will add a button to start the new timeline. You'll add a Surface Suction bus rollover image below the Sloth Child bus rollover image in the Document window. Then you'll add a Play Timeline behavior to the new rollover image.

To add the Play Timeline behavior to the new bus rollover image:

▶ **1.** In the Document window, click to the right of the Sloth Child bus rollover image, and then press the **Enter** key to position the pointer below the Sloth Child button.

▶ **2.** On the **Common** tab of the Insert bar, click the **Rollover Image** button 🖼 in the **Images** list. The Insert Rollover Image dialog box opens.

▶ **3.** Type **SSbusRollover** in the Image Name box, click the Original Image **Browse** button, and then double-click the **SSbusButtonUp.gif** graphic located in the **Tutorial.07\Tutorial** folder included with your Data Files.

▶ **4.** Click the Rollover Image **Browse** button, and then double-click the **SSbusButtonOver.gif** graphic located in the **Tutorial.07\ Tutorial** folder included with your Data Files.

▶ **5.** Click the **Preload Rollover Image** check box to check it, if necessary, and then click the **OK** button. The SSbusRollover button is added to the page.

Next, you will add the Play Timeline behavior to the SSbusRollover image so that the button will trigger Timeline2 to start.

▶ **6.** In the Document window, click the **SSbusRollover** graphic to select it. The Swap Image Restore and Swap Image behaviors already appear in the Behaviors panel.

▶ **7.** In the Behaviors panel, click the **Add Behavior** button ➕ , point to **Timeline**, and then click **Play Timeline**. The Play Timeline dialog box opens.

▶ **8.** Click the **Play Timeline** button, click **Timeline2**, and then click the **OK** button. The Play Timeline behavior is added to the end of the list in the Behaviors panel.

▶ **9.** In the Behaviors panel, select the **Play Timeline** behavior, click the **Events** arrow, and then click **onMouseDown** if it is not already selected. The event is onMouseDown. See Figure 7-35.

Surface Suction bus rollover image ◄ **Figure 7-35**

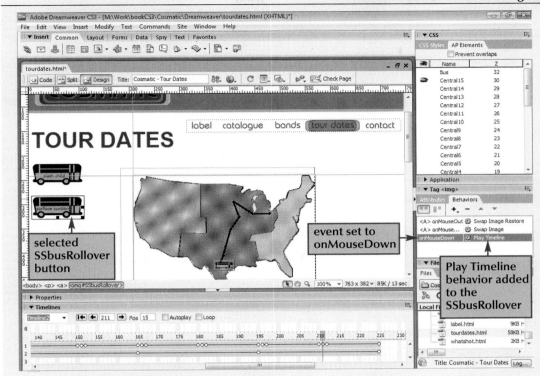

10. Save the Tour Dates page, preview the page in a browser, click the **Surface Suction tour bus** button, watch the animation, and then close the browser.

Next, you will add a Show-Hide Elements behavior to the first frame of Timeline2, add a Show-Hide Elements behavior to the second frame, and then add a Stop Timeline behavior and a Go To Frame behavior to the 245th frame of Timeline2. The Show-Hide Elements behavior will hide all the AP divs in the first frame of the timeline and show the Bus and Central1 AP divs in the second frame so that the animation will be hidden until the button that triggers it is clicked. The Stop Timeline behavior prevents the timeline from continuing to play, and the Go To Frame behavior returns the stopped timeline to the first frame so that it can be played again.

To add a Show-Hide Elements behavior to frame 1 in Timeline2:

1. In the Timelines panel, click in **frame 1** of the Behaviors channel.

2. In the Behaviors panel, click the **Add Behavior** button ⊞ , and then click **Show-Hide Elements**. The Show-Hide Elements dialog box opens.

3. Click **div "Bus"** in the Elements box, and then click the **Hide** button. The word "(hide)" appears beside the selected AP div to indicate that it will be hidden in frame 1.

4. Repeat Step 3 to hide each of the following AP divs: **div "Central1"**, **div "Central2"**, **div "Central3"**, **div "Central4"**, **div "Central5"**, **div "Central6"**, **div "Central7"**, **div "Central8"**, **div "Central9"**, **div "Central10"**, **div "Central11"**, **div "Central12"**, **div "Central13"**, **div "Central14"**, and **div "Central15"**. Do not place anything beside div "USmap" or other elements because they should remain visible, and do not place anything beside the East AP divs because they will be reset by the behaviors in Timeline1.

▶ **5.** Click the **OK** button. The dialog box closes and the behavior is added to the frame.

Next, you will add a Show-Hide Elements behavior to frame 2 of Timeline2.

To add a Show-Hide Elements behavior to frame 2 in Timeline2:

▶ **1.** In the Timelines panel, click **frame 2** in the Behaviors channel.

▶ **2.** In the Behaviors panel, click the **Add Behavior** button ➕ , and then click **Show-Hide Elements**. The Show-Hide Elements dialog box opens.

▶ **3.** Click **div "Bus"** in the Elements box, and then click the **Show** button.

▶ **4.** Click **div "Central1"** in the Elements box, and then click the **Show** button.

▶ **5.** Click the **OK** button. The Show-Hide Elements behavior is added to the second frame of the timeline.

Next, you'll add the Stop behavior and the Go To Frame behavior to the 245th frame of the timeline.

To add the Stop and the Go To Frame behaviors to frame 245 in Timeline2:

▶ **1.** In the Timelines panel, click **frame 245** in the Behaviors channel.

▶ **2.** In the Behaviors panel, click the **Add Behavior** button ➕ , point to **Timeline**, and then click **Stop Timeline**. The Stop Timeline dialog box opens.

▶ **3.** Click the **Stop Timeline** button, click **Timeline2**, and then click the **OK** button. The Stop Timeline behavior is added to the frame.

▶ **4.** In the Behaviors panel, click the **Add Behavior** button ➕ , point to **Timeline**, and then click **Go To Timeline Frame**. The Go To Timeline Frame dialog box opens.

▶ **5.** Click the **Timeline** button, and then click **Timeline2**.

▶ **6.** Type **1** in the Go to Frame box, if necessary, and then click the **OK** button. The Go to Timeline Frame behavior, which will reset the timeline to frame 1 after the animation ends, is added to frame 245.

Before you finish, you'll save the page and then preview it in a browser. Testing the page ensures that both tour bus buttons work. The Sloth Child tour bus button will trigger Timeline1, and the Surface Suction tour bus button will trigger Timeline2.

To preview and test the tour bus animations:

▶ **1.** Save the Tour Dates page, and then preview the page in a browser.

▶ **2.** Click the **Sloth Child tour bus** button. The Timeline1 animation plays.

▶ **3.** Click the **Surface Suction tour bus** button. The Timeline2 animation plays. See Figure 7-36.

Timeline1 and Timeline2 in the Tour Dates page ◄ Figure 7-36

4. Close the browser, and then close the Tour Dates page.

The second timeline for the Tour Dates pages is finished. You will create a third time-line for the Dizzied Connections tour path in the Review Assignments.

Updating the Web Site on the Remote Server

As a final review of the changes you made to the Tour Dates page, you'll update the files for the Cosmatic site on the remote server and review the page over the Web. You need to upload the Tour Dates page and include dependent files so that the new graphics are uploaded to the remote server. Then you'll preview the site on the Web.

To upload the updated Cosmatic site to the remote server:

1. Click the **Connects to Remote Host** button 🖧 on the Files panel toolbar.

2. If necessary, click the **View** button on the Files panel toolbar, and then click **Local View**.

3. Click **tourdates.html** in the Local View list to select the file, and then click the **Put File(s)** button ⬆ on the Files panel toolbar.

4. Click the **Yes** button when asked if you want to include dependent files because you have not yet selected the new dependent files for the site.

5. Click the **Disconnects From Remote Host** button 🖧 on the Files panel toolbar.

6. Click the **View** button on the Files panel toolbar, and then click **Local View**.

Next, you'll preview the updated site in a browser. The site will include all of the new elements that you added to the local version.

To preview the updated Cosmatic site in a browser:

▶ **1.** Open your browser, type the URL of your remote site in the Address bar on the browser toolbar, and then press the **Enter** key.

▶ **2.** Explore the **Tour Dates** page on the remote site from within the browser.

▶ **3.** Click the **Sloth Child tour bus** button and view the animation.

▶ **4.** Click the **Surface Suction tour bus** button and view the animation.

▶ **5.** Close the browser.

Sara likes the animations you created in the Tour Dates page that show the tour paths for two of the Cosmatic bands—Sloth Child and Surface Suction. She is looking forward to seeing the animated tour path for Dizzied Connections.

Review | **Session 7.3 Quick Check**

1. What behavior do you add to a rollover image to start a timeline?
2. Where are behaviors added in the timeline?
3. List one benefit of using behaviors in a timeline.
4. List one benefit of using multiple timelines in a page.
5. How do you switch between timelines?
6. Why is it a good idea to test pages that contain timelines on a variety of computers?

Review | **Tutorial Summary**

In this tutorial, you learned about basic animation and used the Timelines panel to create animations. You added AP divs to a timeline, moved AP divs, and then changed the duration of AP divs. You inserted additional keyframes into animation bars. You moved and resized AP divs, and you changed the visibility and the stacking order of AP divs. You also used a button to start your timeline. You added behaviors to the timeline using the Behaviors channel. Finally, you added multiple timelines to a Web page.

Key Terms

animation	frame	playback head
animation bar	keyframe	playback rate
animation channel	looping	timeline action
Behaviors channel		

Practice	**Review Assignments**

Practice the skills you learned in the tutorial.

Data Files needed for the Review Assignments: DCbusButtonOver.gif, DCbusButtonUp.gif, Dizzied1.gif, Dizzied2.gif, Dizzied3.gif, Dizzied4.gif, Dizzied5.gif, Dizzied6.gif, Dizzied7.gif, Dizzied8.gif, Dizzied9.gif, Dizzied10.gif, Dizzied11.gif, Dizzied12.gif

Brian asks you to create a timeline for the Dizzied Connections tour path in the Tour Dates page of the Cosmatic site. The band is touring the West Coast. Like the timelines for Sloth Child and Surface Suction, the timeline for Dizzied Connections will have an animated tour bus that follows the tour path. You will add a rollover image for the band, add a Play Timeline behavior to the rollover image, and then add the needed behaviors to the new timeline. Some of the Dizzied Connections tour dates are with the Life in Minor Chords band; however, this will not affect the tour path because Life in Minor Chords will have its own animated tour path added to the page as soon as its tour schedule is finalized.

1. Open the **Cosmatic** site that you modified in this tutorial, and then open the **tourdates.html** page in the Document window.
2. In the Timelines panel, add a new timeline, and then rename the new timeline as **Timeline3**, if necessary.
3. Draw a new AP div over the U.S. map (aligning the top and left borders of the new AP div to the guides positioned at the top and left borders of the East1 AP div), insert the **Dizzied1.gif** graphic located in the Tutorial.07\Review folder included with your Data Files into the new AP div, and then resize the AP div to fit snugly against the borders of the graphic.
4. In the AP Elements panel, rename the AP div as **Dizzied1**, and then drag the Dizzied1 AP div to animation channel 1 of Timeline3 in the Timelines panel. (*Hint:* Make sure that Timeline3 is selected in the Timelines list.)
5. Repeat Steps 3 and 4 to create AP divs and add the following graphics, using the graphic name for the AP div name and placing the animation bar for each new AP div to the right of the animation bars already in the animation channel: **Dizzied2.gif**, **Dizzied3.gif**, **Dizzied4.gif**, **Dizzied5.gif**, **Dizzied6.gif**, **Dizzied7.gif**, **Dizzied8.gif**, **Dizzied9.gif**, **Dizzied10.gif**, **Dizzied11.gif**, and **Dizzied12.gif**.
6. Select the Bus AP div in the AP Elements panel, move the Bus AP div over the first point in the Dizzied Connections tour path in the Document window, and then drag the AP div to frame 1 in animation channel 2 in Timeline3.
7. Drag the ending keyframe of the Bus animation bar to frame 180.
8. Select the opening keyframe in the Bus animation bar in Timeline3, and then change the z-index number of the Bus AP div to 45 in the AP Elements panel.
9. Select the ending keyframe in the Bus animation bar in Timeline3, and then change the z-index number of the Bus AP div to 45 in the AP Elements panel.
10. Add a new keyframe in frame 45 of the Bus animation bar, select the new keyframe, and then move the Bus AP div to the second point on the tour path.
11. Place a keyframe in frames 75, 105, 135, and 165 of the Bus animation bar, moving the Bus AP div to the next point on the tour path at each keyframe. Use the keyframe already in frame 180 to set the bus at the final location.
12. Add a new keyframe in frame 2 of the Dizzied1 animation bar, and then set its visibility in the AP Elements panel to visible (the open eye icon appears in the visibility column).
13. Select frame 1 in the Dizzied1 animation bar, and then set its visibility in the AP Elements panel to hidden (the closed eye icon appears in the visibility column).

14. Repeat Steps 12 and 13 for the following animation bars: Dizzied2, Dizzied3, Dizzied4, Dizzied5, Dizzied6, Dizzied7, Dizzied8, Dizzied9, Dizzied10, Dizzied11, and Dizzied12.

15. Click to the right of the Surface Suction bus rollover image, press the Enter key, and then insert a new rollover image named **DCbusRollover**. For the original image, use the **DCbusButtonUp.gif** graphic located in the Tutorial.07\Review folder included with your Data Files. For the rollover image, use the **DCbusButtonOver.gif** graphic located in the Tutorial.07\Review folder included with your Data Files. Preload the rollover image.

16. In the Document window, select the DCbusRollover graphic, add the Play Timeline behavior for Timeline3, and then change the event to onMouseDown.

17. In the Timelines panel, in frame 1 of the Behaviors channel, add the Show-Hide Elements behavior to hide div "Bus" and all the Dizzied AP divs. (*Hint:* Do not place anything beside div "USmap" or other elements because that div should remain visible, and do not place anything beside the East or Central divs because they will be reset by the behaviors in the other timelines.)

18. In the Timelines panel, in frame 2 of the Behaviors channel, add the Show-Hide Elements behavior to show div "Bus" and div "Dizzied1".

19. In the Timelines panel, in frame 200 of the Behaviors channel, add the Stop Timeline behavior for Timeline3.

20. In the Timelines panel, in frame 200 of the Behaviors channel, add the Go To Timeline Frame behavior to go to frame 1 of Timeline3.

21. Save the page, preview the page in a browser, test the animation, and then close the browser and the page.

22. Upload the site to your remote server, and then preview the site over the Web, testing the new animation in the Tour Dates page.

23. Submit the finished files to your instructor, either in printed or electronic form, as requested.

Apply | **Case Problem 1**

Add an animation to a Web site about the small rural communities of northern Vietnam.

Data Files needed for this Case Problem: WASetiquetteButton2.gif

World Anthropology Association   Dr. Olivia Thompson wants you to animate the Etiquette Tips button on the home page of the site to draw attention to the new feature. You will use timelines and behaviors to create a button with a blinking white border that: (1) when moused over, stops blinking but retains the white border, (2) when clicked, opens the Etiquette Tips page, and (3) when moused out, begins blinking again.

1. Open the **DrThompson** site that you modified in **Tutorial 6**, **Case 1**, and then open the **index.html** page in the Document window.

2. In the AP Elements panel, rename apDiv1 as **ETwithRing**.

3. Select the WASettiquetteButton.gif, and then in the Property inspector, change its border to 0.

4. Draw a new AP div on top of the ETwithRing AP div, insert the **WASetiquetteButton2.gif** graphic located in the Tutorial.07\Case1 folder included with your Data Files, set the graphic's border to 0 in the Property inspector, resize the AP div to fit snugly around the graphic, and then align the top and left borders of the AP divs.

5. Rename the new AP div as **ETplain**.

6. Add the ETwithRing AP div to animation channel 1 of the timeline, and then make the animation bar 11 frames long.

7. Add the ETplain AP div to animation channel 2 of the timeline so that the first frame is on frame 4, and then resize the animation bar so it ends on frame 10.

8. Add a new keyframe in the second frame of the ETplain animation bar, and set its visibility to visible.

9. Set the visibility of the first and last keyframes of the ETplain animation bar to hidden, and then verify that the visibility of the second keyframe is visible.

10. Check the Autoplay check box.

11. In frame 10 in the Behaviors channel, add a Go To Timeline Frame behavior that goes to frame 1. This behavior will cause the timeline to loop to the first frame each time the timeline reaches the 10th frame.

12. In frame 11 in the Behaviors channel, add a Stop Timeline behavior for Timeline1. If the timeline goes to frame 11, it will stop and remain on frame 11.

13. Click outside of the Behaviors channel in the Timelines panel, select the WASetiquetteButton2.gif graphic in the Document window, and then add the Go To Timeline Frame behavior to the graphic that goes to frame 11.

14. Change the event to onMouseOver. This will cause the timeline to go to frame 11 and stop when the user mouses over the graphic, causing the white circle to stop blinking when the mouse is over the graphic. (*Hint:* If you don't see the onMouseOver event, change the event settings for 4.0 and later browsers.)

15. With the WASetiquetteButton2.gif graphic still selected in the Document window, add a second Go To Timeline Frame behavior to the graphic that goes to frame 1.

16. Change the event to onMouseOut. When the user moves the mouse away from the graphic, the timeline will go to frame 1 and play, causing the button to resume blinking.

17. Save the page, preview the page in a browser, mouse over the button you added, and then click the button. Because the WASetiquetteButton.gif was already linked, and because the graphic is showing when the mouse is over the graphic, the button opens the etiquette_tips.html page when you click it. Close the browser and the page.

18. Upload the site to the remote server, and then preview the site over the Web.

19. Submit the finished files to your instructor, either in printed or electronic form, as requested.

| Apply | **Case Problem 2** |

Create a slide show of paintings for the home page of a Web site for an art museum.

Data File needed for this Case Problem: SlideShowBG.gif

Museum of Western Art C. J. Strittmatter wants you to add a slide show of paintings to the home page of the Museum site. To create the slide show, you will create new AP divs and then add a painting graphic to each new AP div. You will name the AP divs, align the AP divs, and then add each AP div to an animation channel in the timeline.

1. Open the **Museum** site that you modified in **Tutorial 6**, **Case 2**, and then open the **index.html** page in the Document window.

2. Draw an AP div in the page below the heading, select the body text for the page (not the heading text), and then drag the selected body text into the AP div.

3. Rename the AP div as **Text**, move the Text AP div to position its top border 20 pixels below the Welcome heading text and its left border at 200 pixels, and resize the AP div so that its bottom border is snug against the text and its right border is even with the left border of the navigation bar table.

4. Draw a new AP div in the empty space at the left of the page, rename the new AP div as **Background**, insert the **SlideShowBG.gif** graphic located in the Tutorial.07\Case2 folder included with your Data Files, and then drag the borders of the AP div to fit snugly around the graphic.

5. Use the guides to help reposition the Background AP div 10 pixels below the horizontal rule below the museum logo and 15 pixels from the left edge of the page.

6. Draw a new AP div over the Background AP div, rename the AP div as **Painting1,** insert the AFigureOfTheNight.jpg graphic located in the Graphics folder in the site's local root folder, and then resize the AP div to fit snugly around the graphic.

7. Link the AFigureOfTheNight.jpg graphic to the art.html page, set the border to 2, and then add the image_border style to the image. (*Hint:* Use the Property inspector to make these changes.)

8. Repeat Steps 6 and 7 for the following graphics, naming each AP div with a later number (such asPainting2, Painting3, and so on): **BuffaloRunners.jpg, TheCowPuncher.jpg, AQuietDayInUtica.jpg, CowpunchingSometimes.jpg, DeerInForest.jpg, IndiansHuntingBuffalo.jpg,** and **TheBucker.jpg**.

9. Select all of the Painting AP divs, align the left borders, and then use the Left Arrow and Right Arrow keys to center the paintings horizontally inside the Background AP div.

10. Select each Painting AP div one at a time, and then center it vertically within the Background. Each AP div will have a different vertical alignment based on the size of its painting image. (*Hint:* Use only the Up Arrow and Down Arrow keys so that you do not change the horizontal alignment of the AP div.)

11. Drag the Painting8 AP div so that the first frame of its animation bar is positioned in frame 1 of animation channel 1. (*Hint:* Select the AP div in the AP Elements panel.)

12. Drag the Painting7 AP div so that the first frame of its animation bar is positioned in frame 14 of animation channel 2. The Painting 8 and Painting7 animation bars overlap by two frames.

13. Drag the following Painting AP divs to the specified positions in the timeline:

AP Div	Animation Channel	Beginning Frame
Painting6	3	27
Painting5	4	40
Painting4	5	53
Painting3	6	66
Painting2	7	79
Painting1	8	92

14. Add keyframes to the second frame of the following animation bars: Painting7, Painting6, Painting5, Painting4, Painting3, Painting2, and Painting1.

15. Use the AP Elements panel to set the following visibilities:

Animation Bar	First Keyframe	Second Keyframe	Last Keyframe
Painting8	Visible		Hidden
Painting7	Hidden	Visible	Hidden
Painting6	Hidden	Visible	Hidden
Painting5	Hidden	Visible	Hidden
Painting4	Hidden	Visible	Hidden
Painting3	Hidden	Visible	Hidden
Painting2	Hidden	Visible	Hidden
Painting1	Hidden	Visible	Hidden

Staggering the AP divs' positions in the timeline, and then hiding and revealing the AP divs sequentially, will create an animation that looks like a slide show.

16. Check the Autoplay and the Loop check boxes.
17. Save the page, and then preview the page in a browser. (*Hint:* If the animation is jerky where it loops, the loop behavior was added to frame 107 in the Behaviors channel. Drag the behavior to frame 106 in the Behaviors channel, and then preview the page again.)
18. Upload the site to the remote server, and then preview the site over the Web.
19. Submit the finished files to your instructor, either in printed or electronic form, as requested.

Challenge	**Case Problem 3**

Create an animated link in a Web site for an independent bookstore.

There are no Data Files needed for this Case Problem.

MORE Books   Natalie More wants you to replace the current link to the Featured Book page with a new animated link. The Featured Book heading text will blink once the page is loaded. When the user mouses over the book cover graphic, a yellow tab will slide out and text will appear. When the user clicks the blinking Featured Book text or the book cover, the featured_frameset.html page will open in a new browser window. You will accomplish this by creating two timelines. The FeatureTxt timeline will make the Featured Book text blink, and the SlideOutTab timeline will control the slide-out tab.

1. Open the **MOREbooks** site that you modified in **Tutorial 6**, **Case 3**, and then open the **index.html** page in the Document window.
2. Draw an AP div in the page, drag the Featured Book heading text into the new AP div, apply the more_sub_headings style to the heading text, and then verify that the heading text is linked to the featured_frameset.html page.
3. Resize the AP div so that the text fits on one line, rename the AP div as **FeaturedText**, and then use the guides to help position the AP div so that its top border is at 100 pixels and its right border is at 725 pixels.
4. Draw a new AP div below the FeaturedText AP div, rename the new AP div as **BookCover**, drag the BookCoverPunchSmall.jpg graphic into the BookCover AP div, resize the AP div to fit snugly around the graphic, and then center the BookCover AP div horizontally below the Featured Text AP div.
5. Select the BookCoverPunchSmall.jpg graphic, and then change the border to 2 and link the book cover to the featured_frameset.html page, if necessary.

6. Create a CSS custom style class defined in the site's style sheet that sets the image's border as solid, thin, #CC9933 color, and then apply the style to the book cover graphic.

7. Place the pointer to the left of the NEWS subheading, and then press the Enter key to move the rest of the text in the page down.

8. Draw a new AP div left-aligned and top-aligned with the BookCover AP div that is the same height as the book cover and 10 pixels wide, and then change the AP div's background color to #CC9933 in the Property inspector.

EXPLORE

9. Rename the new AP div as **YellowTab**, and then drag the YellowTab AP div to the bottom of the list in the AP Elements panel so that it becomes 1 in the stacking order.

10. Draw a new AP div the same height as the BookCover AP div, type **Click here to learn more about this amazing new book by Kelly Moore** in the AP div, adjust the width so that all the text is visible, and then move the AP div to the left of the BookCover AP div.

EXPLORE

11. Rename the new AP div as **TabText**, and then drag the AP div in the AP Elements panel until it is 2 in the stacking order.

12. In the Timelines panel, rename the timeline as **FeatureText**.

13. Drag the FeaturedText AP div to frame 1 of animation channel 1 in the timeline, and make the animation bar 10 frames long.

14. Add a new keyframe at frame 5 of the animation bar, and then set the visibility of the AP div to hidden in the new keyframe.

15. Check the Autoplay and Loop check boxes.

16. Save the page, preview the page in a browser to view the blinking Featured Text animation, and then close the browser.

17. Add a new timeline, rename the timeline as **SlideOutTab**, and then drag the YellowTab AP div to frame 1 of animation channel 1 in the timeline.

18. Select the ending frame of the YellowTab animation bar, and then set the AP div's width to 90 pixels in the Property inspector.

19. Press the Left Arrow key to move the YellowTab AP div until its right border is flush against the left border of the BookCover AP div.

20. Drag the TabText AP div to frame 14 of animation channel 2 in the SlideOutTab timeline, and resize the animation bar to end in frame 15.

21. Change the visibility of the opening keyframe in frame 14 of animation channel 2 to hidden, and then change the ending keyframe in frame 15 of animation channel 2 to visible.

22. Add the Play Timeline behavior to the BookCoverPunchSmall.jpg graphic, selecting SlideOutTab from the timeline list, and then change the event to onMouseOver, if necessary.

23. Save the page, and then preview the page in a browser, verifying that the Featured Book heading text blinks when the page is loaded and that the yellow tab slides out when you mouse over the book cover.

24. Upload the site to your remote server, and then preview the site over the Web.

25. Submit the finished files to your instructor, either in printed or electronic form, as requested.

Challenge | Case Problem 4

Create an animated graphic in a Web site for a newly opening sushi restaurant.

Data File needed for this Case Problem: Wasabi2.gif

Sushi Ya-Ya   Mary O'Brien asks you to delete the old Wasabi graphic in the Sushi Ya-Ya home page and replace it with an animated graphic that links to the wasabi.html page. You will create a timeline to animate a tab that moves out when the Wasabi graphic is moused over. Then you will create a second timeline that causes the tab text to blink.

1. Open the **SushiYaYa** site that you modified in **Tutorial 6**, **Case 4**, and then open the **index.html** page in the Document window.

2. Delete the WasabiPictureSmall.gif graphic and the How Hot Is Wasabi?? text from the home page.

3. Draw a new AP div to the left of the heading, rename the AP div as **Wasabi**, insert the **Wasabi2.gif** graphic located in the Tutorial.07\Case4 folder included with your Data Files, and then resize the AP div to fit snugly against the borders of the graphic, and then apply the image border style to the graphic.

4. Position the Wasabi AP div so that its top border is 10 pixels below the horizontal rule and its left border is 10 pixels from the edge of the page.

5. Create an AP div the width of the Wasabi AP div and 10 pixels in height, rename the AP div as **Tab**, and then change the background color for the Tab AP div to #6666FF.

6. Align the Tab AP div so that its bottom and left borders are even with the Wasabi AP div's bottom and left borders.

⊕EXPLORE   7. Drag the Tab AP div to the bottom of the list in the AP Elements panel to change its stacking order.

8. In the Timelines panel, rename the timeline as **Tab**, and then drag the Tab AP div to the first frame of animation channel 1.

9. Add a keyframe in frame 8 of the Tab animation bar, select the new keyframe, move the Tab AP div so that its top border is flush with the bottom border of the Wasabi AP div, and then change the Tab AP div height to 27 pixels.

10. Select the ending keyframe in the Tab animation bar, change the Tab AP div height to 27 pixels, move the Tab AP div so that its top border is flush with the bottom border of the Wasabi AP div (the same position it was occupying in frame 8), and then drag the right border of the Tab AP div until its width is 236 pixels.

11. Draw a new AP div over the extended Tab AP div, and then rename the new AP div as **TabText**.

12. Type **How Hot Is Wasabi??** in the new TabText AP div, apply the sub_headings style to the text, and then link the text to the wasabi.html page, targeting the link to open in a new browser window.

13. Center the TabText AP div text over the extended Tab AP div.

14. Add a new timeline, rename the timeline as **TabText**, and then drag the TabText AP div to the first frame of animation channel 1.

15. Resize the TabText animation bar to end in frame 10, add a new keyframe in frame 5, change the visibility of the AP div to hidden in frame 1 and to visible in frame 5, and then check the Loop check box.

16. Display the Tab timeline, and then add the Play Timeline behavior in frame 10 of the Behaviors channel to play the TabText timeline.

17. Link the Wasabi2.gif graphic to the wasabi.html page and target the link to open in a new browser window. Add the Play Timeline behavior to the graphic, and then set the selector to onMouseOver to play the Tab timeline when the user mouses over the wasabi image.

18. Save the page, and then preview the page in a browser, testing the animated tabs and links.

19. Upload the page to your remote server, and then preview the site over the Web.

20. Submit the finished files to your instructor, either in printed or electronic form, as requested.

Review | Quick Check Answers

Session 7.1

1. a series of graphics or images that appear to move over a period of time
2. move, show/hide, resize, and change stacking order (or z-index)
3. frames
4. 15 frames per second
5. keyframes
6. makes the animation run over more frames, which slows the animation and makes the movement more fluid

Session 7.2

1. in the keyframes
2. Show-Hide Elements, Move Elements, Change Stacking Order (or z-index number), Resize Elements
3. Check the Autoplay check box, or attach a Play Timeline behavior to a button to play a timeline in a browser.
4. Select a keyframe in the timeline, and then type a different z-index number in the Z column of the AP Elements panel.
5. False; to change the dimensions of an image, select the image.
6. False; you can delete an animation.

Session 7.3

1. the Start Timeline behavior
2. in the Behaviors channel and in keyframes
3. You can make things that are not triggered by user interaction happen over time, such as reset the timeline to frame 1 after the animation ended so the timeline can run again.
4. You can control the animations separately. For example, you can use the Start Timeline behavior attached to a button to play one of the timelines.
5. by selecting a timeline with the Timelines list on the Timelines panel toolbar
6. to get an idea of the average speed at which the timeline will run, because timelines run at different speeds on different computers

Adding Rich Media to a Web Site

Inserting Flash, Shockwave, Sound, and Video Elements

Case | Cosmatic

Sara Lynn, president of Cosmatic, has gotten great response to the Sloth Child page. She has received several complimentary e-mail messages and heard many positive comments from fans at local shows. Now she wants to incorporate rich media elements into the Cosmatic site in hopes that the other pages in the site generate the same kind of buzz.

You will replace the current What's Hot section in the home page with a Flash movie that links to the What's Hot page. The Flash movie will draw attention to the new Cosmatic products. Some other team members are creating a Shockwave game, which will be added to the Bands page. Brian wants you to add a Shockwave promo for the game in the spot that the game will eventually occupy. Also, you'll add some audio samples and video clips to the Catalogue page so that users can get a chance to hear and see the bands.

Starting Data Files

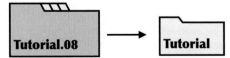

Tutorial
GamePromo.dcr
MP3SoundButton.gif
sunshine.mp3
sunshine.swf
sunshinevideo.flv
whatshot.swf

Review
limcVideo.flv
sunshine_autostart.swf

Case1
WASBreathySample.flv
WASHarshSample.flv
WASHarshwhSample.mp3
WASModalSample.mp3

Case2
museumtour.dcr
MuseumTour.txt

Case3
MOREform.dcr

Case4
sushigame.dcr
wasabisound_autoplay.swf

Session 8.1

Adding Media to a Web Site

Media refers to any special configurable object added to a Web page that needs a player or an application that is not part of the browser (such as plug-ins, ActiveX controls, or helper applications) to display within a browser. The terms *player* and *plug-in* are used in this tutorial to refer generally to the above technologies. Some of the most useful media used in Web pages are Flash, Shockwave, sound, and video. You often need a special software package, separate from the player or plug-in, to create a media component. For example, you create Flash applications and animations in the Adobe Flash software. After you have created a media element, you can insert it into a Web page and users can view it using the player or plug-in. Users view Flash files that you have inserted into your Web pages with the Flash Player.

In this tutorial, you learn about Flash, Shockwave, sound, and video, and then add each type of element to the Cosmatic site.

InSight | **Using Media to Enhance the User's Experience**

No matter what media you add to a site, it is important to make sure that you have a purpose for including that element. The animation, game, audio, or movie must enhance the site, contribute to the user experience, and reinforce the site goals. Be discriminating when adding media to a Web site. You do not want to overwhelm the user with too much glitz on pages. When trying to decide what to add to pages, ask yourself whether the proposed element will enhance the user's ability to grasp the site goals or distract them from focusing on the message. If the element will distract the user, discard it. When you follow these guidelines to determine what media to include in a site, you might find yourself cutting some of the coolest elements created for the site. Even the most innovative or creative element should be cut if it does not reinforce the site goals and enhance the user's experience.

Also consider the technological limitations of the target audience when adding media to a site. Review your research to ensure that the target audience can easily access media elements that communicate necessary information. For example, if you plan to communicate vital information in audio files, make sure that most users will have access to computers with sound capabilities. Most media require some sort of plug-in to run on the client computer. Some plug-ins are included with the latest browsers, whereas others must be downloaded separately by the end user. Before incorporating media into Web pages, learn what plug-in users will need to view each element, determine the likelihood that users have the needed plug-in, and assess how difficult it is for users to get a needed plug-in. Be aware that media elements often use considerable bandwidth. Evaluate the connection speed and the computer speed for your target audience to determine if the client computer can display the media element effectively without prolonged delays. If users have to wait too long to view a page, they often lose interest and move to another site. Users usually wait longer for an item they perceive to be important than for an item they perceive to be unimportant. If you are asking users to wait for your site to load, make sure that the wait is worth their time.

In addition to these general concerns, you should explore the most common use of each media type (for example, Flash is frequently used to create animations and so forth) and consider both the pros and the cons associated with each type of media element.

Understanding Adobe Flash

Flash was one of the first widely used animation programs that used vector-based graphics. Because vector-based graphics can scale and compress to a very small file size without losing quality, Flash has become one of the premier solutions for creating and delivering interactive animations for display on the Web. Over time, Flash development has continued. The latest version of Flash also contains video-handling capabilities, is better at compressing bitmap-based animation, has more developed coding capabilities, and includes excellent audio capabilities. Flash is a good choice for lightweight interactive components (such as an address book or an animated menu system), Web applications, slide show-type presentations, vector-based animation, some bitmap-based animation, video, video that has additional animation or text laid over it, and sound.

Flash is both the name of the software you use to create animations and the name commonly used to refer to the completed animation files. Flash files are also called Flash movies. The types of Flash files that you will see most frequently are:

- **.fla.** The source file used by the Flash program when you create a Flash movie. You edit .fla files when you want to make changes to Flash movies. These authoring files can be opened only in the Flash program. The files must be exported from Flash as .swf files to be viewed on the Web.
- **.swf.** A compressed Flash file that is viewable in a browser and can be previewed in Dreamweaver. You'll use .swf Flash files in the Cosmatic site.
- **.swt.** A Flash template file that enables you to change and replace content in the .swf file. In Dreamweaver, these files are used with the Flash button objects to enable you to update text when you add buttons to a page.
- **.swc.** A compiled clip that you work with in Flash that contains Flash symbols and ActionScript code. The components included with Flash are .swc files that enable you to incorporate mostly prebuilt Web components into pages. Like .fla files, these authoring files must be exported from Flash as .swf files to be viewed on the Web.
- **.flv.** The Flash video file format that enables you to include encoded audio and video for delivery through the Flash Player.

Like every program, there are both positive and negative aspects of using Flash. Figure 8-1 lists these benefits and drawbacks.

Figure 8-1 ▶ **Pros and cons of using Flash**

Pros	Cons
As of Sept. 2007, 99.1% of Internet-enabled desktops in mature markets as well as a wide range of devices have the Flash Player plug-in (it has a 99% browser penetration). Flash Player 9 already has 93.3% penetration as of June 2007. The Flash Player plug-in is included with the latest versions of Internet Explorer and Mozilla Firefox.	The playback speed of a Flash movie may depend on the client computer because older versions of Flash render the movies on the client computer, whereas the newest version of Flash has an option to prerender certain types of frames, which might eliminate this problem.
A Flash movie will look the same in all browsers and across platforms.	There are limitations to the amount of interactivity and control you can achieve with Flash.
Flash compresses movies to a reasonable size.	Although Flash has 99% browser penetration, not all users have the latest version; therefore, problems sometimes arise in playback due to version differences. (You can usually overcome this by making the movie check to see which version the user has and then downloading the current version automatically, if necessary, but you must know Flash to do this.)
You can use any fonts within a Flash movie because Flash is not dependent on the fonts on users' computers.	
Some alternative and portable devices, such as cell phones, PDAs, wireless handsets, and interactive television systems, can play Flash movies.	

You can find additional information and statistics about the pros and cons of using Flash on the Adobe site at *www.adobe.com/products/flashplayer*. The Adobe Flash Player Statistics section provides current statistical data regarding Flash Player browser penetration (and version penetration), a current market breakdown that includes Flash Player and competing technologies, and user profiles.

Before you add a Flash movie to the Cosmatic site, Brian asks you to research the integration of Flash elements into a Web site. You will go to the Adobe site and review the current Flash information and statistics.

To research Flash information and statistics on the Adobe site:

▶ 1. Start your browser, type **www.adobe.com/products/flashplayer** in the Address bar, and then press the **Enter** key. The Adobe Flash Player home page opens.

   Trouble? If the Adobe Flash Player home page does not open, type www.adobe.com in the Address bar, press the Enter key to open the Adobe home page, type flash player in the Search for box, press the Enter key, click a link to the Flash Player in the list of links, and then continue with Step 2.

▶ 2. Click the **Statistics** link. The current statistical breakdown of market penetration for each of the most popular media players appears in the browser window. See Figure 8-2.

Flash Player adoption statistics ◄ Figure 8-2

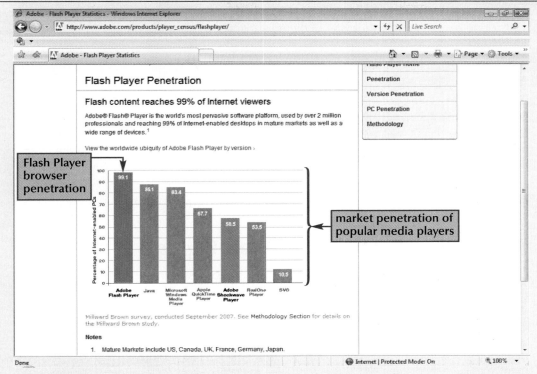

Trouble? If the data you see differs from Figure 8-2, Adobe has updated the data since this tutorial was published. Continue with Step 3.

▶ 3. Review the information, and then click the **Version Penetration** link. The version penetration statistics for Flash Player appear in the browser window. See Figure 8-3.

Flash Player version penetration ◄ Figure 8-3

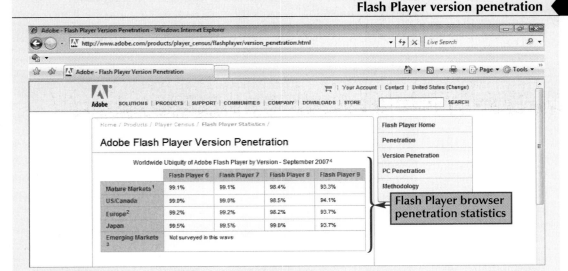

Trouble? If the data you see differs from Figure 8-3, Adobe has updated the data since this tutorial was published. Continue with Step 4.

▶ 4. Close the browser.

The statistics show that the Flash Player has a larger share of the market than any of the competing technologies. It is included with most current browsers. As a result, most end users will likely be able to view any Flash components that you add to a Web site. This is one reason that Flash is one of the most widely used media on the Web.

| InSight | | **Using the Latest Flash Player** |

Although the Flash Player has a 99% browser penetration, not everyone has the latest version of the player installed on their computer. As of June 2007, Flash Player 9 already has 93.3% penetration. As a result, users might encounter some differences in how a Web page displays on their screen. This is generally not a big issue. If a user is connected to the Internet and does not have the latest version of the Flash Player, Flash will generally open a dialog box, prompting the user to install the latest version of the player. The update is quick and easy to install.

Adding Flash Movies to Web Pages

You will add a Flash movie to the home page of the Cosmatic site. When you insert a Flash movie, Dreamweaver places the code for the movie into the page and prompts you to include a copy of the movie in the site's local root folder. You do this so that all the materials for the site are in one place. Be aware that any links to elements outside the local root folder will be incorrect after the site is uploaded to the remote server. If you are using only a few media elements in a site, you can place the files in the Graphics folder. If you plan to use many media elements in a site, it is a good idea to create a new folder for each type of element so that the site remains organized and files are easy to find. You'll create a Media folder to store the Flash, Shockwave, sound, and video files that Brian wants you to add to the Cosmatic site.

A Flash movie appears in the Document window as a gray rectangle with the same dimensions as the Flash movie and a Flash logo in its center. The width and height of the Flash movie is determined when the movie is created, but you can adjust its width, height, scalability, and other attributes in the Property inspector. To view the Flash movie, you must preview the page in a browser or you must select the movie in Dreamweaver and press the Play button in the Property inspector.

| Reference Window | | **Adding a Flash Movie to a Web Page** |

- In the Document window, click in the page where you want to add the Flash movie.
- On the Common tab of the Insert bar, in the Media list, click the Flash button.
- Navigate to the Flash movie file, and then double-click the file.
- Click the Yes button, navigate to the folder in which you want to save the file, and then click the Save button.
- In the Document window, click the Flash movie, and then, in the Property inspector, adjust attributes as needed.

Brian wants you to replace the WhatsHot AP div in the home page of the Cosmatic site with a What's Hot Flash movie created by another member of the design team. You'll delete the existing elements from the page and insert the new Flash movie. You will create a Media folder in the local root folder to store the Flash movie and other media files you will add to the Cosmatic site. When you save the Flash movie, Dreamweaver will save the script that controls the movie in a new Scripts folder. You will learn more about scripts later.

To add the What's Hot Flash movie to the home page:

▶ **1.** Open the **Cosmatic** site that you modified in the **Tutorial 7 Review Assignments**, and then open the **index.html** page in the Document window.

▶ **2.** In the Document window, delete the text and graphic in the WhatsHot AP div. The borders of the AP div remain visible.

Trouble? If elements are still visible at the top of the AP div, you need to delete them. Press the Backspace key.

▶ **3.** Click in the **WhatsHot** AP div, if necessary, and then, on the **Common** tab of the Insert bar, in the **Media** list, click the **Flash** button ▪ . The Select File dialog box opens.

▶ **4.** Double-click the **whatshot.swf** file located in the **Tutorial.08\Tutorial** folder included with your Data Files. A dialog box opens, prompting you to place a copy of the file in the local root folder.

▶ **5.** Click the **Yes** button. The Copy File As dialog box opens.

▶ **6.** Browse to the local root folder of your Cosmatic site, click the **Create New Folder** button ▪ to create a new folder in the local root folder, type **Media** as the folder name, and then press the **Enter** key. The Media folder opens.

▶ **7.** Click the **Save** button. A copy of the whatshot.swf file is placed in the Media folder and a gray rectangle with the dimensions of the Flash movie appears in the WhatsHot AP div in the Document window. See Figure 8-4.

Flash movie inserted in the home page — Figure 8-4

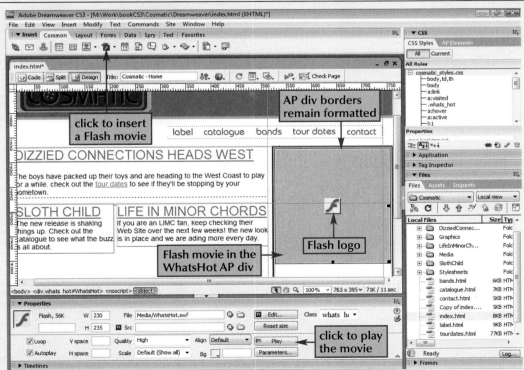

Trouble? If the Object Tag Accessibility Attributes dialog box opens, this option is enabled for your installation of Dreamweaver. In this instance, and each time an Accessibility Attributes dialog box opens when you insert a media file into a Web page in this tutorial, click the Cancel button to close the dialog box.

▶ **8.** Save the home page. The Copy Dependent Files dialog box opens, stating that the pages use an object or behavior that requires supporting files, which have been copied to the local site.

▶ **9.** Click the **OK** button. A new Scripts folder appears in the local root folder and includes the copied file.

▶ **10.** In the Document window, select the **Flash movie**, if necessary, and then, in the Property inspector, click the **Play** button. The Flash movie plays in the Document window, and the Play button changes to a Stop button. See Figure 8-5.

Figure 8-5	Home page with the Flash movie playing

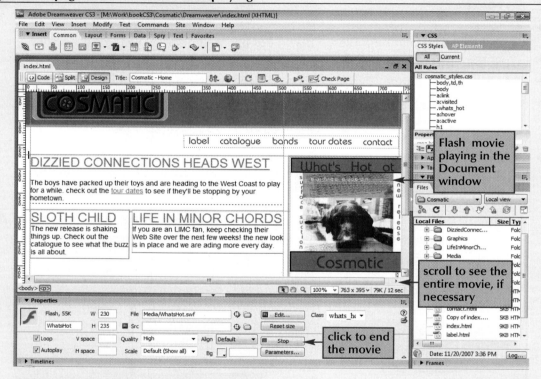

▶ **11.** Watch the movie, and then click the **Stop** button when you are finished.

▶ **12.** Preview the home page in a browser (enabling blocked content as needed whenever you preview pages in this tutorial), and then view the Flash movie. The movie will start automatically when the page is loaded in the browser. See Figure 8-6.

Trouble? If you do not have the latest version of the Flash Player plug-in, a Security Warning dialog box opens when you try to preview the page in a browser. Click the Yes button to update the version. After the new Flash Player is downloaded, the movie will start playing automatically.

Trouble? If the page continues to load for an extended period of time (twice the time it would usually take), you need to download the most recent version of the Flash Player from the Adobe site. Type www.adobe.com/downloads in the Address bar in your browser, press the Enter key, click the Adobe Flash Player link, click the Install Now button, and then click the Yes button in the Security Warning dialog box. Close the browser, and then repeat Step 12.

The AP div border doesn't surround the entire Flash movie. You will resize the AP div to match the movie.

▶ **13.** Close the browser, and then resize the AP div as needed to fit snugly against the borders of the Flash movie.

Trouble? If you cannot fit the AP div snugly against the movie borders, you might have inserted a paragraph tag in the AP div. Select the AP div, click the Code button on the Document toolbar to switch to Code view, locate and delete the opening <p> tag, locate and delete the closing <p> tag, click the Design button on the Document toolbar, and then repeat Step 13.

▶ **14.** Save the home page, and then preview the page in a browser. See Figure 8-7.

Figure 8-7 Resized AP div previewed in a browser

Adjusting Attributes of a Flash Movie

Many attributes of Flash movies can be adjusted within Dreamweaver. Like other elements, you adjust the attributes of a Flash movie in the Property inspector when the movie object is selected. The Flash attributes include:

- **Name.** A unique identifier of the movie for scripting. A movie name can contain letters and numbers. It cannot contain spaces or special characters, and it cannot start with a number.
- **W (Width) and H (Height).** The dimensions of the Flash movie, which are set when the movie is created and measured by default in pixels. You can also measure the movie in picas (pc), points (pt), inches (in), millimeters (mm), centimeters (cm), and percentage of a parent object (%). Changing the width or height of a Flash movie can change the aspect ratio of the movie. It can cause the movie to play more slowly because every frame of the movie must be rendered and changed on the client computer, and it can cause the movie to look distorted, especially if the movie contains a lot of text.
- **File.** The path to the Flash movie file (.swf).
- **Src (Source File).** The path to the Flash source file (.fla) for the .swf movie file in a Web page; available only if Flash is installed on your local computer.
- **Edit.** The button that launches Flash and opens the .fla file specified in the Src box so you can edit the Flash movie. When you save the .fla file, Flash re-exports the .swf movie file with the changes. If Flash is not installed on your local computer, the Edit button is disabled.
- **Reset Size.** The button that returns the Flash movie to its original size if you have altered it.
- **Class.** A list of CSS styles that you can apply to the object.
- **Loop.** The option that, when checked, plays the movie continuously as long as the page is loaded in the browser or, which unchecked, adds code that plays the movie only once.
- **Autoplay.** The option that, when checked, plays the movie automatically when the page is loaded in a browser.

Tip

To size a Flash movie in a unit other than pixels, type the unit abbreviation after the number in the W box.

- **V Space (Vertical Space) and H Space (Horizontal Space).** The number of pixels of white space inserted above and below the movie or to the left and right of the movie. If blank, no code is specified and the browser adds 0 pixels of white space around the movie.

- **Quality.** The amount of anti-aliasing (smoothing of diagonal or jagged lines) that occurs when the movie is played; options include Low, Auto Low, Auto High, and High. Movies with High anti-aliasing look best but require more processing power to render correctly on the screen. Low emphasizes speed over appearance. Auto Low emphasizes speed, but also improves appearance when the speed is acceptable. Auto High emphasizes both appearance and speed, but will sacrifice appearance for speed, if necessary. High emphasizes appearance over speed.

- **Scale.** How the Flash movie displays in the specified W and H dimensions. Default (Show All) displays the movie at the greatest size possible within the designated space while still maintaining aspect ratio and showing all the content; the background color might appear on two sides of the movie. No Borders fits the movie into the designated space so that no borders show and the movie maintains the original aspect ratio (a portion of the movie might not be seen). Exact Fit scales the movie to the exact W and H dimensions, regardless of the aspect ratio of the movie. The entire movie is seen, but it might be distorted to fit in the space.

- **Align.** The alignment of the movie in the page. The alignment options are the same as for an image: Default, Baseline, Top, Middle, Bottom, Text Top, Absolute Middle, Absolute Bottom, Left, and Right.

- **Bg (Background Color).** The color specified for the background of the movie area. This color also appears in the page if the movie is not playing, such as while the page is loading.

- **Play.** The button that starts the movie in Dreamweaver. The movie plays in the Document window and a Stop button, which ends the movie, replaces the Play button.

- **Parameters.** The button that opens a dialog box for entering parameters that are passed to a movie if the movie was designed to receive them. Parameters entered in the Parameters dialog box are placed in the appropriate places in the page code.

Brian wants you to name the Flash movie, and make sure the movie is set to loop and autoplay.

To adjust the attributes of the Flash movie:

1. Click the **Flash movie** to select it, if necessary, and then, in the Property inspector, type **WhatsHot** in the Flash box in the upper-left corner. The Flash movie is named.

2. If necessary, in the Property inspector, click the **Loop** and **Autoplay** check boxes to insert check marks. The movie will play continuously and start as soon as the page is loaded in a browser window.

3. In the Property inspector, click the **Play** button. The WhatsHot Flash movie plays in the Document window. The movie restarts from the beginning after it reaches the end. This continues until you click the Stop button.

4. In the Property inspector, click the **Stop** button. The movie ends and the Play button reappears.

5. Save and close the home page.

Adding Flash Text to Web Pages

You can use a Flash movie to add text that uses designer fonts to a Web page. Because Flash movies are self-contained and do not require fonts to be installed on the client computer, they are a good way to add custom fonts to Web pages. For example, you might use a Flash movie to add page headings that use the logo font to the pages of the Cosmatic site.

The downside to using Flash text is that the text is no longer attached to the style sheet. Therefore, if you change the styles for a site, you must modify each Flash text movie separately. This can be a big job if you are working on a large site that contains many Flash text movies; therefore, it is a good idea to use Flash text sparingly. Also, Flash text sometimes appears poorly rendered in Dreamweaver. You need to preview the page to see the text as it will appear in a browser.

Reference Window | **Adding Flash Text in a Web Page**

- In the Document window, click in the page where you want to add the Flash text.
- On the Common tab of the Insert bar, in the Media list, click the Flash Text button.
- Select the font, size, and color, and then type the text for the Flash text.
- Click the Browse button next to the Save As box, navigate to the folder in which you want to save the Flash text, and then click the Save button.
- Click the OK button.

You can create a small Flash movie that contains text and a link from within Dreamweaver even if you do not have Flash installed on your computer. You set the following attributes for the text in the Insert Flash Text dialog box:

Tip

To edit a Flash text movie, double-click the Flash text and change its attributes in the Insert Flash Text dialog box.

- **Font.** All the TrueType fonts loaded on your computer. A font must be on your local system for you to use that font.
- **Size.** The size of text in points.
- **Bold and Italicize.** Style attributes for text.
- **Alignment.** Text alignment options: left, center, or right.
- **Color.** The text color; type a hexadecimal color code or use the color picker to select a color.
- **Rollover color.** The text color that appears when the pointer is positioned over linked text in a browser; type a hexadecimal color code or use the color picker to select a color.
- **Text.** The text you want in the Flash text movie.
- **Show font.** The option to display the font style in the Text field in the Insert Flash Text dialog box.
- **Link.** A link between the Flash text and another page in the current Web site or in another Web site. Use an absolute link; relative links do not necessarily work with Flash movies and may cause problems with the Flash text feature. To link text to another page in the site, you must use the absolute path (beginning with *http://*) the page will have when it is uploaded to the remote server for the link to work in the remote site. (The absolute path for the link might prevent the link from working when you view the page locally.) You can avoid problems by not creating links to other pages in a site from Flash text.
- **Target.** The target for the linked page: _blank, _parent, _self, or _top.
- **Bg (Background) color.** The color that displays behind the text; type a hexadecimal color code or use the color picker to select a color.

- **Save as.** The option to browse to the save location, name the file, and save the file. When you use the Flash text object to create custom text elements for Web pages, Dreamweaver saves the files as .swf files. Place these files in the folder with your other Flash elements.

Brian thinks that all of the main page headings in the Cosmatic site would look better in the Bauhaus Md BT font (the Cosmatic logo font). Your job is to replace the existing page headings with customized Flash text headings in the Bands page, the Catalogue page, the Contact page, the Label page, and the Tour Dates page.

To add Flash text to the other Cosmatic Web pages:

▶ 1. Open the **bands.html** page in the Document window, select the **COSMATIC BANDS** heading, and then press the **Delete** key. The text is deleted from the page.

▶ 2. On the **Common** tab of the Insert bar, in the **Media** list, click the **Flash Text** button ⬛ . The Insert Flash Text dialog box opens.

▶ 3. Click the **Font** button, and then click **Bauhaus Md BT** or a similar font of your choice.

   Trouble? If you do not have the Bauhaus Md BT font, adjust the font size as needed in Step 4.

▶ 4. Type **55** in the Size box, type **#772300** in the Color box, and then type **COSMATIC BANDS** in the Text box.

▶ 5. Click the **Browse** button next to the Save as box. The Select File dialog box opens.

▶ 6. Navigate to the **Media** folder in the site's local root folder, type **HeadingBands.swf** in the File Name box, and then click the **Save** button. The Select File dialog box closes and Media/HeadingBands.swf appears in the Save as box. See Figure 8-8.

Insert Flash Text dialog box   Figure 8-8

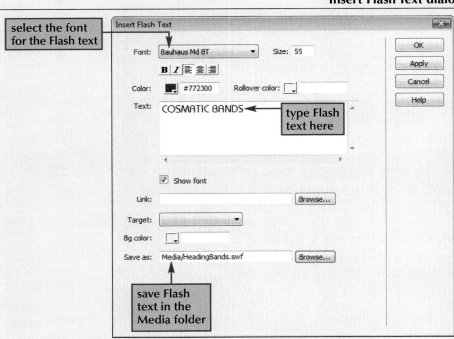

7. Click the **OK** button. The Flash text appears in the Bands page. The text might have some artifacts (be a bit jagged) in the Document window that will not appear in the browser. See Figure 8-9.

Figure 8-9 | **Bands page with the Flash text**

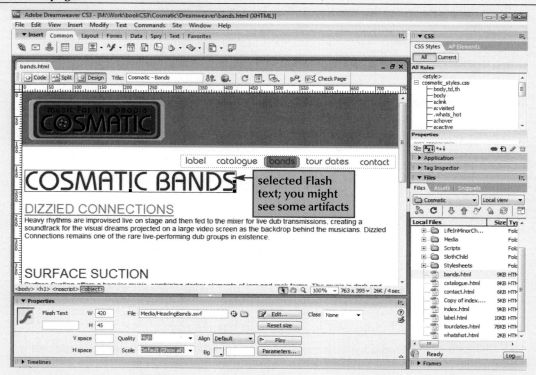

Trouble? If an extra space appears between the new heading text and the Dizzied Connections subheading, you need to delete it. Click in the extra space, and then press the Backspace key.

8. Save the page, and then preview the page in a browser. The text no longer has any artifacts (it is smooth). See Figure 8-10.

Figure 8-10 | **Flash text previewed in a browser**

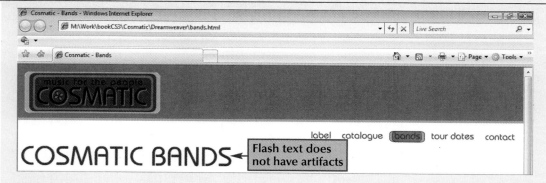

9. Close the browser, and then close the page.

10. Repeat Steps 1 through 9, using the word "Heading" followed by the page name in the filename in Step 6, to add Flash text with the page name in the following pages: **catalogue.html**, **contact.html**, **label.html**, and **tourdates.html**.

Using Flash Buttons

Another way to add motion and excitement to a Web page is to add Flash buttons. Dreamweaver includes a set of predesigned, customizable Flash buttons that you can use in Web pages. First, you select a button style from the Style list the Insert Flash Button dialog box. Then, you can view the various states of the selected button style in the Sample box. Move the pointer over a button in the Sample box to view the Over state, and click the button in the Sample box to view the Down state. After you choose a button style, you can customize the button by typing text for the button, selecting a font and font size, adding a link, specifying a target, and choosing a background color for the button. These customizations do not appear in the Sample box, but they appear in the Document window after you add the button to the page.

There are a few downsides to adding Flash buttons to a Web site. Buttons enable the user to navigate through the site; however, users who do not have the Flash Player will not be able to navigate through the pages of the site. Also, Flash buttons are templates, which means that the same buttons will appear in many sites. If you choose to use a Flash button, your site will look more generic and less like an original, professionally designed site.

Brian asks you to review the available Flash button styles and see whether any are suitable for the Cosmatic site.

To review the Flash button styles:

▶ **1.** Open the **index.html** page in the Document window, and then, on the **Common** tab of the Insert bar, in the **Media** list, click the **Flash Button** button 🔥 . The Insert Flash Button dialog box opens with the first button style selected. See Figure 8-11.

Insert Flash Button dialog box ◀ **Figure 8-11**

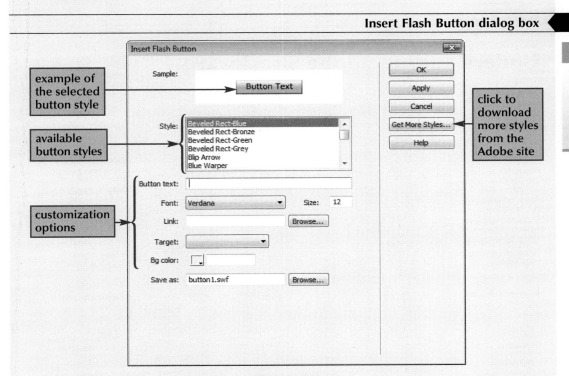

Tip

You can download additional Flash button styles from the Adobe Web site by clicking the Get More Styles button in the Insert Flash Button dialog box.

▶ **2.** In the Style box, click the **Beveled Rect-Bronze** style, and then view the button in the Sample box.

▶ **3.** In the Sample box, move the pointer over the button, and then click the button. The button changes states.

▶ **4.** Review the remaining styles in the Style box.

▶ **5.** Click the **Cancel** button. The dialog box closes without adding a Flash button.

▶ **6.** Close the home page.

None of the button styles are appropriate for the Cosmatic site. To keep the site unique, you won't add any Flash buttons to the text.

So far, you learned about the different media you can add to a Web site. Then, you added a Flash movie and Flash text to the Cosmatic site and reviewed the available Flash buttons. In the next session, you'll add a Shockwave movie and sound to the Cosmatic site.

Review | **Session 8.1 Quick Check**

1. What is media?

2. What will a user need to view media in a browser?

3. What is the file extension for Flash movies that you place in Web pages?

4. True or False? The Flash Player is included with the latest versions of Internet Explorer and Firefox.

5. True or False? You can create Flash text in Dreamweaver only if you have the Flash program installed on your computer.

6. True or False? You can create customizable Flash buttons in Dreamweaver.

Session 8.2

Understanding Adobe Shockwave

Shockwave is the Adobe solution for delivering interactive multimedia on the Web. You use Shockwave for more complex interactive media components, such as games, interactive 3D, database-driven multimedia, multi-user applications, and educational materials.

Unlike Flash files, which are created in the Flash program, Shockwave files are created in Adobe Director. **Director** is a program that is used to create comprehensive multimedia solutions deployable across multiple media, including CD-ROM, DVD, Web, Kiosk, and so on. Most interactive CDs are produced in Director, and many casual Web games are distributed in Shockwave.

Several file extensions are associated with Director, including:

- **.dcr (Shockwave).** A compressed Director file that is viewable in a browser and can be previewed in Dreamweaver. You'll use .dcr files in the Cosmatic site for Shockwave movies.

- **.dir.** The source files used by Director when you are creating movies. These authoring files can be opened in Director. Unlike Flash authoring files, .dir files can be called by Director projectors for playback. (**Director projectors** are standalone executable files that do not need any software or plug-ins to run on the client computer.) Files that are going to be viewed on the Web are usually exported from Director as .dcr files.

- **.dxr.** Director files that are locked for distribution. **Locked files** cannot be opened in the authoring environment. Usually, .dxr files are used with Director projectors to deliver material via CD.

- **.cst.** Cast files that contain additional information used in a .dir or .dxr file.
- **.cxt.** The .cst files that are locked for distribution.

Although Flash and Shockwave files are often used in similar ways, there are some marked differences between them. Because Director movies are prerendered, Shockwave files are less dependent on the processing speed of the user's computer for playback speed than Flash files, which are fully or partially rendered on the client computer. For this same reason, the file size of a Flash movie with vector graphics is usually smaller than the file size of a Director movie with the same content. Shockwave movies tend to process complex coding faster than Flash movies. Shockwave movies can display a wider range of media formats; for example, all Flash video is converted to the .flv video files format, which uses either On2 VP6 or the Sorenson Spark codec, whereas Shockwave can display video in a wide range of native formats. Finally, the Shockwave Player must be installed on the client computer for Shockwave movies to be displayed. Unlike the Flash Player plug-in, the Shockwave Player is generally not distributed with current browsers and must be downloaded separately by end users.

Some positive and negative aspects of using Shockwave are listed in Figure 8-12.

Pros and cons of using Shockwave ◄ **Figure 8-12**

Pros	Cons
Shockwave files are less dependent on the processing speed of the end user's computer for playback speed.	As of September, 2007, only 58.5% of users have the Shockwave Player plug-in (Shockwave has a 59% browser penetration).
Shockwave movies tend to process complex code faster than Flash movies.	The Shockwave Player plug-in is not included with the latest versions of Internet Explorer and Firefox; it must be downloaded by the end user.
Shockwave movies can display a wide range of media formats.	Shockwave file size may be larger than Flash files because the files are prerendered.
Shockwave movies look the same across browsers and across platforms.	
You can use any fonts within a Shockwave movie because Shockwave is not dependent on the fonts on the client computer.	

You can find additional information and statistics about Shockwave on the Adobe site at *www.adobe.com/products/shockwaveplayer*. The Adobe site also provides a Flash and Director comparison and a Shockwave/Flash movie comparison at *www.adobe.com/products/director/resources/integration*.

Brian asks you to research the integration of Shockwave elements in the Cosmatic site. You will go to the Adobe site and review the current Shockwave information and statistics. Then you will review the Shockwave/Flash movie comparisons.

To research current Shockwave information and statistics:

▶ **1.** Start your browser, type **www.adobe.com/products/shockwaveplayer** in the Address bar, and then press the **Enter** key. The Adobe Shockwave Player home page opens in the browser window. See Figure 8-13.

Figure 8-13 | **Adobe Shockwave Player home page**

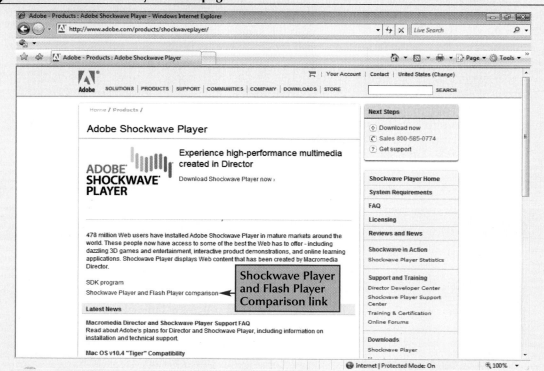

Trouble? If the Adobe Shockwave Player home page does not open, type **www.adobe.com** in the Address bar, press the Enter key to open the Adobe home page, type **Shockwave Player** into the Search for box, press the Enter key, select Products: Adobe Shockwave Player from the list of links, and then continue with Step 2.

▶ **2.** Click the **Shockwave Player and Flash Player comparison** link. The Flash and Director Resource Center page opens.

▶ **3.** Click the **Quick Comparison Chart** link in the Flash and Director Comparison list, read the information, and then click the **Back** button ⬅ on the browser toolbar to return to the list of links.

▶ **4.** Repeat Step 3 for all the links in the list.

▶ **5.** Click the **Shockwave Player Statistics** link located on the right side of the page, read the adoption statistics, and then click the **Version Penetration** link to view browser penetration statistics. See Figure 8-14.

Shockwave Player version penetration | **Figure 8-14**

Trouble? If the data you see differs from Figure 8-14, Adobe has updated the data since this tutorial was published. Continue with Step 6.

6. Click the **Penetration** link to view the technology breakdown statistics for the various multimedia plug-ins. See Figure 8-15.

Shockwave Player adoption statistics | **Figure 8-15**

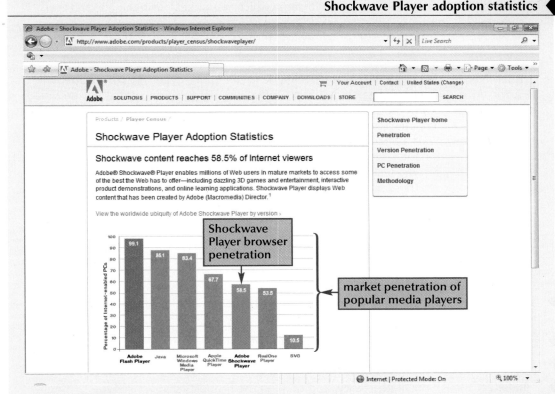

Trouble? If the data you see differs from Figure 8-15, Adobe has updated the data since this tutorial was published. Continue with Step 7.

7. Close the browser.

Adding Shockwave Movies to Web Pages

Adding a Shockwave movie to a Web page is very similar to adding a Flash movie to a Web page. When you insert a movie, Dreamweaver places the code for the movie into the page. When you add a Shockwave movie that is located outside of the site's local root folder to a page, Dreamweaver prompts you to include a copy of the file in the local root folder. You should place a copy of the file in the Media folder in the local root folder for your site so that all the materials for the site are located in one place.

After the Shockwave movie has been added to a page, a small gray rectangle with the Shockwave logo appears in the page. The gray rectangle is 32 x 32 pixels, regardless of the size at which the Shockwave movie was created. (This occurs because a bug in the Shockwave button prevents the program from seeing the correct dimensions of the movie.) You must enter the correct width and height for the movie in the Property inspector to see the movie in a browser or to play the movie from within Dreamweaver. In addition, the Play button in the Property inspector might not start the movie; you might need to preview the page in a browser to see the movie. If you don't see the movie, you might need to install the Shockwave Player.

Reference Window | **Adding a Shockwave Movie to a Web Page**

- In the Document window, click in the AP div where you want to add the Shockwave movie.
- On the Common tab of the Insert bar, in the Media list, click the Shockwave button.
- Navigate to the Shockwave movie file, and then double-click the file.
- Click the Yes button, navigate to the folder in which you want to save the file, and then click the Save button.
- In the Property inspector, adjust Shockwave movie attributes as needed.

Brian has decided to add an interactive game to the Bands page. The new game will be a Shockwave movie. The game is still in production, but the game group has provided an animated promo for the game in the Shockwave format. Although the preview is animation without interactivity and could be delivered as a Flash movie, the team wants to deliver the preview as a Shockwave movie to test for problems that might arise. It is a good idea to use the intended final technology when making placeholder objects because you can test the technology in advance. You will add the Shockwave movie game placeholder to the Bands page.

Before you can add the Shockwave movie to the page, you need to create two new AP div tabs in the page and add the page content to the AP divs. You will use the AP divs to position the text around the Shockwave movie.

To add AP divs in the Bands page:

▶ **1.** If you took a break after the previous session, make sure that the Cosmatic site is open.

▶ **2.** Open the **bands.html** page in the Document window.

▶ **3.** Draw an AP div in the blank area to the right of the page heading.

▶ **4.** Select the AP div, if necessary, and then, in the Property inspector, type **DizziedConnections** in the CSS-P Element ID box. The AP div is renamed.

5. Select the **Dizzied Connections** paragraphs, including the heading and text, drag the text into the DizziedConnections AP div, and then press the **Right Arrow** key to deselect the text. See Figure 8-16.

DizziedConnections AP div selected in the Bands page ◀ Figure 8-16

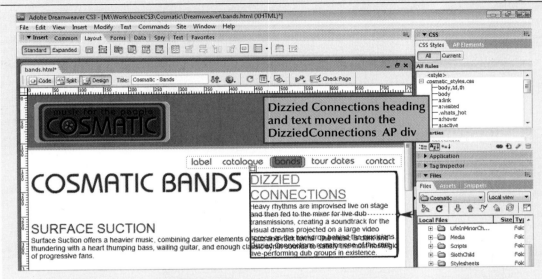

6. Draw an AP div over the page heading, rename the AP div as **RemainingText**, and then drag the remaining text (do not include the page heading, navigation bar, logo, or footer) into the RemainingText AP div.

7. Show the rulers and change the measurement to pixels, if necessary, and then drag a horizontal guide to the **500 pixel** mark and drag a vertical guide to the **5 pixel** mark.

8. Select the **RemainingText** AP div, and then position its upper-left corner where the two guides intersect.

   Trouble? If the RemainingText AP div overlaps the footer (the copyright notice), you need to fix the footer placement. You'll do this after you work with the DizziedConnections AP div.

9. Drag the horizontal guide **25 pixels** below the page heading, select the **DizziedConnections** AP div, position its upper-left corner where the two guides intersect, and then resize the AP div to the same width as the page heading and the same height as the text it contains. See Figure 8-17.

Figure 8-17 ▸ DizziedConnections AP div repositioned in the Bands page

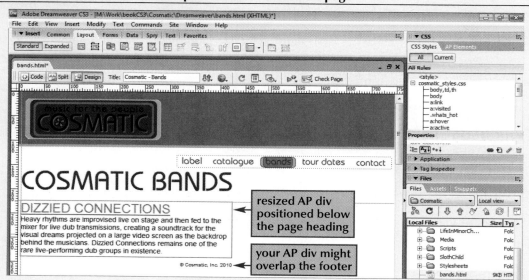

Trouble? If the footer is behind the text in the DizziedConnections AP div, you need to reposition the footer. Click in the page below the page heading, and then press the Enter key until the footer appears below the DizziedConnections AP div.

▸ 10. Select the **RemainingText** AP div, move it **25 pixels** below the DizziedConnections AP div, and then align the RemainingText AP div to the vertical guide.

▸ 11. Select the **RemainingText** AP div, and then drag its right border until it is aligned with the end of the last word in the navigation bar. See Figure 8-18.

Figure 8-18 ▸ RemainingText AP div positioned in the Bands page

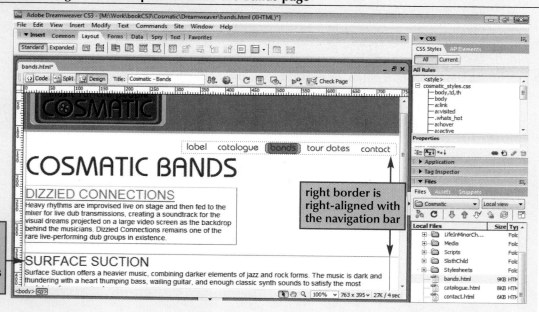

Trouble? If the footer is behind the text in the RemainingText AP div, you need to reposition the footer. Click in the page below the page heading, and then press the Enter key until the footer appears below the RemainingText AP div.

You will add a new AP div next to the page heading, and then insert the Shockwave movie into it.

To insert the Shockwave movie into a new AP div:

▶ 1. In the Document window, draw a small AP div in the blank area to the right of the page heading, and then, in the Property inspector, rename the AP div as **GamePromo**. The AP div appears in the Bands page.

▶ 2. Use guides to help you position the GamePromo AP div **5 pixels** below the navigation bar and **20 pixels** from the right edge of the page heading.

▶ 3. Click in the **GamePromo** AP div, and then, on the **Common** tab of the Insert bar, in the **Media** list, click the **Shockwave** button ▥ . The Select File dialog box opens.

▶ 4. Double-click the **GamePromo.dcr** file located in the **Tutorial.08\Tutorial** folder included with your Data Files, click the **Yes** button in the message dialog box, and then place a copy of the file in the **Media** folder. The GamePromo.dcr Shockwave movie is inserted into the AP div, and a small gray rectangle with the Shockwave logo in the center appears in the GamePromo AP div. See Figure 8-19.

Tip

You can also click Insert on the menu bar, point to Media, and then click Shockwave to insert a Shockwave movie.

Shockwave movie added to the Bands page ◀ **Figure 8-19**

Trouble? If the size of your GamePromo AP div differs from the one shown in Figure 8-19, continue with the tutorial. You will adjust its size in the next set of steps.

Adjusting Attributes of a Shockwave Movie

Shockwave movies have some of the same attributes as Flash movies. You can adjust the attributes in the Property inspector when the Shockwave movie is selected. Shockwave attributes include: Name, W, H, File, Play, Parameters, V Space, H Space, Align, and Bg. For descriptions of these attributes, refer to the "Adjusting Attributes of a Flash Movie" section.

The Shockwave movie embedded in the Bands page is not at the proper size and will not play. You'll change the width and height of the Shockwave movie to its original creation size so that it will display properly in the browser.

To adjust the attributes of the GamePromo.dcr Shockwave movie:

▶ **1.** In the Document window, select the Shockwave movie, if necessary.

▶ **2.** In the Property inspector, type **240** in the W box, type **240** in the H box, and then press the **Enter** key. The gray square increases in size.

▶ **3.** Move the GamePromo AP div so that its right border is aligned with the right border of the RemainingText AP div. See Figure 8-20.

Figure 8-20 ▶ **Edited Shockwave movie**

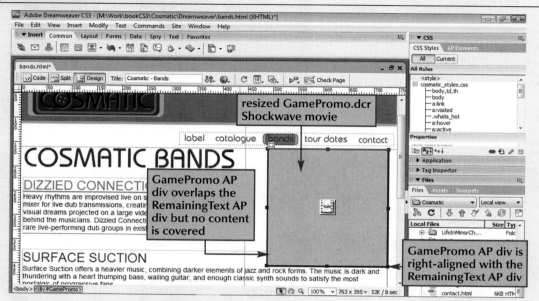

Trouble? If the Shockwave movie obscures any of the text in the other AP divs, you need to reposition those AP divs. Move those AP divs down until all of the text is visible.

▶ **4.** Save the Bands page, and then preview the page in a browser. See Figure 8-21.

Bands page with the Shockwave movie previewed in a browser   Figure 8-21

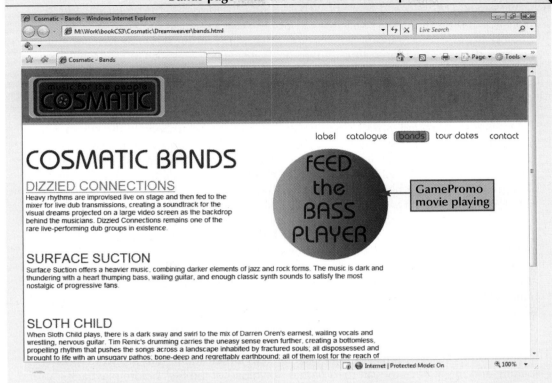

Trouble? If a dialog box opens or an icon appears, prompting you to install the latest version of the Shockwave Player, click the Yes button to install the player. You cannot view the Shockwave movie without the latest version of the player. You might need to close the browser while installing the Shockwave Player, and then preview the page in the browser.

Trouble? If the movie displays poorly (the words are split between lines and so forth), you are probably viewing the Shockwave movie in the wrong font. You are probably logged in to your computer as a restricted user and do not have access to some system folders that are necessary to view the movie in the correct font. This is a potential drawback of using media elements in a Web site. Continue with Step 5.

▶ 5. Close the browser, and then close the Bands page.

Understanding Sound

As you create more advanced Web sites, you might want to include sound on some pages. Some common uses of sound on the Web are music, narration, and sounds paired with user actions, such as sound that plays when the pointer is positioned over a button or other element.

Sound can add richness and depth to Web sites when used wisely. The sound you add to a site should reinforce the site goals and enhance the user's experience. When deciding whether to add sound to a site, first consider whether the target audience even has sound playback hardware and capabilities. If they do, think about issues such as user connection speed and computer speed. You must also determine whether sound is appropriate to the site goals and whether it will truly add value to the site for the end users.

Designers add sound to a site in two ways. Sound can be embedded directly in a page, or sound can be included as a link. With most sound formats, sound streams to the end user's computer. **Streaming** means that sound can begin to play after only a small portion downloads and will continue to play while the rest of the file is downloading. Streaming is especially helpful to users with slow connections because they can begin to hear the sound without waiting for large files to download completely.

When sound is embedded directly in a page, the sound files begin to download to the client computer as soon as the page is loaded. Embedded sound files can either start automatically or be set up to start when the user clicks a start button. Either way, the embedded file begins to download as soon as the page loads, allowing relatively quick automatic playback or preloading so that it starts as soon as the user clicks the start button. However, beginning to download many files that a user might not even play wastes the user's time and consumes unnecessary bandwidth.

Many music sites, which often include a lot of sound files, use links to the sound files. When a page is linked to sound files, the file does not download to the client computer until the user clicks the link. The user then decides which sound files are worth down-loading and might have to wait for a partial download of the files before playback begins. However, the wait time after making a choice can become frustrating, especially on slower connections.

Sound files are created or recorded with programs outside of Dreamweaver, such as SoundForge, Audacity, or ProTools. You can add sound files to Web pages and, in some cases, preview them within Dreamweaver.

Many formats can be used to store and play sound on a computer. Sound files can be fairly large and, like graphics, must be compressed to be delivered over the Web. Remember that compression is the process of eliminating redundant and less important details from a file in order to shrink its size. The different types of compression used for sound are often called **sound formats**. Each sound format uses a different CODEC as the sound is compressed for delivery and decompressed for playback. **CODEC**, short for COmpressor/DECompressor, is the software that converts sound to digital code, shrinks the code to the smallest possible size for faster transmission, and later expands the code for playback on the client computer. Several popular CODECs are used for sound on the Web, including MP3, RealMedia, QuickTime, and Windows Media. In the past, each format was better for some types of sound and worse for others. Today, all the formats provide high-quality sound for nearly any application.

For a client computer to play sound, most sound formats require the end user to download some type of plug-in or player. Plug-ins and players are additional software that interpret the sound format and convert the code back to sound. When a user installs plug-in or player software, it often includes both browser integration (sound that plays from within the browser) as well as a standalone player with its own interface and controls. Most users have several players installed on their systems, and most players work with a wide range of sound formats. For example, the QuickTime Player will work with QuickTime formats as well as with RealMedia and Windows Media formats.

With care, you can make sure that sound will work for the majority of the target audience. However, making sound work the same on all end users' systems is complex and sometimes impossible. The inability to control a user's experience with sound is one of the challenges to adding sound to a Web page. The difficulties depend on the user's installed players and hardware configuration. For example, a single user might have the RealMedia, QuickTime, and Windows Media players installed on his or her system. When the user visits a site that includes a RealMedia Audio clip, any of the installed players might handle the sound. And, depending on configuration, the sound might just play or a separate player window with sound controls (and ads) might pop up, which is often not desirable. Also, depending on configuration, the sound can either start automatically or require the user to click the Play button on the launched player. Another user who has the same players installed might have a different player respond to the RealMedia Audio clip, leading to a completely different experience.

One way to alleviate this confusion and to ensure the same sound experience for all site visitors is to use the Flash format to add sound to Web pages. Many professional sites further ease the potential problems by including a choice between two or more sound formats containing the exact same content. This gives the user more control and increases the potential for trouble-free sound playback.

Embedding a Flash Movie That Contains Sound

Although Flash is more often used to add animation to Web sites, it is also a very consistent and reliable method for adding sound to Web pages. Because the Flash Player is widely installed and does not open a separate application to play sound, Flash will deliver sound without disrupting the aesthetic of Web pages. When you use Flash to add sound to a page, you are simply adding a Flash movie that contains sound with or without images. The process for adding the Flash movie to a page is the same whether the Flash movie contains sound and images or only sound. A Flash movie that contains only sound is generally created at a size of 1 x 1 pixel and with the same background color as the page.

The two types of sound-inclusive Flash movies are those that prevent automatic play and those that play automatically when the page loads. (When creating a Flash movie, a stop action added to the first frame prevents automatic play, whereas omitting this action allows automatic play.) Flash movies that play automatically are used to add background sound to pages. For example, a Web page that loads music when the home page loads in the browser might use a Flash movie that includes only sounds and plays automatically. Flash movies that do not play automatically are often used to provide sounds that the user can activate with the click of a button. You can include the button that starts the audio contained in the Flash movie. For example, when you include multiple Flash movies that contain audio in a page, you can create a Play button in each movie that the user can click to play the audio in that particular movie.

Reference Window | **Adding a Flash Movie with Sound to a Web Page**

- In the Document window, click in the AP div or in the page where you want to add the Flash movie.
- On the Common tab of the Insert bar, in the Media list, click the Flash button.
- Navigate to the Flash movie file, and then double-click the file.
- Click the Yes button, navigate to the folder in which you want to save the file, and then click the Save button.
- In the Property inspector, adjust Flash movie attributes as needed.

Sara wants to add audio files for some of the songs in the Catalogue page. You will add a Flash movie with sound to the page that does not play automatically. The movie will contain a button that users click to start the audio.

To add a Flash movie with sound to the Catalogue page:

1. Open the **catalogue.html** page in the Document window. You'll add the Flash movie in the Sloth Child song list.

2. In the Sloth Child song list, click to the right of the song title "Sunshine," and then press the **Spacebar**.

3. On the **Common** tab of the Insert bar, in the **Media** list, click the **Flash** button. The Select File dialog box opens.

4. Double-click the **sunshine.swf** movie located in the **Tutorial.08\Tutorial** folder included with your Data Files, click the **Yes** button, and then place a copy of the Flash movie in the **Media** folder. A small Flash placeholder image appears beside the "Sunshine" song title. See Figure 8-22.

Figure 8-22 ▶ **Flash movie with sound in the Catalogue page**

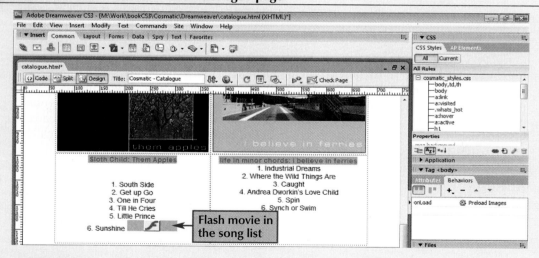

5. In the Document window, click the Flash movie to select it.

6. In the Property inspector, click the **Align** button, and then click **Absolute Middle**.

7. Save the Catalogue page, and then preview the page in a browser.

8. Click the **Flash sound** button to play the audio in the Flash movie. See Figure 8-23.

Tip

You can also right-click the selected Flash movie, point to Align, and then click the alignment you want.

Flash movie with sound in the Catalogue page previewed in a browser ◄ Figure 8-23

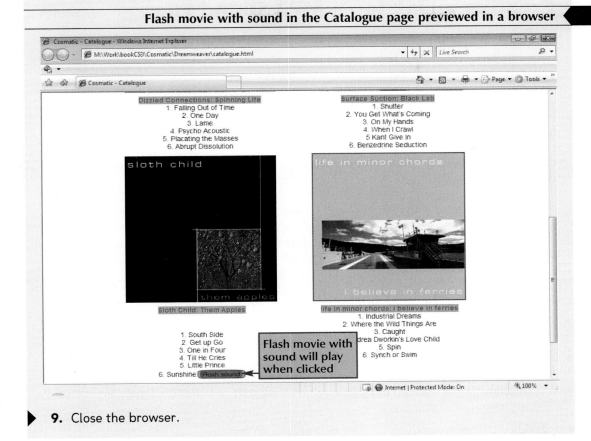

▶ **9.** Close the browser.

Adjusting Attributes of a Flash Movie

After you have added a Flash movie to a Web page, you might need to set some of its attributes in the Property inspector. Most of the settings affect only visual aspects of the Flash movie and don't apply to Flash movies that include only sound. Only the Loop and Autoplay attributes affect the sound of a Flash movie. When using a movie that is designed to prevent automatic play, checking the Loop and Autoplay check boxes have no effect, but they function as usual with a movie that is designed to allow automatic play when the page loads.

You do not need to set any attributes for the Sunshine Flash movie you added to the Catalogue page.

Embedding Other Sound Formats

Embedding other types of sound files (MP3, RealMedia, and so on) is a bit more difficult than embedding a Flash movie because Dreamweaver does not have a custom control for embedding the other types of files. You can use the generic Plugin button in the Media list on the Common tab of the Insert bar, but you must type many parameters to make the sound work, or you must download an extension from the Adobe Exchange. After you have downloaded an extension, embedding other types of sound files follows the same basic process as embedding a Flash movie.

Creating a Link to an MP3 Sound File

MP3 is a common sound format that can contain very high-quality sound with a surprisingly small file size. This is perfect for sending sound over the Web, especially when the end user has a slow connection. It is such a popular format that most computers come preconfigured with a player that will play MP3 files, avoiding the need to download additional software. MP3 files are a good choice when you want to link to a sound file instead of embedding the file in a page because the sound will very likely play as expected even though many different players might handle MP3 on an end user's computer. Using a link, instead of embedding, ensures that whatever player handles MP3 does not display its own sound control interface in the Web page, potentially interfering with the page's design.

Brian wants to provide users with a choice of sound formats. You have already added sound to the page by embedding a Flash movie in the page. Now you will create a link to an MP3 file that contains the same sound content as the Flash file. When the user clicks the link, the sound file will begin to download and will be played back by whatever player is configured to handle MP3s on the end user's computer.

To link to an MP3 sound file to the Catalogue page:

▶ **1.** In the Catalogue page, click to the right of the Flash placeholder image, and then press the **Shift+Enter** keys. The insertion point moves to the next line.

▶ **2.** On the **Common** tab of the Insert bar, in the **Images** list, click the **Image** button 🖼 , and then double-click the **MP3SoundButton.gif** file located in the **Tutorial.08\Tutorial** folder included with your Data Files. The MP3SoundButton image is inserted into the page.

> **Tip**
>
> You can also insert a non-breaking space by clicking the Text tab on the Insert bar, and then, in the Characters list, clicking the Non-breaking Space button.

▶ **3.** Click to the left of the MP3SoundButton image, and then press the **Ctrl+Shift+Spacebar** keys to add nonbreaking spaces until the image is aligned with the Flash placeholder image above it.

▶ **4.** In the Document window, select the **MP3SoundButton** image, and then, in the Property inspector, next to the Link box, click the **Browse for File** button 📁 . The Select File dialog box opens.

▶ **5.** Double-click the **sunshine.mp3** file located in the **Tutorial.08\Tutorial** folder included with your Data Files, click the **Yes** button, and then place a copy of the sunshine.mp3 file in the **Media** folder in the site's local root folder. See Figure 8-24.

MP3 sound button added to the Catalogue page | **Figure 8-24**

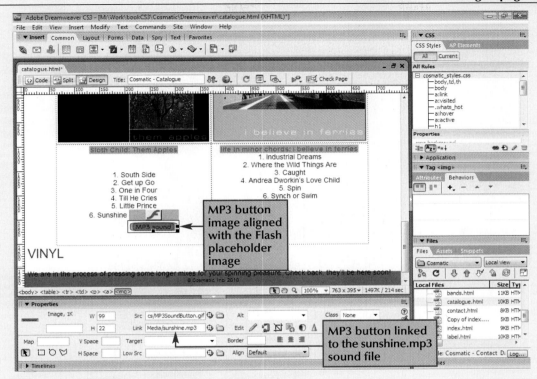

6. In the Document window, select the **MP3SoundButton** image, and then, in the Property inspector, type **0** in the Border box and press the **Enter** key. The colored border no longer appears around the button.

7. Save the Catalogue page, and then preview the page in a browser.

8. Click the **MP3 sound** button. Sound will play and, depending on which player is playing the sound, a number of things could happen: a player could appear in the browser, a player could appear outside the browser, or the sound might simply begin to play without any player opening. See Figure 8-25.

Figure 8-25 ▶ **Windows Media Player**

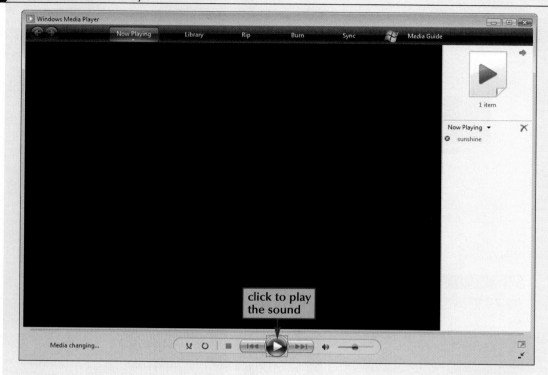

Trouble? If no sound plays and a player opens, you probably need to click the Play button in the player to start the sound. If that doesn't start the sound, you might need to view the page over the Web to hear the sound; sometimes MP3 files do not play locally.

Trouble? If a Media Bar Settings dialog box opens, asking whether Internet Explorer should play this link in its own window so it will be easier to see and hear, you need to determine where you want the player to appear. Click the Yes button to open a side panel with the player in your browser, or click the No button to have the player open in its own window.

Trouble? If a dialog box opens, prompting you to update your media player, a newer version might be available. Click the Yes button to update your media player, or click the No button if you do not want to update the player.

▶ 9. Close the browser, close the player and panel if necessary, and then close the Catalogue page.

Creating Links to Other Sound Files

You can create a link to any of the other commonly used sound file formats, including MP3, RealMedia, QuickTime, and Windows Media. (Generally, it is not a good idea to link directly to Flash movies with only sound; instead, embed these Flash movies in a page so that they play reliably.) You link to the other types of sound files in the same way that you link to an MP3 file. Simply add a button to the page, create a link to the sound file, and include a copy of the sound file in the Media folder in the site's local root folder. One file format will basically work as well as another, and the CODECs needed to play each format are included in all the popular media players.

In this session, you added a Shockwave movie to the Cosmatic site, and you embedded and linked sound files. In the next session, you will add video to the site.

1. What program is used to create Shockwave movies?
2. What is the Shockwave file extension?
3. Define the term *streaming*.
4. What are two ways to include sound in a page?
5. List four popular sound formats.
6. What sound format should you not link directly to?

Session 8.3

Understanding Digital Video

Video files, like sound files, must be compressed to make them small enough to deliver over the Web. Several major factors affect the file size of a digital video clip, including frame size, playback quality, and sound parameters. Some common video frame sizes used on the Web are 320 x 240 pixels and 240 x 180 pixels—the smaller frame size creates a smaller video file. Playback quality for digital video is often adjusted to match the target connection speed and is usually measured in the amount of data that needs to be downloaded per second. For example, 31 kb/s (kilobits per second) might be used with a video clip intended for standard modems, whereas 400 kb/s might be used to provide higher-quality video to users with high-speed connections. Video quality affects the amount of detail and motion in the video image. Higher-quality video contains cleaner, more detailed images and smoother movement than lower-quality video. Sound parameters in digital video include the choice of stereo or mono and the resolution or clarity of the sound. Stereo and high resolution occupy more file space than mono and lower resolution.

To ensure continuous playback of a video clip, it must be **buffered**, which means that the first 5 or 10 seconds of the clip are downloaded before it begins to play. After the clip begins to play, as long as the current download is at or past the current clip playback location, the playback will continue without interruption. A user who has a fast, consistent connection is more likely to be able to download enough of the clip each second to view a continuous playback. If the download does not keep up with the playback (that is, if the next piece of needed file hasn't completed downloading yet), then the video playback will be interrupted. The user may see any of a number of things: the video might stop until the download catches up, the video might become jittery and chunks of it may not play, and sometimes a warning appears telling the user that the download is being interrupted. Any of these things can be annoying and cause the user to leave the page without viewing the entire video clip.

Web sites that include digital video use several solutions to minimize playback interruptions and maximize the end user's viewing experience. These solutions include multiple clip options, multiple formats, and specialized video servers. By offering the same digital video clip in multiple file sizes, a site can satisfy a wide range of visitors. Sites taking this approach often offer each clip in low, medium, and high resolutions. They sometimes instead offer dial-up and broadband sizes, which means that they have used the compression parameters discussed earlier to offer the same clip in lower-quality/ smaller-frame size for user with slower dial-up connections and in higher-quality/larger-frame size for users with faster broadband connections. Some sites also offer different format options, because some users prefer the QuickTime format and player, whereas others might choose RealMedia, Flash video, or Windows Media. In addition, bigger-budget Web sites might use a specialized video server to monitor a user's connection and adjust the video quality to compensate for slowdowns, increasing the likelihood that the user can view the video clip without interruption. Another benefit provided by a video server is the ability to allow thousands of users to view the same clip simultaneously, which is impossible when including video on a standard Web server.

Video files are created or recorded with programs outside of Dreamweaver, such as Avid, Apple Final Cut, and Adobe Premiere, but can be added to Web pages in Dreamweaver.

| InSight | **Choosing When to Include Video in a Site** |

Video can add excitement to a Web page and greatly enhance the experience of site visitors. However, even with compression, video files are relatively large and may be slow to download, especially for users who have dial-up connections. Because video includes moving images and often sound, it requires more focused attention from site visitors. This can be both good and bad. The positive aspect is that video can really reinforce what you are trying to say. Users tend to pay attention, so it is a good way to drive home an important message. The negative aspect is that it is easy to overload users with too much motion in the page. When users are barraged with too much motion or too many messages, the video becomes a distraction and can detract from the effectiveness of the Web site rather than reinforce it. The steeper user requirements (more time to download and more focused attention from the user) associated with video mean that video should be included in a site only when it is truly appropriate for the site goals and the target audience.

When deciding whether to use video in a site, keep in mind that when site visitors must wait for something large to download, their expectations are raised. Or, put another way, site visitors wait for downloads only when they perceive that the content is something worth waiting for.

Reviewing Video File Formats

Digital video can have many different formats. Most of the popular sound formats can also be used for video, including RealMedia, QuickTime, Flash, and Windows Media. As with audio formats, earlier versions of these video formats were preferred for different uses. Although differences still exist, all of these formats provide excellent video performance with a wide range of materials. Today, Web sites that include video often offer the user a choice of formats.

On the Web, these formats are identified by their file extensions. Some of the most common extensions are:

- **.mov.** A QuickTime movie that can contain sound, video, and animation tracks. QuickTime is a very popular cross-platform format from Apple used for both Web and CD-ROM video.
- **.rm.** A RealMedia movie, which is another popular format for Web and intranet streaming video.
- **.smil.** A Synchronized Multimedia Integration Language (SMIL) file used with RealMedia to create time-based multimedia presentations that can include audio, video, graphics, animation, and text.
- **.wmv.** A Windows Media File, which is a format for Web- and CD-based digital video made popular by Microsoft.
- **.avi.** An earlier Microsoft format designation that has largely been replaced by the Windows Media format (.wmv).

- **.mpg.** A format created by the Motion Picture Experts Group that is generally used for CDs, DVDs, and multimedia pieces rather than for Web distribution.
- **.flv.** The Flash video format.

Most of the popular players play back both sound and video. The makers of the RealMedia, QuickTime, and Window Media formats each provide a free player that can be downloaded. And, as with sound, the players include both standalone player functionality as well as browser integration, which allows the browser to play video embedded directly in a Web page. Flash video is played in the latest version of Flash Player, which is included with recent versions of popular browsers. Users who have older browsers can also download the most recent version of Flash Player.

Adding Flash Video to a Web Page

The process for adding Flash video to a Web site is similar to the process for adding other Flash elements to the site. When you add a Flash video clip to your site, you set some attributes that are only applicable to video. Some of these parameters can be set from the Property inspector or the Insert Flash Video dialog box; others, however, can be set only in the Insert Flash Video dialog box when you insert the video clip into the page. Flash video parameters include:

- **Video type.** The two video type options are Progressive Download Video and Streaming Video. Unless you have a streaming video server, you will always select Progressive Download Video.
- **URL.** The path to the video clip, which you set by clicking the Browse button and navigating to the clip you will insert in the page.
- **Skin.** A predefined look that you select for the control bar, which enables users to play, stop, pause, mute, and control the video volume, and is included with the video file when you insert the Flash video in a page. A sample of the skin you select appears below the Skin box. Some skins require that the video clip be a certain minimum width to accommodate the width of the control bar. The minimum width requirements are listed at the right of the selection.
- **Width and Height.** The dimensions of the video clip. You can specify the video clip's width and height or you can click the Detect Size button to have Dreamweaver find the width and height.
- **Auto play.** The option to start playing the video clip automatically when the page is loaded into a browser.
- **Auto rewind.** The option to rewind the video clip to the first frame automatically after it has played.
- **Prompt users to download Flash Player if necessary.** The option to add code to the page that checks whether the user's browser has the correct version of the Flash Player installed. If the user does not have the correct version of the player, an alert dialog box opens and provides the user with the option to download the correct version of the Flash Player.
- **Message.** A custom message you enter that is seen by users who do not have the correct version of the Flash Player installed in their browser. (Some browsers do not allow this message to be displayed and display the default message.)

Tip

In Dreamweaver on a Macintosh, you must use an absolute path if the Flash video file is in a directory two or more levels up from the page in which you are inserting it.

Reference Window | **Adding a Flash Video Clip to a Web Page**

- In the Document window, click in the page where you want to add the video.
- On the Common tab of the Insert bar, in the Media list, click the Flash Video button.
- Navigate to the video file, and then double-click the file.
- Click the Yes button, navigate to the folder in which you want to save the file, and then click the Save button.
- Adjust the video clip attributes as needed.

You will add a Flash video clip with a promo for the upcoming Sloth Child video below the SlothChild AP div in the home page. The video contains audio. The movie does not loop, so it will play only once in the browser.

To add the promotional Flash video clip to the home page:

▶ 1. If you took a break after the previous session, make sure that the Cosmatic site is open.

▶ 2. Open the **index.html** page in the Document window, and then draw a small AP div that is left-aligned and 15 pixels below the SlothChild AP div.

▶ 3. Select the new AP div, and then, in the Property inspector, type **Video** in the CSS-P Element ID box to rename it.

Tip

You can also insert a Flash video clip by clicking Insert on the menu bar, pointing to Media, and then clicking Flash Video.

▶ 4. Click in the **Video** AP div, and then, on the **Common** tab of the Insert bar, in the **Media** list, click the **Flash Video** button 🎞. The Insert Flash Video dialog box opens.

▶ 5. If necessary, click the **Video type** button, and then click **Progressive Download Video**.

▶ 6. Click the URL **Browse** button, double-click the **sunshinevideo.flv** file located in the **Tutorial.08\Tutorial** folder included with your Data Files, click the **Yes** button, and then place a copy of the file in the **Media** folder in the site's local root folder.

▶ 7. If necessary, click the **Skin** button, and then click **Clear Skin 1**. The preview of the skin appears below the Skin box.

▶ 8. Click the **Detect Size** button. Dreamweaver determines the video's width and height (320 x 240) and enters the values in the Width and Height boxes.

▶ 9. Click the **Auto play** check box to insert a check mark, and then click the **Prompt users to download Flash Player if necessary** check box, if necessary, to insert a check mark. See Figure 8-26.

Insert Flash Video dialog box ◀ **Figure 8-26**

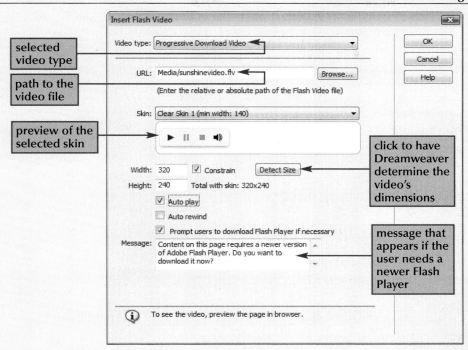

10. Click the **OK** button. A gray rectangle with the Flash video logo appears in the Video AP div in the home page. See Figure 8-27.

Flash video in the home page ◀ **Figure 8-27**

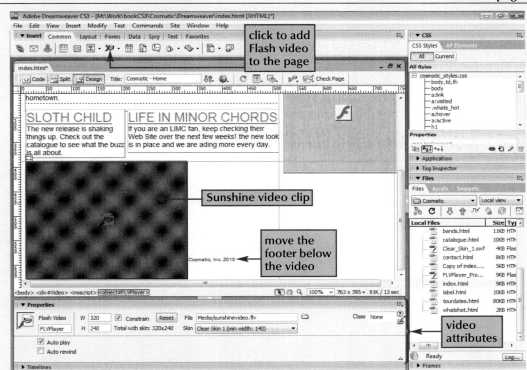

▶ **11.** Click in the page, and then press the **Enter** key until the footer is below the video clip.

▶ **12.** Save the home page, and then preview the page in a browser. See Figure 8-28.

| Figure 8-28 | Home page with the video clip previewed in a browser |

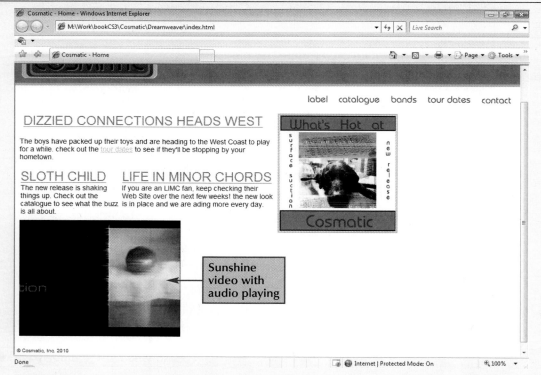

Trouble? If a dialog box opens, prompting you to download a newer version of Flash Player, click the Yes button and update the Flash Player to its most current version.

▶ **13.** Close the browser.

Reviewing the Files and Code Added with Flash Video Clips

When you add a Flash video clip to a page using the Insert Flash Video button, two additional files are added to the site's local root folder. In the Files panel, a Flash file with the name of the skin you selected (Clear_Skin_1.swf) was added to the local root folder of your site. This file contains the information for the look you selected for the control bar that was inserted in the Flash video. The second file inserted into the site's local root folder is the FLVPlayer_Progressive.swf file, which enables the page to play the Flash video file.

You'll review these files now.

To review the files inserted with the Flash video:

▶ **1.** If necessary, expand the **Files** panel, and collapse any other open panels.

▶ **2.** Locate the two files that were added to the local root folder. See Figure 8-29.

Files added to the local root folder with the Flash video **Figure 8-29**

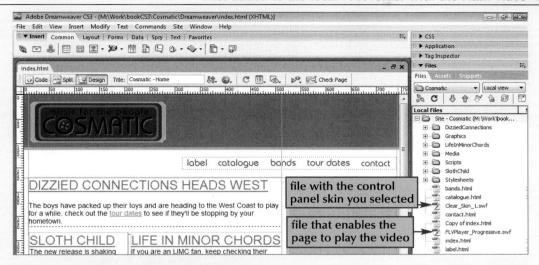

Trouble? If you don't see the new files in the Files panel, click the Refresh button on the Files panel toolbar to update the file list.

In addition to the files, Dreamweaver adds some extra code to the page when a Flash video file is inserted into the page using the Flash Video button. If you check the Prompt users to download Flash Player if necessary check box, code is inserted into the head of the page that detects the version of Flash Player and determines if it is the correct version of Flash Player. The CheckFlashVersion behavior is also added to the page. You can view the behavior in the Behaviors panel when you select the <body> tag.

You'll examine the behavior and code that was inserted in the home page when you inserted the sunshinevideo.flv file.

To examine the behavior and code inserted with the Flash video:

▶ **1.** Expand the **Tag Inspector panel group**, and then click the **Behaviors** tab to open the Behaviors panel.

▶ **2.** Click the **<body>** tag in the status bar. Two onLoad behaviors appear in the Behaviors panel—Preload Images and MM_CheckFlashVersion. See Figure 8-30.

Figure 8-30	Behaviors attached to the <body> tag

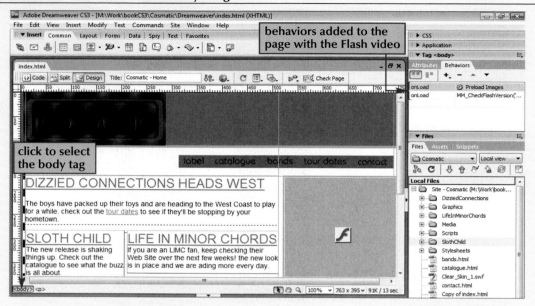

▶ **3.** Click the **Code** button on the Document toolbar, and then collapse the Property inspector. You can now see more of the code at one time.

▶ **4.** Scroll to view the code for the head of the page, and then select the **function MM_CheckFlashVersion** code (from the name to the last closing bracket). You would delete this code from the page if you were to remove the Flash movie. See Figure 8-31.

Figure 8-31	Home page in Code view

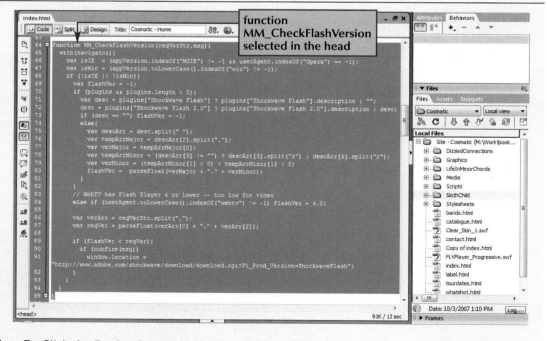

▶ **5.** Click the **Design** button on the Document toolbar. The page returns to Design view.

Deleting Flash Video

If you no longer want a Flash video in a Web page, you can select and delete the video from the AP div. However, deleting the Flash video does not delete the extra code or the behavior that was added when you inserted the Flash video. If you do not manually delete the behavior from the page, the page will continue to check the user's browser for Flash Player and prompt the user to download the correct version, if necessary. To delete the behavior from the page, select the <body> tag in the status bar, select the MM_CheckFlashVersion behavior in the Behaviors panel, and then press the Delete key. It is also a good idea to delete the extra code that was inserted in the head of the page to keep the code from getting cluttered. To delete the code, switch to Code view, and then select and delete the inserted Flash video code.

Adding Mark of the Web

Sometimes Internet Explorer (version 6 and above) prevents you from previewing pages with active content in them or warns that it has restricted the file from showing active content. **Active content** is JavaScript or anything that requires an ActiveX control, such as Flash Player. Originally, this was intended to tighten security because attackers were attempting to take advantage of the fact that active content is displayed in the Local Machine zone by default when run from a local computer (and not over the Web). Because it is inconvenient to upload pages that contain active content every time you want to view those pages in a browser, Dreamweaver includes code called Mark of the Web that you can add to your pages with active content to enable you to safely preview the pages locally. **Mark of the Web** is a special comment that you insert into Web pages to enable Internet Explorer to display active content from a local file without a warning. It is safe because it tells the active content to display in the Internet zone and not in the Local Machine zone.

Adding Mark of the Web to a Web Page | Reference Window

- Open the page to which you want to add Mark of the Web.
- Click Commands on the menu bar, and then click Insert Mark of the Web.
- Save the page, and then preview the page in a browser. The page should display without warnings.

You will add Mark of the Web to the pages in the Cosmatic site.

To add Mark of the Web to the Cosmatic pages:

▶ 1. Preview the **index.html** page in a browser. If you are using Internet Explorer version 6 or later, a warning, such as the one shown in Figure 8-32, might appear in the page.

Internet Explorer active content warning ◀ Figure 8-32

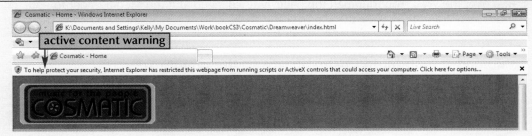

Trouble? If you don't see the active content warning, the default security settings for your browser have been adjusted. Continue with Step 2.

Tip

To remove Mark of the Web code from a page, click Commands on the menu bar, and then click Remove Mark of the Web.

▶ **2.** Close the browser. The index.html page is open in the Document window.

▶ **3.** Click **Commands** on the menu bar, and then click **Insert Mark of the Web**. Mark of the Web code is inserted in the page.

▶ **4.** Save the page, and then preview the page in a browser. The page displays without warnings. See Figure 8-33.

Figure 8-33	Home page with video previewed in a browser

▶ **5.** Close the browser, and then close the page.

▶ **6.** Open each of the following pages and repeat Steps 3 through 5 to add the Mark of the Web to the other top-level pages in the Cosmatic site: **bands.html**, **catalogue.html**, **label.html**, and **tourdates.html**.

Updating the Web Site on the Remote Server

As a final test of the media elements you've added to the Cosmatic site, you'll view the pages over the Web. You'll upload the pages you changed and the Media folder to your remote server, and then view the site over the Web.

To upload the updated Cosmatic site to the remote server:

▶ **1.** Click the **Connects to Remote Host** button on the Files panel toolbar.

▶ **2.** Click the **View** button on the Files panel toolbar, and then click **Local View**.

▶ 3. Select the **index.html**, **bands.html**, **catalogue.html**, **label.html**, and **tourdates.html** files and the **Media** folder in Local view, and then click the **Put File(s)** button 🔼 on the Files panel toolbar.

▶ 4. Click the **Yes** button to include dependent files because you have not selected the new dependent files for the site yet.

A dialog box might open with the message that the requested file is not found.

▶ 5. Click the **OK** button, if necessary.

▶ 6. Click the **Disconnects from Remote Host** button 🔲 on the Files panel toolbar.

▶ 7. Click the **View** button on the Files panel toolbar, and then click **Local View**. The Files panel returns to the Local view.

Next, you'll view the updated remote site in a browser. The remote site will include all of the new elements that you added to your local version of the site.

To view the updated remote site in a browser:

▶ 1. Open a browser, type the URL for your remote site in the Address bar on the browser toolbar, and then press the **Enter** key.

▶ 2. Explore the home page on the remote site from within the browser, being sure to view the Flash movie.

▶ 3. Click the **bands** link to open the Bands page, and then watch the Shockwave movie.

▶ 4. Click the **catalogue** link to open the Catalogue page, and then scroll to the bottom of the Catalogue page.

▶ 5. Click the **Flash sound** button, and listen to the sound clip.

▶ 6. Click the **MP3 sound** button, and listen to the sound clip.

▶ 7. Close the browser.

In this session, you inserted video into Web pages and explored the code that is inserted in the page when you insert Flash video. You added Mark of the Web to all of the pages in the Cosmatic site that use active content. Then you uploaded the site to your remote server and viewed the pages over the Web.

Session 8.3 Quick Check | Review

1. List three things that might affect the file size of a video clip.
2. What is the RealMedia file extension?
3. Why must a video clip be buffered?
4. Name three commonly used video file formats.
5. True or False? Most of the popular sound formats can also be used for video.
6. True or False? Installing a video player on your computer enables all other users to view the video on their computers.

In this tutorial, you explored the benefits and drawbacks of adding media to a site. You added a Flash movie, Flash text, and a Shockwave movie to a Web page. Then, you added sound to a Web page with a Flash movie and an MP3 file. Next, you explored adding video to a site, and then added Flash video to the site. You also learned about Mark of the Web and added it to pages with active content. Finally, you viewed the updated pages and the video over the Web.

Key Terms

active content	Flash	MP3
buffer	locked file	Shockwave
CODEC	Mark of the Web	sound formats
Director	media	streaming
Director projector		

Practice		**Review Assignments**

Data Files needed for the Review Assignments: sunshine_autostart.swf, limcVideo.flv

Brian wants you to add additional media elements to the Cosmatic site. First, you'll change the text in the What's Hot page to Flash text so it displays in the logo font. You'll also add a Flash movie that contains only sound and that is set to play automatically to the Sloth Child page. The movie will add sound to the background of the page. The Life in Minor Chords band is going to be releasing a video of some live performances that were filmed during its most recent tour. The band has created a short promo video to generate some buzz. You will embed the video promo in the tour section of the LIMC page.

1. Open the **Cosmatic** site that you modified in this tutorial, and then open the **whatshot.html** page in the Document window.
2. Delete the text "BLACK LAB: THE LATEST RELEASE FROM SURFACE SUCTION" from the upper-right corner of the What's Hot page.
3. Insert Flash Text using the Bauhaus Md BT font (or a font of your choice that resembles the Cosmatic logo font), size 55, align center, color #772300, and the following text (pressing the Enter key after each line):

   Black Lab:

   The latest

   release

   from

   Surface Suction

4. Save the Flash text in the Media folder with the filename **WhatsHotText1.swf**.
5. View the Flash text in the What's Hot page, and then save and close the page.
6. Open the **sloth_child.html** page located in the SlothChild folder, and then draw an AP div beside the Sloth Child logo.
7. Click in the background AP div, and then insert the Flash movie **sunshine_autostart.swf** file located in the Tutorial.08\Review folder included with your Data Files, placing a copy of the file in the Media folder in the site's local root folder.
8. Select the Flash movie, and then check the Autoplay and Loop check boxes in the Property inspector, if necessary.
9. Add Mark of the Web to the page.
10. Save the page, and then preview the page in a browser. The sound will begin to play when the page is loaded. Close the browser and the page.
11. Open the **limc_content_tours.html** page located in the LifeInMinorChords folder, and then draw an AP div below the page heading.
12. Click in the AP div, insert a Flash video, set the video type to Progressive Download Video, add the **limcVideo.flv** file located in the Tutorial.08\Review folder included with your Data Files, place a copy of the file in the Media folder in the site's local root folder, set the skin to Clear Skin 1, click the Detect Size button, check the Auto play and prompt users to download Flash Player if necessary check boxes, and then click the OK button.
13. Resize the AP div as needed to fit snugly against the borders of the movie.
14. Move the AP div so that its top border is 50 pixels below the page heading and its left border is aligned with the end of the page heading text.
15. Add Mark of the Web to the page, and then save and close the page.
16. Open each limc page (except the frameset page), add Mark of the Web to the page, and then save and close the page.

17. Open the **limc_frameset.html** page in the Document window, preview the page in a browser, click the tour link to view the video, and then close the page. (*Hint:* The video has audio in it.)

18. Upload the site to your remote server, and then preview the site over the Web.

19. Submit the finished files to your instructor, either in printed or electronic form, as requested.

| Apply | **Case Problem 1** |

Add audio and video clips to demonstrate linguistic differences in a Web site about the small rural communities of northern Vietnam.

Data Files needed for this Case Problem: WASHarshSample.flv, WASHarshwhSample.mp3, WASModalSample.mp3, WASBreathySample.flv

World Anthropology Society   Dr. Olivia Thompson has put together two MP3 audio clips and one video clip that demonstrate some of the linguistic differences she found in northern Vietnam. She asks you to place each example in the Linguistic Differences page.

1. Open the **DrThompson** site that you modified in **Tutorial 7**, **Case 1**, and then open the **linguistic_differences.html** page in the Document window.

2. Delete the text in the second row of the table, and then type **Research in process; in the meantime, click on the video and audio files to preview some interesting findings.** in the row.

3. Press the Enter key to create another line in the table row, and then insert a Flash video.

4. Set the video type to Progressive Download Video, set the URL to the **WASHarshSample.flv** file located in the Tutorial.08\Case1 folder included with your Data Files, include a copy of the file in a new folder named **Media** that you create in the DrThompson site, set the skin to Corona Skin 1, have Dreamweaver detect the size, and then click the OK button.

5. Insert 14 nonbreaking spaces in the page to the right of the video. (*Hint:* Press the Ctrl+Shift+Spacebar keys to insert a nonbreaking space.)

6. Type **audio 1**, insert another 14 nonbreaking spaces in the page, and then type **audio 2**.

7. Select the audio 1 text, and link the selected text to the **WASHarshwhSample.mp3** file located in the Tutorial.08\Case1 folder included with your Data Files, placing a copy of the MP3 file in the Media folder.

8. Select the audio 2 text, and link the selected text to the **WASModalSample.mp3** file located in the Tutorial.08\Case1 folder included with your Data Files, placing a copy of the MP3 file in the Media folder.

9. Insert 14 nonbreaking spaces to the right of the audio 2 text.

10. Add Flash video to the page. Set the video type to Progressive Download Video, set the URL to the **WASBreathySample.flv** file located in the Tutorial.08\Case1 folder included with your Data Files, include a copy of the file in the Media folder, set the skin to Corona Skin 1, and have Dreamweaver detect the size.

11. Add Mark of the Web to the page.

12. Save the page, preview the page in a browser, test the audio and video you added to the page, and then close the browser and the page. Sometimes MP3 files will not play locally, although they will play correctly when the page is viewed over the Web.

13. Upload the site to your remote server, and then preview the site over the Web.

14. Submit the finished files to your instructor, either in printed or electronic form, as requested.

| Challenge | **Case Problem 2** |

Add a promotional Shockwave movie and a Flash button to play the movie in a Web site for an art museum.

Data Files needed for this Case Problem: MuseumTour.txt, museumtour.dcr

Museum of Western Art   The Museum of Western Art is sponsoring a regional tour of some of their more popular paintings. C. J. Strittmatter asks you to create a new page to promote the tour. The page will eventually include an interactive educational Shockwave movie that provides information about the paintings and promotes the tour. The team that is creating that movie has made a promotional Shockwave movie to include in the page until the interactive educational movie is complete. You'll add the promotional Shockwave movie to the page. Then you'll add a Flash button to the home page of the site, and link the button to the new page.

1. Open the **Museum** site that you modified in **Tutorial 7**, **Case 2**.
2. In the Files panel, duplicate the location.html page in the site's local root folder.
3. Rename the Copy of Location page as **tour.html**, and then open the **tour.html** page in the Document window.
4. Delete the navigation bar and all the text below the page heading from the page. The page is empty except for the logo, the horizontal rule, and the heading.
5. Change the page title to **Museum of Western Art - Tour**.
6. Change the page heading to **THE TOUR**; and then copy and past the text from the **MuseumTour.txt** file located in the Tutorial.08\Case2 folder included with your Data Files into the new Tour page below the page heading.
7. To the left of the page heading, insert the **museumtour.dcr** Shockwave movie file located in the Tutorial.08\Case2 folder included with your Data Files, placing a copy of the file in a new **Media** folder that you create in the site's local root folder.
8. Select the Shockwave movie, and then, in the Property inspector, set the width (W) to 323, set the height (H) to 240, top align the movie, and set the background color (Bg) to #006666.
9. Save the page, preview the page in a browser, and then close the browser and the page.
10. Open the **index.html** page in the Document window, and then draw a small AP div at the right of the logo and above the horizontal rule.

⊕ **EXPLORE**   11. Click in the new AP div, and then insert a Flash button.
12. Select Simple Tab as the Style, type **Regional Tour** as the button text, select Times New Roman as the font, and then set the size to 15.
13. Link the Flash button to the tour.html page in the site's local root folder, and then set the target to _blank.
14. Click the color picker, and then click the eyedropper on the background of the Tour page to select the background color of the page as the background color for the Flash button.
15. Click the Save As Browse button to open the Select File dialog box, browse to the site's local root folder, type **TourButton.swf** in the File Name box, click the Save button in the Select File dialog box, verify the file path in the Save As box, and then click the OK button. The Flash button is added to the home page.
16. Adjust the borders of the AP div to fit snugly against the edges of the Flash button.
17. Move the AP div so that the button is right-aligned to the 750 pixel mark and its bottom edge touches the top of the horizontal rule. (*Hint:* Use guides as necessary.)
18. Save the page, preview the page in a browser, test the button, and then close the browser and the page.
19. Upload the site to your remote server, and then preview the site over the Web.

20. Submit the finished files to your instructor, either in printed or electronic form, as requested.

| Apply | **Case Problem 3** |

Create an order form with a Shockwave movie in a Web site for an independent bookstore.

Data File needed for this Case Problem: MOREform.dcr

MORE Books   Natalie More wants to increase catalogue orders for her bookstore. Mark Chapman has already created a Shockwave movie that contains a catalogue order form. You will place the Shockwave movie into a new page you create for the site. Then you will add a Flash button to the top of the home page. The Flash button will link to the new page and target the page to open in a new browser window.

1. Open the **MOREbooks** site that you modified in **Tutorial 7**, **Case 3**.
2. In the Files panel, duplicate one of the existing pages to add a new page to the site, rename the new page as **catalogue_order.html**, and then open the **catalogue_order.html** page in the Document window.
3. Delete everything below the navigation bar from the page, and then enter **MORE Books - Catalogue Order** as the page title.
4. In the upper-left corner of the page below the navigation bar, insert the **MOREform.dcr** Shockwave movie file located in the Tutorial.08\Case3 folder included with your Data Files, placing a copy of the file in a new **Media** folder that you create in the site's local root folder.
5. In the Property inspector, set the width of the Shockwave movie to 500 and its height to 330, and then save and close the page.
6. Open the **index.html** page in the Document window, and then draw an AP div at the right of the page above the horizontal rule.
7. In the new AP div, insert a Flash button using the Translucent Tab style, **MORE CATALOGUE** as the button text, Verdana as the font, 10 as the size, catalogue_order.html as the link, _blank as the target, #003366 as the Bg color, and **CatalogueOrderButton.swf** as the Save as name.
8. Move the AP div so that the bottom of the button is touching the horizontal rule and the right border is positioned at 700 pixels. (*Hint:* Use guides as necessary.)
9. Save the page, preview the page in a browser, test the button, and then close the browser and the page.
10. Upload the site to your remote server, and then preview the site over the Web.
11. Submit the finished files to your instructor, either in printed or electronic form, as requested.

| Create | **Case Problem 4** |

Add a Shockwave movie and a sound clip to a Web site for a newly opening sushi restaurant.

Data Files needed for this Case Problem: sushigame.dcr, wasabisound_autoplay.swf

Sushi Ya-Ya   Mary O'Brien has decided to add a Sushi-Shell Game to the Specials page. The game will be a Shockwave movie that e-mails the user a coupon for a free piece of the sushi special if the user finds the wasabi hidden under the sushi. Mary also wants you to add a sound clip to the Wasabi page. The sound file is a Flash movie that will automatically play only sound when the page is loaded.

1. Open the **Sushi Ya-Ya** site that you modified in **Tutorial 7**, **Case 4**.
2. Open the **specials.html** page in the Document window, and then draw an AP div below the table.

3. In the AP div, insert the **sushigame.dcr** Shockwave movie located in the Tutorial.08\Case4 folder included with your Data Files, placing a copy of the file in a new **Media** folder that you create in the site's local root folder.

4. In the Property inspector, set the width of the Shockwave movie to 500 and its height to 330.

5. Save the page, preview the page in a browser, test the game, and then close the browser.

⊕ EXPLORE
6. Adjust the AP div so that the game is placed in an aesthetically pleasing place in the page.

7. Save the page, preview the page in a browser, and then close the browser and the page.

8. Open the **wasabi.html** page in the Document window, and then place the insertion point to the right of the page heading.

9. Insert the **wasabisound_autoplay.swf** Flash movie located in the Tutorial.08\Case4 folder included with your Data Files, placing a copy of the file in the Media folder.

10. In the Property inspector, set the Flash movie to autoplay but not loop.

⊕ EXPLORE
11. Click the Play button to preview the sound.

12. Save the page, preview the page in a browser, and then close the browser and the page.

13. Upload the site to your remote server, and then preview the site over the Web.

14. Submit the finished files to your instructor, either in printed or electronic form, as requested.

Review | **Quick Check Answers**

Session 8.1

1. any special configurable objects that you might add to the pages of your site, which need a player or application that is not part of the browser—such as plug-ins, ActiveX controls, or helper applications—to display within a browser
2. some type of plug-in or player
3. .swf
4. True.
5. False; you can create Flash text in Dreamweaver even if the Flash program is not installed on your computer.
6. True.

Session 8.2

1. Director
2. .dcr
3. Sound can begin to play after only a small portion downloads and will continue to play while the rest of the file continues to download.
4. Embed the sound in the page or link to the sound file. When sound is embedded directly in a page, the sound files in the page begin to download to the client computer as soon as the page is loaded. When you link to sound files, the file does not download to the client computer until the link is clicked.
5. RealMedia, MP3, QuickTime, and Windows Media
6. Flash movies that contain only sound; you should only embed Flash movies in a page.

Session 8.3

1. frame size, playback quality, and sound parameters
2. .rm

3. To ensure continuous playback of a video clip, it must be buffered, which means that the first 5 or 10 seconds of the clip are downloaded before it begins to play.
4. RealMedia, QuickTime, and Windows Media
5. True.
6. False; all users must install a video player on their computer to view the video.

Creating Reusable Assets and Forms

Creating Meta Tags, Library Items, Templates, and Forms

Case | Cosmatic

Brian Lee, public relations and marketing director at Cosmatic, has been reviewing the Cosmatic site and has some additions and changes he wants made. He wants you to add keywords and a meta description to each page, which will be useful when he lists the pages with search engines after the site is launched. He has also decided that you should convert some of the commonly used site elements, such as the footer, into library items. In addition, he wants you to create templates for the site to make it simpler to add new pages and update the look and feel of all the existing pages. Finally, he has decided to gather some additional information about the users of the Cosmatic site, and asks you to add a form to the Contact page that users can fill out and submit.

Starting Data Files

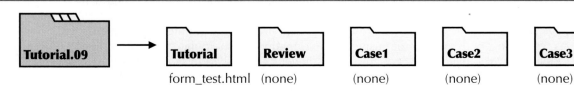

Tutorial.09 → Tutorial   Review   Case1   Case2   Case3   Case4

form_test.html (none)   (none)   (none)   (none)   form_test.html
                                                    sushi_menu.html

Session 9.1

Reviewing Head Content

All Web pages contain head content. Remember that head content refers to anything that is placed within the <head> tags of Web pages. Users usually cannot see elements that are placed in the head of a page when the page is viewed in a browser. Head content typically either adds functionality to a page when viewed in a browser or provides information about the page for search engines. For example, you placed <title> tags in the head of each page to display a page title in the title bar of a browser window. Two tags commonly inserted into the head that add functionality to a page are:

- **Base.** Enters the desired base URL for the page's document relative links.
- **Link.** Links an external style sheet to a page.

Search engines use head content to learn about a page by looking for information in some meta tags included in the head of Web pages. A **meta tag** holds information about the page, gives information to the Web server, or adds functionality to the page. For example, the page description that many search engines display in their search results is pulled from the description meta tag. In addition to the page description, you use meta tags to add information such as keywords, author names, a copyright statement, and so on to the code of a Web page. The exact purpose of each meta tag is defined by its attributes. You can use more than one meta tag in a page. The meta tags buttons in Dreamweaver are:

- **Meta.** Inserts a generic meta tag into the head and enables you to set attributes, values, and content for the meta tag.
- **Keywords.** Inserts a meta tag with the attribute name="keywords" into the head, which enables you to enter keywords for the page. The keywords meta tag is one of the most frequently used meta tags.
- **Description.** Inserts a meta tag with the attribute name="description" into the head, which enables you to enter a description for the page. The description meta tag is one of the most frequently used meta tags.
- **Refresh.** Inserts a meta tag with the attribute http-equiv="refresh" into the head, which enables you to enter amount of delay, in seconds, before the page is refreshed and choose whether to refresh the current page or open a new URL. Refreshing to a new URL is often used when a site has moved, redirecting users who visit the old URL to the new location.

You'll add keywords and a meta description to the head content of Web pages in the Cosmatic site.

Optimizing Web Pages for Search Engine Placement

Optimizing the pages in a Web site for search engine placement is an important part of designing a Web site because search engines enable people to find the site. Optimizing a page means doing everything you can to the page to ensure that it is ranked highly in target search engines. Each search engine has a different set of formulas that determine page placement. These placement formulas change frequently and are a closely guarded secret to prevent designers from using this information to manipulate page placement. Optimizing Web pages does not automatically get them placed in search engines, but it will help a site receive higher listings when it is listed. Having a Web site not listed appropriately with search engines is like having a business located in an unmarked building with no published address: There is no way for people to know about the amazing things inside.

Listing Your Web Site with a Search Engine | InSight

There are hundreds of search engines, but the top three or four major engines direct more than 90% of traffic. Some longer-standing top search engines are Google (63%, September 2007), Yahoo! (22%, September 2007), and MSN (8%, September 2007). Unfortunately, the major search engines sometimes change, making it more difficult to maintain high rankings. The major engines also feed information to many smaller engines. You should concentrate on getting a site placed in the top search engines to get the most listings for the site. To list a site with search engines, go to the Web site for each search engine and follow the guidelines to list pages of the site in that engine. You can also pay a service to list the site for you. In addition, some search engines send out **robots**, software that searches the Web and sends information back to the engine, to compile the information used to list pages in the search engines. However, robots might not find your site on their own (because submitting a site to a search engine just tells the search engine to dispatch a robot to index your site content). To maintain a favorable listing position (a listing within the first page of results), you must list the pages yourself or pay a service to list them for you. Finally, be sure to relist the pages in your site with each engine to maintain a favorable position. Some engines allow you to relist pages monthly, whereas others prefer that you relist only a few times a year. Guidelines for relisting pages can be found with the listing information on the Web site for each major search engine.

Of the many things you can do to optimize Web pages for search engine placement, the two most basic things you should do to every Web page are to add keywords and a meta description to the head of the pages. In this session, you will begin to optimize the pages in the Cosmatic site for search engine placement by adding keywords and a meta description to each page.

Adding and Editing Keywords

Keywords are one of the elements many search engines use to index Web pages, although their importance has diminished. A **keyword** is a descriptive word or phrase that is placed in the meta tag with the attribute name="keywords". You add one keywords meta tag to the head of each page and then list all the keywords for the site in that tag. The keywords you choose should be the words you think most people will type into search engines to look for that site or the words you want people to find the site under. Include all of the words and phrases that your target audience would use to do a general search for your product or service even if they didn't know your company exists. Remember to include the name of the company and products or services in the list. It can also be helpful to include common misspellings of the company or product name. For example, good keywords for the Cosmatic site would be *Cosmatic Records*, the band names, and the album titles.

Keywords can be individual words or short phrases fewer than six words. (Some search engines may penalize you for adding longer phrases by decreasing your ranking order or by dropping your site from the index.) When you use phrases, generally each word is indexed separately and together. For example, if you use the phrase "indie music" for the Cosmatic site, the word *indie* and the word *music* will both be indexed as well as the phrase *indie music*. Also, the root of the word is indexed as well; for example, if you include the word *silky*, the word *silk* is also indexed.

You can use as many keywords as you would like; however, the first 10 words are the most important because many search engines use only those first 10 words in the keywords list to index a site. Additionally, search engines often give higher placement to sites that use the keywords within the page content, page titles, navigation system, text links, and image names, so make sure that the Web site contains the keywords many times. For example, because the Cosmatic site uses the words *indie* and *music* many times within the text of the pages, the pages of the Cosmatic site may be ranked higher in value under these keywords than the pages of a site that uses these keywords but does not use the words in its page content. Another example is if you use the word *hippopotamus* in the keywords list for the Cosmatic pages. The pages in the Cosmatic site may receive a lower ranking under that keyword because the word *hippopotamus* never appears in the page content of the Cosmatic site. Conversely, using the keywords excessively in the page content of a site may lead to penalties, including decreased ranking of the site or complete removal of the site from the index because many search engines see this as an attempt at spamming or artificially attempting to inflate the site's listing position.

InSight | **Researching Search Engine Optimization**

Search engine optimization (SEO) standards are constantly changing. It is a good idea to review current trends before choosing the keywords for a site. You can find current information by using your favorite search engine to search on the following keywords: *current search engine optimization trends* or *seo trends* or *optimization guidelines*. The search results will also include placement companies that have used these keywords to attract new clients.

Some placement techniques are considered unethical (referred to as "black hat") and usually work only until the search engines discover them. Then the search engines disallow these techniques and decrease the ranking of pages that use them. Ethical placement techniques are often referred to as "white hat" techniques.

In recent years, meta keywords have become less important to search engine ranking than page content. You should still include meta keywords when you create a site, because they may still be important to some search engines and they won't hurt your site's ranking.

Adding Keywords and Examining the HTML Code

Although you can type the meta keywords tag directly in Code view, it is simpler to use a dialog box to add keywords to a page and let Dreamweaver create the code. When entering keywords, you should use all lowercase letters because in most search engines, lowercase letters represent both uppercase and lowercase letters, whereas uppercase letters make an item case specific. You should also separate each word or phrase with a comma. When you add keywords to a page, the following code is inserted into the head of the page:

```
<meta name="keywords" content="keyword1, keyword2, keyword3" />
```

Meta tags are unpaired tags, which means that each tag stands alone and not as part of a set of opening and closing tags. Like all tags, the meta tag starts with an opening bracket followed by the name of the tag, meta. The tag name is followed by a series of tag attributes and values. The first attribute in the keywords meta tag is *name* and its value is the type of meta tag, *"keywords"*. The second attribute is *content* and its value is the content of the tag, or the list of keywords. The tag ends with a forward slash and a closing bracket.

Brian asks you to insert the list of keywords into the home page of the Cosmatic site. Then you'll examine the code in Code view.

To add keywords to the Cosmatic home page:

▶ **1.** Open the **Cosmatic** site that you modified in the **Tutorial 8 Review Assignments**, and then open the **index.html** page in the Document window.

▶ **2.** On the **Common** tab of the Insert bar, click the **Head button arrow** 🖸 , and then click the **Keywords** button 🔤 . The Keywords dialog box opens so you can type the words you want. Remember to use all lowercase letters and to separate each word or phrase with a comma.

▶ **3.** Type **cosmatic records, indie music, sloth child, dizzied connections, life in minor chords, surface suction, spinning life, black lab, them apples, i believe in ferries, independent scene, denton music, underground sound** in the Keywords box. See Figure 9-1.

Keywords dialog box ◀ **Figure 9-1**

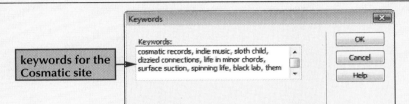

keywords for the Cosmatic site

▶ **4.** Click the **OK** button, and then save the home page. The meta keywords tag is added to the head of the page. Its exact location within the head content can vary, depending on where the insertion point was located in the page when you clicked the Keywords button.

▶ **5.** Click the **Code** button on the Document toolbar to switch to Code view, and then scroll, if necessary, to view the meta keywords tag in the Document window. The tag is located somewhere in the head section of the page.

▶ **6.** In the Code pane, click in the meta keywords tag, and then, in the status bar, click the **<meta>** tag. The <meta> tag is selected in the status bar and the Document window, and the list of keywords appears in the Property inspector. See Figure 9-2.

Tip

You can also enter or edit the keywords list directly in Code view.

Figure 9-2 | Meta keywords tag in Code view

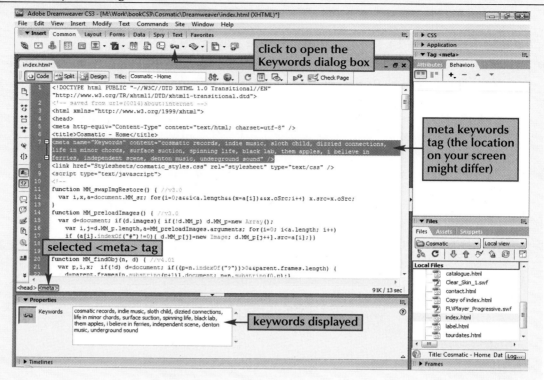

Editing Keywords

Sometimes, you'll want to add another keyword to the list, delete a keyword from the list, or correct the spelling of a keyword in the list. You can do any of these by editing the list of keywords that has already been added to a page in the Property inspector or in the code.

Sara's research shows that Cosmatic is frequently misspelled as *Cosmattic*. You'll add this misspelling to the list of keywords in the home page.

To edit the list of keywords:

▶ **1.** In the Property inspector, click after the last word in the Keywords box, type **,** (a comma), press the **Spacebar**, and then type **cosmattic**. The new keyword is added in the Property inspector, but is not yet added to the code.

▶ **2.** In the Document window, click outside the meta keywords tag, and then click in the meta keywords tag again. The updated keywords list appears in the code and the Property inspector.

▶ **3.** On the status bar, click the **<meta>** tag. The meta keywords tag is selected in the Document window. See Figure 9-3.

Tip

You can also click the Refresh button in the Head list on the Common tab to update the keywords code.

Edited keywords list ◀ Figure 9-3

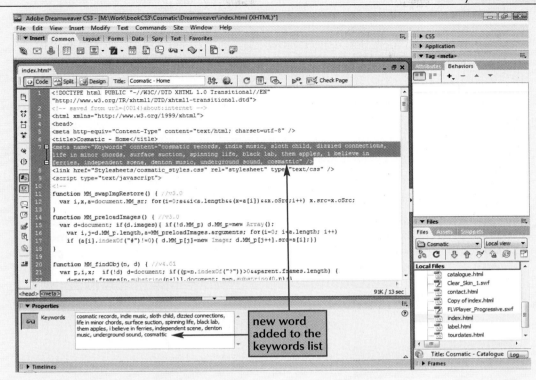

4. Save the home page.

Adding and Editing a Meta Description

Many search engines also use the meta description to index Web pages. A **meta description** is a short summary of the Web page that is placed in the meta tag with the attribute *name="description"*. The description should contain a concise summary of the site's content and goals. For example, the Cosmatic site description will be "Cosmatic is an indie label that has tapped into a vein of post-discord punk music. Our mission is to expose the world to exceptional indie music. Cosmatic promotes bands that we believe will change and infuse the planet with original good music." Some search engines also display the first part of the description in the search results page when a user looks up a word or phrase. Therefore, it is a good idea to use the first line or two of the description as a short caption for the site. Think of it as a newspaper headline, summarizing the highlights of the page content. Some engines also penalize a page with very long descriptions, so you should make your description fairly short—no more than six average lines of text.

Adding a Meta Description and Viewing the Code

When you add the meta description, be sure to use standard capitalization, spelling, grammar, and punctuation for ease of reading. Users quickly scan search results looking for a particular topic or site and might skip difficult-to-read descriptions. The meta description tag is similar to the meta keywords tag:

```
<meta name="description" content="The description text goes here."> /
```

The tag begins with an opening bracket followed by the name of the tag, *meta*. The *name* attribute has the value of *"description"* to specify that this tag provides a summary of the Web site. The value of the *content* attribute is the description text. The tag ends with a forward slash and a closing bracket.

Brian has written a meta description for the Cosmatic site that he wants you to add to the home page.

To add a meta description to the home page:

▶ **1.** In the Document window, click at the end of the meta keywords tag (to the right of "...cosmattic" />"), and then press the **Enter** key. The insertion point is positioned below the keywords, which is where you'll add the meta description.

▶ **2.** On the Common tab of the **Insert** bar, click the **Head button arrow** 🔲 ▾ , and then click the **Description** button 🔲 . The Description dialog box opens.

▶ **3.** Type **Cosmatic is an indie label that has tapped into a vein of post-discord punk music. Our mission is to expose the world to exceptional indie music. Cosmatic promotes bands that we believe will change and infuse the planet with original good music.** in the Description box. See Figure 9-4.

Figure 9-4 ▶ **Description dialog box**

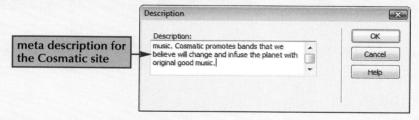

meta description for the Cosmatic site

▶ **4.** Click the **OK** button. The description appears below the keywords in the Document window.

▶ **5.** In the Property inspector, click the **Refresh** button.

▶ **6.** In the Document window, click in the meta description tag, and then, in the status bar, click the **<meta>** tag. The description appears in the Property inspector, and the meta tag is selected in the Document window. See Figure 9-5.

Meta description tag in Code view ◀ Figure 9-5

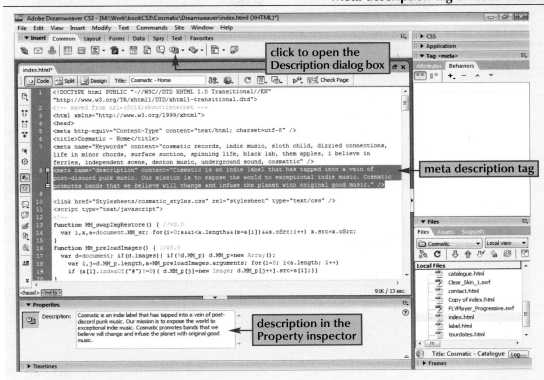

Trouble? If you cannot find the description, click the Refresh button in the Head list on the Common tab to update screen to show the changes, and then repeat Step 6.

▶ **7.** Save the home page.

Editing a Meta Description

Periodically, you might want to update a meta description to reflect changes in the Web site or the company and its products. You can edit a meta description in the same ways that you edit keywords. Click in the description in the Document window in Code view, and then change the description in either the Property inspector or the Document window.

Keywords and descriptions should be added to all the pages of a Web site. You will add them to the remaining pages of the Cosmatic site in the Review Assignments.

Understanding Using Library Items

Sometimes you need to add an element to many pages in a site. Dreamweaver features such as library items help you automate site design and decrease redundant work. A **library item** is a page element (a piece of a Web page) saved in the .lbi file format that can be inserted in more than one page of a site. It is useful to create library items for elements that you intend to reuse or update frequently, such as footers or a list of upcoming events, that will be displayed in several pages of a site. Using a library item not only saves time, but also ensures consistency of that element throughout the site. You can have any number of library items in a site, but making an element a library item is helpful only if you are going to reuse the element a number of times.

A library item can include most elements in the body of a Web page, including bits of code, text, images, tables, forms, formatting, and so on. You can even include a navigation bar in a library item, but you cannot use the Show "Down State" Initially feature effectively because every page that included the library item would show the Down state for the same button. Library items elements are found only in the body of a Web page. You cannot create a library item for head content.

When you include a library item in a Web page, the regular HTML code for the element is inserted into the page along with a hidden link to the library item. When you edit a library item, Dreamweaver updates each page in which the library item is used and changes the code in each Web page. For example, you'll create a library item for the footer in the Cosmatic pages that includes the footer text, formatting, and a link. By making the footer a library item and then inserting the library item in the pages of the site, you can easily change the footer as needed. If, for instance, the footer link changes, you simply change the link once in the library item and Dreamweaver changes the link in every page in which the footer library item is used. This can save a great amount of time in a large site.

Library items are stored in the Dreamweaver library for the site. A **library** is a collection of library items that are located in the Library folder in the site's local root folder. Every site created in Dreamweaver that has library items has a Library folder. You can view the library in the Assets panel when you click the Library button. The library and library items are Dreamweaver authoring tools. This means that unlike other items that you have added to pages, CSS styles for example, libraries and library items do not exist outside Dreamweaver. When you make a change in a library item, Dreamweaver updates each page in which the library item is used and changes the code in each page. When you upload the site to a remote server, you do not need to upload the Library folder because all of the code for each library item has been added to the individual pages in which an instance of that item is found.

The downside to using library items is that you cannot change an individual instance of the item without disconnecting that instance from the library item. For example, if you decide that the footer should be bold in one page of the Cosmatic site, you cannot change the instance of the library item only in that page. Instead, you must delete the library item from that page and create a unique footer. You could also change the library item, which would change the look of the footer on every page in the site. This all-or-nothing aspect of library items can be somewhat limiting.

Creating and Using a Library Item

Tip

Switch to Split view to see the tags that are included in the library item as well as viewing the item in the page.

You can create as many library items as you need for a site. To create a library item, you simply create the element in a page, select the element, and then drag the selected element to the library in the Assets panel. Be sure to select all the text, the formatting elements, and anything else you want to include in the library item. For example, if you want to include a blank line above and below the footer in the library item, you must select the line break above and below the footer when you create the library item. Pay careful attention to what you are selecting because everything you select will be included in the library item. Once all the elements are included in the library item, you name the new library item and it is added to the library. Choose a descriptive name that will help you identify the content of the library item. As with other filenames, use only alphanumeric characters, do not use spaces or special characters, and do not start the name with a number. Every library item is saved in the .lbi file format.

Because library items can contain only elements found in the body of a Web page, they display CSS styles only if a style sheet that has a style definition referenced in the library item code is attached to the page in which it is inserted. Recall that the CSS style sheet code is inserted either in the head of the page or in an external style sheet. When you create a library item from a page that uses CSS styles, the library item will include the code that references the CSS style. As long as the pages in which the library item is inserted are attached to a style sheet that has a style definition for the referenced style, the library item will look the same in the new pages. A library item can be inserted into pages that are attached to different style sheets. Each style sheet can define the style in a different way so that the same library item can look different in different pages.

| **Creating a Library Item** | | Reference Window |

- Create the page element you want as the library item, if necessary.
- Drag the selected page element to the library in the Assets panel.
- Type a name for the new library item, and then press the Enter key.

or

- In the Assets panel, click the New Library Item button in the library.
- Type a name for the new library item, and then press the Enter key.
- In the Assets panel, click the Edit button in the library.
- Create the page element you want as the new library item, and then save and close the library item.

Brian noticed that the footer text within the Cosmatic site is inconsistent. To ensure consistency, you will create a library item that contains footer information, and then use it to replace the existing footers.

To create a library item for the Cosmatic footer:

▶ 1. Click the **Design** button on the Document toolbar, scroll to the bottom of the page, and then select the footer and the blank line above the footer.

▶ 2. Collapse any open panels except the Files panel group, click the **Assets** tab in the Files panel group, and then click the **Library** button 🕮 on the Assets panel toolbar. The library appears in the Assets panel.

▶ 3. Drag the selected footer and blank line to the library. A dialog box opens, warning that the selection may not look the same when placed in other documents because the style sheet information is not copied with it.

Trouble? If the dialog box does not open, the message was disabled for your installation of Dreamweaver. Continue with Step 5.

▶ 4. Click the **OK** button. An untitled library item is added to the library. See Figure 9-6.

Figure 9-6

Library displayed in the Assets panel

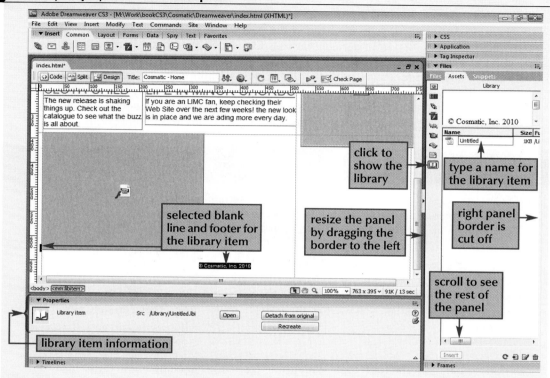

5. Type **cosmatic_footer**, and then press the **Enter** key to name the library item.

6. Click in the Document window, and then press the **Right Arrow** key to deselect the footer. The footer is highlighted in yellow, indicating that it is a library item. See Figure 9-7.

Figure 9-7

Library item created from the footer

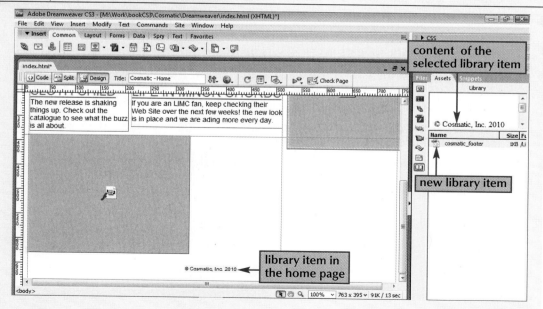

The page contains a link to the library item and must be saved.

▶ **7.** Save and close the home page.

Adding a Library Item to Web Pages

You can add a library item to any page in the Web site. After a library item has been added to a page, you can drag it to any location within the page. You can add the same library item to a page as many times as you want, and you can add as many different library items to a page as you need.

You'll add the cosmatic_footer library item to the other pages of the site.

To add the footer library item to the rest of the Cosmatic pages:

▶ **1.** Display the Files panel, and then open the **bands.html** page in the Document window.

Trouble? If a dialog box opens, indicating that the library item has been changed and prompting you to update all the documents in your site, click the OK button.

▶ **2.** Select the footer at the bottom of the page, and then press the **Delete** key. The footer is removed from the page.

Trouble? If you cannot select the footer, the RemainingText AP div is over it. Select the AP div and drag the bottom selection handle until the bottom border of the AP div is just below the text in the AP div. The footer is now positioned below the AP div. Select the footer and press the Delete key.

▶ **3.** Display the library in the Assets panel.

▶ **4.** Drag the **cosmatic_footer** library item to the bottom of the Bands page below the RemainingText AP div. The cosmatic_footer library item is inserted into the Bands page.

▶ **5.** Press the **Right Arrow** key to deselect the footer. The footer is highlighted in pale yellow.

▶ **6.** Save and close the page.

You need to add the footer to the rest of the pages in the site.

▶ **7.** Repeat Steps 1 through 6 to add the footer library item to each of the following pages: **catalogue.html**, **contact.html**, **label.html**, and **tourdates.html**. (The Tour Dates page is long; to ensure that the anchors in the page work properly, place the footer within the green strip where it will be visible rather than at the bottom of the page.)

Examining the Code for a Library Item

The code for the page elements is added to the page along with a hidden link to the library item. The cosmatic_footer library item has the following code:

```
<!-- #BeginLibraryItem "/Library/cosmatic_footer.lbi" -->
<p > </p>
<span class="cosmatic_footer">© Cosmatic, Inc. 2010</span><br />
<!-- #EndLibraryItem -->
```

The library item starts with a comment tag. Comment tags are unpaired tags that are used to add notes to the code that do not appear in the page or affect the way the html is rendered. For example, you might use a comment tag to add a note that helps you remember the use or purpose of a section of code. Comment tags are used to denote library items because comment tags will not cause problems even when the page is edited in another program. The comment tag begins with an opening bracket followed by an exclamation point and two dashes, <!--, and ends with two dashes followed by a closing bracket, -->. Everything that appears between the dashes is considered a comment and will be ignored by the browser. Every library item begins with a comment tag that tells Dreamweaver that a library item has started, <!--#BeginLibraryItem, includes a path to that library item, "/Library/cosmatic_footer.lbi", followed by two dashes and the closing bracket of the comment tag. All code for the page element in the library item follows the comment tag. Each library item ends with a second comment tag that tells Dreamweaver the library item is ending, <!--#EndLibraryItem-->.

You'll view the code for the cosmatic_footer library item in the Bands page.

To view the cosmatic_footer library item code in the Bands page:

▶ 1. Open the **bands.html** page in the Document window, select the footer, and then click the **Split** button on the Document toolbar. The code for the cosmatic_footer library item is selected in the Code pane. See Figure 9-8.

Figure 9-8 ▶ **cosmatic_footer library item in Split view**

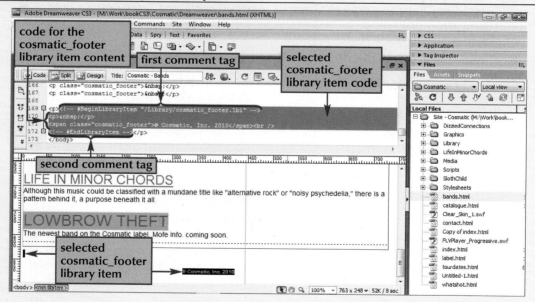

Trouble? If you do not see paragraph tags at the beginning and end of the footer library item code, you probably did not select both the line above the footer and the footer when you created the library item. You can fix this when you edit the library item in the next set of steps by comparing your code to the code shown in Figure 9-11 and typing the missing code.

▶ 2. Identify the first comment tag, the library item path, the page element code, and the second comment tag.

▶ 3. Click the **Design** button on the Document toolbar.

Editing a Library Item

One of the most useful aspects of a library item is that you can update every instance of the item by editing the library item itself. This is much faster, not to mention possibly more accurate, than editing the same element in many pages. To edit a library item, you simply open the library item, make the changes, and then save the library item. A dialog box lists all the pages in which that library item has been used and prompts you to update the files. When you choose to update the files, Dreamweaver makes the changes to the library item in each page that was listed. After the pages are updated, a log might open, showing the history of the changes made to the pages.

Brian wants you to make the footer an e-mail link so users can quickly contact the company.

To edit the cosmatic_footer library item:

1. With the cosmatic_footer library item selected in the page, click the **Open** button in the Property inspector. The cosmatic_footer libarary item opens in the Document window. The text does not have the appropriate style because the style sheet is not attached to the actual library item. When you view the library item from within the pages in the site, it will again display the appropriate style. See Figure 9-9.

Tip

You can also double-click a library item in the library to open the item.

Document window with the cosmatic_footer library item | Figure 9-9

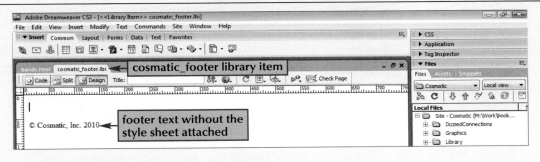

Next, you'll add the e-mail link to the text.

2. In the Document window, select the footer text.

3. In the Property inspector, type **mailto:info@cosmaticnoise.com** in the Link box, press the **Enter** key, and then, in the Document window, deselect the text. See Figure 9-10.

cosmatic_footer library item with linked text | Figure 9-10

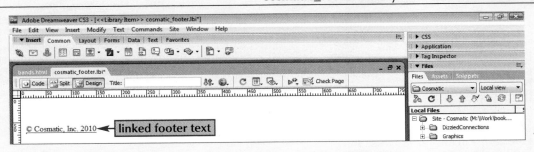

You'll also change the format of the footer text to ensure that the CSS style will be inserted in the paragraph tag, which is a block-level tag. Only block-level tags can be centered.

▶ **4.** In the Document window, select the footer text, and then, if necessary, in the Property inspector, click the **Format** button, and then click **Paragraph**.

▶ **5.** Click the **Split** button on the Document toolbar, and then, if necessary, select **class="cosmatic_footer"**, drag the selected code into the opening paragraph tag, and delete the opening and closing span tags. See Figure 9-11.

Figure 9-11 ▶ **Completed code for the edited cosmatic_footer library item**

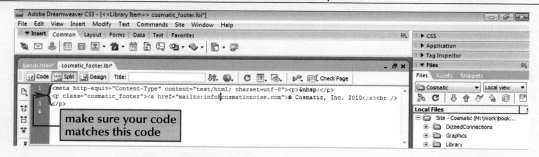

▶ **6.** Save the cosmatic_footer library item. The Update Library Items dialog box opens, listing all the pages that contain the library item. See Figure 9-12.

Figure 9-12 ▶ **Update Library Items dialog box**

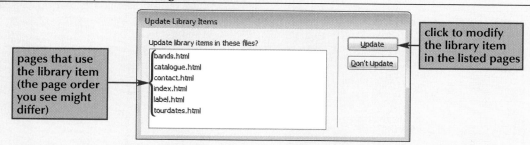

▶ **7.** Click the **Update** button to update the library item in the listed pages. Dreamweaver updates all the pages that contain the library item and the Update Pages dialog box opens.

▶ **8.** Click the **Show log** check box to insert a check mark, if necessary. The dialog box shows a log of the updates. See Figure 9-13.

Figure 9-13 ▶ **Update Pages dialog box**

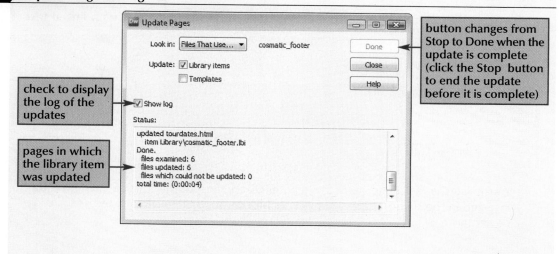

▶ **9.** Click the **Close** button to close the dialog box, and then close the cosmatic_footer library item.

▶ **10.** Scroll to the bottom of the Bands page, if necessary. The footer is a link and is displayed with the appropriate CSS styles.

▶ **11.** Save the page, and then preview the page in a browser. See Figure 9-14.

Bands page with the e-mail link footer previewed in a browser ◀ **Figure 9-14**

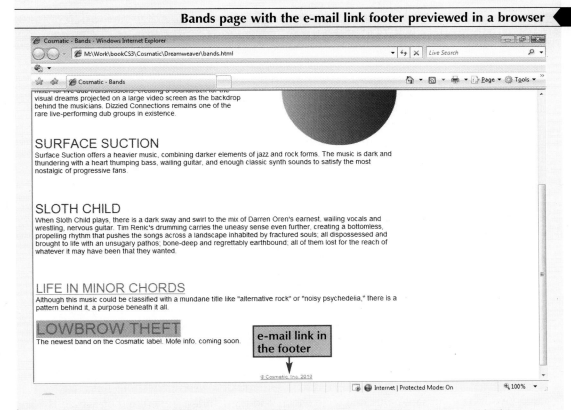

▶ **12.** Click the **footer** link to test the e-mail link (a message window opens with the e-mail addressed to info@cosmaticnoise.com), close the message window, close the browser, and then close the page.

Trouble? If a message window does not open, an e-mail program might not be installed or configured on your computer. Close any dialog boxes and windows that open, and then continue with Step 13, but do not test the footer in the other pages.

▶ **13.** Open each page in the site, preview the page, test the footer, close the message window, and then close the browser and the page.

Deleting a Library Item

You can delete a library item from Web pages or from the library. If a library item is no longer appropriate to include in a specific page, you can quickly delete it from the page by selecting the library item in the page and then pressing the Delete key. That instance of the library item is deleted from the page, but the library item remains available in the library. If a library item is no longer appropriate to include anywhere in a site, you can delete it from the library by selecting the library item in the library and clicking the Delete button 🗑 in the Assets panel. If you delete a library item from the site while it is being used in the pages of the site, the content of the library item will remain in each page in which it was placed, but the items will no longer be library items. It is a good idea to delete unused library items from the library to keep your site uncluttered and well organized.

In this session, you added the keywords and description meta tags to the head content of pages and you added a library item to the Cosmatic site. In the next session, you will create templates for the Web site.

Review | **Session 9.1 Quick Check**

1. What are meta tags?
2. List two frequently used meta tags.
3. Why are keywords important?
4. Where are library items stored?
5. What type of tag begins and ends the code for a library item?
6. What is one of the most useful aspects of a library item?

Session 9.2

Understanding Templates

Professional designers sometimes plan and design Web sites based on templates. A **template** is a special page that enables the designer to separate the look and layout of the page from the content by "locking" the page layout. The designer designates what is locked in a page by creating editable regions and noneditable regions. **Editable regions** are areas that can be changed in the pages created from a template. **Noneditable regions** are areas that can be changed in the template, but cannot be changed in the pages created from a template. You use a template to create multiple Web pages that share the same layout, use the same attached style sheet, and contain the same content, which is placed in the noneditable regions of the template. For example, you can create a template from which to create new pages added to the Cosmatic site. The template should include all the elements that are used in every page—such as the Cosmatic logo, the navigation bar, and the footer—in noneditable regions. The style sheet should also be attached to the template, so that the pages created from the template will have the appropriate style sheet attached. The template should include editable regions for elements that vary from page to page, such as the page heading and content sections of the pages.

Templates are one avenue for creating shared site formatting. However, you should also consider a few other methods when you plan a Web site. In recent years, CSS positioning has become widely supported by all of the commonly used browsers. If you are using templates only to ensure consistent positioning and formatting of the various page elements across all the pages in the site, you can also use CSS style sheets to accomplish this. If you have a large site, you might create a database to store the site content and then add code to the pages that enables the pages to dynamically display the content from the database formatted appropriately for the site design. Brian wants to create a template for the Cosmatic site so that all his employees can update the content of pages without accidentally changing the page layout, look, and so on.

| **Planning a Template** | | InSight |

Creating a template for a Web site requires more planning and forethought than creating individual pages. You need to thoroughly plan the layout of the pages before creating the site to ensure that you have set up the appropriate editable regions—the only regions that can contain unique page content. For example, you need to include an editable region for the page heading in the template for the Cosmatic site because a unique page heading appears in the same location in every page. You also need to include an editable region for page content because each page displays unique content below the page heading. Although it is important to include editable regions for each general area of the page, it is also important not to create too many specific editable regions, which would limit the flexibility of the pages. For example, you do not want to set up separate editable regions for subheadings because subheadings are not used in every page. Adding a separate editable region for a subheading would add a separate subheading region to every page created from the template. Instead, you can include subheadings in pages that require them in the editable region that you set up for content. It is tempting to shortcut the planning phase when designing sites with simple pages that are not template-based. When you begin to design large, professional, template-based sites, the pages are more interconnected and the design requires a great deal of forethought.

Be aware that templates can limit your flexibility to vary the content of pages created from the template. For example, to a large extent, head content is locked in pages created from templates, so you cannot add many common elements that add code to the head of a page to the template-based pages. Also, you cannot add content outside the established editable regions.

Templates, like style sheets, reduce much of the redundant work that goes into creating and maintaining a Web site. You do the work once to set up the page layout, including CSS styles, a navigation bar, and a footer, in a template. You or others can use that template to quickly create any number of pages with that same layout. Anyone can then add content to the pages without affecting the layout or design. If you later decide to modify the layout, you need to make the changes only in one place—the template. Any pages created from a template are connected to that template. If you modify a template, all the pages connected to that template are updated to reflect the changes. This saves you time and ensures consistency across the pages.

A site usually has only one main template, but you can use more than one main template if some pages in the site have distinctly different styles. For example, if Brian wants each band under the Cosmatic label to have a Web page in the Cosmatic site with a completely different look and feel than the other pages in the site, you could create a separate template for those pages. Using more than two main templates in one site is generally not a good idea because the site can get cumbersome and confusing. In addition, it is easy to forget to make changes that affect the whole site to every template.

Creating a Template

Templates can be created from a new blank page or an existing page in a site. When you create a template from a blank page, you must add all the elements that you want to include in pages made from the template to the template page. In the Cosmatic site, for example, you must attach the CSS style sheet to the template and create any new CSS styles you plan to use in the subsequent pages, you must add the Cosmatic logo at the top of the template page to have the logo appear in the new pages, and you must add the keywords and meta description that will be used in the pages. When you create a template from an existing page, all of these shared elements are already in the page. The page from which you created the template is unaffected and is not attached to the template.

InSight | **Creating a New Template for Each Site**

Although you can save a template from one site to another site and use that template to create pages in the other site, it is not a good idea to do so. Copying a template from one site to another causes all of the relative links in the template (including links to graphics and other materials used in the template) to become absolute links. To use the template in the new site, you must change the links to relative links and copy the materials used in the template to the new site's local root directory. Furthermore, choosing a template from another site when you create a new Web page causes these same problems, and it does not move a copy of the template to the new site. Also, if you choose a template from another site and you leave the Update page when template changes check box checked (which is its default state), then the links will be in a locked area of the template and you cannot change them. Thus, you will not be able to view the template content when you post the new page to the Web. Because of these problems, it is a good idea to create a new template for each site.

When you create a new template, you need to save it with a unique name. As with other filenames, use only alphanumeric characters, do not use spaces or special characters, and do not start the name with a number. If you create more than one main template in a site, choose a name that will help you to identify the template. The template file is saved with the .dwt extension in a Templates folder in the site's local root folder. If the Templates folder does not already exist, Dreamweaver creates one. You can view all the templates for a site in the Assets panel when the Templates button is selected.

Reference Window | **Creating a Template**

- Open an existing page, and then, on the Common tab of the Insert bar, click the Make Template button in the Templates list (or in the Assets panel, click the Templates button, and then click the New Template button or click File on the menu bar, click New, click Blank Template, click HTML Template in the Template Type box, click a layout in the Layout box, and then click the Create button).
- Type a name for the template, and then save the template.
- If you created a new template from the Assets panel, select the template in the Assets panel, and then click the Edit Template button.
- Add editable regions to the template using the buttons in the Templates list on the Common tab of the Insert bar.
- Save the template.

You'll create a template for the Cosmatic site based on the existing Label page. You'll use the Label page because it has the most basic layout of all the existing pages—it doesn't contain any special media elements—and will be the easiest page to modify. Brian is developing a series of new pages with information about indie music and the current underground music scene in the United States. The template will be used to create these new pages in the site. Eventually, the existing pages in the Cosmatic site will be converted to the template so that the look of the entire site can be managed and updated more easily.

To create a template from the Label page:

▶ **1.** If you took a break after the previous session, make sure that the Cosmatic site is open.

▶ **2.** Open the **label.html** page in the Document window. This page will be modified to create the template layout.

▶ **3.** On the **Common** tab of the Insert bar, click the **Templates button arrow** 📄▾ , and then click the **Make Template** button 📄 . The Save As Template dialog box opens. See Figure 9-15.

Save As Template dialog box ◀ Figure 9-15

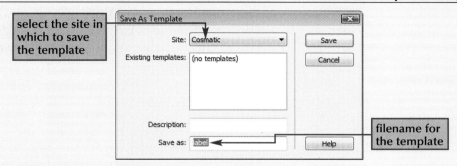

select the site in which to save the template

filename for the template

▶ **4.** If necessary, click the **Site** button, and then click **Cosmatic**. This selects the site in which you will save the template.

▶ **5.** Type **cosmatic_main** in the Save As box, and then click the **Save** button. A dialog box opens, prompting you to update links.

▶ **6.** Click the **Yes** button. Dreamweaver creates a copy of the page with the name cosmatic_main.dwt, creates a Templates folder in the site's local root folder, and then saves the template in that folder.

▶ **7.** In the Files panel, click the **Plus (+)** button ➕ next to the Templates folders to expand the folder, if necessary. See Figure 9-16.

New template page ◀ Figure 9-16

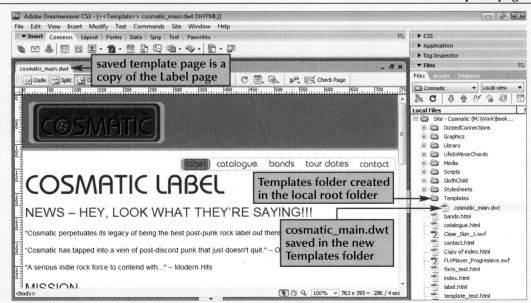

saved template page is a copy of the Label page

Templates folder created in the local root folder

cosmatic_main.dwt saved in the new Templates folder

Adding Regions to a Template

When you create a template, the entire document is locked. In other words, the page is one big noneditable region and only the template itself can be edited. You must add at least one editable region to the template to be able to change page content and other elements in the pages created from the template. Anything outside an editable region can be altered only within the template.

You can add the following types of regions to a template:

- **Editable region.** An area in a template-based page that can be edited. Any area can be defined as an editable region. You can designate either an entire table or a single table cell as editable; however, you cannot designate multiple cells as one editable region. Also, AP divs and their content are separate elements. Designating an AP div as editable enables you to move it. Designating the area inside the AP div as editable enables you to change its content.

- **Optional region.** A noneditable region for which you set conditions for displaying the content in that region in template-based pages. You set parameters for displaying the optional region content when you create the template. The regions are displayed in the pages created from the template only if those conditions or parameters are met.

- **Repeating region.** A region that can be duplicated within the pages made from the template, enabling the region to expand without altering the page design. For example, you can designate a table row as a repeating region, and then you can repeat the table row in the template-based pages to create expanding lists and so forth. The repeating region is used so frequently with tables that the Templates list on the Common tab of the Insert bar includes a Repeating Table button in addition to the Repeating Region button.

- **Editable optional region.** An optional region that is editable.

- **Editable tag attribute.** A tag attribute that you unlock in a template so that the attribute can be edited in the pages created from the template. For example, you can "lock" which graphic appears in the template-based pages, and then create an editable tag attribute that enables the person editing these pages to set the graphic's alignment.

You'll delete the page-specific content from the cosmatic_main template as you create editable regions in the template.

With the exception of the title and a few other page-specific elements, the head content is locked in the pages created from a template. This means that you cannot add navigation bars and many other common elements that place code into the head of the page to template-based pages. Many elements that add code to the head of a page must be added either directly in the template or, sometimes, in a library item that is placed in an editable region.

Regions added to templates are invisible elements. When you show Invisible Elements, a border appears around the regions in both the template and the template-based pages and a tab appears at the top of each region in the Document window. Although the border and tab help you to quickly identify each region, they also interfere slightly with the way the layout appears in the Document window. To see a page as it will appear in browsers, you must hide the invisible elements or preview the page in a browser.

You will show the invisible elements, if necessary, and then add editable regions to the template in the Cosmatic site. You'll begin by creating an editable region named "PageHeading" at the top of the template. You want to make the page heading an editable region so that you can change the heading for each new page created from the template.

To add the page heading as an editable region to the template:

▶ **1.** If necessary, click **View** on the menu bar, point to **Visual Aids**, and then click **Invisible Elements** to check it. You will be able to see any invisible elements you add in the page.

▶ **2.** Select the **Cosmatic Label** Flash text. The page heading is selected.

▶ **3.** On the **Common** tab of the Insert bar, click the **Templates button arrow** 📄 ▾ , and then click the **Editable Region** button 📝 . The New Editable Region dialog box opens.

▶ **4.** Type **PageHeading** in the Name box, and then click the **OK** button. The new editable region is added to the template, and a tab appears over the text.

▶ **5.** Press the **Right Arrow** key to deselect the Flash text. A blue border surrounds the editable region with the page heading text. See Figure 9-17.

Editable region added to the template page | **Figure 9-17**

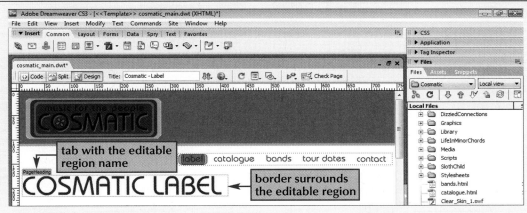

Trouble? If the tab is not visible in the Document window, Invisible Elements are hidden. Click View on the menu bar, point to Visual Aids, and then click Invisible Elements.

You'll change the page heading from the page-specific content to generic placeholder text. You need to create a new Flash text file with the placeholder text, otherwise the Flash text in the Label page will also change because the same Flash text file will be used in both pages.

▶ **6.** Double-click the **Flash text** in the editable region. The Insert Flash Text dialog box opens.

▶ **7.** Type **NEW PAGE HEADING** in the Text box to replace the COSMATIC Label text. This is the generic placeholder text.

▶ **8.** Type **../Media/HeadingTemplate.swf** in the Save As box. The new Flash text file will be saved in the Media folder with the filename HeadingTemplate.swf.

▶ **9.** Click the **OK** button. The placeholder text is saved in the Media folder and appears in the template.

Next, you'll create a repeating region with a table. You will use the Repeating Table button, and the table will be added to the repeating region for you. The Repeating Table button also adds an editable area in the table so that you can add content to the table in pages that are created from the template. Remember that repeating regions can be editable or noneditable. If you plan to add content in the repeating region within the pages created from the template, you must add an editable region within the repeating region.

You'll delete the body text from the template and add a repeating table with an editable region named "Content." You'll use this repeating table to enter the general content for each page that is created from the template.

To create a repeating table in the template:

▶ **1.** Delete all of the text below the page heading and above the footer in the template.

▶ **2.** On the **Common** tab of the Insert bar, click the **Templates button arrow** ⬚ ▾ , and then click the **Repeating Table** button ⬚ . The Insert Repeating Table dialog box opens. See Figure 9-18.

Figure 9-18 ▶ **Insert Repeating Table dialog box**

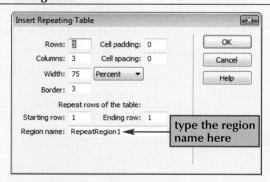

▶ **3.** Type **1** in the Rows box, type **1** in the Columns box, type **100** in the Width box, select **Percent** from the list, if necessary, and then type **0** in the Border box. This will create a borderless one-cell table the full width of the page.

▶ **4.** Type **Content** in the Region name box, and then click the **OK** button. A repeating table named "Content" with an unnamed editable region is placed in the page below the page heading.

▶ **5.** Click in a blank area of the page to deselect the table. See Figure 9-19.

Figure 9-19 ▶ **Repeating table with an editable region**

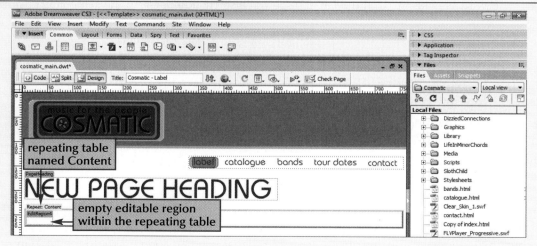

6. Click in the editable region in the repeating table, and then type **Add content here.** (including the period). This placeholder text will act as a reminder to enter appropriate content in the template-based pages.

Finally, you will modify the navigation bar so that no images appear in the Down state when the page is loaded. This is necessary because you cannot modify the navigation bar in the pages created from the template. If the navigation bar was not altered, all the pages created from the template would show the label button in the Down state initially.

To modify the navigation bar in the template:

1. Click **Modify** on the menu bar, and then click **Navigation Bar**. The Modify Navigation Bar dialog box opens.

2. If necessary, click **Label *** in the Nav Bar Elements box.

3. Click the **Show "Down Image" Initially** check box to uncheck it, and then click the **OK** button.

4. Click a blank area of the Document window to deselect all of the page elements, and then save the template. See Figure 9-20.

Template with the modified navigation bar | Figure 9-20

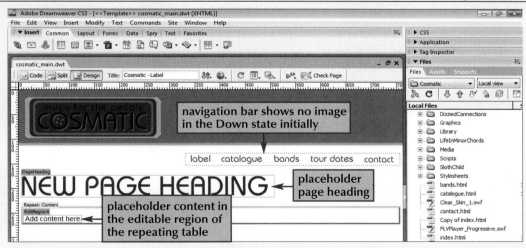

Trouble? If a dialog box opens, stating that you placed the PageHeading editable region inside a block tag and that users of the template will not be able to create new blocks in this region, click the OK button. If additional dialog boxes open, click the OK button to close them. The PageHeading region is inside <h1> tags (which are block tags); any text entered in the field will have the h1 style, which is good, in this case, because the heading text had the h1 style applied to it. Because the heading is now Flash text, the tags do not affect it. This dialog box may open whenever you save the page; if it does, click the OK button each time.

5. Close the cosmatic_main page.

Creating Web Pages from a Template

After you create a template, you should test it by creating a page from the template. There are two ways to create a Web page from a template. You can create a new page based on the template and then add the appropriate content to the editable regions, or you can apply the template to an existing page that already contains content.

Creating a New Template-Based Page

Creating a new page from a template is similar to creating a new, blank page as you have done before. The only difference is that you select the template you want to base the page on. After the page is created, you add content to the editable regions, and then save the page as usual.

Reference Window | **Creating a Template-Based Page**

- Click File on the menu bar, and then click New.
- Click Page from Templates in the New Document dialog box.
- Select the current site, and then select the template from which you want to create the page.
- Click the Create button.
- Enter the appropriate content into the editable regions of the page, and then save the page.

Brian wants to see a sample page from the new template before more pages are added to the Cosmatic site. You will create a new page from the cosmatic_main template, and then add a new page heading and some content to the test page.

To create a new Web page from the cosmatic_main template:

▶ **1.** Click **File** on the menu bar, and then click **New**. The New Document dialog box opens.

▶ **2.** Click **Page from Template**. The Page from Template options appear in the dialog box. See Figure 9-21.

Page from Template options in the New Document dialog box ◀ **Figure 9-21**

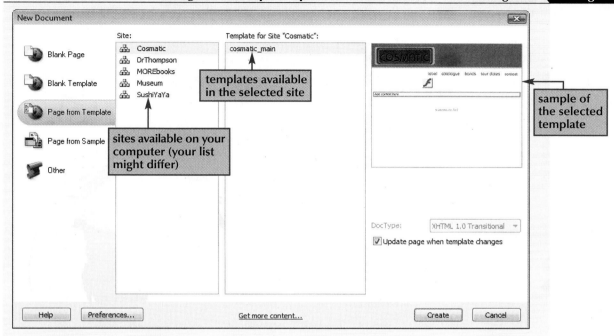

3. If necessary, click **Cosmatic** in the Site box, and then click **cosmatic_main** in the Template for Site "Cosmatic" box. A preview of the selected template page appears in the dialog box.

4. Verify that the **Update page when template changes** check box is checked.

5. Click the **Create** button. A new page based on the cosmatic_main template opens in the Document window. See Figure 9-22.

Page created from the cosmatic_main template ◀ **Figure 9-22**

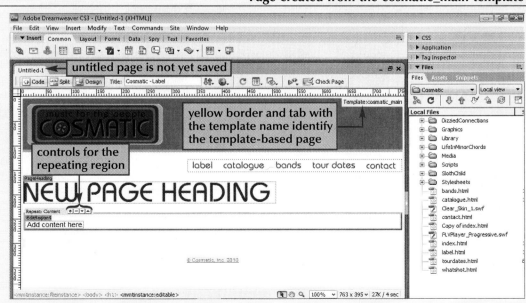

6. Save the page as **template_test.html** in the site's local root folder.

As a further test, you'll add content to the editable regions in the new template-based page. You'll create a new Flash text file for the modified page heading, add multiple rows of content to the repeating table, and update the page title.

To add content to the editable regions in the Test page:

▶ 1. In the Title box on the Document toolbar, select **Label**, type **Test**, and then press the **Enter** key. The page title changes to reflect the content of the new page.

▶ 2. Double-click the **PageHeading** editable region. The Insert Flash Text dialog box opens.

▶ 3. Select the text in the Text box, if necessary, and then type **TEMPLATE TEST PAGE**.

▶ 4. Click the Save As **Browse** button, navigate to the **Media** folder, if necessary, type **HeadingTest.swf** in the File name box, and then click the **Save** button. The page heading of the test page is saved as a new Flash text file. (Remember, each time you create a page from the template, you must save the Flash text with a new filename.)

▶ 5. Click the **OK** button. The new heading appears in the PageHeading region.

▶ 6. Select **Add content here.** in the editable region in the repeating table Content, and then type **Placeholder text for the test page.** (including the period).

You'll test the repeating table by adding a second row to the table.

▶ 7. In the Repeat: Content tab, click the **Plus** button ⊞. A second editable region appears in the page.

▶ 8. Select the text in the new editable region, if necessary, and then type **More text will be placed here.** (including the period). See Figure 9-23.

Figure 9-23 ▶ **Test page with new content**

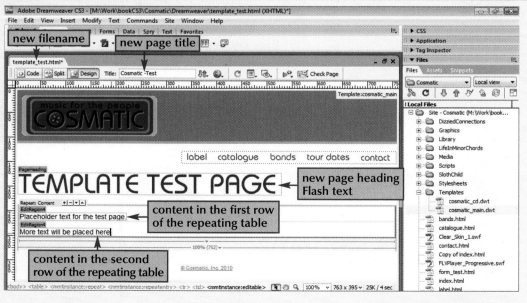

▶ 9. Save the Test page, and then preview the page in a browser. See Figure 9-24.

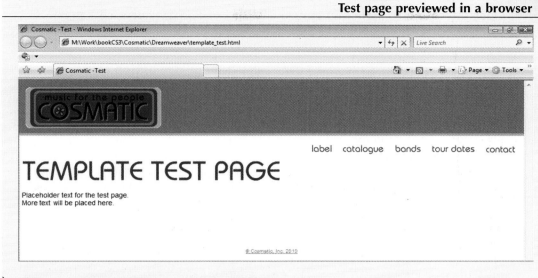

Test page previewed in a browser | Figure 9-24

▶ **10.** Close the browser, and then close the page.

Applying a Template to an Existing Web Page

If you already have a page with content, you can apply a template to it. When you apply a template to an existing page, the page uses the layout of the template page and a dialog box opens so you can designate into which regions the existing content will be placed. This can get a bit confusing, especially with complex pages that contain a lot of content. It is usually easier to create a new template-based page and move the content from the existing page into the new page.

Editing a Template

One of the most powerful aspects of using templates is that you can adjust all of the template-based pages in a site at once by editing the template. This ability to make a change once saves you time and ensures that all of the pages maintain a consistent design, which is similar to the benefits of using CSS styles. Adjusting elements in the editable regions of a template affects only new pages created from that template. Pages that were already created are not affected because updating content in editable regions to reflect the modified template would overwrite any new content you added to the template-based pages. However, repositioning existing editable regions, adding new editable regions, or adjusting anything in a noneditable region affects all existing template-based pages, as well as any new pages created from the template. You can also delete the various regions from the template. When you delete an editable region from the template, you choose what happens to the content in that region in the existing template-based pages. You can either move any content from that region to another editable region or you can delete the content in that region from the page. You can add, edit, or delete content from the noneditable regions. Any changes made to the noneditable regions in the template affect all of pages created from the template—whether new or existing.

Brian noticed that every page in the Cosmatic site has a subheading below the page heading. He wants you to add an editable region named "SubHeading" for the subheading to the template.

To edit the cosmatic_main template:

1. Open the **cosmatic_main.dwt** template in the Document window, click in the blank area to the right of the PageHeading region, and then press the **Enter** key. A new line is created below the PageHeading region.

2. On the **Common** tab of the Insert bar, click the **Templates button arrow** ⊞ ▾ , and then click the **Editable Region** button 📝 . The New Editable Region dialog box opens.

3. Type **SubHeading** in the Name box, and then click the **OK** button. The new editable region appears in the site.

   Trouble? If the SubHeading text is not visible, it is blocked by the tab of the Content repeating table and you need to hide the invisible elements. Click View on the menu bar, point to Visual Aids, and then click Invisible Elements to hide the tab and view the text, complete Step 4, and then show the invisible elements.

4. Select the **SubHeading** placeholder text in the SubHeading region, and then, in the Property inspector, click the **Format** button and click **Heading 2**. The SubHeading text is formatted.

5. Click the **Right Arrow** key to deselect the SubHeading text. See Figure 9-25.

Figure 9-25 ▸ **Edited template page**

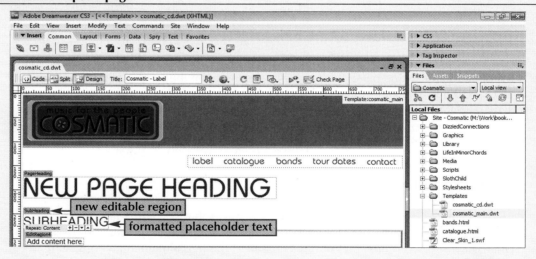

---

6. Save the template. The Update Template Files dialog box opens, asking whether to update the pages created from the template to reflect the changes in the template. You want this change to appear in the existing template-based pages—in this case, the template_test.html page.

   Trouble? If a dialog box opens, stating that the PageHeading region is in a block tag, click the OK button. This dialog box might open whenever you save the page; if it does, click the OK button each time.

7. Click the **Update** button to update the page, review the changes in the Update Pages dialog box when the update is complete, and then click the **Close** button.

8. Close the cosmatic_main template, and then open the **template_test.html** page. The subheading has been added to this page, which you earlier created from the template.

9. Select the placeholder text in the SubHeading region, and then type **template test subheading**. The text appears in all capital letters, as specified in the style.

10. Save the Test page, and then preview the page in a browser. See Figure 9-26.

Figure 9-26 **Edited Template Test page previewed in a browser**

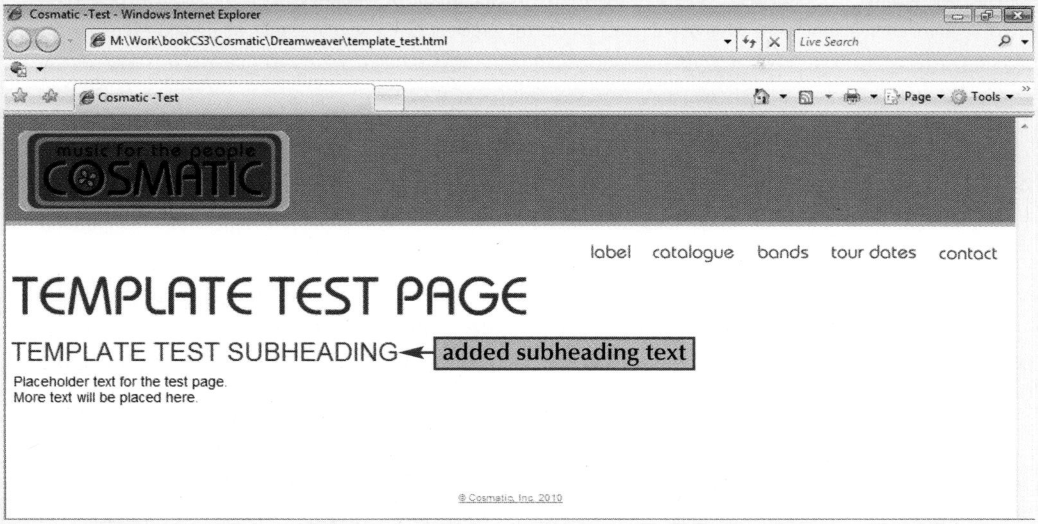

11. Close the browser, and then close the page.

Deleting a Template

If a template is no longer relevant for a site, you can delete the entire template. You delete an entire template from a site by selecting the template in the Assets panel and clicking the Delete button . When you delete a template, the pages that were created from that template still contain the template mark-up code. You must also detach the pages from the attached template to make them regular Web pages.

Tip

To detach a page from a template, open the template-based page, click Modify on the menu bar, point to Templates, and then click Detach From Template.

Creating Nested Templates

Nested templates are templates created from the main template so that you can create a more defined structure for some pages of a site. Each nested template inherits all the features of the main template. In other words, each nested template contains the same editable and noneditable regions as the main template and is linked to the main template. You can add additional editable regions to the nested template, but only within the editable regions that exist in the main template. Any change you make to the main template affects all the nested templates as well as any pages created from the main template and the nested templates. Any change you make to a nested template affects only the pages created from that nested template.

Nested templates enable you to maintain even greater control over the look of the pages in a site because you further limit the choices people have when they input content into those pages. For example, because many pages in the Cosmatic site have subheadings below the page heading followed by a paragraph of text and another subheading, you could create a nested template with an editable region for a subheading followed by an editable region for text within the editable region that is designated for content in the main template.

| InSight | | **Using Nested Templates** |

Nested templates are also useful when a Web site includes more than one major style of page. For example, consider a site with both informational pages and product pages. If informational pages have one style and product pages have a different style but the same basic page properties (CSS styles, navigation bar, and so on), you can create a main template for the site and a nested template for each type of page. Another example is a site that has the same basic layout for all pages, but uses a different background color for each major section of the site. You might create a nested template for each section and change only the background color. You save time and eliminate work because the basic layout for each type of page is already designed and all your pages are still connected to the same main template.

At some point, Brian plans to add a new page to the site for every CD that Cosmatic produces. All the new CD pages will have the same layout. You'll create a nested template based on the main template with the special layout Brian wants to use for these pages.

To create a nested template for the cosmatic_main template:

▶ 1. Create a new page from the cosmatic_main.dwt template.

▶ 2. On the **Common** tab of the Insert bar, click the **Templates button arrow** 🗒 ▾ , and then click the **Make Nested Template** button 🗒 . The Save As Template dialog box opens.

▶ 3. Type **cosmatic_cd** in the Save As box, and then click the **Save** button to save the nested template.

▶ 4. Delete all the text in the EditRegion within the Repeat:Content region. You'll create a table in this editable region.

▶ 5. On the **Common** tab of the Insert bar, click the **Table** button 🖩 , create a table with 2 rows, 2 columns, 100% width, 0 border thickness, 0 cell padding, 0 cell spacing, Top header, and then click the **OK** button. The new table appears in the nested template.

▶ 6. Merge the bottom cells, top-align both cells in the top row, and then left-align the upper-right cell.

▶ 7. In the upper-left cell, type **Add content here.** (including the period).

▶ 8. In the upper-right cell, insert the **DCcd300.jpg** graphic located in the **Graphics** folder in the site's local root folder.

▶ 9. In the bottom cell, type **Add additional content here.** (including the period). See Figure 9-27.

Nested template page | Figure 9-27

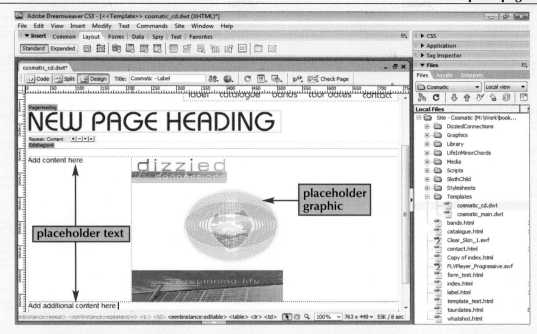

10. Save the nested template, and then, if necessary, click the **Yes** button in the dialog box that opens to update all the documents in your local site that use the template. The Update Pages dialog box opens.

11. Click the **Close** button once the pages are done updating, if necessary. The nested template appears in the Templates folder in the Files panel.

Trouble? If you don't see cosmatic_cd.dwt in the Templates folder, you may need to refresh the Files panel. On the Files panel toolbar, click the Refresh button ⟳ to display the new template in the Templates folder.

12. Close the nested template.

You create pages from a nested template in the same way that you create pages from the main template. The changes you make to the main template flow through to nested templates.

Brian decided that including the SubHeading editable region in the main template for the Cosmatic site is too restrictive. He asks you to delete the region from the cosmatic_main template. When you delete a region from a template, you must decide where to move the text that was located in that region in the existing template-based pages. You can choose to move the content either to another editable region that is in the page or nowhere, which then deletes the content from the pages.

To delete the SubHeading editable region from the cosmatic_main template:

1. Open the **cosmatic_main.dwt** template in the Document window, select the **SubHeading** editable region, and then press the **Delete** key. The region is removed from the template.

2. Save the template. The Update Template Files dialog box opens.

▶ **3.** Click the **Update** button to update the nested template and the page you created from the template. The Inconsistent Region Names dialog box opens. See Figure 9-28.

Figure 9-28 | **Inconsistent Region Names dialog box**

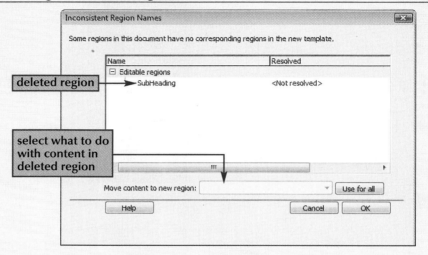

▶ **4.** Click **SubHeading** (the region that was deleted from the template) in the Name list, click the **Move content to new region** button, click **Nowhere**, and then click the **OK** button. The text that was in the SubHeading region is cleared from the nested template and the template-based page.

▶ **5.** Click the **Close** button in the Update Pages dialog box, and then close the template.

▶ **6.** Open the **cosmatic_cd.dwt** nested template in the Document window, verify that the SubHeading region was deleted from the nested template, and then close the nested template.

▶ **7.** Open the **template_test.html** page in the Document window, verify that the text from the SubHeading region was deleted from the page, and then close the page.

In this session, you created a template, added editable regions to the page, and then created a new page based on the template. You also created a nested template and edited the main template. In the next session, you'll add a form to the Contact page.

Review | **Session 9.2 Quick Check**

1. Does creating a template-based site require more or less planning than creating a regular Web site? Explain your answer.

2. What are noneditable regions?

3. How does editing a template affect pages that were created from that template?

4. What is a nested template?

5. True or False? Nested templates inherit all the characteristics of the main template.

6. What happens when you delete an editable region from the main template?

Session 9.3

Understanding Forms

Forms have become an important element in Web design because they provide a way to interact with users. A **form** is a means of collecting information from users. You can use forms to gather information about the user, create a user log in, gather user feedback, and so on. Forms encourage user interaction because they enable the user to enter and send information over the Web without leaving the Web site. The user inputs information into the Web page by typing requested data into designated fields or clicking check boxes, option buttons, lists, and so forth to make selections. Once the form is filled out, the user submits the information, which sends the information somewhere, usually to the server, for processing. Forms do not process information. After the form information is processed, the server (or information-processing destination) sends requested information back to the user, such as search information, or performs tasks based on the collected information, such as logging in a user.

Several steps must occur for a form to work:

- The designer creates a form in a Web page.
- The designer installs a script or application in the designated information-processing destination, which is usually a server, to process the form information. (Most forms cannot work without server-side scripts or applications that process the information.)
- The user fills out the form and clicks the Submit button.
- The information-processing destination, such as a server, receives the information and a server-side script or application processes the information.
- The server or information-processing destination sends requested information back to the user or performs an action based on the form's information.

You will create a form in the Contact page to enable site visitors to communicate with Cosmatic and Cosmatic to gather information about the site visitors.

Creating a Form

You can create a form in any Web page. Before you create a form, you should plan what information you want to collect, how the form should be designed to best collect that information, and in which page to create the form. For example, Sara wants to collect information from users to determine which bands they are listening to and what types of music they like as well as collect their mailing address and e-mail information. The form will be in the Contact page.

Reference Window | **Creating a Form**

- Add the script that will process the form data to the server or information-processing destination.
- Open the page in which you want a form, position the insertion point at the location you want to insert the form, and then on the Forms tab of the Insert bar, click the Form button.
- Set the form attributes, including Form Name, Action, Method, Enctype, and Target.
- Add form objects and explanations for each form object to the form, and then set the attributes for each form object, including a name.
- Add a Submit button to the form.
- Add the Verification behavior to the form.
- Test the form in a browser.

The general process for creating a form is to add a form to a Web page, set form attributes, add form objects, and then validate form data.

Adding a Form to a Web Page

The first step in creating a form is to add the form to a page. Basically, adding a form to a Web page places a container in the page for the form content that you will add. You should try to add the form at the page location where you want the form to appear, but you can reposition the form later if you change your mind. When you add a form to a Web page, Dreamweaver inserts <form> </form> tags in the code for the page, and a red dotted line appears in the Document window in Design view. The red line designates the form area in Dreamweaver and is invisible in the browser window.

You'll add a form at the bottom of the Contact page.

To add a form to the Contact page:

▶ 1. If you took a break after the previous session, make sure that the Cosmatic site is open.

▶ 2. Open the **contact.html** page in the Document window, click in the blank line below the Directions content, and then press the **Shift+Enter** keys to create a new line. You'll insert the form on this new line.

   Trouble? If there is no blank line below the Directions content, you need to add one. Click at the end of the paragraph below the Directions heading, press the Shift+Enter keys twice to insert two new lines, and then continue with Step 3.

▶ 3. Click the **Forms** tab on the Insert bar, and then click the **Form** button 🔲 . A red dotted line that designates the form area appears in the Contact page below the content. See Figure 9-29.

Form added to the Contact page Figure 9-29

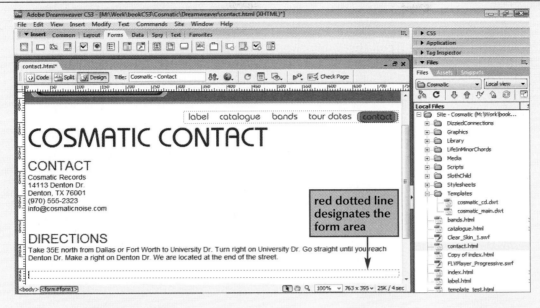

4. Save the Contact page.

Setting Form Attributes

After you have added a form to a page, you can adjust the form attributes in the Property inspector when the form is selected. You must set all of the form attributes except the Target attribute, which is optional. Form attributes include:

- **Form name.** A unique name for the form. The form name enables the form to be referenced or controlled with a scripting language. If you do not name the form, Dreamweaver generates a unique name for it. The form name can include alphanumeric characters, but cannot begin with a number and include spaces or special characters.

- **Action.** The path to the location of the script you will use to process the form data. You must install the script or create the page in the desired location prior to setting the Action. You can also type "mailto:" followed by an e-mail address in the Action box to send the form information to a specified e-mail address (the mailto: link works only if the user is on a computer configured to send e-mail), or you can type the name of a JavaScript function in the Action box if you are using a JavaScript to process the form.

- **Method.** The way form data will be sent to the location specified in the Action box. POST embeds form data in an HTTP request. When you use the POST method, the form data is not visible. POST is the preferred method for most forms. GET appends the form data to the end of the path specified in the Action box. When you use the GET method, form data is limited to 8,192 characters of information and is visible because it is added to the end of the URL. GET is frequently used for search engine requests. Default uses the browser default of the user's browser to send form data. The script or application you use to process form data may affect the method that you will need to use to send the form data.

- **Target.** The target destination for any response from the form. For example, if the script attached to the form sends a response to the user such as "Thank you for filling out the form. We have received your information.", that response will appear in the target destination. Target options are the usual _blank, _parent, _self, and _top.
- **Enctype (Encoding Type).** The Multipurpose Internet Mail Extensions encoding type (MIME type) for the form data. The MIME type is a file identification based on the MIME encoding system, which is the standard for identifying content on the Internet. Most forms use the application/x-www-form-urlencoded MIME type. The multipart/form-data MIME type is used for uploading files, such as when you use a file-upload field in a form.

You'll set each of these attributes for the form in the Contact page. You'll use "Contact-Form" as the form name. The action will eventually point to a script placed on the server to process the form data. The programming team is writing the script, but is waiting for information from the ISP. In the meantime, they have created a Web page with a script that will enable you to test the form by displaying the data that the form will send to the server when the Submit button is clicked. For now, you will place a copy of the test script Web page in the local root folder of the Cosmatic site and set the action to form_test.html. GET is the method for data delivery. The enctype is application/x-www-form-urlencoded. The target is _blank.

To set up the form in the Contact page:

▶ 1. Copy the **form_test.html** file located in the **Tutorial.09\Tutorial** folder included with your Data Files, and then paste it in the site's local root folder.

▶ 2. In the Contact page, click the red dotted line to select the form. The form attributes appear in the Property inspector.

▶ 3. Type **ContactForm** in the Form name box.

▶ 4. Type **form_test.html** in the Action box.

▶ 5. Click the **Method** arrow, and then click **GET**.

▶ 6. Click the **Enctype** arrow, and then click **application/x-www-form-urlencoded**.

▶ 7. Click the **Target** arrow, and then click **_blank**. See Figure 9-30.

Form attributes added to the form | Figure 9-30

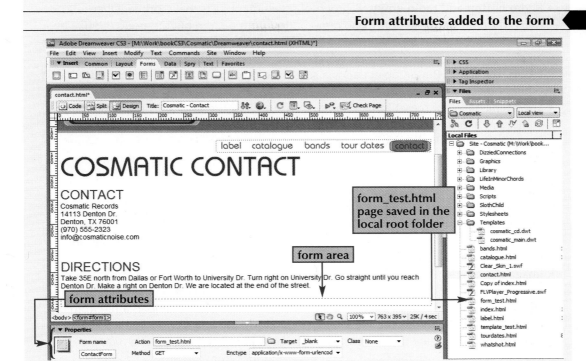

8. Save the page.

Adding Form Objects

You must add form objects to a form to make it useful. **Form objects** are generally the mechanisms that enable users to interact with a form. Each form object has a specific function:

- **Text fields and text areas.** A box into which a user can type input in a form. Text fields are usually used for short-answer input. Text areas are usually used for long-answer input. Text fields are displayed as a single-line box, whereas text areas are displayed as a multiple-line box. Both can accept either single or multiple lines of input. The input can be displayed as typed or as a series of dots or asterisks to protect private information. For example, a password is usually displayed as a series of asterisks when typed into a browser window.

- **Hidden fields.** Fields used to include information in a form that will be sent along with the form data to the server or designated processing location and which the user cannot see. For example, if a site has more than one form, you can use a hidden field to send the name of the form with the collected form data.

- **Checkbox.** A predefined toggle selection object in a form. Each checkbox can be toggled "on (checked)" or "off (unchecked)." A checkbox is toggled on or off independently, enabling the user to check as many items in a series of checkboxes as is appropriate. For example, you might use a series of checkboxes to have a user select all the types of music he or she listens to.

- **Radio button and radio group.** A group of selection objects that work together in a form. The user can select only one radio button from a radio button group. Unlike a checkbox, which can be toggled on and off independently, a selected radio button can be deselected only when the user selects another radio button within the radio button group. The Radio Button object adds a single radio button at a time, whereas the Radio Group object inserts an entire radio button group.
- **List/Menu.** A list of preset input choices in a form. List presents a list of possible input choices in a designated area, providing a scroll bar, if necessary, that enables users to navigate through the list. The user can select multiple items in a list. Menu presents the user with a list of choices in a drop-down menu. The user can select only one item from a menu.
- **Jump menu.** A special menu that contains a list of active links to other pages, graphics, or any type of file that can be opened in a browser. When a user selects an item from the jump menu, the new page or document opens. Unlike other form objects, the jump menu can be used within or outside a form because it includes form tags and a Submit button.
- **Image field.** A graphic used as a Submit or Reset button in a form. You can also use graphics as buttons that perform other tasks by adding behaviors.
- **File field.** A file upload field in the form that enables the user to upload a file from the client computer to the server. The file field contains a Browse button and a text box. The user can select the file using the Browse button or by typing the file path into the text box. You must use the POST method to send files from the browser to the server, and your Web server must be set up to handle this type of file upload.
- **Button.** A button in the form that performs the behavior you specify. The button can be designated as a Submit button or a Reset button, or it can have no designation at all. A Submit button sends the form data to the location you designated for processing. A Reset button clears any content that the user added to or modified in the form so that the user can start over. You can also add behaviors to the button, enabling it to perform other functions.

You'll use text fields, checkboxes, radio buttons, a list, a Submit button, and a Reset button in the Contact page form.

You set the attributes for a form object in the Property inspector when that object is selected in the form. Each type of object has a unique set of attributes. However, every object has a name attribute. It is important to name every form object because the scripting language uses this name to identify the form object. If you do not name an object, Dreamweaver names it for you, using the object type and a number as its name. It is better to name form objects yourself because the field name will be paired with the data from that field when it is sent to the processing destination. When you view the data collected from forms, you use the field name to identify the information beside it. If the name does not identify the field, you may have trouble understanding the information you collect. For example, you'll name the text field where users input their last name "LastName" so that when you view the data you see LastName beside the data captured in the last name field. Without this descriptive name, you might have trouble distinguishing the user's first name from the user's last name.

Creating the Form Structure

You want to add form objects to a form in logical groupings. For example, all similar or related information should be placed together so users can enter that data, such as all their personal information, at the same time. You should also include a label with brief instructions or a description of the information being requested for each object so users know what to do.

Organizing a Form's Structure | InSight

The requested information should be organized clearly within the form. You can use line breaks, paragraph breaks, tables, and so on within forms to lay out the form objects. However, a table is usually the simplest way to keep forms fairly clean. For example, you could insert a two-column table in a form that includes a separate row for each form object. Then, you can right-justify the form labels in the left column and left-justify the corresponding form objects in the right column. This creates a form that is well organized and easy to follow. It also creates a form that is fairly stable across browsers. Different versions of browsers sometimes display form objects in slightly different ways. Putting form objects in a table helps to keep them in the same place in a page regardless of how a user's browser displays the form. However, the form layout might still vary slightly in different browsers.

You'll use a two-column table without a border to organize the form in the Contact page.

To add a table to the Contact form:

▶ 1. Click in the form area, click the **Common** tab on the Insert bar, and then click the **Table** button 🔳 . The Table dialog box opens.

▶ 2. Create a table with 9 rows, 2 columns, 100% width, 0 border thickness, 10 cell padding, 0 cell spacing, and Top header.

▶ 3. Align the left column to the **Right** and the **Top**.

▶ 4. Align the right column to the **Left** and the **Top**.

▶ 5. Merge the cells in the top row.

You'll add the form heading to this merged row.

▶ 6. Type **Cosmatic – Contact Form** in the top row, center the form heading text, format the heading text in the Heading 2 style, and then deselect the text. See Figure 9-31.

Contact form with the inserted table | Figure 9-31

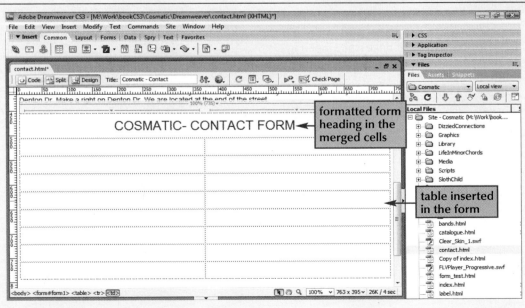

Inserting Text Fields and Areas into a Form

Text fields and areas are used to gather information that a user types. Most commonly, they are used for collecting name, address, and e-mail address information. You can set a number of attributes to control how each text field or area appears and functions in the form. In addition to Name, the attributes include:

- **Char width (Character Width).** The maximum number of characters that can be displayed. When the character width value is smaller than the maximum characters value, the text field or area will not display all the input without scrolling.
- **Max chars (Maximum Characters)/Num Lines (Number of Lines).** The maximum number of characters that the user can input into a single-line text field or the height of a multiple-line text area. You can use Max Chars to limit a user's response. For example, you can limit the number of characters in a text field used to input zip code information to five characters.
- **Type.** The designated appearance. Single line creates a text field that is one line in height. Multi Line creates a text area that is more than one line in height and has scroll bars. Password displays the data as dots or asterisks to protect the data.
- **Init val (Initial Value).** Text that is displayed until the user types new input.

You'll add single-line text fields for collecting the user's first name, last name, and e-mail address. Then you'll add a multi-line text area for collecting user comments.

To add text fields to the Contact form:

▶ 1. Click in the upper-left cell of the table below the form heading, type **First Name:** to enter the label for the first text field, and then press the **Tab** key to move the insertion point to the next cell.

▶ 2. Click the **Forms** tab on the Insert bar, and then click the **Text Field** button 🖵 . A text field is inserted in the cell. You'll set its attributes in the Property inspector.

Trouble? If the Input Tag Accessibility Attributes dialog box opens, the Accessibility preferences are not set to disable this prompt. Click the Cancel button to close the dialog box here and each time this dialog box opens when you insert a field.

▶ 3. In the Property inspector, type **FirstName** in the TextField box, type **50** in the Char width box, type **100** in the Max chars box, and then click the **Single line** option button, if necessary. See Figure 9-32.

Text field added to the form | Figure 9-32

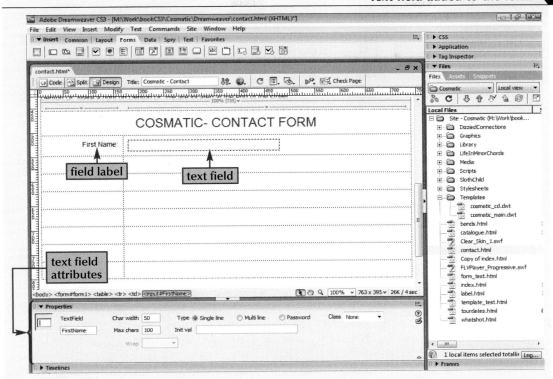

Next, you'll add the LastName label and text field to the third row of the table.

▶ **4.** Click in the left column of the third row of the table, type **Last Name:** to enter the label, and then press the **Tab** key to move the insertion point to the next cell.

▶ **5.** On the **Forms** tab of the Insert bar, click the **Text Field** button 🔲 to insert another text field, and then in the Property inspector, type **LastName** in the TextField box, type **50** in the Char width box, type **100** in the Max chars box, and click the **Single line** option button, if necessary.

You'll add the EmailAddress label and text field to the fourth row of the table.

▶ **6.** Click in the left column of the fourth row, type **E-mail Address:** to enter the label, and then press the **Tab** key to move the insertion point to the next cell.

▶ **7.** On the **Forms** tab of the Insert bar, click the **Text Field** button 🔲 to insert another text field, and then, in the Property inspector, type **EmailAddress** in the TextField box, type **50** in the Char width box, type **100** in the Max chars box, and click the **Single line** option button, if necessary.

You'll add the Comments label and text area to the fifth row of the table.

▶ **8.** Click in the left column of the fifth row, type **Comments:** to enter the label, and then press the **Tab** key to move the insertion point to the next cell.

▶ **9.** On the **Forms** tab of the Insert bar, click the **Text area** button 🔲 to add a multi-line text area to the cell, and then, in the Property inspector, type **Comments** in the TextField box, type **44** in the Char width box, type **10** in the Num lines box, and click the **Multi line** option button, if necessary. See Figure 9-33.

Tip

You can change a text field to a text area by changing the Type attribute from Single line to Multi line in the Property inspector.

Figure 9-33	Form with text fields

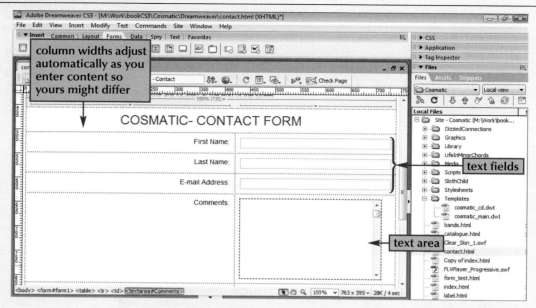

10. Save the Contact page, preview the page in a browser (the form has three text fields and one text area), and then close the browser.

Inserting Checkboxes into a Form

Checkboxes have only two attributes in addition to Name. Because some forms use many checkboxes, it is often convenient to use a code, instead of a name, in the script to process them. The other attributes are Checked Value and Initial State. Checked Value is where you can assign a value or a numeric code for a checkbox. The Checked Value is sent to the processing location along with the name when the checkbox is checked. Nothing is sent to the processing location if the checkbox is unchecked. Initial State sets whether the checkbox starts out checked or unchecked when a user first views the form.

Sara wants to find out what styles of music users like. You will insert a series of check-boxes into the form to enable users to select the types of music they enjoy. You will not include a checked value for these checkboxes.

To add checkboxes to the Contact form:

1. Click in the left column of the sixth row, type **Check all of the musical styles that interest you.** (including the period), and then press the **Tab** key to move the inser-tion point to the next cell.

2. On the **Forms** tab of the Insert bar, click the **Checkbox** button ☑ to insert a checkbox in the cell.

3. In the Property inspector, type **Punk** in the Checkbox name box, and then click the **Unchecked** option button, if necessary.

4. Click to the right of the checkbox in the table, type **Punk**, and then press the **Shift+Enter** keys to create a new line in the cell.

▶ **5.** Repeat Steps 2 through 4 to create the following checkboxes: **Alternative**, **Trance**, and **Jazz**. See Figure 9-34.

Form with checkboxes | **Figure 9-34**

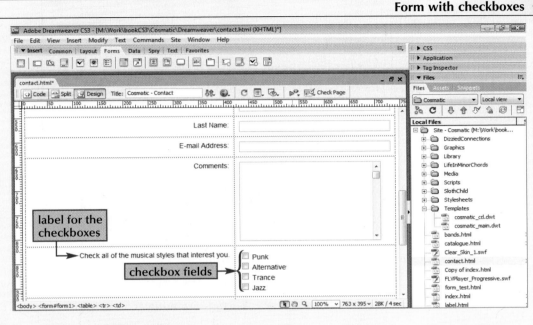

▶ **6.** Save the Contact page.

Adding Radio Buttons to a Form

Radio buttons are a group of selection objects that work together in a form. Users can select only one radio button from a radio button group. You can insert a group of radio buttons into your form using the Radio Group button. When you click the Radio Group button, a dialog box opens so you can name the radio group, label each radio button with the text you want to appear beside it in the form, and enter a value for the Checked Value of each button. Unlike checkboxes, the label information for a selected radio button does not appear when the information is sent to the processing location. You must enter a unique value for each radio button to distinguish which radio button was selected. When you click the OK button, the radio group is added to the form. When you select a radio button in a form, the name of the radio group to which the button belongs appears in the Radio Button box, its value appears in the Checked Value box, and you can choose Checked or Unchecked as the initial state for the button.

Brian has decided to start a newsletter and he wants to give users the option to join the newsletter mailing list. You'll add a radio group with two radio buttons to the form to collect this information.

To add a group of radio buttons to the Contact form:

▶ **1.** Click in the left column of the seventh row, type **Would you like to receive a monthly newsletter with updates about the Cosmatic bands?**, and then press the **Tab** key to move the insertion point to the next cell.

▶ **2.** On the **Forms** tab of the Insert bar, click the **Radio Group** button [≣]. The Radio Group dialog box opens. See Figure 9-35.

| Figure 9-35 | Radio Group dialog box |

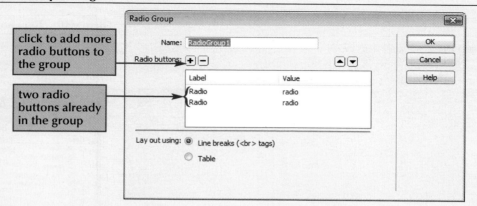

▶ 3. Type **Newsletter** in the Name box, click **Radio** in the first row of the Label column, type **Yes**, click **radio** in the first row of the Value column, and then type **Yes**.

▶ 4. Click **Radio** in the second row of the Label column, type **No**, click **radio** in the second row of the Value column, and then type **No**.

▶ 5. In the Lay out using group, click the **Line breaks** option button, if necessary.

▶ 6. Click the **OK** button. The Yes and No radio buttons are added to the form.

　You want the Yes radio button to be selected initially, so you'll change its initial state.

▶ 7. In the Document window, select the **Yes** radio button, and then, in the Property inspector, click the **Checked** option button in the Initial state group. See Figure 9-36.

| Figure 9-36 | Contact form with a radio group |

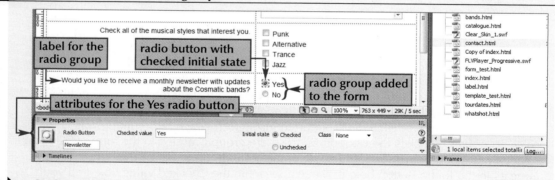

▶ 8. Save the Contact page.

Adding Lists to a Form

Lists are another way to enable users to choose several items from a group. There are a few attribute choices associated with lists. Height enables you to set how many rows are visible in the list box. You can add as many items to the list as you want. If the list includes more items than are visible in the list box, scroll bars enable the users to view all of the selections. The Selections check box enables you to set whether users can select only one item in the list (unchecked) or more than one item in the list (checked). The List Values button opens the dialog box in which you type the items that will appear in a list or edit existing items in a list. You can also associate a value with each item, which can be used by a script to identify the list item. The Initially Selected list enables you to select one or more items from the list to appear selected in the list. This option is often used to create a default selection, such as selecting Dallas from a list of cities because Cosmatic is based near Dallas and it is assumed that more users will be from that area. If you prefer the list to appear as a menu, click the Menu option button in the Type section.

Sara wants to know which bands users listen to. You will add a list field to the form that includes all the Cosmatic bands.

To add a list to the Contact form:

▶ 1. Click in the left column of the eighth row, type **Select all of the bands that you enjoy from the list.** (including the period), and then press the **Tab** key to move the insertion point to the next cell.

▶ 2. On the **Forms** tab of the Insert bar, click the **List/Menu** button 📄 to insert a list in the cell. A small list box appears in the form.

▶ 3. In the Property inspector, type **BandsList** in the List/Menu box, click the **List** option button in the Type group, type **3** in the Height box, and then check the **Allow multiple** check box in the Selections group. The Cosmatic bands list will be three rows high, and the user can select more than one band from the list.

▶ 4. In the Property inspector, click the **List Values** button. The List Values dialog box opens. See Figure 9-37.

List Values dialog box ◀ **Figure 9-37**

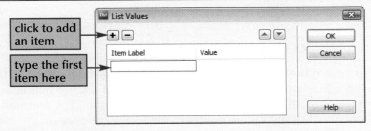

▶ 5. In the first row of the Item Label column, type **sloth child**, click in the first row of the Value column, and then type **sloth child**.

▶ 6. Click the **Add Item** button ➕ to add another item, and then type **dizzied connections** in each column.

▶ 7. Repeat Step 6 to add **Life in Minor Chords** and **surface suction** to the list.

▶ 8. Click the **OK** button. The items appear in the list. See Figure 9-38.

Tip

You can press the Tab key to move between columns and add another item in the List Values dialog box.

Figure 9-38 | **Completed list/menu box**

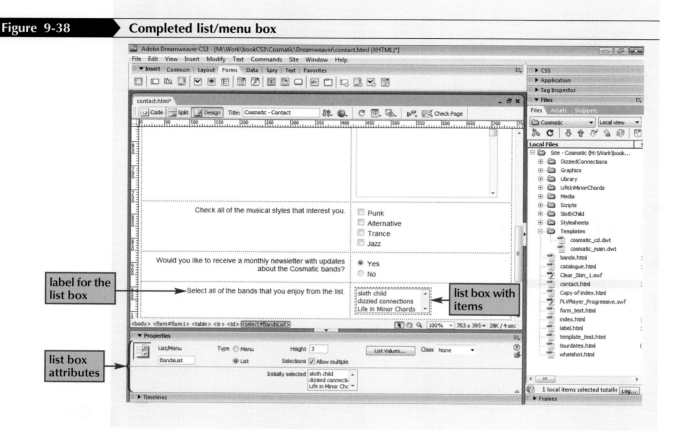

Adding Buttons to a Form

You must add a Submit button to a form to enable users to send the form data to the location where it will be processed. It is a good idea to add a Reset button as well so that users can clear any data they input into the form with one click and start over, if necessary. When you click the Button button in the Forms category on the Insert bar, it defaults to the Submit form action, which creates a Submit button. You can also choose the Reset Form action to create a Reset button, or you can choose None and then add other behaviors to the button. In addition to an action, you should type a name and a value for the button. The value will appear as text on the button, and the name is used to reference the button in the code.

You'll add a Submit button and a Reset button to the form.

To add a Submit button and a Reset button to the Contact form:

▶ **1.** Click in the left column of the last row, and then, on the **Forms** tab of the Insert bar, click the **Button** button ▢ . A Submit button appears in the form. See Figure 9-39.

Form with one button ◀ Figure 9-39

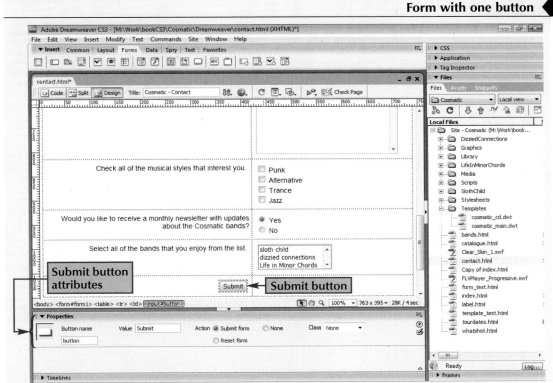

Trouble? If the button on your screen is not a Submit button, you need to adjust the button attributes. You'll do this in the following steps; continue with Step 2.

▶ **2.** If necessary, in the Property inspector, click the **Submit form** option button in the Action group, type **Submit** in the Button name box, and then type **Submit** in the Value box.

▶ **3.** In the Document window, click in the blank space to the right of the Submit button, and then, on the **Forms** tab of the Insert bar, click the **Button** button ▢ to insert another button.

▶ **4.** In the Property inspector, click the **Reset form** option button in the Action group, type **Reset** in the Button Name box, and then type **Reset** in the Value box, if necessary. The Reset button is added to the form. See Figure 9-40.

Figure 9-40 **Form with two buttons**

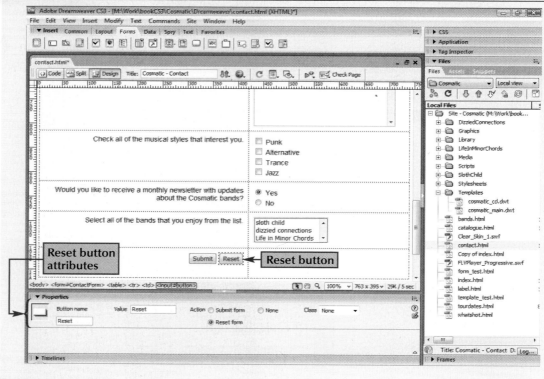

5. Save the Contact page.

Validating Form Data

The **Validate Form behavior** enables you to create requirements/limits that check the form data before the form is submitted. When you click Validate Form in the Behavior list, a dialog box opens so you can select each form object and then set limits/requirements. When the user clicks the Submit button, the data is checked to make sure the data meets the limits/requirements that were set for each object in the Validate Form behavior. If information is missing or is not within the set limits, a dialog box opens, prompting the user to change incorrect information or add missing information and then click the Submit button again.

The Validate Form dialog box displays all of the form objects in the Named Fields list box. You select a field from the list and then set the requirements/limits for that field. You first set whether the selected field is required or optional by checking or unchecking the Required check box in the Value section. The user must enter information into a required field in order to submit the form. If the field is optional, the form will be submitted even if the user does not enter information in that field. You can also set a variety of limits for the data the user enters into the selected field in the Accept section of the dialog box. Accept limits include:

- **Anything.** Allows the user to enter anything into the selected field.
- **Number.** Allows the user to enter only numeric values into the selected field. This limit is often used in fields that are used to input phone numbers or zip codes.

- **Email address.** Allows the user to enter only information that follows the format of an e-mail address (for example, something@something.topleveldomain). This limit does not ensure that the user has inserted a valid e-mail address, only that the submitted address is in the correct format.
- **Number from.** Enables you to set a range of acceptable numeric values for the field. The first box is the lowest acceptable numeric value for the field, and the second box is the highest acceptable numeric value for the field. For example, you might use this limit when you ask a question such as "How old is your teenager?" The lowest value would be 13 and the highest value would be 19. If a user inputs a number below 13 or above 19, the Validate Form behavior would inform the user that the data was outside the acceptable range, and then prompt the user to input an acceptable value and resubmit the form.

You'll add the Validate Form behavior to the form. You'll make the FirstName, Last-Name, and EmailAddress fields required fields and set the Email address limit for the EmailAddress field to ensure that all submitted addresses are in the correct format.

To add the Validate Form behavior to the contact form:

▶ **1.** On the status bar, click the **<form#ContactForm>** tag to select the form.

▶ **2.** Expand the **Tag Inspector panel group**, and then click the **Behaviors** tab to open the Behaviors panel.

▶ **3.** In the Behaviors panel, click the **Add Behavior** button ✚ , and then click **Validate Form**. The Validate Form dialog box opens. See Figure 9-41.

Tip

To select a difficult-to-select element, click its corresponding tag in the status bar.

Validate Form dialog box ◀ **Figure 9-41**

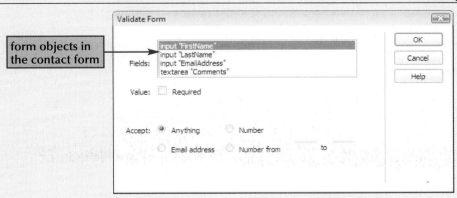

Trouble? If the Validate Form behavior is not available, you probably selected the table, a cell, or another part of the form rather than the form itself. Click in the Document window, and then repeat Step 1. You know the form is selected when the form attributes appear in the Property inspector.

▶ **4.** Select **input "FirstName"** in the Fields box, if necessary, and then check the **Required** check box. The text "(R)" appears after the field name to indicate that the field is required.

▶ **5.** Select **input "LastName"** in the Fields box, and then check the **Required** check box to make the field a required field.

▶ **6.** Select **input "EmailAddress"** in the Fields box, and then check the **Required** check box to make the field a required field.

▶ 7. In the Accept group, click the **Email Address** option button to set a limit requiring the data to follow the standard e-mail format. The text "(NisEmail) appears after the field name to indicate that the field is required and must be in the e-mail format.

▶ 8. Click the **OK** button. The Validate Form behavior appears in the Behavior list in the Behaviors panel.

▶ 9. In the Behaviors panel, click the **Events** arrow, and then click on **Submit**, if necessary. The behavior will run when the Submit button is clicked.

▶ 10. Save the Contact page.

Testing a Form

You should test a form to ensure that it displays properly in a browser and to ensure that the form functionality is working. You should view the form locally to verify that the form objects are laid out properly, and then you should upload the site and test the functionality of the form over the Web. It is sometimes possible to test the functionality of a form locally, but often, when the form-processing script resides on a Web server, the script will not work properly until the site is posted to the remote server. In this case, the script is located in a Web page and is set up to test the form. When you click the Submit button, the script will display the information that would be sent to the server if the script were located there.

InSight	Testing a Form

When you test a form, you should input data in each field to verify that it is functioning and then submit the form to verify that the processing script is working properly and that any requested information is returned to the end user. If the form returns an error, you should check the form attributes to make sure that the action, method, and enctype are correct. If you are still having problems, check the script to make sure that it is in the correct location and that it has been configured correctly.

You will test the form in the Contact page. Because the script is in a Web page, you can test the form locally. The process for testing the form is the same as it would be if you were testing the form over the Web.

To test the Contact form:

▶ 1. Preview the Contact page in a browser.

▶ 2. Type your first name in the First Name text box.

▶ 3. Type your last name in the Last Name text box.

▶ 4. Type **potato** in the E-mail Address text box.

▶ 5. Type **testing** in the Comments text area.

▶ 6. Check the **Punk** check box.

The Yes radio button is already selected because its initial state is set to checked.

▶ 7. Click **sloth child** in the bands list. See Figure 9-42.

Tip

To select multiple entries in the list, press the Ctrl key as you click each additional entry.

Contact page with the completed form | Figure 9-42

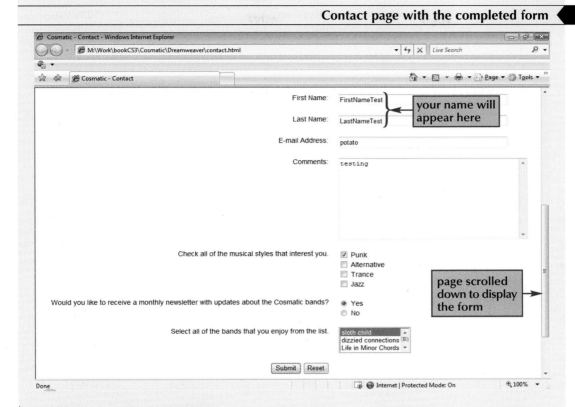

8. Click the **Submit** button. A dialog box opens, explaining that the E-mail Address box must contain an e-mail address. This means that the Validate Form behavior determined that "potato" is not in the correct format for an e-mail address.

9. Click the **OK** button, type your e-mail address in the E-mail Address box, and then click the **Submit** button. The test script opens another browser window with the form data that would be submitted to the server. See Figure 9-43.

Form data that would be sent to the server | Figure 9-43

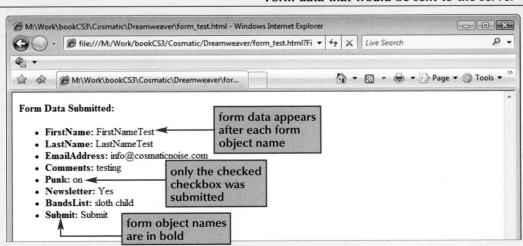

Trouble? If you do not have an e-mail address, type **info@cosmaticnoise.com** in the Email Address box.

▶ **10.** Close the browser window with the form data, click the **Reset** button in the form to clear the information from the form, and then close the browser and close the Contact page.

Updating the Web Site on the Remote Server

You'll upload the site to the remote server and preview the site over the Web. This way, you can see all the changes you made to the Cosmatic site, including the library item footer and the form.

To upload the Cosmatic site to your remote server:

▶ **1.** Click the **Connects to Remote Host** button 🔩 on the Files panel toolbar.

▶ **2.** Click the **View** button on the Files panel toolbar, and then click **Local View**.

▶ **3.** Select the **index.html**, **bands.html**, **catalogue.html**, **form_test.html**, **contact.html**, **label.htm**, and **tourdates.html** files in Local view, and then click the **Put File(s)** button ⬆ on the Files panel toolbar.

▶ **4.** Click the **Yes** button when prompted to include dependent files because you have not selected the new dependent files for the site yet.

▶ **5.** Click the **Disconnects from Remote Host** button 🔩 on the Files panel toolbar.

▶ **6.** Click the **View** button on the Files panel toolbar, and then click **Local View**. The Files panel returns to the local view.

Next, you'll preview the updated site in a browser. The site will include the new footer and the form that you added to the local version of the Cosmatic site.

To preview the updated Cosmatic site in a browser:

▶ **1.** Open a browser, type the URL of your remote site into the Address bar on the browser toolbar, and then press the **Enter** key.

▶ **2.** Click the **bands** link to view the Bands page, and then click the **footer** link to test it.

▶ **3.** Close the message window that opens.

▶ **4.** Click the **contact** link to view the Contact page, and then enter information in the form to test it.

▶ **5.** Submit the form.

▶ **6.** Close any open browser windows.

In this tutorial, you added keywords and a meta description to the head content, created and used library items in pages, created and used templates, and added a form to the Cosmatic site.

Session 9.3 Quick Check | Review

1. What is a form?
2. True or False? Forms process data.
3. What is a form object?
4. List three types of form objects.
5. Which behavior do you add to the form that enables you to create requirements/limits that check the form data before the form is submitted?
6. What is the final step in creating a form?

Tutorial Summary | Review

In this tutorial, you explored the head content for a page. You learned how to optimize a page for search engine placement, and then you added keywords and a meta description to the pages. You created a library item and added it to the pages. You created a template and then you created a new page based on the template. You also created a nested template. Finally, you created a form, added form attributes and form objects, and then validated the form data.

Key Terms

editable region
form
form object
keyword
library

library item
meta description
meta tag
nested template
noneditable region

robot
template
Validate Form behavior

Practice	**Review Assignments**

Practice the skills you learned in the tutorial.

There are no Data Files needed for the Review Assignments.

Brian asks you to add the list of keywords and the meta description to every page of the Cosmatic site. You'll also add the keywords and description to the template so that future pages will have this head content. Then, you'll create a form in the tour section of the Life in Minor Chords page to enable users to be placed on a list to receive notice when the new tour video is released. You'll use the form_test.html file already in the Cosmatic site as the form action so that you can test the form.

1. Open the **Cosmatic** site that you modified in this tutorial, and then open the **bands.html** page in the Document window.
2. Click the Keywords button in the Head list on the Common tab of the Insert bar, and then type **cosmatic records, indie music, sloth child, dizzied connections, life in minor chords, surface suction, spinning life, black lab, them apples, i believe in ferries, independent scene, denton music, underground sound, cosmattic** into the Keywords box. (*Hint:* Use all lowercase letters and separate each word or phrase with a comma.)
3. Select the entire list of keywords in the Keywords box, copy the list, click the OK button to add the keywords to the page, and then save and close the page.
4. Open each of the following pages in the Document window, open the Keywords dialog box, paste the list of keywords in the Keywords box, click the OK button to add the list to the page, and then save and close the page: **catalogue.html**, **contact.html**, **label.html**, **tourdates.html**, **whatshot.html**, and **cosmatic_main.dwt**. (*Hint:* When you add the keywords to the template, update the pages made from the template.)
5. Open the **bands.html** page in the Document window, click the Description button in the Head list on the Common tab of the Insert bar, and then type **Cosmatic is an indie label that has tapped into a vein of post-discord punk music. Our mission is to expose the world to exceptional indie music. Cosmatic promotes bands that we believe will change and infuse the planet with original good music.** in the Description box.
6. Select the text in the Description box, copy it, click the OK button, and then save and close the page.
7. Open each of the following pages in the Document window, open the Description dialog box, paste the description in the Description box, click the OK button, and then save and close the page: **catalogue.html**, **contact.html**, **label.html**, **tourdates.html**, **whatshot.html**, and **cosmatic_main.dwt**. (*Hint:* When you add the description to the template, update the pages made from the template.)
8. Open the **limc_content_tours.html** page located in the LifeInMinorChords folder, click outside the AP div in the page, and then press the Enter key until the pointer is positioned below the movie in the page.
9. Click the Form button on the Forms tab of the Insert bar to add the form area to the page.
10. Type **LIMCvideoForm** in the Form Name box, click the Browse For File button next to the Action box, and then double-click the form_test.html page in the site's local root folder.
11. Click GET in the Method list, click application/x-www-form-urlencoded in the Enctype list, and then click _blank in the Target list to set the form attributes.

12. Click in the form area, click the Table button on the Common tab of the Insert bar, and then create a table with 5 rows, 2 columns, 100% table width, 0 border thickness, 0 cell spacing, 10 cell padding, and no header.

13. Align the left column of the table to the Right and Top, and then align the right column of the table to the Left and Top.

14. Click in the upper-left cell, type **first name:**, press the Tab key to move the insertion point to the next cell, click the Text Field button on the Forms tab of the Insert bar to add a text field into the form, and then type **firstname** in the TextField box in the Property inspector. Use the default character width and maximum characters values.

15. Click in the left cell of the second row, type **last name:**, press the Tab key, click the Text Field button on the Forms tab of the Insert bar, and then type **lastname** in the TextField box in the Property inspector. Use the default character width and maximum characters values.

16. Click in the left cell of the third row, type **email address:**, press the Tab key, click the Text Field button on the Forms tab of the Insert bar, and then type **email** in the TextField box in the Property inspector.

17. Click in the left cell of the fourth row, type **Notify me when the new video is released.**, press the Tab key, click the Radio Group button on the Forms tab of the Insert bar, type **notify_video_release** in the Name box in the Radio Group dialog box, click the first row in the Label column and type **yes**, click the first row in the Value column and type **Yes**, click the second row in the Label column and type **no**, click the second row in the Value column and type **No**, click the Lay out using line breaks option button, and then click the OK button to insert the radio group.

18. Select the Yes radio button in the form, and then click the Checked option button in the Property inspector.

19. Click in the lower-right cell, click the Button button on the Forms tab of the Insert bar to insert a Submit button, and then click the Button button again to insert a second button.

20. Select the second button, click the Reset form option button in the Property inspector, type **Reset** in the Button name box, and then type **Reset** in the Value box, if necessary.

21. Select the form, click the Add Behavior button in the Behaviors panel, and then click Validate Form.

22. Click input "firstname" in the Fields box, and then check the Required check box.

23. Click input "lastname" in the Fields box, and then check the Required check box.

24. Click the input "email" in the Fields box, check the Required check box, click the Email address option button in the Accept group, and then click the OK button.

25. Save the page, preview the page in a browser, test the form, and then close the browser windows and the page.

26. Upload the site to your remote server, preview the site over the Web, and then test the form.

27. Submit the finished files to your instructor, either in printed or electronic form, as requested.

Apply | **Case Problem 1**

Add keywords, a meta description, and a footer library item to a Web site about the small rural communities of northern Vietnam.

There are no Data Files needed for this Case Problem.

World Anthropology Society Dr. Olivia Thompson wants you to add keywords and a meta description to the pages of the site to help optimize the pages for search engines. She also wants you to create a library item for the footer, and then add the library item to every page of the site.

1. Open the **DrThompson** site that you modified in **Tutorial 8**, **Case 1**, and then open the **index.html** page in the Document window.

2. Open the Keywords dialog box, and then type **world anthropology society, social anthropology, northern vietnam, linguistic differences, cultural cross-pollination, rituals, olivia thompson, anthropological research** in the Keywords box.

3. Copy the words in the Keywords box, click the OK button in the Keywords dialog box, and then save and close the page.

4. Open each of the following pages in the Document window, open the Keywords dialog box, paste the list of keywords into the Keywords box, click the OK button, and then save and close the page: **contact.html, cultural_cross_pollination.html, linguistic_differences.html, etiquette_tips.html, dr_thompson.html,** and **rituals_and_practices.html**.

5. Open the **index.html** page in the Document window, open the Description dialog box, and then type **Research and study of the language and rituals of peoples of Northern Vietnam by Dr. Olivia Thompson of the World Anthropology Society.** in the Description box.

6. Copy the text in the Description box, click the OK button in the dialog box, and then save and close the page.

7. Open each of the following pages in the Document window, open the Description dialog box, paste the description into the Description box, click the OK button, and then save and close the page: **contact.html, cultural_cross_pollination.html, linguistic_differences.html, etiquette_tips.html, dr_thompson.html,** and **rituals_and_practices.html**.

8. Open the **linguistic_differences.html** page in the Document window, scroll to the bottom of the page, and then select the footer.

9. Click the Library button on the Assets panel toolbar, drag the footer to the panel, and then name the library item **footer**.

⊕ **EXPLORE** 10. Double-click the footer library item in the Assets panel to open it, select the text, and then click the Align Center button in the Property inspector.

11. Save and close the footer library item, updating as needed, and then save and close the page.

12. Open each of the following pages in the Document window, drag the footer library item from the Assets panel to the bottom of the page, and then save and close the page: **contact.html, cultural_cross_pollination.html, index.html, etiquette_tips.html, dr_thompson.html,** and **rituals_and_practices.html**. (*Hint:* If a page already has a footer, delete the existing footer before adding the footer library item to the page. In the etiquette_tips.html page, place the library item in the AP div.)

13. Open the **index.html** page, preview each page of the site in a browser, and then close the browser and close the page.

14. Upload the site to your remote server, and then preview the site over the Web.

15. Submit the finished files to your instructor, either in printed or electronic form, as requested.

| Apply | **Case Problem 2** |

Create a template and a footer library item for a Web site for an art museum.

There are no Data Files needed for this Case Problem.

Museum of Western Art   C. J. Strittmatter has decided to make the Museum site a template-based site, which will make it faster to update the site. C.J. asks you to create a template for the site based on the Museum page and include a footer library item, which you need to create. There is no need to add the footer library item to the existing pages of the site because you will move the existing pages over to the template once it is approved.

1. Open the **Museum** site that you modified in **Tutorial 8**, **Case 2**, and then open the **museum.html** page in the Document window.
2. Click the Make Template button in the Templates list on the Common tab of the Insert bar.
3. Save the new template as **museum_main** and update links.
4. Select the page heading in the museum_main.dwt template, insert an editable region, and then name the region **PageHeading**.
5. Type **PAGE HEADING** as placeholder text for the page heading.
6. Delete all the text below the page heading and navigation bar.
7. Insert an editable region, and then name the region **Content**.
8. Move the insertion point to the line below the editable region, insert the © symbol, and then type **copyright Museum of Western Art, 2010.**
9. Center align the copyright text.
10. Drag the selected copyright text to the library in the Assets panel, and then name the new library item **footer**.
11. Save and close the template.
12. Create a new page from the template.
13. Type **TEST PAGE** in the PageHeading editable region, type **Test Content** in the Content editable region, change the page title to **Museum of Western Art – Template Test**, and then save the page as **template_test.html** in the site's local root folder.
14. Preview the page in a browser, and then close the browser and close the page.
15. Upload the site to your remote server, and then preview the site over the Web.
16. Submit the finished files to your instructor, either in printed or electronic form, as requested.

| Apply | **Case Problem 3** |

Create a template for a Web site for an independent bookstore.

There are no Data Files needed for this Case Problem.

MORE Books   Mark Chapman asks you to create a template for the MORE Books site and then apply the template to the Contact page. Once this page is approved, the template will be applied to the other existing pages of the site.

1. Open the **MOREbooks** site that you modified in **Tutorial 8**, **Case 3**, and then open the **contact.html** page in the Document window.
2. Make a template from the page, save the template as **more_main**, and then update links.
3. Create an editable region from the page heading named **PageHeading**.
4. Select the text in the PageHeading region, and then type **Page Heading** to insert placeholder text.

5. Delete the text below the PageHeading region, insert an editable region, and then name the region **PageContent**.

6. Click to the right of the new editable region, and then press the Enter key to move to the next line.

7. Insert the © symbol, press the Spacebar, type **copyright MOREbooks, Inc. 2010.**, center the text, and then save and close the page.

8. Open the **contact.html** page, and then delete the navigation bar and the logo from the page because those elements already exist in the template.

⊕ EXPLORE

9. Click the Templates button on the Assets panel toolbar, select more_main in the templates list, and then click the Apply button at the bottom of the Assets panel. The Inconsistent Region Names dialog box opens. (*Hint:* If the Assets list is blank, click the Refresh button at the bottom of the Assets panel to refresh the list.)

10. Click the Document Body region in the Editable Regions list, and then click PageHeading in the Move Content to New Region list.

11. Click the Document Head region in the Editable Regions list, and then click Head in the Move Content to New Region list.

12. Click the OK button to connect the Contact page to the template; the page content moves into the PageHeading region.

13. Select the text below the page heading, drag it into the PageContent region, delete the placeholder text from the PageContent region, and then, if necessary, remove any extra spaces from the PageHeading region.

14. Save the page, preview the page in a browser, and then close the browser and close the page.

15. Upload the site to your remote server, and then preview the page over the Web.

16. Submit the finished files to your instructor, either in printed or electronic form, as requested.

Create | **Case Problem 4**

Create an online order form for a Web site for a newly opening sushi restaurant.

Data Files needed for this Case Problem: form_test.html, sushi_menu.html

Sushi Ya-Ya   Mary O'Brien asks you to create an online order form for the Menu page of the Sushi Ya-Ya site. Because the server-side script is still being finalized, you'll add the form_test.html page to the site so you can test the form.

1. Open the **SushiYaYa** site that you modified in **Tutorial 8**, **Case 4**.

2. Copy the **form_test.html** page located in the Tutorial.09\Case4 folder included with your Data Files to the site's local root folder.

3. Open the **menu.html** page in the Document window, delete the Coming Soon! text, and then insert a form into the page.

4. In the Property inspector, change the form's name to **Menu**, set the Action to the form_test.html page in the site's local root folder, set the Target to _blank, change the Method to GET, and then set the Enctype to application/x-www-form-urlencoded.

5. Type **Menu** in the form area, and then apply the sub_headings style.

6. Copy the **sushi_menu.html** page located in the Tutorial.09\Case4 folder included with your Data Files to the site's local root folder, and then open the page in the Document window.

7. Copy the table from the Sushi Menu page into the form below the Menu text in the Menu page.

8. Apply applicable CSS styles to the table as needed.

9. Insert a text field in the cell in the first column of the second row.

10. In the Property inspector, name the text field **KappaRoll**, set the character width to 6, and then set the maximum characters to 2.

11. Insert a text field in the cell in the first column of the next row, type the sushi name as the text field name, set the character width to 6, and then set the maximum characters to 2. (*Hint:* Do not include spaces in the field name.)

12. Repeat Step 11 to add text fields for the remaining sushi.

13. Insert a button in the lower-right cell, verify that "Submit" appears in the Button Name and Value boxes, and then set the Action to Submit Form.

14. Insert a second button, change the Action to Reset Form, and then type **Reset** in the Button name box.

15. Add the Validate Form behavior from the Behavior list in the Behaviors panel to the form.

✦ EXPLORE 16. In the Validate Form dialog box, select the first item in the Fields list (input "KappaRoll"), click the Number From option button in the Accept group, and then type **1** and **10** in the boxes.

17. Select each of the remaining items in the Fields list, set a number limit from 1 to 10, and then click the OK button.

18. Save the page, preview the page in a browser, test the form, and then close the browser and close the page.

19. Upload the site to your remote server, preview the site over the Web, and then test the form.

20. Submit the finished files to your instructor, either in printed or electronic form, as requested.

| Review | | **Quick Check Answers** |

Session 9.1

1. Tags used in the head of a page to record information about the page or to give information to the server. The exact purpose of the meta tag is defined by its attributes.

2. keywords meta tag and description meta tag

3. Keywords are one of the elements some search engines use to index Web pages; the keywords you choose should be the words you feel most people will type into search engines to look for the site or the words you want people to find your site under.

4. in the library, which you can access from the Assets panel or in the Library folder in the root folder for the site

5. A comment tag is placed at the beginning and end of every library item.

6. You can update every instance of the item by editing the library item itself.

Session 9.2

1. More; when you begin to design large, professional, template-driven sites, the pages are more interconnected and the design requires a great deal more forethought than designing a regular Web site.

2. areas that can be changed in the template but cannot be changed in the template-based pages

3. When you edit a template, the changes are also made in all the pages that were created from that template.
4. a template that is created from the main template, which enables you to create a more defined structure for some pages of the site
5. True.
6. The region is also deleted from the nested template, and you can select whether to move the content to another editable region on pages created from the template or nested template.

Session 9.3

1. A form is a means of collecting information from users. A user can input information into the Web page by typing into designated fields or clicking various elements to make selections. Once the form is filled out, the information is submitted to a server (or other information-processing location) for processing.
2. False; forms collect information from users.
3. a mechanism that enables users to interact with a form
4. any three of the following: text fields (text areas), hidden fields, checkboxes, radio buttons (radio groups), menus/lists, jump menus, file fields, image fields, and buttons
5. Validate Form behavior
6. testing the form

Objectives

Session 10.1
- Learn about Spry elements
- Add and format a Spry widget
- Add a Spry effect
- Learn about creating dynamic database content for Web pages

Session 10.2
- Create database-driven pages using MySQL and PHP for a Linux server
- Create a database on a remote Linux server
- Connect a Web site to a database
- Add server behaviors to Web pages
- Create pages to view data in a database
- Create a Login page

Session 10.3
- Create database-driven pages using Access and ASP for a Windows server
- Upload a database to a remote Windows server
- Connect a Web site to a database
- Add server behaviors to Web pages
- Create pages to view data in a database
- Create a Login page

Adding Spry Elements and Database Functionality

Adding Spry Elements and Collecting and Viewing Form Data in a Database

Case | Cosmatic

Sara Lynn, president of Cosmatic, believes that the site could be enhanced with some Spry elements. User feedback has indicated that the directions provided on the site are confusing. To alleviate the confusion, Sara wants to add the Spry Accordion widget to the Contact page and include tabs for directions from Dallas as well as from Fort Worth. The Accordion element will enable Sara to add the information to the Contact page without pushing the contact form out of sight. She also wants to add some panache to the site by adding the Spry Shake effect to the Catalogue page.

In addition, Sara believes that Cosmatic could benefit from the collection of some user data. She thinks it would be helpful to collect the data that is received from users who complete and submit the form in the Contact page. Brian Lee, public relations and marketing director, asks you to create a database to store the information collected from the form and connect the form in the Contact page to the database. He also wants you to create pages that enable you to view the data collected in the database. Finally, he asks you to create a Login page and connect the pages that display collected database information to the Login page so that users must have a valid login and password to view the data.

Starting Data Files

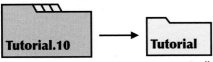

Tutorial	Review	Case1	Case2	Case3	Case4
cosmaticdb.mdb	(none)	wasdb.mdb	museumdb.mdb	moredb.mdb	sushidb.mdb
cosmaticdb.sql		wasdb.sql	museumdb.sql	moredb.sql	sushidb.sql
Directions.doc					

Session 10.1

Understanding Spry

The **Spry framework for AJAX** is a JavaScript and CSS code library that enables Web designers to more easily add advanced functionality to Web pages. **AJAX (Asynchronous JavaScript and XML)** is a concept for using various techniques to update Web page content and targeted pieces of content within a page without visible refreshes and without browser add-on technologies. Adobe created the Spry framework library to help Web designers add AJAX into Web pages without having to learn to write the code. After developing the Spry framework as a standalone library, Adobe added a limited version of the library to Dreamweaver CS3 and created a visual interface to enable designers to integrate the Spry elements into Web pages. **Spry elements** are chunks of prewritten, reusable code such as behaviors that were written using the Spry framework library and available in Dreamweaver CS3 to add specific functionality to Web pages. For example, the Accordion widget enables you to add a set of collapsible panels to a page. Users who view the page can click a panel tab to view the content in that panel. Dreamweaver places Spry elements in three categories. Widgets are page elements such as the Accordion widget that add interactive components to pages. XML Data Sources display data from an XML source, which is similar to displaying data from a database. This enables user input to trigger a data update elsewhere in a page without a full-page refresh. Finally, effects are visual enhancements that change elements of a page over time. For example, the Fade effect causes an image to fade from 100% to 0 visibility over time when a page is loaded into the browser window.

You will add the Accordion widget to the Contact page of the Cosmatic site, and then you will apply the Shake effect to the CD cover images in the Catalogue page.

InSight	**Checking the Usefulness of a Spry Element**

Before you insert a Spry element into a Web page, take a moment to check that the element you plan to insert adds needed and useful functionality to the Web site. You should also make sure that the element you want to use complements the look and feel of the site, keeping in mind that you can modify the element's styles. Finally, it is also a good idea to gather all of the content required for the element before you begin to create it.

Adding a Spry Widget to a Web Page

Widgets are reusable, prebuilt page elements that enable user interaction. Dreamweaver includes the widgets described in Figure 10-1. You can also create widgets yourself using the Spry framework if you are familiar with AJAX. The Validation Text Field, Validation Text Area, Validation Select, and Validation Checkbox widgets are used in data collection, and are similar to the fields you used when you created a regular form. You can use these widgets to create a Spry form. A major difference between these Spry widgets and their HTML counterparts that you used when you created a regular form is that the Spry widgets can check for validation and can collect information without causing the entire page to refresh.

Widget	Description
Accordion	A set of expandable/collapsible panels that is inserted into a page to hold content. Only one panel in the set is visible at any given time. This enables you to insert a large amount of related content in a small amount of space.
Collapsible Panel	A single-tabbed panel that can expand to reveal content or collapse to hide content. The panel tab runs the width of the panel.
Menu Bar	A series of buttons, each of which displays a submenu on hover. Submenus contain text links that enable the user to navigate throughout the site.
Tabbed Panel	A multi-tabbed panel that remains a consistent size. When a tab is clicked, the content related to that tab becomes visible in the panel and the tab moves to the front.
Validation Checkbox	A check box or group of check boxes that validates whether a user has selected one check box or the specified number of check boxes.
Validation Select	A drop-down menu that validates whether a user has made a selection from the list.
Validation Textarea	A text area that validates whether a user has entered data in a specified format.
Validation Text Field	A text field that validates whether a user has entered data in a specified format.

All widgets have three parts: container, behavior, and styling. The widget container is HTML code that defines the structural composition of the widget. When you place content into a widget you are placing it in the HTML container. The widget behavior is JavaScript that controls how users interact with the widget. The widget styling is a set of CSS styles that specify the appearance of the various elements of the widget. The JavaScript and CSS for Spry elements you add to Web pages in Dreamweaver are stored in separate files in a SpryAssets folder. Dreamweaver creates the SpryAssets folder in the site's root folder the first time you add a Spry element to the site. Any time you add a Spry widget to the site, files with the corresponding code and style sheets are added to the SpryAssets folder.

To add a Spry widget to a Web page, you first insert the widget you want to use into the page, then you add appropriate content to the widget, and finally you style the widget to fit the look and feel of the site.

Adding a Spry Widget to a Web Page | Reference Window

- In the Web page, position the pointer where you want the Spry widget to appear.
- Click the Spry tab on the Insert bar, and then click the appropriate Spry widget button.
- Add content to the widget.
- Style the widget as needed.

Inserting a Spry Widget

You will add the Accordion widget in the Contact page to provide the user with complete driving directions to the company from both Dallas and Fort Worth without increasing the length of the page. You will then modify the styles of the Accordion widget to fit the look and feel of the Cosmatic site. In this case, the Spry element is both useful and aesthetically cohesive.

To insert the Accordion widget in the Contact page:

▶ **1.** Open the **Cosmatic** site that you modified in the **Tutorial 9 Review Assignments**, and then open the **contact.html** page in the Document window.

▶ **2.** Click in the blank line above the DIRECTIONS header, and then press the **Shift+Enter** keys. A blank line is added to the page.

▶ **3.** Press the **Up Arrow** key. The insertion point moves to the new, blank line.

▶ **4.** Click the **Spry** tab on the Insert bar, and then click the **Spry Accordion** button 📄 . The Accordion widget is inserted in the blank line, and its properties appear in the Property inspector. See Figure 10-2.

Figure 10-2 ▶	Accordion widget in the Contact page

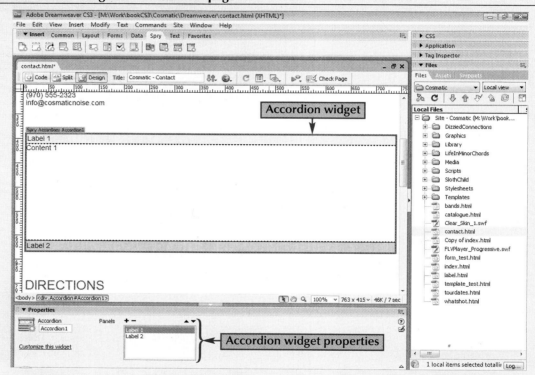

▶ **5.** Save the Contact page. The Copy Dependent Files dialog box opens, indicating that you need to copy the files that contain the widget's JavaScript and the CSS style sheet to the site.

▶ **6.** Click the **OK** button. The SpryAssets folder and its content are added to the site.

▶ **7.** In the Files panel, click the **Plus (+)** button ⊞ next to the SpryAssets folder to display the two files it contains. See Figure 10-3.

SpryAssets folder added to the site ◄   Figure 10-3

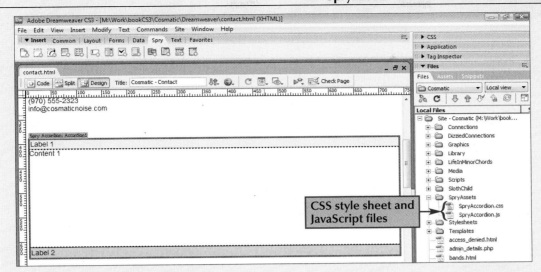

▶ **8.** In the Files panel, click the **Minus (–)** button ⊟ next to the SpryAssets folder to hide the two files it contains.

Adding Content to a Spry Widget

After you insert a Spry widget in a Web page, you can customize the container and add content to make it useful and relevant for the site. The Accordion widget you inserted in the Contact page is an empty container that has two panel tabs. To make the component useful, you need to add content and labels that are specific and meaningful to your site. You can also add panel tabs, remove panel tabs, and reorder the panel tabs.

You'll change the Accordion widget label placeholder text to "Directions from Dallas" and "Directions from Fort Worth," which are more relevant to Cosmatic users. You'll add the appropriate driving directions into the content area of each panel tab. You will first name the Accordion widget in the Property inspector. It is a good idea to name any components you add to a site because behaviors and other advanced coding components use that name to refer to the element. The names are especially helpful if a page includes several similar elements.

To name and add content to the Accordion widget:

▶ **1.** If necessary, click the **Spry Accordion: Accordion1** tab to select the Accordion widget container in the page. The properties for the widget appear in the Property inspector.

▶ **2.** In the Property inspector, type **Directions** in the Name box, and then press the **Enter** key. The Accordion widget is renamed with a descriptive name, which appears in both the Property inspector and in the widget's tab in the Document window.

▶ **3.** In the top panel tab of the Accordion widget, select **Label 1**, and then type **Directions from Dallas**. The first panel tab is updated.

   Trouble? If you pressed the Enter key, a new line was added in the top panel tab. Press the Backspace key to delete the unneeded line.

▶ **4.** In the lower panel tab of the Accordion widget, select **Label 2**, and then type **Directions from Fort Worth**. The second panel tab is updated.

▶ **5.** Click the **Spry Accordion: Directions** tab to select the widget. The panel tab names are updated in the Property inspector. See Figure 10-4.

Figure 10-4	Accordion widget with new names

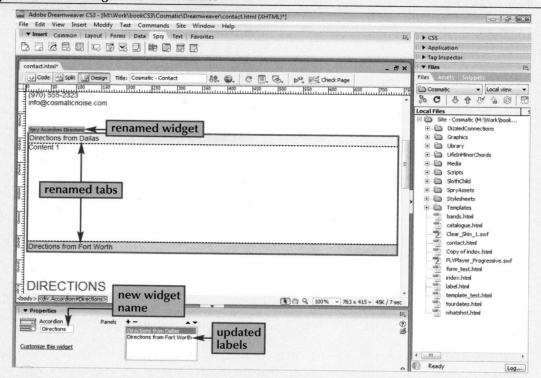

▶ **6.** Open the **Directions.doc** file located in the **Tutorial.10/Tutorial** folder included with your Data Files in Word or another word processing program, and then copy the content under the Directions from Dallas heading.

▶ **7.** In the Document window, in the Accordion widget, select **Content 1**, and then paste the directions into the content area of the widget.

▶ **8.** Point to the **Directions from Fort Worth tab**. An eye icon 👁 appears at the right of the panel tab. See Figure-10-5.

Accordion widget with content

Figure 10-5

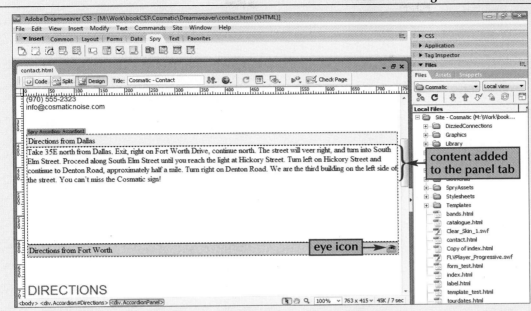

9. Click the **eye** icon 👁 that appears at the right of the Directions from Fort Worth tab. The content area of the Directions from Fort Worth tab opens and the content in the tab as well as the content in the content area are selected.

10. In the Directions.doc document, copy the content under the Directions from Fort Worth heading, and then close the document.

11. In the Document window, select **Content 2**, and then paste the Fort Worth directions into the widget.

12. Save the Contact page, and then preview the page in a browser. See Figure 10-6.

Figure 10-6   **Widget previewed in the Contact page**

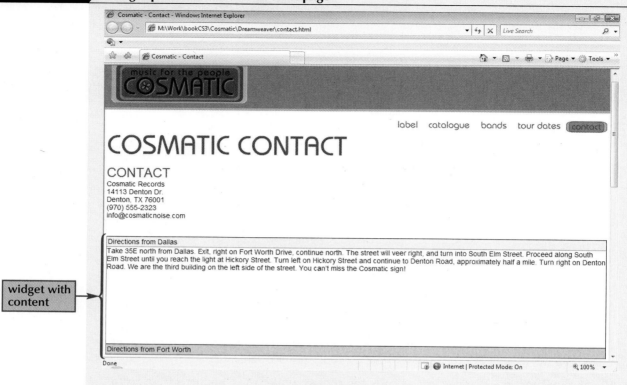

widget with content

13. Click the **Directions from Fort Worth** tab. The Accordion widget becomes active and its default CSS styles are visible. Also, the Directions from Fort Worth tab moves to the top of the widget area and the driving directions in its content appear. See Figure 10-7.

Figure 10-7   **Widget with the default CSS styles**

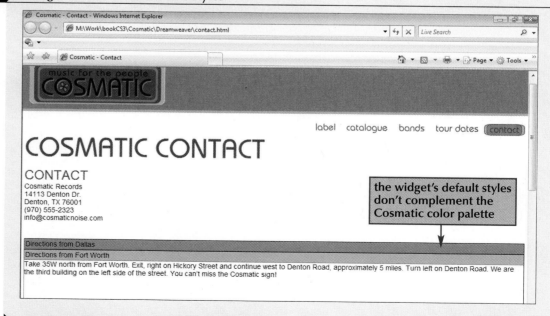

the widget's default styles don't complement the Cosmatic color palette

14. Click the **Directions from Dallas** tab to reveal its content, and then close the browser.

Formatting the CSS Styles of a Spry Widget

The look of any widget you add to a Web page should be formatted to complement the aesthetics of the page in which it appears. You format widgets by modifying the existing CSS styles that are applied to it or by creating new CSS styles for the widget. Each widget has its own style sheet that is added to the site's SpryAssets folder when you first save the widget. You modify the widget's default styles by editing the code directly in the style sheet or by adjusting the styles in the CSS Styles panel. Dreamweaver Help provides a list of styles used by each widget with information about what those styles affect. You should read this information before modifying the CSS styles of a widget.

You'll read the appropriate Help topic to learn about the CSS styles applied to the Accordion widget.

To research the default CSS styles of the Accordion widget:

▶ **1.** In the Document window, click the **Spry Accordion: Directions** tab to select the widget container. The widget's properties appear in the Property inspector.

▶ **2.** In the Property inspector, click the **Customize this widget** link. The Adobe Help Viewer opens to the Customize the Accordion widget page, which includes an Accordion widget to organize information. See Figure 10-8.

Customize the Accordion widget Help page ◀ **Figure 10-8**

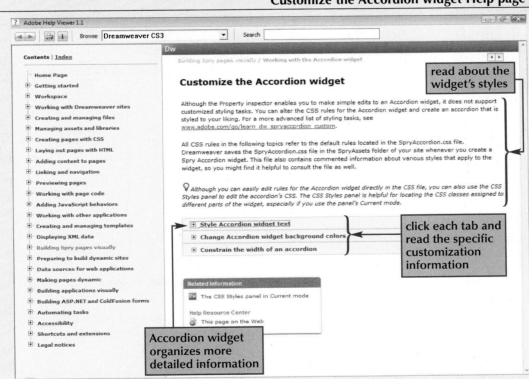

▶ **3.** Read the content in the page.

▶ **4.** In the Accordion widget in the Help page, click the **Style Accordion widget text** tab to display its content, and then read the information.

▶ **5.** Repeat Step 4 for each of the other tabs of the widget, and then close the Adobe Help Viewer.

As you read in the Constrain the width of an accordion panel, you change the Accordion widget's width by changing the width property for the accordion container, which is located in the .Accordion CSS rule. This rule, along with all the other styles for the Accordion widget, is located in the SpryAccordion.css style sheet, which is saved in the SpryAssets folder in the site's root folder. You will use the CSS Styles panel to change the widget's width property in the .Accordion rule and its height property in the .AccordionPanelContent rule. The new dimensions will better fit the content you added to the widget.

To change the Accordion widget's dimensions in the CSS Styles panel:

▶ 1. Expand the **CSS Styles panel**, and then, in the All Rules pane, click the **Minus (–)** button ⊟ next to cosmatic_styles.css to collapse the site's style sheet and click the **Plus (+)** button ⊞ next to SpryAccordion.css, if necessary, to expand the widget's style sheet. All of the styles in the SpryAccordion.css style sheet are visible.

▶ 2. In the CSS Styles panel, click the **Show List View** button ᴬᶻ↓, if necessary, to switch to list view.

▶ 3. In the All Rules pane of the CSS Styles panel, click **.Accordion**. The properties for the selected .Accordion style appear in the Properties pane. See Figure 10-9.

| Figure 10-9 | **Properties for the .Accordion rule** |

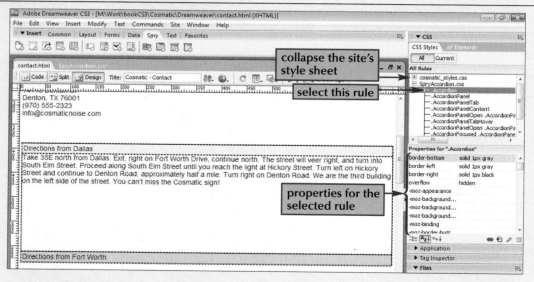

Trouble? If the Fort Worth directions appear on your screen instead of the Dallas directions, click the Directions from Dallas tab.

▶ 4. Scroll to the end of the Properties list to locate width, click in the width property's right column, type **600**, and then press the **Enter** key. The Accordion widget becomes 600px wide.

You'll repeat this process to change the widget's height, which is located in the .AccordionPanelContent rule.

▶ 5. In the CSS Styles panel, click the **.AccordionPanelContent** rule in the All Rules pane.

▶ 6. At the top of the Properties pane, click in the height property's right column, select **200** in the first box, type **100**, and then press the **Enter** key. The widget's height changes to 100px. See Figure 10-10.

Accordion widget with new width and height ◄ **Figure 10-10**

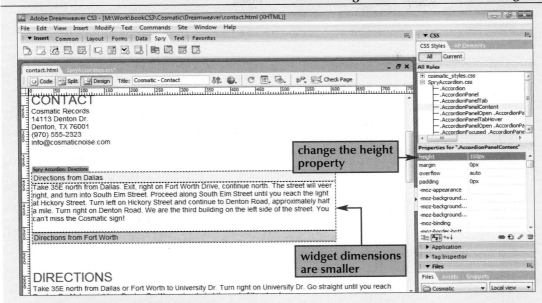

7. Click the **SpryAccordion.css** tab, and then save the style sheet. You don't need to save the Contact page because all of the changes you made were in the style sheet.

You can customize the aesthetic look of the widget either by adjusting the CSS rules that affect the aesthetic display of the widget or by creating and applying new styles to different elements of the widget. The rules in the SpryAccordion.css page are annotated to provide information about what elements each rule effects. You will review the SpryAccordion.css page, and then continue to customize the Accordion widget.

To modify rules in the SpryAccordion.css style sheet:

1. If necessary, click the **SpryAccordion.css** tab to make the page active. The page is color-coded. Each rule is pink and its corresponding properties are blue. Notes describing each rule appear above the rule in gray.

2. Read the gray notes above the .Accordion rule.

3. In the Document window, click the **.Accordion** rule. In the CSS Styles panel, the rule is selected in the All Rules pane and its properties appear in the Properties pane. See Figure 10-11.

Figure 10-11 SpryAccordion.css page

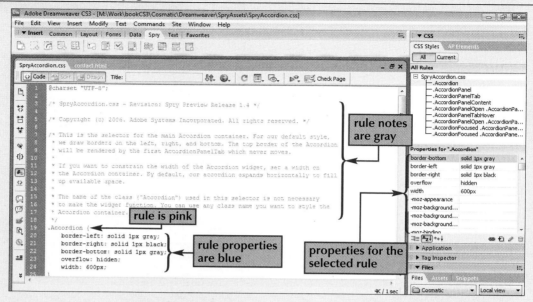

You can change properties for the widget's rules in the CSS Styles panel as you did for the widget's width and height, or you can modify them directly in the style sheet.

4. In the .Accordion rule, locate the border-left property, select **1px gray**, type **2px #878816**, and then press the **Enter** key. The properties are changed in the style sheet, and the style is updated in the CSS Styles panel. See Figure 10-12.

Figure 10-12 Border-left property updated

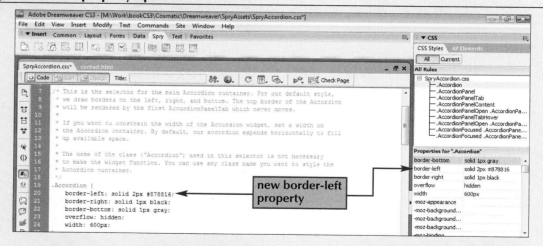

Trouble? If the properties are changed in the style sheet, but not in the CSS Styles panel, you need to update the CSS Styles panel. In the CSS Styles panel, click the Refresh button.

5. Modify the rule properties shown in Figure 10-13 from either the CSS Styles panel or directly in the style sheet.

Rules and properties to modify in the SpryAccordion.css style sheet ◀ **Figure 10-13**

Rule	Properties
.Accordion	Border-right: solid 2px #E0AE4D; Border-bottom: solid 2px #E0AE4D;
.AccordionPanelTab	Background-color: #E0AE4D; Border-top: solid 2px #E0AE4D; Border-bottom: solid 2px #E0AE4D; Color: #772300; Font-size: 16px; Text-transform: uppercase;
.AccordionPanelOpen .AccordionPanelTab	Background-color: #878816;
.AccordionPanelTabHover	Color: #878816;
.AccordionPanelOpen .AccordionPanelTabHover	Color: #772300; Text-decoration: underline;
.AccordionFocused .AccordionPanelTab	Background-color: #878816;
.AccordionFocused .AccordionPanelOpen .AccordionPanelTab	Background-color: #B9B91E;

▶ **6.** Save the SpryAccordion.css page, and then click the **contact.html** tab to view the Contact page. See Figure 10-14.

Form in the Contact page ◀ **Figure 10-14**

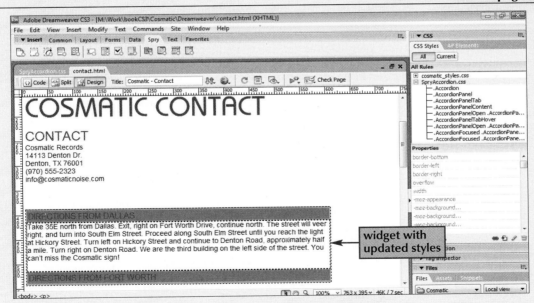

▶ **7.** Collapse the CSS panel group, preview the Contact page in a browser, and then click the **Directions from Fort Worth** tab. The changes you made to the Accordion widget are visible. See Figure 10-15.

Figure 10-15 | **Modified Accordion widget previewed in the Contact page**

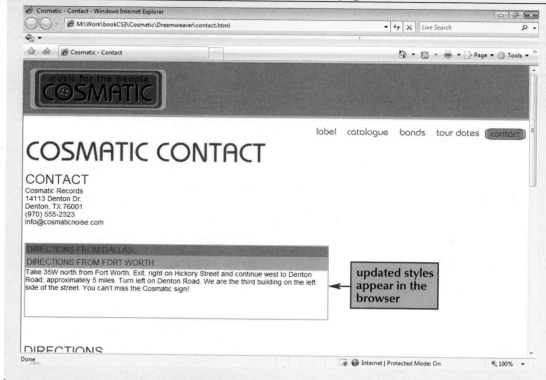

8. Click the **Directions from Dallas** tab to reveal its content, and then close the browser.

9. Close the SpryAccordion.css style sheet and the Contact page.

Using Spry Effects

Spry effects are visual enhancements that you can apply to the various elements in Web pages. The Spry effects available in Dreamweaver are described in Figure 10-16. These effects are usually used to call attention to a page element, animate a page element, or alter a page element visually over a period of time. For example, you could make an image fade from 0% transparency to 100% transparency once the page is loaded in the browser, or you could have an image slide into place on the screen.

Figure 10-16 | **Spry effects available in Dreamweaver**

Spry Effect	Description
Appear/Fade	Changes the visibility of an element over a period of time.
Highlight	Changes the background color of a selected element.
Blind up/down	Hides or reveals an element in a motion that simulates the opening or closing of a window blind.
Grow/Shrink	Increases or decreases the size of an element.
Shake	Moves the element left and right in the page over a period of time to simulate a shaking motion.
Squish	Causes the element to disappear into the upper-left corner of the page.

You should use Spry effects only when they will enhance the user's experience. An effect should draw attention to an important piece of information or enable you to transition between two important points. It is easy to overdo the use of effects in a page. They should be used sparingly.

You will add the Shake effect to the dizzied connections CD cover image in the Catalogue page to draw attention to it and add some movement to the page.

To add the Shake effect to the Catalogue page:

▶ **1.** Open the **catalogue.html** page in the Document window, and then select the dizzied connections album cover.

▶ **2.** Expand the Tag Inspector panel group, and then open the **Behaviors** panel.

▶ **3.** In the Behaviors panel, click the **Add Behavior** button ✚ , point to **Effects**, and then click **Shake**. The Shake dialog box opens. See Figure 10-17.

Shake dialog box ◀ Figure 10-17

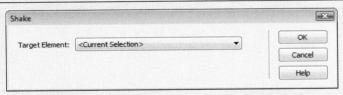

▶ **4.** Click the **Target Element** button, and then click **<Current Selection>**, if necessary.

▶ **5.** Click the **OK** button. Shake is listed in the Behaviors panel.

Next, you'll change the event to onLoad so that the behavior will occur when the page opens in a browser.

▶ **6.** In the Behaviors panel, click in the **Events** box, click the **Events** arrow, and then click **onLoad**. The album cover will shake when it is loaded in the browser window.

▶ **7.** Save the Catalogue page, and then click the **OK** button in the Copy Dependent Files dialog box that opens. The SpryEffects.js file is saved in the SpryAssets folder.

▶ **8.** Preview the Catalogue page in a browser. The dizzied connections CD cover shakes briefly after the page is loaded.

Trouble? If the surface suction album cover also shakes, the effect was applied to both top images because they are next to each other in the page. Continue with Step 9.

▶ **9.** Close the browser, and then close the page.

So far, you added a Spry widget to the Contact page, modified its properties to match the Cosmatic styles, and then added a Spry effect to the Catalogue page. Next, you will create a database page.

Exploring Databases and Dynamic Page Content

One of the best ways to extend the functionality of a Web site is to connect the site to a database. A **database** is a collection of information that is arranged for ease and speed of search and retrieval and is usually associated with a specific software package such as Microsoft Access or a specific database server such as MySQL. A database can be a simple list of people's names or it can be a large collection of complex information such as product inventory. A **database-driven Web site** is a Web site that uses a database to gather, display, or manipulate information. For example, e-commerce sites often use a database to store online orders and billing information, and weather sites often retrieve current weather conditions from a database and display it in a Web page. The Cosmatic site will use a database to store the information collected from the form in the Contact page.

There are different ways to create database-driven Web sites; the method depends on the amount of data being served out, the number of users potentially accessing that information simultaneously, the budget available, and the technology already being used. Some large companies, such as Panasonic and LG Electronics, Inc., use expensive database software like Oracle or DB2 to serve out massive amounts of data to multiple users. If you plan to serve out massive amounts of information to thousands of users simultaneously and have access to a large budget, this is a great solution. However, many large companies are turning to other solutions. If you are creating a medium or small database-driven site, these other database software solutions are more accessible.

The two database software packages that are most frequently used with medium and small Web sites are MySQL and Microsoft Access. MySQL is a free open-source database engine that was designed specifically for Web use. Both Google and Yahoo use MySQL as their database engine. It is usually installed by default on Linux servers. MySQL can also be installed on Windows servers. Additional information about MySQL is available at *www.mysql.com*. Access is a database management program that is part of the Microsoft Office suite. Windows servers can serve out Access files by default if the permissions are set correctly for the database file.

In addition to selecting a database, you must also select the programming or scripting language that you will use to create server behaviors. **Server behaviors** are behaviors that run on the Web server before the Web page is sent to a user's browser and are written in PHP, ASP, ASP.NET, JSP, or ColdFusion. You will use server behaviors to communicate with a database (send data and retrieve data) and to turn data into plain HTML that can be displayed in a browser as part of a Web page.

All server behaviors use SQL when addressing databases. **SQL (Structured Query Language)** is a specialized language used for working with databases. When Web pages display data stored in a database, they are said to be **dynamically generated**. You will use server behaviors to process data collected from the form in the Contact page and stored in the database to create HTML that will display an overview of the data stored in the database in the database.php page, and to display the details of selected records in the database_details.php page. Using server behaviors to generate dynamic pages is much more efficient than updating content manually each time the information changes.

This tutorial provides two methods for creating the database-driven pages in the Cosmatic site. If you are working with a Linux server, you will use a MySQL database and PHP to create the database-driven pages. If you are working with a Windows server, you will use an Access database and ASP to create the pages. Each method requires different steps and methodologies, both of which are provided in this tutorial.

Regardless of which method you use, the general process for creating the database-driven pages in the Cosmatic site is:

- Adjust the form in the Contact page.
- Create the Web pages you will need.
- Place or create the database on the remote server.
- Add server behaviors to the form to connect the database.

- Add server behaviors to view the data collected in the database from within the designated Web pages.
- Format the Login page.
- Set the database pages to display only when a user has logged in.

If you are working on a Linux server with MySQL and PHP, continue with Session 10.2. If you are working on a Windows server with Access and ASP, continue with Session 10.3. If you are unsure which type of server you are using or if you do not have access to a server, check with your instructor or technical support person before continuing with this tutorial.

Session 10.1 Quick Check | Review

1. What is the Spry framework?
2. What is AJAX?
3. What is a Spry widget?
4. Name the three parts of a widget.
5. Explain what a Spry effect might be used for.
6. What is a database?
7. What are two popular databases used by medium and small Web sites?

Session 10.2

Creating Database-Driven Pages Using MySQL and PHP

Adding database functionality to a Web site can be quite complex. Just as it is a good idea to make a plan prior to creating a Web site, it is also a good idea to plan the database-driven portion of the site in advance. Brian has created a site plan for the new portion of the Cosmatic site.

Based on his plan, the Cosmatic technical team will create the SQL for a database that stores the information collected from the form in the Contact page. You'll modify the form to work with the database. You'll create the pages that you will need for the new portion of the site: thankyou.html, access_denied.html, database.php, database_details.php, and login.php. You'll create the database on the remote server using the SQL provided by the technical team, and then you'll connect the site to the database. Next, you'll add server behaviors to the pages you created to enable the form data to be sent to and stored in the database and to enable the database.php and database_details.php pages to display the information stored in the database. Finally, you'll create a login.php page and add code to the backend pages that will prevent unauthorized users from viewing the content of those pages.

When the database-driven pages are complete, the survey information received from users who completed the form in the Contact pages will be stored in a database that only authorized users can access.

Reference Window | **Creating Database-Driven Pages for a Linux Server**

- Create the Web pages you need.
- Create a database on your remote server.
- Add server behaviors to connect the site to the database.
- Add server behaviors to store submitted data in the database and to view the data collected in the database from within designated Web pages.
- Create a Login page.
- Add code to the backend pages to prevent unauthorized users from viewing the content of those pages.

Modifying the Form

Before you create the database-driven pages of the Cosmatic site, you'll modify the form in the Contact page to work with the database that you will create on your remote server. You will delete the list box with the band names from the form, and then create a series of checkboxes to collect this same information. You are replacing the list box to keep things simpler because it requires more steps and custom scripts to process data from a list box for storage in a database.

To modify the form in the Contact page:

▶ 1. If you took a break after the previous session, make sure that the Cosmatic site is open.

▶ 2. Open the **contact.html** page in the Document window, select the list box in the right column near the bottom of the form, and then press the **Delete** key. The list box is removed from the form in the page.

▶ 3. Click the **Forms** tab on the Insert bar, click the **Checkbox** button ☑ to insert the first checkbox, type **sloth_child** in the Checkbox name box in the Property inspector, click to the right of the checkbox to deselect the checkbox, type **sloth child** beside the checkbox, and then press the **Shift+Enter** keys to move the insertion point down one line. You've entered the first checkbox and label in the form.

Trouble? If the Tag Input Accessibility Attributes dialog box opens, click the Cancel button here and each time you insert a new form object in this tutorial.

▶ 4. Repeat Step 3 to create checkboxes and labels for the following bands, replacing the spaces in the band names with underscores in the Checkbox name box: **dizzied connections**, **Life in Minor Chords**, and **surface suction**.

▶ 5. Select the sentence in the left column next to the new checkboxes, and then type **Check all of the bands that you enjoy.** (including the period). See Figure 10-18.

Modified form | Figure 10-18

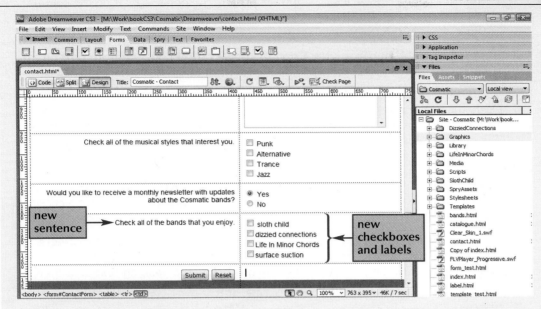

> **6.** Save and close the Contact page, and then upload the page to your remote server.

Creating New Pages

You need five pages for the database-driven portion of the site. You will create all of these pages now so that they will be available when you need them. According to Brian's plan for the database-driven portion of the Cosmatic site, you will create the following pages:

- **thankyou.html** — A page thanking the user for his or her submission that appears when the user submits the form in the Contact page.
- **access_denied.html** — A page informing the user that the wrong user name or password has been entered that appears when a user attempts to log in on the Login page with incorrect information or if a user attempts to access a password-protected page without logging in. After a four-second delay, the user is returned to the Login page.
- **database.php** — A page showing an overview of the data stored in the database. After the Login page is created, users cannot access this page unless they log in.
- **database_details.php** — A page showing the details of a selected record that appears when a user clicks a record in the Database page. After the Login page is created, users cannot access this page unless they log in.
- **login.php** — A page in which a user enters his or her user name and password and then clicks the Login button. If the information is correct, the Database page appears; if the information is incorrect, the Access Denied page appears.

Three of the pages you will create are PHP pages. You can create a PHP page by typing .php as the file extension when you name the page.

To create the pages for the database-driven portion of the Cosmatic site:

▶ 1. In the Files panel, right-click the **contact.html** page, point to **Edit** on the context menu, and then click **Duplicate**. A new page named Copy of contact.html appears at the bottom of the list in the Files panel.

▶ 2. In the Files panel, right-click the **Copy of contact.html** page, point to **Edit** on the context menu, click **Rename**, type **thankyou.html**, and then press the **Enter** key. The page is renamed.

▶ 3. Open the **thankyou.html** page in the Document window, select **Contact** in the Title box on the Document toolbar, type **Thank you**, and then press the **Enter** key. The new page title appears.

▶ 4. Double-click the page heading. The Insert Flash Text dialog box opens.

▶ 5. Select the text in the Text box if necessary, type **COSMATIC THANK YOU**, select the text in the Save As box, type **Media/HeadingThankyou.swf**, and then click the **OK** button. The Flash text heading is updated.

▶ 6. Select all the content below the heading and above the footer, press the **Delete** key to remove it from the page, type **Thank you for submitting your information.** (including the period) in the line below the heading text, and then, if necessary, format the sentence in the **Paragraph** format.

▶ 7. Click **Modify** on the menu bar, and then click **Navigation Bar**. The Modify Navigation Bar dialog box opens.

▶ 8. Click **Contact** in the Nav Bar Elements list, click the **Show "Down image" initially** check box to uncheck it and remove the asterisk from Contact in the Nav bar elements box, click the **OK** button, and then click in the Thank You page to deselect the navigation bar element. The Contact button is no longer displayed in the Down state. See Figure 10-19.

| **Figure 10-19** | **New thankyou.html page** |

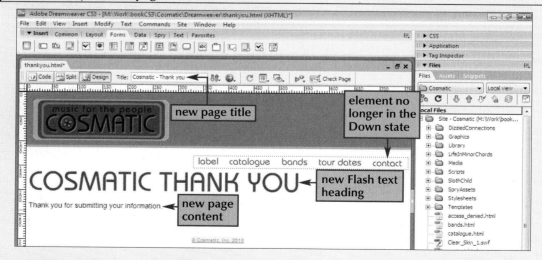

▶ 9. Save and close the page, and then upload the page to your remote server.

You'll use the same process to create the rest of the pages, except you will add content to the pages later (so you will not type any text in Step 6).

▶ **10.** Repeat Steps 1 through 9 to create the following pages, typing .php as the file extension for the last three pages in Step 2 and not typing any new page content in Step 6:

Filename	Page Title	Page Heading	Save Page Heading As
access_denied.html	Cosmatic - Access Denied	Cosmatic Access Denied	Media/Heading AccessDenied.swf
database.php	Cosmatic Database	Cosmatic Database	Media/Heading Database.swf
database_details.php	Cosmatic - Database Details	Cosmatic Database Details	Media/Heading Database Details.swf
login.php	Cosmatic - Login	Cosmatic Login	Media/Heading Login.swf

Now that you have modified the form and created the new pages, you are ready to create the database on your remote server.

Creating a Database on a Remote Server

You must create the database on the remote server so it can send data to and receive data from Web pages or Web applications. For example, in the Cosmatic site, the form in the Contact page will send data to the database that you create on the remote server.

If your instructor has already created the database on your remote server, you should read but not complete the next set of steps. In this case, you will be sharing the same database with your classmates, so you might see data that you did not add in the database or data you added might be removed. If you are creating the database on your remote server, you will need to contact your ISP (or your IT department) and have them create an empty MySQL database, name the empty database "cosmaticdb," and provide you with access information. Once the empty database is available on your remote server, you will use the administrative tools your host provides to:

- Log in to the database management interface (use the information and steps provided by your ISP or IT department).
- Run the statements that are provided as SQL in the cosmaticdb.sql file located in the Tutorial.10\Tutorial folder included with your Data Files. (The steps will vary depending on the system your ISP or IT department uses.) Running the statements will create the database that will be used in this tutorial by filling the empty database on the remote server with the structure and content that the Cosmatic technical team provided.

The following are the steps the authors' ISP provided to log in to the empty database and run the cosmaticdb.sql file using phpMyAdmin as the database management interface. phpMyAdmin is the most frequently used database management interface for MySQL databases. Additional information about phpMyAdmin can be found at *www.phpmyadmin.net*. If your ISP or IT department uses a different interface or if the interface is configured differently, your steps will differ slightly; contact your ISP or IT department for the exact steps you should follow. If your instructor has already created the database for you, read the following steps, and then continue working in the Connecting a Web Site to a Database section.

To log in to the database management interface and run the SQL file:

▶ **1.** Open a browser window, type the URL provided by your ISP or IT department in the Address bar, and then press the **Enter** key. A page or dialog box opens in which you enter login information.

▶ **2.** Type the user name and password information provided by your ISP or IT department in the appropriate boxes, and then click the **OK** button. The default page of
the database management interface that your ISP or IT department uses appears
in the browser window. Figure 10-20 shows the default page for the phpMyAdmin
database management interface.

Figure 10-20 ▶ **phpMyAdmin default page**

Trouble? If your screen does not match Figure 10-20, your ISP or IT department
uses a different interface or has phpMyAdmin configured differently. The same
general steps should work. However, if you have difficulty, ask your instructor,
technical support person, ISP, or IT department for instructions.

▶ **3.** Click the **Databases** arrow, and then click **cosmaticdb**, if necessary. The
cosmaticdb detail page is displayed. See Figure 10-21.

Figure 10-21 ▶ **cosmaticdb detail page**

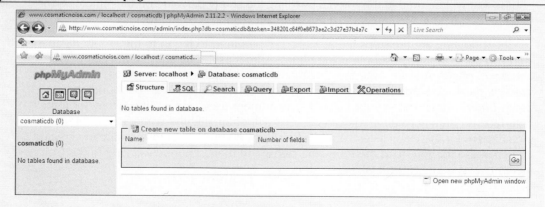

▶ **4.** Click the **SQL** tab at the top of the page. The SQL page opens in the browser
window.

▶ **5.** Navigate to the **Tutorial.10\Tutorial** folder included with your Data Files, open the **cosmaticdb.sql** file in Notepad, and then copy all of the content and paste it into the **Run SQL query/queries on database cosmaticdb** text area.

▶ **6.** Click the **Go** button. The database management interface runs the SQL, the database structure is created, and a list of the tables in the database appears at the left of the browser window below the database name. See Figure 10-22.

Database created on the remote server ◀ Figure 10-22

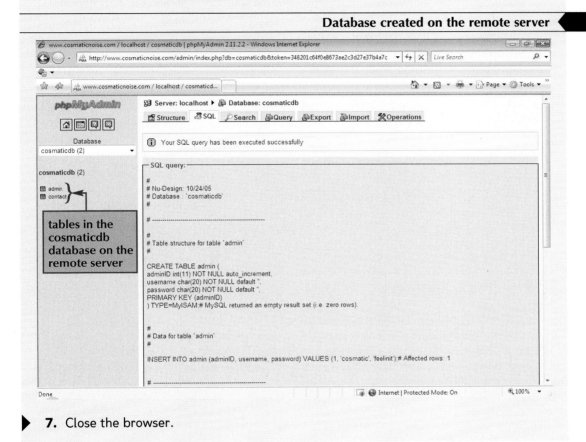

tables in the cosmaticdb database on the remote server

▶ **7.** Close the browser.

Connecting a Web Site to a Database

The database is created on the remote Web server, and you are ready to connect the site to the database. When you open a Web page in the Document window that is not connected to the database, the Server Behaviors panel displays an interactive list of steps for setting up Dreamweaver to connect the site to the database. Clicking the linked text in each step opens the dialog boxes needed to complete that step. A check mark appears at the left of each step to indicate that all the necessary information has been entered and the step is completed.

The three main steps for connecting a Web page to the database are:

1. **Create a site for this file.** This step is checked because you have already set the local and remote information for the site when you created the site definition.

2. **Choose a document type.** In this step, you specify which document type you are using to create server behaviors. When you click the link text in Step 2, the Choose Document Type dialog box opens, and you can select ASP JavaScript, ASP VBScript, ASP.NET C#, ASP.NET VB, ColdFusion, JSP, or PHP MySQL as the document type. For the Cosmatic site, you will use PHP.

3. **Set up the site's testing server.** In this step, you specify the testing server in the site definition. You cannot preview dynamic pages from within Dreamweaver until you specify a folder in which the dynamic pages can be processed. Dreamweaver uses this folder to generate dynamic content and connect to the database while you work. For the Cosmatic site, you will use the root folder you created on the remote server for your Cosmatic site because the server usually runs an application server that can handle the dynamic pages. You can, however, specify a different location for the testing server as long as it can handle dynamic pages. When you set up the testing server for a professional site that is already live, you might designate a separate folder on another server where you can test the pages without affecting the live site. When you click the link text in Step 3, the Site Definition dialog box opens to the Testing Server category. The information for the remote server is displayed by default, but you may need to delete the first part of the file path in the URL prefix box.

InSight	**Comparing Modified Times of Local and Server Files**

Some of the files required for server-sided processing are located outside of the Web page. Therefore, whenever you upload pages to your remote or testing server, you must also upload dependent files. As you upload files, a dialog box may open indicating that you are trying to overwrite newer files with older files. This occurs because Dreamweaver has a feature that compares the modified time of local files with the modified time of server files. If the time on either the server or your computer is inaccurate and your local computer time is behind the server time, then Dreamweaver sees the file on the server as newer and notifies you that you are overwriting a newer file with an older file. Click the OK button each time you see this message.

You'll open the Contact page and complete Steps 2 and 3 in the Server Behaviors panel.

To select the document type and set the testing server:

▶ 1. Open the **contact.html** page in the Document window, expand the **Application panel group**, click the **Server Behaviors** tab, and then click the **document type** link in the Server Behaviors panel. The Choose Document Type dialog box opens. See Figure 10-23.

Choose Document Type dialog box ◀ Figure 10-23

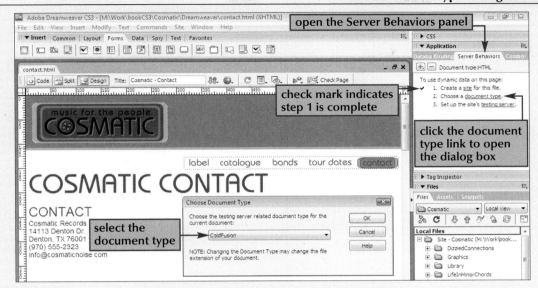

▶ **2.** Click the document type button, click **PHP**, and then click the **OK** button. The Update Files dialog box opens. You want to update the links in all the listed files.

▶ **3.** Click the **Update** button to update the links. The file extension for the Contact page changes to .php, and the Update Files dialog box opens, indicating that the contact.php page could not be updated. You will update the link in the contact.php page yourself.

▶ **4.** Click the **OK** button. A check mark appears in the Server Behaviors panel beside Step 2 to indicate that this step is complete (the check mark may not appear immediately).

▶ **5.** Click **Modify** on the menu bar, click **Navigation Bar**, click **Contact** in the Nav bar elements list, select **html** in the When clicked, Go to URL box, type **php** to change the file extension, and then click the **OK** button. The link for the Contact element of the navigation bar is updated.

▶ **6.** Save the page, and then upload the page to your remote server, including the dependent files. (The contact.html page remains in the site's root folder but is no longer used.)

Next, you'll complete Step 3.

▶ **7.** In the Server Behaviors panel, click the **testing server** link in Step 3. The Site Definition for Cosmatic dialog box opens with the Advanced tab displayed and Testing Server selected in the Category box.

▶ **8.** Click the **Server model** button, click **PHP MySQL**, click the **Access** button, and then click **FTP**. Additional FTP options appear in the dialog box, displaying the information you entered in the Remote Info category.

▶ **9.** Delete all the file path information in the URL prefix box, and then type the URL for your posted site. See Figure 10-24.

Figure 10-24 | **Completed Testing Server information**

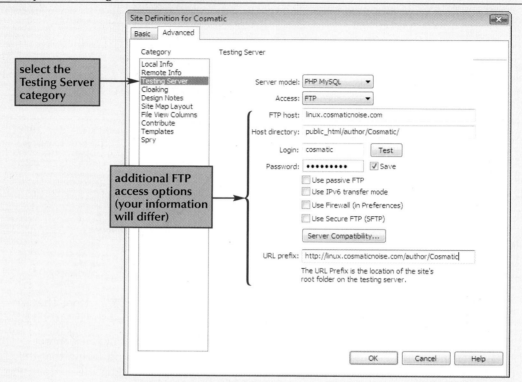

Trouble? If you do not know the URL for your remote site, ask your instructor, technical support person, or ISP for this information.

▶ **10.** Click the **OK** button. The Testing Server information is set, and a check mark appears beside Step 3 in the Server Behaviors panel.

Trouble? If a dialog box opens saying that the site URL prefix for the testing server does not match the site URL prefix specified in the HTTP address for the site, your server includes a public_html directory that stores all the content that viewers can access to view with a Web browser. However, when visitors view the Web site, the URL they enter does not include the public_html directory. Therefore, these paths are different. Click the OK button here and whenever this dialog box appears.

Adding Server Behaviors

Dreamweaver provides a list of prewritten server behaviors in the Server Behaviors panel after the page is connected to the database. You include these server behaviors in the page to extend the functionality of the page and to enable you to retrieve and display the data from the database.

You will include the following two server behaviors in the contact.php page:

- **Recordset.** The Recordset behavior enables you to specify which data you want to retrieve from the database and display in the Web page. A **recordset** is a temporary collection of data retrieved from a database and stored on the application server that generates the Web page when that page is loaded in a browser window. You specify the database and the records (or data) to include in the recordset when you set the parameters for the behavior. A recordset can include all the data in the database or a subset of the data. You must add the server-side behaviors that will create the recordset in which to store and retrieve data before you can use a database as a content source for a dynamic Web page. The server discards the recordset when it is no longer needed.
- **Insert Record.** The Insert Record behavior enables you to specify what will happen to the information collected from the Web page (in this case, when the form is submitted). You can specify in which database the data will be placed, where the data will be stored in the database, what columns will be included, and so on. It also enables you to select the page that appears in the browser window once the form is submitted.

You'll create a recordset for the contact.php page.

To create a recordset:

▶ 1. At the top of the Server Behaviors panel, click the **Add Behavior** button ➕ , and then click **Recordset**. The Recordset dialog box opens. See Figure 10-25.

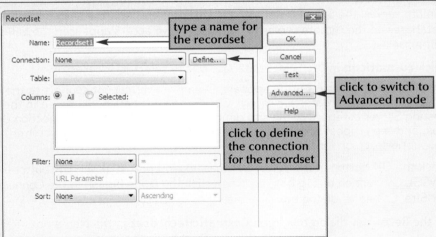

▶ 2. Click the **Advanced** button (if necessary to switch the Recordset dialog box to Advanced mode), and then click the **Define** button next to the Connection box. The Connections for Site 'Cosmatic' dialog box opens.

▶ 3. Click the **New** button. The MySQL Connection dialog box opens. See Figure 10-26.

| Figure 10-26 | MySQL Connection dialog box |

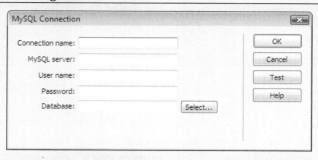

4. Type **CosmaticDBconnection** in the Connection name box. This is an internal name that will be visible only when you are working in Dreamweaver.

5. Type **localhost** in the MySQL server box if your database server is on the same server as your Web server; otherwise, type the database server URL provided by your ISP when you requested access information.

   Trouble? If you are using a different testing server than the remote server, you will need different information for this step. Ask your instructor or technical support person for help.

6. Type your database user name in the User name box, and then type your database password in the Password box. You'll need to obtain this information from your instructor, technical support person, ISP, or IT department.

7. Click the **Select** button next to the Database box. Dreamweaver connects to the remote server, the Select Database dialog box opens, and the names of all the databases on the remote server to which you have access appear in the Select Database list.

8. Click **cosmaticdb** in the Select database box to select it, if necessary.

   Trouble? If an error message appears, Dreamweaver cannot connect to the database on the remote database server. Check the information you typed in the Testing Server category of the site definition and in the MySQL Connection dialog box, and then repeat Step 8. If you still have trouble, ask your instructor or technical support person for help.

9. Click the **OK** button in the Select Database dialog box, click the **OK** button in the MySQL Connection dialog box, and then click the **Done** button in the Connections for Site 'Cosmatic' dialog box. The dialog boxes close.

10. In the Recordset dialog box, type **CosmaticRecordset** in the Name box.

11. Click the **Connection** button, click **CosmaticDBconnection**, expand the **Tables** list in the Database items box, click **contact**, click the **SELECT** button, and then click the **OK** button. The Recordset behavior is added to the page and appears in the Server Behaviors panel. See Figure 10-27.

Recordset behavior added to the contact.php page ◄ Figure 10-27

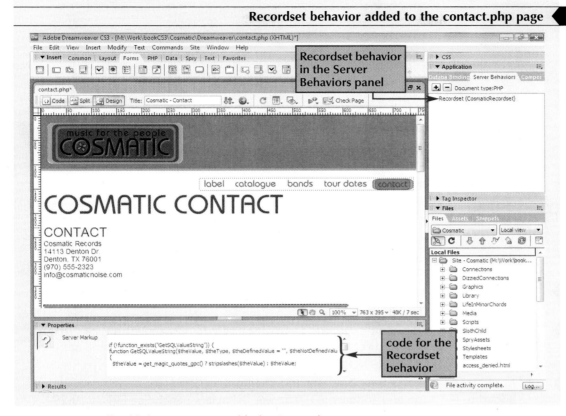

Next, you'll add the Insert Record behavior to the page.

To add the Insert Record behavior:

▶ **1.** At the top of the Server Behaviors panel, click the **Add Behavior** button ➕ , and then click **Insert Record**. The Insert Record dialog box opens.

▶ **2.** Click the **Submit values from** button and click **ContactForm**, if necessary, click the **Connection** button and click **CosmaticDBconnection**, and then click the **Insert table** button and click **contact**. The columns in the contact table are displayed in the Columns box. See Figure 10-28.

Figure 10-28   Insert Record dialog box

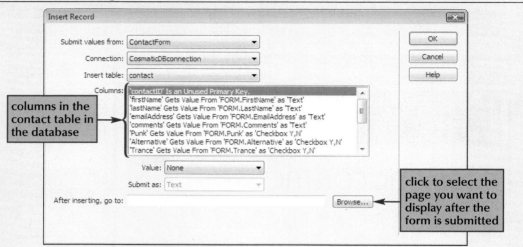

columns in the contact table in the database

click to select the page you want to display after the form is submitted

▶ **3.** Click the **Browse** button next to the After inserting, go to box. The Select a redirect file dialog box opens.

▶ **4.** Click the **thankyou.html** page in the site's local root folder, and then click the **OK** button. The Select a redirect file dialog box closes, and the page filename appears in the After inserting, go to box.

▶ **5.** In the Insert Record dialog box, click the **OK** button. The Insert Record behavior is added to the page and appears in the Server Behaviors panel. See Figure 10-29.

Insert Record behavior added to the contact.php page

Figure 10-29

Before continuing, you'll test the Insert Record behavior you added to the contact.php page. You need to upload the page to the remote server, preview the page in a browser, and then complete and submit the form. The Thank You page should then display.

To test the Insert Record behavior:

1. Save the page, and then upload the page to the remote server. The Dependent Files dialog box opens.

2. Click the **Yes** button to update the dependent files.

3. Preview the contact.php page in a browser. The Update Copy on Testing Server dialog box opens.

4. Click the **Yes** button to update the file on the testing server, and then click **Yes** in the Dependent Files dialog box, if necessary.

5. Scroll down to view the form in the Contact page, enter appropriate information in the form, and then click the **Submit** button to submit the form. The Thank You page appears in a new browser window.

6. Close the browser.

The page is connected to the database, and the behaviors have been added to the page. Next, you will create pages that enable you to view the data collected in the database.

Creating Backend Pages for Viewing Data in a Database

Pages that are intended for internal use are usually called **backend pages**. For the Cosmatic site, the Database and Database Details pages are backend pages. You will set the database.php and database_details.php pages to display the data that you collect in the database. The Master Detail Page Set button in the Data category on the Insert bar enables you to create a set of pages that present information in two levels of detail. The master page (in this case, the database.php page) lists all the records in the recordset that you create for the page. The detail page (in this case, the database_details.php page) displays the detail of the selected record. You determine which fields of information are displayed in the master page and which fields of information are displayed in the detail page when you set the parameters for the pages. In addition to creating all the code needed to display the dynamic content in the pages, Dreamweaver also adds server behaviors to create a page navigation bar that enables you to move between the dynamic records if there are more records in the database than are displayed in the page. The navigation bar includes First Page, Last Page, Previous Page, and Next Page buttons. The pages also include Display Record Count server behaviors to indicate which records are visible in the page and the total number of records in the database (Records *x* to *y* of *z*).

To create the master page:

1. In the Server Behaviors panel, click **Recordset**, right-click the selected behavior, and then click **Copy** on the context menu.

2. Open the **database_details.php** page, right-click in the Server Behaviors panel, and then click **Paste** on the context menu. The Recordset behavior is pasted in the Database Details page.

3. Place the insertion point in the heading line after the heading text, press the **Right Arrow** key to move the insertion point past the heading text, and then press the **Enter** key to move the insertion point to the next line.

   Trouble? If Dreamweaver locks up, then you've encountered a bug in Dreamweaver that causes the program to lock up if you place the insertion point in the line below the heading and then press the Enter key when using server behaviors. End the program, restart the computer, and then repeat Steps 1 through 3.

4. Open the **database.php** page in the Document window, right-click in the Server Behaviors panel, click **Paste** on the context menu to paste the Recordset behavior into the page, place the insertion point in the heading line, press the **Right Arrow** key to move the insertion point past the heading text, and then press the **Enter** key to move the insertion point to the next line.

5. Click the **Data** tab on the Insert bar, and then click the **Master Detail Page Set** button 🖺 . The Insert Master-Detail Page Set dialog box opens. See Figure 10-30.

Insert Master-Detail Page Set dialog box ◄ Figure 10-30

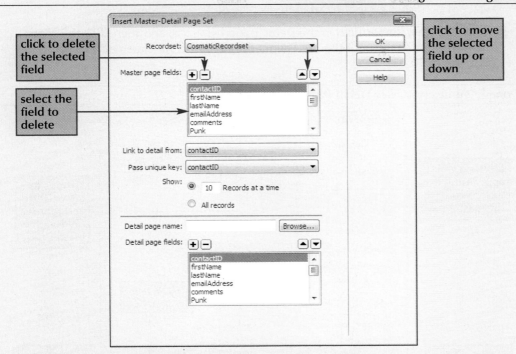

You will remove the fields from the Master page fields box that you do not want to display in the master page. You'll also change the field order so that the last name will appear in the first column.

▶ **6.** Click **contactID** in the Master page fields box, if necessary, and then click the Master page fields **Remove Item** button ⊟ . The selected field name is removed from the list.

▶ **7.** Repeat Step 6 to remove the following field names: **comments**, **Punk**, **Alternative**, **Trance**, **Jazz**, **sloth_child**, **dizzied_connections**, **Life_In_Minor_Chords**, and **surface_suction**. Only the names of fields that will be visible in the Database page appear in the Master page fields box.

▶ **8.** Click **lastName** in the Master page fields box, and then click the Master page fields **Move Item Up** button ▲ until the lastName field is at the top of the list. The fields will display in the page in the same order they appear in the list.

▶ **9.** Click the **Link to detail from** button, and then click **lastName**. The data from the lastName field in the Database page is now linked to the record details, which will display in the Database Details page.

You'll set the record details to display in the database_details.php page. As with the master page, you'll delete unneeded fields and change the field order for the detail page.

To create the detail page:

▶ **1.** Click the **Browse** button next to the Detail page name box, click the **database_details.php** page in the Select File dialog box, and then click the **OK** button. The page name appears in the Detail page name box.

▶ **2.** Click **contactID** in the Detail page fields list, if necessary, and then click the **Remove Item** button ⊟. The field name is removed from the list and the field will not be displayed in the Database Details page.

▶ **3.** Click the **Newsletter** field in the Detail page fields list, and then click the **Move Item Up** button ▲ until the field name is directly below the emailAddress field. See Figure 10-31.

Figure 10-31 ▶ **Completed Insert Master-Detail Page Set dialog box**

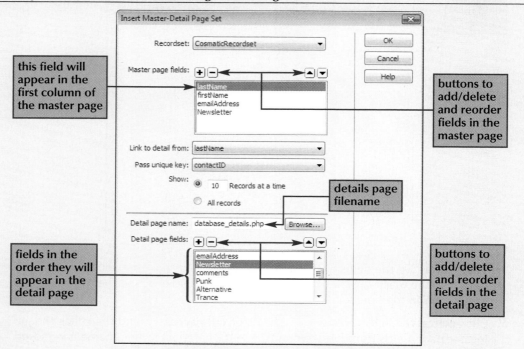

▶ **4.** Click the **OK** button. The dialog box closes, and the master/detail pages are complete.

Dreamweaver adds elements to the pages that will enable you to view the data collected in the database, as well as the details of selected records. Before continuing, you'll upload the pages to the remote server and preview the pages in the browser.

To view the Database Details page:

▶ **1.** Save the Database page, and then upload the page to your remote server. Dreamweaver adds elements to the page that will enable you to view the data collected in the database. See Figure 10-32.

Database page Figure 10-32

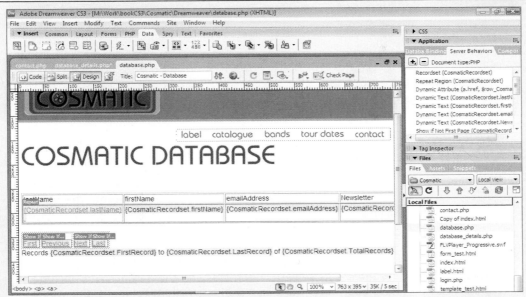

▶ **2.** Click the **database_details.php** tab to view the Database Details page. Dreamweaver has also added elements to this page that will enable you to view the details of records selected in the Database page. See Figure 10-33.

Database Details page Figure 10-33

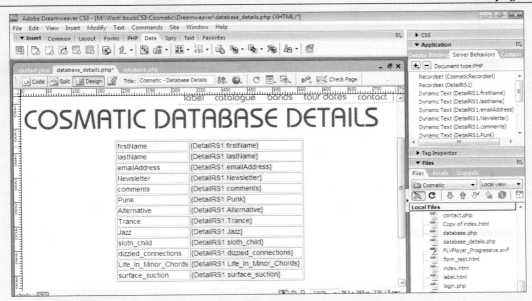

Trouble? If Dreamweaver inserted the table below the footer in the page, select the table and drag it above the footer in the page.

▶ **3.** Save the Database Details page, and then upload the page to your remote server.

▶ **4.** Click the **database.php** tab, and then preview the page in a browser, clicking the **No** button when Dreamweaver asks you to update the files on the testing server because you have already done that. The data that you collected from the form in the Contact page appears in the browser window. See Figure 10-34.

Figure 10-34 Database page previewed in a browser

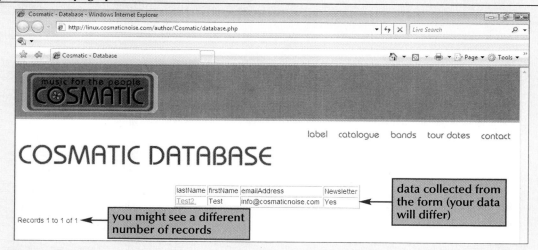

Trouble? If you see more than the one record you entered into the contact form, then you're sharing the database with classmates and the database will include all the entries that have been submitted. In a professional environment, this would probably not be the case.

▶ **5.** Click a link to view the details of a record. The details are displayed in the Database Details page.

▶ **6.** Click the **Back** button ⬅ on the browser toolbar to return to the Database page, and then click another record, if available.

▶ **7.** Close the browser, and then close all the pages.

InSight | **Copying and Pasting Code**

As you use more advanced techniques, you will begin to work with code more frequently. When you want the same functionality in two different places, a good technique is to copy the code from one location and paste it in the other location. Not only does this technique save you time, it also eliminates the chance of mistyping the code. It is also acceptable technique to copy and paste code from other code sources that are "available to the public" such as example code sites and books that teach coding techniques. When copying and pasting code from one source to another, it is a good idea to paste the copied code into a style-free text editor such as TextPad or Notepad and remove any formatting from the text before pasting it into the code of your Web pages. This prevents hard-to-trace code errors that arise from pasting formatted text in code.

Creating a Login Page to Protect Backend Pages

Data collected from a Web site and stored in a database is often displayed in Web pages. This convenience enables you to view the data from any computer that is connected to the Internet. However, most businesses do not want the general public to have access to this type of proprietary information. One way to restrict the access to Web pages is to require users to log in before they can view the pages. This protects the data from unauthorized access. To add this functionality, you must:

- **Create a table in the database that holds user names and passwords.** The team that created the SQL that you used to create the database included an administrative table with columns to collect user names and passwords. They also added one user name (cosmatic) and one password (feelinit) in the table. You will use the user name and password included in the database to create and test the Login page.
- **Create a page that enables users to create accounts by entering a unique user name and password.** Because only one member of the Cosmatic staff is in charge of monitoring and reporting the information collected in the database, you won't create this page now. The team member will use the supplied user name and password to log in to protected pages. Because you eventually want to enable other users to log in to the site, you will create additional pages that will enable users to create unique user names and passwords in the Review Assignments.
- **Create a page that enables users to log in to the site.** You have already created the Login page. Now you will create a form in the Login page that enables users to input their user name and password information. You will also add the Log In User server behavior to the page, which will check the database when a user submits the form to ensure that the user name and password are valid. If login is successful, the Database page will appear in the user's browser window. If login is unsuccessful, the Access Denied page will be displayed in the browser window.
- **Restrict access to the pages.** You add the Restrict Access To Page server behavior to the pages that you want to protect, in this case, the Database and Database Details pages. After this behavior is added to the pages, users who are not logged in will be sent to the Access Denied page.

You'll create the form in the Login page, and then add the Log In User server behavior to the page.

To add content to the Login page:

1. Open the **login.php** page in the Document window, place the insertion point in the heading line, press the **Right Arrow** key until the insertion point is positioned at the right of the heading text, and then press the **Enter** key. The insertion point moves to the next line.

2. Click the **Forms** tab on the Insert bar, and then click the **Form** button ▢ . The code for a form is inserted into the page.

3. In the Property inspector, type **loginform** in the Form name box. For this form, it is not necessary to enter information for the other attributes in the Property inspector because you will add behaviors to control the form.

4. Click inside of the form area (the dotted red lines), click the **Common** tab on the Insert bar, and then click the **Table** button ▦ . The Table dialog box opens.

5. Type **3** in the Rows box, type **2** in the Columns box, type **80** percent in the Table width boxes, type **2** in the Cell padding box, type **0** in the Border thickness box, type **2** in the Cell spacing box, click **None** in the Header box, and then click the **OK** button. A table with three rows and two columns is inserted into the form.

6. Select the left column of the table, click the **Horz** button in the Property inspector and click **Right**, click the **Vert** button and click **Top**, select the right column of the table, click the **Horz** button in the Property inspector and click **Left**, and then click the **Vert** button and click **Top**.

▶ **7.** Click in the first cell of the table, type **User name:** (including the colon), and then press the **Tab** key to move the insertion point to the upper-right cell.

▶ **8.** Click the **Forms** tab on the Insert Bar, and then click the **Text Field** button 🔲 to insert a text field.

▶ **9.** In the Property inspector, type **username** in the TextField box, type **40** in the Char width box, and then type **20** in the Max chars box.

▶ **10.** Click in the middle-left cell of the table, type **Password:** (including the colon), and then press the **Tab** key to move the insertion point to the next cell.

▶ **11.** On the Forms tab of the Insert bar, click the **Text Field** button 🔲 , and then, in the Property inspector, type **password** in the TextField box, type **40** in the Char width box, and type **20** in the Max chars box.

▶ **12.** Click in the bottom-right cell of the table, click the **Button** button 🔲 on the **Forms** tab of the Insert bar, type **Login** in the Button name and Value boxes, and then press the **Enter** key. See Figure 10-35.

Figure 10-35	Form in the Login page

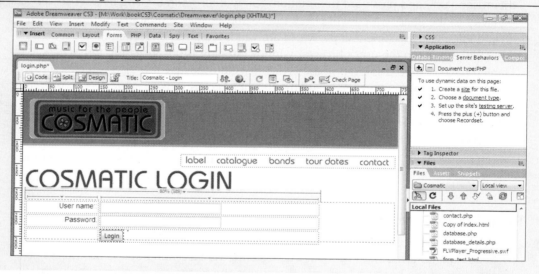

Next, you'll add the Log In User server behavior to the page, which will verify the submitted user name and password.

To add server behaviors to the Login page:

▶ **1.** Select the **Login** button in the form, click the **Data** tab on the Insert bar, click the **User Authentication button arrow** 🔒▾ , and then click **Log In User**. The Log In User dialog box opens.

▶ **2.** Click the **Validate using connection** button, click **CosmaticDBconnection**, click the **Table** button, click **admin**, click the **Username column** button, click **username**, click the **Password column** button, and then click **password**.

▶ **3.** Click the **Browse** button next to the If login succeeds, go to box, click the **database.php** page in the Select File dialog box, and then click the **OK** button. This sets the Database page to display in the browser window if the submitted user name and password are listed in the database.

▶ **4.** Click the **Browse** button next to the If login fails, go to box, click the **access_denied.html** page in the Select File dialog box, and then click the **OK** button. This sets the Access Denied page to display in the browser window if the submitted user name and password are not listed in the database. See Figure 10-36.

Log In User dialog box ◀ Figure 10-36

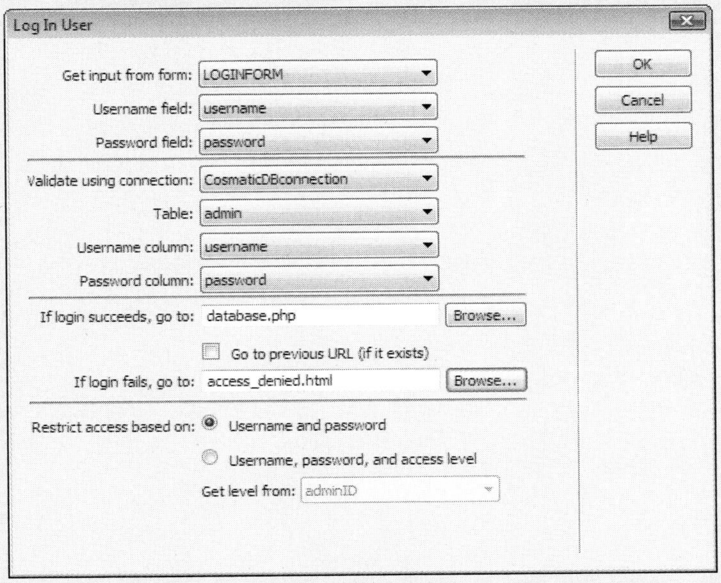

▶ **5.** Click the **OK** button. The Log In User server behavior is added to the page.

▶ **6.** Save the page, and then upload the page to your remote server.

You'll add a meta refresh tag to the Access Denied page, which tells the browser to automatically refresh the page (by reloading the current page or going to a different page) after a certain amount of time. You'll also add text to indicate that access was denied to that user.

To add a meta refresh tag and text to the Access Denied page:

▶ **1.** Open the **access_denied.html** page in the Document window.

▶ **2.** Click the **Common** tab on the Insert bar, click the **Head button arrow** , and then click **Refresh**. The Refresh dialog box opens.

▶ **3.** Type **4** in the Delay box, and then type **login.php** in the Go to URL box. See Figure 10-37.

Refresh dialog box ◀ Figure 10-37

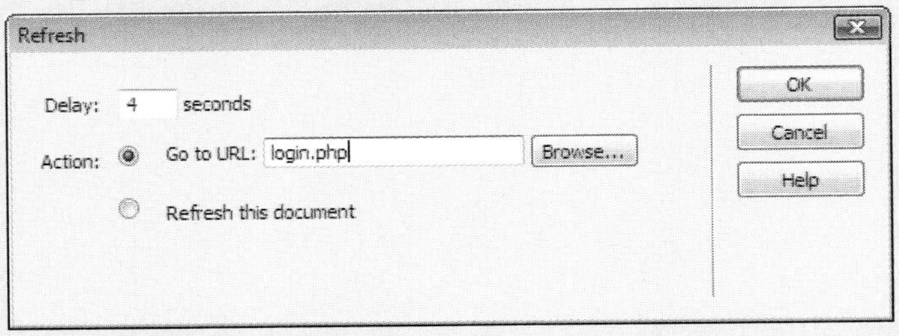

▶ **4.** Click the **OK** button, place the insertion point after the heading text, press the **Enter** key, and then type **Your access was denied. Please enter your login ID and password again.** (including the period).

▶ **5.** Save the page, and then upload the page to your remote server.

Before you continue, you'll test the Login page and the behaviors you added to the Database and Access Denied pages.

To test the Login page:

▶ **1.** Preview the login.php page in a browser. The Update Copy on Testing Server dialog box opens.

▶ **2.** Click the **Yes** button to ensure that the most recent copy of the page is on both the testing and remote servers. The Dependent Files dialog box opens.

▶ **3.** Click the **Yes** button to ensure that all the dependent files are current on both the testing and remote servers. The Login page appears in the browser window.

Trouble? If the message, "Warning: session_start():" followed by a file path and "failed: Permission denied" appears when you test the page on your remote server, you may need to adjust the permissions on your Web server's temporary directory (usually tmp) so that it is writable by the server. Contact your ISP or technical support person for assistance.

You'll enter an invalid user name and password.

▶ **4.** Type **test** in the User name box, type **random** in the Password box, and then click the **Login** button. The login information is invalid, so the access_denied.html page is displayed in the browser window. After four seconds, the Login page is redisplayed.

Now, you'll enter a valid user name and password.

▶ **5.** Type **cosmatic** in the User name box, type **feelinit** in the Password box, and then click the **Login** button. The Database page is displayed in the browser window.

▶ **6.** Close the browser, and then close the pages.

Finally, you will protect the Database and Database Details pages from unauthorized access by adding the Restrict Access server behavior to the pages.

To restrict access to pages:

▶ **1.** Open the **database.php** page in the Document window.

▶ **2.** Click the **Data** tab on the Insert bar, click the **User Authentication button arrow** , and then click **Restrict Access To Page**. The Restrict Access To Page dialog box opens.

▶ **3.** Type **access_denied.html** in the If access denied, go to box. See Figure 10-38.

Restrict Access To Page dialog box | Figure 10-38

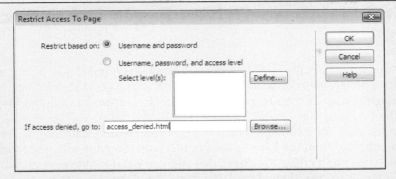

4. Click the **OK** button, save the page, and then upload the page to your remote server and update the copy on the testing server if asked.

5. Open the **database_details.php** page in the Document window, and then repeat Steps 2 through 4 to restrict access to that page.

   You'll test the behavior you added to the pages.

6. Preview the database.php page in a browser. Because you are not logged in, the Database page will not display in the browser window. Instead, the Access Denied page is displayed for four seconds, and then the Login page is displayed.

   Trouble? If the Database page does appear, you did not close the browser window after you logged in and you are still logged in. Close any open browser windows, and then repeat Step 6.

7. Close the browser, and then close the pages.

In this session, you created database-driven Web pages for the Cosmatic site using MySQL and PHP for a Linux server. The database functionality will enable Sara and Brian to collect data about their customers' preferences. Analyzing this data will help them shape future marketing plans for Cosmatic.

Session 10.2 Quick Check | Review

1. In addition to selecting a database, you must also select a(n) _____ that you will use to create server behaviors.
2. What language do you use to create server behaviors when you use a MySQL database?
3. What is a server behavior?
4. Why do you need the Recordset behavior?
5. Why would you create a Login page?
6. What is the purpose of the meta refresh tag?

Session 10.3

Creating Database-Driven Pages Using Access and ASP

Adding database functionality to a Web site can be quite complex. Just as it is a good idea to make a plan prior to creating a Web site, it is also a good idea to plan the database-driven portion of the site in advance. Brian has created a site plan for the new portion of the Cosmatic site.

Based on his plan, the Cosmatic technical team will create a database to store the information collected from the form in the Contact page. You'll modify the form to work with the database. You'll create the pages that you will need for the new portion of the site: thankyou.html, access_denied.html, database.asp, database_details.asp, and login. asp. You'll upload the database file provided by the technical team to the remote server, and then you'll connect the site to the database. Next, you'll add server behaviors to the pages you created to enable the form data to be sent to and stored in the database and to enable the database.asp and database_details.asp pages to display the information stored in the database. Finally, you'll create a login.asp page and add code to the backend pages that will prevent unauthorized users from viewing the content of those pages.

When the database-driven pages are complete, the survey information received from users who completed the form in the Contact page will be stored in a database that only authorized users can access.

| Reference Window | **Creating Database-Driven Pages for a Windows Server** |

- Create the Web pages you need.
- Upload a database file in which to store data to your remote server.
- Add server behaviors to connect the site to the database.
- Add server behaviors to store submitted data in the database and to view the data collected in the database from within designated Web pages.
- Create a Login page.
- Add code to the backend pages to prevent unauthorized users from viewing the content of those pages.

Modifying the Form

Before you create the database-driven pages of the Cosmatic site, you'll modify the form in the Contact page to work with the database that you will place on your remote server. You will delete the list box with the band names from the form, and then create a series of checkboxes to collect this same information. You are replacing the list box to keep things simpler because it requires more steps and custom scripts to process data from a list box for storage in a database.

To modify the form in the Contact page:

▶ 1. If you took a break after the previous session, make sure that the Cosmatic site is open.

▶ 2. Open the **contact.html** page in the Document window, select the list box in the right column near the bottom of the form, and then press the **Delete** key. The list box is removed from the form in the page.

▶ **3.** Click the **Forms** tab on the Insert bar, click the **Checkbox** button ☑ to insert the first checkbox, type **sloth_child** in the Checkbox name box in the Property inspector, click to the right of the checkbox to deselect the checkbox, type **sloth child** beside the checkbox, and then press the **Shift+Enter** keys to move the insertion point down one line. You've entered the first checkbox and label in the form.

> **Trouble?** If the Tag Input Accessibility Attributes dialog box opens, click the Cancel button here and each time you insert a new form object in this tutorial.

▶ **4.** Repeat Step 3 to create checkboxes and labels for the following bands, replacing the spaces in the band names with underscores in the Checkbox name box: **dizzied connections, Life in Minor Chords**, and **surface suction**.

▶ **5.** Select the sentence in the left column next to the new checkboxes, and then type **Check all of the bands that you enjoy.** (including the period). See Figure 10-39.

Modified form ◀ **Figure 10-39**

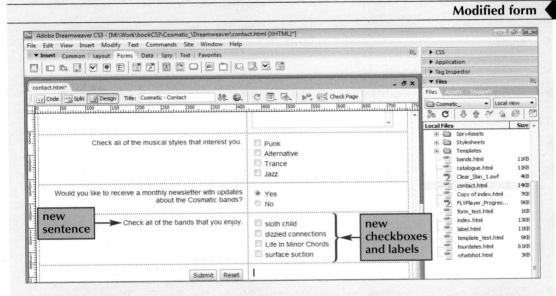

▶ **6.** Save and close the Contact page, and then upload the page to your remote server.

Creating New Pages

You need five pages for the database-driven portion of the site. You will create all these pages now so that they will be available when you need them. According to Brian's plan for the database-driven portion of the Cosmatic site, you will create the following pages:

- **thankyou.html** — A page thanking the user for his or her submission that appears when the user submits the form in the Contact page.
- **access_denied.html** — A page informing the user that the wrong user name or password has been entered that appears when a user attempts to log in on the Login page with incorrect information or if a user attempts to access a password-protected page without logging in. After a four-second delay, the user will be returned to the Login page.
- **database.asp** — A page showing an overview of the data stored in the database. After the Login page is created, users cannot access this page unless they log in.

- **database_details.asp** — A page showing the details of a selected record that appears when a user clicks a record in the Database page. After the Login page is created, users cannot access this page unless they log in.
- **login.asp** — A page in which a user enters his or her user name and password and then clicks the Login button. If the information is correct, the Database page appears; if the information is incorrect, the Access Denied page appears.

Three of the pages you will create are ASP pages. You can create an ASP page by typing .asp as the file extension when you name the page.

Tip

You can also press the Ctrl+D keys to duplicate the selected page.

To create pages for the database-driven portion of the Cosmatic site:

▶ **1.** In the Files panel, right-click the **contact.html** page, point to **Edit** on the context menu, and then click **Duplicate**. A new page named Copy of contact.html appears at the bottom of the list in the Files panel.

▶ **2.** In the Files panel, right-click the **Copy of contact.html** page, point to **Edit** on the context menu, click **Rename**, type **thankyou.html**, and then press the **Enter** key. The page is renamed.

▶ **3.** Open the **thankyou.html** page in the Document window, select **Contact** in the Title box on the Document toolbar, type **Thank you**, and then press the **Enter** key. The new page title appears.

▶ **4.** Double-click the page heading. The Insert Flash Text dialog box opens.

▶ **5.** Select the text in the Text box if necessary, type **COSMATIC THANK YOU**, select the text in the Save As box, type **Media/HeadingThankyou.swf**, and then click the **OK** button. The Flash Text heading is updated.

▶ **6.** Select all the content below the heading and above the footer, press the **Delete** key to remove it from the page, type **Thank you for submitting your information.** (including the period) in the line below the heading text, and then, if necessary, format the sentence in the **Paragraph** format.

▶ **7.** Click **Modify** on the menu bar, and then click **Navigation Bar**. The Modify Navigation Bar dialog box opens.

▶ **8.** Click **Contact** in the Nav Bar Elements list, click the **Show "Down image" initially** check box to uncheck it and remove the asterisk from Contact in the Nav bar elements box, click the **OK** button, and then click in the Thank You page to deselect the navigation bar element. The Contact button is no longer displayed in the Down state. See Figure 10-40.

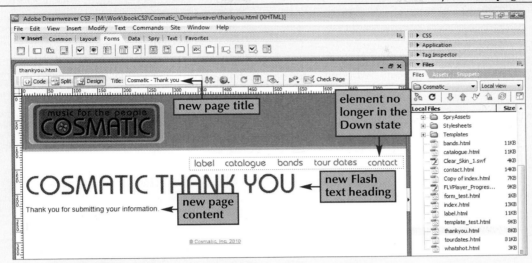

New thankyou.html page | Figure 10-40

▶ **9.** Save and close the page, and then upload the page to your remote server.

You'll use the same process to create the rest of the pages, except that you will add content to the pages later (so you will not type any text in Step 6).

▶ **10.** Repeat Steps 1 through 9 to create the following pages, typing .asp as the file extension for the last three pages in Step 2 and not typing any new page content in Step 6:

Filename	Page Title	Page Heading	Save Page Heading As
access_denied.html	Cosmatic - Access Denied	Cosmatic Access Denied	Media/HeadingAccessDenied.swf
database.asp	Cosmatic - Database	Cosmatic Database	Media/HeadingDatabase.swf
database_details.asp	Cosmatic - Database Details	Cosmatic Database	Media/HeadingDatabaseDetails.swf
login.asp	Cosmatic - Login	Cosmatic Login	Media/HeadingLogin.swf

Now that you have modified the form and created the new pages, you are ready to upload the database to your remote server.

Uploading a Database to a Remote Server

You must upload the database for the Cosmatic site to your remote server so it can send data to and receive data from Web pages or Web applications. For example, in the Cosmatic site, the form in the Contact page will send data to the database that you place on the remote server.

If your instructor has already uploaded the database to your remote server, you should read but not complete the next set of steps. In this case, you will be sharing the same database with your classmates, so you might see data that you did not add in the database or data you added might be removed. If you are uploading the database on your remote server, you will need to contact your ISP (or your IT department) and have them create a directory named "Database" on the remote server and provide you with the exact file path to the directory, as well as the FTP host, host directory, login, and password you should use. The directory must be writable by the IUSR account. (Instructors should verify that the new directory is accessible to all of their students.) Once the database directory has been created, you can then upload the cosmaticdb.mdb file located in the Tutorial.10\Tutorial folder included with your Data Files to the database directory on the remote server.

The following steps show how to use Dreamweaver to FTP the database file to your remote server. If your instructor has already uploaded the database for you, read the following steps and then continue working in the Connecting a Web Site to a Database section.

To upload the database to the remote server:

▶ **1.** Click **Site** on the menu bar, and then click **Manage Sites**. The Manage Sites dialog box opens.

▶ **2.** Click the **New** button, and then click **FTP & RDS Server**. The Configure Server dialog box opens. See Figure 10-41.

Figure 10-41 ▶ **Configure Server dialog box**

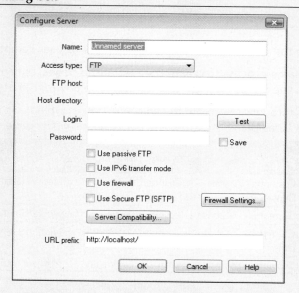

Trouble? If a dialog box opens to remind you that server connections allow you to work directly on the server but do not allow you to perform sitewide operations, click the OK button to close the dialog box. The Configure Server dialog box then opens. Continue with Step 3.

▶ **3.** Type **RemoteCosmaticFTP** in the Name box, click the **Access type** button, click **FTP**, if necessary, and then type the FTP host, host directory, login, and password that your ISP provided into the appropriate boxes (make sure the host directory ends with /Database/).

▶ **4.** Click the **Use passive FTP** check box to insert a check mark, click the **OK** button in the Configure Server dialog box, and then click the **Done** button in the Manage Sites dialog box. The new FTP connection is open in the Files panel. See Figure 10-42.

FTP connection to the remote server ◀ Figure 10-42

Trouble? If the FTP connection is not open in the Files panel, click the Site button, click ftp://RemoteCosmaticFTP, and then continue with Step 5.

5. In the Files panel, click the **Site** button, navigate to the **Tutorial.10\Tutorial** folder included with your Data Files, right-click the **cosmaticdb.mdb** file, point to **Edit** on the context menu, and then click **Copy** to copy the file.

6. In the Files panel, click the **Site** button, and then click **ftp://RemoteCosmaticFTP**. The FTP connection is listed in the Files panel.

7. Right-click **ftp://RemoteCosmaticFTP** in the file list, point to **Edit** on the context menu, and then click **Paste**. The cosmaticdb.mdb database file is uploaded to the remote server and is listed in the Files panel. See Figure 10-43.

Database copied to the remote server ◀ Figure 10-43

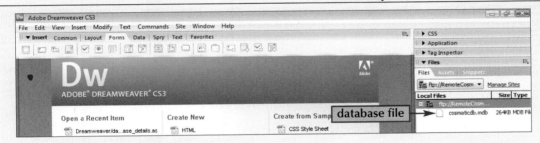

Trouble? If the database file is not listed, right-click ftp://RemoteCosmaticFTP in the files list, and then click Refresh on the context menu. The Files panel refreshes, and the cosmaticdb.mdb file appears in the list.

8. In the Files panel, click the **Site** button, and then click **Cosmatic**. The local root folder for your Cosmatic site is listed in the Files panel.

Connecting a Web Site to a Database

The database is copied to your remote server, and you are ready to connect the site to the database. When you open a Web page in the Document window that is not connected to the database, the Server Behaviors panel displays an interactive list of steps for setting up Dreamweaver to connect the site to the database. Clicking the linked text in each step opens the dialog boxes needed to complete that step. A check mark appears at the left of each step to indicate that all the necessary information has been entered and the step is completed.

The three main steps for connecting a page to the database are:

1. **Create a site for this file.** This step is checked because you already set the local and remote information for the site when you created the site definition.

2. **Choose a document type.** In this step, you specify which document type you are using to create server behaviors. When you click the link text in Step 2, the Choose Document Type dialog box opens, and you can select ASP JavaScript, ASP VBScript, ASP.NET C#, ASP.NET VB, ColdFusion, ColdFusion component, JSP, or PHP as the document type. For the Cosmatic site, you will use ASP JavaScript.

3. **Set up the site's testing server.** In this step, you specify the testing server in the site definition. You cannot preview dynamic pages from within Dreamweaver until you specify a folder in which the dynamic pages can be processed. Dreamweaver uses this folder to generate dynamic content and connect to the database while you work. For the Cosmatic site, you will use the root folder you created on the remote server for your Cosmatic site because the server usually runs an application server that can handle the dynamic pages. You can, however, specify a different location for the testing server as long as it can handle dynamic pages. When you set up the testing server for a professional site that is already live, you might designate a separate folder on another server where you can test the pages without affecting the live site. When you click the link text in Step 3, the Site Definition dialog box opens to the Testing Server category. The information for the remote server is displayed by default, but you may need to delete the first part of the file path in the URL prefix box.

InSight | **Comparing Modified Times of Local and Server Files**

Some of the files required for server-sided processing are located outside the Web page. Therefore, whenever you upload pages to your remote or testing server, you must also upload dependent files. As you upload files, a dialog box may open indicating that you are trying to overwrite newer files with older files. This occurs because Dreamweaver has a feature that compares the modified time of local files with the modified time of server files. If the time on either the server or your computer is inaccurate and your local computer time is behind the server time, then Dreamweaver sees the file on the server as newer and notifies you that you are overwriting a newer file with an older file. Click the OK button each time you see this message.

You'll open the Contact page and complete Steps 2 and 3 in the Server Behaviors panel.

To select the document type and set the testing server:

▶ 1. Open the **contact.html** page in the Document window, expand the **Application panel group**, click the **Server Behaviors** tab, and then click the **document type** link in the Server Behaviors panel. The Choose Document Type dialog box opens. See Figure 10-44.

Choose Document Type dialog box ◄ **Figure 10-44**

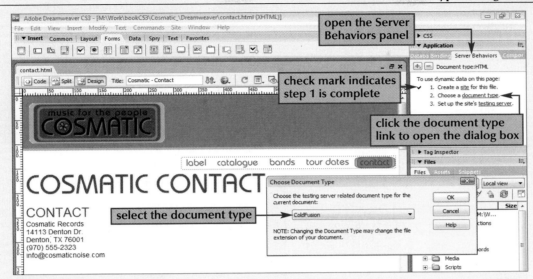

Trouble? If the document type in your list is different than the document type in the figure, your default is set differently. You will select the document type in Step 2.

▶ **2.** Click the document type button, click **ASP JavaScript**, and then click the **OK** button. The Update Files dialog box opens. You want to update the links in all the listed files.

▶ **3.** Click the **Update** button to update the links. The page extension for the Contact page changes to .asp and the Update Files dialog box opens, indicating that the contact.asp page could not be updated. You will update the link in the contact.asp page yourself.

▶ **4.** Click the **OK** button. A check mark appears in the Server Behaviors panel beside Step 2 to indicate this step is complete (the check mark may not appear immediately).

Trouble? If the background image disappears from the pages of your site when you view them in Dreamweaver, don't worry. The background image will be visible when you preview the page in a browser and when you view the pages over the Internet.

▶ **5.** Click **Modify** on the menu bar, click **Navigation Bar**, click **Contact** in the Nav bar elements box, select **html** in the When clicked, Go to URL box, type **asp** to change the file extension, and then click the **OK** button. The link for the Contact element of the navigation bar is updated.

▶ **6.** Save the page, and then upload the page to your remote server, including the dependent files. (The contact.html page remains in the site's root folder but is no longer used.)

Next, you'll complete Step 3.

▶ **7.** In the Server Behaviors panel, click the **testing server** link in Step 3. The Site Definition for Cosmatic dialog box opens with the Advanced tab displayed and Testing Server selected in the Category box.

▶ **8.** Click the **Server model** button, click **ASP JavaScript**, click the **Access** button, and then click **FTP**. Additional FTP options appear in the dialog box, displaying the information entered in the Remote Info category.

▶ **9.** Delete the entire file path information in the URL prefix box, and then type the URL for your posted site. See Figure 10-45.

Figure 10-45 ▶ **Completed Testing Server information**

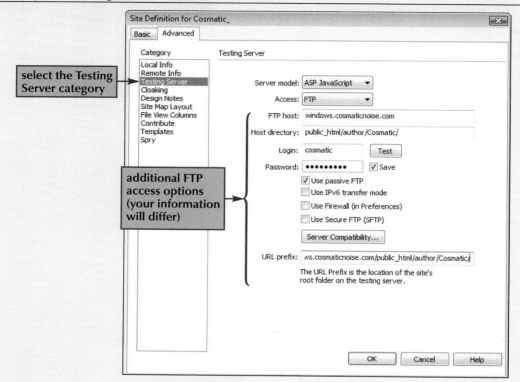

Trouble? If you do not know the URL for your remote site, ask your instructor, technical support person, or ISP for this information.

▶ **10.** Click the **OK** button. The Testing Server information is set, and a check mark appears beside Step 3 in the Server Behaviors panel.

Trouble? If a dialog box opens saying that the site URL prefix for the testing server does not match the site URL prefix specified in the HTTP address for the site, your server includes a public_html directory that stores all the content that viewers can access to view with a Web browser. However, when visitors view the Web site, the URL they enter does not include the public_html directory. There-fore, these paths are different. Click the OK button here and whenever this dialog box appears.

Adding Server Behaviors

Dreamweaver provides a list of prewritten server behaviors in the Server Behaviors panel once the page is connected to the database. You include these server behaviors in the page to extend the functionality of the page and to enable you to retrieve and display the data from the database.

You will include the following two server behaviors in the contact.asp page.

- **Recordset.** The Recordset behavior enables you to specify which data you want to retrieve from the database and display in the Web page. A **recordset** is a temporary collection of data retrieved from a database and stored on the application server that generates the Web page when that page is loaded in a browser window. You specify the database and the records (or data) to include in the recordset when you set the parameters for the behavior. A recordset can include all the data in the database or a subset of the data. You must add the server-side behaviors that will create the recordset in which to store and retrieve data before you can use a database as a content source for a dynamic Web page. The server discards the recordset when it is no longer needed. When you use ASP and an Access database, you must input a custom connection string that Dreamweaver inserts into the page's server behaviors to set up the recordset. A **connection string** is all the information that a Web application server needs to connect to a database. The connection string begins and ends with quotation marks. The connection string has two parts:
  - **Provider.** The name of the interface that provides ASP pages with access to the specific type of database you are using.
  - **Data Source.** The complete path to the database on the server.
- **Insert Record.** The Insert Record behavior enables you to specify what will happen to the information collected from the Web page (in this case, when the form is submitted). You can specify in which database the data will be placed, where the data will be stored in the database, what columns will be included, and so on. It also enables you to select the page that appears in the browser window once the form is submitted.

You'll create a recordset for the contact.asp page.

To create the recordset:

1. At the top of the Server Behaviors panel, click the **Add Behavior** button +, and then click **Recordset (Query)**. The Recordset dialog box opens. See Figure 10-46.

Recordset dialog box | **Figure 10-46**

2. Click the **Advanced** button, if necessary, to switch the Recordset dialog box to Advanced mode, and then click the **Define** button next to the Connection box. The Connections for Site 'Cosmatic' dialog box opens.

▶ **3.** Click the **New** button, and then click **Custom Connection String**. The Custom Connection String dialog box opens. See Figure 10-47.

Figure 10-47 **Custom Connection String dialog box**

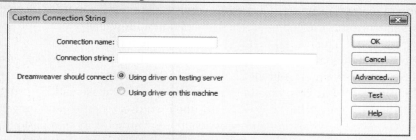

▶ **4.** Type **cosmaticdb** in the Connection name box. This is an internal name that will be visible only when you are working in Dreamweaver.

▶ **5.** In the Connection string box, type **"Provider=Microsoft.Jet.OLEDB.4.0;data source=** followed by the exact file path to your database, and then type **"** (closing quotation marks).

▶ **6.** Click the **Using driver on testing server** option button, if necessary, and then click the **Test** button. A dialog box opens, stating that the connection was made successfully.

Trouble? If error messages appear when you click the Test button, you probably mistyped the connection string. Click the OK button to close the message dialog box, delete the text in the Connection string box, retype the information, and then repeat Step 6. If the test is still unsuccessful, verify the file path for your database with your instructor or technical support person and verify the information in the Testing Server category in the Site Definition dialog box. If you still are having trouble, use an outside FTP program to upload the _mmServerScripts folder to the root directory on your remote server and on your testing server if you are using a separate testing server. In addition, verify that the IUSER has been given write permission to the database.

▶ **7.** Click the **OK** button to close the message dialog box, and then click the **OK** button to close the Custom Connection String dialog box. The database name appears in the Connections for Site 'Cosmatic' dialog box.

▶ **8.** Click the **Done** button in the Connections for Site 'Cosmatic' dialog box. The dialog box closes.

▶ **9.** In the Recordset dialog box, type **CosmaticRecordset** in the Name box.

▶ **10.** If necessary, click the **Connection** button, and then click **cosmaticdb**.

▶ **11.** In the Database items box, click the **Plus (+)** button next to Tables to expand the list, click **contact** to select the database table, click the **SELECT** button to add the information to the SQL box, and then click the **OK** button. The Recordset behavior is added to the page and appears in the Server Behaviors panel. See Figure 10-48.

Recordset behavior added to the contact.asp page | **Figure 10-48**

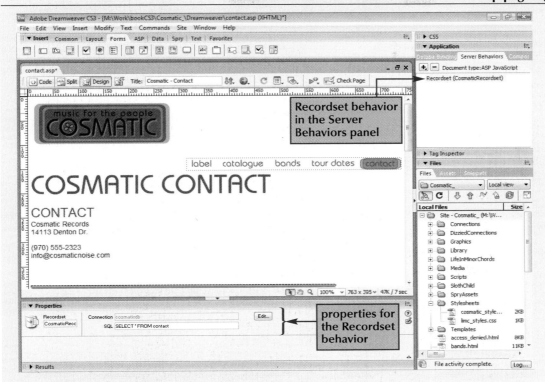

Next, you'll add the Insert Record behavior to the page.

To add the Insert Record behavior:

▶ **1.** At the top of the Server Behaviors panel, click the **Add Behavior** button ➕ , and then click **Insert Record**. The Insert Record dialog box opens.

▶ **2.** Click the **Connection** button, click **cosmaticdb** to select the connection to the database, click the **Insert into table** button, and then click **contact** to select the contact table in the database.

▶ **3.** Click the **Browse** button next to the After inserting, go to box. The Select File dialog box opens.

▶ **4.** Click **thankyou.html** in the site's local root folder, and then click the **OK** button. The Select File dialog box closes, and the page filename appears in the After inserting, go to box.

▶ **5.** Click the **Get values from** button, and then click **ContactForm**, if necessary. The contact form's elements appear in the Form elements box, and the column headings in the contact table are displayed in the Column list. See Figure 10-49.

| Figure 10-49 | Insert Record dialog box |

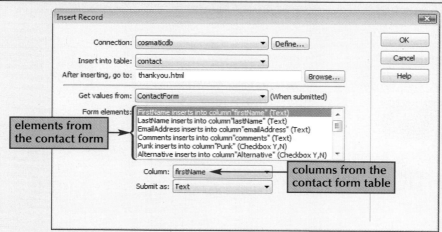

6. In the Insert Record dialog box, click the **OK** button. The Insert Record behavior is added to the page and appears in the Server Behaviors panel. The red exclamation mark that appears next to Insert Record means that Dreamweaver is having trouble distinguishing the two Newsletter radio buttons. See Figure 10-50.

| Figure 10-50 | Insert Record behavior added to the contact.asp page |

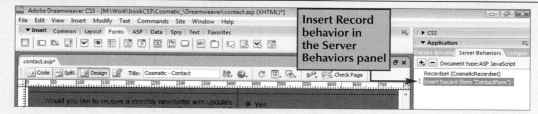

7. In the Document window, select the **Yes** radio button, switch to Code view, find Newsletter_0 in the highlighted text, and then delete **_0** from the code.

8. Find Newsletter_1 four lines down, delete **_1** from the code, and then return to Design view. The red exclamation mark disappears from the Server Behaviors panel.

Before continuing, you'll test the Insert Record behavior you added to the contact.asp page. You need to upload the page to the remote server, preview the page in a browser, and then complete and submit the form. The Thank You page should then display.

To test the Insert Record behavior:

1. Save the page, and then upload the page to your remote server (update the page on the testing server, if necessary).

2. Preview the contact.asp page in a browser.

▶ **3.** Enter appropriate information in the form, and then click the **Submit** button to submit the form. The Thank You page appears in a new browser window.

   Trouble? When you save an .html file as an .asp page, Dreamweaver does not insert code that may be necessary to identify the ASP scripting language at the top of the page. If you have an ASP JavaScript site, an .asp file requires the following code at the top of the page: <%@LANGUAGE="JAVASCRIPT"%>. Without this code, the page might not function on the server, and Dreamweaver might not recognize or add server behaviors correctly. Close the browser, switch the contact.asp page to Code view, type the missing code at the top of the page, save and close the page, reopen the contact.asp page in Dreamweaver, and then repeat Steps 1 through 3.

▶ **4.** Close the browser.

The page is connected to the database, and the behaviors have been added to the page. Next, you will create pages that enable you to view the data collected in the database.

Creating Backend Pages for Viewing Data in a Database

Pages that are intended for internal use are usually called **backend pages**. For the Cosmatic site, the Database and Database Details pages are backend pages. You will set the database.asp and database_details.asp pages to display the data that you collect in the database. The Master Detail Page Set button on the Data tab of the Insert bar enables you to create a set of pages that present information in two levels of detail. The master page (in this case, the database.asp page) lists all the records in the recordset that you create for the page. The detail page (in this case, the database_details.asp page) displays the detail of the selected record. You determine which fields of information are displayed in the master page and which fields of information are displayed in the detail page when you set the parameters for the pages. In addition to creating all the code needed to display the dynamic content in the pages, Dreamweaver also adds server behaviors to create a page navigation bar that enables you to move between the dynamic records if there are more records in the database than are displayed in the page. The navigation bar includes First Page, Last Page, Previous Page, and Next Page buttons. The pages also include Display Record Count server behaviors to indicate which records are visible in the page and the total number of records in the database (Records x to y of z).

To create the master page:

▶ **1.** In the Server Behaviors panel, click **Recordset**, right-click the selected behavior, and then click **Copy** on the context menu.

▶ **2.** Open the **database_details.asp** page in the Document window, right-click in the Server Behaviors panel, and then click **Paste** on the context menu. The Recordset behavior is pasted in the Database Details page.

▶ **3.** Place the insertion point in the heading line after the heading text, press the **Right Arrow** key to move the insertion point past the heading text, and then press the **Enter** key to move the insertion point to the next line.

   Trouble? If Dreamweaver locks up, then you've encountered a bug in Dreamweaver that causes the program to lock up if you place the insertion point in the line below the heading and then press the Enter key when using server behaviors. End the program, restart the computer, and then repeat Steps 1 through 3.

▶ **4.** Open the **database.asp** page in the Document window, right-click in the Server Behaviors panel, click **Paste** on the context menu to paste the Recordset behavior into the page, place the insertion point in the heading line, press the **Right Arrow** key to move the insertion point past the heading text, and then press the **Enter** key to move the insertion point to the next line.

▶ **5.** Click the **Data** tab on the Insert bar, and then click the **Master Detail Page Set** button 🖼 . The Insert Master-Detail Page Set dialog box opens. See Figure 10-51.

Figure 10-51   **Insert Master-Detail Page Set dialog box**

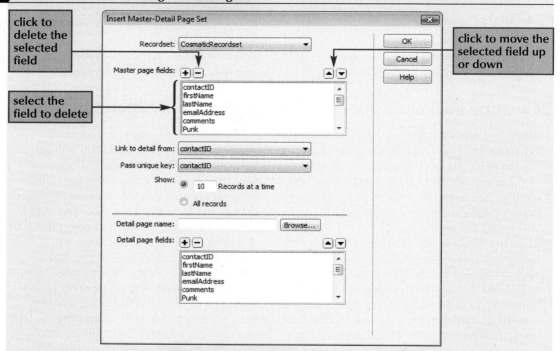

You will remove the fields from the Master page fields box that you do not want to display in the master page. You'll also change the field order so that the last name will appear in the first column.

▶ **6.** Click **contactID** in the Master page fields box, and then click the Master page fields **Remove Item** button ⊟ . The selected field name is removed from the list.

▶ **7.** Repeat Step 6 to delete the following field names: **comments**, **Punk**, **Alternative**, **Trance**, **Jazz**, **sloth_child**, **dizzied_connections**, **Life_In_Minor_Chords**, and **surface_suction**. Only the names of fields that will be visible in the Database page appear in the Master page fields box.

▶ **8.** Click **lastName** in the Master page fields box, and then click the Master page fields **Move Item Up** button ▲ until the lastName field is at the top of the list. The fields will display in the page in the same order they appear in the list.

▶ **9.** Click the **Link to detail from** button, and then click **lastName**. The data from the lastName field in the Database page is now linked to the record details, which will display in the Database Details page.

You'll set the record details to display in the database_details.asp page. As with the master page, you'll delete unneeded fields and change the field order for the detail page.

To create the detail page:

▶ **1.** Click the **Browse** button next to the Detail page name box, click the **database_details.asp** page in the Select Detail Page dialog box, and then click the **OK** button. The page name appears in the Detail page name box.

▶ **2.** Click **contactID** in the Detail page fields box, and then click the **Remove Item** button 🔲. The field name is removed from the list and the field will not be displayed in the Database Details page.

▶ **3.** Click the **Newsletter** field in the Detail page fields box, and then click the **Move Item Up** button 🔺 until the field name is directly below the emailAddress field. See Figure 10-52.

Completed Insert Master-Detail Page Set dialog box Figure 10-52

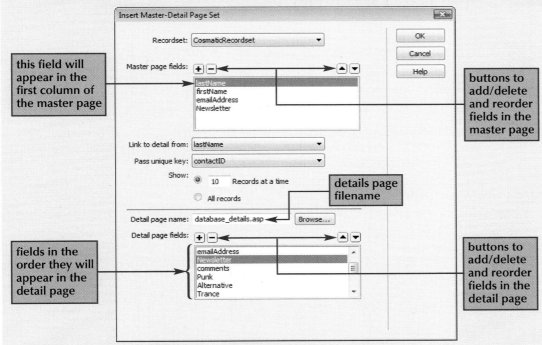

▶ **4.** Click the **OK** button. The dialog box closes, and the master/detail pages are complete.

Dreamweaver adds elements to the pages that will enable you to view the data collected in the database as well as the details of selected records. Before continuing, you'll upload the pages to the remote server and preview the pages in the browser.

To view the Database Details page:

▶ **1.** Save the Database page, and then upload the page to your remote server. Dreamweaver adds elements to the page that will enable you to view the data collected in the database. See Figure 10-53.

Figure 10-53 | **Database page**

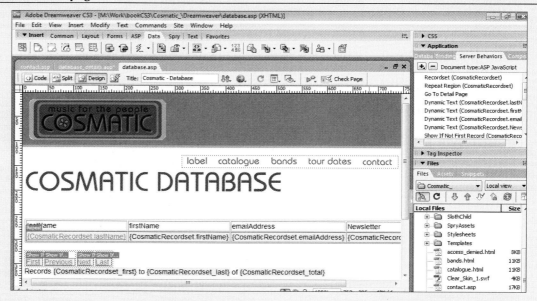

▶ **2.** Click the **database_details.asp** tab to view the Database Details page. Dreamweaver has also added elements to this page that will enable you to view the details of records selected in the Database page. See Figure 10-54.

Figure 10-54 | **Database Details page**

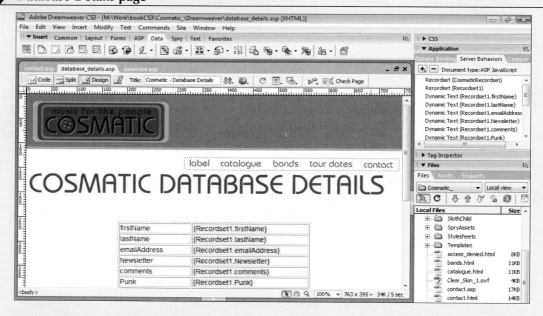

Trouble? If Dreamweaver inserted the table below the footer in the page, select the table and drag it above the footer in the page.

▶ **3.** Save the Database Details page, and then upload the page to your remote server.

▶ **4.** Click the **database.asp** tab, and then preview the page in a browser, clicking the **No** button when Dreamweaver prompts you to upload the changes to the testing server because you have already done that (remember, your testing server and remote server are the same). The data you collected from the form in the Contact page appears in the browser window. See Figure 10-55.

Database page previewed in a browser ◀ **Figure 10-55**

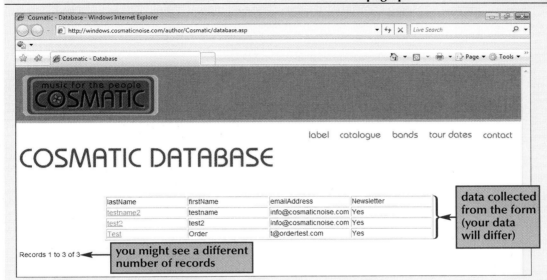

Trouble? When you save an .html file as an .asp page, Dreamweaver does not insert code that may be necessary to identify the ASP scripting language at the top of the page. If you have an ASP JavaScript site, an .asp file requires the following code at the top of the page: <%@LANGUAGE="JAVASCRIPT"%>. Without this code, the page may not function on the server, and Dreamweaver might not recognize or add server behaviors correctly. Close the browser, switch to Code view, type the missing code at the top of the file, save and close the page, reopen it in Dreamweaver, and then repeat Steps 1 and 4.

Trouble? If you see more than the one record you entered into the contact form, then you are sharing the database with classmates and the database will include all the entries that have been submitted. In a professional environment, this would probably not be the case.

▶ **5.** Click a link to view the details of a record. The details are displayed in the Database Details page.

▶ **6.** Click the **Back** button 🔙 on the browser toolbar to return to the Database page, and then click another record, if available.

▶ **7.** Close the browser, and then close all the pages.

As you use more advanced techniques, you will begin to work with code more frequently. When you want the same functionality in two different places, a good technique is to copy the code from one location and paste it in the other location. Not only does this technique save you time, it also eliminates the chance of mistyping the code. It is also acceptable technique to copy and paste code from other code sources that are "available to the public" such as example code sites and books that teach coding techniques. When copying and pasting code from one source to another, it is a good idea to paste the copied code into a style-free text editor such as TextPad or Notepad and remove any formatting from the text before pasting it into the code of your Web pages. This prevents hard-to-trace code errors that arise from pasting formatted text in code.

Creating a Login Page to Protect Backend Pages

Data collected from a Web site and stored in a database is often displayed in Web pages. This convenience enables you to view the data from any computer that is connected to the Internet. However, most businesses do not want the general public to have access to this type of proprietary information. One way to restrict the access to Web pages is to require users to log in before they can view the pages. This protects the data from unauthorized access. To add this functionality to pages you must:

- **Create a table in the database that holds user names and passwords.** The team that created the database included an administrative table with columns to collect user names and passwords. They also added one user name (cosmatic) and one password (feelinit) in the table. You will use the user name and password included in the database to create and test the Login page. You will create additional pages that will enable users to create unique user names and passwords in the Review Assignments.
- **Create a page that enables users to create accounts by entering a unique user name and password.** Because only one member of the Cosmatic staff is in charge of monitoring and reporting the information collected in the database, you won't create this page now. The team member will use the supplied user name and password to log in to protected pages. Because you eventually want to enable other users to log in to the site, you will create additional pages that will enable users to create unique user names and passwords in the Review Assignments.
- **Create a page that enables users to log in to the site.** You have already created the Login page. Now you will create a form in the Login page that enables users to input their user name and password information. You will add the Log In User server behavior to the page, which will check the database when a user submits the form to ensure that the user name and password are valid. If login is successful, the Database page will appear in the user's browser window. If login is unsuccessful, the Access Denied page will be displayed in the browser window.
- **Restrict access to the pages.** You add the Restrict Access To Page server behavior to the pages that you want to protect, in this case, the Database and Database Details pages. Once this behavior is added to the pages, users who are not logged in will be sent to the Access Denied page.

You'll create the form in the Login page, and then add the Log In User server behavior to the page.

To add content to the Login page:

▶ 1. Open the **login.asp** page in the Document window, place the insertion point in the heading line, press the **Right Arrow** key until the insertion point is positioned at the right of the heading text, and then press the **Enter** key. The insertion point moves to the next line.

▶ 2. Click the **Forms** tab on the Insert bar, and then click the **Form** button ▣ . The code for a form is inserted into the page.

▶ 3. In the Property inspector, type **loginform** in the Form name box. For this form, it is not necessary to enter information for the other attributes in the Property inspector because you will add behaviors to control the form.

▶ 4. Click inside of the form area (the dotted red lines), click the **Common** tab on the Insert bar, and then click the **Table** button ▦ . The Table dialog box opens.

▶ 5. Type **3** in the Rows box, type **2** in the Columns box, type **80** percent in the Table width boxes, type **2** in the Cell padding box, type **0** in the Border thickness box, type **2** in the Cell spacing box, click **None** in the Header box, and then click the **OK** button. The table is inserted into the form.

▶ 6. Select the left column of the table, click the **Horz** button in the Property inspector and click **Right**, click the **Vert** button and click **Top**, select the right column of the table, click the **Horz** button in the Property inspector and click **Left**, and then click the **Vert** button and click **Top**.

▶ 7. Click in the first cell of the table, type **User name:** (including the colon), and then press the **Tab** key to move the insertion point to the upper-right cell.

▶ 8. Click the **Forms** tab on the Insert Bar, and then click the **Text Field** button ▣ to insert a text field.

▶ 9. In the Property inspector, type **username** in the TextField box, type **40** in the Char width box, and then type **20** in the Max chars box.

▶ 10. Click in the middle-left cell of the table, type **Password:** (including the colon), and then press the **Tab** key to move the insertion point to the next cell.

▶ 11. On the Forms tab of the Insert bar, click the **Text Field** button ▣ , and then, in the Property inspector, type **password** in the TextField box, type **40** in the Char width box, and type **20** in the Max chars box.

▶ 12. Click in the bottom-right cell of the table, click the **Button** button ▣ on the **Forms** tab of the Insert bar, type **Login** in the Button name and Value boxes, and then press the **Enter** key. See Figure 10-56.

Figure 10-56 ▶ **Form in the Login page**

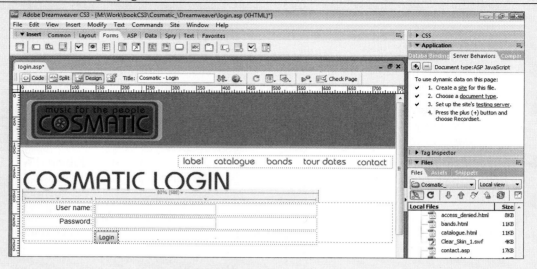

Next, you'll add the Log In User server behavior to the page, which will verify the submitted user name and password.

To add server behaviors to the Login page:

▶ **1.** Select the **Login** button in the form, click the **Data** tab on the Insert bar, click the **User Authentication button arrow** 📇▾, and then click **Log In User**. The Log In User dialog box opens.

▶ **2.** Click the **Validate using connection** button, click **cosmaticdb**, click the **Table** button, click **admin**, click the **Username column** button, click **username**, click the **Password column** button, and then click **password**.

▶ **3.** Click the **Browse** button next to the If login succeeds, go to box, click the **database.asp** page in the Select File dialog box, and then click the **OK** button. This sets the Database page to display in the browser window if the submitted user name and password are listed in the database.

▶ **4.** Click the **Browse** button next to the If login fails, go to box, click the **access_denied.html** page in the Select File dialog box, and then click the **OK** button. This sets the Access Denied page to display in the browser window if the submitted user name and password are not listed in the database. See Figure 10-57.

Log In User dialog box ◄ **Figure 10-57**

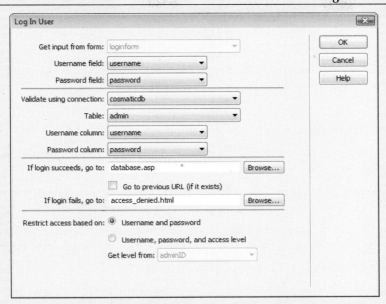

▶ **5.** Click the **OK** button. The Log In User server behavior is added to the page and appears in the Server Behaviors panel.

▶ **6.** Save the page, and then upload the page to your remote server.

You'll add text and a meta refresh tag to the Access Denied page, which tells the browser to automatically refresh the page (by reloading the current page or going to a different page) after a certain amount of time. You'll also add text to indicate that access was denied to that user.

To add content and a meta refresh tag to the Access Denied page:

▶ **1.** Open the **access_denied.html** page in the Document window.

▶ **2.** Click the **Common** tab on the Insert bar, click the **Head button arrow** 📋 ▾ , and then click **Refresh**. The Refresh dialog box opens.

▶ **3.** Type **4** in the Delay box, and then type **login.asp** in the Go to URL box. See Figure 10-58.

Refresh dialog box ◄ **Figure 10-58**

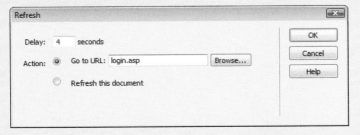

▶ **4.** Click the **OK** button, place the insertion point after the heading, press the **Enter** key, and then type **Your access was denied. Please enter your login ID and password again.** (including the period).

▶ **5.** Save the page, and then upload the page to your remote server.

Before you continue, you'll test the Login page and the behaviors you added to the Database and Access Denied pages.

To test the Login page:

▶ **1.** Preview the login.asp page in a browser. The Update Copy on Testing Server dialog box opens.

▶ **2.** Click the **Yes** button to ensure that the most recent copy of the page is on both the testing and remote servers. The Dependent Files dialog box opens.

▶ **3.** Click the **Yes** button to ensure that all the dependent files are current on both the testing and remote servers. The Login page appears in the browser window.

You'll enter an invalid user name and password.

▶ **4.** Type **test** in the User name box, type **random** in the Password box, and then click the **Login** button. The login information is invalid, so the access_denied.html page appears in the browser window. After four seconds, the Login page is redisplayed.

Now, you'll enter a valid user name and password.

▶ **5.** Type **cosmatic** in the User name box, type **feelinit** in the Password box, and then click the **Login** button. The Database page is displayed in the browser window.

▶ **6.** Close the browser, and then close the pages.

Finally, you will protect the Database and Database Details pages from unauthorized access by adding the Restrict Access server behavior to the page.

To restrict access to pages:

▶ **1.** Open the **database.asp** page in the Document window.

▶ **2.** Click the **Data** tab on the Insert bar, click the **User Authentication button arrow** , and then click **Restrict Access To Page**. The Restrict Access To Page dialog box opens.

▶ **3.** Type **access_denied.html** in the If access denied, go to box. See Figure 10-59.

Restrict Access To Page dialog box | **Figure 10-59**

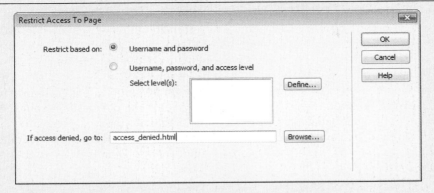

4. Click the **OK** button, save the page, and then upload the page to your remote server.

5. Open the **database_details.asp** page in the Document window, and then repeat Steps 2 through 4 to restrict access to that page.

You'll test the behavior you added to the pages.

6. Preview the database.asp page in a browser. Because you are not logged in, the Database page does not open in the browser window. Instead, the Access Denied page appears for four seconds, and then the Login page appears.

Trouble? If the Database page does appear, you did not close the browser window after you logged in and you are still logged in. Close any open browser windows and repeat Step 6.

7. Close the browser, and then close the pages.

In this session, you created database-driven Web pages for the Cosmatic site using Access and ASP for a Windows server. The database functionality will enable Sara and Brian to collect data about their customers' preferences. Analyzing this data will help them shape future marketing plans for Cosmatic.

Session 10.3 Quick Check | Review

1. In addition to selecting a database, you must also select a(n) _____ that you will use to create server behaviors.
2. What language do you use to create server behaviors when you use an Access database?
3. What is a server behavior?
4. Why do you need the Recordset behavior?
5. Why would you create a Login page?
6. What is the purpose of the meta refresh tag?

Review | **Tutorial Summary**

In this tutorial, you learned about adding Spry elements to Web pages. You inserted a Spry widget, added content to the widget, and then customized the look of the widget to better match the Web site. You added a Spry effect to add motion to a Web page. You learned about creating database-driven Web sites working with a Linux server and a Windows server. Then, you created database-driven Web pages for the Cosmatic site using MySQL and PHP for a Linux server or using Access and ASP for a Windows server. To do this, you created the Web pages you needed, you placed or created the database on your remote server, you added server behaviors to connect the database to the form, you added server behaviors to Web pages to view the data collected in the database, you added content to the Login page, and then you set the Database and Database Details pages to display only when a user has logged in to the site with a valid user name and password.

Key Terms

AJAX (Asynchronous
  JavaScript and XML)
backend page
connection string
database

database-driven Web site
dynamically generated
recordset
server behavior
Spry effect

Spry element
Spry framework for AJAX
SQL (Structured Query
  Language)
widget

Practice	**Review Assignments**

Practice the skills you learned in the tutorial.

There are no Data Files needed for the Review Assignments.

Sara and Brian want you to create a Login Admin page that will enable users who already have user names and passwords to create new user accounts and create a page to display record details. You'll also create a master/detail page set, using the Login Admin page as the master page so that you can view the user account information as soon as you create a new account. Finally, you will restrict access to the new pages so that only users that already have user accounts can enable other users to view the information. Sara also wants you to add the Spry Shake effect to all of the CD covers in the Catalogue page, and then remove the effect from the page if motion makes the page look too busy.

If you are using MySQL and PHP on a Linux server, complete the following steps:

1. Open the **Cosmatic** site that you modified in the tutorial, and then duplicate the login.php page in the Files panel.
2. In the Files panel, rename the Copy of login.php page to **login_admin.php**.
3. Open the login_admin.php page in the Document window, and then change the page title to **Cosmatic - Login Administration**.
4. Double-click the page heading to open the Insert Flash Text dialog box, change the heading text to **COSMATIC LOGIN ADMIN**, and then save the file as **Media/HeadingLoginAdmin.swf**.
5. Repeat Steps 1 through 4 to create an **admin_details.php** page, using **Cosmatic - Login Administration Details** as the page title, **COSMATIC LOGIN ADMIN DETAILS** as the page heading, and **Media/HeadingLoginAdminDetails.swf** as the page heading filename.
6. Select the form in the login_admin.php page, and then enter **loginadminform** as the form name.
7. Click the Login button, and then enter **Add** as both the button name and the value.
8. In the Server Behaviors panel, click the Log In User server behavior, and then remove the behavior.
9. In the Server Behaviors panel, add the Recordset behavior to open the Recordset dialog box, type **loginadmin** in the Name box, click CosmaticDBconnection in the Connection list, click admin in the Table list if necessary, click the Select button, and then click the OK button.
10. In the Server Behaviors panel, add the Insert Record behavior to open the Insert Record dialog box, click CosmaticDBconnection in the Connection list, click admin in the Insert table list, if necessary, type **login_admin.php** in the After inserting, go to box (because you will display the results in this page), and then click the OK button.
11. Display the admin_details.php page in the Document window, remove the Log In User server behavior from the Server Behaviors panel, and then select and delete the form in the page. (*Hint:* The details table will be inserted in the blank line below the heading text where the insertion point is located in the page.)
12. Display the login_admin.php page in the Document window, click in the blank line below the form, and then click the Master Detail Page Set button on the Data tab of the Insert bar.

13. Click adminID in the Master page fields box, remove the item, name the detail page as **admin_details.php**, and then click the OK button. The admin_details.php page displays, and the details table and server behaviors have been added to the page. (*Hint:* If the admin_details.php page does not display, click the admin_details.php tab to view the page in the Document window. If the table displays at the bottom of the page, select the table and drag it above the footer.)

14. Save the page, and then upload the page and its dependent files to your remote server.

15. Display the login_admin.php page in the Document window and see an overview of the admin table content in the database below the loginadmin form.

16. Save the page, upload the page and its dependent files to your remote server, and then preview the page in a browser.

17. Type a user name and a password in the appropriate boxes, click the Add button (your new user name and password appear in the table below the form), click your new user name to display the admin_details.php page, and then close the browser. (*Hint:* If the new username and password are not added to the table, Dreamweaver added two sets of single quotation marks in the code. Close the browser, switch the login_admin.php page to Code view, open the Find and Replace dialog box, and then search for **insertSQL** in the Source Code of the Current Document, which should be in approximately line 40 in the code. On the same line to the right, locate "*admin*" and then remove the outside single quotation mark from each side of the word *admin*, save the page, upload the page to your remote server, preview the page in a browser, and then add a new username and password.)

18. Click Restrict Access To Page in the User Authentication list on the Data tab of the Insert bar to open the Restrict Access To Page dialog box, type **access_denied.html** in the If access denied, go to box, click the OK button, save the page, and then upload the page to your remote server. Users who do not already have user accounts cannot access this page.

19. Display the admin_details.php page in the Document window, and then repeat Step 18 to restrict access to that page.

20. Display the login_admin.php page in the Document window, place the insertion point to the right of the heading text, press the Enter key to move the insertion point to the next line, type **To the database page**, and then create a hyperlink from the text you just typed to the database.php page. Save the page, upload the page to your remote server, and then close the page.

21. Open the database.php page in the Document window, place the insertion point to the right of the heading text, press the Enter key to move the insertion point to the next line, type **To the login admin page**, and then create a hyperlink from the text you just typed to the login_admin.php page. Save the page, upload the page to your remote server, and then close the page.

22. In the admin_details.php page, place the insertion point to the right of the heading text, press the Enter key to move the insertion point to the next line, type **To the login admin page**, and then create a hyperlink from the text you just typed to the login_admin.php page. Save the page, upload the page to your remote server, and then close the page.

23. Preview the login.php page in a browser, enter your user name and password in the appropriate boxes, click the Login button, click the To the login admin page link in the Database page, create a new user account by adding a new user name and password, and then close the browser and any open pages.

24. Open the **catalogue.html** page in the Document window, select the surface suction CD cover, and then add the Shake effect, making sure the target element is the current selection. (*Hint:* In the Behaviors panel, click the Add Behavior button, point to Effects, and then click Shake.)

25. In the Behaviors panel, change the event to onLoad.

26. Repeat Steps 24 and 25 to add the Shake effect to the sloth child and the Life in Minor Chords CD covers.

27. Save the page, and then preview the page in a browser, uploading the page and its dependent file when prompted. The excessive motion will probably distract users and become annoying for users who visit the page frequently. You will remove the effect from the CD covers.

28. Select the dizzied connections CD cover, select Shake in the behaviors list of the Behaviors panel, and then press the Delete key to remove the effect. Repeat to remove the Shake effect from the surface suction, sloth child, and Life in Minor Chords CD covers.

29. Save the page, upload the page and its dependent files to the remove server, and then preview the page in a browser.

30. Submit the finished files to your instructor, either in printed or electronic form, as requested.

If you are using Access and ASP on a Windows server, complete the following steps:

1. Open the **Cosmatic** site that you modified in the tutorial, and then duplicate the login.asp page in the Files panel.

2. In the Files panel, rename the Copy of login.asp page to **login_admin.asp**.

3. Open the login_admin.asp page in the Document window, and then change the page title to **Cosmatic - Login Administration**.

4. Double-click the page heading to open the Insert Flash Text dialog box, change the heading text to **COSMATIC LOGIN ADMIN**, and then save the file as **Media/HeadingLoginAdmin.swf**.

5. Repeat Steps 1 through 4 to create an **admin_details.asp** page, using **Cosmatic - Login Administration Details** as the page title, **COSMATIC LOGIN ADMIN DETAILS** as the page heading, and **Media/HeadingLoginAdminDetails.swf** as the page heading filename.

6. Select the form in the login_admin.asp page, and then enter **loginadminform** as the form name.

7. Click the Login button, and then enter **Add** as both the button name and the value.

8. In the Server Behaviors panel, click the Log In User server behavior, and then remove the behavior.

9. In the Server Behaviors panel, add the Recordset behavior to open the Recordset dialog box, type **loginadmin** in the Name box, click cosmaticdb in the Connection list, click admin in the Table list, click SELECT, if necessary, and then click the OK button.

10. In the Server Behaviors panel, add the Insert Record behavior to open the Insert Record dialog box, click cosmaticdb in the Connection list, click admin in the Insert into table list, if necessary, type **login_admin.asp** in the After inserting, go to box (because you will display the results in this page), and then click the OK button.

11. Display the admin_details.asp page in the Document window, remove the Log In User server behavior from the Server Behaviors panel, and then select and delete the form in the page. (*Hint:* The details table will be inserted in the blank line below the heading text where the insertion point is located in the page.)

12. Display the login_admin.asp page in the Document window, click in the blank line below the form, and then click the Master Detail Page Set button on the Data tab of the Insert bar.

13. Click adminID in the Master page fields box, remove the item, name the detail page as **admin_details.asp**, and then click the OK button. The admin_details.asp page displays, and the details table and server behaviors have been added to the page. (*Hint:* If the admin_details.asp page does not display, click the admin_details.asp tab to view the page in the Document window. If the table displays at the bottom of the page, select the table and drag it above the footer.)

    Brian realized that one of the column names used in the database (password) is a reserved word in the most recent version of Access. This means that the word *password* is used internally by the system and is not available for external use. You must revise the code to make the old database work with the current system. In business, technology consistently changes and it is sometimes necessary to find a workaround solution. In this instance, you will search for the word *password* in the code of the page and then add code to make the database use of the word *password* distinct from the Access internal use.

14. Display the login_admin.asp page in the Document window, switch to Code view, open the Find and Replace dialog box.

15. Type **password** in the Find box, click Current Document in the Find in list, select Source Code in the Search list, and then click the Find All button. The Results panel opens and displays the search results. The search term *password* is underlined in red.

16. Double-click the underlined password in the first line of the list; the line should start with:

    ```
    MM_editCmd.CommandText = "INSERT INTO [admin] (username,
    ```

17. In the Document window, type an opening bracket at the beginning of the word *password* and type a closing bracket at the end of the word. The line should look as follows:

    ```
    MM_editCmd.CommandText = "INSERT INTO [admin] (username,
    [password]) VALUES (?, ?)";
    ```

18. Close the Results panel.

19. Save the page, and then upload the page to your remote server.

20. In the login_admin.asp page in the Document window, an overview of the admin table content appears in the database below the loginadmin form.

21. Save the page, upload the page to your remote server, and then preview the page in a browser.

22. Type a user name and a password in the appropriate boxes, click the Add button (your new user name and password appear in the table below the form), click your new user name to display the admin_details.asp page, and then close the browser.

23. Click the Restrict Access To Page button in the User Authentication list on the Data tab on the Insert bar to open the Restrict Access To Page dialog box, type **access_denied.html** in the If access denied, go to box, click the OK button, save the page, and then upload the page to your remote server. Users who do not already have user accounts cannot access this page.

24. Display the admin_details.asp page in the Doucment window, and then repeat Step 23 to restrict access to that page.

25. Display the login_admin.asp page in the Document window, place the insertion point to the right of the heading text, press the Enter key to move the insertion point to the next line, type **To the database page**, and then create a hyperlink from the text you just typed to the database.asp page. Save the page, upload the page to your remote server, and then close the page.

26. Open the database.asp page in the Document window, place the insertion point to the right of the heading text, press the Enter key to move the insertion point to the next line, type **To the login admin page**, and then create a hyperlink from the text you just typed to the login_admin.asp page. Save the page, upload the page to your remote server, and then close the page.

27. In the admin_details.asp page, place the insertion point to the right of the heading text, press the Enter key to move the insertion point to the next line, type **To the login admin page**, and then create a hyperlink from the text you just typed to the login_admin.asp page. Save the page, upload the page to your remote server, and then close the page.

28. Preview the login.asp page in a browser, enter your user name and password in the appropriate boxes, click the Login button, click the To login admin page link in the Database page, create a new user account by adding a new user name and password, and then close the browser and any open pages.

29. Open the **catalogue.html** page in the Document window, select the surface suction CD cover, and then add the Shake effect, making sure the target element is the current selection. (*Hint:* In the Behaviors panel, click the Add Behavior button, point to Effects, and then click Shake.)

30. In the Behaviors panel, change the event to onLoad.

31. Repeat Steps 29 and 30 to add the Shake effect to the sloth child and the Life in Minor Chords CD covers.

32. Save the page, and then preview the page in a browser. The excessive motion will probably distract users and become annoying for users who visit the page frequently. You will remove the effect from the CD covers.

33. Select the dizzied connections CD cover, select Shake in the behaviors list of the Behaviors panel, and then press the Delete key to remove the effect. Repeat to remove the Shake effect from the surface suction, sloth shild, and Life in Minor Chords CD covers.

34. Save the page, upload the page to the remove server, and then preview the page in a browser.

35. Submit the finished files to your instructor, either in printed or electronic form, as requested.

Challenge | Case Problem 1

Add database-driven pages to display Dr. Olivia Thompson's journal entries in a Web site on the small rural communities in northern Vietnam.

Data File needed for this Case Problem: wasdb.mdb or wasdb.sql

World Anthropology Society   Dr. Olivia Thompson is reviewing her research on the rituals and practices of the small rural communities in northern Vietnam and has decided that site visitors would be interested in seeing some of her notes. She wants to be able to make ongoing journal entries that will automatically display in the Rituals and Practices page. You'll create database-driven pages to create a tool that will enable her to do this. As part of the tool you will create a form that will enable her to enter journal entries. This form will use the Spry Validation Textarea widget to ensure that no empty entries are posted to the site accidentally.

If you are using MySQL and PHP on a Linux server, complete the following steps:

1. Open the **DrThompson** site that you modified in **Tutorial 9, Case Problem 1**.
2. In the Files panel, duplicate the contact.html page, rename the copied page as **journal.php**, and then update the links in the file.
3. Open the **journal.php** page in the Document window, change the heading text to **Journal Entry**, replace the word *Contact* in the page title with **Journal Entry**, and then delete the content between the heading text and the footer in the page.
4. Insert a form in the page, enter **journalentry** as the form name, and then insert a table with 2 rows, 2 columns, 90% table width, 0 border thickness, 3 cell padding, 0 cell spacing, and no header in the form.
5. In the upper-left cell, type **journal entry**, and then align the text to the Right and Top.

⊕ **EXPLORE**

6. With the insertion point in the upper-right cell of the table, click the Spry Validation Textarea button on the Forms tab or the Spry tab of the Insert bar to insert the widget, and then click the Spry Textarea tab to select the widget. In the Property inspector, enter **journalentryvalidate** in the Spry textarea box, and then check the Required check box, if necessary. In the Document window, click the scroll bar of the widget to display the text field properties. In the Property inspector, enter **journalentry** in the TextField box, enter 80 in the Char width box, and then enter 10 in the Num lines box. In the lower-right cell of the table, insert a Submit button, and then save the page.
7. Modify the navigation bar to no longer display the Contact Information element in the Down state initially.
8. Ask your instructor for the information you need to connect to an existing database or create the database on your remote server using the **wasdb.sql** file located in the **Tutorial.10\Case1** folder included with your Data Files. (*Hint:* Obtain the information you need from your instructor or technical support person.)
9. Expand the Server Behaviors panel in the Application panel group, click the document type link in Step 2, select PHP as the document type, and then click the OK button.
10. In the Server Behaviors panel, click the testing server link in Step 3, select PHP MySQL as the server model, select FTP as the access, delete all the file path information from the URL prefix box, type the URL for your remote site, and then click the OK button.

11. In the Server Behaviors panel, add the Recordset behavior, type **WASRecordset** as the name, click the Define button next to the Connection box, click the New button, type **WASDBconnection** as the connection name, type **localhost** or the database server URL as the MySQL server, type your user name and password, click the Select button to display a list of databases, click wasdb in the list, click the OK button, click the OK button, click the Done button, select WASDBconnection as the connection, click journal in the Tables list, click the SELECT button, and then click the OK button. The Recordset behavior is added to the page and appears in the Server Behaviors panel.

12. In the Server Behaviors panel, add the Insert Record behavior, submit values from journalentry, select WASDBconnection as the connection, click journal in the Insert table list, select 'journal' does not get a value in the Columns list, select FORM. journalentry in the Value list, click Text in the Submit as list, if necessary, click the Browse button, click the rituals_and_practices.html page in the site's local root folder, and then click the OK button in each dialog box. The Insert Record behavior is added to the page and appears in the Server Behaviors panel.

13. Save the page, upload the page to your remote server (include dependent files), preview the page in a browser, updating the page and the dependent files on the testing server, if necessary, and then close the browser.

14. Open the rituals_and_practices.html page, click the document type link in the Server Behaviors panel, select PHP in the list, click the OK button, click the Update button to update the links in the pages, click the OK button in the message dialog box, and then update the Rituals & Practices element in the navigation bar in the rituals_and_practices.php page so that rituals_and_practices.php appears in the When clicked, go to URL box.

15. Click the journal.php tab, right-click the Recordset behavior in the Server Behaviors panel, click Copy on the context menu, click the rituals_and_practices.php tab, right-click in the Server Behaviors panel, and then click Paste on the context menu to paste the Recordset behavior into the page.

⊕ EXPLORE   16. Double-click the Recordset behavior in the Server Behaviors panel to open the Recordset dialog box, click the Simple button, click the Selected option button in the Columns section, click journal in the Columns box, and then click the OK button.

⊕ EXPLORE   17. Delete the "Research in process, check back soon." text, click the Dynamic Table button in the Dynamic Data list on the Data tab of the Insert bar, click the All records option button, set the border to 0, set the cell padding to 3, and then click the OK button.

⊕ EXPLORE   18. Save the page, upload the rituals_and_practices.php page to your remote server (include dependent files), preview the journal.php page in a browser (updating the page and dependent files on the testing server, if necessary), click the Submit button to test that the Spry Validation Textarea widget is working (a message appears, stating that "A value is required."), type a test entry in the form, and then click the Submit button to submit the form. The rituals_and_practices.php page with the new entry opens in the browser window. (*Hint:* If you are sharing a database with classmates, you may see additional entries in the database.)

19. Submit the finished files to your instructor, either in printed or electronic form, as requested.

If you are using Access and ASP on a Windows server, complete the following steps:

1. Open the **DrThompson** site that you modified in **Tutorial 9, Case Problem 1**.

2. In the Files panel, duplicate the contact.html page, rename the copied page as **journal.asp**, and then update the links in the file.

3. Open the **journal.asp** page in the Document window, change the heading text to **Journal Entry**, replace the word *Contact* in the page title with **Journal Entry**, and then delete the content between the heading text and the footer in the page.

4. Insert a form in the page, enter **journalentry** as the form name, and then insert a table with 2 rows, 2 columns, 90% table width, 0 border thickness, 3 cell padding, 0 cell spacing, and no header in the form.

5. In the upper-left cell, type **journal entry**, and then align the text to the Right and Top.

⊕ EXPLORE

6. With the insertion point in the upper-right cell of the table, click the Spry Validation Textarea button on the Forms tab or the Spry tab of the Insert bar to insert the widget, and then click the Spry Textarea tab to select the widget. In the Property inspector, enter **journalentryvalidate** in the Spry textarea box, and then check the Required check box, if necessary. In the Document window, click the scroll bar of the widget to display the text field properties. In the Property inspector, enter **journalentry** in the TextField box, enter 80 in the Char width box, and then enter 10 in the Num lines box. In the lower-right cell of the table, insert a Submit button, and then save the page.

7. Modify the navigation bar to no longer display the Contact Information element in the Down state initially.

8. Ask your instructor for the information you need to connect to an existing database or upload the database on your remote server using an FTP program and the **wasdb.mdb** file located in the **Tutorial.10\Case1** folder included with your Data Files. (*Hint:* Obtain the information you need from your instructor or technical support person.)

9. Expand the Server Behaviors panel in the Application panel group, click the document type link in Step 2, click ASP JavaScript in the list, if necessary, and then update the links.

10. In the Server Behaviors panel, click the testing server link in Step 3, select ASP JavaScript as the server model, select FTP as the access, delete all the file path information from the URL prefix box, type the URL for your posted site, and then click the OK button.

11. In the Server Behaviors panel, click the Add Behavior button, click Recordset, type **WASRecordset** as the name, click the Define button, click the New button, click Custom Connection String, type **WASDBconnection** as the connection name, type **"Provider=Microsoft.Jet.OLEDB.4.0;data source=** and the exact file path to your database followed by **"** (closing quotation mark) as the connection string, click the Using Driver on Testing Server option button, if necessary, click the Test button, click the OK button to close the dialog box that indicates the connection was made successfully, click the OK button to close the Custom Connection String dialog box, click the Done button in the Connections for Site 'DrThompson' dialog box, select WASDBconnection as the connection, click journal in the Tables list, click the SELECT button, and then click the OK button. The Recordset behavior is added to the page and appears in the Server Behaviors panel. (*Hint:* If you do not know the exact path to your database, ask your instructor or technical support person. If the test is unsuccessful, double-check the connection string and file path for your database or use an outside FTP program to upload the _mmServerScripts folder to the root folder on your remote server and your testing server if you're using a separate testing server.)

12. In the Server Behaviors panel, add the Insert Record behavior, select WASDBconnection as the connection, click journal in the Insert into table list, click the Browse button, click the rituals_and_practices.html page in the site's local root folder, click the OK button, click journalentry in the Get values from list, if necessary, click journal in the Column list, click journalentry inserts into column "journal" (Text) in the Form elements list, and then click the OK button. The Insert Record behavior is added to the page and appears in the Server Behaviors panel.

13. Save the page, upload the page to your remote server (include dependent files), preview the page in a browser, and then close the browser.

14. Open the rituals_and_practices.html page, click the document type link in the Server Behaviors panel, select ASP JavaScript in the list, click the OK button, click the Update button to update the links in the pages, click the OK button in the message dialog box, and then update the Rituals & Practices element in the navigation bar in the rituals_and_practices.asp page so that rituals_and_practices.asp appears in the When clicked, go to URL box.

15. Click the journal.asp tab, right-click the Recordset behavior in the Server Behaviors panel, click Copy on the context menu, click the rituals_and_practices.asp tab, right-click in the Server Behaviors panel, and then click Paste on the context menu to paste the Recordset behavior into the page.

⊕ EXPLORE

16. Double-click the Recordset behavior in the Server Behaviors panel to open the Recordset dialog box, click the Simple button, click the Selected option button in the Columns section, click journal in the Columns box, and then click the OK button.

⊕ EXPLORE   17. Delete the "Research in process, check back soon." text, click the Dynamic Table button in the Dynamic Data list on the Data tab of the Insert bar, click the All records button, set the border to 0, set the cell padding to 3, and then click the OK button.

⊕ EXPLORE   18. Save the page, upload the rituals_and_practices.asp page to your remote server (include dependent files), preview the journal.asp page in a browser (updating the page and dependent files on the testing server, if necessary), press the Submit button to test that the Spry Validation Textarea widget is working (a message appears, stating that "A value is required."), type a test entry in the form, and then click the Submit button to submit the form. The rituals_and_practices.asp page with the new entry opens in the browser window. (*Hint:* If you are sharing a database with classmates, you may see additional entries in the database.)

19. Submit the finished files to your instructor, either in printed or electronic form, as requested.

| Apply | Case Problem 2 |

Add database-driven pages to collect and display a tally of visitors' votes for favorite paintings in a Web site for an art museum.

Data File needed for this Case Problem: museumdb.sql or museumdb.mdb

Museum of Western Art   C. J. Strittmatter wants visitors to the Museum site to be able to vote for their favorite painting. You will create a form in the home page that enables visitors to vote for a painting. The form will be connected to a database that stores the votes, and the vote tally will be displayed below the form in the home page.

If you are using MySQL and PHP on a Linux server, complete the following steps:

1. Open the **Museum** site that you modified in **Tutorial 9, Case Problem 2**, and then open the index.html page in the Document window.

2. Insert blank lines until you are below the last line of text (and outside of the AP div), insert a form into the page, enter **voteform** as the form name, and then insert a table with 3 rows, 1 column, 40% table width, 0 border thickness, 2 cell padding, 2 cell spacing, and no header cells in the form.

3. In the top row, type **Select your favorite painting**, and then align the text to the Left and Top.

4. Add a radio group in the second row, name the radio group **vote**, replace "Radio" with **The Cow Puncher** in the first row of both the Label and Value columns, replace "Radio" with **A Figure of the Night** in the second row of both the Label and Value columns, click the Plus (+) button to add a new row, replace "Radio" with **A Quiet Day in Utica** in the third row of both the Label and the Value columns, and then click the OK button.

5. Add a Submit button in the third row of the table, typing **Submit** as the button name and the value, if necessary, and then save the page.

6. Ask your instructor for the information you need to connect to an existing database or create the database on your remote server using the **museumdb.sql** file located in the **Tutorial.10\Case2** folder included with your Data Files. (*Hint:* Obtain the information you need from your instructor or technical support person.)

7. In the Server Behaviors panel, click the document type link in Step 2, click PHP in the list if necessary, click the OK button, update the links; click the OK button to confirm that the index.php page could not be updated, save the index.php page, update the link for the MuseumLogoRollover to the index.php page, and then save the page again.

8. Click the testing server link in Step 3, select PHP MySQL as the server model, select FTP as the access, delete all the file path information from the URL prefix box, type the URL for your posted site, and then click the OK button.

9. In the Server Behaviors panel, add the Recordset behavior, name the recordset **MuseumRecordset**, click the Define button, click the New button, type **MuseumDBconnection** as the connection name, type **localhost** or the database server URL in the MySQL server box, type your user name and password, click the Select button to display a list of databases, select the museumdb database from the list, click the OK button twice, click the Done button, click the Simple button, click MuseumDBconnection in the Connection list, click vote in the Tables list, click the Selected option button, click vote in the Columns list, and then click the OK button. The Recordset behavior is added to the page and appears in the Server Behaviors panel.

10. In the Server Behaviors panel, add the Insert Record behavior, click voteform in the Submit values from list, if necessary, click MuseumDBconnection in the Connection list, click vote in the Insert Table list, click 'vote' Gets Value From 'FORM.vote' as 'Text' in the Columns list, click FORM.vote in the Value list, click Text in the Submit as list if necessary, click the Browse button, click the index.php page in the site's local root folder (because the totals will be displayed in this page), and click the OK button in each dialog box. The Insert Record behavior is added to the page and appears in the Server Behaviors panel.

11. Save the page, upload the page to your remote server (include dependent files), preview the page in a browser (update the page and dependent files on the testing server), and then close the browser.

⊕ EXPLORE 12. In the Server Behaviors panel, double-click the Recordset behavior to open the Recordset dialog box, click the Advanced button, delete all the text in the SQL box, type the following code exactly as it appears, and then click the OK button to enter a query that will enable the vote tally to be displayed in a dynamic table.

> **SELECT vote AS Painting, count(vote) AS Votes**
> **FROM vote**
> **GROUP BY vote**
> **ORDER BY vote**

13. Place the insertion point in a blank line below the form, click Dynamic Table in the Dynamic Data list on the Data tab of the Insert bar, click the All records button, set the border to 0, set the cell padding to 3, and then click the OK button.

14. Create a new CSS style for the table heading text, apply the style to the heading text in the form and the dynamic table, and then save and close the style sheet (or use the subheading style).

15. Save the index.php page, upload the page to your remote server (include dependent files), preview the page in a browser (update the page and the dependent files on the testing server, if necessary), click an option button in the form, and then submit the form. The new vote tally appears below the form in the page. (*Hint:* If you are sharing a database with classmates, you may see additional entries in the database.)

16. Submit the finished files to your instructor, either in printed or electronic form, as requested.

If you are using Access and ASP on a Windows server, complete the following steps:

1. Open the **Museum** site that you modified in **Tutorial 9, Case Problem 2**, and then open the index.html page in the Document window.

2. Insert blank lines until you move down in the page after the last line of text (and outside of the AP div), insert a form into the page, enter **voteform** as the form name, and then insert a table with 3 rows, 1 column, 40% table width, 0 border thickness, 2 cell padding, 2 cell spacing, and no header cells in the form.

3. In the top row, type **Select your favorite painting**, and then align the text to the Left and Top.

4. Add a radio group in the second row, name the radio group **vote**, replace "Radio" with **The Cow Puncher** in the first row of both the Label and Value columns, replace "Radio" with **A Figure of the Night** in the second row of both the Label and Value columns, click the Plus (+) button to add a new row, replace "Radio" with **A Quiet Day in Utica** in the third row of both the Label and the Value columns, and then click the OK button.

5. Add a Submit button in the third row of the table, typing **Submit** as the button name and the value, if necessary, and then save the page.

6. Ask your instructor for the information you need to connect to an existing database or upload the database to your remote server using an FTP program and the **museumdb.mdb** file located in the **Tutorial.10\Case2** folder included with your Data Files. (*Hint:* Obtain the information you need from your instructor or technical support person.)

7. In the Server Behaviors panel, click the document type link in Step 2, click ASP JavaScript in the list, click the OK button, update the links in the files, click the OK button to confirm that the index.asp page could not be updated, save the index.asp page, update the link for the MusuemLogoRollover to the index.asp page, and then save the page again.

8. Click the testing server link in Step 3, select ASP JavaScript as the server model, select FTP as the access, delete all the file path information from the URL prefix box, type the URL for your posted site, and then click the OK button.

9. In the Server Behaviors panel, add the Recordset behavior, name the recordset **MuseumRecordset**, click the Define button, click the New button, click Custom Connection String, type **MuseumDBconnection** as the connection name, type **"Provider=Microsoft.Jet.OLEDB.4.0;data source=** and the exact file path to your database followed by **"** (closing quotation mark) in the Connection String box, click the Using Driver on Testing Server option button, if necessary, click the Test button, click the OK button to close the dialog box stating that the connection was made successfully, click the OK button to close the Custom Connection String dialog box, click the Done button, click MuseumDBconnection in the Connection list, click vote in the Table list, click the Selected option button, click vote in the Columns list, and then click the OK button. The Recordset behavior is added to the page and appears in the Server Behaviors panel. (*Hint:* If you do not know the exact path to your database, ask your instructor or technical support person. If the test is unsuccessful, double-check the connection string and file path for your database or use an outside FTP program to upload the _mmServerScripts folder to the root folder on your remote server and your testing server if you're using a separate testing server.)

10. In the Server Behaviors panel, add the Insert Record behavior, click MuseumDBconnection in the Connection list, click vote in the Insert into table list, click the Browse button, click the index.asp page in the site's local root folder (because the totals will be displayed in this page), click the OK button, click vote-form in the Get values from list, if necessary, click vote in the Column list, click vote inserts into column "vote" (Text) in the Form elements list, and then click the OK button. The Insert Record behavior is added to the page and appears in the Server Behaviors panel. A red exclamation mark may appear, although the behavior works correctly.

11. Save the page, upload the page to your remote server (include dependent files), preview the page in a browser, and then close the browser.

⊕ EXPLORE   12. In the Server Behaviors panel, double-click the Recordset behavior to open the Recordset dialog box, click the Advanced button, delete all the text in the SQL box, type the following code exactly as it appears, and then click the OK button to enter a query that will enable the vote tally to be displayed in a dynamic table.

> **SELECT vote AS Painting, count(vote) AS Votes**
> **FROM vote**
> **GROUP BY vote**
> **ORDER BY vote**

⊕ EXPLORE   13. Place the insertion point in a blank line below the form, click Dynamic Table in the Dynamic Data list on the Data tab of the Insert bar, click the All records button, set the border to 0, set the cell padding to 3, and then click the OK button.

14. Create a new CSS style for the table heading text, apply the style to the heading text in the form and the dynamic table, and then save and close the style sheet (or use the subheading style).

15. Save the index.asp page, upload the page to your remote server (include dependent files), preview the index.asp page in a browser, click an option button in the form, and then submit the form. The new vote tally appears below the form in the page. (*Hint:* If you are sharing a database with classmates, you may see additional entries in the database.)

16. Submit the finished files to your instructor, either in printed or electronic form, as requested.

| Apply | **Case Problem 3** |

Display news items stored in a database in the home page of a Web site for an independent bookstore.

Data File needed for this Case Problem: moredb.sql or moredb.mdb

MORE Books   Mark Chapman asks you to create a section that displays news items at the bottom of the home page. You will create a News Admin page and then add a form in the page that enables employees to enter content. To ensure that employees don't accidentally submit forms with empty entries, you will use the Spry Validation Textarea, which allows forms to be submitted only when the text area contains content. The form will be connected to a database. Finally, you will add code at the bottom of the home page that will display content stored in the database.

If you are using MySQL and PHP on a Linux server, complete the following steps:

1. Open the **MOREbooks** site that you modified in **Tutorial 9, Case Problem 3**.

2. In the Files panel, duplicate the links.html page, rename the copied page as **news.php**, and then open the news.php page in the Document window.

3. Change the heading text to **News Input**, replace "Links" in the page title with **News Input**, and then delete the content in the page.

4. Insert a form in the page, enter **newsform** as the form name, and then insert a table with 2 rows, 2 columns, 90% table width, 0 border thickness, 3 cell padding, 0 cell spacing, and no header cells in the form.

5. Type **input news** in the upper-left cell, and then align the text to the Right and Top.

⊕ EXPLORE

6. Insert a Spry Validation Textarea widget in the upper-right cell, enter **newsvalidate** as the Spry Textarea name, and then check the Required property, if necessary. Click the scroll bar to select the text area, enter **news** as the field name, set the character width to 80, and then set the number of lines to 10. Add a Submit button in the lower-right cell, and then save the page. Click the OK button in the Copy Dependent Files dialog box to add the SpryAssets folder and files to the site.

7. Ask your instructor for the information you need to connect to an existing database or create the database on your remote server using the **moredb.sql** file located in the **Tutorial.10\Case3** folder included with your Data Files. (*Hint:* Obtain the information you need from your instructor or technical support person.)

8. In the Server Behaviors panel, select PHP as the document type in Step 2.

9. Set up the testing server in Step 3, selecting PHP MySQL as the server model and FTP as the access, and entering the URL for your posted site in the URL prefix box.

10. In the Server Behaviors panel, add the Recordset behavior, click the Simple button, if necessary, name the recordset **moreRecordset**, click the Define button, click the New button, type **moreDBconnection** as the connection name, type **localhost** or your database server URL as the MySQL server, type your user name and password, click the Select button to display a list of databases, click the moredb database, click the OK button twice, click the Done button, click moreDBconnection in the Connection list, click news in the Table list, click the Selected option button, click news_text in the Columns list, and then click the OK button. The Recordset behavior is added to the page and appears in the Server Behaviors panel.

11. In the Server Behaviors panel, add the Insert Record behavior, click newsform in the Submit values from list, if necessary, click moreDBconnection in the Connection list, click news in the Insert table list, click 'news_text' does not get a value in the Columns list, click FORM.news in the Value list, click Text in the Submit as list, if necessary, click the Browse button, click the index.html page in the site's local root folder, and click the OK button in each dialog box. The Insert Record behavior is added to the page and is visible in the Server Behaviors panel.

12. Save the page, upload the page to your remote server (include dependent files), and then preview the page in a browser (update the page and the dependent files on the testing server, if necessary).

13. Copy the Recordset behavior in the Server Behaviors panel, and then close the page.

14. Open the **index.html** page, select PHP as the document type in Step 2 in the Server Behaviors panel, update the links in the file, paste the Recordset behavior into the Server Behaviors panel in the page, save the index.php page, update the MORE logo rollover to link to the index.php page, save the page again, and then upload the page to your remote server.

15. Select the first quote in the NEWS section, copy the text, delete the text from the page, save the page, preview the news.php page in a browser, paste the text into the input news box, click the Submit button, repeat this process to copy the second quote in the NEWS section of the home page to the database, and then close the browser.

EXPLORE 16. Make sure the insertion point is below the NEWS heading in the home page, click the Dynamic Table button in the Dynamic Data list on the Data tab of the Insert bar, click the All records option button, set the border to 0, set the cell padding to 5, click the OK button, and then delete the first row of the dynamic table (the row that shows "news_text").

17. Save the index.php page, upload the page to your remote server (include dependent files), preview the news.php page in a browser (update the files and dependent files on the testing server, if necessary), type a test entry in the form followed by your name, and then click the Submit button. The index.php page with the news entries appears in the browser. (*Hint:* If you are sharing a database with classmates, you may see additional entries in the database.)

18. Submit the finished files to your instructor, either in printed or electronic form, as requested.

If you are using Access and ASP on a Windows server, complete the following steps:

1. Open the **MOREbooks** site that you modified in **Tutorial 9, Case Problem 3**.

2. In the Files panel, duplicate the links.html page, rename the copied page as **news.asp**, and then open the news.asp page in the Document window.

3. Change the heading to **News Input**, replace "Links" in the page title with **News Input**, and then delete the content in the page.

4. Insert a form in the page, enter **newsform** as the form name, and then insert a table with 2 rows, 2 columns, 90% table width, 0 border thickness, 3 cell padding, 0 cell spacing, and no header cells in the form.

5. Type **input news** in the upper-left cell, and then align the text to the Right and Top.

EXPLORE 6. Insert a Spry Validation Textarea widget in the upper-right cell, enter **newsvalidate** as the Spry Textarea name, and then check the Required property, if necessary. Click the scroll bar to select the text area, enter **news** as the field name, set the character width to 80, and then set the number of lines to 10. Add a Submit button in the lower-right cell, and then save the page. Click the OK button in the Copy Dependent Files dialog box to add the SpryAssets folder and files to the site.

7. Ask your instructor for the information you need to connect to an existing database or upload the database to your remote server using an FTP program and the **moredb.mdb** file located in the **Tutorial.10\Case3** folder included with your Data Files. (*Hint:* Obtain the information you need from your instructor or technical support person.)

8. In the Server Behaviors panel, select ASP JavaScript as the document type in Step 2.

9. Set up the testing server in Step 3, selecting ASP JavaScript as the server model and FTP as the access, and entering the URL for your posted site in the URL prefix box.

10. In the Server Behaviors panel, add the Recordset behavior, click the Simple button in the Recordset dialog box, if necessary, name the recordset **moreRecordset**, click the Define button, click the New button, click Custom Connection String, type **moreDBconnection** as the connection name, type **"Provider=Microsoft.Jet.OLEDB. 4.0;data source=** followed by the exact file path to your database and **"** (closing quotation mark) as the connection string, click the Using Driver on Testing Server option button, click the Test button, click the OK button to confirm the connection was made successfully, click the OK button, click the Done button, click moreDBconnection in the Connection list, click news in the Table list, click the Selected option button, click news in the Columns list, and then click the OK button. The Recordset behavior is added to the page and appears in the Server Behaviors panel. (*Hint:* If you do not know the exact path to your database, ask your instructor or technical support person. If the test is unsuccessful, double-check the connection string and file path for your database or use an outside FTP program to upload the _mmServerScripts folder to the root folder on your remote server and your testing server if you're using a separate testing server.)

11. In the Server Behaviors panel, add the Insert Record behavior, click moreDBconnection in the Connection list, click news in the Insert table list, type **index.asp** in the After inserting, go to box, click newsform in the Get values from list, if necessary, click news in the Column list, click news inserts into column "news" (Text) in the Form elements list, and then click the OK button. The Insert Record behavior is added to the page and appears in the Server Behaviors panel.

12. Save the page, upload the page to your remote server (include dependent files), and then preview the page in a browser.

13. Copy the Recordset behavior in the Server Behaviors panel, and then close the page.

14. Open the **index.html** page, select ASP JavaScript as the document type in Step 2 in the Server Behaviors panel, update the links in the pages, click the OK button to confirm that the index.asp page could not be updated, paste the Recordset behavior into the Server Behaviors panel, save the index.asp page, update the MOREbooks logo rollover to link to the index.asp page, save the page again, and then upload the page to your remote server (include dependent files).

15. Select the first quote in the NEWS section, copy the text, delete the text from the page, preview the **news.asp** page in a browser, paste the text into the input news box, click the Submit button, repeat this process to copy the second quote in the NEWS section of the home page to the database, and then close the browser.

✦ EXPLORE   16. Make sure the insertion point is below the NEWS heading in the home page, click the Dynamic Table button in the Dynamic Data list on the Data tab of the Insert bar, click the All records option button, set the border to 0, set the cell padding to 5, click the OK button, and then delete the first row of the dynamic table (the row that shows "news").

17. Save the index.asp page, upload the page to your remote server (include dependent files), preview the news.asp page in a browser (update the files and dependent files on the testing server, if necessary), type a test entry in the form followed by your name, and then click the Submit button form. The index.asp page with the news entries appears in the browser. (*Hint:* If you are sharing a database with classmates, you may see additional entries in the database.)

18. Submit the finished files to your instructor, either in printed or electronic form, as requested.

| Create | **Case Problem 4** |

Create database-driven pages to collect and display customer comments in a Web site for a newly opening sushi restaurant.

Data File needed for this Case Problem: sushidb.sql or sushidb.mdb

Sushi Ya-Ya Mary O'Brien wants to add a form in the Contact page that includes a comments section. After you create the form, you will connect the form to a database and then add code to the home page that will enable the page to display customer comments.

1. Open the **SushiYaYa** site that you modified in **Tutorial 9, Case Problem 4**, and then open the **contact.html** page in the Document window.

⊕ **EXPLORE**

2. Create a form in the Contact page that enables customers to enter comments. The form should have a text area for comments and a Submit button for submission. (*Hint:* Use a table to create the form structure and use the Spry Validation Textarea widget to verify that users have entered content into the text area before they submit the form.)

3. If your instructor has not already done so, upload the database on the remote server using the **sushidb.sql** file (if you are using MySQL and PHP) or create the database on your remote server using the **sushidb.mdb** file (if you are using Access and ASP) located in the **Tutorial.10\Case4** folder included with your Data Files. (*Hint:* Obtain the information you need from your instructor or technical support person.)

4. Connect the Web site to the database by completing Steps 2 and 3 in the Server Behaviors panel. (*Hint:* Remember to update the link on the contact.php or contact. asp page.)

5. Add the Recordset and the Insert Record server behaviors to the Contact page.

6. Copy the Recordset server behavior from the Contact page, open the **index.html** page, and then paste the Recordset server behavior in the home page.

⊕ **EXPLORE**

7. Add a customer comments heading below the existing page content, and then add a dynamic table that displays customer comments in the page. (*Hint:* To add a dynamic table, click the Dynamic Table button in the Dynamic Data list on the Data tab of the Insert bar.)

8. Save the pages, upload the pages to your remote server, and then test the pages.

9. Submit the finished files to your instructor, either in printed or electronic form, as requested.

| Review | **Quick Check Answers** |

Session 10.1

1. a JavaScript and CSS code library that enables Web designers to more easily add advanced functionality to Web pages

2. Asynchronous JavaScript and XML is a concept for using various techniques to update Web page content and targeted pieces of content within a page without visible refreshes and without browser add-on technologies.

3. a reusable, prebuilt page element that enables user interaction

4. container, behavior, and styling

5. a visual enhancement you can apply to various elements in Web pages; usually used to call attention to a page element, animate a page element, or alter a page element visually over a period of time

6. a collection of information that is arranged for ease and speed of search and retrieval

7. MySQL and Access

Session 10.2

1. language
2. PHP
3. a behavior that runs on the Web server before the Web page is sent to a user's browser and is written in PHP, ASP, JSP, or ColdFusion
4. to specify which data you want to retrieve from the database and display in the Web page
5. to protect the data from unauthorized access
6. to tell the browser to automatically refresh the page (by reloading the current page or going to a different page) after a certain amount of time

Session 10.3

1. language
2. ASP
3. a behavior that runs on the Web server before the Web page is sent to a user's browser and is written in PHP, ASP, JSP, or ColdFusion
4. to specify which data you want to retrieve from the database and display in the Web page
5. to protect the data from unauthorized access
6. to tell the browser to automatically refresh the page (by reloading the current page or going to a different page) after a certain amount of time

Reality Check

Dreamweaver is the industry-standard tool for professional Web design, but it also has a wide user base beyond the professional world. Consider these examples. Individuals use Dreamweaver to create personal Web sites, small businesses use Dreamweaver to create and maintain online catalogues, educational institutions use Dreamweaver to create promotional information and Web applications. The possibilities are infinite.

In this exercise, you will use Dreamweaver to plan and create a personal Web site with information of your choice, using the Dreamweaver skills and tools presented in Tutorials 1 through 10. Use the following steps as a guide to completing your Web site.

Note: Do **not** include any personal information of a sensitive nature in any Web sites that you create to be submitted to your instructor for this exercise. Later, you can update the Web sites with such information, but remember that any Web sites you post to a Web server are visible to anyone who has Internet access and a Web browser.

1. Create a list of site goals; review the list for order of importance and wording.
2. Define your target audience, researching the target audience as needed, and create a user profile for the site.
3. Conduct market research to gather information about three similar Web sites, and analyze them.
4. Develop two end-user scenarios for your site.
5. Design the information architecture for the site.
6. Draw a flow chart for the site so that you can visualize the site navigation and page connectivity.
7. Develop a site concept and metaphor.
8. Choose a color palette, fonts, and graphic style for the site. (*Hint:* you might want to create a document that identifies all of your choices, including hexadecimal color codes for each color as well as a breakdown of font attributes by family, font size, color, and style for body text, links, headings, subheadings, and so on.)
9. Create a layout design for the pages of the site.
10. Gather relevant content materials and write the page content for the pages. Consider including a page heading and a summary sentence at the top of each page, and then break page content into smaller chunks with subheadings that will guide the target audience through the page.
11. Create a local site definition and a remote site definition.
12. Create a main template for the site. Add editable regions to the template and insert placeholder text as appropriate. Add background and colors to the template as appropriate based on your site plan.
13. Design the site navigation system, and then add a navigation bar to the template, creating appropriate elements. (*Hint:* If you do not have access to a graphics program, you can create a series of text links for the site navigation instead of inserting a navigation bar.)
14. Add an appropriate list of keywords to the head content of the template.
15. Add an appropriate description of the site to the head content of the template.
16. Create the CSS styles for your site, export the styles to an external style sheet, and then link the style sheet to each page in your site.

17. Create at least two library items for elements that you intend to reuse or update frequently, such as footers or information that will appear in more than one page.

18. Use the template to create the pages of your site in the local root folder, and name each page with a descriptive filename.

19. For each page in your site, enter an appropriate page title, add content and graphics, and then apply appropriate CSS styles to format the content.

20. After you have created all the pages for the site, modify the navigation bar in the template to link each element to the appropriate page, and then save the template and update the pages.

21. Create an image map in at least one Web page.

22. Add a rollover button in at least one Web page.

23. Create an animation in at least one page. Use the timeline and behaviors to make images move over a period of time.

24. Insert Flash text, movie or sound into at least one page.

25. Include at least one Spry element in your pages.

26. Save the pages, and preview them in a browser. Adjust the pages, as needed.

27. Upload the site to a remote server, and then preview the site over the Web. Test each page of the site, and adjust the pages in Dreamweaver as needed.

28. Save and close your site, and then submit the completed Web site to your instructor, in printed or electronic form, as requested.

Additional Case 1

Objectives

- Plan and design a Web site
- Create a template
- Create and use library items
- Create and use a CSS style sheet
- Create template-based Web pages that include text, images, an image map, and a rollover button
- Create and test a form
- Insert a Flash movie, Flash text, a Shockwave movie, a Flash video, or a sound in a Web page
- Preview and test each page in a Web site

Building a Web Site with a Form

Case | Coffee Lounge

The Coffee Lounge is an all-night coffee bar located on Exposition Parkway at the heart of the Dallas punk music scene. The lounge features live, alternative, and punk music on the weekends; an improvisational psychedelic jazz jam on Thursday nights; poetry slams on Wednesday nights; experimental film screenings on Tuesday nights; and a book club for cyberpunk titles on Monday nights. In addition, the Coffee Lounge encourages public art by allowing patrons and local artists to use the various pens, markers, and paints scattered throughout the club to add their mark to the walls and tables.

Coffee Lounge owner, Tommy Caddell, has decided that the lounge could benefit from a Web site. He wants to use the site as a marketing tool to promote featured events, the monthly special—a different coffee blend is featured each month—and sales. Tommy also wants to include a page that features a different Dallas-based non-profit organization each month. The page should include a blurb about the organization, contact information and, if possible, a link to the organization's Web site. He wants to be able to update this page himself.

1. Create a list of site goals; review the list for order of importance and wording.
2. Define a target audience and create a user profile for the site. (*Hint:* Research the target audience as needed.)
3. Conduct market research to gather information about at least four competing Web sites or other Web sites that cater to the target audience, and then write a paragraph summarizing your findings.
4. Develop two end-user scenarios for the site.
5. Create an information category outline for the site.
6. Create a flowchart for the site.
7. Develop a site concept and a metaphor for the site. Write a paragraph explaining your choices.
8. Choose a color palette, fonts, and a graphic style for the site. Write a paragraph explaining your choices.
9. Create rough sketches of two layouts for the site. Write a paragraph explaining which layout you prefer and why.
10. Check the layout of the design you prefer for logic, and verify that your design reinforces the site goals and supports the site metaphor.

Starting Data Files

AddCases

CoffeeLoungeFormTest.html

11. Create a local site definition and a remote site definition.
12. Create a main template for the site.
13. Add editable regions to the template and insert placeholder text as appropriate.
14. Add a background and colors to the template as appropriate based on your site plan.
15. Add an appropriate list of keywords to the head content of the template.
16. Add an appropriate description of the site to the head content of the template.
17. Create at least three CSS styles to format the text in the site; refer to your site plan for the appropriate colors, fonts, and so forth.
18. Insert a navigation bar into the template, and create appropriate elements. You will not create links in the navigation bar at this time because the pages have not yet been created; you will modify the template and add the links later. (*Hint:* If you do not have access to a graphics program, you can create a series of text links for site navigation instead of inserting a navigation bar.)
19. Create at least two library items for elements that you intend to reuse or update frequently, such as footers or an upcoming events list that will be displayed in more than one page.
20. Use the template to create a Web page.
21. Rename the Web page with a descriptive filename. (*Hint:* Remember to use index.html or index.htm as the filename for the home page.)
22. Set an appropriate page title for the Web page you created.
23. Open the Web page, type an appropriate page heading and text content, and then apply appropriate CSS styles, if necessary, to format the content.
24. Add at least one image to the Web page. (*Hint:* If you don't have an image file to insert, you can use any of the image files included with your Data Files.)
25. Save the page, and then preview the page in a browser.
26. Repeat Steps 20 through 25 to create a home page and at least three first-level pages for the site based on your site plan.
27. After you have created all the pages for the site, open the template and modify the navigation bar, selecting each element and adding the link to the appropriate page.
28. Save the template, and then update the pages.
29. Create an image map in at least one Web page.
30. Copy the **CoffeeLoungeFormTest.html** file located in the AddCases folder included with your Data Files to the site's local root folder. This will enable you to test the form.
31. Open the CoffeeLoungeFormTest.html file in the Document window, add the Mark of the Web to the page, and then save the page.
32. Add a rollover button to at least one Web page.
33. Create a form in one Web page to collect appropriate data from visitors. Use a table to organize the form objects. Add at least four different types of Spry validation widget form objects to the form. Using the Spry form objects will enable you to validate form content before submitting the form.
34. Preview the form in a browser, and then test the form.
35. Insert a Flash movie, Flash text, a Shockwave movie, a Flash video, or a sound into at least one page. (*Hint:* If you don't have one of these types of files to insert, you can use any of the files in the Tutorial.08 folders included with your Data Files as placeholders.)
36. Preview the site in a browser.
37. Upload the site to a remote server, and then preview the site over the Web.
38. Test each page of the site.
39. Submit the finished files to your instructor, either in printed or electronic form, as requested.

Objectives

- Plan and design a Web site
- Creat and use a CSS style sheet
- Create Web pages that include text, images, an image map, and a rollover button
- Insert a navigation bar
- Create and use library items
- Create an animation that uses the Timeline and behaviors
- Use Spry effects
- Insert a Flash movie, Flash text, a Shockwave movie, a Flash video, or a sound
- Preview and test each page in the Web site

Building a Web Site with Animation

Case | Framed

Framed is a frame shop that specializes in creating contemporary, one-of-a-kind frames for traditional western art. The shop also displays the work of local western artists. Located in Sundance Square in the heart of cow town (Fort Worth, Texas) Framed caters to young, upwardly mobile city dwellers who want to combine their western roots with urban style. The site will be used for marketing purposes and to let people know about upcoming events. In the future, if the site is a success, the owners would like to add an e-commerce section.

1. Create a list of site goals; review the list for order of importance and wording.
2. Define a target audience and create a user profile for the site. (*Hint:* Research the target audience as needed.)
3. Conduct market research to gather information about at least four competing Web sites or other Web sites that cater to the target audience, and then write a paragraph summarizing your findings. (*Hint:* Look at Web sites such as *www.cowboycool.com.*)
4. Develop two end-user scenarios for the site.
5. Create an information category outline for the site.
6. Create a flowchart for the site.
7. Develop a site concept and a metaphor for the site. Write a paragraph explaining your choices.
8. Choose a color palette, fonts, and a graphic style for the site. Write a paragraph explaining your choices.
9. Create rough sketches of two layouts for the site. Write a paragraph explaining which layout you prefer and why.
10. Check the layout of the design you prefer for logic, and verify that your design reinforces the site goals and supports the site metaphor.
11. Create a local site definition and a remote site definition.
12. Create a home page for the site. Name the Web page with a descriptive filename and save the page. (*Hint:* Remember to use index.html or index.htm as the filename for the home page.)
13. Create a style sheet and attach the page to the style sheet.
14. Add CSS styles to the style sheet for background, links, font colors, headings, and so forth based on what is appropriate for your site.
15. Add an appropriate list of keywords to the head content of the page.

Starting Data Files

There are no starting Data Files needed for this Additional Case.

16. Add an appropriate description of the site to the head content of the page.
17. Set an appropriate page title for the Web page you created.
18. Insert a navigation bar into the page, and create appropriate elements. (*Hint:* If you do not have access to a graphics program, you can create a series of text links for site navigation instead of inserting a navigation bar.)
19. Type an appropriate page heading and text content in the Web page, and then apply appropriate CSS styles to format the content.
20. Add at least one image to the Web page. (*Hint:* If you don't have an image file to insert, you can use any of the image files included with your Data Files.)
21. Repeat Steps 12 through 20 to create at least three additional first-level pages for the site based on your site plan, but attach the style sheet you created in Step 13 to the subsequent pages.
22. Create at least two library items for elements that you intend to reuse or update frequently, such as footers or upcoming sales information that will be displayed in more than one page. Add the library items to the pages of your site.
23. Save the pages, and then preview the pages in a browser.
24. Create an image map in at least one Web page.
25. Add a rollover button to at least one Web page.
26. Save the pages, and then preview the pages in a browser.
27. Create an animation in one page. Use the timeline and behaviors to make images move over a period of time. (*Hint:* You can create your own graphics to animate, or you can use any of the images in the Cases folder included with your Data Files for Case Problem 2 Museum of Western Art, which includes images of original western paintings.)
28. Preview the animation in a browser.
29. Add Spry effects to animate at least two images.
30. Insert a Flash movie, Flash text, a Shockwave movie, a Flash video, or a sound into at least one page. (*Hint:* If you don't have one of these types of files to insert, you can use any of the files in the Tutorial.08 folders included with your Data Files as placeholders.)
31. Preview the site in a browser.
32. Upload the site to a remote server, and then preview the site over the Web.
33. Test each page of the site.
34. Submit the finished files to your instructor, either in printed or electronic form, as requested.

Objectives

- Plan and design a Web site
- Create a template
- Create and use a CSS style sheet
- Insert the Spry Menu Bar widget
- Create and use library items
- Create template-based Web pages that include page headings, text, images, an image map, and a rollover button
- Create and test a form
- Insert a Flash movie, Flash text, a Shockwave movie, a Flash video, or a sound in a Web page
- Preview and test each page in a Web site

Building a Web Site with Database Functionality

Case | Tweetie

Sonia Orozco, known as Tweetie, is a band promoter of indie music. She has decided to create a monthly online zine called D-zine. Each issue will include band interviews, a calendar of local performances and events, reviews of local performances and new CD releases, and reader reviews and comments. The zine will also include a "wanted" section for bands looking for new members and a section that features a local venue.

1. Create a list of site goals; review the list for order of importance and wording.
2. Define a target audience and create a user profile for the site. (*Hint:* Research the target audience as needed.)
3. Conduct market research to gather information about at least four e-zine Web sites as well as two Web sites that promote local venues and bands, and then write a paragraph summarizing your findings.
4. Develop two end-user scenarios for the site.
5. Create an information category outline for the site.
6. Create a flowchart for the site.
7. Develop a site concept and a metaphor for the site. Write a paragraph explaining your choices.
8. Choose a color palette, fonts, and a graphic style for the site. Write a paragraph explaining your choices.
9. Create rough sketches of two layouts for the site. Write a paragraph explaining which layout you prefer and why.
10. Check the layout of the design you prefer for logic, and verify that your design reinforces the site goals and supports the site metaphor.
11. Create a local site definition and a remote site definition.
12. Create a main template for the site.
13. Add editable regions to the template and insert placeholder text as appropriate.

Starting Data Files

zine.mdb
zine.sql

14. Add a background and colors to the template as appropriate based on your site plan.

15. Add an appropriate list of keywords to the head content of the template.

16. Add an appropriate description of the site to the head content of the template.

17. Create at least three CSS styles to format the text in the site; refer to your site plan for the appropriate colors, fonts, and so forth.

18. Insert the Spry Menu Bar widget into the template to add a navigation system for the site. Create appropriate elements.

19. Create at least two library items for elements that you intend to reuse or update frequently, such as footers or an upcoming events list that will be displayed in more than one page.

20. Use the template to create a Web page.

21. Rename the Web page with a descriptive filename. (*Hint:* Remember to use index.html or index.htm as the filename for the home page.)

22. Set an appropriate page title for the Web page you created.

23. Open the Web page, type an appropriate page heading and text content, and then apply appropriate CSS styles, if necessary, to format the content. (*Hint:* You can use the Cosmatic bands as featured bands.)

24. Add at least one image to the Web page. (*Hint:* If you don't have an image file to insert, you can use any of the image files included with your Data Files.)

25. Save the page, and then preview the page in a browser.

26. Repeat Steps 20 through 25 to create a home page and at least three first-level pages for the site based on your site plan.

27. After you have created all the pages for the site, open the template and modify the navigation bar, selecting each element and adding the link to the appropriate page.

28. Save the template, and then update the pages.

29. Create an image map in at least one Web page.

30. Add a rollover button to at least one Web page.

31. Create a form in one Web page to collect comments from visitors. Use a table to organize the form objects and buttons. Don't forget to include a Submit button. (The zine database located in the AddCases folder included with your Data Files includes a full_name field, a comment field, and an e-mail address field.)

32. Upload the **zine** database file located in the AddCases folder included with your Data Files to your remote server if you are using ASP, or create the database on your remote server if you are using PHP.

33. Connect the site to the database, and then connect the form page to the database.

34. Add server behaviors to a Web page that will enable users to view the comments that are collected in the database.

35. Upload the site to your remote server, if necessary.

36. Preview the form in a browser, and then test the form by entering appropriate information and submitting the form.

37. Preview the Web page in which comments are displayed.

38. Insert a Flash movie, Flash text, a Shockwave movie, a Flash video, or a sound into at least one page in the site. (*Hint:* If you don't have one of these types of files to insert, you can use any of the files in the Tutorial.08 folders included with your Data Files as placeholders.)

39. Preview the site in a browser.

40. Upload the site to a remote server, and then preview the site over the Web.

41. Test each page of the site.

42. Submit the finished files to your instructor, either in printed or electronic form, as requested.

Objectives

- Insert a Photoshop file into a Web page
- Learn about optimization settings
- Opening and changing a Photoshop file
- Copy and paste a Photoshop file to update an image in a Web page
- Insert part of a Photoshop file into a Web page

Integrating Photoshop and Dreamweaver

Adding Images to a Web Page   .

Case

Indyview

Indyview is a Web site that provides reviews of the latest indy music releases. The site has a strong following and is linked to by many sources. A review of the newest sloth child CD is being readied for the indyview site. The sloth child CD cover is available as a Photoshop file. You will insert the entire Photoshop file into the weekly cd review page. You will paste multiple layers from the CD cover Photoshop file directly into the page. You will optimize the image for Web display in Dreamweaver without altering the original image. Finally, you will select the image in Dreamweaver and then open and edit the original image in Photoshop. When you are finished editing the original image in Photoshop, you will update the image displayed in the Web page in Dreamweaver.

Starting Data Files

Appendix.A

Understanding Photoshop and Its Integration with Dreamweaver

Dreamweaver CS3 provides enhanced integration with **Adobe Photoshop CS3**, the industry-standard software for editing and working with graphic images. This integration enables you to insert Photoshop files or parts of Photoshop files into Web pages you are creating in Dreamweaver. You can then use Dreamweaver to optimize the image for Web display. In Dreamweaver, the optimized image in a Web page remains linked to the original image that was created in Photoshop. This link enables you to select and change the original image and then copy the changes to the Web site. This is extremely helpful because Web site content can change frequently. Every time you modify a compressed image and resave that image, the file is compressed again. Each time this occurs, the image is further degraded and looks worse because the types of compression that are used for the Web are often lossy forms of compression. Recall that lossy compression discards (or loses) some of the image information to compress the image. However, if you modify an original Photoshop file and save that file, the image does not degrade because Photoshop files are not compressed at all. By linking the images in Web pages to the original Photoshop files, Dreamweaver makes it simple to edit the original files when you need to make changes.

Tip

The native Photoshop file format is .psd.

InSight | **Integrating Photoshop with Dreamweaver Effectively**

Dreamweaver, the industry-standard Web authoring tool, and Photoshop, the industry-standard image editing tool, are part of the Adobe Creative Suite. This allows integration between the two programs, providing for basic image editing and compression that is controlled directly within Dreamweaver but that is actually accomplished in the background by Photoshop. Although this feature makes high-quality compression simple to accomplish, professional Web designers usually design and plan their sites completely before they begin to work in Dreamweaver. As a result, for the most part, professional designers have all of the images and graphics created, scaled, and compressed, ready for inclusion in the Web site, before they even begin to work with Dreamweaver. However, Web sites are frequently updated, and the integration feature can be handy for doing quick updates and changes.

Inserting a Photoshop File in a Web Page

There are two ways to insert a Photoshop file into a Web page in Dreamweaver. You can insert the file into a Web page using the Image button in the Images list on the Common tab of the Insert bar just as you did when you inserted JPEG and GIF images into the pages of the Cosmatic site. You can also copy an image that is open in Photoshop, and then paste the image into a Web page in Dreamweaver.

Inserting a Photoshop File into a Dreamweaver Web Page | Reference Window

- In the Document window, click where you want to insert the image.
- On the Common tab of the Insert bar, click the Images button arrow, click Image, and then double-click the image to insert (or copy the image in the Photoshop window, and then paste the image in the Web page in Dreamweaver).
- Select optimization settings in the Image Preview dialog box, and then click the OK button.
- Enter a filename and storage location in the Save Web Image dialog box, and then click the OK button.

When you insert a Photoshop file in a Web page, Dreamweaver opens the Image Preview dialog box so you can optimize the image for Web display. The goal of optimizing an image for Web display is to create the smallest possible file size so that the image loads in a user's browser quickly while still maintaining good image quality so that the image looks like you intended it to look in the Web page. The basic process for inserting the image is:

1. Select the format in which to save the optimized image; you can choose GIF, JPEG, or PNG.
2. Select the optimization settings, which are specific for each format because each format compresses the file differently.
3. Name and save the optimized image to the Graphics folder in the site's local root folder.

Optimizing an Image | InSight

Image optimization can be a trial-and-error process. For each image, you want to find the smallest file size that still looks good when displayed on the user's screen. To do this, you select an image format (GIF, JPEG, or PNG), and then you adjust the settings and preview the image until you are satisfied with the results. If you are unsure which format will be best for an image, you can switch between the formats while the Image Preview dialog box is open to compare image quality and file size. Keep in mind that the smaller the file size, the faster the image downloads when users load the page in their browser.

Figure A-1 describes the basic optimization settings for each format. The Image Preview dialog box includes other buttons and settings, but the settings described below are the basic settings that you will need for image optimization.

Figure A-1 | **Basic image optimization settings**

Format	Setting	Description
JPEG	Quality	Adjusts the quality of the image. A setting of 80 provides very good quality with a fairly low file size, but you can adjust to find the optimal setting for the image.
	Smoothing	Blurs the edges of the image, making it look softer or slightly out of focus. Also decreases the image's file size. Unless you want the soft look that smoothing provides, leave it off.
	Progressive browser	Displays the image in a Web page at a low resolution and then progressively increases the image to high resolution. With slower connections, the image will begin to appear sooner in the user's browser.
	Sharpen color edges	Makes the edges of the image sharper, creating the illusion that the image is more in focus. This setting increases the image's file size significantly and should be used sparingly.
	Matte	Sets the color that will fill in any transparent areas of the image.
	Remove unused colors	Deletes any unused colors, reducing the image's file size. Use this setting unless the resulting image has a blocky color display instead of smooth.
GIF/PNG8	Palette	Sets the colors used in the image's compression. Because GIF/PNG8 images can include a maximum of 256 colors, you must select the specific colors used to display the image. Adaptive often provides best results because it enables Dreamweaver to select the best 256 colors for the image's compression.
	Loss	Removes spots of color, decreasing the image's file size. This usually looks more like an image effect and should be avoided unless you want a stylized look.
	Maximum number of colors	Adjusts the image's quality/file size because GIF and PNG8 formats compress images by adjusting the number of colors in the image. The maximum number of colors is 256, but you can decrease the number of colors in the color palette as long as the image retains its visual quality in the preview.
	Dither	Simulates additional colors that are not included in the palette by creating patterns of related colors that resemble the desired color. This usually does a poor job and increases the image's file size.
	Transparency	Enables you to set index, alpha, or no transparency for the image. The gray/white checked pattern in the background of the image denotes the transparent area.
	Remove unused colors	Deletes any unused colors from the image color palette, reducing the image's file size. Use this setting unless the resulting image has a blocky color display instead of smooth.
	Interlaced browser display	Displays the image in a Web page at a low resolution and then progressively increases the image to high resolution. Although this setting can decrease the image's file size, it may not provide the desired look when the user loads the page.
	PNG24	No real settings for this format.
	PNG32	No real settings for this format.

You will create a site definition for the new indyview site so that you can work with the site in Dreamweaver. Then, you'll open the weekly cd review Web page and insert a Photoshop file in the page.

To open the indyview site and insert the CD cover graphic in the Web page:

▶ **1.** Create local and remote site definitions to the **indyview** site located in the **Appendix.A** folder included with your Data Files, using **indyview** as the site name, **indyview\ Dreamweaver** as the local root folder, **indyview\Dreamweaver\Graphics** as the default images folder, set links relative to document, use case-sensitive link checking, and enable cache.

▶ **2.** Open the **index.html** page in the Document window, place the insertion point after the *sloth child : this bite makes you smaller* heading, and then press the **Enter** key. You'll insert the image on this line.

▶ **3.** On the **Common** tab of the Insert bar, click the **Images button arrow** 🖼▾, click the **Image** button 🖼 to open the Select Image Source dialog box, navigate to the **Appendix.A** folder included with your Data Files, click the **ThisBite.psd** file, and then click the **OK** button. After a few moments, the Image Preview dialog box opens. See Figure A-2.

Image Preview dialog box ◀ **Figure A-2**

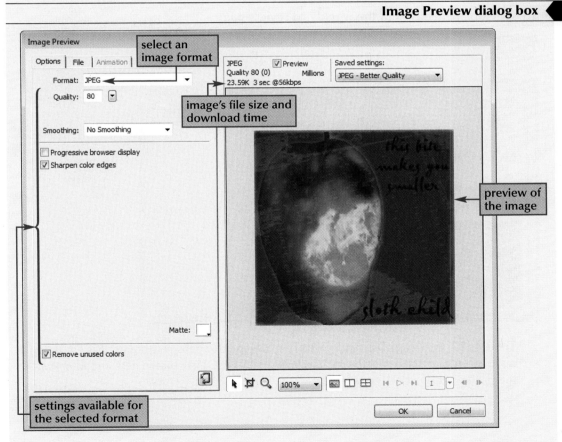

▶ **4.** If necessary, click the **Format** arrow, and then click **JPEG**. The CD cover has many gradient colors, like a photograph does, and will compress better in this format.

▶ **5.** View the image in the Preview box. With the standard quality of 80%, some artifacts are visible around the letters and the letters look a bit fuzzy. You'll increase the quality to eliminate this problem.

▶ **6.** Type **90** in the Quality box. The artifacts disappear and the letters are in sharper focus. Also, the image's file size increases, lengthening the download time for the image.

▶ **7.** If necessary, click the **Smoothing** arrow, and then click **No Smoothing**. The image remains crisp and in focus.

▶ **8.** If necessary, click the **Progressive browser display** check box to remove the check mark. The image will appear only in high resolution when the Web page loads.

▶ **9.** If necessary, click the **Sharpen color edges** check box to remove the check mark. The image is already sharply in focus, so you don't need to unnecessarily increase the image's file size.

▶ **10.** If necessary, click the **Remove unused colors** check box to insert a check mark. Any unneeded colors are eliminated, reducing the image's file size.

▶ **11.** View the image in the Preview box, and then click the **OK** button. The Save Web Image dialog box opens.

▶ **12.** Save the image as **ThisBite** in the **indyview\Dreamweaver\Graphics** folder. The sloth child CD cover is inserted into the page. See Figure A-3.

Figure A-3 ▶ **ThisBite image inserted in the weekly cd review page**

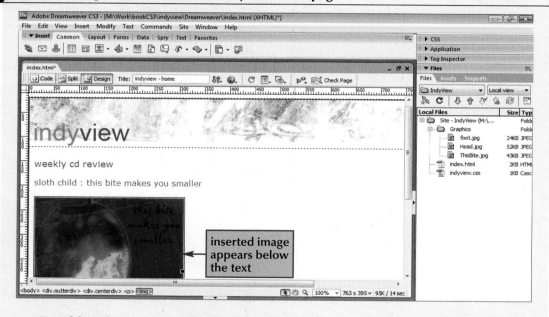

Trouble? If the Image Description (Alt Text) dialog box opens, this prompt has not been disabled on your installation of Dreamweaver. Click the Cancel button here and whenever this dialog box opens in this appendix.

As with any other image you insert in a Web page, you can use CSS styles to format the graphic. For the weekly cd review page, you'll create a new CSS style that enables the text to flow around the graphic.

To create a CSS style for the ThisBite graphic:

1. In the CSS Styles panel, click the **New CSS Rule** button ⊞, and then create a custom style class named **.cds** and defined in the **indyview.css** style sheet. The CSS Rule Definition dialog box opens.

2. In the **Box** category, set Float to **left**, set Top in the Padding group to **10 pixels**, click the **Same for all** check box in the Padding group to insert a check mark if necessary, and then click the **OK** button. This style moves the image to the left of the screen, adds an invisible 10 pixel border around the image, and wraps the text around the image.

   You'll apply the cds style to the cover image you just inserted in the weekly cd review page.

3. In the Document window, select the **ThisBite** image, and then, in the Property inspector, click the **Class** arrow and click **cds**. The cds style is applied to the sloth child CD cover and the text moves up in the page. (The footer div appears to the right of the image in Dreamweaver but it will be displayed correctly in the browser.) See Figure A–4.

Image with cds style applied ◄ **Figure A-4**

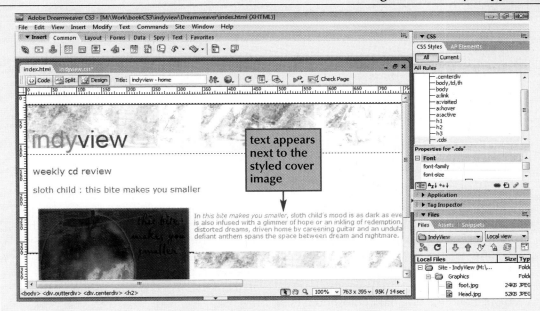

4. Save the page, save and close the indyview.css page, and then preview the page in a browser. See Figure A-5.

Figure A-5 ▶ **Weekly cd review page previewed in a browser**

▶ **5.** Close the browser.

Opening and Changing an Original Photoshop File

One of the benefits of Web pages is that you can quickly and regularly update their content and styles as needed. Although Web pages can continuously change, you should not modify and then resave Web graphics. Each time you resave a compressed image file, the file compresses further and degrades the image quality. Instead, you should make changes to the original, uncompressed image file, and then recompress the updated image. This preserves the quality of the artwork in the Web pages. This process is fairly simple because Dreamweaver preserves the link between the compressed image inserted in a Web page and the original Photoshop file.

Because Photoshop is an image processing program, you can change just about anything in the image. For example, you can change the image size or color, you can rotate and bend an image, you can add text and textures to an image, you can combine multiple images, and so on. The editing capabilities increase exponentially when an image is created with layers. In Photoshop, **layers** enable you to separate the elements that make up your image. Layers stack the elements of an image one on top of another to create the complete image. You can think of layers as pieces of acetate that are stacked to form a cell of a cartoon animation. Areas of a layer that do not contain image elements are transparent, so you can see the elements that appear on the layers below that one. Additionally, you can move or change elements in one layer without changing or moving elements in other layers.

You will open the original file for the sloth child CD cover, and then modify the album cover artwork in the original Photoshop file.

To open and edit the original image file in Photoshop:

▶ **1.** In the Document window, right-click the **ThisBite** image, point to **Edit Source With** on the context menu, and then click **Photoshop**. The ThisBite.psd image opens in the Photoshop program window. See Figure A-6.

Original ThisBite image in Photoshop | Figure A-6

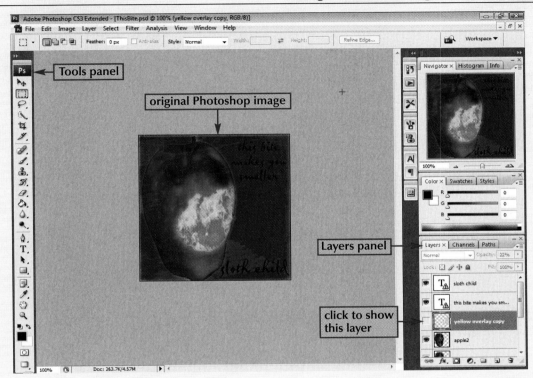

Trouble? If a dialog box opens, warning that some text layers contain fonts that are missing, the font used in the album cover image is not installed on your computer. Click the OK button, and be careful not to double-click any layers that contain fonts.

Trouble? If the Photoshop program window on your screen looks different than the one shown in the figure, Photoshop is not set to its default configuration on your computer. To set Photoshop to its default workspace setup, click the Workspace button on the toolbar, and then click Default Workspace.

▶ **2.** In the Layers panel, click to the left of the yellow overlay copy layer. The eye icon appears in the box, and the yellow overlay copy layer becomes visible. See Figure A-7.

Figure A-7 | **Original Photoshop image modified**

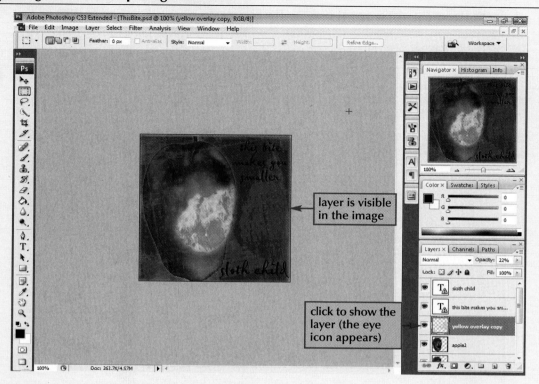

3. Click **File** on the menu bar, and then click **Save**. The changes you made to the image are saved.

Updating an Image in Dreamweaver

After you have modified and saved the original Photoshop file, you can copy and paste the updated image into the Web page in Dreamweaver. First, you select and copy the file in Photoshop. Then, in the Document window in Dreamweaver, you select the compressed image you want to update and paste the updated image into the Web page. The optimization settings you selected for the image are applied to the updated image when it replaces the earlier version. The updated image has the same name and remains linked to the original Photoshop file.

You will update the ThisBite.jpg with the changes you made to the Photoshop file.

To update the ThisBite image in the weekly cd review page:

Tip

You can also press the Ctrl+A keys to select the entire image.

1. In Photoshop, click **Select** on the menu bar, and then click **All**. The entire image is selected and a dotted border is visible around the image.

2. Click **Edit** on the menu bar, and then click **Copy Merged**. The selected image is copied to the Clipboard.

3. In Dreamweaver, right-click the **ThisBite.jpg** image to open the context menu, and then click **Paste**. The image is updated to reflect the changes you made in Photoshop.

4. Press the **Right Arrow** key to deselect the image. See Figure A-8.

Photoshop image copied and pasted in the weekly cd review page ◄ Figure A-8

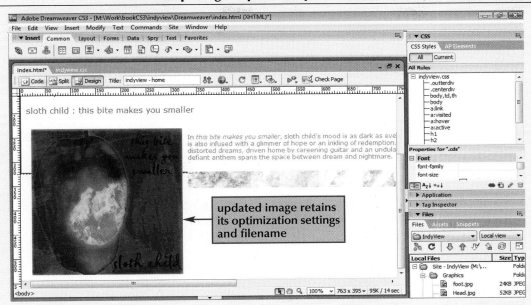

5. Save the page, and then preview the page in a browser. See Figure A-9.

Weekly cd review page with updated image previewed in browser ◄ Figure A-9

6. Close the browser.

Inserting Part of a Photoshop File in Dreamweaver

You can also insert part of a Photoshop file into a Web page. This is helpful when you design the layout of an entire Web page in Photoshop but create the working page in Dreamweaver. With this method, you copy only the images you need from the Photoshop document and recreate the other elements such as the page layout, background color, and text in CSS or HTML in Dreamweaver.

You will copy the sloth child band name from the ThisBite image, and then paste it into the weekly cd review page. This logo image will later be linked to the sloth child Web site.

To insert the sloth child name from the ThisBite image:

▶ **1.** In Photoshop, deselect the image, and then, in the Layers panel, click the **sloth child** layer to select it. This layer contains the text of the band name.

▶ **2.** In the Tools panel, click the **Rectangular Marquee Tool** [⬚] to select it.

▶ **3.** In the Document window, draw a rectangle around the sloth child band name. Only part of the image is selected. See Figure A-10.

Figure A-10 ▶ **Sloth child logo selected**

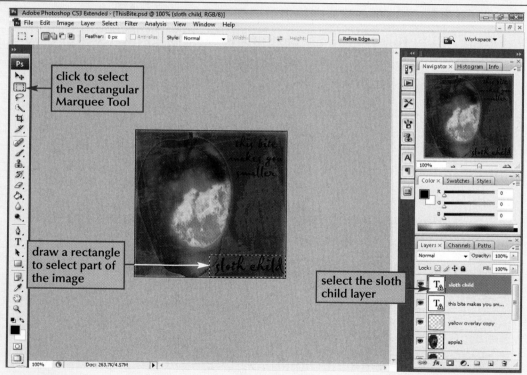

▶ **4.** Click **Edit** on the menu bar, and then click **Copy**. The selected area of the image is copied to the Windows Clipboard.

5. In Dreamweaver, click to the right of the *sloth child : this bite makes you smaller* heading, and then press the **Spacebar**. You'll paste the sloth child logo in this location.

6. Right-click the space next to the heading to open the context menu, and then click **Paste**. The sloth child logo appears in the Image Preview dialog box, so you can modify its settings.

7. Click the **Format** arrow, and then click **GIF**. The optimization settings change to reflect the selected format. You'll use GIF format because this image has only a few simple colors, lending itself to GIF compression. See Figure A-11.

Image Preview dialog box with the sloth child logo Figure A-11

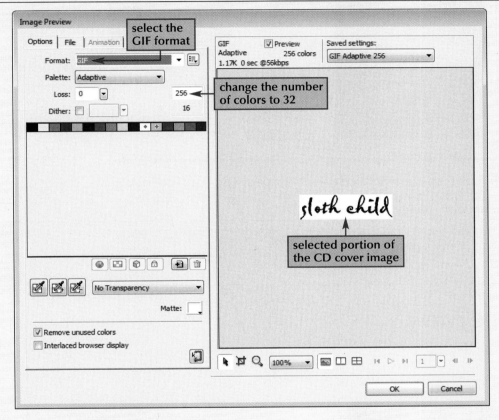

8. Click the **Maximum number of colors** arrow, and then click **32**. Although the text looks black and white, it has some gradient color around the edges to smooth the jagged edges (called anti-aliasing). The setting of 32 ensures the text displays clearly in the Web page.

The rest of the default settings are fine for this image.

9. Click the **OK** button to open the Save Web Image dialog box, and then save the image as **ThisBite** in the **Graphics** folder in the local root folder. The logo appears in the page.

10. If necessary, press the **Right Arrow** key to deselect the logo image. See Figure A-12.

Figure A-12 ▶ **Sloth child logo inserted in the weekly cd review page**

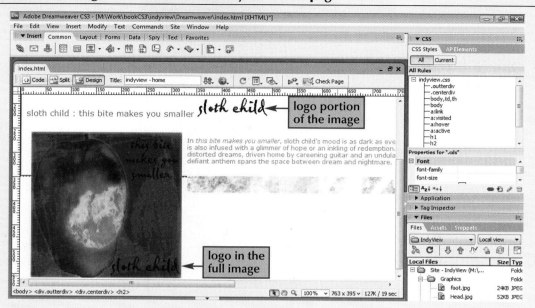

11. Save the page, and then preview the page in a browser. See Figure A-13.

Figure A-13 ▶ **Completed weekly cd review page**

12. Close the browser, upload the site to your remote server, and then view the **index.html** page to ensure that it displays properly.

In this appendix, you inserted a Photoshop image into a Web page in Dreamweaver. You modified the original Photoshop image, and then updated the Web page image. You also inserted part of a Photoshop image into the Web page.

Review | **Appendix A Quick Check**

1. What type of software is Photoshop?
2. What are the two ways to insert a Photoshop file into a page in Dreamweaver?
3. What is the goal when you optimize an image for Web display?
4. What is a layer used for in Photoshop?
5. True or False? You can paste a single layer from a Photoshop image into a Web page in Dreamweaver.

Review | **Appendix A Summary**

In this appendix, you learned how to integrate Photoshop and Dreamweaver. You inserted a Photoshop image into a Web page. You modified the original Photoshop image, and then updated the Web page image. You also inserted part of a Photoshop image into the Web page.

Key Terms

Adobe Photoshop CS3
layers

Appendix A

1. image processing software
2. using the Image button in the Insert list on the Common tab of the Insert bar; copy the image from Photoshop and paste it into the page in Dreamweaver
3. to obtain the smallest possible file size while retaining good visual image quality
4. to separate and stack elements of an image
5. True

Glossary/Index

external, 127–133

formatting tables with, 209–211

introduction to, 116

page layout with, 302–308

prebuilt CSS layout pages, 302–303

viewing code for, 134–137

case sensitivity

of filenames, 74

of links, 16

cell padding, 191, 223

cell The container created by the intersection of a row and a column in a table, 190

adding content to, 193–195, 228–230

column span of, 205–206

drawing in Layout mode, 216–217

formatting, 203–205

modifying attributes, 226–228

modifying layout of, 203–205

moving and resizing, 225–226

row span of, 205–206

selecting, 196–197, 219

working with, in Layout mode, 225–230

cell spacing, 191, 223

cell tags, 211

CERN (European Council for Nuclear Research), 3

Char width attribute, 504

checkboxes, 501, 506–507

Class attribute, 319

Clear column widths attribute, 200

Clear row heights attribute, 200, 223

client The person or persons for whom you are working, 44. *See also* Web client

Clip attribute, 320

Close command, 35

code

added with Flash video clips, 450–452

for AP div tags, 321–324

copying and pasting, 560, 584

for CSS styles, 134–140

viewing HTML, 77–78, 148–149, 211–213

CODEC (COmpressor/DECompressor) The software that shrinks the digital sound and or video to the smallest possible size for faster transmission, and later expands it for playback on the client computer. Several different popular CODECs are used for sound and video on the Web, including MP3 (sound only), RealMedia, QuickTime, and Windows Media., 438

Coder workspace environment, 13

Code view, 23–25

frame tags in, 284–286

table tags in, 212

ColdFusion, 13

Collapsible Panel widget, 527

colors

additive, 58

background, 79

font, 62, 78–79, 105

hexadecimal, 79

hexadecimal codes, 60

link, 63

RGB, 58–59

selection of, 58–61

subtractive, 58

columns The vertical structure of a table, 190

adding/deleting, 208–209

resizing, 207–208

selecting, 197–198

working with, 207–209

column span The width of a cell measured in columns, 205–206

comment tag An unpaired tag that is used to add notes to the code of an HTML page that do not appear in the rendered page. Generally used to add a note to help you recall the use or purpose of a section of code but can also be used to hide newer tags and technologies from older browsers that do not support them, 134

company logos, 9

competitors, Web sites of, 50

compression A process that shrinks the file size of a graphic, sound or video by using different types of encoding to remove redundant or less important information. The smaller the file size, the faster it will load in a browser.

of graphics, 164–165

lossless, 166

lossy, 166

for sound files, 438

of video files, 445

comp A comprehensive, fully developed, detailed drawing that provides a complete preview of what the final design will look like; also called storyboard, 65

connection strings All the information that a Web application server needs to connect to a database, 575

consistency, 64

contact forms. *See* forms

container

widget, 527

content The information presented in a Web page; can be a combination of text, graphics, and multimedia elements such as video, animation, or interactive content.

adding

to AP div tags, 313–319

to cells, 228–230

to editable areas of template, 490

to frames, 274–276

to Spry widgets, 529–532

NoFrames, 254, 277–278

organization of, 56

reusing, 193

reviewing, 11

of Web pages, 10–11

context-sensitive Help, 35

contrast, 176

Convert table heights to percent attribute, 200

Convert table heights to pixels attribute, 200

Convert table widths to percents attribute, 200

TASK	PAGE #	RECOMMENDED METHOD
Alternate text, add to graphic or link	DRM 175	Select link or graphic, type text in Alt box in Property inspector
Animation bar, delete	DRM 390	In Timelines panel, select animation bar, press Delete
Animation bar, move to another animation channel	DRM 373	In Timelines panel, select animation bar, drag to new channel
Animation bar, move within animation channel	DRM 375	In Timelines panel, select animation bar, drag to right or left as needed
Animation bar, resize	DRM 375	In Timelines panel, select a keyframe, drag selected keyframe to right or left
Animation bar, select	DRM 374	In Timelines panel, click between keyframes of animation bar
AP div content, add	DRM 313	Click in AP div, enter content as usual
AP div properties, adjust	DRM 319	Select AP div, set attributes in Property inspector
AP div stacking order, adjust	DRM 324	In AP Elements panel, drag AP div to new position
AP div stacking order, adjust in timeline	DRM 382	See Reference Window: Adjusting AP Div Timeline Stacking Order
AP div visibility, adjust in Timelines panel	DRM 378	Click keyframe where visibility changes, click visibility column in AP Elements panel until 👁 or 👁 appears
AP div, add to Timelines panel	DRM 369	Drag selected AP div from Document window to desired position in Timelines panel
AP div, insert	DRM 308	On Layout tab of Insert bar, click 📄, drag in Document window to draw AP div
AP div, make active	DRM 309	Click in AP div
AP div, move	DRM 309	Select AP div, drag with AP div selection handle to new position
AP div, nest	DRM 331	In AP Elements panel, select AP div to nest, press and hold Ctrl, drag selected AP div over parent AP div
AP div, reposition over time	DRM 386	In Timelines panel, select keyframe and drag AP div to new position, repeat for each keyframe where AP div moves, adding keyframes as needed
AP div, resize	DRM 309	Select AP div, drag resize handle
AP div, resize over time	DRM 388	In Timelines panel, select keyframe, drag AP div resize handles to resize AP div, deselect AP div
AP div, select	DRM 309	In AP Elements panel, click selection handle of active AP div or click AP div name
AP div, unnest	DRM 331	In AP Elements panel, select nested AP div to unnest, drag selected AP div to top of list
AP divs, align	DRM 329	Select first AP div, press and hold Shift, click AP div to align to, click Modify, point to Arrange, click alignment
AP Elements panel, display	DRM 326	Expand CSS panel group, click AP Elements tab
Behavior, add to object with Behaviors panel	DRM 342	Select object to apply behavior to, click ➕ in Behaviors panel, click action, click Event arrow, click event
Behavior, delete	DRM 350	In Behaviors panel, select behavior, click ➖
Behavior, edit in Behaviors panel	DRM 350	Select object with behavior to edit, click behavior in Behaviors panel, click Events arrow, click new event
Behaviors panel, display	DRM 342	Expand Tag Inspector panel group, click Behaviors tab

TASK	PAGE #	RECOMMENDED METHOD
Behaviors, add to Behaviors channel	DRM 393	See Reference Window: Adding Behaviors to Behaviors Channel
Browser window, close	DRM 11	Click ⬛X on browser title bar
Cell attributes, modify in Layout mode	DRM 226	Select cell, set desired attributes in Property inspector
Cell, draw in Layout mode	DRM 216	On Layout tab of Insert bar, click 📧, drag ┼ to draw cell
Cell, move in Layout mode	DRM 225	Select cell, drag cell perimeter to new location
Cell, resize in Layout mode	DRM 225	Select cell, drag resize handles
Cell, select in Layout mode	DRM 220	Click perimeter of cell
Cell, select one or more in Standard mode	DRM 196	Ctrl+click a cell or drag across multiple table cells
Cells, merge	DRM 203	Select cells to merge, click 🔲 in Property inspector
Code view, display page in	DRM 24	Click Code button on Document toolbar
Column span, adjust	DRM 205	Right-click cell in column, point to Table, click Increase Column Span or Decrease Column Span
Column, delete	DRM 208	Select column, right-click selected column, point to Table, click Delete Column
Column, insert	DRM 208	Select column to right of column you want to insert, right-click selected column, point to Table, click Insert Column
Column, resize	DRM 207	Drag column border
Column, select in Standard mode	DRM 197	Click in table, click arrow button above top border of column, click Select Column
Copyright symbol, add to page	DRM 133	On Text tab of Insert bar, click ©️ in Characters list
Custom script, add to page	DRM 346	On Common tab of Insert bar, click 🔷 in Script list, select language, enter content, click OK
Custom style class, apply	DRM 123	Select text, click Style arrow in Property inspector, click style name
Custom style class, create	DRM 122	See Reference Window: Creating a Custom Style Class
Database, connect Web site to	DRM 547, DRM 571	In Server Behaviors panel, click document type link to select document type, click testing server link to set testing server in site definition
Database, create on remote Linux server	DRM 545	Log into database management interface, run SQL statements to create database
Database, upload to remote Windows server	DRM 569	Click Site, click Manage Sites, click New, click FTP & RDS Server, enter server information, click OK, click Done
Database-driven pages, create for Linux server	DRM 542	See Reference Window: Creating Database-Driven Pages for a Linux Server
Database-driven pages, create for Windows server	DRM 566	See Reference Window: Creating Database-Driven Pages for a Windows Server
Design view, display page in	DRM 23	Click Design button on Document toolbar
Div tag content, add	DRM 305	Select placeholder text in div, enter text or image as usual
Div tag, insert	DRM 304	On Layout tab of Insert bar, click 📧, click Insert, click At insertion point, create new CSS style if needed, click OK
Document window, change window size	DRM 27	Click Window Size button on status bar, click desired size
Dreamweaver, exit	DRM 35	Click File, click Exit

TASK	PAGE #	RECOMMENDED METHOD
Dreamweaver, start	DRM 13	Click Start, click All Programs, click Adobe Design Premium CS3, click Adobe Dreamweaver CS3
Editable region, add to template	DRM 485	On Common tab of Insert bar, click 📝 in Templates list
Editable region, delete from template	DRM 495	Open template in Document window, select editable region, press Delete, save template, click Update, resolve inconsistent region names, click OK, click Close
E-mail link behavior, add to hotspot	DRM 345	Click hotspot, double-click Link box in Property inspector, type mailto: and e-mail address, press Enter
Expanded Tables mode, switch to	DRM 198	On Layout tab of Insert bar, click Expanded button
External style sheet, attach to Web page	DRM 131	See Reference Window: Attaching an External Style Sheet to a Web Page
External style sheet, create	DRM 127	See Reference Window: Moving Styles to a New External Style Sheet
External style sheet, define new style in	DRM 132	See Reference Window: Defining a Style in an External Style Sheet
File list and site map, view in Files panel	DRM 19	See Reference Window: Viewing the File List and Site Map in the Files Panel
File, close	DRM 35	Click ✖ on Document window title bar
File, open in Document window	DRM 21	In Files panel, double-click filename
Files panel, expand or collapse	DRM 21	Click 🗗 on Files panel toolbar
Flash button, add to Web page	DRM 427	On Common tab of Insert bar, in Media list, click 🎬, click button style, review button states in Sample box, type button text, select customization options, click OK
Flash movie attributes, adjust	DRM 422	Select Flash movie, change attributes in Property inspector
Flash movie with sound attributes, adjust	DRM 441	Select Flash movie, change attributes in Property inspector
Flash movie with sound, embed in Web page	DRM 440	See Reference Window: Adding a Flash Movie with Sound to a Web Page
Flash movie, add to Web page	DRM 418	See Reference Window: Adding a Flash Movie to a Web Page
Flash text, add to Web page	DRM 424	See Reference Window: Adding Flash Text in a Web Page
Flash video, add to Web page	DRM 448	See Reference Window: Adding a Flash Video Clip to a Web Page
Flash video, delete	DRM 453	Select Flash video clip in AP div, press Delete, select <body> in status bar, select MM_CheckFlashVersion behavior in Behaviors panel, press Delete, switch to Code view, delete Flash video code from head of page
Flash, find information and statistics	DRM 416	In browser, type www.adobe.com/products/flashplayer in Address bar, press Enter, click links
Form attributes, add to form	DRM 498	Select form, set attributes in Property inspector
Form data, validate	DRM 512	On status bar, click form tab, in Behaviors panel, click ➕, click Validate Form, set validation options, click OK, in Behaviors panel, click Events arrow, click Submit
Form object, add to form	DRM 501	Click in form, click appropriate button on Forms tab of Insert bar, type object name and set attributes in Property inspector
Form, add to Web page	DRM 498	Click in page in location for form, on Forms tab of Insert bar, click 🔲
Form, create	DRM 498	See Reference Window: Creating a Form

TASK	PAGE #	RECOMMENDED METHOD
Formatting, remove from text	DRM 121	Select text, click Format button in Property inspector, click None
Frame borders, display	DRM 257	Click View, point to Visual Aids, click Frame Borders
Frame, adjust properties	DRM 266	Select frame, click Page Properties button in Property inspector, adjust properties as needed, click OK
Frame, create in Web page	DRM 257	See Reference Window: Creating a Web Page with Frames
Frame, save	DRM 264	See Reference Window: Saving a Frame
Frames panel, open	DRM 269	Click Window, click Frames
Frameset properties, adjust	DRM 272	Select frameset, adjust properties in Property inspector as needed
Frameset, save	DRM 265	See Reference Window: Saving a Frameset
Graphic, add to Web page	DRM 168	See Reference Window: Adding a Graphic to a Web Page
Graphic, align to left, center, or right	DRM 183	Select graphic, click ▤, ▤, or ▤ in Property inspector
Graphic, apply CSS style to	DRM 172	Select graphic, click Class arrow in Property inspector, click style
Graphic, change brightness and contrast	DRM 179	Select graphic, click ◑ in Property inspector, click OK, drag Brightness and/or Contrast slider, click OK
Graphic, crop	DRM 178	Select graphic, click ⊠ in Property inspector, click OK, drag resize handles to set crop area, press Enter
Graphic, resample	DRM 177	Select graphic, click ▣ in Property inspector
Graphic, resize	DRM 178	Select graphic, drag resize handles or click ▣ in Property inspector
Graphic, sharpen	DRM 180	Select graphic, click △ in Property inspector, click OK, drag Sharpen slider, click OK
Grid, display or hide	DRM 330	Click View, point to Grid, click Show Grid
Guide, display or hide	DRM 311	Drag to or from horizontal or vertical ruler
Guide, reposition	DRM 311	Drag to new location in Document window
Header row, create	DRM 207	Select row, check Header check box in Property inspector
Help, get in Dreamweaver	DRM 32	See Reference Window: Getting Help in Dreamweaver
Hotspot, create	DRM 183	Click ▭, ◯, or ▽ in Property inspector, drag in Document window to create hotspot
Hotspot, move, resize, or reposition point	DRM 185	Click ▶ in Property inspector, drag hotspot or point on hotspot
HTML tag, modify	DRM 118	See Reference Window: Modifying an Existing HTML Tag
HTML tags, examine in Web pages	DRM 112	See Reference Window: Examining HTML Tags
Hyperlink, create from graphic	DRM 180	Select graphic, click ▢ next to Link box in Property inspector, double-click file to link to
Hyperlink, create from text	DRM 109	Select text in Document window, drag ⊕ from Property inspector to filename of page to link in Files panel
Hyperlink, customize appearance of	DRM 125	See Reference Window: Using the Advanced Style for Hyperlinks
Hyperlink, delete	DRM 246	Select link, press Delete
Hyperlink, set target	DRM 230	Select link, click Target arrow in Property inspector, click target option
Hyperlink, use	DRM 9	Click link in browser window
Image map, create	DRM 181	See Reference Window: Creating an Image Map
Keyframe, add to animation bar	DRM 376	See Reference Window: Adding Keyframes to an Animation Bar

TASK	PAGE #	RECOMMENDED METHOD
Keywords, add to Web page	DRM 465	On Common tab of Insert bar, click 🔤 in Head list, type keywords, click OK
Keywords, edit	DRM 468	In Document window in Code view, click in keywords list, make changes to keywords as needed in Property inspector or Document window
Layout mode, switch to	DRM 215	Click View, point to Table Mode, click Layout Mode
Layout table, delete	DRM 224	Select layout table, press Delete
Library item, add to Web page	DRM 475	Drag library item from library in Assets panel to desired location in page
Library item, create	DRM 473	See Reference Window: Creating a Library Item
Library item, delete from library	DRM 479	Select library item in library, click 🗑 in Assets panel
Library item, delete from page	DRM 479	Select library item in page, press Delete
Library item, edit	DRM 477	Open library item, make changes as needed, save library item, click Update, click Close
Library item, open	DRM 477	Double-click library item in Assets panel
Local site definition, create	DRM 15	See Reference Window: Creating a Local Site Definition
Local Web page, open in browser	DRM 7	See Reference Window: Opening a Local Web Page in a Browser
Mark of the Web, add	DRM 453	See Reference Window: Adding Mark of the Web to a Web Page
Meta description, add to Web page	DRM 469	On Common tab of Insert bar, click 🖹 in Head list, type description, click OK
Meta description, edit	DRM 471	In Document window in Code view, click in description, make changes to description as needed in Property inspector or Document window
Navigation bar, copy and paste	DRM 250	Select navigation bar, click Edit, click Copy, place insertion point at destination, click Edit, click Paste
Navigation bar, create	DRM 242	See Reference Window: Creating a Navigation Bar
Navigation bar, modify	DRM 252	See Reference Window: Modifying a Navigation Bar
Nested table, remove	DRM 224	Select nested table, click 🖼 in Property inspector
Nested template, create	DRM 493	Create new page from main template, click 🖺 in Templates list on Common tab of Insert bar, type template name, click Save, add or modify template content as needed, save page, click Yes, click Close
NoFrames content, add	DRM 277	See Reference Window: Adding NoFrames content
Nonbreaking space, insert	DRM 108	On Text tab of Insert bar, click 📥 in Characters list
Page properties, export to external style sheet	DRM 267	Right-click style in Code view, point to CSS Styles, click Move CSS Rules, create or select style sheet, click Save or OK
Page properties, set	DRM 79	Click Modify, click Page Properties, set desired properties, click OK
Page title, add	DRM 75	Type page title in Title box on Document toolbar
Password, delete from remote site definition	DRM 88	Click Site, click Manage Sites, click Web site name in list, click Edit, click Remote Info in Category box, uncheck Save check box, click OK, click Done
Photoshop file, insert in Web page	DRM A3	See Reference Window: Inserting a Photoshop File into a Dreamweaver Web Page
Photoshop file, insert part in Web page	DRM A12	In Photoshop, click layer in Layers panel, click 🖼 in Tools panel, draw rectangle to select area of layer, click Edit, click Copy; in Dreamweaver, right-click location for partial Photoshop file, click Paste, click Format arrow, click format, select optimization settings, click OK

TASK	PAGE #	RECOMMENDED METHOD
Photoshop file, open original	DRM A8	In Document window, right-click image, point to Edit Source With, click Photoshop
Photoshop file, update in Dreamweaver	DRM A10	In Photoshop, click Select, click All, click Edit, click Copy Merged; in Dreamweaver, right-click compressed image to update, click Paste
Prebuilt CSS layout page, create	DRM 302	Click File, click New, click Blank Page, click HTML page type, click layout, click Create
Preview list, add browser to	DRM 84	Click File, point to Preview in Browser, click Edit Browser List, click ⊞, type browser name in Name box, click Browse, navigate to browser to add, click Open, check Primary browser or Secondary browser check box, click OK, click OK
Previously viewed Web pages, display in browser	DRM 10	Click ⬅ or ➡ on browser toolbar
Remote host, connect	DRM 87	Click 🔌 on Files panel toolbar
Remote host, disconnect	DRM 88	Click 🔌 on Files panel toolbar
Remote site definition, create	DRM 69	See Reference Window: Creating a Remote Site Definition for FTP Access
Remote Web page, open in browser	DRM 5	See Reference Window: Opening a Remote Web Page in a Browser
Repeating table, add to template	DRM 486	On Common tab of Insert bar, click 🔲 in Templates list, set table options, click OK
Rollover, copy and paste	DRM 188	Select rollover, click Edit, click Copy, place insertion point at destination, click Edit, click Paste
Rollover, insert	DRM 186	See Reference Window: Inserting a Rollover
Row span, adjust	DRM 205	Right-click cell in row, point to Table, click Increase Row Span or Decrease Row Span
Row, delete	DRM 208	Select row, right-click selected row, point to Table, click Delete Row
Row, insert	DRM 208	Select cell or row below row you want to insert, right-click selected cell or row, point to Table, click Insert Row
Row, resize	DRM 207	Drag row border
Row, select in Standard mode	DRM 197	Click ➡ outside left border of row
Rulers, change to pixel measurement	DRM 202	Click View, point to Rulers, click Pixels
Rulers, show or hide	DRM 202	Click View, point to Rulers, click Show
Shockwave movie attributes, adjust	DRM 435	Select Shockwave movie, change attributes in Property inspector
Shockwave movie, add to Web page	DRM 432	See Reference Window: Adding a Shockwave Movie to a Web Page
Shockwave, find information and statistics	DRM 430	In browser, type www.adobe.com/products/shockwaveplayer in Address bar, press Enter, click links
Show-Hide Elements behavior, add	DRM 334	See Reference Window: Adding the Show-Hide Elements Prewritten Behavior
Sound file, link to Web page	DRM 442	Select graphic, click 📁 next to Link box in Property inspector, double-click sound file
Spelling, check in page	DRM 102	Click Text, click Check Spelling
Split view, display page in	DRM 24	Click Split button on Document toolbar

TASK	PAGE #	RECOMMENDED METHOD
Spry effect, add to page element	DRM 538	Select element in Document window, click ➕ in Behaviors panel, point to Effects, click effect, select options in dialog box, click OK, modify event in Behaviors panel as needed
Spry widget styles, edit in CSS Styles panel	DRM 534	Click widget in Document window, click style in All Rules pane of CSS Styles panel, modify rule properties as needed
Spry widget styles, edit in style sheet	DRM 535	Click widget in Document window, open widget style sheet, modify rule properties as needed
Spry widget styles, research	DRM 533	Click widget in Document window, click Customize this widget link in Property inspector, read content in Adobe Help Viewer
Spry widget, add to Web page	DRM 527	See Reference Window: Adding a Spry Widget to a Web Page
Standard mode, switch to	DRM 199	On Layout tab of Insert bar, click Standard button
Style, define in external style sheet	DRM 132	See Reference Window: Defining a Style in an External Style Sheet
Style, delete	DRM 129	In CSS Styles panel, select style, click 🗑
Style, edit in All Rules pane of CSS Styles panel	DRM 141	See Reference Window: Editing a Style
Style, edit in Current Selection mode in CSS Styles panel	DRM 142	Select text with style to edit in page, click Current button in CSS Styles panel, click 🔲, click value for attribute, enter new value, press Enter
Styles, delete from within document	DRM 129	In CSS Styles panel, select <style>, click 🗑
Styles, move to external style sheet	DRM 127	See Reference Window: Moving Styles to a New External Style Sheet
Table attributes, modify in Layout mode	DRM 222	Select layout table, set desired attributes in Property inspector
Table attributes, modify in Standard mode	DRM 199	Select table, change desired attributes in Property inspector
Table, add content to cells	DRM 193	Click in table cell, type text, press Enter to add paragraph within cell, press Tab to move to next cell
Table, create in Layout mode	DRM 215	See Reference Window: Creating a Table in Layout Mode
Table, create in Standard mode	DRM 190	See Reference Window: Inserting a Table
Table, delete structure and content	DRM 203	Select table, press Delete
Table, format with CSS styles	DRM 209	Create CSS styles as needed, select table cell, row, or column to format, click Style arrow in Property inspector, click style
Table, import tabular data	DRM 193	Click in cell, click File, point to Import, click Tabular Data, set data file, delimiter, and table settings, click OK
Table, move in Layout mode	DRM 221	Drag Layout Table tab to new location
Table, move in Standard mode	DRM 203	Select table, drag with ⬚ from upper-left corner of table to new location
Table, resize in Layout mode	DRM 221	Select layout table, drag a resize handle
Table, resize in Standard mode	DRM 202	Select table, drag a resize handle or type value in W box in Property inspector
Table, select in Layout mode	DRM 219	Click Layout Table tab
Table, select in Standard mode	DRM 195	Right-click table, point to Table, click Select Table
Template region, add to template	DRM 484	On Common tab of Insert bar, click appropriate button in Templates list
Template, apply to existing Web page	DRM 491	Open page in Document window, select template in Assets panel, click Apply, designate in which regions to place existing content

TASK	PAGE #	RECOMMENDED METHOD
Template, create	DRM 482	See Reference Window: Creating a Template
Template, delete	DRM 493	Select template in Assets panel, click 🗑
Template, edit	DRM 491	Open template in Document window, add, remove, and change elements as needed, save template, click Update, click Close
Template-based page, detach from template	DRM 493	Open template-based page, click Modify, point to Templates, click Detach From Template
Text, align to left, center, or right	DRM 108	In Document window, select text; in Property inspector, click ☰, ☰, or ☰
Text, copy from another file and paste in Web page	DRM 101	Open file, select text, press Ctrl+C, place insertion point in Web page in Dreamweaver, click Edit, click Paste Special
Text, find and replace in page	DRM 103	Click Edit, click Find and Replace
Text, format using Property inspector	DRM 106	See Reference Window: Formatting Text Using the Property Inspector
Text, format in HTML mode	DRM 150	See Reference Window: Formatting Text in HTML Mode
Text, indent or outdent	DRM 276	Select text, click ⬚ or ⬚
Timeline, preview in browser	DRM 380	Check Autoplay check box on Timelines panel toolbar, click OK to confirm Play Timeline action added to Web page, preview page in browser
Timeline, preview in Document window	DRM 379	Click and hold ➡ on Timelines panel toolbar while viewing animation in Document window
Timeline, start with a button	DRM 391	Select button in Document window, click ➕ in Behaviors panel, point to Timeline, click Play Timeline, select timeline in Play Timeline list, click OK, select Play Timeline behavior in Behaviors panel, click Events arrow, click desired event, uncheck Autoplay check box on Timelines panel toolbar
Timelines panel, open or close	DRM 366	Click Window, click Timelines
Timelines, create multiple	DRM 396	In Timelines panel, right-click blank frame, click Add Timeline, rename timeline
Timelines, toggle between	DRM 397	Click Timelines arrow on Timelines panel toolbar, click timeline name
Web page, create from template	DRM 488	See Reference Window: Creating a Template-Based Page
Web page, create new	DRM 72	See Reference Window: Creating HTML Pages in a Site
Web page, open in Document window	DRM 21	Double-click filename in Files panel
Web page, preview in browser	DRM 86	Open page to preview, click File, point to Preview in Browser, click browser name
Web page, save existing	DRM 75	Click File, click Save
Web page, save new	DRM 74	Click File, click Save As, navigate to save location, type filename in File name box, click Save
Web site plan, create	DRM 44	See Reference Window: Creating a Plan for a New Web Site
Web site, design	DRM 56	See Reference Window: Designing a Web Site
Web site, preview on Web from remote location	DRM 88	Start browser, type URL of remote site in Address bar, press Enter
Web site, upload to remote location	DRM 87	See Reference Window: Uploading a Web Site to a Remote Location
Web site, upload to remote server	DRM 151	See Reference Window: Uploading a Site to the Remote Server
Workspace environment, select	DRM 13	Click Window, point to Workspace Layout, click desired environment